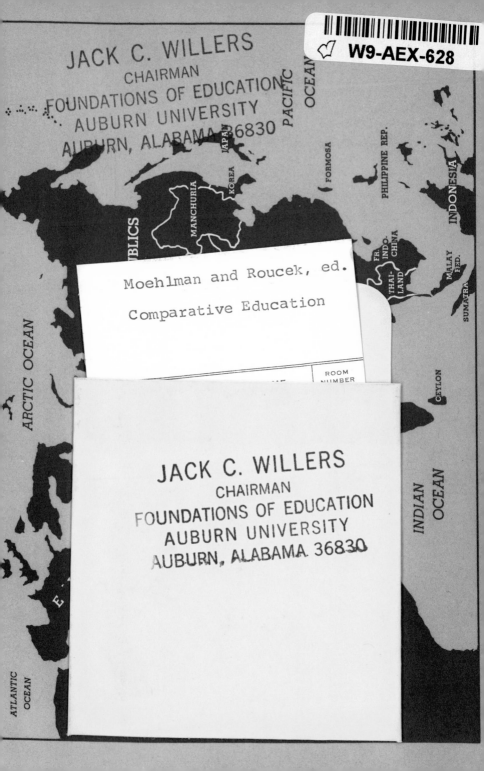

W9-AEX-628

JACK C. WILLERS
CHAIRMAN
FOUNDATIONS OF EDUCATION
AUBURN UNIVERSITY
AUBURN, ALABAMA 36830

Moehlman and Roucek, ed.

Comparative Education

ROOM
NUMBER

JACK C. WILLERS
CHAIRMAN
FOUNDATIONS OF EDUCATION
AUBURN UNIVERSITY
AUBURN, ALABAMA 36830

Dryden Professional Books in Education

ARTHUR HENRY MOEHLMAN
Professor of the History and Philosophy of Education, State University of Iowa

GEORGE I. SÁNCHEZ
Professor and Consultant in Latin American Education and Chairman, Department of the History and Philosophy of Education, University of Texas

HERBERT SCHUELER
Associate Professor of Education and Director of the School of General Studies, Queens College

SAMUEL J. HURWITZ
Department of History, Brooklyn College

GEORGE F. KNELLER
Visiting Professor of American Education, Institute of Education, University of London

JOSEPH S. ROUCEK
Professor of Sociology and Political Science and Chairman, Departments of Sociology and Political Science, University of Bridgeport

WILLIAM H. E. JOHNSON
Associate Professor of Psychology and Education, Carnegie Institute of Technology

M. M. CHAMBERS
Formerly of the American Council on Education, Washington, D. C.

DOUGLAS RUGH
Professor of Education and Psychology and Chairman, Department of Education and Psychology, Teachers College of Connecticut, New Britain

THEODORE HSI-EN CHEN
Professor of Education and International Relations, University of Southern California

EMIL LENGYEL
Professor of Education, School of Education, New York University

COMPARATIVE EDUCATION

EDITED BY

ARTHUR HENRY MOEHLMAN

Professor of the History and Philosophy of
Education · The State University of Iowa

JOSEPH S. ROUCEK

Chairman, Departments of Sociology and Political
Science · The University of Bridgeport

THE DRYDEN PRESS · NEW YORK 19

First Printing, December 1951
Second Printing, July 1953

Copyright, 1951, by The Dryden Press, Inc.
The Dryden Press Building
31 West 54th Street, New York 19, N. Y.

The photographs on the front cover are reproduced by
permission of and special arrangement with Acme
Newspictures, Black Star, Dan Klugherz, and UNations.

FORMAT

The text has been set in Baskerville type, with chapter titles and
display in Electra and Deepdene. Designed by Stanley Burnshaw.
Maps drawn by John O'Rourke. Manufactured by The
Haddon Craftsmen, Scranton, Pennsylvania.

TO

CONRAD HENRY MOEHLMAN
Scholar and Statesman in Education

AND

JAMES H. HALSEY
Guiding Spirit of the University of Bridgeport

Table of Contents

LIST OF MAPS

Comparative Education

1 · EDUCATION IN

Various Cultures

ARTHUR HENRY MOEHLMAN

A nation possesses the key to its future if it understands the purposes and inner logic of its own culture. Education, when used intelligently, is the means for obtaining that key. There is no pat formula for an educational solution which applies everywhere and at all times. It is necessary to study a system of education in its own culture pattern, using a check list or morphology covering philosophy, people, land, historical determinants, and technology in relation to educational development. The use of such a morphology facilitates a comparative study of education which is not dogmatic or narrow, a study in which the wide variety in the patterns is examined from the point of view of relativism. There are innumerable combinations and variations, each of which may be wise for its own area in terms of that area's time, space, technology, and philosophy. It is essential to recognize that contact and interchange of cultures, or acculturation, must proceed on the basis of understanding, tolerance, and patience. It is also essential to understand that the civilizations of today are part of the great cultural shift of the nineteenth and twentieth centuries and of a conflict between force and freedom. The point of view emphasized in this book is that we as human beings live in a symbolic universe that we create ourselves, and that universal education offers the best opportunities to create a wise and realistic symbolic world rather than one which is manipulated by the dead hand of the past.

Each of the succeeding chapters follows a basically similar structure or morphology which relates the pattern of education to a time-space continuum in a specific cultural region with due regard to certain historical determinants. As a consequence, it is inevitable that there will be a wide range in treatment as dictated by the area investigated and the unique nature of the educational pattern.

—A. H. M.

Education has become a major instrument in cultural change. The evidence becomes increasingly clear that human nature *can* be changed and that education is a prime factor in this process. Education, both formal and informal, has accelerated the shift from rural to highly industrialized nations or cultures in the time span of a few generations.

Humankind is unique in that it can construct its own dimensions of life. It lives in a world of symbols, which it has created itself: language, number, and formulae. Education is the great instrument for training human beings in the use of symbols basic to their survival and progress.

Nations and culture areas around the world have changed at different rates of speed with regard to control of this symbolic world. The systems of education which they use to survive and progress cover a wide range. We are all passengers on the same planet but we follow very different paths, educationally and culturally speaking. The United States, Canada, and a few other countries have pioneered in universal education, or a "one-track" type, in which many have an opportunity to receive the same amount of education. Most nations have held in the past to an elite, or "two-track," system of education, in which a few are highly educated but the great majority are educated to a very limited degree. Only recently have these nations begun the process of change toward universal education.

It becomes increasingly obvious that educators can no longer content themselves with a narrow national view of education. In fact, every citizen is faced with a need for knowing more about how other peoples are educated, so that he may understand their way of life and the choices that they tend to make in work and play, in peace and war.

Our own country, the United States, is a nation of immigrants. Our culture is an amalgam of contributions from all over the world. It is vital that we know the sources of our immigrant-created culture pattern. We are engaged in making decisions which will determine our future in relation to the other peoples of the world. These decisions must be based not only upon the values which we ourselves consider important but upon an appreciation of those which people in foreign countries esteem. Study of other cultures on a comparative basis with special emphasis upon the indigenous patterns of education which help to create and maintain those cultures is of the essence in the modern world.

What do we mean by comparative study of education? It is the systematic examination of cultures and in particular their systems of education in order to discover resemblances and differences. This method may be used destructively or constructively. Sneering comparisons have brought conflict in everything from personal to national relations. There is a whole literature of international slurs with regard to language, religion, dress, food. Constructive comparison is quite otherwise. The student or researcher with an especial interest in education sets up a structural outline or morphology which he uses to study each system of education in its culture pattern with regard to its time, space, and people. He may thus view each system of education in its own cultural setting—historical, social, economic, and political. The use of the same morphology for each investigation facilitates constructive comparative study of education in various cultures. It becomes evident that no one has a monopoly upon an intelligent educational system. Each culture pattern has its peculiar problems, which it has attempted to solve in its own way.

The thoughtful student begins to see that much of our advance in living comes from the interchange of diverse cultural elements —i.e., the process of acculturation. Symbols are exchanged or transmitted ranging from Arabic numerals to the processes of printing and the scientific method.

Before we attempt to examine the essential character of the major educational patterns of the world, it would seem wise to examine the basic cultural shifts of the nineteenth and twentieth centuries, which were global in scope and to a greater or smaller extent affected the philosophy and practice of education in all culture areas.

BASIC CULTURAL CHANGES IN THE NINETEENTH CENTURY

The world of the nineteenth century was much more complex intellectually than that of any preceding period. The causes of this complexity may be visualized as follows. The coming of the power age, based upon the steam engine, enabled the Atlantic Community to expand frontiers of settlement into vast areas of new land. The Atlantic Community is defined as including Europe and the new republics on this side of the Atlantic. At the same time that the Russians expanded across the land mass of Asia on interior lines of communication, the other members of the Atlantic Community utilized the sea lanes to found frontiers of settlement on the edges of every continent. The new republics of the Americas pushed frontiers of settlement inland and utilized the sea lanes for cultural contact with the rest of the world. Meanwhile the rapid growth of power-machine mass production in Europe and the United States accelerated the growth of cities and supercities. Accompanying changes in the social structure increased the size and power of the middle classes and accentuated the conflict between labor and capital.

Above all, the rise of huge national powers influenced the intellectual pattern of the period. England and France expanded their colonial possessions and created the symbolisms of modern empires. After a lag in industrial development and national unity, Germany and Italy sought for a place in the sun. The United States and Russia began their race toward the Pacific with their frontiers of settlement backed by a growing industrial framework. The extension of settlement into new land and the growth of metropolitan areas acted as a great stimulus for the growth of national philosophic patterns and national systems of education. A striking illustration of Old World growth is to be seen in the intellectual prominence of German philosophy and in the development in Germany of an elite school system which trained a social pyramid of soldiers and workers with its apex in a few bureaucrats, industrialists, and Army officers.

In contrast to Europe, with its growth of elite national systems of education, the United States engaged in a great cultural experiment in democracy which was supported by a growing system of universal education. It is true that in the Atlantic Community across the water many pioneers, from Condorcet and Pestalozzi to Herbart and Huxley, favored the extension of education universally; but the weight of the crystallized European culture pattern was against them. Their most trenchant and forceful ideas migrated to this side of the Atlantic and were combined with the indigenous proposals of the Americans to produce what is perhaps the United States' most important cultural contribution—universal education.

In the nineteenth century, scientific research made a tremendous impact upon all phases of human life—from geology, chemistry, and physics to biology, anthropology, and the social sciences. It was during this period that intellectual forces began in earnest to wear away the deposit of myth, theological and philosophical, which restrained free inquiry for the truth. The work of Lyell in geology showed the great age of the earth and its life forms. The contributions of Charles Darwin concerning the evolution of life upon this planet were revolutionary. The publication of Darwin's *Origin of Species* in 1859 and *Descent of Man* in 1871 touched off an explosive phase in the warfare between science and theology and aided the growth of the new critical realism.[1]

The great chemists and physicists began to explore the entire realm of matter in detail, both in university and industrial laboratories. The biologists and in particular the microbiologists investigated the microbes and bacteria which can destroy or aid human life. Pasteur and Koch, Bruce and Ross pioneered in the control of "this world of the very little." At the same time astronomers and mathematicians were probing time and space and discovering the vast extent of the universe. Social scientists began to examine everything from primitive communities to highly complex urban agglomerations. These researchers criticized particularly the exploitation of both natural and human resources. They indicated that what man has done man can undo, and they suggested that solution of our critical problems lay in the realm of a broadly conceived process of education, based upon scientific humanism.

In general this period when most nations were ruled by conservative and reactionary governments was characterized also by a very complex intellectual revolt against tradition—a revolt which was expressed in every field from the fine arts to philosophy, from

[1] H. W. Schneider, *A History of American Philosophy* (New York: Columbia University Press, 1946), pp. 346-347.

politics to education. This intellectual revolt assumed two quite different forms, one rationalistic and realistic and the other romantic and idealistic; both attacked a vast range of institutions, beliefs, and social procedures which up to that time had been regarded as impregnable. The revolt of the rationalists passed from its beginning with the philosophers of the French Revolution through the philosophical radicals in England to Comte and the positivists in France. The revolt of the romanticists began with Rousseau and Goethe and moved on through Byron and Schopenhauer to Nietzsche.

The nineteenth century began a trend with which the succeeding century has been dangerously entangled. It was a trend toward a tremendous increase in the sense of human power, both of individuals and groups. This new faith in power included both the power to control nature completely and the power of rulers to control vast numbers of human beings by means of a pattern of education which was really scientific propaganda. The nineteenth century was a formative period, intellectually and educationally speaking, which set in motion the dynamisms of man against the universe and man against himself and posed the problem of a new ethics and a new education—i.e., of a new purpose and a new method of attaining it.

BASIC CULTURAL SHIFTS IN THE TWENTIETH CENTURY

The intellectual world of the twentieth century faced a series of colossal challenges which had emerged in the preceding formative period. Human beings in the first half of the twentieth century could no longer take refuge in valleys, islands, or "Shangri-La's." Time and space were for practical purposes rapidly eliminated by the proliferation and acceleration of channels of communication and means of transportation. In these fifty years the primitive airplane accelerated to aircraft driven by chemical jets or rockets which may at any time become space-free by means of atomic power. The radio and telephone accelerated to fabulous electronic devices which now include automatic linkages of radar, television, and computers which expand the mental horizon of man into the infinite.

The rapid advances of science in the control of the universe may lead either to "scientism" and "mechanization" or to humanization and a new, complete life. The world is beginning to face the fact that human beings live in a symbolic world which they themselves create. The mathematical measurements, the art forms, the methods of instruction, the formulae for control of disease and infection can all be ultimately traced to this symbol-making process. As a distinguished American man of letters, James Branch Cabell, pointed out, "Man alone of animals plays the ape to his dreams." Human beings can actually dream a dream or set up a hypothesis and then bring it into three-dimensional reality by the use of a whole set of symbols. Furthermore, humanity has begun to realize that unless everyone has access through universal education to this rich heritage of human symbols coming out of the past and reaching forward into the future, there will continue to be the wasteful and all-embracing cultural and class conflicts which have destroyed civilizations from within or smashed them from without.[2]

One of the outstanding cultural shifts of the twentieth century has been the growth of ideologies which have cut the world into large compartments. Russia represents one pole of thought, in which a complicated doctrine drawn from Hegel by Marx and revised by Lenin and Stalin decrees the future of millions of people. The intellectual level of peasants, according to this doctrine, can be transformed in a generation by governmental decree implemented by educational processes. A people's pattern of thinking can be completely prescribed and circumscribed. State planning, the uses of secret police, and imperial expansion controlled by dictatorship have been demonstrated in detail by the Russian experiment in the twentieth century.

In contrast, the American experiment has been in the direction of a democratic synthesis of the cultures of the world, within the framework of a federal republic under judicial review and implemented by mass production, individualized universal education, and humanized scientific research. According to the American experiment, there is not one predestined pattern of living but rather a range of choice in which the power of the few and the apathy of the masses of the old elite culture may be eliminated in favor of equal opportunity for everyone—the concept of the common man.

In other words, humanity has come to the crossroads in its self-

[2] Ernst Cassirer, *An Essay on Man* (New Haven: Yale University Press, 1944), pp. 25 and 41.

constructed symbolic world. Some would have us hold to the old myths of the classical or medieval past, to those that were part of the imperialist phase, or to the new and violent myths of Communism or Fascism. Others believe that free human beings may live together in mutual understanding in this rapidly expanding symbolic world in which time and space are conquered, if they think in global terms rather than in narrow ideological compartments and if they are capable of formulating for human relations a modern code of ethics, to be implemented by universal education.

ELITE AND UNIVERSAL SYSTEMS OF EDUCATION

The pattern of education utilized by a nation or culture area is of vital importance, since education is of increasing significance as an instrument in cultural change. Education may be used to build up dictatorships based upon force, fear, and suppression of the individual. It may be utilized to maintain social stratification, sharpen class conflict, and handicap the individual because of his social, religious, racial, or economic background. On the other hand, education may be used to build democracies based upon search for truth, trust in human integrity, and stimulation of the growth of the individual. Education may be used to provide equal opportunity and social mobility by giving full scope to the talent and ability of the individual. In general there are two major types of educational pattern: the elite and the universal.

The elite, or "two-track," system of education has been the characteristic pattern followed in the past. The elite system of centralized control and division into two channels, one for the minority of rulers and the other for the majority of mechanics, farmers, etc., has had a profound influence on many countries throughout the world. The French, Italian, German, Russian, and English systems have been, in the main, variations of this one. An essential characteristic of the system has been the determination of future educational experiences and in fact the lifework and position in society at approximately the eleventh year—that is, at the onset of adolescence. In each of these major European countries a set of examinations (and, of course, the social and economic position of the parents) determined who was to receive secondary and higher education. Another factor has been the heavy emphasis upon the so-called humanities—that is, classical languages and national literature—with only a recent intrusion of the sciences and arts.

The general story of education in Europe has been that of a conflict between two poles of educational thought, conservative and liberal. The conservatives wished to hold on to the old forms and maintain a stable class structure in which only those of wealth or position had much opportunity for education. The elite, or "two-track," system of education was at once a product of a stratified culture pattern and a very efficient instrument for blocking social mobility and preserving a crystallized structure.

The universal, or "one-track," system of education represented the other pole of thought, that of the liberals who believed in the integrity and worth of all individuals and felt that there should be an aristocracy of talent drawn from all backgrounds. Their plan moved in the direction of equal opportunity for all. This is evident in the propaganda and enthusiasm for the *école unique* in France, for the *Einheitsschule* in Germany, for the *scuola unica* in Italy, and for the Education Act of 1944 in England. These ideas were proposed as early as the French Revolution by Condorcet and others in France, but they were not utilized to any degree until the close of the nineteenth century, and it was only in the period following World War I that any real changes were made. The appearance of dictatorships submerged the movement again; it reappeared on the statute books after World War II, but is yet to be fully realized. The Children's Charter of 1944 in England, the Langevin Reform of 1947 in France, and the postwar reforms in Italy are indicative of the recency of the movement toward "one-track" education in Europe. In fact, it is only in the twentieth century that movements toward universal education have taken hold in Europe, Asia, Africa, and South America.

The following section attempts to summarize main currents in educational growth in the major areas of the world and to provide a key to an understanding of the more detailed interpretations of educational patterns in the chapters that follow.

EDUCATION IN THE UNITED STATES

What is the pattern of education in the United States? Have we been able to create an education for a classless society or is our educational system creating conflicting classes? Does the United States represent a conflict between the frontier pattern of the three R's and an integrated educational pattern carried out by professionals?

The structure of education in the United States includes both the formal pattern of the public schools and higher education and the informal pattern of such channels as newspapers, films, museums, and libraries. The public schools operate in a decentralized, regional pattern, with a wide variety and at the same time a basic agreement in their philosophy, curriculum, methods, and administration.

From the beginning Americans have been engaged in an experiment in universal education which they felt was the basis and essence of the democratic way of life. Such men as Jefferson, Franklin, and Washington wished to take advantage of the talents present in all walks of life, which are wasted if not sought out and cultivated. There have been certain major historical determinants in the growth of the present pattern of American education. Above all, American culture and education have been based upon a tension between the westward-moving frontier of the New World and the European culture of the Old World. America has been a nation of immigrants who brought with them their ideas and languages and tools and within two hundred years pushed a frontier of settlement across the continent. Historically speaking, the United States missed almost completely the stage of feudal medievalism and stepped almost directly into the modern period of belief in the worth and integrity of the individual and the right of everyone to "life, liberty, and the pursuit of happiness."

The story of American education may be divided into three major periods: the Dawn Period (1600-1800), the Formative Period (1800-1900), and the Period of Midpassage (1900-   ). In the Dawn Period the technology was based upon muscle, wind, and water power and the pattern of life was, in the main, self-sufficient, rural, and agricultural. The educational pattern became that of the district school and control of education by the local community. The three R's, learned by rote, constituted the curriculum; the family and apprenticeship systems taught all the necessary techniques of survival. The leaders of the Revolution saw the need for universal education if democracy was to survive and if the various immigrant stocks were to be consolidated. Education was not mentioned in the Constitution, however. Its control was left to state and local authority.

It was only in the Formative Period of the nineteenth century that the pattern of universal education was outlined and implemented. A technology of coal and steam power rapidly changed the country in the direction of industrial cities and an expanding network of transportation and communication superimposed upon the rural areas. The farmers of the frontier which raced to the Pacific in this period and the workers of the cities had little patience with a "two-track" system supporting and perpetuating classes. By the close of the century, together with professional and government leaders they had fought and won the battle for universal education, including public tax support of elementary, secondary, and higher education, separation of church and state, and improvement of curriculum, methods of instruction, and teacher-training programs. By the end of the Formative Period the American schools had a "one-track" system of education which included the eight-year elementary school, the four-year high school, and the four-year college.

The Period of Midpassage which followed the turn of the century was characterized by new power technology and brought about a further extension of universal education in the United States and improvement of its structure and procedures. By World War I the system was changing to 6-3-3-4, or a six-year elementary school, a three-year junior high school, a three-year high school, and a four-year college; this provided a better relationship between childhood and the elementary school and the onset of adolescence and the secondary school. Furthermore, the state and private universities had expanded in their capacity for research and were able to accommodate increasing numbers of students from all walks of life. The curriculum moved in the direction of youth's needs and interests and also provided preparation for vocations and for citizenship in a democratic society. A general or comprehensive curriculum was extended upward from the elementary school through the secondary school to the college.

What was the pattern of education as it operated in the American culture in the middle of the twentieth century? Over 150 million Americans lived in a continental area in the central part of North America. They constituted about one fifteenth of the world population and possessed about one fifteenth of its natural resources in a well-balanced pattern. The United States produced approximately one third of the world's goods from its powerful technology of production, distribution, transportation, and communication, which was based upon well-organized scientific research. The educational system was concerned with some 30 million individuals enrolled as follows: approximately 21 million in elementary schools, 7 million in high schools, and 2 million in universities and colleges. The system of public education in the United States was decentralized and basically organized into forty-eight state school systems. There was no central ministry of education exercising direct control over the forty-eight state systems. The federal authority in the U. S. Office of Education was confined to research and advisory functions except for direct control of schools in territories under federal jurisdiction. The state school systems derived their authority from the state legislatures and operated in quasi corporations called school districts.

This "school state," or independent school system, which has grown out of the little red schoolhouse of the frontier and the American condition of local control of education, has sometimes been called the fourth dimension of government. Local taxation has furnished the major support of education, with most of the burden falling upon real property. This has made for an uneven distribution of financial support. The programs of the schools ranged from a relatively narrow type of instruction in the poorer areas to the enriched and broad programs of the wealthier areas. Teacher preparation and salaries were directly related to the size and financial support of the school district. The public-school plant included some 200,000 school buildings.

Analysts of the American educational scene have raised certain major criticisms. They feel that education may not provide sufficient social mobility, with careers open to all. These critics also are concerned by the cultural lag of the content of the curriculum in relation to the demands of everyday life. There is probably not enough emphasis upon basic health, social relationships, recreational choices, and career planning and too much emphasis upon certain subject matter traditionally taught or required by colleges that train for the professions. It is also possible that the emphasis upon a general education creates a "cult of the average," which makes everyone con-form to an average pattern and provides insufficiently for gifted individuals and for those with greater than average interest in intellectual pursuits. The school schedule and routine may be too much a reflection of mass-production methods, of too many students in one building, of overorganized administrative chain of command, of insufficient opportunity for individual variation and insufficient preparation for the world outside the school walls.

These criticisms do not mean that the United States has failed in universal education but rather that it is keenly alive to the unending challenge which must be faced if the country's record of educational pioneering is to continue. Despite the criticisms, there is a very real pride in public education in the United States. The great majority of educators and lay citizens appreciate how much has been accom-plished. The United States does possess a universal educational system extending from the kindergarten through the university. It is a powerful structure which thus far has generally maintained its freedom from corrupt politics and from pressure-group control, whether it be religious, governmental, or economic. The majority of American children complete high school, in which they partici-pate in essentially the same comprehensive course of general educa-tion. Approximately one third of the age group eligible for higher education receives training in the colleges, universities, and allied institutions of higher education. The informal pattern of education, which includes libraries, museums, art galleries, and to a smaller extent the press, radio, and television, is definitely connected with the formal pattern of the schools and colleges. Educators have played a direct role in all these fields. In fact, more and more pro-fessionals in the area of media of mass communication are being trained in the institutions of higher education. Education in the United States has become all-pervading and performs a primary function in the advance of the American democracy.

EDUCATION IN MEXICO

The culture and education of Mexico are resultants of four phases in Mexican growth: the Indian base, the Spanish Conquest, the revolution for independence, and the Revolution of 1910 for economic, educational, and political democracy.

The old Indian culture was rural and self-sufficient. The Indians moved with an easy tempo as they made their own clothing and houses and raised their own food.

Into the Indian way of life came the Spaniard with his medieval way of life. Knights on horseback and priests ruled the workers on the land. The Spaniards brought with them draft animals, such as the horse and the ox, and the institutions of the large hacienda (or landed estate), the mission, and the presidio (or military fort).

The nineteenth century brought the impact of the American and European revolutions. A succession of Mexicans fought for their own freedom against native and foreign dictatorship. Figures such as Zapata moved through the country with the war cry "Land for the landless." At the end of the period an uneasy peace was instituted by Díaz, whose despotism led observers to coin the phrase "Diazpotism." The country's transport, industry, oil, minerals, cities, and ports were developed with foreign capital.

The ferment and conflict finally led to the Revolution of 1910, in which Mexicans resumed control of their own country, eliminating foreign financial, religious, and political control. This new democracy was strongly supported by a movement toward universal education in the federal elementary schools. Actually in 1910 there began a series of continuing revolutions with regard to the agrarian problem, industrialization, separation of church and state, and education. Mexico's problems centered in the people on the land. At least fifty-four different Indian languages persisted nearly four centuries after the Conquest. Mexico represented a tremendous mixture of race, language, and culture. The Mexicans were a complex people, neither Spanish nor Indian but a new race with a new culture. They were, in the main, rooted to the land as an agricultural people. Mexico was a country with limited resources in both minerals and agriculture and a seriously inadequate water supply. The fundamental problem was to improve rural life.

The revolutionary movements of a Juárez and a Zapata did not meet these problems. They had to be met by the people as a whole through an educational process, and the Revolution of 1910 had as a war cry *"Educar es redimir"* ("to educate is to redeem"). Following 1920 the elementary schools entered upon a period of rapid growth; 80 percent of these schools were rural and 70 percent of these were federal. However, there was great variety in the curriculums, since they had to be adapted to the particular needs of the regional environment. Secondary education began at the end of the sixth year of the elementary program. The five years of the secondary program were organized as follows: the first three were general and the last two were divided into specialized vocational and preprofessional schools, really the lower college of the university. Whereas the elementary schools reached large numbers of the children of school age, the secondary schools reached only a small segment of the population. Mexico illustrates the major phases in Latin American development and the expanding role of education as an instrument in cultural change.

EDUCATION IN ENGLAND

The British have demonstrated a great deal of adaptability in their history, changing as they have from a feudal agricultural country to a heavily industrialized welfare state and shifting from the point of view of a colonial empire to that of a commonwealth of independent and cooperative nations. The British have referred to this adaptability as a process of "muddling through" which conserved certain values out of the past, such as constitutional monarchy and local autonomy, and at the same time permitted new solutions for social problems, such as the trade unions. It was characteristic that the English retained the old social classes and ways of doing things and also permitted the bold experimentation of a labor government that assumed responsibility for social medicine and nationalization of industry.

The British educational system has changed relatively slowly and, in fact, has demonstrated considerable cultural lag. Until recently the British have shown marked resistance to change in education despite the criticisms and pressures exerted by their educational pioneers. Until World War II Great Britain had an elite, or "two-track," system of education which produced a limited number of competent leaders and professionals but provided little opportunity for the mass of children to go beyond the elementary school, with the result that a great deal of youthful talent was, so to speak, plowed under. In the nineteenth century Great Britain changed rapidly from an island of farmers and seafarers to a densely populated, heavily industrialized world center, but there was no corresponding advance in education. Britain's leaders in war and peace were trained by the great "public schools," which were privately controlled and financed and attended by children from families of wealth and position. Despite the agitation of scientists such as Huxley and statesmen such as Disraeli and Brougham, the mass of young people were educated as "cipherers" and "scribblers," if at all. Statutes were passed favoring the extension of public education, but they were not implemented; in fact, England could not be described as having a definite educational system, such was the diversity of church-supported schools, private foundations, schools with some public support, etc.

Until the Education Act of 1944 and its successive extensions, England educated a minority of children, almost exclusively from the upper classes, to go on to secondary schools and higher education. The majority of the children attended elementary school, receiving a limited amount of training from the ages of eleven and a half to fourteen in a senior division of the elementary school. Only 15 percent, as a result of competitive examinations and inability to pay tuition costs, passed over into secondary schools.

The Education Act of 1944 broke completely with this tradition of permitting only an elite to go to secondary school and the university. The school-leaving age was raised by 1947 to fifteen years and all children were to attend some type of secondary school between the ages of eleven and fifteen. All these secondary schools were to have social equality, whether their program was academic, vocational, technical, or general. The intent was to give opportunity wherever there was ability.

The Education Act of 1944 was in effect a Children's Charter which provided not only for the three R's but for attention to the three A's, defined as age, aptitude, and ability. According to the Act, general primary schools were to furnish education for children from five to eleven years of age. At eleven, instead of the old, grueling Special Place Examination, with about 15 percent surviving to enter secondary schools, a new approach was required. The Special Place Examinations were to be eliminated and children were to pass on to secondary schools with curriculums better adjusted to their needs. The British tended to separate the secondary educational pattern into four major types of specialization. One was the grammar school linked to preparation for college, for those who wished to emphasize the training of the mind. Another type was the technical school, for those who wished to go on to industry, commerce, or business. A third type was the agricultural school, designed primarily for those who liked the land and farming. The fourth was a general type of school for the great majority, offering a curriculum which combined training for family life, work, and social relations. The change has been gradual, with continuance of the private types of school, local independence for educational authorities, and, in general, freedom from official direction for teachers. There has also been pressure in the direction of extending higher educational facilities by continuation of education in regional colleges and by increased scholarships for able individuals wishing to attend the university. The British have also developed an excellent network of informal education ranging from the radio programs of the British Broadcasting Corporation to various types of adult education.

EDUCATION IN THE BRITISH COMMONWEALTH AND COLONIES

When British colonists settled in new lands they brought with them the educational system that then existed in the British Isles. It should be remembered that the pattern of education in Scotland differed from that of England in that it had a parish school which provided both elementary and secondary education. In contrast, the English tended to make a very sharp separation between elementary and secondary education. The environment and historical development of the British colonies which later became dominions had varied effects upon education. Canada was colonized by French and English, South Africa by Dutch and English, Australia by English and Irish, and New Zealand by English and Scottish settlers. The educational variations in these commonwealths should be carefully studied.

The general educational policy of the British and their colonial dependencies has differed greatly from that of the Dutch and French. The Dutch favored two separate education systems in their colonies, one for the Europeans and another for the natives. They did not attempt to superimpose their culture upon native society. At the same time, they permitted mobility to the natives and considered as European all persons of mixed blood and natives living as Europeans. The French have regarded their native subjects as potential French citizens. They have not been sympathetic to native aspirations for independence. The educational system was set up to make the natives into Frenchmen and citizens of the Republic.

In the past Great Britain did seek to superimpose European government and education upon the natives. The educational system was a reflection of the system existing in England at the time. For example, Macaulay and others transplanted the English elite system with its classical emphasis to India. The objectives were to spread education as widely as possible among the native peoples of the colonies so as to provide for social progress. At the same time the British policy was to train as many natives as possible for government service, the professions, and business and labor leadership. Great emphasis was placed upon strengthening cultural and other links between Western civilizations and the dependent territories. The British emphasis has been in the direction of persuading the natives that European methods are superior to those of the native culture.

Under the pressures of native aspirations for national independence, the British colonial educational policy has changed in recent years. In the colonies there has been the same gradual transition from privately supported schools, both church and secular, to publicly supported schools. The curriculums have changed in the direction of utilitarian training to meet the actual needs of the natives. Legal school-attendance standards are far from being implemented by financial support and enforcement. Increasing emphasis has been placed upon the mass education of adults not only in literacy but in better farming methods, sanitation, and hygiene. The neglect of technical education has created a serious problem and it has only recently been attacked. The tremendous variation in native languages has presented serious difficulties. In general the British have favored the use of English as the basic language of commerce, science, and industry in their colonies.

EDUCATION IN FRANCE

The educational system of France has been of vital significance not only because of its own changes in pattern but also because of its world-wide influence. France was one of the first unified nations in Europe. France tended to be a leader in educational thought and experimentation but was among the slowest to adopt many of the new findings in her own educational system. Certain historical determinants brought about this contradiction. From the beginning, ecclesiastical thought had great control. Scholasticism and a desire for pure knowledge via the Aristotelian method was of the first importance. The French concentrated upon skill in speech and discussion—*l'art de persuader*. Subject matter also became important as a thing in itself. The regulations of the Ministry of Education left no detail untouched, from courses and hours to texts and detailed inventories of materials of instruction, including the last pen point.

French lay thinkers have challenged this conservatism from the Renaissance through the modern period. Montaigne and others protested against the artificiality of French education and as humanists emphasized the worth of the individual and called for the humanization of curriculum and instruction. In the Revolutionary period the French contributed many of our modern educational ideas. The Encyclopedists brought in new and accurate data that could be read and used by all. Rousseau saw the child as a growing individual rather than a miniature adult and understood the values of direct contact with nature and reality. Condorcet drew a blueprint for French education which began to be realized only 150 years later. However, the influence of Napoleon and the church blocked educational reforms and moved toward a tremendous centralization of educational control. This centralized and conservative education, with its rigid intellectualism and classicism, had a world-wide influence.

At the end of the nineteenth century and the beginning of the twentieth century, the French became more and more conscious of the shortcomings of a centralized, rigid "two-track" educational system. The few received a highly intellectual advanced education, whereas the masses were severely restricted and did not necessarily get a balanced education even in the time which they were permitted. The agitation and propaganda for the unified school, or *école unique*, increased. The idea was to organize a single educational "ladder" system whereby elementary education would be basic to all training for all the people. Separate elementary schools preparing for secondary schools and universities were to be discouraged. The new plans came to the fore after World War I and especially in the Langevin Reform after World War II.

The French educational system has certainly produced many distinguished and competent individuals and has been a model for many other countries. What, then, were the criticisms which have forced the French to move more rapidly in the direction of universal education? French schools were solidly grounded in philosophy, literature, and intellectualism and produced brilliance in those fields; but schools have other obligations involving the total life of the individual and the nation. French education did not provide for experience with the handicrafts and practical arts. The high level of French production was maintained only through the apprenticeship system. Furthermore, a great vacuum existed in the training of French youth for civic responsibilty. There was a strong tendency toward hereditary transmission of professional activities, including participation in politics. France's leaders did not represent or speak for the rank and file of the people. The schools did not provide for citizenship training for the middle and lower classes in town and country. Few sons of French workers or farmers thought in terms of political participation because they were not born in the right surroundings.

The Langevin Reform moved in the direction of meeting these weaknesses, insisting that "educational justice" required that all children be entitled to a maximum development of their personalities through general education with broad cultural emphasis. The school was to become a center for the dissemination of general culture, with the curriculum to be modified by the needs of the individual locality. This meant that the various levels of education would follow a single unified plan, that more children were to go on to secondary education, and that all children were to receive a common background in communication, social problems, citizenship, and vocational training. It meant also that all education must be free, with every student considered a potentially productive member of society. The French were accompanying their democratic point of view with the essential mechanism of universal education.

EDUCATION IN ITALY

The long Italian peninsula thrusting southward into the sunlit Mediterranean has been a land and sea corridor for a series of phases of acculturation, or contact and exchange of cultures. A major role has been played by the classical Greek and Roman culture, to which the Greeks contributed the tradition of individualistic city-state control, later repeated in the Renaissance flowering of the cities, and the Romans contributed the imperial tradition, later repeated by the Fascists. The situation has been complicated by Italy's central role in the development of the Catholic church as a world power, by the Moslem drive from the south, by the conflict with German imperial ambitions, and, more recently, by the liberal, democratic tendencies coming out of the revolutionary nineteenth century.

Culturally speaking, Italy is an amalgam, then, of the classical, of the feudal Middle Ages with Moslem intrusions, of the Renaissance fragmentation into city-states, and of a very late start toward industrialization and world influence. The total result has been the building up of a rich and significant literature, art, science, and industry, a great heritage of the remote and immediate past. However, the recent story of Italy has been that of land and forest exhaustion, of overpopulation, of great migrations to the New World, and of very costly wars to gain international prestige. Furthermore, great regional differences have been built up. The north is urban, relatively heavily industrialized, and relatively well educated. The south is poverty-stricken, heavily overpopulated, agricultural with an antiquated land system, and ill-educated.

The educational pattern of Italy has been that of a "two-track" system; this is quite understandable in a land traditionally divided into lords, peasants, and workers. Balancing this trend has been the series of drives for school reform. In the main, advance toward universal education began in the second half of the nineteenth century with the rise of Italy as a unified national power, but real progress did not occur until after World War I. The centralization principle was adopted early, in the Casati Law of 1859, which organized the school system along the same lines as that of France. The church was excluded, in principle, from educational control, but religious instruction was preserved in the schools. The administration of elementary schools, first delegated to the *commune,* (the smallest administrative district), was taken away in 1911 because of mismanagement and given to the provinces. The basic problem was lack of money; the allocation for education never exceeded 5 percent of the total budget, and the bulk of the funds went to institutions of higher education. The collapse and depression following World War I accentuated this economic problem, as did the high birth rate. Above all, the general curriculum was derived from the classical past and was little related to life needs and daily problems.

The Fascists did not find a well-organized school system awaiting them. They installed Gentile as Minister of Education. He made great progress in liberalizing elementary education, but he continued to keep secondary and higher education as the aristocratic preserve of the chosen few. After a few years the Fascists discharged him and increased central ideological control with the slogan "Believe, obey, fight." They installed the Bottai Reform of 1939, which was never put into full effect but which did emphasize some of the ideals of the *scuola unica*, or universal school, in the elementary field. It also created the middle schools, which helped postpone occupational decisions from age eleven to age fourteen. Nevertheless, further education was still reserved for the few and a distinctly military and Fascist curriculum was emphasized. Fascism never went more than skin deep in educational reform and did not attack the real problems which result from an age-long gap between Italy's fine aspirations and her physical capacity to fulfill them.

Despite the substitution of a democratic philosophy for Fascism, the primary problems of low income, overpopulation, and need for basic reform of the curriculum and methods of teaching have still not been faced. The elementary school is inadequate, consisting of only the first four grades. Vast numbers never finish and a great majority never advance beyond it. The curriculum is still authoritarian and little related to basic needs with regard to work, home life, and literacy. An intense campaign is needed to put all of Italy's children in schools. Vocational, technical, and agricultural work must be made as respectable as that of the classical variety. The secondary area must be liberalized in the direction of functional courses and better articulated with elementary and higher education. Higher education must train more teachers, social scientists, physicians, and dentists and fewer classicists and academic humanists. Above all, the schools must be organized together with media of mass communication to combat the illiteracy and belief in myth and magic characteristic of the backward areas. None of this can be done without improvement of tax collection and provision of a better financial base for the schools. Both these reforms rest upon general improvement of the national economy.

EDUCATION IN GERMANY

The study of education in Germany provides an example of the conflict between force and freedom and also of the impact of technology upon an educational system. Furthermore, German educational pioneers, although often unrecognized at home, had a dynamic influence upon the general progress of world education.

The major shifts in ways of living during the nineteenth and twentieth centuries were accentuated and magnified in Germany. Above all, the conflict between force and freedom in human affairs was very clear-cut in Germany and was reflected in a series of educational changes. During the nineteenth century the German drive for the freedom of the individual flared in the revolutions of 1830 and 1848 and then was suppressed. Force won out, symbolized by the "blood and iron" policy of Bismarck in Prussia. In the twentieth century a new drive for freedom was made by the Weimar Republic and was wrecked by another dictatorship of force, that of the Nazis.

In addition, the Germans made the shift from an agricultural, feudal way of life to that of a highly industrialized and centrally controlled monarchy or dictatorship. Behind all this social change, and permeated by it, was the educational pattern. Germany's liberals and pioneer thinkers tried many times to bring about a system of universal education which would open opportunities to all in terms of their ability. Such men as Froebel, founder of the kindergarten movement, and Herbart, who advocated the reorganization of curriculum and method, were honored abroad sooner than in their own country.

The German educational system was molded into a "two-track" system. A few were trained as rulers, officers, professors, and manufacturing and business leaders in a system of advanced education. The masses were trained to be good farmers, workers, and soldiers in a separate system extending as far as the twelfth year and supplemented beyond that by special vocational-training schools.

The coming of mass production in Germany was not accompanied by the growth of a system of universal education, as it was in the United States. Instead the class lines were drawn even more firmly with the addition of a new and powerful group, the leaders of industrial cartels, to the older ones of the nobility, the army, and the church. The Germans provided a revealing example of human fragmentation into classes and groups—a fragmentation that was facilitated by a "two-track" educational system.

The short-lived Weimar Republic attempted to set up a universal system of education (*Einheitsschule*) and did improve structure, curriculum, and method. But the pressures of the past were too strong and the Nazi party reinstituted an elite education for its own destructive ends. The Nazi suppression of human freedom and the war's destruction have further handicapped the Germans' capabilities for universal education.

EDUCATION IN THE SOVIET UNION

The Soviet Union is strategically situated in the center or Heartland of the major land mass, Eurasia. Its area equals one sixth of the land surface of the world and its population amounts to approximately one eighth of the world's total population. In a few generations this area has been changed from an overwhelmingly agricultural peasant land to an increasingly industrialized and urban civilization. The Soviet Union is the world center of Communism as a militant ideology of social, economic, political, and religious change.

Many features of the Communist dictatorship are not new to Russia. Historical determinants, the far from dead hand of the past, have merely been linked to a new authoritarianism. The historical determinants are very old and very deep in Russia. The drive of the Slav peasant for freedom was suppressed from the time of the foundations of Russia. The connections with the Byzantine Empire contributed a fundamental base in religion, art, culture, and pattern of autocratic rule. The Mongol invasion of the thirteenth century added to the Oriental influence already exerted by Byzantine culture. A resultant was the rise of the dukes of Moscow to drive back the Mongols and to lay the foundations for the Russian czardom. The czars were not only dictators but imperialists; they expanded in every direction toward warm-water ports on the Baltic and Mediterranean and, above all, the Indian and Pacific oceans— that is, toward the outer edge of the strategic rim of Eurasia. Autocracy and imperialism have been the distinguishing characteristics of the Soviet dictatorship at home and the Cominform abroad.

The primary philosophy has been an interpretation of Marxism. It is a cosmic jest that the teachings of Karl Marx, a German Jew who despised the Russians, contributed the pattern of their present ideology. These basic ideas were formulated by Marx around a metaphysics in which matter, not spirit, is basic. More precisely for Marx, man's relationship to matter and especially his mode of production or economics is the driving force. The Marxist believes that the broad outline of any period in human history—its politics, philosophy, and art—is an outcome ultimately of its methods of production; this doctrine is referred to by Marxists as the "materialist conception of history." Marx believed that class warfare was inevitable and would bring about the dictatorship of the proletariat, or working class. He thought that he was making socialism scientific; actually he was merely expressing a reaction that was natural to a middle-class German Jew rebelling against certain aspects of the nineteenth century.

In Russia a very complex series of political phases in which Lenin and Stalin played leading roles led to a dictatorship of the Communist party, whose rule was based upon military and police power and supported by propaganda and educational controls. The Five-year Plans changed Russia from a nation of peasants to a modern industrial power with regional nuclei of production in central and southern Russia, the Urals, and the Amur region. At the same time the mechanisms of propaganda and education recast Russian habits of thought from the cradle to the grave. In addition, the Russian Communists set up nuclei throughout the world, rigidly disciplined and adhering strictly to the party line. From the Heartland of Russia, central Asia, and Siberia, the Russian Communists moved tenaciously outward to control the strategic rim of Eurasia and the world beyond. The Soviet state is a modern form of the ancient Asiatic "god-king" idea. The Byzantine emperor, the Muscovite duke, the Russian czar, and the Generalissimo of the U.S.S.R. were all forms of the "god-king" approach, which brought with it enslavement of the individual and the plunder of surrounding territories.

The Soviet system of education has been a part of the great propaganda machine, the media of mass communication, utilized by the relatively small Communist party to control and direct the great masses of Russians. In general the Russians have set up an elite system of education, although they claim to have organized a universal system. Their elementary schools of four grades have constituted a primary step toward universal education, but the secondary school, which begins at the eleventh year, is in general limited to towns and cities and consists of only an additional three years. In other words, separation into a "two-track" system still exists and begins about the eleventh chronological year. Furthermore, an increasing tendency toward segregation of the sexes in the secondary field, probably directly related to the needs of military training, has been noted. The existing situation with respect to education in the secondary schools, the technical schools, and the universities indicates merely that the Communist party elite has replaced the old czar's elite.

Heaviest emphasis has been upon the Russian language and upon mathematics and political indoctrination. The secondary schools moved rapidly in the direction of specialization and training in technical subjects. Above all, the curriculum is to a large degree controlled by the party line and indoctrination in the Stalinist interpretation of Marxism. In the early phases of the revolution, there was considerable liberalism in the curriculum and an attempt was made to experiment, but this was generally condemned as deviationist. The experimental liberal approaches, some of which came from America, were eliminated with the coming of Stalin. The methods changed in the direction of a very stiff discipline and a reiterated secular worship of Stalin as the Russian leader. In addition the textbooks and reference materials on all levels of education were continually reviewed and rewritten according to the party line. Perhaps the most significant example of this was the relatively recent Lysenko case, which eliminated all the carefully collected modern experimental data on genetics and heredity, to which Russians had made large contributions, and in their place put Lysenko's party-line doctrine of environmental factors as primary. The Soviet Union provides a vital lesson in the interrelationship of culture and education in a crucial geographical location, the crossroads of Europe and Asia. The Russians have demonstrated the very great effectiveness of a modernized system of elite education in building and maintaining an aggressive dictatorship. They have not yet tried the universal system, which requires respect for the truth and for the integrity of the individual.

EDUCATION IN AFRICA

The emphasis in our analysis will be placed upon problems and progress in the education of native peoples of all parts of Africa except Egypt and South Africa. Certain primary factors in the situation should be noted. The African native peoples present a tremendous range in physical appearance, language, and cultural patterns, a fact which has resulted in major conflicts and problems. The Zulus of the south, the Bantu peoples of the center, and the Sudanese toward the north, together with smaller tribal groups, have until the present engaged in a succession of intertribal wars. This situation was complicated by the slave trade, which was directed by the Arabs and supported by tribal chiefs for their own gain. There were some four hundred oral languages with no writing in French West and Equatorial Africa alone. In general the societies were tribal and pastoral and centered in village life. They had a primitive type of education which was adjusted to primitive needs and carried on by the family and the tribe.

During the nineteenth and the twentieth centuries the Western industrial and technological culture made a series of increasingly forceful intrusions into this already complicated cultural complex. At first the pattern was one of colonial exploitation with a tendency to educate a few scribblers and cipherers for use in a native bureaucracy, but of recent years the trend has been in the direction of saner and more humane views of progress and an appreciation of the tremendous problems of native peoples. The new approach was based upon an understanding of the difficulties of life in a tropical climate, such as the high incidence of malaria and other diseases; upon acceptance of such fundamental scientific truths as the equality of ability in all races; and upon recognition of the necessity for extension of universal education.

There were some difficult choices to be made in major policy. With regard to language, the choice was between using a European language as the medium of instruction in the elementary schools and reducing selected native languages to written form and using them in the schools. Increased ease of cultural contact and avoidance of enormous labor and expense favored the first choice. Psychologists offered some evidence indicating that elementary education carried on in a European language contributed to the tangles of verbalism separating pupils from the tribal background and that the native languages were thus the preferable choice. Furthermore, there was increasing emphasis upon education related to local needs in agriculture, herding, health, and family life. This included a heavy emphasis upon adult education, so that the present population might benefit by new ideas in production and health. The work in Africa of such men as Frank Laubach in literacy and Emory Alvord in agricultural education is an example of this trend and was certainly of enormous importance, since the African population was 95 percent illiterate. The impact of industrial technology accentuated the need for extending compulsory education and articulating the entire ladder of education. The movement of native families into concentrations in mining or other industrial areas broke up the traditional family and tribal setting. This led to the neglect of children and moral degeneration, together with a breakdown of adult society. Education in Africa has become a matter of primary concern, since it constitutes an extensive and major experiment in acculturation.

EDUCATION IN ARAB COUNTRIES OF THE NEAR EAST AND IN TURKEY

The Near East has always been a great land bridge between the West and the East for movements of population, ideas, symbols, religions, and technologies. No informed person can afford to overlook its present significance, which is closely linked with the relationship among education, technology, and culture pattern. Furthermore, this is the world of Islam, which is not only a religion but a culture that must be understood in terms of its own history. Two of the major groups of this area are the Arabs and the Turks. Their educational situations are quite different. Since 1928 the Turks have moved rapidly toward a system of universal education. The Arabs are just now beginning their advance toward universal education and away from an elite system.

In general both these groups are concerned with the great change going forward in Asia today: an awakening to Asia's own enormous possibilities and problems, a revolt against the West's penetration and, at the same time, against the sordid conditions of Asiatic life that have existed for centuries.

In the Arab areas of the Near East there are certain major determinants that should be mentioned. The Arab areas are located strategically at the crossroads of three continents and have always been a battleground. Today the new discovery of vast mineral wealth accentuates this historical trend. A nationalism which began to rise in World War I has been further stimulated by the violent birth of the new state of Israel. Perhaps the most critical factor affecting education is the very low standard of living and the backward agricultural economy upon which it is based. Absentee landownership together with high birth rate and incidence of disease handicap any move toward improvement of education. The lack of an industrial base and intelligent taxation further complicates the situation. In every other country there has been a middle class of substantial size and force which has been a dominant influence toward universal education; here there is no real middle class. (By middle class we mean skilled workers, professional people of all types, businessmen, independent farmers.) Above all, the Near East is the birthplace of the world's three great monotheistic religions: Judaism, Christianity, and Islam. Islam is the dominant and official religion in all the areas except Lebanon, which has a majority of Christians. Islam is a way of life, a culture in which the Koran and its teachings order everyone's daily life, including the profession of faith in no God but Allah, prayer toward Mecca five times daily, the giving of alms, fasting, and pilgrimage to Mecca.

The Near East stands between the old culture and the Western influences which media of mass communication, transportation, and foreign industry have injected into the cultural stream. Education in this area is an amalgam of the Islamic base with an importation of a wide variety of Western curriculums and methods, of "two-track" education from France, and, to a smaller extent, of "one-track" education from the United States.

Arabic has two channels of language: the spoken colloquial and the written classical, which is based upon the Koran. Officially elementary education is compulsory. Actually compulsory education is only partly effective, because of lack of appropriation of sufficient money and inability of peasants to take advantage of what facilities exist. In addition, the large proportion of illiterate adults constitutes a major problem and is being attacked by a program of adult education.

Another key problem is curriculum revision. The teaching of the three R's based upon memorization of the Koran was not sufficient to meet the real needs of the school population and the nation. The schools have not yet made real moves in the direction of curriculums based upon pupils' local and national needs. In fact, the schools are often separated from the community. In contrast, in Egypt, in Lebanon, and in Iraq, a drive has been made for new types of rural elementary schools dealing with the handicrafts, farming, health and sanitation, and the needs of the home. It should be realized that both the indigenous educational tradition and the imported elite influence emphasized education for a few and that education was on an academic, classical level, for those intending to enter the professions or the bureaucracy. Education related to agriculture, labor, and the daily needs of the masses was frowned upon; a stigma was attached to work with the hands. In addition, only recently have girls and women begun to be free of restrictions which treated them as inferior beings. The attitude has changed, but it has still not been implemented in the Arab areas. The teacher-training situation is very bad, and the status of the teacher tends to be quite low.

In contrast to the Arab areas, Turkey carried out a tremendous drive for the improvement of education following 1928. The Turks live in the strategic central plateau of Anatolia. It is mainly agricultural, its great mineral resources and its industrial potentialities being as yet undeveloped. In contrast to the Arabs with their Semitic strains, the Turks are in the main allied with the early Hittite amalgam. The great figure in Turkish educational change was Kemal Atatürk. He is considered the savior who not only preserved the nation as a revolutionary leader and served as president of the republic but gave the Turks democracy and education. The basic philosophy today is scientific realism in a republican state in which the citizen is of primary importance. Education is regarded as a major instrument in the hands of citizens for implementing this philosophy. A system of education was instituted with central control in the hands of a Minister of Instruction; the scope of the system has been steadily extended.

EDUCATION IN THE FAR EAST

Certain basic determinants should be borne in mind when one visualizes the relationship of education and the culture pattern in the Far East. The Far East is defined as including India, southeast Asia, China, and Japan. More than half the world's population lives in the Far East, including more than a half billion Chinese and Japanese and a half billion Indians and Indonesians. They live southeast of the line drawn from the Indus River to the Amur River in the valleys and the mountain ranges radiating outward from the mountain-hearted continent of Asia. Some 2.5 acres of arable land are necessary for the adequate support of one human being in terms of food, shelter, etc. The Far East in the main has less than one acre of arable land per person. The introduction of modern health and sanitation together with opposition to birth control have created a serious overpopulation problem which will not be solved by famine, immigration, or wars of conquest.

Another major determinant has been the indigenous religious point of view concerning the "god-king," which, despite many protestations about basic democracy in the Indian village or the Chinese village, tends to reappear in new forms. The "god-king" idea in brief is that the ruler, by a variety of types of magic, is transformed into a god. The Hindu version of the idea utilized the Brahman ritual, the Chinese the "son of heaven" approach, and the Japanese the "descendant of the sun goddess" approach. The Communists have adapted this old idea and implemented it with modern propaganda. A colonial type of contact with western Europe has had some questionable results for both participants and has caused a very definite irritation on the part of Asiatics toward European political control. Last and by no means least has been the contact of the Far East with the technology and education of the West, leading to a relatively delayed industrial revolution and interest in universal education.

The three major culture areas of the Far East analyzed in *Comparative Education* are India, China, and Japan. Each of these presents an illuminating and basic variation in the over-all problem of understanding education as an instrument in cultural change.

India. The story of education and culture in India has been one of successive intrusion and synthesis. The first great phase was the coming of the Indo-European warriors and herdsmen from the grass plains of the north into the fertile warm valleys of India and the driving of the darker-skinned Dravidian natives south of the Satpura line. From the beginning an elite system of education evolved. The caste system was organized in such a way that the highest caste, the Brahmans, had a monopoly upon knowledge and learning, together with religious control on the basis of the "god-king" idea. There was a series of attempts to break this educational and religious monopoly. Buddhism, with its doctrine of the "middleway," was one of these attempts, but it became crystallized into a whole new set of idols and rituals and an elite monastic education. The intrusion of the Mohammedans brought a new culture, a new language, and insistence upon individual freedom and a casteless society, but it too failed to bring any basic trend toward universal education.

The English intrusion of the eighteenth and nineteenth centuries merely brought an elite classical literary education from Europe and tended to produce the educated native bureaucrat, or *babu*. Indian nationalism brought with it an increasing emphasis upon universal education but met with many obstacles. Chief among them were poverty, rapid population increase, at least three major native languages, and a tendency to seek refuge in the old village agricultural system. The problem is a difficult one. Universal education in terms of the Indian population's production, health, political, and other needs is essential but is dependent upon an improved economic base, which the country's poverty blocks to a major degree. The hand of the past in terms of religious tradition and intellectualism as against science and utility of training also constitutes a major difficulty. Yet the human and cultural resources are present and what is done about education will determine whether they are wasted or constructively employed.

China. The great cultural area of China with its some 463 million population, which is chiefly agricultural, has been moving in the direction of a great economic, political, and educational revolution. The educational story can be divided into two major phases: before and after 1911.

Before 1911 China's educational history was that of an elite "two-track" system controlled by the "god-king" idea and administered by a mandarin elite trained primarily upon a classical literary base. China has been a nation of villages and some large administrative and cultural centers living on a very narrow margin between famine and bare existence. The trend toward overpopulation; the presence of some six major languages with one common written language, Mandarin, consisting of a multitude of difficult ideographs rather than a simple alphabet; and a delayed development of industrial technology have all constituted major problems.

With the Revolution of 1911 the Chinese moved in the direction of democratic government and universal education under the leadership of Sun Yat-sen. This was a complex and difficult change undertaken against the tradition of thousands of years and against the growth of war lords who controlled separate regions in a medieval atmosphere, wasting natural and human resources. The school system was reorganized in harmony with the new ideals of the Chinese Republic; in general the major features of the American school system were adopted. China followed the American example when the United States began to shift toward the 6-3-3-4 system of school organization, providing for a six-year elementary school, a three-year junior middle school, a three-year senior middle school, and a four-year college and university. Normal schools and vocational schools of different grades paralleled these middle schools. With slight modification this system has continued to the present day. This was part of a broad movement of intellectual awakening and cultural advance which has been called the Chinese Renaissance, including a Student Movement and Literary Revolution. A language reform known as the *pai-hua*, or vernacular movement, was the basis of the Literary Revolution. Its leaders proposed to eliminate the difference between the vernacular spoken language and the classical written language and to write according to the spoken language. This new style of writing "plain talk" enabled the Chinese to write just as they would speak, in a style readily intelligible to a much larger portion of the population. Hu-Shih, one of the leaders in the movement, together with a host of new writers, produced plays and poems that brightened the intellectual horizon enormously.

The Nationalists, who came to power with the revolution, were keenly aware of the power of universal education in producing national strength and progress, but national poverty and political waste prevented implementation of the fine program of education proposed. The economy was not able to support an effective program of universal education despite brilliant efforts, especially in simplification of the language and in adult education.

The war with Japan had very serious effects upon educational progress in China, and the aftermath of depression and conflict further retarded the progress of universal education. The rise to power of the Communists in the People's Republic has created a series of new and difficult problems for Chinese education. The duties of the school are defined as political indoctrination in Marxist materialism and education for national reconstruction, including national defense against future aggression. Heavy emphasis has been placed upon party loyalty and brotherly love for the Soviet Union and seeing through the hypocrisy and aggressive design of American imperialism. At the same time, the educational program has concentrated not only upon learning but upon engaging in a productive agricultural and industrial activity. New training schools for elite cadres were established in 1950 in order to provide adequate Communist leadership throughout the country. All education is firmly under the control of the state and closely coordinated with its ideology and program. A very close connection has been established with Soviet Russia's science, art, literature, films, and language.

Japan. The educational pattern in Japan is a very important example of what centralized control of education may accomplish in a relatively brief time. Before the coming of Perry's "black ships," Japan was a feudal society with an extremely limited elite type of education. Thereafter the Japanese in two generations were able to set up a "two-track" system of education which educated rulers and masses efficiently enough to establish the nation as an industrial and military power. Japan defeated Russia, expanded out over the continent of Asia and into the Pacific, and was halted only by the combined powers of the Western industrialized world. The Japanese, like other cultures, faced the problems of rapid overpopulation, a relatively small amount of arable land upon its rocky islands, and the need of industries to produce machines and process raw materials.

The system set up to deal with the various problems of education was largely borrowed from western Europe and controlled by a Ministry of Education which attended to detail to an even greater extent than did the French Ministry of Education. The system merely perpetuated the ruling groups of Japan and did not to any marked degree offer real opportunity where there was ability. The loss of the war by Japan has brought about a reorientation in terms of a more democratic form of government and a greater extension of universal education. The success of this system is contingent upon Japan's ability to cope with a number of problems, including the persistence of feudal and class traditions, economic difficulties, and the threat of Communism. The language difficulty stemming from the ideographs constitutes another obstacle to universal education. The Japanese have demonstrated an enormous capacity for progress in the past and it is quite possible that they may overcome their linguistic, political, and economic handicaps.

BIBLIOGRAPHY

Annuaire international de l'éducation et de l'enseignement (Geneva: Bureau International d'Education, 1933-1939, 1945-1947; beginning in 1948-1949, published jointly with UNESCO). Also published in English under the title *International Yearbook of Education.*

CHAMBERS, M. M., ed., *Universities of the World Outside U. S. A.* (Washington, D. C.: American Council on Education, 1950).

Education Abstracts (Paris: Education Clearing House, UNESCO). Issued monthly.

KANDEL, I. L., ed., *Educational Yearbooks of the International Institute* (New York: Teachers College, Columbia University, 1921-1944). An annual review of education.

World Handbook of Educational Organization and Statistics (Paris: Education Clearing House, UNESCO, 1951). A new edition will be published every two years.

The Year Books of Education (London: Evans Brothers Ltd.). Published annually since 1932 (except during the war period). A picture of educational developments around the world.

2 · EDUCATION IN THE

United States of America

ARTHUR HENRY MOEHLMAN

The United States has a total population of over 150 million and an area of 3,022,387 square miles with a density of about forty-nine people per square mile. The population is three-fifths urban and two-fifths rural. The country is highly industrialized but has a low population density and is capable of feeding itself. The ratio between people and acres of arable land is favorable, being close to 2.5 acres per person. The civilization is not military or ecclesiastical but is a new experiment in democracy supported by universal education, separation of church and state, and highly efficient mass production and technology. The population is extremely diverse and represents a synthesis of immigrants to the New World. The illiteracy rate is 2.7 percent.

The educational pattern from the time of the foundation of the nation has moved with increasing rapidity in the direction of universal, or "one-track," education. By World War I the majority of children of school age received twelve years of education—that is, into the secondary level; by World War II this level had been raised to include the first two years of college. The curriculum was generalized and comprehensive, providing training not only in the three R's but in citizenship, health, vocations, and home life.

—A. H. M.

NORTH AMERICA

The way of life in the United States cannot be clearly understood without a careful analysis of the system of education, both formal and informal. The profile and pattern of the American way of life may be said to have the following major characteristics: (1) a federal republic or democracy combining forty-eight states; (2) a system of universal free public education constructed on the "one-track" principle; (3) a basic bill of rights and freedoms guaranteed by a system of judicial review culminating in the Supreme Court; (4) a highly developed system of mass production based upon scientific research; (5) separation of church and state so as to guarantee freedom of conscience and faith and noninterference in the public welfare by any religious hierarchy; (6) a nation of immigrants representing a synthesis of many culture patterns, races, languages, and creeds; (7) a highly developed network of media of mass communication and transportation facilities.

The United States is a complex country. Foreigners have difficulty in reconciling certain paradoxes which they have observed. To the outside world, the United States seems to be a closely knit unity; yet at the same time it is a union of states which enjoy far-reaching independence. The people of the United States do not seem to be very articulate about their basic philosophy of living. Nevertheless, anyone who lives with us for some time becomes convinced of a tough, tenacious, and clear-cut philosophy of life which includes the above-mentioned seven major characteristics. The Constitution contains no decrees concerning the schools and educational system. Yet Americans are very clear in their own minds concerning the need for free public education which is controlled on a state, regional, and local community basis. Despite some who think that universal education has failed, Americans in general are convinced that the universal system of education is fundamental to democracy, since it encourages equal opportunity, social mobility, and an aristocracy of talent rather than one of class or special privilege.

Because education operates as a major instrument in cultural change, it is particularly vital that Americans analyze their indigenous system of universal education. What is the true picture? Have we been able to create an education for a classless society or is our educational system perpetuating or creating conflicting classes such as have brought about the disintegration of other civilizations? Does the United States represent an educational conflict between the frontier pattern of the three R's and the college of hard knocks on one hand and an integrated educational pattern carried out by professionals on the other?

From the beginning Americans have been engaged in a unique experiment in universal education, which they felt was the basis and essence of the democratic way of life. Americans have been charged with a "lust for money" from the first years of the Republic. In contrast, the really great drives in American growth have been a passion for freedom of the mind linked to a faith in universal education and careers open to all through the medium of education. The American citizen was once described by the historian Henry Adams as follows: "European travelers who pass through America notice that everywhere, in the White House at Washington and in the log cabins beyond the Alleghenies, except for a few federalists, every American from Jefferson and Gallatin down to the poorest squatter, seemed to nourish an idea that he was doing what he could to overthrow the tyranny which the past had fastened on the human mind."

Jefferson himself spoke of the basic faith of the common people in universal education. "The ultimate result of the whole scheme of education would be the teaching of *all* the children of the state, reading, writing and common arithmetic." Furthermore, he believed in the crucial importance of opening all careers freely to all the talented. He wished, "instead of an aristocracy of wealth, of more harm and danger than benefit to society, to make an opening to the aristocracy of virtue and talent which nature has wisely provided for the direction of the interests of society and scattered with an equal hand through all its conditions." He said further, "We hope to avail the state of those talents which nature has sown as liberally among the poor as the rich but which perish without use if not sought for and cultivated." Since Jefferson's original visualization of our faith in free public education as the foundation of freedom of the mind, the democratic way of life, and careers open to all, we have driven steadily forward with our unique educational experiment. It has been an unceasing struggle against the forces of class snobbery, Old World fatigue and pessimism, would-be dictators, and special interest.

The educational scene in the United States, broadly defined, is made up of (1) formal education in the public and private schools from the first grade to the graduate colleges of the university and (2) informal education, including channels of mass communication, such as the newspaper, films, and radio, libraries and museums, and informal educational groups ranging from service clubs to professional societies. This great stream of formal and informal education is characterized by certain main currents including the following: equality of opportunity for all persons, no matter what their race, sex, social status, or economic status; a balanced educational experience; local educational responsibility and authority; public tax support of the schools, with no diversion of funds to religious or private schools; exclusion of church influence from the schools; and participation in the planning and operation of education by teachers, parents, and students.

THE DAWN PERIOD OF EDUCATION

The American system of universal education was a reflection of and at the same time a catalyst in the major phases of cultural growth in the United States. These periods may be defined as follows: the Dawn Period (1500-1800), the Formative Period (1800-1900), and the Period of Midpassage (1900-   ).

In the Dawn Period of American education we find the genesis and development of certain ideas which are the essence of our culture and education. Fortunately for us, liberal ideas from the Old World of the growing Atlantic Community were transplanted and flourished, being further stimulated by the westward-expanding frontier of settlement. From the tension between the two poles of the frontier and the Atlantic Community grew the nation's native ideals and the realistic instruments—above all, that of universal education—so necessary to their attainment.

It was extraordinary that we escaped the "dead hand of the past" —the Old World pessimisms, the conservatism, and an elite, or "two-track," educational pattern tied to and perpetuating a class system which restrained the talents and abilities of the population.

To the north of us the French introduced a cultural pattern which was basically feudal and preserved the world of lord and peasant, from which the only escape was fur trading in the forest wilderness of the Great Lakes, the Canadian Shield, and the Mississippi. The church controlled education, in the main, and the scholastic philosophy in medieval universities was the educational basis for training the leaders.

To the south of us the Spaniards founded a Hispanic-American culture which was an amalgam of the Amerind base and a super-imposed feudal culture. The institutions of the presidio, or military post, and the mission were utilized as controls in building up a ranching and mining frontier which expanded rapidly into the Great Plains, the Southwest, and California. This frontier brought a rich heritage in informal education, particularly in the art of cattle ranching as practiced by the *vaquero* (herdsman), but formal education was again limited to the upper strata of society and based upon medieval scholastic philosophy in contrast to the new, liberal ideas.

The first Americans on the east coast of North America were, however, able to break away from the Old World pattern of stratification and reaction comparatively rapidly. The combination of liberal ideas from Europe with the great area of free land, rapidly peopled by the westward-moving frontier, provided social mobility in all fields of human living. Liberal ideas drawn from the Atlantic Community were of major importance in shaping the way of life and in particular the pattern of education. The English group of thinkers, especially John Locke, contributed to the main currents of American thought, emphasizing the integrity and dignity of the individual and his rights in organized society. The French thinkers also contributed to the American fight for freedom in contrast to the prevailing belief of the Old World in force. The realists, Diderot and Condorcet, assisted American thought in the direction of scientific analysis of data. At the same time the romantic idealists, Rousseau and others, stimulated understanding of the importance of the individual and his freedom to grow.

The Americans of the Dawn Period blended liberal European ideas with their own experiences in the conquest of a continent to create a new pattern of living, based upon freedom and posing a never-ending threat, implicit in the mere existence of the nation, to tyranny and force of any kind. Above all, the Americans began to fashion a new system of education to support democracy in both a formal and an informal pattern. Some of the outstanding contributions in formal education included the setting up of district schools by the community, especially in New England. At the same time universities were founded from Massachusetts to Georgia. In addition, the Americans experimented in the secondary-school area. Notable were Benjamin Franklin's proposals with regard to the foundation of an Academy in 1749; it was to have a greatly broadened curriculum directly related to the life of the people.

In the realm of informal education Americans believed in functional vocational training for everyone, whether it be father-son, mother-daughter, or master-apprentice training, and whether it be in the handicrafts or the domestic arts. Furthermore, there was an enormous activity in the direction of the importing and printing of books, pamphlets, and newspapers, all of which served as the "school of the people." Handbooks on agriculture, architecture, cabinet-making, and shipbuilding were of vital importance to the craftsmen of early America.

The concept of American universal education was beginning. Such major thinkers as Jefferson, Washington, and John Adams, together with Benjamin Franklin, understood the need for universal education, spoke forcefully in its favor, and contributed directly to its growth and development, despite reactionary opposition. American education began to move in the direction of public tax support, separation of church and state, functional curriculums, and opportunity for all. Around the end of the eighteenth century, following the Revolution and the founding of the Republic, a transition occurred from the Dawn Period to the Formative Period, when the battles were fought—and to a large degree won—for the major distinguishing characteristics of our unique system of universal education.

How did the district school system begin? The early colonial legislatures used the town as a unit of local school administration. The town was defined as a civil subdivision including some 20 to 40 square miles and was not necessarily a central village or aggregation of people. The town meeting was the authority for administering schools. Gradually the elected officers of the town took over decisions previously made in town meetings, such as whether the town would have a school or pay the fine imposed upon it for not having one, the location of the school, the means of supporting the teachers and supplying materials for instruction.

It is important to understand the district system because from the beginning it has been the basis of our decentralized school control—

what the late educator Henry Suzzallo referred to as "folk-made schools." The district system separated the schools from municipal administration and laid a basis for some 100,000 school districts scattered throughout forty-eight states. This was in complete contrast to the European operation of education by means of a single authoritative system under a central ministry of education. The district system developed in connection with the widely dispersed population and the growth of local government and democracy. The early Americans built their homes around the village center—for example, the New England town common, with its church, its town hall, and perhaps a schoolhouse. But, as the population increased, the settlers moved on and formed outlying settlements which soon demanded local self-government, including their own church parishes and road districts. These outlying districts often had a private school kept by a master in winter and a "dame school" in summer. This cut down the tax support of the town school. A compromise known as the moving school was often the outcome. The schoolmaster spent a few weeks at each settlement, the length of his stay depending upon the amount of taxes paid for school purposes into the town treasury. The moving school was obviously very unsatisfactory. In central and western Pennsylvania, neighborhood schools serving all faiths were in the majority. These were indigenous schools built by the contributions of the frontier farmers. Soon after the Revolution the district system was written into law by Massachusetts and by other states in New England and beyond.

In the United States the middle class rose to great importance; today we might be described as a nation in which the majority belongs to the middle class and extremes of poverty and wealth have steadily decreased. The new middle class of the American republic, made up of small farmers and artisans as well as merchants and manufacturers, insisted that the opportunities for education be shared by all. The district school was a means of achieving a higher degree of educational opportunity for all, but the education was very thin, the three R's at best.

The pattern of education was directly related to the general way of life in this Eotechnic Period. The technology of the time was one of simple tools and machines operated by muscle, wind, and water power. The pace was slow and sure, that of a handicraft society in which articles were made to last a long time and in which families were the primary unit and were, to a large degree, self-sufficient. Elementary education was made up of two rather sharply differentiated compartments: formal education, consisting of the three R's, with emphasis on reading and writing and very little attention paid to figuring; and informal education, the education of the head and hand in the everyday pursuits of life. The latter type was carried out mostly by means of a father-son, mother-daughter relationship or by means of an apprenticeship to the blacksmith, the shipwright, or the wheelwright. Apprenticeship did not preclude formal education; in fact it usually required training in "learning and labor"—specifically, in "ability to read." Formal elementary education, which was carried on in a wide variety of neighborhood, church, and district schools, by no means reached all children. The school year was short, often totaling less than three months. In general, formal secondary and higher education were transplanted out of the Middle Ages and Renaissance of the Old World; the heavy emphasis upon classical languages and the glories of antiquity was retained. This education was largely male, aristocratic, European, and little suited to the climate of opinion in the Americas.

Education in the Dawn Period was a great experiment in acculturation. In each region an attempt was made to relate a transplanted Old World education to the demands of a new land with an indigenous frontier culture. In New England a theocracy survived for a while but soon gave way to a form of government under which merchant, manufacturer, artisan, farmer, and seaman wrote the laws and demanded a new type of education for the sea, the farm, and business. The middle area of New York, Pennsylvania, etc. pointed like a double derringer pistol toward the west. The great cities of New York and Philadelphia funneled trade and people toward the Mohawk Valley and the Great Lakes, the Juniata and the Ohio-Mississippi country. The people constituted language and culture blocs ranging from the Dutch, English, and Scotch-Irish to Palatinate Germans. Education was faced with major problems raised by language, religion, and customs. South of the Potomac was the land of Dixie. The small, yeoman farms were in the majority, but larger plantations developed with the increased use of slaves. An educational conflict evolved between the aristocratic tidewater area and the equalitarian Piedmont and frontier to the west. The stage was set for a new experiment in universal education, although another hundred years would be necessary to complete its outline.

THE FORMATIVE PERIOD OF EDUCATION

In great measure, the Formative Period of the nineteenth century determined the profile and pattern of American education for a long time to come. America had the good fortune to succeed in establishing public, free, tax-supported, nonsectarian, universal education. In contrast to Europe, we drove forward a "one-track" pattern of education, whereas the Old World set up a "two-track" system for the elite and the masses, which was to help produce a wide range of social conflict.

America's educational growth was directly related to major changes in the culture pattern—in the climate of thought, in the growth of cities and regions, in the expansion of the frontier, and in the rapid acceleration of technology. The steam engine was used as the basis of transportation and production. Sooty cities and metropolises connected by a network of railroads were a characteristic outgrowth of this Paleotechnic Period. Vast numbers of immigrants, speaking a wide range of languages, moved across the American continent to settle in rural areas or to swell the size of cities. The educational system had to do more than teach them the three R's: it had to Americanize them socially, economically, and culturally.

There was also a surge forward in fundamental knowledge. The impact of "evolution" after the publication of Darwin's *Origin of Species,* in 1859, gave science a forward drive, lessening the influence of the theology of the Middle Ages and the classicism of the Renaissance. Americans studied abroad and at home and came to maturity in the field of original research.

This was a time of important original thinking ranging from science and research to creative literature and art. A great mechanism for mass communication of ideas grew up based upon the new libraries, penny newspapers, and such periodicals as *Harper's, The Atlantic Monthly,* and *Popular Science Monthly.* In this period, the Romantic Revolution and its ideas of progress blended with the new critical realism arising from the study of science and the inequalities accompanying the Paleotechnic Industrial Revolution. The succeeding period, the Neotechnic, was already on the horizon, created by Edison's electric light and dynamo, Selden's automobile patent, Hoe's rotary press, Bell's telephone, and Sholes's typewriter.

Since it was simple, democratic, and subject to local control, the district school served fairly well for a widely scattered farm population. But in the rapidly growing cities and towns of the nineteenth century, it was impossible for the ungraded district school to work at all satisfactorily. In these new urban communities demands were made for the extension of education to all elements of the population—to those interested in manufacturing, in trading, in farming. Furthermore, hundreds of children were gathered together in a single building in these urban communities; obviously a new type of organization had to appear. However, only late in the nineteenth century was a graded elementary school of eight years introduced. A hundred years ago our leading educators were assembling children of four to sixteen and sometimes over to be instructed by a single master, in a single room, in all studies from "alphabet of knowledge up to the higher branches of mathematics."

The general form of the American system of education was almost complete by the close of the nineteenth century. It included kindergarten, eight-year elementary school, four-year high school, and college. It was a universal system aiming at adequate education for all at all levels. The elementary school was a major factor in educational progress, owing to the work and influence of a wide range of able people. Before the Civil War, Mann, Barnard, and others pushed forward toward an improved elementary school. Following the Civil War, even more marked advance took place, partly as a result of Pestalozzian influence and object teaching at Oswego. This approach utilized collections of objects of all sorts for teaching reading matter, number, natural history, etc., as suited to the children's ages. In the nineties the Herbartians contributed enormously to the progress of education. DeGarmo, the McMurrys, and others utilized and transformed the ideas of Herbart into improved methods and curriculum. Furthermore, the use of the nature-study approach was advanced by such leaders as H. H. Straight in Illinois and Anna B. Comstock in New York State. The Quincy, Massachusetts, experiment of Francis W. Parker and his later work in the Cook County, Illinois, schools introduced an enriched curriculum for elementary-school children, not only in the three R's but also in the arts, physical education, geography, and nature study.

The rapid change toward city life under the pressure of industrialization concentrated the population and increased wealth. The need for child labor was lessened by better machinery, and more children were freed to go to school. The increasing number of children attending school and the increasing length of attendance forced a change in the direction of a broader program in the schools, since the home and work activities no longer supplemented the three R's.

The graded school developed in the rapidly growing communities together with an articulation or fitting together of schools so as to provide a regular progression from elementary school to high school to college. The grading of pupils according to age and the use of a fixed curriculum and fixed examinations were improvements over the helter-skelter mixing of all ages in the district school. Nevertheless, this system rapidly became a "school machine." The difficult promotion examinations at the end of each year's work resulted in the failure of many pupils. They had to take over not merely the studies failed but the complete work of the year. This resulted in a great deal of retardation and the repetition by many pupils of fifth- or sixth-grade work until the school-leaving age.

Furthermore, the 8-4-4 articulation conflicted with the new scientific findings concerning the onset of adolescence and the need for instruction with greater depth in subject-matter areas. Social change ranging from city growth to new data from scientific research produced pressure upon the schools, but human inertia made for slow change in the schools, worrying both educators and parents. Too many children failed to make progress or were cut off from development of special talents and left school even before completing the elementary program. By the turn of the century, despite the reactionary resistance, educators, communities, and school boards began to make new adjustments to social change.

THE PERIOD OF MIDPASSAGE

The beginning of the twentieth century was a Period of Midpassage in the culture pattern of the American people as they attempted to make intelligent adjustments to the new power machines and the new philosophy of living, which changed the old ways of life with explosive speed. The compact power machines created new relationships between people and their surroundings. Scientific research and technology accelerated geometrically in the United States. The new centers of mass production, producing everything from heavy machinery and structural materials to automobiles and light consumer goods, were directly connected with private research laboratories and with the scientific facilities of a rapidly growing system of higher education.

In relation to the over-all culture pattern, this period may be referred to as the Neotechnic, since it was based on the application of a new technology of compact power machines, ranging from the electric motor and internal-combustion engine to the diesel motor and jet, rocket, and atomic power units. Each one of the compact power machines changed the pattern of living radically. The internal-combustion engine, when applied to the automobile, facilitated the growth of a new network of roads and the expansion of city suburbs, consolidated schools, brought about dietary changes, and revised moral standards. The use of the internal-combustion engine in the airplane not only shrank the size of the world but made possible more destructive methods of warfare than had ever before been known. The release of atomic power through nuclear fission brought this trend to a head; it symbolized the ability to unleash enormous power and thereby either reach out toward the stars or cripple and perhaps destroy our major cultural advances.

Furthermore, these power machines could now be controlled securely and automatically in a tremendous variety of sequences, whether it was for the high-speed manufacture of automobile frames or for the production of radio and electronic tubes. In fact, humanity was now able to realize in three dimensions a world which it had only dreamed about before. In the past fifty years we have built extensions of all the human receptors, or senses, and effectors, or activators of action, ranging from the electronic microscope to the 200-inch telescope, from the television tube to radar, and from robot rockets to electronic computers. Education has been faced with the most rapid change in human history, a change so great that unless everyone understands the common human values necessary to cooperation and survival and can manipulate the basic symbols of transport, communication, exchange, and government, the outlook is one not of progress but rather of conflict and destruction. Specifically, the Neotechnic speed-up has merely accentuated the age-old conflict between force and freedom, between fear and truth, and between the rights of the individual and the methods of the dictator.

Because of the great acceleration in science, technology, and invention, the first half of the twentieth century has been characterized by a wide range of social and cultural shifts occurring at high speed. Modern living has been confused and complicated everywhere, but especially in the United States. Our culture pattern has had an amazing flexibility, owing to rapid population growth, immigration from many lands, high social mobility, and a marked tendency to devise and utilize many new types of power machines.

Unequal rates of change in the various life activities have resulted in points of tension and zones of danger. Our ability to produce has changed faster than our capacity to consume through adequate buying power; the reorganization of international relations lags behind intercontinental communication. The rapid moves forward and the marked lags in our way of life may be compared to the parts of an automobile operating at unsynchronized speeds with resulting friction and explosion.

Population movement has been an illustration of this often dangerous mobility. In the nineteenth century the frontier moved westward and disappeared. In the twentieth century a ceaseless shift of population across the face of the continent continued in a multitude of directions—from rural areas to cities, from cities to satellite suburbs, from South to North, from harsher northern climate areas to milder southern climate areas, from the drought areas to the Pacific coast. For the educator such population mobility is of the utmost importance. Excellent school systems are at times overcrowded because of the addition of students from educational areas with limited opportunities.

Observers of American education from abroad have expressed critical views of the effectiveness of American education in the twentieth century. Some believe that we place too much emphasis upon a "cult of the average" which emphasizes basic skills and "book larnin'" and distrusts outstanding intellectuals and geniuses. They charge that we make everyone conform to an average pattern and do not provide for gifted individuals and for those with greater than average interest in the intellectual pursuits.

One observer points to the conflict between the frontier pattern of the three R's as against an integrated educational pattern carried out by professionals. This observer feels that American education has failed to meet the challenge of the cosmos of the generation before 1914, a cosmos which has been transformed into today's near chaos. He believes that John Dewey's great statement that the schools must be life itself has not been met. The school curriculum has not been made flexible enough to help people adapt to new social and economic conditions, and has not provided a serious training for citizenship. Furthermore, the gap between what is being taught and the tremendous body of new knowledge is far too large. The contours of our world have been reshaped by the social and natural sciences, but the curriculum has not humanized that knowledge. Finally, there has not been sufficient recognition of the tremendous changes in the life of youth with regard to the institutions of the church and the family, effected in part by the automobile and the motion picture. In general, the American philosophy of the complete life, recreationally, vocationally, and politically, has not been clarified in the schools in terms of the pressures of the present day.

Another analyst feels that the figures on United States education are impressive—over 28 million in elementary and secondary schools and 2 million in colleges—but that the real level of education is less impressive than the numbers. He understands that it was necessary to use the school as a melting pot for the children of immigrants from Polish ghettos, Sicilian villages, and north-European towns; but he thinks that the social life is exaggeratedly intense and that the children from the "wrong side of the tracks" are penalized. Furthermore, it seems to him that the little red schoolhouse has outlived its day and that a great weakness of the American system of education is the huge number of independent school authorities. He feels that there is class bias in American as well as in English education, with a tendency for those who can afford it to send their children to private schools.

A competent German observer noted his reactions to American education, writing at the close of the liberal Weimar period, before the coming of the Nazis. Above all, he was impressed by the "one-track" system of universal education, and by the lack of any central ministry of education and the placing of responsibility instead upon the individual states and local school boards. It was surprising to him that in spite of the lack of central ministerial control of education the spirit and purpose of the schools were in strong agreement across the face of the continent. He was struck, however, by the lack of democracy in school administration, feeling that the school administrator had absolute sovereignty in hiring and firing teachers, whereas in the European system life-tenure was gained after teachers' examinations were passed. This observer was impressed by the separation of church and state in the public schools in contrast to religious control and instruction by Lutherans in the north and Catholics in the south of Germany. Above all, he felt that the aim of education was very unusual in the United States because the way of life was unique. The American philosophy seemed to require education of the masses first, and education of the most talented second. Furthermore, American education appeared to train for intelligent action rather than for aesthetics and analysis of ideas, as in Germany. He felt that the result of education in Germany was all too often a retreat from reality into an unreal world of ideas. On the other hand, American education did not withdraw one's vision from reality with all its conflicts but instead gave a robustness and ability to work with optimistic courage for the accomplishment of a better reality.

Many American analysts have felt that in the twentieth century American education expanded greatly in terms of opportunity for all and experience with humanity and its surroundings. More and more schools burst the bonds of one-room, one-teacher, memory learning. Teachers such as John Dewey brought the world into the schoolroom. Better working space, laboratories, libraries, and above all audio-visual materials and humanized books enriched the learning and growth of youngsters. At the same time teachers such as Anna Comstock took the children out of the classroom and into the world to study their natural surroundings. The accent was not only upon the three R's but upon the three H's of Pestalozzi and Geddes: the head, the heart, and the hand.

The school experience was better planned and articulated so as to relate not only to individual differences but to the process of human growth. The introduction of the 6-3-3-4 or variations of it corresponded more closely with the growth stages of childhood, adolescence, and young adulthood. By 1900 the junior high school was under way and by the close of World War I it had become established. Nuclei of first-class schools were established which were better adjusted to the demands of the technology and culture of the twentieth century—the automobile and air age, with its city life and fluid movement of families across the country and into foreign areas.

People desired to obtain the best possible education for their children. The process of social change underlined the vast difference between the meager and limited one-teacher, one-room three R's education and the functional and enriched many-teacher, laboratory, library, broad-experience type of education. A district school might be suited to a frontier type of rural life with two to four people per square mile. But a one-room school was a dangerous vestige of the past, a vermiform appendix in a high-speed, complex, industrial way of life. It could not provide the education needed for modern life—a life in which people do not stay in the same place but move around and must be competent to cope with conditions of life on their own continent and in the world beyond.

MID-CENTURY PATTERN OF EDUCATION IN THE UNITED STATES

A survey of the pattern of universal education in the United States is essential to an understanding of the American way of life. Our educational system is one of the great social institutions of our nation and perhaps our most important cultural contribution. Its significance lies not only in its size, structure and extensive activities but also in its philosophy, curriculum, method, and general cultural influence. As we have seen, American universal education did not arise through revolution or governmental decree but instead was a developmental process intimately connected with the American experiment in the democratic way of life.

Americans often take for granted the magnitude of the nation's educational undertaking, without having a clear picture of its actual scope. In 1950 the population enrolled in the educational system—elementary, secondary, and higher—totaled over 30 million, or one in five in a population of over 150 million. Of the children five to seventeen years of age more than 90 percent attended school, a ratio far higher than that in any other country. The school-leaving age was sixteen in forty of the states and seventeen or eighteen in the remainder. The majority of the states required school attendance from age seven through sixteen. Approximately 21 million pupils were enrolled in elementary schools, 7 million in high schools, and 2 million in colleges and universities. Over 5 million children, or more than Switzerland's total population, were transported in school buses every school day.

Approximately a million teachers were required to teach this great number of students, and almost as many persons were engaged in nonteaching school services. Over 3 percent of the nation's total working force earned its living in educational work.

By mid-century more than 6 billion dollars was being spent annually for the operation of the school system. The school plant, including equipment, land, and more than 200,000 school buildings, represented an investment of over 12 billion dollars.

The American dream of a universal education giving every individual "equality of opportunity" has been clearly stated in the report of the White House Conference of 1930 summarized in a nineteen-point document known as the Children's Charter.

THE CHILDREN'S CHARTER

The White House Conference on Child Health and Protection, recognizing the rights of the child as the first rights of citizenship, pledges itself to these aims for the Children of America.

I. For every child spiritual and moral training to help him to stand firm under the pressure of life.

II. For every child understanding and the guarding of his personality as his most precious right.

III. For every child a home and that love and security which a home provides; and for that child who must receive foster care, the nearest substitute for his own home.

IV. For every child full preparation for his birth, his mother receiving prenatal, natal, and postnatal care; and the establishment of such protective measures as will make child-bearing safer.

V. For every child health protection from birth through adolescence, including: periodical health examinations and, where needed, care of specialists and hospital treatment; regular dental examinations and care of teeth; protective and preventive measures against communicable diseases; the insuring of pure food, pure milk, and pure water.

VI. For every child from birth through adolescence, promotion of health including health instruction and a health program, wholesome physical and mental recreation, with teachers and leaders adequately trained.

VII. For every child a dwelling-place safe, sanitary, and wholesome, with reasonable provisions for privacy; free from conditions which tend to thwart development; and a home environment harmonious and enriching.

VIII. For every child a school which is safe from hazards, sanitary, properly equipped, lighted, and ventilated. For younger children nursery schools and kindergartens to supplement home care.

IX. For every child a community which recognizes and plans for his needs, protects him against physical dangers, moral hazards, and disease; provides him with safe and wholesome places for play and recreation; and makes provision for his cultural and social needs.

X. For every child an education which, through the discovery and development of his individual abilities, prepares him for life; and through training and vocational guidance prepares him for a living which will yield him the maximum of satisfaction.

XI. For every child such teaching and training as will prepare him for successful parenthood, homemaking, and the rights of citizenship; and, for parents, supplementary training to fit them to deal wisely with the problems of parenthood.

XII. For every child education for safety and protection against accidents to which modern conditions subject him—those to which he is directly exposed and those which, through loss or maiming of his parents, affect him indirectly.

XIII. For every child who is blind, deaf, crippled, or otherwise physically handicapped, and for the child who is mentally handicapped, such measures as will early discover and diagnose his handicap, provide care and treatment, and so train him that he may become an asset to society rather than a liability. Expenses of these services should be borne publicly where they cannot be privately met.

XIV. For every child who is in conflict with society the right to be dealt with intelligently as society's charge, not society's outcast; with the home, the school, the church, the court and the institution when needed, shaped to return him whenever possible to the normal stream of life.

XV. For every child the right to grow up in a family with an adequate standard of living and the security of a stable income as the surest safeguard against social handicaps.

XVI. For every child protection against labor that stunts growth, either physical or mental, that limits education, that deprives children of the right of comradeship, of play, and of joy.

XVII. For every rural child as satisfactory schooling and health services as for the city child, and an extension to rural families of social, recreational, and cultural facilities.

XVIII. To supplement the home and the school in the training of youth, and to return to them those interests of which modern life tends to cheat children, every stimulation and encouragement should be given to the extension and development of the voluntary youth organizations.

XIX. To make everywhere available these minimum protections of the health and welfare of children, there should be a district, county, or community organization for health, education, and welfare, with full-time officials, co-ordinating with a statewide program which will be responsive to a nationwide service of general information, statistics, and scientific research. This should include:

(a) Trained, full-time public health officials, with public health nurses, sanitary inspection, and laboratory workers.
(b) Available hospital beds.
(c) Full-time public welfare service for the relief, aid, and guidance of children in special need due to poverty, misfortune, or behavior difficulties, and for the protection of children from abuse, neglect, exploitation, or moral hazard.

FOR EVERY CHILD THESE RIGHTS, REGARDLESS OF RACE, OR COLOR, OR SITUATION, WHEREVER HE MAY LIVE UNDER THE PROTECTION OF THE AMERICAN FLAG.

The nineteen objectives of the Children's Charter depict the broad range of educational and other needs in a democracy, which must be met by the schools, by the channels of communication, by the libraries and museums, and by the institutions of the family, community, and church.

Educators in the organized schools face the continuing challenge of translating the objectives of the Children's Charter into realistic, evolving programs. The school's span of responsibility extends from infancy to maturity. This means that the schools must provide educational opportunities for a population of over 150 million. These 150 million Americans live in a continental area of over 3 million square miles—an area which ranges from a cold climate in the Great Lakes region of the North to a subtropical climate in the South. The United States is well balanced both in natural resources, including food, wood, water power, coal, oil, and minerals, and in its powerful technology of production, distribution, transportation, communication, and fundamental scientific research. The United States under its democratic way of life has conquered this continent in the last 150 years. The new country exploited its natural resources ruthlessly and combined many races in a cultural melting pot. Today the American way of life faces the new challenges of global responsibility and a new level of technology based upon exploration of the atom, the galaxies, and living cells. Education has been a primary instrument in past cultural change in America, and it faces increasing responsibility in the future.

Basically, our system of public education is organized into forty-eight state school systems with a total of more than three thousand county educational organizations and some 100,000 school districts. We do not have a central ministry of education exercising direct control over these forty-eight state systems. The federal authority in the Office of Education is confined mainly to research and advisory functions except for direct control of schools in territories under federal jurisdiction. The state school systems derive their authority from the state legislatures and operate in quasi corporations called school districts. This is a unique development of folk-made schools which gives great flexibility and power and at the same time has certain dangers. This "school state," or independent school system, growing out of the little red schoolhouse of the frontier and the American condition of local control of education has sometimes been called the fourth dimension of government. Local taxation furnishes the major support of education, with the burden falling upon real property. This has made for an uneven distribution of financial support, owing to the great variation in property value from area to area. The programs of the schools range from a relatively narrow type of instruction, barely covering basic tools of learning, in the poorer rural areas to the enriched and broad programs of the wealthy city areas. Teacher preparation and salary are directly related to the size and financial support of the school district. The basic instructional aid used by teachers is the textbook, but instruction has been enriched by the growing use of school libraries, audio-visual aids, and field trips.

Self-education through a variety of media has been a long-standing tradition and activity in the United States. This informal education existed on the frontier and in the early urban communities at the beginning of our republic and has swept forward with steadily increasing force. Instruments of informal education in the middle of the twentieth century include such groups as the family, the church, and service clubs; the libraries, art galleries, and museums and the means of communicating the printed word; the techniques of films, radio, and television and other means of communicating the spoken word. The informal education groups (family, church, service clubs, etc.) have had a particularly great impact on the growth and development of the American people.

Fraternal organizations and service clubs are as much a part of the American scene as pork chops and corn on the cob. The social emphasis of these various organizations has been much emphasized, but their educational implications have been overlooked. All these groups are laboratories for experience in democratic techniques of living. Masons, Kiwanians, Rotarians, Moose, Elks, Lions, and various types of women's clubs are all vitally interested in the problems of the day and conduct an informal educational program nearly every week in the year, bringing speakers on every possible facet of human existence. This informal educational organization is really unique. It not only interests members in economic, social, political, and aesthetic problems but also provides channels for formulating future policies of vital educational importance.

American libraries, museums, and art galleries have provided an avenue for self-education which has been unmatched upon the planet. The American public library, whether stationary or on wheels, has been an especially potent force in the intellectual and technological advance of our population. After all, books are the magic casements that open to reveal new vistas of individual growth and development.

The art galleries have provided us with a means for examining and understanding the aesthetic contributions of the past and present in all the visual fields. Today an art gallery is not merely a storage and display area for the great creative works of art but also a studio and laboratory for the development of the aesthetic interests of young and old, of professionals and amateurs. The new museums, which have gone far beyond the earlier experiments in collecting items, are vast, intelligently organized centers of educational growth and development. Modern museums depict in working models every aspect of human activity and development. They contain not only habitat groups of animals, birds, plants, and trees as they occur in nature but also three-dimensional working models of the human ear and eye, of the growth of human beings, of the movement of the stars and galaxies, of mining deep in the earth, and of the uses of minerals, fibers, and the entire periodic table of elements.

The channels of communication, some people say, threaten to engulf us with their emphasis upon the tawdry, the destructive and the evil or in the facility of control which they offer to power-mad dictators. On the other hand, when intelligently directed in terms of the individual's health, wisdom, creative work, friendship, and love, the channels of communication can humanize our existence and direct it toward complete living.

The motion-picture industry has to its credit many great pictures which have probed into the limitless possibilities of human development. Radio and television presents—in addition to soap operas and who-dun-it's—on-the-spot broadcasts of significant human change, thrilling and accurate analyses of the cavalcade of human history, and great symphonies and plays. The newspapers have always served as a school of the people, reporting the most recent scientific and cultural developments in both word and picture. In fact, the people of the United States have better access than any other nation of the world to the facts of the time.

Publishing of books and periodicals has been one of the great techniques of informal education in the United States. These organs have brought continuing insight, tragic and comic, to Americans as they faced the challenges of daily existence. American publishers have never hewed to a party line but have produced books which investigated the entire range of American experience. They have dealt with suppressed sharecroppers, with politicians in search of power, with explorers of the human mind and spirit at their best. In fact, the books published in America provide a humanized geography of every region of our country, of every manner and class of people. Furthermore, textbooks and reference books in all the fundamental disciplines have been a major contribution of book publishing.

The main currents of education in the United States are those of a free people in courageous pursuit of the good life through the intelligent solution of the challenges of human existence, utilizing both formal and informal education from infancy to death. Such a pattern of education is an index to the condition of humankind in the United States. For perhaps the first time in human existence, there is the promise of a people's possessing insight into their past and present and planning intelligently for the future, because of a universal and individualized education which operates throughout all life—not only through the schools but through the channels of communication and the vast cultural mechanisms open to all manner and kinds of people.

BIBLIOGRAPHY

BEARD, CHARLES A., and MARY R. BEARD, *A Basic History of the United States* (Philadelphia: The Blakiston Company, 1944). An invaluable analysis of social, cultural, and political change in United States history. The last historical judgment of the Beards after some forty years of research.

BEARD, CHARLES A., and MARY R. BEARD, *The Rise of American Civilization* (New York: The Macmillan Company, 1939), Vols. I, II, and III. The classical analysis of the genesis and growth of the American experiment in civilization.

BUTTS, R. FREEMAN, *Cultural History of Education* (New York: McGraw-Hill Book Company, Inc., 1946). A thoughtful and scholarly interpretation of the development of education in relation to cultural growth.

COOK, L. A., and E. F. COOK, *A Sociological Approach to Education* (New York: McGraw-Hill Book Company, Inc., 1950). A balanced analysis of education in relation to community backgrounds, with a good evaluation of the class-caste controversy.

CURTI, MERLE, *The Social Ideas of American Educators* (New York: Charles Scribner's Sons, 1935). A scholarly study of the main currents of thought expressed by outstanding American educators in relation to the American culture pattern in space and time.

GOOD, H. G., *A History of Western Education* (New York: The Macmillan Company, 1947). A clear and authoritative study which contains one of the best brief narratives of the development of American education.

KALLEN, H. M., *The Education of Free Men* (New York: Farrar, Straus & Co., Inc., 1949). An outstanding and interesting analysis of the philosophy and practice of American education by one of the scholars in the field.

LASKI, HAROLD J., *The American Democracy* (New York: The Viking Press, 1948). This book is the culmination of Laski's long and scholarly study of democracy in the United States. He analyzes every aspect of the American culture pattern and includes a very valuable chapter on education.

MOEHLMAN, ARTHUR B., *School Administration* (Boston: Houghton Mifflin Company, 1951). A scholarly and lucid study of the philosophy and practice of school administration in the United States, by one of the outstanding contributors to the field.

MOEHLMAN, CONRAD H., *The Wall of Separation Between Church and State* (Boston: The Beacon Press, Inc., 1951). The definitive study of the American doctrine of separation of church and state with special reference to universal public education, by the *doyen* of research in the field.

MUMFORD, LEWIS, *Technics and Civilizations* (New York: Harcourt, Brace and Company, Inc., 1934). An original analysis of the relationship between cultural growth and technology by a pioneer in aesthetics, education, and planning.

Recent Social Trends in the United States (New York: McGraw-Hill Book Company, Inc., 1933), Vols. I and II. An invaluable reference source in all fields of American growth in the twentieth century, written by outstanding experts in the various fields.

3 · EDUCATION IN *Latin America*

GEORGE I. SÁNCHEZ

Latin America constitutes a cultural unit with an inner logic of its own drawn from certain major sources. Its philosophy has come from the American Indian and from the successive intrusions from Spain and Portugal, France, and North America. Latin America has pursued an ideal of freedom derived from the American Indian, from the American experiment to the north, and from the continental revolutions in thought and economics.

The region is extremely diverse in the size, population, and technology of its various nations, despite their common inheritance in philosophy, religion, language, and education. The nations vary greatly in size; Brazil, the largest, has a total area of 3,286,170 square miles (it is larger than the United States), and Uruguay, the smallest, has a total area of about 72,153 square miles (it is about twice the size of the state of Pennsylvania). The density of population is relatively low, since the area is primarily agricultural and is just beginning to enter upon a large-scale industrialization, chiefly in certain coastal areas. The total population of Latin America is about 130 million. Brazil has about 49,800,000, Argentina about 16 million. Other population totals in round numbers are, in descending order: Colombia, 11 million; Peru, 8 million; Chile, almost 6 million; Venezuela, 4½ million; Bolivia, almost 4 million; Uruguay, 2½ million. One of the smallest countries, Uruguay, has the heaviest population density, about thirty-five people per square mile; most of the other countries have fewer than six people per square mile. Latin America faces some difficult problems with regard to its land, people, and technology. Superficially South America resembles North America: both continents are triangles and have a range of new mountains on the west and two blocks of older mountains on the east separated by major river systems. But actually there are great contrasts. The lowest mountain pass and the first one traversed by railroad in the Andes of South America—Uspallata Pass, east of Santiago de Chile—is as high as the peaks of the Rockies. Furthermore, the greater part of the continent is located over the equator and has consequent problems of heat and rainfall. The mineral resources are rich—there is much oil, copper, tin, and iron—but often not easily accessible or of the wrong type (for example, there is a scarcity of coking coal for steel manufacture). Despite these disadvantages the rise of technology and industrialization has been marked in the twentieth century, especially in Mexico, Brazil, Uruguay, Argentina, Chile, Colombia, and Venezuela.

Latin American political history has been characterized by a great deal of instability and a tendency to use revolution as a means of election or change of government. Latin America in general has been tolerant in the past in terms of the color line but there has been little further opening of the gates to immigration from Asia or Africa. Argentina is proud of its "European" ancestry. European immigration has been very important in forming the culture pattern since the days of the Spanish and Portuguese. In fact, there has been a development of national colonies in many Latin American countries; for example, the Italians in Argentina and the Germans in southern Brazil.

All these historical determinants have affected the development of education in Latin America. In general the tradition has been that of an elite, or "two-track," education. However, the process of change toward a universal, or "one-track," system of education has been under way from the beginning of the twentieth century, especially in Mexico, Uruguay, and Brazil. Such leaders as Sarmiento in Argentina made a beginning in the nineteenth century, but lack of an appropriate financial base, political instability, tradition, and the wide variety of native languages has made progress difficult.

Writing a chapter on Latin American education presents a particularly difficult problem in educational analysis. Since one is concerned with a vast territory consisting of twenty nations,

SOUTH AMERICA

obviously none can be dealt with in adequate detail; instead one must rely upon exploration of certain major currents in development.

—A. H. M.

———————

Latin America comprises twenty sovereign nations whose populations total more than 130 million people. These countries cover almost 8 million square miles of land; their northernmost point is roughly 6000 miles from the most southern; and they extend over some 6000 miles of longitude. In this vast spread of territory is to be found virtually every extreme of climate and geography, an imposing variety of plants and animals, and a great diversity of peoples and cultures. The histories of these nations reveal great individual differences. The development of their institutions—educational, political, economic—has responded to these differences, and the institutions reflect the variety and the individuality of the settings out of which they arose.

Education as Social Development. Educational institutions, like all other social institutions, are cultural products—the expression of social development in a circumstance. The factors that operate in that circumstance, such as time, place, resources, tools, and peoples, are determinants and conditioners of social development and of social institutions. This is as true of each Latin American country as it is of Germany, of France, of the United States, or of any other nation. Therefore, given the individual character of each Latin American nation and recognizing the numerous differences that are evident in the cultural development of the twenty nations, it is obvious that only in a very limited sense can one examine education in Latin America as a whole.[1]

It becomes apparent also that the limited space available here make it impossible to present a satisfactory description and interpretation of "education in Latin America" or of education in each of the twenty nations comprising Latin America—even if one could make the farfetched assumption that any author was competent to treat adequately and authoritatively so broad and complex

[1] Concha Romero James, "Latin American Trends," *Among Us,* No. 1 (Washington, D. C.: October 1942), p. 1.

a field. As a consequence, the writer is limited to a presentation that is simply introductory and that deals almost exclusively with general features that are more or less common to the Latin American countries. Fortunately for such a purpose, in the background of Latin American development there are common features which are highly significant in the interpretation of contemporary institutions and practices.

Cultural Affinity Among Latin Americans. An understanding of the cultural affinity that exists among Latin Americans is basic to an understanding of the similarities in the educational developments that have taken place in Latin America. That affinity and the common experiences behind it have far-reaching implications in the interpretation of many salient features of educational organization, of educational policy, and of educational achievement. It is only in the light of this fundamental cultural fact that students of comparative education may discern the meanings of the differences or similarities that are found to exist between the educational institutions and practices of one country, say the United States, and those of any one or all of the countries of Latin America.

The backgrounds for this cultural affinity, with its educational implications, may be examined most conveniently by historical periods, although it must be recognized that a chronological relation of events is subject to many limitations. For our purposes, cultural development in Latin America may be studied in terms of pre-Columbian antecedents, of the salient events and accomplishments of the colonial period, and of developments after the attainment of independence. Out of each of these large areas of history arise the foundations upon which cultural affinity is based—and upon which rest important parts of the present-day educational programs. Although the examination of these common backgrounds will not explain the structure and other details of the educational program of any one country, it does establish the frame of reference within which the interpretation of educational development in each country must be made. These backgrounds constitute the circumstance to which Latin American peoples have reacted in the creation of their educational programs, and only in terms of an understanding of that circumstance do those programs have meaning.

Indigenous Factors. The pre-Columbian antecedents of Latin American cultural affinity are to be found not only in Europe but in America as well. Before the coming of Europeans, the New World was neither wholly a wilderness nor a cultural vacuum. Indigenous people have been on this hemisphere for more than ten thousand years, and through the centuries they have developed ways of life of their own—cultures that, before 1492, were deeply rooted and solidly established. Those cultures have carried over, in varying degrees, to the present time—contributing to the cultural flow that has streamed off to produce a Mexico, a Peru, a Chile, a Paraguay. The extent of this carry-over of peoples and cultures is easily appreciated when one examines a detailed report, such as that of Basauri (for Mexico), on the current status of indigenous peoples.[2]

Before the conquest there were millions of Indians in Mexico and Central America. Other millions were in South America. Nearly everyone has heard of the advanced civilizations of such peoples as the Aztecs, the Mayas, and the Incas. There were many other less well-known but no less important peoples—in Chile, in Colombia, in the La Plata area, and, in fact, up the length and along the breadth of the hemisphere. These peoples were not exterminated by the Conquest. They have persisted to the present time—many as Indians, many more as mestizos or otherwise "assimilated." These Indian and Indo-European peoples constitute the great mass of the Latin American population, and they have conditioned, in highly significant ways, the growth and development of educational institutions.[3]

Although it is evident that the Indian peoples are not evenly distributed over Latin America, who will deny that all of Latin America partakes in some measure of the Indian cultural influences —or, at the very least, of the carry-over of colonial policies which responded to the fact that there were millions of indigenous peoples in the New World? It is not difficult to find tangible evidence of

[2] Carlos Basauri, *La población indígena de México* (Mexico City: Secretaría de Educación Pública, 1940), Vols. I and II.

[3] Donald D. Brand, "The American Indian: Forgotten Man of Four Centuries," in *Latin America in Social and Economic Transition* (Albuquerque: University of New Mexico Press, 1943), pp. 23-24.

these influences—in language, in customs and foods, in arts and crafts, and so on.[4] Much more subtle, but no less real, are the effects produced by Indian cultures on current psychological patterns, on schemes of values, on social and economic institutions.

Impact of Indian Cultures. Cultural developments in such countries as Mexico and Ecuador, which have felt a particularly strong impact of Indian cultures, reflect vividly the indigenous contribution, both in what has been accomplished and in what has been left undone. In such countries, large-scale immigration from Europe was neither desirable nor feasible, among the important reasons being the fact that the resources were barely sufficient to maintain existing Indian populations. The establishment of social institutions has been handicapped by (1) the relative paucity of resources (schools and other institutions constitute an "overhead" cost that, in these countries, could not be borne without a fatal impairment of vital functions) and (2) the slowness of the process of incorporating into European patterns Indian populations that far outnumbered their European fellow citizens. On the other hand, the cultural patterns that did evolve reflected the effects of acculturation—the Indian, while being modified by European patterns, in turn modified the imported culture.

Educational thought in Mexico (and to an increasing degree in Peru, Guatemala, and other Indo-Hispanic countries) is not simply an American evolution of Spanish and other European prototypes. Those prototypes have been modified through interaction with new, non-European peoples. Literacy programs, for example, must be adjusted to the Indian and his languages. The European concept of literacy itself changes in the face of non-European schemes of values, of a radically different cultural experience.[5] Too, because of large non-Christian populations, greater than normal emphasis was placed on the missionary, religious aspect of education—an emphasis which explains many of the basic achievements and deficiencies of colonial and nineteenth-century education. Modern schools have been much influenced by both the successes and failures incident to this religious emphasis.

[4] Samuel Guy Inman, *Latin America* (Chicago: Willett, Clark and Company, 1937), pp. 76-78.
[5] I. L. Kandel, *Education in the Latin American Countries* (New York: Teachers College, Columbia University, 1942), pp. xii-xiv.

Spanish policy, of both state and church, encouraged the fusion of Spaniards and Indians. "The cultural penetration of Spain in America was aided by a policy constantly favorable to the marriage of Spaniards and Indians. This policy was not only authorized by kings but was stimulated by them from the beginning."[6]

Cultural Diversity. No one cognizant of the cultural diversity of pre-Columbian America will make the error of claiming that the Indian influences were the same on all the Latin American countries or that they produced uniform effects. The number and concentration of Indian populations was not uniform; acculturation took place at varying rates; and so on.[7] Nonetheless, it is not farfetched to assume that exposure to indigenous cultures—to a higher or lower degree, directly or indirectly—has contributed in an important way to the current cultural affinity among Latin Americans. Speaking of the source of American art Justino Fernández says, "From the welding of two races, from the conquered world, from the imposed culture, a new art began to flourish; it was not a degenerated art . . . but a new artistic phenomenon, emerging from a conscience that was taking form in America."[8]

Manuel Toussaint, Mexico's leading art critic, writes to the same effect; and he points out that, as a result of the interaction of the European culture and the new environment, "America is born in twenty branches from the same prolific trunk—Spain."[9]

In the same manner were born the social institutions of Latin America. The acculturation of Spaniard and Indian, of Portuguese and Indian, of later immigrants and the Indians and mestizos gave birth to new American peoples and American ways. The common experience of dealing and associating with Indians and of operating under policies which took account of Indian populations—to say nothing of such post-Columbian developments as intermarriage and

[6] Fernando de los Ríos, "The Action of Spain in America," in Charles C. Griffin, ed., *Concerning Latin American Culture* (New York: Columbia University Press, 1940), p. 74.

[7] Samuel Guy Inman, *op. cit.*, p. 44.

[8] Justino Fernández, "The Source of American Art," in *Cultural Bases of Hemispheric Understanding* (Austin: Institute of Latin-American Studies, University of Texas, 1942), p. 22.

[9] Manuel Toussaint, "A Defense of Baroque Art in America," in *Inter-American Intellectual Interchange* (Austin: Institute of Latin-American Studies, University of Texas. 1943), p. 162.

mestizaje (the mixing of races and cultures) in general—does establish that, in this respect, there is a community of cultural antecedents for Latin Americans that contributes in no small way to their present cultural affinity. These common cultural antecedents have highly similar effects upon the programs of education of the several countries.

THE EUROPEAN

Latin American cultural affinity has significant antecedents in pre-Columbian Europe and in later European events and values closely associated with pre-Columbian factors. In examining this affinity and its implications for education, it is very important to recognize this fact—for therein is to be found the basis of interpretation of many Latin American ways and institutions. Much of the cultural foundation of Latin America was laid upon medieval norms; note, for example, the carry-over of the medieval university, of medieval tools and methods, of a medieval fusion of church and state. On the other hand, the fact that the basic settlement of Latin America took place largely during the Golden Age (1450-1650) of the people of the Iberian Peninsula—at the height of the Southern Renaissance—explains the traditional heavy emphasis on humanism in Latin America and the enthusiasm of early colonial effort. Similarly, medieval religious fervor and the Counter Reformation combined to give educational efforts in Latin America a special religious and authoritarian flavor. A brief examination of a few phases of Iberian history before 1492 and of developments closely allied with pre-Columbian history will suffice to illustrate our point.

First of all it must be remembered that the people of Spain and Portugal have a long background of contact with a variety of cultures—Western and non-Western. Before and after the coming of the Romans, the Iberian Peninsula had important contacts with the civilizations of northern Africa. Later, the Visigothic invasion left marked impressions on the peoples of Spain and Portugal. Seven centuries of occupation by the Moors brought the peninsula in direct contact with the Moslem world and with much of the East. All these contacts conditioned Spaniards and Portugese to other races and cultures. It is not surprising, then, to find Portuguese and Spaniards taking their contacts with the indigenous peoples of

America in stride. It is not surprising, either, that this background should cause Latin Americans to eschew racism and color lines. Therefore, it is not miraculous that the president of a great school in Colombia is what in the United States we would call a Negro; that a great educator and political reformer in Venezuela also has Negro antecedents; that one of the greatest presidents of Mexico was a fullblood Indian; that the phrase *la raza* is used in Latin America to mean "our people," rather than "the race"; and that Brazil should be frankly espousing miscegenation to produce a "cosmic race."

Among the best expositions of the results of the racial tolerance of Iberian peoples in the New World is that made for Brazil by Gilberto Freyre in his various works. In one of them he states, "On the large sugar-cane plantations, and later in the mining fields, the coffee plantations, and the towns of colonial Brazil, race mixture went on freely through irregular sexual relations, and European culture came into close contact with Indian and African cultures."[10]

Freyre goes on to point out that it was in the plantation area that Brazilian music, domestic architecture, and cuisine were born and that the Portuguese language developed its best Brazilian flavor. Many past and current cultural achievements in Brazil are a result of the new ethnic and cultural combinations made possible by the typically Iberian racial tolerance of the Portuguese. In the next chapter we shall see how similar factors have created a new Mexican people, the predominant mestizo.

One of the most potent factors in the molding of Spanish and Portuguese character was the epic struggle with Islam. The occupation of large portions of the Iberian Peninsula by the Moors, beginning in the eighth century and terminating in the fifteenth, was an event of incalculable significance in the cultural development of the peoples of that region. The acculturation that took place over a period of seven centuries is clearly evident in Spain and Portugal in a great variety of fields.[11] What is more important to us, the effects of the acculturation were carried over to the New

[10] Gilberto Freyre, "Some Aspects of the Social Development of Portuguese America," in Charles C. Griffin, ed., *op. cit.*, p. 102.

[11] Fernando de los Ríos, "Spain in the Epoch of American Colonization," in Charles C. Griffin, ed., *op. cit.*, pp. 25 and 26-27.

World, and they are clearly evident in the growth of Latin American cultures.

It is impossible to understand fully the conquest of America unless one understands the long-range indoctrination for conquest that had gone on in Spain for hundreds of years before Columbus. In view of their cultural antecedents, it is not remarkable that Cortés undertook the conquest of Mexico with a mere six hundred Spanish soldiers and that Cabeza de Vaca would stick to his tremendous hike from Galveston to the Gulf of California (and come back for more, when he returned from Spain for a similar jaunt in South America). In view of their cultural antecedents, it would have been remarkable if they had failed to go on. They and their ancestors had come to accept that kind of behavior as the norm rather than the exception.

The history and the lore of Spain and Portugal before 1492 are full of prototypes of the conquistadors and their deeds—particularly the history of the centuries-long struggle against the Moors. Those antecedents give meaning to much of what Spaniards and Portuguese did in America, and they explain in part the present-day cultural affinity of Latin Americans.

The Spanish church, for example, which laid much of the cultural foundation of Latin America, was deeply and peculiarly influenced by the long struggle against the fanaticism of the Moslems. It was inevitable that, through the centuries, the Spanish church should partake of that same kind of ardor, of a militant zeal which led it to spread its faith and the culture it represented from New Mexico to southern Chile all in the course of less than one hundred years. That achievement was more than mere religious "conversion" of Indians —it constituted *la piedra angular*, the keystone, of the development of Spanish institutions. Those institutions, with local variations, became the foundation of Latin American institutions. Much that is good in Latin America, and much that some believe is bad, stems from the role played by the Spanish church in colonial days. The good and the bad contribute to the sense of community that exists among Latin Americans—for they all have the Spanish church as a common heritage.

The union of church and state in Spain and in colonial Latin America and the bearing of this union upon the meaning of the Conquest and the establishment of educational and other institutions are little understood in the United States. As Fernando de los Ríos makes clear, the state recognized that only on the basis of spiritual values could the Conquest be justified—and those values called for the humanitarian incorporation of the natives.[12]

There are other significant features of Latin American culture that depend for interpretation upon an understanding of Spanish history. Some are quite obvious—the direct influence of the Southern Renaissance on language and learning, the direct borrowing of laws and political institutions from old Spain, the transplantation in America of the Spanish medieval university, to mention but a few. All these and others serve as strands which bind together, in a cultural sense, nations as diverse as Argentina and Mexico, Cuba and Chile.

THE COLONIAL PERIOD

Rise of Cultural Affinity. The circumstances of colonial life did much to develop cultural affinity in Latin America and to condition the character of education. The common experiences of waging a relentless struggle against a forbidding environment; the common political status and relationships with the mother countries; and the ever-growing consciousness of an independent, American way of life all contributed to the development of common perspectives and led to highly similar accomplishments. Although separated by geographic barriers and limited means of communication, by political restrictions, and by the exigencies of divergent economies, all the American colonies of Spain and Portugal were much alike in their development and in their ways of life.

The fact that the Iberian Peninsula did not have an excess of population, coupled with the fact that much of the New World was heavily populated by native peoples, placed the burden of Europeanizing Latin America on a remarkably small number of persons. Portugal, with about one million people in 1500, sent only 25,000 colonists to Brazil in the first century of colonization. Only 300,000 Spaniards came to New Spain during the three colonial centuries. In both instances few women were among the colonizers, and *mestizaje* began from the earliest days of the Conquest. In areas

[12] Fernando de los Ríos, "The Action of Spain in America," in Charles C. Griffin, ed., *op. cit.*, pp. 55-56.

such as Brazil and Cuba, where large numbers of Negro slaves were imported to labor on plantations, this *mestizaje* soon included these people as well as the Indians. The task of cultural growth and development, then, quickly began to assume characteristics that were less and less European and more and more American—less and less Spanish, Portuguese, Negro, and Indian, and more and more Mexican, Brazilian, Cuban, Colombian, etc. This metamorphosis modified the impact of the imported institutions and values and set the stage for a slow and difficult process of acculturation.

Early Contributions. The fervor of the early colonial effort performed wonders in the introduction of European ways to the New World. Although handicapped by geography, by the limitations of the tools and techniques of the time, by the smallness of the European contingent and the overwhelming numerical majority of non-European peoples, and by similar factors, the early colonists saw Latin America take on many basic European ways. By 1600 the Spanish and Portuguese languages were firmly entrenched in key centers throughout Latin America. Also by 1600, numerous institutions of higher learning, including several full-fledged universities,[13] to say nothing of institutions for less advanced learning, were to be found in Santo Domingo, Mexico, Argentina, Chile, and Peru. Christianity had established a firm foothold throughout the length and breadth of the colonial area (with the exception of a few isolated regions), as had the political institutions of the conquerors.

There is widespread evidence today of the hectic and highly successful cultural conquest that followed immediately upon the heels of the achievements of the conquistadors. Monuments to this early endeavor are widely in evidence. In the next chapter will be found mention of some of those that are to be observed in Mexico. By and large, it can be said that the basic elements of the cultural foundations of Latin America were laid during the early period, and those elements have played a significant role in the development of education.

Interest in Education. It is a widespread misconception about education in Latin America that the conquerors had little interest in education and that there were no "public schools" prior to the period of independence. Nothing could be further from the truth.

[13] *Higher Education in Latin America* (Washington, D. C.: Division of Intellectual Cooperation, Pan American Union, 1943-1949), Vols. 1-7.

One of the most remarkable aspects of colonial endeavor in many parts of Latin America was the tremendous amount of energy and funds expended in the establishment of schools. Among the very first steps taken after the Conquest was the founding of a large variety of schools—from the nursery school through the university level. In many instances these schools were especially concerned with the native mestizo populations. In some, the schools were exclusively for Europeans. In some areas the schools were primarily for the training of members of the clergy; in others the educational purpose was broader. As already noted, some of the educational effort was represented by formal schools. However, much of that effort was expressed in more general, less formal ways.

The work of the churches, and particularly of the missions, represented educational endeavor of the highest significance. It is to be noted that, whether the educational purpose was to train religious leaders or whether it aimed at a broader range of leadership, whether the educational endeavor concerned itself with academic subject matter or with the inculcation of Christianity, with "community education," and with the teaching of simple trades and skills, the entire program *was an educational one* and should be recognized as such.

Castañeda's[14] thesis (see quotation on p. 102) as to the strong interest in higher education in Mexico can be amply supported with the facts of the history of the universities elsewhere in Latin America. Santo Domingo had a university in 1538,[15] Cuba in 1728,[16] Argentina in 1614,[17] and so on. A great variety of colleges, some of which later became universities, existed in many parts of Latin America before 1600. Throughout the colonial period there was a persistent interest in the establishment of schools of many kinds and levels. Although this interest could not accomplish the impossible—the complete Europeanization, by a relative handful of persons, of millions of culturally diverse Indians scattered over millions of square miles of territory that was tremendously difficult to traverse—it did leave indelible marks on the Latin American

[14] Carlos E. Castañeda, *The Beginnings of University Life in America* (Austin: Texas Catholic Historical Society, 1938), pp. 7-8.
[15] *Higher Education in Latin America,* Vol. 4, p. 49.
[16] *Ibid.,* p. 1.
[17] *Ibid.,* p. 1.

scene, marks that quickly become apparent when one examines the total cultural development of any one of the Latin American nations. This writer has often thought that a comparison of the education of "white" Latin Americans with that of "white" U. S. Americans, during the same period of colonial history, would not show education in colonial Latin America at a disadvantage.

"Public" *Education.* In the United States, as a result of our historical background, we have come to make a hard and fast distinction between "public" and "private" education. Because of the separation of church and state here, education supported on a denominational basis is classed as "private" and, therefore, not "public." On the other hand, "public" education is not administered through the instrumentality of a church (with some rare exceptions). In colonial Latin America, however, the close association of church and state places an entirely different connotation on the concept of "public" education. There, the church was the principal avenue through which the state expressed its interest in education. The state made grants-in-aid to the church schools; the church joined with the state in founding and supervising educational institutions not under the immediate direction of the clergy; the state assigned to the church a variety of educational projects; the entire population was Catholic (or in the process of conversion from non-Christian ways)—in sum, most of the state's support of education was channeled through the agencies of the church, and that interest embraced all the people. "Religious education" under those circumstances *is* "public" education, not "private."

Under this program of church-state education, millions of non-European people were incorporated into the fold of the Spanish and Portuguese empires—as subjects of the crown ("citizens"), as Christians, speaking the language of their conquerors, using their ways and tools, and participating in their institutions. Under this same program, thousands of Latin Americans enjoyed the privileges of advanced formal education. Attention must be called again to the fact that this was taking place long before the founding of Jamestown in Virginia; that full-fledged universities, not to mention numerous colleges, had been operating with a high degree of success for more than eighty years before the establishment of Harvard College, in 1636, and for more than two centuries before there was a university in the United States.

It is particularly important to emphasize that, unlike the educational efforts in the English colonies that became the United States—where the Indian remained a foreigner, was dealt with as an outsider through treaties, and was not looked upon as worthy of incorporation (becoming a citizen only after 1925)—a large portion of educational endeavor in Latin America was concerned with the Indian's conversion and incorporation into the new society. This concern placed a tremendous load on the whole educational process, with a consequent impairment of results. One may gain an appreciation of this fact by comparing the incorporation of Indians in the United States today (some 500,000 including those in Alaska) with that of the 2 million Indians and 14 million mestizos of Mexico. (The figure for Indians is variously estimated at 2 to 6 million, depending on what percentage of the mestizo population is considered Indian.) The contrast becomes more striking when one takes into account the per-capita wealth of the two countries, the proportion of "whites" to Indians, and related factors. The whole point of such a comparison is to reveal that, in judging colonial education in Latin America, which went far in bringing the Indian into the fold, one must recognize the magnitude of the task undertaken and the widespread, if nonacademic, results attained.

The fact to be kept in mind is that the object of church endeavor in Latin America in colonial days was education, "public" education—whether this endeavor was represented in the establishment of missions among the Pueblo Indians of our Southwest, in the founding of seminaries in the Andean region, or in the operation of colleges and universities in Santo Domingo, in Peru, in Mexico, and elsewhere. Furthermore, the achievements of this educational endeavor must be judged not only by the formal degrees conferred or the books written but also by the spread of Christianity and of European ways; by the use of new plants, tools, and techniques by Indians and mestizos everywhere; and by the incorporation of widely scattered and culturally diverse peoples into foreign political and economic institutions.

The Religious Orders. The educational work of the colonial period was carried on principally by religious orders. These orders, notably the Franciscans, Dominicans, Augustinians, and Jesuits, manned many of the schools and missions. Although the work of the other orders should not be minimized, it is to be noted that the influence of the Jesuits was particularly strong and lasting. This is explained in large part by the outstanding preparation of the Jesuits as teachers and by the progressive character of their school curriculum.[18]

The Compañía de Jesús was established early in the sixteenth century for the express purpose of educating Catholic leadership. Through a long and meticulous training of a carefully selected membership, the order developed a dynamic teaching personnel of the highest quality and clarity of purpose. These highly trained teachers offered a *ratio studiorum*, or plan of studies, that was based on humanism, a new intellectual trend that constituted a breaking away from scholasticism and from the other educational norms of the Middle Ages. Thus the order was able to compete successfully with the programs offered by the older, more traditionally minded orders, such as the Augustinian and Dominican.

The Jesuit secondary schools and colleges in the New World were firmly entrenched throughout a period of two hundred years—from shortly before 1600 until the late eighteenth century, when the order was suppressed. During this period, the humanistic and verbalistic features of the Jesuit curriculum became the norm—a norm that has persisted to the present time. Although various tendencies, notably positivism and French influences in the nineteenth century, have modified the humanistic bent given to education (particularly secondary education) by the Jesuits, those tendencies were in turn modified by the older pattern. Only in the last few years have humanism, verbalistic encyclopedism, theoretical and classical education—all products, in whole or in part, of the Jesuit influence or of a subsequent confusion of humanism, positivism, and French romanticism—begun to give ground to laboratory sciences, to vocational courses, and to a more broadly social and practical concept of the purposes of the school.

INDEPENDENCE

Period of Gestation. The persistence of colonial educational norms, such as those of the Jesuits, is not to the discredit of those norms; rather it is a reflection of the slowness of Latin America's

[18] Frederick Eby and Charles Flinn Arrowood, *The Development of Modern Education* (New York: Prentice-Hall, Inc., 1934), pp. 191-198.

transition from a colonial status to that of independence. This slowness is reflected not only in the failure of the new republics to put forth large-scale educational efforts but in their inability to salvage much from the educational programs that had been carried on by the church.

The separation of church and state and the more or less general antagonism of the new governments to the clergy resulted in the neglect and disappearance of many colonial educational institutions. More important still, it resulted in the loss for the new states of the educational training and professional "know-how" of the religious teaching orders. This, in turn, left the establishment of schools for the new nations in professionally untrained and inexperienced hands. Elsewhere this writer has said:

> One salient characteristic of the educational practices inherited from the nineteenth century can be seen in a failure to develop education as a professional career. This failure is not peculiar to Mexico but is evident in most of the countries of Latin America. From the very beginnings of public education in Mexico, school administration and the formulation of educational policy has been in the hands either of political figures who have had only a passing interest in education as a career or of those academic specialists whose limited experience as teachers was seldom supplemented by a broad study of educational theory and practice. The administrative and directive positions in education, instead of being filled by trained and experienced educators from the ranks of a teaching profession, have been assigned as rewards to those in the political world or, on occasion, to some learned person who had attained distinction as a literary figure—to a lawyer, a physician, or someone in a field of endeavor which, though of value in its own right, can seldom constitute a wholly adequate background for the successful discharge of the functions involved in educational administration. This practice has produced a distressing and puzzling lack of continuity in Mexican education. Each administrator or administration, because of this very lack of professional background in education, has relied on individual intuition and untrained interpretation in making far-reaching decisions as to the course which education should take. Each succeeding administration has felt it incumbent upon it to modify the program of its predecessor to conform to its peculiar, and usually equally untrained, viewpoint.[19]

[19] George I. Sánchez, *The Development of Higher Education in Mexico* (New York: King's Crown Press, 1944), p. 84.

Political and economic limitations slowed down the adjustment to independence and handicapped the establishment and support of schools. Outside the religious orders there were virtually no teachers and a great scarcity in all the other essentials of schools— books, other instructional materials, buildings. The new nations were exceedingly poor and unsettled.[20]

Slow Rise of Modern Education. The unsettled political situation persisted into the twentieth century. Although important steps in laying the foundation of modern programs of education were taken by some countries, notably Argentina and Chile, in the nineteenth century, as a general rule until the last two or three decades Latin America has been too poor, too disorganized, and too unconcerned with popular education to make the effort necessary for the establishment of the sort of educational programs which were required to capacitate the masses of the people for democratic self-rule and for material progress.

Latin America has had numerous exponents of educational reforms. From the very inception of independence, some of the leaders recognized the need to establish national systems of schools.[21] Later, such men as Domingo Faustino Sarmiento (Argentina and Chile) and Justo Sierra (Mexico) undertook to modernize education and to spread it more widely. Nevertheless, it was not until recent years that their dreams have begun to be realized.

The Modern Period. Out of the struggles of a century of adjustment to independence there has gradually arisen a consciousness of nationality, a new outlook on cultural values, and a recognition of the important place that stable and widespread programs of modern education have in national growth. Kandel summarizes this clearly when he says:

> It would be surprising if, in the profound crisis which is affecting the whole world, the republics of Latin America remained unaffected. It would be equally surprising if the crisis failed to direct the attention of these countries to the importance of reexamining their educational foundations. There is a ferment in education in the Latin-American republics which has no parallel in their history, but it is too early to note any great or far-reaching reforms in Latin-American education. The ferment is there, but

[20] Amanda Labarca Hubertson, "Educational Development in Latin America," in Charles C. Griffin, ed., *op. cit.,* pp. 218-219.

[21] *Ibid.,* p. 218.

it will be some time before the obstacles in the way of serious changes can be overcome. These obstacles which are due to a vast complex of causes—geography, lack of adequate means of communication and transportation, social attitudes and traditions, economic and political conditions, composition of population, and religious influences—are too great to be overcome in a few years. The immediate ferment may be new, but there is hardly any one of the Latin-American republics which has not produced educational theorists in the nineteenth century and in increasing numbers in the present century who rank as high as any who have written on education in other parts of the world. The difficulty has always been, however, that the leaders of educational thought have not always possessed that capacity for political leadership which would enable them to translate their theories into practice. There have been and there are many educators who, in the expression of educational ideals, could rank with Sarmiento; but the number who possess his political ability has on the whole been small. It is not without significance, perhaps, that professional organizations in Argentina have in the past two years been warned and many teachers and educators suspended or dismissed from their positions when they sought to pay homage to the memory of Sarmiento or to give expression to the ideals for which he stood in education.

The educational ferment will not be checked, for it had its first beginnings not in the current world crisis but in a new dawn of national and cultural self-consciousness which antedated this crisis. Education in the Latin-American republics has been one of the least Latin-American institutions in the sense of being adapted to the Latin-American environment. It has been an amalgam of various influences—North American in elementary education; French in secondary education; German in vocational and technical education. Education, like culture, was expressed in foreign molds. It has only been in recent years that the creative writers and artists have turned to the Latin-American scene with new eyes and have discovered there something that demands forms of expression more appropriate to itself. Such a transformation seems to have been inevitable in all recently settled countries. The cultural leaders of Latin America were not different from their confreres in the United States, New Zealand, or Australia. It may be some time, perhaps, before the Latin-American republics reform their educational systems and attune them to the pressing

needs of their environment, but here lies one of the chief problems now confronting the educational leaders of these republics.[22]

The transformation that Kandel speaks of has gone on rapidly in
most of the Latin American nations in the last twenty years. Mexico,
through gigantic efforts stimulated by a truly popular revolution, is
carrying out a remarkable program of national education. Venezuela
has made beginnings in the establishment of modern schools. Argentina and Uruguay, melting pots for European immigrants, have
begun the reform of old programs and the expansion of education.
The enthusiasm for economic development has stimulated Brazil's
laying of foundations in education, particularly along technological
lines in the upper educational levels. Growing political and economic stability in Cuba has been accompanied by a genuine concern
for education, and her public schools have shown a healthy growth
during the past twenty years. Similar progress may be noted in many
of the other nations.

Many difficult problems face Latin America in the development
of national systems of modern schools. The incorporation of large
masses of indigenous peoples is still in process. Poverty is widespread, and only very slowly are ways and means of raising living
standards being discovered. Geographic barriers and the uneven distribution of population handicap the extension of educational
facilities. Bitter political factionalism, inept leadership, and the
lack of sound political orientation of the masses in most of the
countries has subjected those countries to frequent turmoil and to
governmental instability. The creation of an educational profession
is a long-time job, and most of the Latin American nations have
been at that job only a short time. These obstacles, and others like
them, stand between the beginings that have been made and the
attainment of adequate educational programs.

BIBLIOGRAPHY

Basauri, Carlos, *La población indígena de México* (Mexico City:
Secretaría de Educación Pública, 1940), Vols. I and II. A descrip-

[22] I. L. Kandel, "Problems and Trends of Education in the Latin-
American Republics," in *Intellectual Trends in Latin America* (Austin:
Institute of Latin-American Studies, University of Texas, 1945), pp. 82-83.

tion of the cultures of present-day Mexican Indians. Offers a large amount of material and statistical data and interprets current issues and developments. Reveals the wide distribution, variety, and complexity of Indian cultures.

CASTAÑEDA, CARLOS E., *The Beginnings of University Life in America* (Austin: Texas Catholic Historical Society, 1938). Castañeda has made numerous contributions in the field of Mexican history, particularly the history of the missions in Texas. This pamphlet, one of several short studies that he has made of the early colonial history of Mexico, reveals that great educational efforts were made by the first Spaniards.

Cultural Bases of Hemispheric Understanding (Austin: Institute of Latin-American Studies, University of Texas, 1942). From time to time the Institute sponsors lecturers on Latin American affairs. Through its publications, the Institute presents the papers delivered at such lectures, as well as researches conducted by its students and faculty. This particular publication, in addition to the lecture on art by Fernández, includes those of Charles A. Thomson (on inter-American solidarity), Julio Jiménez Rueda (on Latin American literature), Pablo Max Ynsfran (on Pan-Americanism), and Federico de Onís (on Spain and the Southwest).

EBY, FREDERICK, and CHARLES FLINN ARROWOOD, *The Development of Modern Education* (New York: Prentice-Hall, Inc., 1934). One of the best histories of education available. However, as with all other such texts in the United States, little space is devoted to the educational history of southern Europe and none to that of Latin America. Chap. VI, "The Catholic Reformation and Education," (pp. 189-199) gives a brief insight into a few of the special factors that entered into education in Catholic countries.

GRIFFIN, CHARLES C., ed., *Concerning Latin American Culture* (New York: Columbia University Press, 1940). The papers read at a series of conferences sponsored by the National Committee of the United States on International Intellectual Cooperation. A valuable series of interpretations by highly responsible and competent specialists. The particular lectures cited are those by Fernando de los Ríos, formerly Minister of Education of the Spanish Republic and Spanish Ambassador to the United States; by Gilberto Freyre, the great Brazilian sociologist; and by Amanda Labarca Hubertson, a distinguished Chilean educator. Other very worth-while chapters are included—on art, music, Indian cultures, literature, etc.

Higher Education in Latin America (Washington, D. C.: Division of Intellectual Cooperation, Pan American Union, 1943-1949), Vols I-VII. A series of bulletins giving a brief history of each Latin American university, with a detailed presentation of organization and plans of studies. The series is still in process of completion.

INMAN, SAMUEL GUY, *Latin America* (Chicago: Willett, Clark and Company, 1937). Inman has devoted many years to the interpretation of events in Latin America. In this book he gives an overall analysis of Latin America's place in world life.

Intellectual Trends in Latin America (Austin: Institute of Latin-American Studies, University of Texas, 1945). A series of lectures (see above) by William Spence Robertson (historiography), Russell H. Fitzgibbon (government), Theodore Apstein (theater), Gilbert Chase (music), Samuel Ramos (philosophy), Isaac L. Kandel (education), Eastin Nelson (economics), Fernando de los Ríos (Spanish refugees), Rex D. Hopper (sociology), Martin E. Erickson (Central-American literature), Antonio Castro Leal (poetry), and Erico Verissimo (Brazilian literature).

Inter-American Intellectual Interchange (Austin: Institute of Latin-American Studies, University of Texas, 1943). The papers read at an Institute conference by Samuel Guy Inman, Donald Coney, Sturgis E. Leavitt, Risieri Frondizi, Fefferson Rea Spell, Ezequiel Ordóñez, Arturo Torres Rioseco, Carlos E. Castañeda, Arturo Arnáiz y Freg, Arthur P. Whittaker, Hugo Leipziger, Robert C. Smith, and Manuel Toussaint.

JAMES, CONCHA ROMERO, "Latin American Trends," *Among Us*, No. 1 (Washington, D. C.: October 1942), pp. 1-3. Mrs. James, Chief of the Division of Intellectual Cooperation of the Pan American Union, has done much to disseminate information about intellectual endeavor in Latin America. In this short article she summarizes some of the common trends in education.

KANDEL, I. L., ed., *Education in the Latin American Countries* (New York: Teachers College, Columbia University, 1942). This is an educational yearbook of the International Institute of Teachers College. Kandel's introduction leads into a brief exposition, by an expert from each country, of current developments in education in the twenty Latin American nations. This valuable work is typical of the numerous contributions made to the study of Latin American education by, or under stimulation and direction of, the dean of comparative education—Professor Kandel.

Latin America in Social and Economic Transition (Albuquerque:

University of New Mexico Press, 1943). The lectures by Donald D. Brand on the American Indian and on strategic materials were part of a series which includes papers on land and on economic problems, by Richard F. Behrendt; on malnutrition, by Michel Pijoán; on humanistic solidarity, by Stuart Cuthbertson; on Chile, by Erna Fergusson; and on Mexico, by George I. Sánchez.

SÁNCHEZ, GEORGE I., *The Development of Higher Education in Mexico* (New York: King's Crown Press, 1944). A review of the backgrounds for higher education in Mexico, with an interpretation of present status and major issues.

SMITH, T. LYNN, and ALEXANDER MARCHANT, eds., *Brazil: Portrait of Half a Continent* (New York: The Dryden Press, 1951). A useful volume of essays by both North American and Latin American scholars on Brazil's history, geography, population, culture, economy, institutions, and civilization. Includes a valuable chapter on education.

4 · EDUCATION IN *Mexico*

GEORGE I. SÁNCHEZ

Mexico has for many years been a bridge between the cultures of North America and Latin America. It retains the more leisurely tempo, courtesy, and aesthetic sensitivity of Latin America and, at the same time, has applied the technology of North America to mineral resources, agriculture, and industry. Furthermore, Mexico has experimented with and made marked progress in the field of universal education, especially in the twentieth century. Mexico has an area of approximately 764,000 square miles, or is about one fourth the size of the United States. As Stuart Chase has pointed out, the country is shaped like a cornucopia open toward the north; it is bordered by high mountains on the west and east, and the central plateau rises to about 8000 feet. The population is approximately 24,448,000, almost twice that of Canada, and the density is about thirty people per square mile.

Mexico must deal with certain major problems, including the tradition of political instability and of control essentially by a small elite in which the army plays an important role. The country has great natural resources, including soil, but it also suffers from widespread poverty, since land utilization is poor. Mexico's history has been marked by a series of revolutions, the greatest of which occurred in the twentieth century and included demands for land reform, national control of mineral resources, separation of church and state, and extension of education for the masses. Despite her extensive problems, Mexico has made great progress in health, agriculture, production, industrialization, and, above all, in the direction of universal education.

—A. H. M.

Education in Mexico today is peculiarly identified with the social and economic forces which have played back and forth for centuries across a scene in which the variety and contrasts of the land have been matched by exotic and variegated culture contacts. The Mexican past is found to a surprising degree in the present; and the educational experience of yesterday, which responded to the circumstances of that period, is a vital part of today's school. In the milieu of that school the Mexican historical experience—the Conquest, the Indian, independence, the Revolution of 1910—lives again and weighs heavily in molding the character of educational theory and practice.

The Mexican scene, the setting for the schools of today and of tomorrow, has often been described.[1] One of the most penetrating interpreters of the scene was Moisés Sáenz who, speaking of rural education, once said:

> This, then, is the human scene upon which the rural school must act: an abrupt and gloomy land, indomitable mountain range, thirsty steppe, sweet plateau, virgin forest, torrential ravine, a provident clime; a people learned in the wisdom of many races, with a memory of many traditions, tired at times, more often with virginal strength; a confused murmuring of strange tongues, kaleidoscopic coursing of lives and customs; a fluid race, flowing constantly, pure here, turbid there; the complex mentality of the Indian, Moor, and Castilian; a strange religion which sprays the pagan petals of the *zempatzúchil* before the Christian cross; a country of many peoples, united in sentiment, divided in ideas; a soul in the making, and upon this cosmos the gust of a revolution which has passed leaving the boughs of the trees still waving, the leaves of the forest still trembling, and the consciences awakened and awed, lifting their eyes and seeing a heaven upon which a new sun shines. A magnificent scene upon which the rural teacher comes as a product of that community, planted in

---

[1] See George I. Sánchez, *Mexico—A Revolution by Education* (New York: The Viking Press, 1936), pp. 3-53.

that ground, awakened also and excited by the same hurricane which upset every one, tremulous by the very desire to become.[2]

This statement by Sáenz points out the fluid and variable character of Mexican culture—"flowing constantly, pure here, turbid there"—and suggests that Mexican social institutions, responding to the continuous impact of culture contacts and conflicts, are constantly in the process of change. If there is any one outstanding characteristic of Mexican culture, it is that of change, of transition. From time immemorial until the present, the people of Mexico have been subjected to periodic and often brusque cultural changes. These have not been the changes which are normally experienced by a society in the course of its cultural development. They have not been simply those incident to the normal adjustment of cultures. Rather, the people of Mexico have time and again felt the rude shock of major cultural upheavals; the history of Mexican culture is made up of a series of crises which have left the effects of their passing deeply and indelibly etched upon the human scene.

Let us visualize life in pre-Columbian Mexico. First we have a hazy view of simple peoples wandering southward after their ancestors had crossed the Bering Strait from Asia. Some of these primitive, nomadic tribes finally find a resting place somewhere in Mexico, where they remain. Some who preceded them have gone to other parts of the hemisphere. Those who remain in Mexico continue their several ways of life; some settle down to agricultural pursuits. The early people of Mexico soon feel the impact of new peoples coming from the north. These new peoples incorporate the older cultures as they build new ways of life. They, in turn, are overrun by other waves that in successive periods move southward.

These culture contacts produced fundamental transitions in the ways of life of these early peoples. The fusion of cultures brought about through this process produced such famous civilizations as those of the Mayas and the Aztecs. The pre-Columbian cultures of Mexico were the products of contacts among many peoples of varying ways of life. Every stage in the growth of those cultures constituted an important social and economic change for the peoples involved. One can say, then, that even before the coming of the Europeans the peoples of Mexico were growing in response to

[2] Moisés Sáenz, *La educación rural en México* (Mexico City: Secretaría de Educación Pública, 1928), p. 27.

successive cultural crises which produced fundamental transitions in their ways of life.

The rudest shock and the most far-reaching transition was occasioned by the coming of Europeans in the sixteenth century. This event produced a cultural crisis among all the peoples of Mexico, and it brought about changes in the way of life of every tribal group in every section of the region. The spread of Christianity, of the Spanish language, and of European ways, tools, techniques, and institutions brought about the adjustments which constitute the foundation stones of the Mexican nation of today.

The adjustments necessitated by this major cultural transition were spread over a period of three hundred years. The colonial period of New Spain was essentially a period during which the peoples of Mexico sought to adapt themselves to the fusion of European and indigenous cultures. This process of adaptation had within it the germ of later crises and transitions. The growth of the mestizo, the rise of the church as an economic and political power, the conflicts between *criollos* (Creoles: Spaniards born in the New World) and *peninsulares* (Spaniards born in the Spanish peninsula), etc. during these three centuries presaged later cultural upheavals.

These later upheavals began with the war for independence. Independence from Spain did not bring a satisfactory answer to the issues which had arisen during the adjustment process represented by the colonial period. The adjustment to independence itself required another century—a period of transition from colonial status to nationality, which was filled with major crises of all kinds.[3]

The enthusiasm for French culture throughout Latin America during the nineteenth century was strengthened in Mexico by Maximilian's empire. This enthusiasm tended to lure the interest of Mexican leaders—novelists, artists, politicians, educators—away from native values and basic reforms to the worship of foreign forms and to a superficial and unrealistic sophistication. This, in turn, led to a growing unrest among the masses and among those leaders who would look for the inspiration and materials of nationality in the Mexican scene itself.

[3] Nathaniel Weyl, "Mexico, European and Native," in Charles C. Griffin, ed., *Concerning Latin American Culture* (New York: Columbia University Press, 1940), pp. 136-137.

The century after independence was attained did not serve as a wholly successful transition. The process of adjustment to independence bore within it the germ of revolution—the Revolution of 1910-1920. Thus we find Mexico resorting to violence, as it had done one hundred years before, in seeking a settlement of the cultural issues which centuries of evolution had not succeeded in settling. But a successful revolution, although it was the great crisis of Mexican history, could not by itself achieve a full-fledged and well-balanced Mexican cultural personality. The winning of the Revolution of 1910-1920 by the Mexican masses simply set the stage; the basic adjustments and transitions were yet to be made and the fundamental cultural issues were yet to be met.

The period from 1920 to the present has been one of constant crisis and of numerous transitions. From Carranza and Obregón to Cárdenas, to Avila Camacho, and to Alemán there is evidence of a never-ending succession of crises and a kaleidoscopic series of basic social transitions. It is important to observe that the administrations of every one of these men represents a phase of the transition from the Revolution to the future Mexican nation. The particular phase of the transition chosen by each as the administration's program of work—education, the church-state issue, the agrarian problem, industrialization, etc.—must be recognized as such, simply a phase of the total transition. It is only by taking all the administrations from 1920 through the present time and examining them as though they constituted a unit that one may observe the process which reflects the will of the people of Mexico in their attempt to attain balanced nationality.

As we shall see, much has been accomplished by the educational reforms of the last thirty years. But a staggering task still lies ahead. José Santos Valdés in 1943 recognized the inadequacy of recent accomplishments, and he urged a more militant attack on basic problems. Reviewing the historical battles, largely successful, waged to free the fatherland from oppression, he stated:

> Nevertheless, the majority of the people—the immense majority —needs to be snatched from the darkest dungeons of history: those of ignorance. Millions of Indians need, joined to political and economic liberty, the truth that science gives. Too, millions of mestizos need the light of literacy to be able to penetrate the dominion of a free and democratic life in which man's conscience

is cultivated precisely so that, living within that dominion, it may at the same time be the most zealous defender and the most powerful impeller of that way of life. We can begin to wage that battle right now, and right now begin to assure victory for ourselves.[4]

The causes of ignorance, of illiteracy, and of economic backwardness in Mexico are many. A review of the major factors which have operated to handicap the growth of the nation will reveal that in Mexico poverty and ignorance have deep roots. Such an examination will reveal, too, the genesis of the educational changes by which the people of Mexico are seeking to overcome the handicaps of their heritage.

THE MEXICAN HERITAGE

The People. It is impossible to understand education in Mexico without a prior understanding of the evolution of the Mexican people, a people whose biological complexities are more than matched by their cultural variety. This is suggested by the fact that today there are some 2½ million Mexicans who speak one of fifty-four Indian languages. The persistence of these languages, more than four centuries after the Conquest, is highly significant to the educator. More significant, however, is the cultural diversity which this linguistic variety represents. As Robert Redfield puts it, "The 'fifty-four' different languages in terms of which the census enumerates the Indian-speaking population are not to be taken as a definite and exhaustive list. . . . The fact of consequence is the great linguistic diversity, with the cultural separateness that accompanies it."[5]

The persistence of Indian languages and Indian ways has led many authorities to insist that Mexico is Indian. This would imply that cultural development in Mexico is simply the process by which the European and his institutions have become, or are becoming, Indianized. By the same reasoning, education is reduced largely

---

[4] José Santos Valdés, *La batalla por la cultura* (Mexico City: Ediciones Morelos, 1943), pp. 7-8.

[5] Robert Redfield, "The Indian in Mexico," in Arthur P. Whittaker, ed., *Mexico Today, Annals of the American Academy of Political and Social Science,* Vol. 208 (March 1940), p. 135.

to a process by which the Indian culture is brought up to date, injected with the vitamins of modern technology, and inoculated against the virus of the indigenous deficiencies. Such an interpretation is much too simple, and it ignores the fact that the typical Mexican, representing the vast majority of the population, is not Indian but mestizo.

Mexican *mestizaje* (the mixing of races and cultures) is cultural as well as biological. The development of the *mestizaje* had its beginning in the first days of the Conquest, and it is still in progress. At the outset there were several million Indians and a few hundred Europeans. Only some 300,000 Spaniards came to New Spain during the three colonial centuries, and subsequent immigration was not particularly heavy. The biological crossing of the races that has taken place between this large number of Indians and the comparatively very small number of Spaniards has, in truth, "Indianized" the latter—if by that we mean that the mestizo has a lot of Indian blood. Today there are in Mexico 2-4 million Indians, 16-18 million mestizos, and 2-4 million "whites." That is to say that, biologically, around 90 percent of the Mexican people have some degree of Indian blood, and probably 75 percent are more "Indian" than "white."

These biological estimates can, however, be highly misleading. The very fact that, although the vast majority of the people are largely Indian in the biological sense, less than 10 percent speak an Indian language (and less than 5 percent speak only an Indian language) is indicative of the process of acculturation that has produced the typical Mexican—the mestizo. The Mexican government recognizes the fallacy of biological classification,[6] as do students of Mexican problems such as Nathan L. Whetten.[7] The great majority of the people of Mexico (including a large percentage of pure-blood Indians), their biological make-up notwithstanding, do not live as Indians. They speak Spanish; they are Christians; their institutions are basically Western. But they are not Spaniards—for their language, their religion, and their institutions have taken on a local flavor—the flavor of Indian values transformed by accultura-

---

[6] *México en cifras, atlas estadístico* (Mexico City: Secretaría de la Economía Nacional, 1934), pp. 13-15.

[7] Nathan L. Whetten, *Rural Mexico* (Chicago: University of Chicago Press, 1948), pp. 50-63.

tion. Culturally, the Mexican is neither Spanish nor Indian. With the cultural contributions supplied by both his progenitors he has built a new culture, reminiscent now of one and now of the other but integral and Mexican, or mestizo, withal.

The variety of Indian cultures involved in this blending, the varied settings and circumstances within which the blending has taken and is taking place, and similar factors give Mexico's *mestizaje* a multiformity beyond description—and rule out the assumption that the Mexican school can be uniform. In response to this multiformity, educational policies and practices follow diverse, and sometimes divergent, courses. Concern for Indian culture goes hand in hand with *castellanización,* the conversion from Indian languages to Spanish; coeducation has been eliminated in certain schools in spite of inability to support duplications and in face of the over-all tendency to get away from reactionary norms; the clergy operate some schools, in spite of express constitutional prohibition; and so on.

All this means that it is hazardous to generalize about the Mexican people or their schools from a limited observation; what is true in one region may not hold in another. As we have seen, the people of Mexico are not culturally homogeneous. Furthermore, since their diversity is based on heterogeneous manifestations of *mestizaje,* the cultural blend peculiar to a given area will affect the school policy and program there in ways that are not necessarily common to other areas.

The Land. The Mexicans are an agricultural people, rooted to the land, and the problems of land use and management and the fundamental problems of the national economy. By the same token, it is inevitable that Mexican educational reforms should be closely identified with the problems facing rural peoples: illiteracy, isolation, poor health, outmoded techniques, and the like. Whetten says:

> Rural Mexico is geographically and culturally isolated from the general life of the nation. This is due partly to the mountainous nature of the country and partly to the lack of development of transportation and communication facilities for connecting the rural areas with the large centers of population. Mexico has made considerable progress in recent years in extending her system of trunkline highways, which link some of her principal urban centers. In a mountainous country, road

building is expensive, and, although the federal government is spending about fifty million pesos a year (about $10,309,279, or 5 per cent of the total federal budget) on her highways, there is still almost complete absence of village-to-market roads connecting the farm population with the trunk highways, railway stations, or marketing centers. Rural people are still dependent on the burro, the mule, or the human beast of burden to transport their goods to and from the markets. In many areas markets of any appreciable size are so far away that perishable products cannot be marketed at all, and the marketing of staple products becomes an expensive and time-consuming process. This is one of the reasons—the other is lack of control of tropical diseases— why vast areas of the potentially more productive coastal regions have remained practically undeveloped.

Culturally, the rural people are so isolated that they have little opportunity to share in the advantages which modern science and education have brought to the homes and lives of many urban dwellers and to less isolated rural people. Having little contact with newer ideas and ways of doing things, they continue to live according to the customs and traditions of their forefathers, without any realization that more efficient ways and techniques may have been discovered.[8]

Mexico's rurality is made particularly significant by the meagerness of her agricultural resources and by the natural obstacles to increased productivity. Less than 8 percent of her area is crop land. Elsewhere this writer has pointed out:

It takes no elaborate analysis to demonstrate Mexico's agricultural poverty. Her agricultural area totals less than fifteen million hectares, only eleven per cent of the area of the nation. This represents less than one hectare per capita. Of this area, less than 60 per cent is under cultivation and, of that, only about 80 per cent is harvested. This means that there is less than half a hectare of productive land per capita. Add to this the fact that the productivity of much of it is seriously limited by such factors as inadequate water supply and poor soil conditions, and it will be evident that, though agriculture is Mexico's primary economic base, Mexican agriculture does not constitute the foundation for an abundant economy.[9]

[8] *Ibid.*, pp. 8-9.
[9] George I. Sánchez, *The Development of Higher Education in Mexico* (New York: King's Crown Press, 1944), p. 7.

"Mexico is not a rich country, but an extremely poor one," says the Mexican economist Federico Bach. He notes that Mexico is extremely poor in both minerals and agriculture and that only an enormous investment of money will help overcome the great scarcity of water.[10]

This means that the development of educational institutions has been founded upon inadequacy and poverty. It means, also, that the fundamental educational issue in Mexico is that of improving rural life and helping to supplement the basic agricultural economy. This, in large measure, is the essence of the educational reform movement which has been under way since 1920; and it is the pressing nature of this issue that has stimulated government, particularly the federal government, to stress expansion of realistic rural education—through rural elementary schools, normal schools, agricultural schools, and cultural missions. It has also stimulated the establishment, by the Federation, states, municipalities, and private agencies, of new types of technical and vocational schools at all levels, as well as the increasing modification of urban schools to the end that realistic studies may have a more important place in curriculums which, traditionally, have been humanistic and verbalistic.

The Revolution.   Numerous authorities have written extensively of the Revolution of 1910-1920. Although minor differences of interpretation may be noted in these accounts, there is general agreement that this popular upheaval was the product of (1) the poverty and land hunger of the masses and (2) the long-standing insensitivity and unresponsiveness of governments to the basic material and spiritual facts of life of the great majority of the Mexican population—the mestizos and the Indians. It is also agreed that the Revolution symbolizes the hopes and aspirations of the Mexican masses to belong and to have status, and serves as the inspiration and driving force behind the major reforms that have been under way in Mexico since that time. In 1936 this author wrote:

> For more than four hundred years passions have burned or smouldered. Occasionally a burst of flame has sought to give direction to the emotional urge for relief. Sometimes a common

[10] Federico Bach, "The Distribution of Wealth in Mexico," Arthur P. Whittaker, ed., *op. cit.*, p. 77.

enemy has driven Mexicans to make a united effort, but just for a brief period and only to falter and fall apart, leaving Mexico but little farther along the road to national unity. The successful stroke for independence from Spain; the tremendous loss of territory to the United States; and the repulsion of the French-inducted Emperor, Maximilian, were but temporary stimulants to the flagging national hopes of a strife-born Mexico. Through all strife there has been evidence only of unrest, of uncertainty, of vague hopes of the unfulfilled wish to be free. Always the desire to be free, but never a clear vision as to ultimate national freedom. Always the search for redemption, but never a national consciousness as to wherein redemption lay.

The sporadic brilliance of an Hidalgo, of a Juárez, of a Madero—yes, even of a Zapata and a Villa—in desperate thrusts at restraining shackles, sought to unfetter the hands and the souls of the Mexicans. These efforts, while successful perhaps in an historical sense, were to no immediate avail in freeing Mexico from the chains of national cultural lethargy. The smouldering mass that has been Mexico has lacked unity, has lacked vision. The motley hordes that flocked to the standards of revolt have been driven to arms and rebellion by inarticulate hopes—by a blind and purely emotional search for release. The *pelado* (poor man) wanted lands, the *indio* (Indian) wanted justice, the *cura* (priest) wanted converts and power, the *politico* (politician) wanted autonomy . . . the Mexican people did not know what they wanted. In fact, the Mexicans as a People have not existed! That is the crux of the problem that was Mexico— that is the basic cause for the turmoil of yesterday.

Independence from Spain in 1821 severed the legal ties that bound colonial Mexico to a foreign power but it did not sever the bonds of exploitation and oppression. Change in form did not change the kind of malady that afflicted the people and, to all intents and purposes, Mexico remained the "mother of the world and the stepmother of Mexicans."

The armed Revolution of 1910 was a bloody expression of thwarted hopes. It was a magnificent gesture of disorganized intolerance. It was the impatient emotional explosion of a long-suffering people aroused to a frenzied revolt against its inheritance of subjugation, exploitation, and discrimination. This gesture, this explosion, was chaotic and brutal and it left Mexico physically exhausted and prostrate. To its everlasting glory, however, it left Mexicans with a vision, with a great National

hope, and with the glimmerings of an insight into the fundamental ills that had plagued them. The Revolution left Mexicans
on the road to national recovery. It left them with the courage to
embark upon a new voyage, with renewed hopes, in a new day.
The indomitable spirit of the Mexican was not crushed. Physically exhausted, he has borrowed vigour from his trials and suffer-
ings to undertake the road to freedom.

The Mexican mêlée arose from intolerance, ignorance, fanaticism, and racial and geographic provincialism. It arose from the
myriad clashes incident to the subjugation of the many by a
few—from the disorganized cross purposes of a multitude of
contacts among a conglomeration of cultures. The Revolution
of 1910 brought the mêlée to a climax by submitting the rights
and needs of the masses to the test of war and blood. By 1917
the proletariat had achieved its place of recognition and prestige
in the Mexican sun. After the bloody Revolution, the people—
not the *cura* [the hierarchy] or the *militar* [the military], not the
patrón [the entrepreneur] or the *hacendado* [the landowner]—
held the destiny of Mexico.

The Revolution did not end with the silencing of guns and
the sheathing of swords. The victory of the masses made it
imperative that the Revolution continue, for the injustices of
the past had made it impossible for the people to seize the
fruits which victory normally would have made possible. Reform,
redemption, restitution, and retribution could not await the
tedious process of evolution. The Revolution had to go on if
the shambles of 1910-1917 were not to be in vain.

Zapata's cry of *"Tierra y Libertad"*—"Land and Liberty"—
during the armed revolution finds echo in the present-day peaceful agrarian revolution. The political and economic dominance
of the Church has been broken by a forceful application of the
inherent right of the State to control national economy and
policy. By peaceful revolution Mexico is striving to overcome in
the space of a few years the handicaps it has inherited from
centuries of neglect.

Neither the gust of a revolution that has passed nor the dreams
of a victorious proletariat can overcome the handicaps of the
past in the face of the ignorance of the masses. The cry of the
Revolution for the enlightenment of the masses, *"Educar es
redimir"*—"To educate is to redeem"—struck at the fundamental
cause of the Mexican mêlée, ignorance. The major fruit of
victory was the recognition of the rights of the *indio*, of the

pelado, of the *campesino* (peasant), to enlightenment and culture and to the right to participate and belong in a changing social order. Education, formerly the privilege of the few, by virtue of the popular conquest became a national medium of revolution— a fire to forge a Mexican nation.[11]

A similar interpretation has been made by Samuel Guy Inman:

> The most tremendous event on the American continent during the last two decades has been the Mexican revolution. Like the upheavals in Russia, Turkey and China, it is notable for its fundamental rethinking and reorganization of all life. Its originality is shown in the fact that it preceded the Russian revolution, to which it is often erroneously traced, by some eight years. In its early days, under the leadership of Madero, it was principally interested in political questions but, under a group of young idealists who surrounded Carranza, it soon adopted the socialistic program which was officially set down in the Constitution of Querétaro in 1917. It must therefore be considered not a military event, but a social upheaval, a triumph of idealism, a revolution of the public mind.
>
> Probably not since the founding of the democracy of the United States has anything more original been undertaken in the New World. A white European-North American capitalistic regime is being replaced by an Indian communal system. Private property and the machine are not being eliminated, but are distinctly being subordinated to the welfare of the community as a whole. The fundamental place of land in Mexican life is being emphasized.
>
> The movement has been so incomprehensible to foreigners and to those Mexicans who cling to the ideals of European culture, precisely because all fundamental human desires have been channeled into an urge for a new Indo-Americanism. Loyalty to native values has been made primal. Faced with the probability of being ever more cruelly exploited, Mexico resolved to change wholesale formerly accepted principles of social life. Irrespective of customs, traditions and surface appearances, she has committed herself to a complete reorientation of political, social, educational and spiritual values.
>
> In the early days of the revolution a new respect for work and a love for play began to develop. The old worship of the hidalgo, the "son of something," and the wasteful expenditure by govern-

[11] George I. Sánchez, *Mexico—A Revolution by Education*, pp. 4-7.

ment and by individuals were frowned upon. The Indian, who had been forbidden in the time of Díaz to appear in the cities in native garb, was now encouraged to live his own life, and the young people of the cities staged attractive Indian plays glorifying the life of the Aztecs, the Mayas, the Zapotecas and the Yaquis. Opposed to the *científicos*, [the intellectuals] who had ruled in a lofty manner in utter disregard of the common people, the young revolutionists encouraged the rule of the middle and proletarian classes. They fled from the dominance of French art, of Roman religion and of North American industrialism. A new order of crusaders developed in all fields, including education, labor, agriculture, sanitation, art and literature. Discussions with government leaders in Mexico City and in some of the state capitals during the 1920's often made the visitor feel that he was interviewing the successors of Old Testament prophets.[12]

These interpretations suggest that educational policy in Mexico is not, as in the United States, the outgrowth of a long educational tradition. Although traditional factors—the brilliant contributions of the clergy in the sixteenth century, the humanistic influence, the nineteenth-century influence of the positivists, and the like—enter into it, the program of Mexican schools is of recent creation. In response to the critical issues raised by the Revolution, new constitutional provisions and other laws on education were written expressly to meet needs hitherto unrecognized. The application of the new principles set forth in these laws was, of necessity, a matter of improvisation, and educational method has been, to a large degree, opportunistic—particularly in fields for which satisfactory patterns did not exist elsewhere, such as rural education, mass literary programs, elementary practical agriculture, the education of isolated Indian groups, and community education.

SCHOOLS OF THE REVOLUTION

Elementary Schools. Because the Revolution made educational reform a crucial national issue, the federal government (through the Secretariat of Public Education, headed by a Secretary in the Cabinet of the President) has taken on a major share of the responsi-

[12] Samuel Guy Inman, *Latin America* (Chicago: Willett, Clark and Company, 1937), pp. 375-376.

bility for the spread of education. Article 3 of the Constitution of 1917 (amended in 1946)[13] gives the Federation authority to participate in education, along with the states and municipalities, and vests broad powers in Congress for the regulation of the three-way responsibility for public education. This authorization enabled the central government, which before that time was involved in education only in the Federal District (Mexico City and suburbs) and the Territories, to inaugurate a program which has grown to the point where 60 percent of the more than 20,000 public elementary schools (grades one to six) in the nation are federal schools. These federal elementary schools enroll some 1,200,000 pupils, whereas state and municipal elementary schools enroll 700,000 children. Federal participation in education is on the increase. Unfortunately, this increase is accompanied by a decrease in state and municipal effort and a consequent reduction in the net gains that might otherwise have been expected.[14]

One of the notable achievements of federal participation in education has been the establishment of rural schools. Whereas rural schools were virtually nonexistent before 1920, today 80 percent of the public elementary schools (with almost half of the public elementary-school enrollment) are rural schools. Of the rural schools, 70 percent are federal, 24 percent state and municipal, and 8 percent private or of mixed private and government support. All schools in Mexico are required to adapt the common curriculum to the particular needs of their environment. This results in a great variety of school and community programs designed to improve rural life. In one place the program may involve a school garden and emphasis on the improvement of local agriculture. In another, the stress may be in the field of public health. Elsewhere, a rural school may be pointing its efforts toward recreation and adult education.

There are still many rural areas without elementary schools, and many of the existing schools offer instruction only in the first two or three grades. This, together with the inadequacy of the urban programs, explains in part why more than 2 million children of school age are not in school. This in turn augments the illiteracy

[13] Nathan L. Whetten, *op. cit.,* pp. 430-431.
[14] José Santos Valdés, *op. cit.,* pp. 58-60.

statistics (51.6 percent for the nation), which are based on the population of ten years of age and over.[15]

The states and municipalities support about 40 percent of the public elementary schools. These nonfederal public schools are about equally divided between rural and urban areas. They enroll almost a half million urban children and over 200,000 rural children. There are a total of a little over one thousand private elementary schools, with an enrollment of 167,000 pupils—146,000 urban and 21,000 rural. In addition, a similar number of schools are supported jointly by private and government agencies. These schools enroll over 100,000 urban children and 50,000 rural children.

Secondary Schools. Secondary education begins at the termination of the six-year elementary program; and, from the point of view of the United States, it may be thought of as continuing for the following five years. In Mexico, however, *educación secundaria* refers only to the first three of these five years. The last two years are covered by separate and specialized vocational schools and by preprofessional schools. The latter, the *preparatorias*, constitute the lower college of the university and, to all intents and purposes, must be considered a phase of higher education; the former consist of a small number of trade and technical schools, with both terminal and continuation features, located in a few of the larger cities.

The plan of operation of these three-year post-elementary schools has been changed several times, and there has been a steady growth in their number (from four in 1926 to 273 in 1946). At present their curriculums and plans of work are much like those of the U. S. high school. Of these schools, 134 are public schools and 139 are private. The total enrollment is around 50,000, almost half of which is concentrated in schools located in the Federal District.

There are seventeen agricultural schools that offer both upper-elementary and secondary courses. The total enrollment in these schools is around two thousand students. Also, the first three years of all the normal schools comprise a specialized sort of *educación secundaria*.

As can be seen, secondary education in Mexico is reaching but a

[15] Nathan L. Whetten, *op. cit.*, pp. 416-424.

small segment of the population. While much progress has been made in the establishment of *secundarias*, this program is still in its infancy and will have to be much expanded if a real dent is to be made in Mexico's widespread educational deficiency. Inevitably, the success of social and economic reforms will be determined by the extent to which mass education is extended beyond the elementary school.

Teacher Education. The lack of trained teachers has been a principal drawback in the development of schools in Mexico. Great efforts have been made in trying to meet this lack. There are now eighteen rural normal schools, fifteen urban normal schools, one superior normal school, and several institutes and agencies for part-time and in-service training of teachers. As a rule, except for the superior normal school, these institutions are unisexual.

The rural normal schools, all federal, enroll around four thousand students, most of whom are men. These schools are six-year post-elementary schools located in rural areas. They emphasize activities related to rural life—in agriculture for boys, in home-making for girls. All are boarding schools, and most of the students are subsidized by the government.

The normal schools in urban centers, enrolling over five thousand students, are of the same level as the rural normal schools; but, instead of concentrating on agricultural or homemaking activities, they emphasize classroom studies. The Superior Normal School in Mexico City enrolls around one thousand students, and it is comparable to teachers' colleges in the United States. This school is directing its efforts toward the training of secondary-school teachers and supervisory, administrative, and other special personnel. The universities also offer professional education courses.

Cultural Missions and Rural Education. The *misión cultural,* the rural school, and the rural normal school are distinctly Mexican creations, and they constitute outstanding contributions to education. With all their material lacks, and even though they often suffer from inadequate professional resources, these institutions have produced noteworthy results in the improvement of rural life in Mexico. Their "grass-roots" approach to the problem of rural education is simple, direct, well-rounded, and in complete rapport with the culture of the local community.

The plan of operation of the cultural missions has been revised

several times. They used to operate as traveling normal schools.[16]
Since 1942, the rural missions (about forty in number now) have
been dedicated to community education, and they stay in a locality
for one to three years.[17] Their purpose, as Whetten puts it, is ". . . to
improve the economic, social, and cultural conditions of rural
communities in some of the more backward areas of Mexico and
to shorten the distance which separates the rural inhabitants
culturally from the national life."[18]

A rural cultural mission is composed of a staff representing the
fields of public health, agriculture, constructions, trades and industries, music, recreation, and rural mechanics. The staff members
insinuate themselves into the life of the community and quickly
begin stimulating activities in their respective fields. As a rule they
work in close cooperation with local teachers and governmental
agencies. The missions constitute a department of the national
Secretariat of Public Education, and they are controlled and supervised directly from Mexico City.

Higher Education. Mexico has a long and highly interesting
history of higher education.[19] A college for Indians was established
in 1536; a school, still in operation as the lower college of the
University of Michoacán, was founded in 1540; the origins of the
National University go back to the Royal and Pontifical University
founded in 1551; and a variety of other institutions of higher learning operated in Mexico during the colonial period, some surviving
the wars of independence. Castañeda, taking strong issue with the
notion that there was little interest in education in colonial Latin
America, used Mexico to illustrate his thesis.

Let us take a glance at the relative progress of education
in Mexico and the thirteen English colonies at the beginning of
the American Revolution. By 1776, the year of the Declaration
of Independence, the Royal and Pontifical University of Mexico
had been in continuous operation for two hundred and twenty-
three years. During that time it had granted 1,162 doctors' and
masters' degrees in all four faculties: Theology, Arts, Canon Law

---

[16] George I. Sánchez, *Mexico—A Revolution by Education,* pp. 63-95.
[17] Nathan L. Whetten, *op. cit.,* pp. 433-453.
[18] *Ibid.,* p. 433.
[19] See George I. Sánchez, *The Development of Higher Education in Mexico.*

and Civil Law; and it had granted 29,882 bachelors' degrees, besides numerous licentiates' not recorded. At that time there were
in Mexico, in addition to the university, fourteen different colleges or general houses of study of similar rank, many of whose
students took graduate courses in the university. Now if we turn
to the thirteen American colonies we find that there were nine
colleges, not one of which could rightly be called a university.
Not until 1779, as a result of the efforts of Thomas Jefferson, was
the College of William and Mary, which had been originally
granted a charter in 1692 but which did not actually open until
1693, reorganized as a university. The colleges founded within
the present United States were: Harvard, in 1636; William and
Mary, in 1693; Yale, in 1701; the College of Philadelphia, now
the University of Pennsylvania, in 1749; King's College, now
Columbia University, in 1754; Brown, in 1764; Dartmouth, in
1769; Queen's Rutgers, in 1766; and Hampden-Sidney, in 1776.
In sharp contrast we find seven colleges had been established
in Mexico City alone before the end of the sixteenth century:
Santa Cruz de Tlaltelolco (1536); San Juan de Letrán (1548);
Santa María de Todos Santos (1573); San Pedro y San Pablo
(1573); San Ildefonso (1573); San Gregorio (1575); and San
Bernardo y San Miguel (1576). These were not seminaries or
theological schools but colleges in the medieval sense of the
word; that is, centers of general studies. In addition to these
colleges the various religious Orders in Mexico maintained special
houses of study for those who were destined for the priesthood.
This clearly indicates an interest in education not suspected by
many American scholars and almost totally ignored up to the
present."[20]

During the nineteenth century, all fields of education were at
low ebb, and little was accomplished toward the modernization of
higher education. Many of the colonial institutions were abandoned,
a few were converted into state schools, and small beginnings were
made in founding a few new professional schools (largely law and
medical schools) here and there over the nation. Unsettled political
conditions, the poverty of the nation, and lack of experienced
professional leadership handicapped the development of these
schools.

Stimulated by the establishment of the National University in

[20] Carlos E. Castañeda, *The Beginnings of University Life in America*
(Austin: Texas Catholic Historical Society, 1938), pp. 7-8.

1910 (really a reorganization and re-establishment of the old university, suppressed in 1865), other schools were founded and the older schools reformed to bring their curriculums and procedures more up to date. The Revolution interrupted these reforms, and it is only since 1920 that much headway has been made in converting higher education from the old tradition to a more modern one in which humanism is balanced by laboratory and social sciences and in which the prestige of law and medicine is beginning to be shared by engineering and by research in specialized fields of science and technology.

Every state in the nation has some kind of institution of higher learning (at least five full-fledged state universities, two private universities, and one private polytechnic institute). The nation subsidizes the now autonomous National University and operates a Worker's University and the National Polytechnic Institute. The latter school enrolls some 12,000 students and is the most important institution of its kind in the nation. In addition, the government operates the National School of Agriculture at Chapingo, 25 miles from Mexico City, and two smaller agricultural colleges. As already noted, the Superior Normal School in Mexico City is a national school of higher education for educators.

Much progress has been made in higher education in the past three decades, and efforts in this direction—by the Federation, by the states, and through private initiative—are rapidly expanding and modernizing schools of higher learning. As noted for secondary education, however, these accomplishments can hardly be considered as satisfying Mexico's great need for well-trained leadership—particularly in technological and social-welfare fields. It is doubtful that 4000 university titles and degrees are conferred in Mexico in any one year. Many more trained leaders, with an increasing percentage in fields other than law and medicine, are prerequisite to a successful attack on the pressing problems that face the nation.

BASIC EDUCATIONAL ISSUES

Educational thought in Mexico is plagued by the persistence of practices and ideas inherited from the colonial period and from the nineteenth century—practices and ideas not fully compatible with Mexico's new reform movement. Foremost among these disturbing features is the conflict between church and state, manifested in a variety of ways and illustrated best by the successful attack on coeducation during the Avila Camacho administration (1940-1946). Unisexual schools are a response to reactionary norms; they are a result of the domination of progressive education programs by dogmatic criteria that do not jibe with present realities. Coeducation is not incompatible with any phase of Christianity (except for purely authoritarian dicta)—or with any other faith known to this writer. Mexico's submission to dogmatic controls, at a time when realism and scientific procedures are essential and when duplication of facilities and the stratification of society (whether by races, economic classes, or sexes) can least be afforded, represents an important step backward in the highly realistic and democratic educational reform movement inaugurated in 1921. Mexico's current wavering between the educational values represented by the Revolution and those represented by the Díaz regime (1885-1910) is a disappointment to those who had hoped that, as regards public education, the church-state issue had been settled.

Illustrative of another type of inheritance is the resistance to the professionalization of secondary- and university-level teachers. It is exceedingly doubtful that post-elementary schools can do justice to their responsibilities with part-time, piecework instructors. The monthly remuneration per class taught is often so low that teachers are forced to seek more classes than they can teach efficiently and teaching becomes a side line for professional people who have full-time responsibilities away from the schools. Some progress has been made in eliminating these practices, but further reform is called for before the majority of faculty members in secondary and higher schools are full-time, professional teachers who can not only do a better job of teaching but who can serve also as the leaders in educational thought and reforms.

This lack (except in elementary education) of professional leadership has many ramifications. Because of the absence of an effective educational profession, nonprofessional forces have had an undue influence in educational matters. The exaggerated part played by university students in determining educational policy and practice of higher institutions is the result, in large part, of the deficiencies of the system of part-time teachers. It seems almost certain that a well-trained educational profession could win the day even for such reforms as coeducation. Certainly the professionalization of teaching at the secondary and higher levels would go far toward counteracting the errors resulting from educational improvisation. It would also tend to substitute professional principles for the purely political and personalistic expediency which now so often is a determinant in the formulation of educational policy.

Without doubt the spread of elementary education among the Mexican masses is a matter of major national concern. Half the school-age children are not enrolled in school, attendance is poor, and more than half the population ten years of age and over is illiterate. Elementary schooling could go far in removing the isolation and provincialism of a large sector of the population, and it could provide the Mexican masses with those knowledges and skills indispensable to the reduction of current social and economic backwardness. But this fundamental need to give the masses a primary education is matched by the need to extend education upward— the need to train large numbers of men and women for leadership in all fields, with stress on those which may lead toward social and economic rehabilitation. Mexico's poverty and the unusual handicaps to progress presented by her geography and by the composition of her population call for an especial and realistic emphasis on secondary and higher education.

It is the opinion of this writer that Mexico's revolutionary period in education ended in 1940, with the conclusion of the Cárdenas and the beginning of the Avila Camacho administrations. The "middle of the road" educational policies of the latter were really reactionary, and they dealt a serious blow to educational progress. To obscure the ascendancy of dogmatism and of what the revolutionaries used to call "*la burguesía*," that administration made a great to-do about a superficial illiteracy campaign and about "the school of love." The basic tendencies of the Avila Camacho policies have persisted, and since then Mexican educational thought has been in a plateau reminiscent more of the days of Díaz than of those of Obregón or Cárdenas. It is also the considered opinion of this writer that the basic ills of Mexico will not respond to the slow, unimaginative, evolutionary educational policies inaugurated during 1940-1946. Rather, the Mexican circumstance calls for a much more dynamic and forthright attack through education. Evidence that the energy and the creativeness called for by such an approach exist in Mexico will be found when one examines the rural school, the rural normal school, and the cultural mission— all creatures of the 1920-1939 period. It is to be hoped that similar energy and creativeness will be manifested soon; the Mexican heritage is such that only through the expression of these qualities can the Mexican nation hope to attain a secure well-being.

BIBLIOGRAPHY

CASTAÑEDA, CARLOS E., *The Beginnings of University Life in America* (Austin: Texas Catholic Historical Society, 1938). Described on p. 82 of the present volume.

GRIFFIN, CHARLES C., ed., *Concerning Latin American Culture* (New York: Columbia University Press, 1940). Described on p. 82 of the present volume. See Nathaniel Weyl's contribution, "Mexico, European and Native."

INMAN, SAMUEL GUY, *Latin America* (Chicago: Willett, Clark and Company, 1937). Described on p. 83 of the present volume.

México en cifras, atlas estadístico (Mexico City: *Secretaría de la Economía Nacional*, 1934). Statistical charts based on the 1930 census. A reliable source of great value when compared with the 1940 census data and later statistics.

SÁENZ, MOISÉS, *La educación rural en México* (Mexico City: Secretaría de Educación Pública, 1928). This bulletin is No. 20 of Vol. XIX of the Publicaciones de la Secretaría de Educación Pública. Other studies and reports by Sáenz, who was the outstanding interpreter of rural education in Mexico, will be found in this series.

SÁNCHEZ, GEORGE I., *Mexico—A Revolution by Education* (New York: The Viking Press, 1936). An interpretative review of the development of education in Mexico. Particular attention is given to the early colonial period and to the reform movement begun in 1921.

SÁNCHEZ, GEORGE I., *The Development of Higher Education in Mexico* (New York: King's Crown Press, 1944). Described on p. 84 of the present volume.

SANTOS VALDÉS, JOSÉ, *La batalla por la cultura* (Mexico City: Ediciones Morelos, 1943). A critique of recent developments in education. The author urges renewed efforts in the establishment of schools, the training of teachers, etc. Presents valuable statistics on elementary education.

WHETTEN, NATHAN L., *Rural Mexico* (Chicago: University of Chicago Press, 1948). An authoritative, well-documented, and exceedingly valuable reference work. A great variety of objective data are presented, and a thoroughgoing analysis is made of all aspects of rural life in Mexico.

WHITTAKER, ARTHUR P., ed., *Mexico Today* (Philadelphia: American Academy of Political and Social Science, 1940). This is Vol. 208 (March 1940) of the *Annals* of the Academy. Seventeen authorities, among them Robert Redfield and Federico Bach (quoted above), have written chapters on their respective specialties.

5 · EDUCATION IN THE *United Kingdom of Great Britain*

HERBERT SCHUELER

The United Kingdom, a relatively small area (less than 94,000 square miles) with a population of over 50 million, has exerted an enormous influence on the rest of the world politically, economically, culturally, and educationally. Its population density of over 530 persons per square mile is one of the highest in the world; in Europe it is exceeded only by that of Belgium and the Netherlands. Some analysts have referred to Britain as the unknown isle, since her culture pattern is complex and far from easy to understand. The British have been markedly adaptable and have utilized sea power as a primary instrument to national power both when the island was mainly agricultural and when it became heavily industrialized. Reliance upon a democratic philosophy supported by the common law formed the basis for parliamentary government and growing interest in the extension of education. In Britain, as in other countries, the educational system has mirrored and reflected cultural change. The educational pattern has been in the process of slow change from a "two-track" to a "one-track" system, the latter beginning in the early twentieth century. Furthermore, the system has been so diverse that some students have referred to it as having very little definite pattern.

The United Kingdom is made up of four countries, so that there is a range in educational growth, just as in the United States. Scottish education is most similar to that of the United States, being "single-track" and quite different from that of England. Since World War II and the Education Act of 1944, however, England has been swinging more in the direction of universal education. The Scottish educational system may be summarized as democratic: the laird's and the laborer's sons go to the same school in the same parish. Some 70 percent of all Scottish children reach the end of the third year of secondary school, and many go on to the university and college.

Before World War II and the Education Act of 1944, British education was quite different from what it is today. Before 1944 British education had at least three separate channels. One was the council school, for ages five to twelve, in which a boy's way was paid; another was the church school. This brought about a dualism of council and church schools. The third type was the "public school," really a private school, for ages five to nine and then nine to eighteen. Money was needed to get into these schools despite scholarships, and the schools catered to an elite group.

During World War II England wanted a more nearly equal chance for everyone. For a time it even seemed possible to de-emphasize the church and private schools, but a reaction set in and entrenched interests won. The Education Act of 1944 moved ahead to a certain extent but in general children are still allocated at age eleven plus to one of three schools: 15 percent to the old classical grammar school (prestige still is here); 15 percent to the technical high school; and the great mass, 70 percent, to a secondary modern school.

A revolutionary change for the British has been the introduction of the concept of the three A's—age, aptitude, and ability. There has been official recognition that children's needs differ and that training should be adjusted to their needs. Furthermore, the English are moving in the direction of the idea that where there is talent there should be opportunity.

There is some question as to the wisdom of using age twelve as a selection point for the whole future educational career. Is it too early? The English and the Scotch feel that by the time the child is twelve, by means of careful records and tests they can find out

EUROPE

enough about his health, intellectual ability, and parental background to tell whether he will be capable of meeting the high standards of education in the college and university. In other words, the United Kingdom feels that it cannot afford to waste its limited higher educational facilities. At the same time, it cannot afford to waste intellectual ability. The children are the great resource of the future.

In general, Britain has begun relatively recently to move in the direction of universal education, and the trend is still complicated by many factors.

—A. H. M.

———————

The United Kingdom, comprising England, Wales, Scotland, and Northern Ireland, is the motherland of a vast but shrinking empire with divisions all over the world; the British king is the nominal head of the autonomous nations encompassed in the British Commonwealth of Nations. The United Kingdom is quite small, geographically speaking, with a land area not quite as large as that of Oregon; but it has a population of over 50 million people crowded more than 530 persons to the square mile. Its chief economic strength has long lain in its foreign trade and in its industries. However, with its strength seriously sapped by the long years of World War II, and its foreign empire shrunk by the loss of India, Burma, and Ceylon, its status as a world power, once supreme, has been greatly reduced; the United Kingdom now occupies a secondary position, behind the United States and the Soviet Union. Its economic recovery, harried by the dollar shortage and an unfavorable trade balance, has been slow and painful. The burden of a program of austerity has continued to weigh heavily on a people who, although victorious in heroic defense of their own land and in counter-attack on foreign soil, still bear the deep scars of war.

The government of Britain is a constitutional monarchy buttressed by a deeply rooted devotion to the individual freedoms that is the very essence of the democratic philosophy of government. This tradition of freedom and local autonomy has found application in what is for Europe a unique balance between national authority vested in a universally elected Parliament and local government organized on the basis of popularly elected county councils. A distrust of strong centralized authority and its bureaucratic impedimenta is at the core of British thought and has had, as we shall see later, a determining effect on some of the most characteristic features of British education. This devotion to freedom and natural leaning toward *laissez faire* in government have had to learn to live with an ever-sharpening social conscience, which, since the reign of Victoria, has found increasing expression in the development of collective responsibilities for social welfare. At the mid-century mark, Great Britain stood as an outstanding Western example of the welfare state, with a system of social insurance and a socialistic nationalization of communications, power, and banking which if transplanted to the United States would have been considered revolutionary in the extreme. Indeed, the platform of the Conservatives in the Parliamentary elections of 1950 was in many respects to the left of any program that the Democratic party had ever offered to the people in an American election. The Labour party of Britain won a smashing victory in the Parliamentary elections of 1945 on a platform of socialization and, although its drastically curtailed majority in the 1950 elections halted its program short of full realization, the party set a new pattern of nationalization of fundamental services, which most informed observers believe will persist in essence regardless of normal political fluctuations.

Whether the program of nationalization and social welfare of the Labour party would have succeeded in attracting the support it did had there been no destructive war and its aftermath of austerity is one of those questions that is too glibly answered in retrospect. It is true, however, that democratic socialism and its principal exponent, the Labour party, were by no means impotent in the years between the two wars. The privation of World War II provided the spark that ignited a well-laid fire. Indeed, when the mighty Beveridge report, with its eloquent indictment of "Want, Squalor, Disease, and Ignorance," appeared, its recommendations for government assumption of responsibility in combating these evils found their way into the election platforms of not only the Labour party but the other two major parties as well.

The British government has been known, however, to have two faces, one for domestic and another for foreign affairs, and the two have often affected contrasting expressions. In the years just after World War II, the world saw evidence that the foreign policy of the Labour government bore a closer relationship to old-line imperialism than to democratic socialism. British criteria for action in foreign affairs have always been based in large measure on the realization that it was physically impossible, given its dense population, for the homeland ever to approach self-sufficiency. The welfare of each individual Briton is inextricably bound up with the lands of the Empire, where the natural wealth of Britain lies, and with trade on favorable terms with the other nations of the British Commonwealth and with the rest of the world. This explains why even a Labour government, however devoted to cooperative social welfare in domestic affairs, will act very much like a conservative one, even to the point of favoring traditional imperialist policies, in foreign affairs.

The education of a country is usually an outgrowth of the cultural, economic, and social status of a people, subject to a cultural lag. In Britain the lag between aspiration and achievement in the setting up of a coherent system of education has been considerable. In addition, the British have until recently shown a conservatism and resistance to change in education that is even stronger than what can normally be expected in so traditionally conservative an institution as the school. It seems that the tradition of *laissez faire* and the fear of bureaucratic control that is an ever-present factor in government support, coupled with this natural bent toward educational conservatism, outweighed the people's developing acceptance of the desirability of governmental assumption of responsibility for social welfare. For example, England has lagged behind her sister democracies in extending the bounty of public funds to education, preferring until recently to leave a considerable portion of the support of education to private initiative. In addition, it was not until 1947 that the minimum school-leaving age was raised to fifteen, a standard of minimum education that was commonplace in the United States decades before.[1]

In fact, it is sometimes difficult for the American educator to understand why it has taken the British so long to establish a system

---

[1] It must be remembered, however, that this provision for raising the school-leaving age to fifteen was first embodied in the Education Act of 1936 and that only the outbreak of the war prevented its realization.

of universal public education more in keeping with the democratic ideal of equalization of opportunity. It is a peculiar social and cultural phenomenon that the American finds it quite in the democratic nature of things to have a socialized, publicly controlled and supported school system, but resists the extension of such ideas of public control and support to his economic life, whereas the Briton is more disposed to accept advanced social-insurance provisions and the nationalization of railroads, but is inclined to resist rapid extension of public support and control of education.

The signs are unmistakable, however, that in public education Britain is catching up. In successive stages from the Education Act of 1902, through the Education Acts of 1918, 1921, and 1936, and culminating in the revolutionary Education Act of 1944, the government, first local and then national, assumed progressively more responsibility for the support of education as the need for expanded educational opportunity intruded itself more and more into the national consciousness. This gradual injection of government into education was based only partly on the financial inability of private agencies to expand facilities in proportion to expanding need. It was also the result of a growing realization of the necessity of bringing into some rational order a profusion of variegated schools and school systems which had the virtues that come with freedom to develop in their own way, but were by their very diversity ill-adapted to provide for the expansion that extended universal education inevitably requires.

Few areas in the world can match the diversity of educational institutions that existed in Britain before 1944. Not only were there private schools and schools run by public authority; there were also private schools that received public support and public schools that received private support. Not only were there primary schools and secondary schools; there were also elementary schools that taught on the secondary level and secondary schools that taught on the elementary level. This diversity was largely a natural result of the characteristic British devotion to local autonomy and private initiative in education and the corollary reluctance of national bodies to impose their will. To speak of a British system of education was an almost impossible task before 1944, so luxuriantly variegated was the picture. So strong is this desire for diversity and this resistance against uniformity and conformity that, even after the Education Act of 1944 attempted to establish a logical order and some standard characteristics for education in England and Wales, British authorities left unmodified in an official information handbook the three basic principles of British education which they felt best described their educational system. These three principles are: (1) the decentralization of administration, (2) the prominent part played by voluntary (private) agencies, and (3) the fact that teachers are not subject to official direction relating to curriculums, syllabuses of instruction, and methods of teaching.[2]

It is quite true that, in principle at least, the Education Act of 1944 does not seriously compromise the traditional principle of decentralization and local autonomy in education or the right of voluntary agencies to continue to take as much responsibility for education as they are able. However, the economic dislocation of the postwar period has seriously inhibited the financial ability of private organizations to continue to support their educational endeavors in sufficient degree. As will be explained in more detail later, the way is thus open for subsidy and a measure of control from public sources. Much more important, however, are the provisions of the Act that attempt to establish and implement the principle that there is to be equality of opportunity for all and that all children between the ages of eleven and fifteen (ultimately sixteen) are entitled to secondary education, thereby finally removing, in principle at least, the persistent inequity of the traditional dual system. (Under the old program, two conceptions of education—one for the elite and one for the masses—were applied in separate systems of school types with widely differing standards and widely differing cultural and social prestige.) It is these provisions that constitute what is perhaps the greatest break with tradition in postwar British education; their far-reaching effects have been held by some to represent a profound social revolution for the British people. This is all the more significant because the Act was passed while Parliament was under the control of a Conservative majority.

In England, as in other European countries, provisions for formal education had their origin in private initiative. On one hand there were the schools for the children of the social elite, culminating in Britain in the still powerful and influential "public schools"

---

[2] *Education in Britain: An Outline of the Educational System,* rev. ed. (London: Reference Division, British Information Services, May 1948), p. 3.

(which are private boarding schools of a conservative, classical cast), and on the other hand there were the schools for the poor, established first by religious bodies and charitable organizations for the children of paupers. The state entered the picture when voluntary organizations found themselves unable to cope with the rising demand for education for the lower social and economic classes, for whom the schools for the elite were socially and economically unattainable. This dual tradition of a system of schools for the masses separate and distinct from a system of schools for the elite has been a tenacious one in British educational history. Although it is true that progressively more far-reaching steps have been taken in our century to modify the concept of "elite" to include not only the socially but the intellectually elite, the fact remains that, until the Education Act of 1944, secondary education was considered by tradition to be selective in character and not a stage of education within the reach of all. As a result, before 1944 the great majority of children did not go into a secondary school, but received their education from the age of eleven and a half to the age of fourteen in a "senior" division of the elementary school; only 15 percent, as a result of the combination of competitive examinations and tuition costs, passed over into secondary schools. With this tradition the Education Act of 1944 broke completely. The specific ramifications in school organizations, facilities, and curriculums involved therein will be taken up later in this chapter, but the Act is mentioned here to illustrate a long-coming—and, some might say, long-delayed— change in the social thinking of the British people. The word "elementary" as applied to schools in Britain has always had a low social and intellectual status, as has the pupil (and his class was in the majority) who finished his schooling in the "senior" division of an elementary school. The word has now been removed from the official vocabulary of the school regulations, and all schools encompassing in their student bodies the age levels between eleven plus and fifteen or sixteen as a minimum are to be designated as secondary schools, and, no matter what their programs or purposes— liberal, vocational, or technical—they are to be brought to a stage of parity. A secondary education, then, with all that it implies socially, is to be the privilege of all, not just a few.

There are other, equally important aspects of the dual system. The part played by voluntary or private agencies in the support and control of many schools remains an important characteristic of British education, although its strength seems to be waning fast in the face of depleted private financial resources, making government support and qualifying government controls increasingly significant with each passing year. There are several types of such schools at all levels, subject to varying degrees of public control and support, from almost complete independence to virtually complete dependence. The picture is so complex that it almost defies orderly analysis, but certain general types can be described, with the caution that exceptions and modifications abound.

Most familiar to students of the history of English education are the independent schools, with the so-called "public schools" at their head. They are classified as independent because they receive no grant of public money and are considered to be outside the statutory system of education. These schools are of many types, with the great "public schools" known best by non-British educators for their venerable traditions and their long and honorable record of having contributed to the education of many of the leaders of British thought and action. Administered by private trusts and private governing bodies, these "public schools," together with the preparatory institutions associated with them, are the most influential of the independent schools, but they are far outnumbered by a profusion of others whose exact number and types seem not to have recently been determined. It was estimated in 1948 that their total number was in excess of 10,000 and that they enrolled at least 400,000 students.[3] Some have entered into contract with local communities to provide some part of the education of young people whose education is paid for out of public funds. Although classified as "independent," these schools are all subject to inspection by public authorities.

All other schools are state-aided and therefore subject to closer public control. Very roughly speaking, these schools can be divided into two main types: (1) those which are directly maintained by public authorities and are therefore under their complete control and (2) those which are assisted by public funds and are subject to varying degrees of public control. Of the latter type the most numerous are the denominational schools, about 11,000 of them enrolling in the neighborhood of one third the total school population at the primary level (where they are strongest) in England

[3] *Ibid.*, p. 15.

and Wales. Since 1902, when local government authority was first given control over secular instruction in such schools, these denominational schools, once independent of all government controls, have gradually yielded to the necessity of accepting both the financial assistance and the supervisory control of public authorities. The Education Act of 1944 attempted to fit these schools more closely than ever before into the public system of education. Under the terms of the Act, they are required to meet a specified standard of building and facilities. If a school can meet half the capital cost involved in alteration or in new construction, the local government education authorities will furnish the other half and the school retains substantial rights over the management of its own affairs. If it cannot meet half the cost of bringing its plant to the approved standard and keeping it there, the entire financial burden and much of the control passes into the hands of local government authorities. Since it seems likely that most Church of England and some Roman Catholic schools will be unable to meet these requirements,[4] the control of public authorities over denominational schools will probably increase.[5]

One can therefore conclude that, although the heritage of private control and support—a dominating characteristic of British educational history—remains significant, the trend toward greater public controls will undoubtedly continue, as a part of the growing activity of the British government in social welfare and accelerated by the inability of many private agencies to carry their share of the costs. It is doubtful, however, that this trend will ever reach a point at which it will be fundamentally in conflict with the traditional British principle of *laissez faire* in education. Significantly enough, this intrusion of public controls is concerned with physical considerations, such as buildings and equipment, rather than with considerations of curriculum and quality of instruction.

ADMINISTRATION OF THE PRESENT SYSTEM OF EDUCATION

We have seen how a deeply rooted devotion to the individual freedoms has found expression in Britain in an unusual degree of

[4] Sir Fred Clarke, "Recent Reforms in English Education," *Educational Forum*, Vol. XI, No. 3 (March 1947), pp. 289-294.
[5] The effect of this trend on religious instruction will be taken up in the section called "Religious Education in the Schools."

local autonomy in government. This principle of decentralization is nowhere more characteristically embodied than in the administration of education. This is true in spite of the fact that the Education Act of 1944 greatly simplified the structure of education and established a system of administrative responsibility that is far simpler and more direct than that which prevailed before.

The Local Education Authorities. The responsibility of providing schools rests predominantly with the Local Education Authorities, of which there are 146 in England and Wales. These L.E.A.'s, as they are popularly abbreviated, are quite different from the Boards of Education in the United States. They are the popularly elected governing bodies (councils) of the counties and the boroughs, whose educational function is but one of the many governmental services that they perform. Each council establishes an education committee, on which both council members (who must be in the majority) and invited members of the community who are experienced in the field of education serve. The committee members are not paid for their work, but a permanent paid staff works under them.

The function of the L.E.A.'s is to make provision for a full range of educational opportunity through the stages of primary, secondary, and further education set up under the Act in their areas. Although they are responsible to the Ministry for the conduct of the schools in their district, they have a very real power. It is typical of the working of British government that the local and national authorities have a working relationship based more on consultation and cooperation than on a hierarchy of power, with both local and national agencies subject to acts of Parliament.

The Ministry of Education. The central authority over education in England and Wales is the Ministry of Education, with the politically chosen Minister of Education, a member of the Cabinet, at its head, assisted by a Parliamentary Secretary, also a member of the government with a seat in Parliament. The staff of the Ministry consists of permanent civil servants divided into two groups— those who serve at the administrative central headquarters and those who act as Inspectors assigned mostly to the areas administered by the Local Education Authorities.

The function of the Ministry is to supervise the carrying out of national policy in the schools. The Ministry does not maintain, provide, or directly control any kind of school. Yet it exercises considerable power through the inspectional and advisory function of His Majesty's Inspectors. The work of the Inspectors can be classified into three general areas:

1. Inspecting the schools. This consists not only of inspection and report but also of consultation with school authorities and with teachers and, where necessary, giving advice. Before 1944 only state-aided schools were subject to inspection; under the terms of the Act all schools, including the independents, are open to inspection and must conform to minimum requirements.
2. Representing the Minister in local areas on administrative matters.
3. Advising the Minister in matters of educational theory and practice and being responsible for the Ministry's publications on aspects of school practice.

In addition, two Central Advisory Councils, one for England and one for Wales, have been established, which are available to the Minister for advice on educational theory and practice and which may take the initiative in making recommendations to the Minister.

Comparison with the United States and Other Countries. It will be seen that, although the United States and England share a devotion to the principle of decentralization of educational administration, their ways of working out the principle are fundamentally different. American local Boards of Education have some powers and responsibilities analogous to those enjoyed by the L.E.A.'s but are independent, officially nonpartisan bodies with no governmental responsibilities save the direction of education. The same holds true of state Boards of Education in the United States. Similarly, there is no body in the United States analogous to the British Ministry of Education, with its two political heads, the Minister and the Parliamentary Secretary. In this respect the British system of tying in the national educational policy making with the political party in power is comparable to other European systems, especially those organized within a parliamentary scheme of government. The United States Office of Education parallels the British Ministry of Education only in its fact-finding and study function. It enjoys no such significant privilege as, for example, that of inspecting and giving advice on the national system of schools.

Finance.[6] Significant, too, is the comparison with the United States in the proportion of support of education expected of local communities. On the average, the American local unit is expected to provide two thirds of the cost of running its schools out of local revenues; this is a much larger proportion than that expected of the average British community, and it paves the way for greater inequalities, which depend on the wealth or poverty of the local community.

Education in Britain is financed partly by Parliamentary grants taken out of national tax revenues and partly by local tax resources of the L.E.A.'s. The proportion of grants by the national Ministry to the L.E.A.'s varies according to the need and the resources of the L.E.A.'s. In general, however, national funds provide almost two thirds of the total expenditure for education in each L.E.A. area. Of the estimated expenditure of the L.E.A.'s in 1948-1949, the Ministry was expected to grant 132 million pounds sterling out of national funds and the L.E.A.'s were expected to pay out of local taxes the balance of 83 million. In the face of so large a proportion of financial support by the national government, the degree of local control and autonomy enjoyed by the L.E.A.'s is remarkable and attests to the strength of the British tradition of decentralization.

The rise in expenditure for education reflects rising costs and the expansion of facilities called for in the Education Act of 1944. In the decade of the forties, expenditures for education more than doubled and national income did not keep pace with them. The percentage of the national income devoted to education increased from 1.44 percent in 1944-1945 to 2.24 percent in 1946-1947.

PRIMARY EDUCATION

Under the revised organization of schools, primary education covers all provisions for children below the age of eleven. As previously noted, the term "elementary" has been removed from official education terminology by the Act of 1944. The old "ele-

[6] The principal source of current statistical material for this and other aspects of education is *Education in 1948,* Report of the Ministry of Education (London: His Majesty's Stationery Office, June 1949).

mentary" school, as the inferior half of the old dual system of schools, bore the stigma of social and educational inferiority. The "elementary" schools represented in the dual tradition a system of schools apart, reserved largely for those of lower social class and lower intellectual attainment. The British social climate had long developed beyond the philosophy of special privilege embodied in this inherited educational structure, but so tenacious was the structural inheritance that it was not until 1944 that a break was made. This removal of the term "elementary" was therefore symbolic of the intent of the British people to substitute the principle of equality of opportunity in education for the traditional principle of special privilege based on social and economic class. This meant much more than the mere changing of labels, however. It meant enlargement, reorganization, and improvement of facilities, involving not only physical plant and equipment but the training and retraining of personnel and the enrichment and reorientation of curriculum, at a time of painful austerity after an exhausting war. The gap, therefore, between intent and realization, usually considerable in the best of circumstances, can be expected to be particularly large in this case.

Since this reorganization of British education is an outstanding example of the attempt of a people to give belated structural implementation to a long-held social principle, the various parts of the British school system are discussed in some detail in this section and those that follow.

Infant and Nursery Schools. Public provision of facilities for children below the age of six has been much more a part of education in England than it has been in the United States. Under the Education Act of 1918, Local Education Authorities were empowered to establish day nurseries for infants ranging in age from one month to three years, and nursery schools for children from two to five. Although the depression that followed World War I prevented the full development of these schools, the desirability of such an extension of the ladder of public education downward continued to receive recognition, and the Education Act of 1944 required the L.E.A.'s to provide infant- and nursery-school facilities where they were needed. The facilities are provided either in separate schools (the plan preferred by the Ministry) or in separate classes in the regular primary schools. In 1948 the L.E.A.'s maintained 398 separate nursery schools enrolling 20,343 children (an increase of approximately 12 percent over the previous year), and almost 180,000 children under five were enrolled in the regular primary schools. As was to be expected, the increase in facilities for children under five was usually concentrated in areas where married women with children were employed in industry.

The work of the infant schools has largely developed away from the formal heritage of the three R's handed down from the nineteenth-century infant-school movement, and away from the more formal aspects of the practices of Froebel and Montessori. Emphasis is placed on play and games (especially those that can be conducted in the open air), development of good habits of health and safety, and social activities. Regular medical inspections and the responsibility of keeping a record of each child's physical and mental growth are features of the program.

Primary Schools. Primary schools are now to furnish the education for children from five to eleven years of age, and at eleven plus there is to be a complete break, with the student entering a secondary school. This is the goal of the Act of 1944, but the necessary reorganization will take many years to complete. Before 1944, the elementary school for the great majority of English children extended to the then terminal year of compulsory schooling. Only about 15 percent entered secondary schools after their eleventh year, as a result of tuition costs and a grueling set of Special Place Examinations (to qualify for a relatively small number of "special" openings in secondary schools). These examinations had the dual effect of restricting entrance to secondary schools to the intellectual elite and of restricting the elementary-school curriculum in accordance with the demands of preparation for the examinations. The Special Place Examinations are now a thing of the past, and, although there still remain many unreorganized elementary schools embodying "senior" programs to the age of fourteen and even fifteen, their days are numbered. In the beginning of 1948, 79.6 percent of the pupils in publicly maintained and assisted schools were enrolled in separate primary and secondary schools.

Although the Ministry of Education does not prescribe the exact curriculum to be followed, except in physical education, the following subject areas are ordinarily included: English language, handwriting, arithmetic, drawing, nature study, geography, history, music, hygiene, physical training, handicrafts, domestic subjects, and religious instruction. (For the last-named, see the section on religious education.) However, a publication of the 1931 Board of Education (now the Ministry of Education) emphasizes that "the curriculum of the primary school is to be thought of in terms of activity and experience rather than of knowledge to be acquired and facts to be stored."[7] Accordingly, many primary schools have experimented successfully with newer concepts of curriculum and method, such as the Dalton plan, the project method, and community-centered studies.[8]

SECONDARY EDUCATION

It is on the level of secondary education that England has always shown the greatest diversity and it is on that level that the most far-reaching changes are under way. So great is the diversity and so very much in a state of transition is the secondary-school system that it is difficult to give a reasonably inclusive picture of the present status. The discussion that follows is an attempt to sketch the fundamentals as they are being developed on the basis of the blueprint set down by the Education Act of 1944. Since the minimum school-leaving age has now been raised to fifteen (later to be raised to sixteen) and since an education truly secondary in nature is to be the right of every adolescent, not only is the number of facilities to be increased but the nature of the facilities is undergoing basic changes in keeping with the new demands. The main types of secondary schools have been defined, which, under the terms of the Education Act of 1944, the L.E.A.'s are obliged to provide, either as separate schools or in any combination of multilateral or comprehensive schools that local conditions and preferences may warrant. These three types are grammar schools, modern schools, and technical schools.

Grammar Schools. The grammar schools are in the main an outgrowth of the schools that once formed the bulk of "secondary" education and were provided by the L.E.A.'s since 1902. They offer a nonvocational, liberal general education, "especially suited for

[7] *The Primary School,* Report of the Board of Education (London: His Majesty's Stationery Office, 1931).

[8] H. C. Dent, "Progressive State Education in Britain," *Educational Forum,* Vol. X No. 2 (January 1946).

children with an interest in learning for its own sake." In these schools children up to the age of eighteen (many leave, however, at the age of sixteen after having taken a secondary certificate examination nationally administered by the Ministry) are prepared for university entrance and for the professions. The grammar schools, although less tradition-bound in curriculum and method than the independent "public schools," which are described below, are similar to the latter in purpose. Their curriculum, once officially recognized as the only one other than that of the "public schools" that was worthy of the label "secondary," and still so esteemed by many, is academic and subject-matter centered, with emphasis on foreign languages (if more than one foreign language is offered, at least one is Latin or Greek), English language and literature, history, geography, mathematics, and science. There is, in addition, physical training, some type of manual instruction for boys, and domestic science for girls. In January 1948, these schools, numbering over 1200 units, enrolled more than a half million students. In addition, most of the private schools at the secondary level are of the grammar-school type; some of them are independent and some are in receipt of public grants (see the discussion below on the "public schools").

Modern Schools.   The modern school is destined to become the secondary school for the majority of students up to the minimum school-leaving age. Modern schools are an outgrowth of the former "senior" divisions of the elementary school, and their number has been increasing steadily since the Hadow report, which recommended that the "senior" divisions of elementary schools be reorganized into separate schools or divisions, was made official.[9] In January 1948 there were more than three thousand such schools enrolling just short of a million students. The curriculum is a combination of general education (usually concentrated in the early years and paralleling that of the grammar schools, to make transfers possible) and practical education geared to individual and local employment interests, needs, and opportunities. In not being tied to the requirements for university entrance or to the special requirements incumbent upon a technical or vocational school, these

[9] *Education of the Adolescent,* Report of the Consultative Committee, Sir W. H. Hadow, Chairman (London: His Majesty's Stationery Office, 1926).

schools have the greatest leeway in developing programs geared to the interests and needs of their students and their communities. Significant in that respect is the widespread development of school activity known as "local studies." The "local studies," which are actively encouraged by the Ministry, are similar in conception to American "core" programs centering in problems of community life and involving the active cooperation of the community and extensive out-of-school activity. The 1948 report of the Minister of Education[10] goes out of its way to describe some of these activities and to emphasize that those mentioned are typical rather than outstanding:

> Actual examples of such projects undertaken by schools in 1948 include an investigation by a girls' secondary school into the costume, furniture, industry, and habits of the people over a specified period of time. Much of the work was done at the Geffrye Museum in London, with the help of the Curator. Two secondary schools in a midland town "adopted" a farm. In another area a boys' secondary school undertook an ambitious piece of study in connection with an agricultural estate. The work lasted a year and involved a wider use of mathematics and science than is usual in the secondary modern school course. A girls' school made a study of local housing, both new and old, and visits were made to new estates and sites to study methods of construction and the planning of services. With the good will of tenants, small groups of older girls visited occupied houses of various kinds. . . .

The modern schools usually offer, in addition to the general curriculum, some specialized work in the last year of a student's course (at latest). For the girls there are classes in cooking, home management, dressmaking, laundering, needlework, art, etc., and for the boys classes in wood and metal work, technical and machine drawing, physics, chemistry, etc.

Technical Schools. The secondary technical schools are an outgrowth and extension of the junior technical schools, which provided a two- or three-year course for boys and girls after their graduation from the elementary schools, and which have existed since 1905. These schools work in close relationship with the principal industry or business of the community they serve, and they are

---

[10] *Education in 1948*, pp. 32-34.

intended to give a general education related to the future occupations of their students. It is repeatedly emphasized, however, that these schools are not intended to be trade or vocational schools but schools "in which the bias, especially in such fields as the sciences and mathematics, lies toward their practical application."[11] There are as yet relatively few such schools in existence; in January 1948 they numbered a little more than three hundred and enrolled about 70,000 students.

Multilateral and Comprehensive Schools. As an alternative to establishing separate schools for each of the three courses—grammar, modern, and technical—several L.E.A.'s, notably the London county council, have established multilateral schools, somewhat like the American comprehensive high school, in which all the secondary students of a district are taught together. Such schools follow a general core for the first two years, after which the students are placed in the special program for which they are best fitted.

Another alternative is to arrange various types of secondary schools together on one campus so that the advantages of both heterogeneous social grouping and homogeneous educational grouping may be achieved.

The "Public Schools." The "public schools," which are not owned by the state, are traditionally the most respected of all English secondary schools. Predominantly boarding schools, they form the backbone of the English aristocratic educational tradition. Some of the more famous, such as the nine "Great Schools," Charterhouse, Eton, Harrow, Merchant Taylor's, Rugby, St. Paul's, Shrewsbury, Westminster, and Winchester, all established before the end of the sixteenth century, are familiar to all readers of English literature. Offering a combination of classical and liberal studies aimed at university preparation, and dedicated to the kind of character building and social realism that is expected to build the English "gentleman," their work has recently been much praised and much criticized. On one hand they are extolled for their character building and thorough intellectual training. On the other hand they are criticized for their educational conservatism and social exclusiveness. In general, the "public schools" are of two types: those which are

[11] Mervyn W. Pritchard, "The Challenge of Secondary Education in Postwar England," *Bulletin, National Association of Secondary-School Principals,* Vol. 33, No. 162 (April 1949), pp. 67-73.

classified as "independent" and those which receive substantial direct grants from the Ministry of Education. They were made the subject of a comprehensive report by the Fleming Committee in 1942,[12] in which the particular kind of social and scholastic training offered in these schools was extolled as being of very high educational value, especially in its emphasis on the humane studies and in its training for responsibility. The Committee accordingly recommended that such training as these schools are especially equipped by tradition and competence to offer be made available to all pupils who would profit by it, regardless of whether their parents could afford the considerable costs of tuition and maintenance. The boarding feature of the public schools was considered to be particularly valuable—so valuable, in fact, that the Committee's recommendation that boarding-school facilities be made available to all pupils who could profit by them was incorporated into the Education Act of 1944. Since the L.E.A.'s have not seen fit to undertake the founding of new boarding schools on any significant scale, they are making increasing use of the device of paying for the maintenance at private boarding schools of selected students from their districts.

The programs of the "public schools," as well as those of the many preparatory schools associated with them, are decidedly conservative, with a traditional emphasis on the ancient classics, modified less than in other types of British schools by twentieth-century social and economic change. Methods are conservative, with great emphasis on the discipline of periodic examinations. Stress is laid, in addition, on sports and games and education for character. The corporate life of the school community is controlled with a view to the development and cultivation of the qualities that make a gentleman.

It is significant for an understanding of British educational philosophy to note that, in spite of the criticism heaped upon them, the public schools have not only retained the respect accorded them traditionally by the British people but have become the recipients of increasing public financial support.

Problems of Transition. Many more years will be required for the satisfactory application of the blueprint for secondary education set down by the Act of 1944, with its provision for an unprecedented

[12] *The Public Schools and the General Education System* (London: His Majesty's Stationery Office, 1944), pp. 27-257.

expansion of facilities and for the inclusion of many diverse elements in one coherent pattern. A major problem is still the establishment of separate secondary schools in place of the upper years of the old-line all-age elementary schools. In January 1948 there were still over eight thousand such undifferentiated all-age schools enrolling over a million pupils. One of their greatest problems was that of providing an extra year of education for the fourteen-year-olds who were for the first time required to stay in school until the age of fifteen. The quality of this extra year's schooling was admittedly not as high in the all-age schools as it was in the secondary schools,[13] possibly because of the nonsecondary orientation of the teachers in the all-age schools. A more serious problem, stemming from the same fundamental causes, is to equalize in effect as well as in law the professional and public esteem accorded the various types of education now called secondary. There has been the inevitable friction between "old" and "new" secondary schools and secondary teachers. True parity of standards and esteem cannot be achieved by law alone, and one of the great educational tasks of the leaders of English education is to break down the still prevailing hierarchy of esteem ranging from the traditionally respected "public school" at the top down to the lowly senior elementary school at the bottom.[14]

FURTHER EDUCATION

The term "further education" is used by the British to describe all education beyond the minimum required by law. It includes postsecondary vocational education as well as cultural and recreational education for young people and adults beyond the minimum school-leaving age. The L.E.A.'s have for some time had the power to establish and administer further education, but under the terms of the Act of 1944 they are enjoined to provide such education in a manner and extent approved by the Ministry. In postsecondary vocational and technical training, there has been expansion since the end of the war as the result of a realization that public and private provision for such training has lagged far behind that prevailing in the United States; in public postsecondary and adult

[13] *Education in 1948,* pp. 9-11.
[14] Sir Fred Clarke, "Recent Reforms in English Education," *Educational Forum,* Vol. XI, No. 3 (March 1947), pp. 289-294.

recreational and social education, the plans of the British are ahead
of those prevailing in most countries.

According to the law, all young people must receive some form of
education to the age of eighteen, and educational facilities must be
made available to all persons above that age who desire them. All
young people below the age of eighteen who are not in full-time
attendance at some school must receive part-time education. In addition, adequate vocational, cultural, and recreational facilities must
be developed by the L.E.A.'s in cooperation with one another, with
the universities, and with private agencies which have been active
in these fields.

Vocational Education.   Three main types of postsecondary vocational education are in operation: (1) full-time training in technical
and commercial colleges and art schools; (2) part-time day courses,
for which young people are released by their employers; and (3)
evening classes at colleges and evening institutes. Of these three
types, the last has been attended by most students, but the number
of students taking advantage of full-time and part-time day courses
is increasing with the evident approval of the Ministry and responsible representatives of industry and business. The L.E.A.'s have
been required to submit to the Ministry for approval plans for establishing and maintaining vocational training within the reach of
all who need it, so that it will be financially possible for anyone to
"equip himself for employment without the need to resort to evening classes after a hard and possibly exhausting day."[15]

Assisting in the evaluation of existing provisions for vocational
education and in the planning of new provisions are regional advisory councils, regional academic boards, and a National Advisory
Council on Education for Industry and Commerce, which is comprised of seventy-two members chosen partly by the regional advisory councils and partly by the Ministry and representing universities, L.E.A.'s, teachers, employers, and employees. The effect
of these bodies has yet to be seen; the National Advisory Council
has been meeting only since June 1948. The statistics for 1948,
however, show a significant increase in both full-time and part-
time day enrollments. Most crucial is the need for buildings and
equipment, which were already inadequate in 1939, before the
devastation of war decimated facilities.

[15] *Education in Britain.*

County Colleges. The Fisher Act of 1918 required that every child between the ages of fourteen and eighteen attend a part-time continuation school, but this provision, along with others, turned out to be far ahead of both the educational ideas and the financial resources of its time, and it was finally discarded. The provision for part-time schooling up to the age of eighteen was retained by some L.E.A.'s, however, and was reaffirmed by the Act of 1944. The Act called for the creation of county colleges, which are expected to cater to the needs of approximately a million and a half students. The schools are to be attended one day a week for forty-four weeks each year, or the equivalent. The curriculum is expected to be of a general and avocational nature, with some additional training to help the students in their vocations. Here, too, the need for new buildings and equipment is seriously holding back the realization of the plans; however, the purpose of the provision and the nature of the work being carried on and contemplated make the county colleges one of the most forward-looking and interesting developments in English postwar education.

Youth Service. The Youth Service, concerned with the leisure activities of young people between fifteen and twenty, is a joint enterprise of the Ministry and the L.E.A.'s and is assisted by voluntary organizations. The Service assists many local youth clubs with money, facilities, and counsel, and it is now considered an integral part of the educational system. An idea of the importance of the Service can be derived from the fact that, in spite of shortages and the higher priority that had to be given to other activities, the L.E.A.'s expended £1,550,000 on it in 1948.

Adult Education. Adult education is another activity in which the L.E.A.'s assume primary responsibility, with much moral and some financial support from the Ministry. Activities are varied and many, including courses given by universities in extension programs and at special summer schools, by units of the Workers' Educational Association, and by more than twenty residential colleges. In 1948 the Workers' Educational Association alone sponsored almost six thousand courses with an attendance of more than 65,000 students.

The Workers' Educational Association deserves special mention as a significant force in adult education. Founded in 1903 as a means of educating underprivileged workingmen in the ways of social action aimed at improving their lot, it has steadily increased the scope of its activities. Its courses include a broad range of fields, from economics to the fine arts; about 12 percent are intensive tutorial classes that make unusually high demands of the students. Significantly enough, the proportion of manual laborers among the students, once dominant, has decreased from one in three in the decade before the war to one in five in 1949.[16]

THE UNIVERSITIES

Britain, in sharp contrast with other European countries and with the United States, has no state universities. The twelve universities in England and the five in Scotland and Northern Ireland are autonomous institutions, subject to no significant control but their own. This autonomy, which embraces all aspects of university life—appointments, scholastic requirements, curricular and methodological policies, disbursements of funds, etc.—has not been compromised by increasing government subsidies in the last decade. At the present time, more than half the income of the universities is in the form of Parliamentary grants, and another considerable portion stems from the L.E.A.'s.

In following the discussions on current university developments in British journals, one finds the leitmotif of government support without government control affirmed so absolutely by educational, government, and lay spokesmen that one feels oneself to be in the presence of a firmly rooted principle which the dislocations of war and its aftermath have not weakened. No set of educational institutions—indeed, no set of institutions in the entire British social structure—illustrates so well this principle of paying the piper without dictating his tune.[17]

[16] S. G. Raybould, *The Next Phase* (London: Workers' Educational Association, 1949). This book, written primarily for students and members of the W.E.A., is summarized and reviewed in "The Case for the W.E.A.," *London Times Educational Supplement,* July 15, 1949, p. 489.

[17] (a) *University Development from 1935 to 1947,* Report of the University Grants Committee (London: His Majesty's Stationery Office, 1948). This report documents the increasing dependence of British universities on financial support from the government and the continued autonomy of the universities.

(b) "The Universities and the Nation," *New Statesman and Nation,* December 11, 1948, pp. 516-517. A discussion of the implications of the University Grants Committee report mentioned above.

The universities in Britain fall into several distinct categories. Most familiar to people in other lands are the universities of Oxford and Cambridge, both dating from the twelfth century and both unique in their organization and practices, not only in the educational world at large but in Britain as well. They are organized in a number of relatively small residential colleges and societies with their own buildings and staffs. In addition, there is a central university in both Oxford and Cambridge which offers lectures open to all students. The method of education by which Oxford and Cambridge are most widely known is the tutorial system of individual instruction, which remains without a significant, comparable counterpart in other countries. Associated mainly with instruction in the arts, the method consists of weekly conferences with a tutor based on essays prepared by the student on some designated aspect of his required course. This emphasis on individual contact between tutor and student, reinforced by the inevitable closeness of contact that results from residence in a small academic community (the average number of students resident in an Oxford college is 170, in a Cambridge college, 270), is a function of the time-honored objective of personal character development, which, of all objectives, British educators have always put first.

A second general category of institutions of higher education is represented by the nine provincial or civic universities in England (Birmingham, Bristol, Durham, Leeds, Liverpool, Manchester, Nottingham, Reading, and Sheffield), the four Scottish universities (Aberdeen, Edinburgh, Glasgow, and St. Andrews), and the two universities in Wales. These are largely unitary in pattern rather than loose federations of constituent colleges, nonresidential (with the exception of St. Andrews and Edinburgh), and set in large centers of population from which they draw a high proportion of their students and to which they are bound in increasingly intimate bonds of community contact.

The University of London alone comprises the third category. It is both a federation of colleges and schools, about thirty in all, and an examination and degree-granting body for these constituent schools and for "external" students from all over England and overseas whose home schools do not enjoy the degree-granting privilege. Its constituent schools embrace a large variety of types—for example, the Imperial College of Science and Technology, an institute of education, a number of medical schools, a school of economics, and several general colleges such as University College and King's College. Among the institutions which offer university-grade instruction but do not grant degrees, and whose students receive degrees from the University of London, are local university colleges in cities and towns (Southampton, Exeter, etc.) which someday may become full-fledged universities along the lines of precedent set by such former university colleges as the Universities of Birmingham, Manchester, and Nottingham. (The newest of these, the University of Nottingham, changed its status from university college to chartered university in 1948.)

A fourth category includes the many institutions of university grade serving the fields of technology and agriculture, which are predominantly independent of the universities and grant their own degrees and diplomas. The question of whether such institutions should be closely related to specific universities (as is the Manchester College of Technology to the University of Manchester or an American college of engineering to a comprehensive university) or separate (as is the Massachusetts Institute of Technology, in the United States) has been a subject of lively controversy for many years, especially since the postwar need for technical training has made expansion in this field acutely necessary.[18]

Enrollment and Admissions. Much has been made of comparative enrollment statistics which seem to show that the proportion of the population attending institutions of higher education is about nine times higher in the United States than in Britain. Such statistics are misleading for several reasons. First and foremost is the fact that the British secondary-school course is longer than the American and, consequently, the first semesters of the American college are comparable—chronologically speaking, at least—to the upper forms of the British secondary school. Allied to this circumstance is the fact that in the American college only one out of every two entering freshmen will earn his degree, whereas most of the students entering British universities succeed in earning their degrees. Reasons for this lack of "wastage" in British as compared with American uni-

---

[18] "The Case for the Technical University," *London Times Educational Supplement,* January 20 and 27 and February 3, 1950. A series of three articles by a number of authorities analyzing the many factors involved in this problem.

versities lie in differences of kind rather than in quality of student population and in differences in courses offered. The British university, with its rigid and exacting academic curriculum, its limited range of offerings, and its tendency to favor intense specialization, attracts a smaller proportion of secondary-school graduates than does the much more comprehensize American college or university, with its emphasis on general education and its wide choice of areas of specialization. In the United States the student enters college expecting guidance as to his academic and professional choice, because that is one of the objectives which a college education is expected to fulfill; the British student entering the university, however, has already made his choice and, since he has been selected on the basis of exacting entrance-examination requirements, is reasonably sure to persist in his goal of graduation.

Although the more exclusively academic nature of British higher education will in all probability prevent expansion on a scale comparable with that in the United States, there has been spectacular development in the years following World War II. Enrollment has more than doubled, and the pressures resulting from the beginning of equalization of opportunity at the secondary level on one hand and the ever-increasing need for trained people in the higher professions on the other hand will inevitably result in trends toward even higher enrollment in the second decade after the war. It is significant, however, that, in the face of pressures toward larger enrollments, the average American university looks happily toward a building program, a larger staff, and the opportunity to serve a greater number of students, whereas its British counterpart is disposed rather to see in expanded enrollments dangers to the maintenance of proper intellectual standards, and looks forward hopefully to a "stabilization" of enrollment at a figure nearer to the prewar status, so that the proper traditions of scholarly intimacy can be restored.

Admission to a British university is by examination only. Beginning in 1951, the basis is the "general examination" administered by university examining boards to students finishing their secondary preparation. This examination may be passed at three levels—ordinary, advanced, and scholarship, and the universities will require a significant proportion of the student's grade to be at the advanced level, in addition to requiring a certain distribution of subject-matter areas.[19]

Curriculums and Standards. Typical of the British universities, and peculiar to them, is the offering of two types of courses in the faculties of arts and science—an honors course and a pass, or general, course. The honors course provides for intensive specialization pursued on a high and exacting standard. The pass course provides for more general studies pursued with somewhat less intensity and on a somewhat lower standard. Even though a bachelor's degree is offered for both, the pass degree compares roughly with the American bachelor's degree, whereas the honors degree is roughly comparable in standards and kind of attainment to a superior master's degree in the American universities.[20]

Universities in England favor the honors degree, and the majority of students enroll and succeed in honors; the Scottish universities, on the other hand, favor the general degree, with many more students enrolling in the general than in the honors course. The question of intensive specialization versus a broader competence has caused lively controversy among British educators in the last decade, much as the issue of general education versus specialized education has been in the forefront of academic discussions in the United States. The issue is complicated in Britain by the fact that narrow specialization has traditionally been linked with the academically more desirable honors degree, whereas a more integrated, broader pursuit has suffered from being linked with the less desirable pass standard. It has been felt by many that the intense specialization of the average honors program is achieved at the expense of broad cultural and citizenship development. Proposals and experimental programs to meet this challenge include (1) establishment of new degree courses, both at the honors and pass level, in such broad fields as "Philosophy, Natural and Human" and

[19] Prior to 1951, university examining boards administered two separate examinations. The first was the School Certificate Examination, taken at the age of fifteen or sixteen and regarded as a school-leaving examination. The second was the Higher Certificate Examination, taken at the age of seventeen or eighteen and regarded as a qualifying examination for the professions and for university entrance. Both were replaced in 1951 by the single "general examination" mentioned above.

[20] I. L. Kandel, "Great Britain and Northern Ireland," in *Universities of the World* (Washington: American Council on Education, 1950), p. 439.

(2) provision for courses in the humanities and social sciences for science students and courses in the method and function of science in the modern world for arts students.[21]

World War II and its aftermath made the British leaders acutely aware of the need for greater numbers of trained people in the scientific professions, and led, as in the United States, to a boom in the fields of natural science and technology, with the inevitable accompanying decline in relative popularity of the humanities. This circumstance, in a land of dominant humanistic traditions in higher education, has had the impact of a revolution on the universities of Britain. The problem of achieving university programs in keeping with national needs of trained professionals, without unduly sacrificing cultural breadth and citizenship objectives, has become an issue of national concern and has found expression even in debates in Parliament. The University Grants Committee, which disburses the national funds now forming a dominant proportion of the British university budgets, has been most careful not to earmark the bulk of its disbursements, preferring, in the familiar British tradition, to leave such decisions to the universities themselves. There is real question, however, whether more central planning will not inevitably develop and compromise to some extent the unique autonomy which the universities have traditionally enjoyed. At present certain funds are earmarked to encourage development in certain directions, especially in the fields of science and technology. Whether this is indeed a temporary, emergency expedient, as has been officially indicated by the University Grants Committee, or whether it will be found necessary to continue such earmarking with its accompanying effect on the determination of which types of program will flourish and which will find themselves hard put to survive, remains to be seen. The problem is similar in some respects to the one brought about in the United States by federal research grants in the applied sciences, which stimulate university activity in technical fields while the humanities, faced with this competition from a suddenly affluent academic neighbor, find themselves on the defensive.

The Students. Traditionally, the universities in England belonged to the private system of schools rather than to the state-aided

---

[21] Ernest Barker, *British Universities* (London: Longmans, Green & Company, 1946), pp. 18-19.

system and recruited their student body largely from those classes that were served by the private schools. Although this did not mean that the universities were the exclusive preserve of the aristocracy, it did mean that the larger segment of the population was, by the existence of the dual system of schools, prevented from obtaining the advantage of a university education for its able sons and daughters. To be sure, scholarships have always been available, and the scholarship examinations have always been open to all those with the necessary qualifications; yet the graduates of the private schools, especially the hallowed "public schools," were always in a favored position because of the orientation of their schools toward university preparation. However, with the equalization of opportunity at the secondary level and with the attainment of educational dignity by the state-aided schools, more and more students from the state-aided schools are finding their way into the universities, and much of the future expansion of enrollment will consist of such students. It is the intent of British educators and government leaders—not without opposition, however—to make higher education available to all on the basis of interest and ability alone. The fruition of this ideal must of course await a full realization of equality of opportunity at the secondary level, but efforts are being made to remove at least a part of the serious economic barrier that stands in the way of university education for sons and daughters of lower- and middle-income groups. In 1945 about half the students in the universities were "assisted" in one way or another; it has been proposed that financial assistance to two thirds of the students would more nearly approximate the need. Typically enough, the logical next step—to make the universities free to all, using public funds to pay the bill, has not been seriously considered. The British fear of government domination and the uncompromising devotion to private, institutional autonomy have effectively inhibited any such proposals.

Additional Problems. With its universities, as with its entire program of educational endeavor, England is plagued with an acute shortage of the materials—both human and otherwise— needed to put its ambitious plans into operation. There is a severe shortage of university facilities throughout the nation, and even where money is available the competition for building materials and labor with the even more crucial need for housing is frustrating. In addition, there is a severe shortage of teaching personnel. Partly because faculty salaries are low in relation to salaries in other professions, there has been a serious reluctance among university students to enter into a teaching career. It is hoped that the new salary scales established in March 1949 will increase the number of worthy aspirants to a university career.

Since the need for trained persons in the fields of science and technology is greater than the available supply, there is no problem of post-university unemployment for students specializing in these fields. But the problem of unemployment among arts graduates is serious. A movement toward steering them, after additional training, into the public services, business, and industry is being considered. However, in contrast to the United States, where B.A.'s are increasingly welcome in these fields (a New York department store recently advertised for Phi Beta Kappa's and got them!), in England it will take time before certain prejudices against the academic tradition can be eliminated.[22]

TEACHER EDUCATION

It was inevitable that with the revolutionary expansion of education provided for by the Education Act of 1944, and with the resultant change in basic characteristics of the educational program, the problem of teacher training would need complete evaluation and drastic alteration. Such evaluation and modification was long due, for, even without the changes of the Education Act and the dislocation of supply and training of teachers by the war, there was widespread dissatisfaction with the prevailing system of training. A committee of the Ministry made the needed thoroughgoing study and brought in recommendations; some of them, however, could not be carried out because of the sustained teacher shortage.[23]

The Situation Before 1945. Before 1945 there were two types of teacher-training institutions. The first type, and the older, consisted of the training colleges, which exhibited much diversity of program

---

[22] I. L. Kandel, *loc. cit.*

[23] *Teachers and Youth Leaders,* Report of the Committee Appointed to Consider the Supply, Recruitment, and Training of Teachers and Youth Leaders, Sir Arnold McNair, Chairman (London: His Majesty's Stationery Office, 1944), pp. 27-260.

and sponsorship. Some were church foundations; some were set up by L.E.A.'s; some were controlled by private bodies. Most of them received grants of public money. Candidates had to be eighteen years of age and graduates of a satisfactory secondary-school course. The training course lasted two years and prepared teachers mainly for the elementary schools.

The second type of training institution was the university training department, which provided a one-year course of professional training for students who had already spent three or four years obtaining a regular university degree. Graduates of the U.T.D.'s usually prepared for secondary teaching, but in the years immediately preceding 1944, because the number of available positions in secondary schools was insufficient, two thirds of the graduates had to accept placement in elementary schools. The situation was further complicated by the fact that a university graduate could be accepted in the secondary schools without any professional training at all.

These training arrangements were unsatisfactory because (1) there was little organic relationship between the training colleges and the university departments, (2) the former were lower in public and professional esteem than the latter, and (3) the supply of teachers from these two sources fell far short of the expanded need of the postwar years.[24]

The Current Situation. Both short-term and long-term measures were taken as a consequence of the McNair report. The principal short-term measure was the creation of fifty-five emergency colleges offering an intensive training course of one year (to be followed by two years of probationary service in the schools) to men and women who had been in some form of national service. In the first four years of operation more than 18,000 teachers were graduated from these emergency colleges, and intensive recruitment was being undertaken in 1948 to increase the number of applicants for this training. It was estimated by the Ministry that the number of teachers in primary and secondary schools in 1948—196,000— would have to be increased to 237,500 by 1953 to take care of the increased need.

[24] Sir Fred Clarke, "Preparing Teachers in England and Wales," *Educational Forum*, Vol. X, No. 2 (January 1946), pp. 151-159.

In order to provide a system of teacher training with more organic unity, Area Training Organizations have been established.
These organizations involve the pooling of resources and facilities
by the universities, the training colleges, and the L.E.A.'s into a
teacher-training center usually based administratively in a university and comprising a system of schools, institutes, faculties, and
teachers in service working together. By 1948 every university in
England and Wales except Oxford had become the administrative
center of such an area organization. The functions of the universities in these organizations are fivefold: (1) to supervise the
courses of training in member institutions, (2) to recommend qualified graduates of the training courses for certification as teachers,
(3) to plan the development of further training facilities in the
area, (4) to provide an education center not only for teachers in
training but also for teachers in service, (5) to provide facilities
and opportunities for further study and refresher courses for teachers in service.

Teachers in publicly maintained primary and secondary schools
are appointed by the L.E.A.'s, but must meet national standards
for qualification. They are paid according to a national single salary
scale which makes no distinction between primary- and secondary-
school teachers. (The adoption of the single salary scale in England
provoked fully as much and the same kind of controversy as did
similar adoptions in recent years in some states of the United States.)
Full-time teachers are enrolled in a national pension system, contributions to which are paid by the teachers and the L.E.A.'s.

RELIGIOUS EDUCATION IN THE SCHOOLS

Perhaps the most striking contrast between schools in the United
States and in England is the integral part that religious instruction
and worship plays in England's schools. In fact, the Education Act
of 1944 went further in that respect than did any of its predecessors. It provides that every day in every state-aided primary and
secondary school shall begin with a corporate act of worship, and
that religious instruction shall be a part of the school program of
every child. This religious instruction will be "nondenominational"
and will follow an Agreed Syllabus approved by the important re-

ligious groups in each area, teachers' associations, and the L.E.A.'s.[25] (The Roman Catholic groups do not cooperate.) The traditional "conscience clause" (dating back to 1870) remains in effect, however, and provides that children of parents who so request may be excused from attending religious worship and instruction. Similarly, teachers may not be penalized for refusing to attend religious worship or to give religious instruction, but religious beliefs of teachers may be taken into account by schools and by L.E.A.'s in making appointments. Denominational schools which have been able to meet 50 percent of their maintenance costs (as already described) may continue their denominational teaching; in those schools which have been assimilated by the L.E.A.'s by virtue of being unable to meet 50 percent of their costs, two hours a week of denominational instruction may be retained, with all students of other faiths to be taught according to the Agreed Syllabus.

INFORMAL EDUCATION

The BBC: A Case in Point. The discussion thus far has been confined largely to the formal school system of Britain, since it is precisely in the changes in the system that have been wrought and planned since 1944 that the belated application of a long-developing and profound change in the social and educational thinking of the British can best be seen. However, the educational climate of a people is the composite of many forces, not the least of which are exemplified by those great media of modern mass communication the newspapers, films, periodicals, and radio. It is the last that is chosen here to furnish the student with an example of informal education, that better than anything else can be pointed to as representing much that is peculiar to, and characteristic of, a dominant aspect of British educational and social thought.

About 95 percent of British homes are equipped with at least one radio. No commercial advertising is allowed, and the cost of broadcasting is met chiefly by an annual license charge for each

[25] The basis for the Agreed Syllabus is an outline for religious instruction compiled by a committee of Anglicans and Free Churchmen, the National Union of Teachers, and members of L.E.A.'s. It is called *A National Basic Outline of Religious Instruction* (London: National Union of Teachers, 1945).

radio in use and partly by a weekly journal, the *Radio Times*, which in 1948 had a circulation of 7 million copies.[26] British radio is administered and controlled by the British Broadcasting Corporation, a public corporation created by Royal Charter, whose Board of Directors consists of seven persons appointed by the King upon nomination by the Prime Minister. This Board, while operating under a government-approved constitution, is actually an autonomous body with virtually complete delegation of power. The BBC under its charter has a government-granted monopoly over broadcasting in Britain, is the sole beneficiary of a government-imposed license tax, and yet is as much the master of its policy and operations as any American private commercial broadcasting company. We have here another, and perhaps the most dramatic, example of governmental benevolence without assumption of active governmental controls, a feature which seems to be characteristic of the British philosophy of government, at least in the realm of education.

How, then, is this monopoly over one of the principal media of informal education used? The way it is used is in itself unique and, some say, typical of the British educational climate. The BBC has a definite policy of raising the cultural level of the public through controlled programming. It offers program services for three levels of taste and enlightenment: (1) a "light" program featuring popular music and entertainment; (2) a "home" program featuring more serious music, a larger percentage of serious dramatic and documentary fare, and public-service talks and discussions; and (3) a "third" program, featuring talks, plays, and music of the highest cultural level, aimed frankly at the elite of public taste. There is much overlapping within these services, especially between the first two, and the whole is frankly administered along the lines of a policy of raising the public taste. This policy was described in the following terms by the Director General of the BBC, Sir William Haley:

> It rests on the conception of the community as a broadly based cultural pyramid slowly aspiring upwards. This pyramid is served by three main programs, differentiated but broadly over-lapping

[26] Charles A. Siepmann, *Radio, Television, and Society* (New York: Oxford University Press, 1950), p. 121. This excellent volume contains a comparison of the British and American systems of radio and their respective social and educational significance.

in levels and interest, each program leading on to the other, the
listener being induced through the years increasingly to discriminate in favor of the things that are more worthwhile. Each program at any given moment must be ahead of its public, but not
so much as to lose their confidence. The listener must be led
from good to better by curiosity, liking, and a growth of understanding. As the standards of the education and culture of the
community rise so should the program pyramid rise as a whole.[27]

There seems to be abundant evidence that the British listener,
who listens to the radio as much as the American does, is taking
well to this controlled experiment to raise his cultural level. The
estimated audience for programs which would be considered of
highly questionable public appeal by American broadcasting net-
works—such as talks delivered by university professors and full-
length productions of classics—number many millions. The British
public does not seem to be chafing under the effort of the BBC to
give it what its governors think it should have. This is in marked
contrast to the preoccupation of American broadcasters with the
least common denominator of public taste, depressed several more
levels just to make sure.

There have been criticisms, to be sure, of the educational policies
of the BBC. In seeking to establish goals, it has frankly used standards which bear the stamp of cultural conservatism. The goal seems
to be related predominantly to the intellectual atmosphere of the
traditional "public school" curriculum, with its preference for the
classics and the "high-brow" in literature, music, and art. This is
not at all surprising, since it is still a characteristic of British
culture that the leaders, not only in the humanities but in public
affairs as well, and certainly among the personnel of the BBC, are
predominantly products of the traditional "public school" and
can therefore be expected to seek to perpetuate and expand its
cultural climate. It is difficult for the American to understand, for
example, why the BBC does not try to do more with current social
and political issues in its programs—why, to cite a particularly apt
example, election controversies may not be aired thoroughly over
the BBC during election campaigns. However, on the positive side,

[27] "The Responsibilities of Broadcasting," Lewis Fry Memorial Lectures
delivered in the University of Bristol, May 11 and 12, 1948 (quoted in
Siepmann, op. cit., pp. 127 and 128).

there is no government-sponsored program of informal mass education anywhere else in the world that combines so successfully a planned program of raising the cultural level of a people with the principle of governmental benevolence without dictation.

In passing, the relationship between the schools and the radio must at least be mentioned. In no other country in the world is so much use of the radio made in the schools as in Britain. This too is part of BBC policy. A considerable part of its broadcasting is intended for school use, and the schools are given every help in making best use of the medium.[28]

Visual Aids. The British have long been noted for their outstanding documentary films, and it is in keeping with this tradition that outstanding services have been set up for the production and distribution of films and other visual aids. Coordinating committees representing all those concerned, from the Ministry to the film producers, have been established to ensure a worthy supply of such aids. The newest such organization is the Educational Foundation for Visual Aids, established in 1948 with the aid of a large loan from public funds, which is to promote the preparation, distribution, maintenance, and use of visual aids, and through which ultimately all necessary materials and apparatus will be purchased for the schools by the L.E.A.'s. Certainly in the preparation of films designed specifically for use in classrooms the English educational authorities are far ahead of those in other European countries.

INTERNATIONAL EDUCATION

Two efforts at international education are cited here that are illustrative of the increasing attention that this field is receiving.

UNESCO. The activities of UNESCO and the part played by England in furthering its activities receive prominent mention in each annual report of the Ministry. Eight national advisory committees with a membership of about 250 representatives from scientific, cultural, and educational fields are active. They correspond to the program sections of UNESCO: Education, Mass Communication, Natural Sciences, Social Sciences, Arts and Letters, Libraries and Museums, Philosophy, and Humanistic Studies. In addition, three "National Centres" were established in 1948: a National

[28] R. Palmer, *School Broadcasting in Britain* (BBC, no date).

Book Centre, maintained by an exchequer grant, which handles book exchanges between the United Kingdom and other countries; a Central Bureau for Educational Visits and Exchanges to stimulate educational visits and exchanges of students with foreign countries; and the British Centre of the International Theatre Institute.

In addition to cooperating with UNESCO in projects held in other lands, British authorities assist prominently by holding international seminars and summer institutes. Examples of such activities in 1948 were a seminar on the education and training of teachers and an international summer school for librarians.

Interchange of Teachers.   Interchange of teachers takes place predominantly with other members of the Commonwealth and with the United States. Since such interchange is handicapped by the higher cost of living usually prevailing in the other countries, the Ministry attempts to assist by making supplementary grants. Between 1946 and 1948, 193 teachers had been exchanged with the Commonwealth countries and 313 with the United States.

A unique method of international cooperation is the employing of young university graduates from France and from German-speaking countries to assist in foreign-language conversation in secondary schools. This arrangement is usually reciprocal, with young English graduates employed abroad for help in English conversation.

A NOTE ON SCOTLAND AND NORTHERN IRELAND

There are three separate systems of public education in the United Kingdom: one in England and Wales, covering by far the largest number of people and to which the discussion above was largely confined, another in Scotland, and a third in Northern Ireland. Scotland and Northern Ireland have participated in the postwar urge to democratize education and to provide a greater measure of educational opportunity for all, but because of their respective histories and unique conditions there remain certain factors which keep their systems distinct from that of England and Wales.

Education in Scotland is administered separately from that of England and Wales, but the same Parliament legislates for all three. The Education (Scotland) Act of 1945 applied to Scotland the national educational policy applied to England and Wales in the Act of 1944. However, there were some significant differences, especially those referring to religious matters, and because Scotland was already ahead of England and Wales in certain respects, the Act of 1945 made fewer innovations. As early as 1872 Scotland had legislated for a "one-track" system of schools administered by local school boards and maintained out of public funds. Almost all children went to the local public schools. Furthermore they went on to the same comprehensive, or "omnibus," secondary schools. In England and Wales in 1944, many cumbersome dualisms remained to be resolved. Scotland did not have this problem. All that was needed was to simplify somewhat the local administration of schools and to provide for the expansion of facilities so that not only the spirit but the letter of compulsory education at primary and secondary levels would be enforced. The law for Scotland was introduced "to amend" existing provisions, not "to reform" them, as was the case with England and Wales.[29]

The Secretary of State for Scotland is the national administrative officer for the schools and his functions are analogous to those of the Minister of Education for England and Wales. As in England and Wales, the direct responsibility for directing and maintaining schools rests with local boards. (There is evidence, however, that the teachers would rather have the direction of schools in the hands of a national commission.)

In the field of religious education there is a significant difference between Scotland and England. The principle of religious freedom is strictly adhered to. This means that there is absence of control, direction, or regulation of religious instruction by the Secretary of State. No inspections of religious instruction and no grants for religious instruction can be made by the Office of the Secretary. This does not mean, however, that there is no religious instruction in the schools; it simply means that religious instruction is completely under the aegis of local bodies. A Joint Committee on Religious Education has published syllabuses of religious instruction which are generally used in schools. However, a "conscience clause" gives any parent the right to withdraw his child from the religious instruction.

[29] H. C. Dent, "Educational Reconstruction in Great Britain," *Educational Forum*, Vol. IX, No. 4 (May 1945).

The situation in Northern Ireland is somewhat different. The Education Act (Northern Ireland) of 1947, while embodying the main principles of the Act of 1944, does not go as far in certain respects. The problem is a special one mainly because Northern Ireland was separated from Ireland and made autonomous in 1920, and has ever since been faced with the problem of remodeling its school system. It is now concentrating on establishing sufficient primary and secondary facilities and cannot for the present enforce compulsory part-time education up to the age of eighteen. Like England, it has a heritage of a denominational system of schools; in fact, in 1946, the majority of the schools were owned by denominations. So strong is the denominational control that the secondary system is largely independent, and the provision to establish new public secondary schools to provide a greater measure of equality of opportunity has first priority.

It is important to note, however, that, in spite of certain differences, the basic education provisions for all countries of the United Kingdom—England, Wales, Scotland, and Northern Ireland—are motivated by the same fundamental principle of equalization of educational opportunity, with the removal, by public subsidy, of economic and social barriers to enable each child to receive as much education and the kind of education for which his abilities and his interest fit him.

SOME CONCLUDING GENERALIZATIONS AND COMPARISONS

The British blueprint for education, if fully realized, will give Britain for the first time in its history an organization of education closely consistent with the democratic ideal of equality of opportunity regardless of economic and social circumstances. That progress in carrying out the plan has been limited is due primarily to the financial difficulties of a nation faced with the problems of reconstruction in an insecure postwar world. Until the plan is realized, British education will continue to present a confusing picture of many school types, based largely on the traditional "dual-track" system, which separated the education of the elite from the education of the masses, to the social and cultural detriment of the latter.

This change to a socially and educationally more equitable

"single-track" system is still in a very early stage, but even in its beginnings it is making itself felt not only as a move that will require enormous expansion in facilities and teaching personnel but as a profound social revolution which is elevating the educational level of significant portions of the population whose opportunity was once undemocratically limited. This equality of opportunity in education is a long-delayed outgrowth of the general movement of social reform which reached its climax in the controversial program of nationalized social insurance and nationalized utilities of the postwar Labour government. However, this basic reform in education has the support of all major parties and was made into law during the tenure of a Conservative government. It can be assumed, therefore, that the equalization of educational opportunity, with its accompanying revolutionary expansion and reorganization, is an ideal accepted in principle by the British people without significant opposition.

In contrast to the continental-European pattern of centralization, the British favor a decentralized education with maximum autonomy at the local level. This is a natural result of the typically British strength of local government. In spite of the fact that almost two thirds of the support of public education comes from the national government, the primary control of education rests with the popularly elected Local Education Authorities, with the national Ministry of Education exercising general powers of inspection and charter. An extreme example of support without accompanying control is the relationship between the national government and the universities, which maintain their traditional freedom from outside control even though they are becoming more and more dependent on national funds.

As in the United States, private schools, both denominational and nondenominational, enjoy coexistent status with the public schools. In Britain, however, nonpublic schools may receive financial support from public funds, either directly or through student scholarships. Once dominant in numbers and in prestige, many of these private schools are finding it increasingly difficult to maintain themselves, and some are being forced to yield much of their financial independence, and in some cases a share of their autonomy, to public authorities. All schools, public and private, as in the

United States, are subject to standards regulated by public authorities.

Religious instruction, safeguarded by conscience clauses, is a part of all public education and is regulated by an "agreed" syllabus set by religious authorities. This is in the tradition of countries with an official state religion, and in contrast to the United States, where religious instruction, owing to the strict separation of church and state, plays a very small role in the public-school curriculum.

Through the establishment of the county colleges, unfortunately still largely on paper, Britain is embarking on a promising experiment in part-time compulsory education beyond the full-time compulsory education limit. In their emphasis on avocational education, civic education, and education specifically geared to the individual's needs, and in their planned close relationship to the community, these institutions will occupy a place unique in the educational world.

Britain shares with the rest of the world an urgent need for trained persons in the higher branches of technology and applied science. This has resulted, as in the United States, in an unprecedented expansion of enrollment in institutions of higher education and a crucial taxing of university resources, both human and material. Of the problems arising from this expansion, the following seem to be felt most seriously: (1) the problem of maintaining the traditional high standards of student achievement, (2) the weakened status of the arts and the bleak employment outlook for arts students, (3) the training and recruitment of teaching personnel, and (4) the problem of the threatened replacement of the small, intimate academic community and its most famous manifestation, the tutorial method, by large classes and an impersonal relationship between faculty and students. The average British university community looks askance at the large-scale educational enterprise that is becoming so much a part of the American scene.

The participation of the lay public in education is high. Programs of adult education flourish and are administered partly and often conjointly by the L.E.A.'s and voluntary organizations, such as the Workers' Educational Association. In addition, to judge by frequent debates in Parliament, the establishment of many government educational commissions, and the frequency with which educational news and issues are considered in lay publications, there is abundant evidence of a growing public interest in matters educational. Conversely, members of the educational profession are participating increasingly in civic affairs. (In the national election of 1950, 140 of the candidates for Parliament were members of the teaching profession. The political affiliation of these candidates was reported in the *Times Supplement* of February 17 as follows: Labour, 89; Liberal, 27; Conservative, 15; others, 9.)

It is evidence of high democratic purpose indeed that, in the face of tragic problems of reconstruction and the necessity for stringent austerity, Britain is embarking on an ambitious plan for the democratization of its school system. To be sure, it had been lagging in making educational application of its philosophy of social welfare, but its all-out effort to catch up is exciting the admiration of democratic peoples.

BIBLIOGRAPHY

ADAM, SIR RONALD, *Higher Education in Great Britain and Ireland: A Handbook for Students from Overseas* (New York: Longmans, Green & Company, 1918).

ADAMSON, J. W., *English Education, 1789-1902* (London: Cambridge University Press, 1930). A standard reference for the early history of English education.

BARKER, ERNEST, *British Universities* (Longmans, Green & Company, 1946). A short work by a veteran university professor and administrator, giving an overview of the history and function of British universities.

BIRCHENOUGH, C., *History of Elementary Education in England and Wales from 1800 to the Present Day* (University Tutorial Press, 1938).

"The Case for the Technical University," *London Times Education Supplement*, January 20 and 27 and February 3, 1950. A series of three articles by various authorities discussing the question of the independent technical university versus the university-affiliated technical school.

CLARKE, SIR FRED, "Preparing Teachers in England and Wales," *Educational Forum*, Vol. X, No. 2 (January 1946), pp. 151-159. An account of the problems involved in implementing the plans for teacher education embodied in the McNair report.

———, "Recent Reforms in English Education," *Educational*

Forum, Vol. XI, No. 3 (March 1947), pp. 289-294. An account of the problems involved in carrying out the reform of 1944.

DENT, H. C., "Educational Reconstruction in Great Britain," *Educational Forum*, Vol. IX, No. 4 (May 1945), pp. 395-399. An account of the problems of application of the reforms of 1944 in all four countries of the United Kingdom.

————, "Progressive State Education in Britain," *Educational Forum*, Vol. X, No. 2 (January 1946), pp. 161-168. An attempt to show that public control does not necessarily make for conservatism in the schools. Gives significant examples of educational experimentation in schools run by L.E.A.'s.

Education Act, 1944 (London: His Majesty's Stationery Office), Chapter 31. The official text of the basic educational law.

Education of the Adolescent, Report of the Consultative Committee (London: His Majesty's Stationery Office, 1926), pp. 27-170. The text of the Hadow report, which first recommended the principles of reorganization of secondary education which are now being followed.

Education in Britain: An Outline of the Educational System, rev. ed. (London: Reference Division, British Information Services, May 1948). A useful summary containing, along with descriptive and statistical material, a helpful glossary of British educational terms.

Education in 1948, Report of the Ministry of Education and the Statistics of Public Education for England and Wales (London: His Majesty's Stationery Office, June 1949). The annual reports of the Ministry provide the most reliable accounts of current trends and are the most valuable sources of information.

Education in Scotland in 1948, Report of the Secretary of State for Scotland (Edinburgh, His Majesty's Stationery Office, 1949).

Educational Reconstruction (London: His Majesty's Stationery Office, July 1943). The white paper of educational reconstruction which became the basis for the Education Act of 1944.

GRAVES, J., *Policy and Progress in Secondary Education, 1902-1942* (London and Edinburgh: Thomas Nelson & Sons, 1943).

KANDEL, I. L., "American and English Education Compared," *Educational Forum*, Vol. XVII (November 1946), pp. 421-423 and 450.

————, "Great Britain and Northern Ireland," in *Universities of the World* (Washington: American Council on Education, 1950), pp. 439 ff. A descriptive directory of British universities, preceded by an informative and critical essay on the basic character of British universities set against the background of the over-all status of British education.

————, *History of Secondary Education* (Boston: Houghton Mifflin Company, 1930). The chapter on organization in England gives one of the best short accounts of the development of secondary education to 1930 that is available anywhere. Kandel favors the education of an elite and opposes the comprehensive Secondary School for all.

————, ed., *Educational Yearbooks of the International Institute*, (New York: Teachers College, Columbia University). Articles on current developments in England were contained in the Yearbooks of 1924, 1925, 1926, 1927, 1928, 1929, 1930, 1932, 1935, 1936, 1938, 1939, 1940, 1943, and 1944.

London Times Education Supplement. A weekly supplement, appearing Fridays, to the *London Times*. The best up-to-the-minute source on current educational developments. Contains both news and critical articles and reviews.

LOWNDES, G. A. N., *The Silent Social Revolution: An Account of the Expansion of Public Education in England and Wales* (London: Oxford University Press, 1937).

MEYER, ADOLPH E., *The Development of Education in the Twentieth Century*, 2nd ed. (New York: Prentice-Hall, Inc., 1949). The chapter on English education gives a concise account of the significant trends in education up to the Education Act of 1944.

MORGAN, A., *Rise and Progress of Scottish Education* (Edinburgh: Oliver and Boyd, 1927).

MURRAY, JOHN, "Educational Trends in England," *Association of American Colleges Bulletin*, Vol. XXXIII (October 1947), pp. 493-502.

PALMER, R., *School Broadcasting in Britain* (BBC, no date).

The Public Schools and the General Education System (London: His Majesty's Stationery Office, 1944), pp. 27-261. The text of the Fleming report, which recommended ways to bring the private schools into the education system and extolled the virtues of boarding-school education.

The Purpose and Content of the Youth Service, Report of the Youth Advisory Council (London: His Majesty's Stationery Office, 1943), pp. 27-267.

RAYBOULD, S. G., *The Next Phase* (London: Workers' Educational Association, 1949). A work written chiefly for students and members of the W.E.A., which summarizes the past history, present status, and aims for the future of the W.E.A.

ROSS, ELLA VIRGINIA, "English Secondary Education: The Present

Scene," *Harvard Educational Review*, Vol. XV (May 1945), pp. 220-225.

School and Life, Report of the Central Advisory Council for Education (England) (London: His Majesty's Stationery Office, 1947), pp. 27-273. One of a series of reports by the major consultative and advisory body to the Ministry.

Teachers and Youth Leaders, Report of the Committee Appointed by the President of the Board of Education to Consider the Supply, Recruitment, and Training of Teachers (London: His Majesty's Stationery Office, 1944), pp. 27-260. The McNair report, which became the basis for current reforms in teacher education.

"The Universities and the Nation," *New Statesman and Nation*, December 11, 1948, pp. 516-517. A summary and review of the 1948 report of the University Grants Committee. (See the appropriate reference below.)

University Development from 1935 to 1947, Report of the University Grants Committee (London: His Majesty's Stationery Office, 1948). The most significant official postwar report on British university status. Documents the increasing dependence on government subsidies and the reluctance of the government to impose controls.

WOOD, S. H., "England's Emergency Colleges for Training Teachers," *Educational Forum*, Vol. XII (November 1947), pp. 85-86.

Youth's Opportunity: Further Education in County Colleges (London: His Majesty's Stationery Office, 1945). An account of the purposes and plans of the new county colleges.

The following films on education in Britain are available from the British Information Services:

"Children's Charter" (1 reel, 16 min.). An analysis of the implications of the Education Act of 1944.

"Lessons from the Air" (1 reel, 14 min.). A description of the BBC broadcasts to the schools.

"Near Home" (1 reel, 25 min.). A film showing the actual progress of a "local study" project in a school. One of the outstanding documentaries showing newer methods of instruction.

"3 A's" (1 reel, 19 min.). An excellent film showing the philosophy and practice of the 3 A's—age, aptitude, and ability—in a Yorkshire county modern school.

6 · EDUCATION IN THE *British*

Commonwealth and Colonies

SAMUEL J. HURWITZ

The commonwealth of nations which developed under the leadership and guidance of Great Britain encircles the world and has divisions on all the continents. The total population of the British Commonwealth, including the Republic of India and the Dominion of Pakistan, is almost 600 million, and the total land area is over 13 million square miles. The Commonwealth includes the great Dominions, such as Canada, South Africa, Australia, New Zealand, and Pakistan, and also colonies which vary widely in size, from Nigeria, in Africa, to the little islands of the Bahamas, in the West Indies. Parliamentary government, common law, world trade, and high-level technology, together with a great respect for the British tradition, permeate the Dominions and some of the colonies. British education, language, and literature have become an integral part of the cultural life of the entire area.

At the same time, there has developed a great independence and freedom, especially in the Dominions, each of which has created its own cultural pattern, educational pattern, and foreign policy although remaining closely connected to the British crown and operating under the Statute of Westminster, a momentous Parliamentary act (1931) conferring equal status upon the Dominions. In

North America, Canada has an area of close to 4 million square miles, one fourth again as large as the area of the United States, and a population of less than 14 million. The density of population is very low except in major cities along the St. Lawrence, the Great Lakes, and the coast; for the entire country it is only about three persons per square mile. The population is almost equally divided into rural and urban components. Canada's industrialization and transportation are very advanced, especially along the southern boundary. Her educational system is primarily of the "one-track" type, with a very strong tradition in favor of good education. The illiteracy rate is quite low, under 3 percent, and is partly explained by the Indian and Eskimo populations to the north.

The Union of South Africa has an area of a little less than 500,000 square miles and a population of close to 12 million. The density of population in general is very low, since the population is two-thirds rural. The educational system is an amalgam of the British and Dutch cultural background and is elite in type. There is a definite limitation upon opportunity for the Negro population.

Australia has a total area of about 3 million square miles, almost that of the United States, and a population of approximately 8 million—that is, a relatively low density of about three persons per square mile. Over two thirds of the population is urban, the major concentration being in large cities around the coast. Australia is just now entering a period of industrial expansion which supplements her previous emphasis upon wool and minerals. The educational system tends to be universal in type. Near-by New Zealand has a total area of about 104,000 square miles and a population of approximately 2 million, which is two-thirds urban and one-third rural. The educational system is also of the universal type. Illiteracy is very low in both cases.

In the British colonies the emphasis has been upon strengthening ties between the natives and Great Britain and educating the natives for government, professional, and labor leadership. At the same time, British education has been imposed in its current form, so that in the colonies as in Britain itself education has been in the process of change from an elite to a universal type.

This chapter is concerned with a tremendous range of educational problems which span the globe and which have perforce been related to the particular problems of the indigenous area concerned but always bear the impress of the British pattern of the time. In investigating so great a span of educational patterns, the treatment has been necessarily limited to certain major generalizations.

—A. H. M.

The educational systems of the British Commonwealth and colonies have their roots in Great Britain. Oliver Wendell Holmes observed, in *The Autocrat of the Breakfast Table*, that the education of a child begins at least one hundred years before he is born. So, indeed, it may be said that the educational systems of the British territories did not spring up full blown, as Athena sprang from the head of Zeus, but began before the first settlers from Britain ever set foot on these "new" lands.

The British colonists sought, for diverse reasons, to "escape" from the Old World. But in a deeper sense it was not an escape, for few colonists renounced entirely the basic values of their home country. Theirs was more a search, a quest for that land where they would be freer (economically, politically, and socially) to attain those values which they, as well as the countrymen they left behind, held so dear. Many of the settlers sought an opportunity to better themselves, to get on more successfully in the world, but few sought consciously to develop completely new cultural patterns. Thus, in building an educational system for their children, the colonists were less interested in adapting it to the new environment than in fashioning a link with the "old" country.

The British pioneers did not proceed, at the outset, to develop for their children an educational philosophy and system related to the hard realities of their everyday life. These immigrants, with much of their past training of little help in meeting the problems offered by a new and hazardous environment, could not instantaneously shed their past and simultaneously develop a new philosophy of life. Although occupied with practical problems which left little room for intellectual subtleties, and forced to struggle each day so that they could live the next, the settlers could not forget their past nor the aspirations and inspirations that arose out of that past.

In a strange and often hostile environment, the colonists sought security in cultural continuity, in surrounding themselves as best as they could with the institutions and ideas that had been the framework for their lives in the homeland. They attempted to model their educational systems, along with other social institutions, on a fixed ideal rather than in accordance with their changed situation. Looking fervently forward, they also kept glancing nostalgically backward, and never forgot completely their cultural background. Hence the educational systems of the Dominions originally mirrored very strongly, and still reflect in a measure, not the practical life of the colonists but, rather, their heritage. In the more immediate and practical sense, these cultural possessions were often of doubtful value in the new environment; indeed, they were perhaps more in the nature of excess baggage, encumbrances which were best discarded. But to the settlers from Great Britain, these possessions were their birthright, their spiritual treasure, to be cherished all the more in the strange, new world.

Nevertheless, contradictory forces could not be neatly contained. Loyalty and tradition were balanced—or, rather, unbalanced—by the demands of the new environment. The persistent pressures of geography and climate often posed unanticipated problems. Sometimes, too, there were conflicts of cultures, religions, and peoples. Reluctant as the newcomers were to alter the accepted pattern of their lives, they were forced to make changes in order to function successfully in the new milieu. The modifications that were made varied with the circumstances and the nature of the institutions, but rarely were they integrally related. More so than perhaps any other people, the British are pragmatic; they attempt to meet each problem as it arises, without reference to general theories. The result, as may be expected, has been that the educational systems of the British Dominions and colonies do not lend themselves to precise categorization. In the more practical concerns of providing food, clothing, and shelter, adaptation to local circumstances is obviously necessary for survival. Here the need is immediately apparent, and adjustment must be—and is—more thorough and complete. New ways and new values replace the old; transition is swift and relatively smooth, friction is reduced to the minimum, and accommodation is generally made without stress or strain.

Educational systems, however, which along with certain other social institutions are somewhat removed from day-to-day necessities, are conditioned more by the forces of history and less by immediate needs. Such institutions are influenced by traditions handed down from the past and are accepted with little thought of how they fit into the new ways of life. With time, the incongruity becomes obvious and inevitably results in friction, if not outright clash. Then, as the need for reform becomes more evident and pressing, as the social strains and tensions increase, some attempt at readjustment is made. Yet the "cultural lag" which operated at the start still persists, and rarely is the reorganization of existing institutions complete. Since the reform is, therefore, generally belated and fragmentary, the "reconstructed" institution is immediately in need of further "reconstruction." Thus the race is not only "between education and disaster" but also between reform and disaster.

The educational systems of the British Dominions show the effects of institutions and values transported from Great Britain, bravely and sometimes defiantly set up in strange worlds, but modified inexorably, if not promptly, under the pressure of new needs. Many of these changes arose because of local conditions; others, however, have been the consequence of world-wide developments, for, broadly speaking, the problems and purposes of education have been somewhat similar in most countries. Many peoples have come to regard education as the touchstone of individual advancement; there is everywhere increasing recognition of the significance of education for national welfare. It is a truism that the school reflects, and is the channel for, the social and political ideals of each society. Education has become an instrument of social control not only because it upholds the existing order but because, in a changing world, it must also serve as an important medium for social reconstruction. To the extent that all countries are faced with somewhat similar problems, the demands upon the educational systems and the need for reforms are the same. Almost everywhere the normal period of education has been extended at both ends, and some look forward to the time when education, like an ideal system of social security, will extend from "the cradle to the grave." Increasingly, attempts have been made to offer educational opportunities to all, regardless of economic status. The phrases "equality of access to educational resources" and "equality of educational opportunity" have become something more than pious expressions, although much remains to be done before practices approximate ideals. The raising of the school-leaving age, the extension of secondary and higher education, the development and expansion of facilities for technical and vocational education in order that they may serve the needs of a changing technology, recognition of individual differences—all these, and more, are problems which must be met by all educational systems. But the distinctive character of each national system of education is determined by political, economic, cultural, and social forces, and the attempted solutions to general and specific problems are influenced by differences of tradition and culture.

The educational systems of the British Dominions have been influenced by the history and traditions of two rather different lines of development, which may be described as the English tradition and the Scottish tradition. In England, elementary education was originally viewed only as preparation for secondary education and was therefore planned for, and limited to, pupils who expected to enter secondary schools. Early in the nineteenth century, however, as the modern concept of popular education gradually developed, elementary schools for the children of the "masses" were introduced. In the course of the century they became increasingly important. Yet, as the children who attended them were not expected to continue their education beyond the elementary level, these newer schools were set up without reference to the existing secondary-school system. As late as 1902, when a new public secondary-school system was created for the benefit of selected elementary-school pupils who, it was hoped, would be able to continue their education, no attempt was made to fit the secondary school into its logical position in relation to the elementary school.

In Scotland, where the parish school provided both elementary and secondary education, the educational ladder was constructed in a more logical fashion. The more promising elementary-school graduates went on to the local secondary school, where they were prepared for entrance into the universities. In proportion to population the school attendance was much higher in Scotland than in England. The merits of the Scottish system of education—at least in terms of extensive coverage—had long been recognized among educational reformers everywhere.

The Scottish school system, moreover, was better adapted than the English to meet the needs as well as the aspirations of the colonists. Vast spaces, sparse population, and limited means of communication in the new lands made it necessary that a single schoolhouse serve both for elementary and secondary instruction. At the same time, with almost every colonist viewing his new country as a "land of opportunity," it was deemed but natural that pupils should be given the opportunity to continue their studies beyond the elementary-school level. It was inevitable, therefore, that the elementary- and secondary-school systems be integrated.

One historical tradition inherited from Britain could not be transplanted successfully into the new territories. The policy of nonintervention by the central government, which left control of education in the hands of self-governing local communities, tended to result in extreme decentralization of administration and finance. But this policy, although initially instituted in the Dominions, could not be long continued. Only the large cities had a sufficient number of students to permit separate schools for postprimary education and were therefore able to build local coordinated school systems. The isolated rural communities could barely afford to maintain one-teacher primary schools. Consequently, in keeping with the demand for wider postprimary education, the rural districts had to be consolidated into larger units and the administrative system had to be more centralized. Thus, inherited historical traditions came into conflict with opposing forces of geographical conditions, reinforced by new ideals and aspirations.

The old English policy of "fertilizing agents," or grants-in-aid to voluntary agencies, dominated educational finances in the nineteenth century and was adopted by all the English colonies. The Calvinist identification of church and state also exercised a strong influence. The Calvinist churches, which had powers of assessment for educational and religious needs, started the first public school systems in the British Commonwealth. Being decentralized, the Calvinist churches based their financial policy on local units. This practice was in turn carried on by the loyalist and Scottish settlers in Canada, the Scottish colonists in Otago, New Zealand, and the Dutch Calvinists in South Africa. But here, too, new conditions forced changes, changes which were resisted but which had to be made nonetheless.

Generalizations concerning the educational systems of the British Dominions are, however, apt to be misleading. For history and environment were not always and everywhere the same. British education was itself undergoing changes and colonists who left Great Britain at different times did not necessarily carry with them precisely the same traditions. It must be remembered, too, that the colonists in the Dominions had various European ties. Australia was colonized by English and Irish settlers, Canada by English and French, New Zealand by English and Scottish, and South Africa by Dutch and English. Their individual adjustments determined the new cultural patterns. Furthermore, although the four Dominions to be treated here—Australia, Canada, New Zealand, and the Union of South Africa—offer many similarities with respect to physical environment, the differences in basic institutions are striking. Even more important are the differences in the "sociological climate," which have decidedly influenced the educational philosophy even where the educational structure remains apparently unaffected. Whether as a preparation for life or, as John Dewey holds, as part of life itself, the schools reflect the hopes and aspirations of the society of which they are a part. Likewise, despite other influences, the educational system tends to reflect the political evolution of each state; control of education is generally vested in the political unit which each society considers most important in regulating the day-to-day activities of its citizens. Where state power is centralized, a more centralized educational system may be expected; where local "liberties" are held to be most important, there may be expected a greater dependence on a local system of supervision and control. It must be noted, however, that no more than life itself is the educational system of even the most organized of societies as tidy as the blueprints may demand.

AUSTRALIA

Since Australia was for many years merely an outpost of the "Old World," it is not surprising that the basic patterns of the educational systems of Australia have been taken over from Great Britain. In the course of years, however, modifications have been made as a result of Australia's social environment and as a result of influences which have come from the United States.

The Australian Commonwealth, established in 1900, is a federation of six states. These states were orginally independent of each other, but within each there is a tradition of centralized authority arising out of the system of penal settlement. Later, when the original *raison d'être* had disappeared, centralization was not challenged by the thinly populated areas which found themselves unable to carry on governmental activities on their own. The total population of Australia, which has an area almost the size of that of the United States, is about 8 million, of whom about half live in the six capital cities. Thus Australia is undoubtedly "underpopulated"; but, as at least one third of its area is desert—"the dead heart of Australia"—and as its natural resources are rather limited, there is little likelihood of a growth in population comparable to that of the United States.

In the field of education, centralization within each state became the rule when denominational education was found to be unsatisfactory. With the local authorities possessing neither the knowledge nor the resources to operate schools properly, no other course was possible. This system of centralized control by the states has continued down to the present day, and no fundamental change is likely to take place unless Australia undergoes a phenomenal growth in population.

Federation of the states into the Commonwealth of Australia has had little effect on education. Under the Act of 1900, the federal government has only such powers as are expressly conferred upon it, and, since control of education was not surrendered to the federal government, authority has continued to be vested in the states. There are thus six autonomous and centralized systems of education in Australia. Although some variations are present in each state, the essential characteristics are similar. Great advances have been made in all the states in providing equal educational opportunities for all children and in attempting to provide an education for each child in accordance with his abilities and interests.

Moreover, all schools, whether in city or country, are staffed by teachers of uniform preparation and training. Any community with about ten pupils is eligible for a school and a regularly qualified teacher. Furthermore, teachers are protected in their positions and are guaranteed equality of salaries and opportunities for promotion according to achievement.

There is almost a complete absence of educational activity or responsibility on the part of local authorities, although individual schools have parent organizations which often raise funds for the purchase of supplies and equipment not supplied by the state. All normal costs of education are met by state funds, and all teachers are trained, appointed, promoted, supervised, and paid by the state Departments of Education. Each state maintains at least one teachers' college. Teachers are public servants holding their positions for life, subject to good behavior; they are supervised by a professional staff consisting of persons who have risen through the ranks of the teaching service. The Director of each state Department of Education is a professionally trained executive and is under the authority of the Minister of Education, who is the head of the Department and a member of the state Cabinet. Within each state there are no great variations in standards and facilities. The standards are high, and it is generally acknowledged that the Australian states, faced with special problems, have performed a magnificent task in extending education to all. A tendency toward overcentralization and overconformity has, however, been alleged. It is charged that initiative and constructive criticism tend to be discouraged and that the schools are too widely thought of as "government" schools rather than as belonging to the people of the locality.

The scope of federal activities in education has increased in recent years. The Australian Council for Educational Research, originally set up with the aid of an endowment from the Carnegie Corporation, is now subsidized by the Commonwealth. The Commonwealth Office of Education was established in 1945. Its functions, like those of the United States Office of Education, are chiefly advisory. In addition, it conducts educational research and serves as liaison between the Commonwealth and the states on educational matters. The federal government also provides educational "bursaries" (allowances) for veterans and for some other groups and since 1947 has been making subventions to the state universities.

In 1946 Australia passed legislation for the establishment of a national university, scheduled to open in 1951. As defined by the Act of Parliament the national university has the following functions: (1) to encourage, and provide facilities for, postgraduate research and study; (2) to provide facilities for university education for eligible persons; (3) subject to the Statutes, to award and confer degrees and diplomas. In the first instance it will concentrate on research in the four fields of study specified in the Act of Parliament.

These are the physical sciences, medical research, the social sciences, and Pacific studies.

The national university is to follow the pattern of control of the state universities. It will be governed by a Council of not more than thirty members elected by and representing various groups within and without the university. Two members will be elected from each of the two houses of Parliament; from four to eight members will be appointed by the Commonwealth Governor-General; between five and nine members will be elected by the alumni; two members will be selected by the students, three by the faculty, and not more than three by the Council itself.

From kindergarten to university, the emphasis in Australia is on public education. But private schools play an important role, especially in the field of secondary education. About one third of all students receiving secondary education attend private schools—most of which are church schools modeled after the English "public schools." Although twice as many students attend state secondary schools, university matriculants are about equally divided between graduates of the public and the private secondary schools.

In the field of primary education, the private schools play a less important role. In fact, 50 percent of the pupils attending private secondary schools come from the public elementary schools, from which they transfer at about the age of twelve. The private primary schools are mostly for Roman Catholics, who constitute about 25 percent of the total population of Australia. About 77 percent of all students in private schools are educated in Roman Catholic schools.

Education is compulsory for all children, generally from the ages of six to fifteen. The state schools are free and nondenominational, Australia having departed from the English tradition by secularizing education. Religious instruction is permitted in the schools only after regular school hours. Because of the scattered population, education for pupils in outlying areas has received special attention, and these children are educated through correspondence and radio. A movement to consolidate the schools and convey the children to a central school by bus has also taken hold in Australia. A very interesting and successful experiment has been the Tasmanian Area Schools, the first of which was established in 1936. Children are conveyed distances up to 25 miles by busses. Each school has from 30 to 100 acres of land and the development of this area as an estate is the focal point of the school activities. Each school has a forge and facilities for leatherwork, carpentry, metalwork, cooking, laundry, and needlework. Extensive farming and stock raising are carried on. Older pupils spend two days a week outside the classroom on these activities and three days in the classroom. These schools have aroused great interest and have been rapidly expanded. In all the school systems the stress is changing from the traditional to the functional and the curriculum is being revised so as to emphasize more practical activity.

At the age of about twelve, children generally transfer to technical or other secondary schools. For the most part, secondary education, like elementary education, is free.

Australian universities are modeled on the British universities, except that there are practically no residential colleges. Each of the six states has at least one university. The receipts of the universities are derived principally from government grants, students' fees, and income from private endowments.

Admission to the universities is by state-wide examinations. The first examination (known in most states as the Intermediate Certificate and given on the secondary level) is taken by students of an average age of about fifteen and a half years; the second examination, which admits to the university, requires another two years of study. Normally, therefore, entrance into the university follows six years of secondary education. There is in Australia no institution corresponding to the American "college." The final year of secondary schooling and the first two years of undergraduate study at the university correspond in scope and difficulty with the work covered in the American college. Specialization is much more pronounced than in the American colleges. In each university the student commences his professional studies immediately after matriculation. The main emphasis, as in Great Britain, is more on examinations than on classwork, and examinations are held at the end of each year. Tuition is charged in all universities except the University of Western Australia.

Education for adults is also available outside the universities. The Workers' Educational Associations, first founded in Australia in 1913, ten years after they had been established in Great Britain, and by the same individual, Dr. Albert Mansbridge, have had a wide influence. The universities, in conjunction with the Workers' Educational Associations and Adult Education Boards, have set up tutorial classes and discussion groups and have organized public lectures, conferences, and week-end schools.

CANADA

Education in Canada, as in Australia, is the function of the provinces (called states in Australia) and not of the national government. Under the British North America Act of 1867, each province has complete control over most of its educational activities. Government departments have been organized in each of the ten provinces (including Newfoundland, which gave up her independence and became a province in 1949). In most provinces a Minister of Education, who is an elected member of the provincial legislature, sits in the provincial Cabinet. In Quebec, a system of dual control (to permit the Roman Catholics to administer the schools for children of their faith) is in operation. Here, although the Superintendent of Education is the titular head of the department, two committees, which constitute the Council of Education, formulate policy and superintend administration of all educational matters. One of these committees directs education for all except Roman Catholics, while the other is in charge of the education of Roman Catholics throughout the province. Thus in Quebec there is both a French-language system (for Roman Catholics) and an English-language system (for those who are not Roman Catholics), with each committee responsible for the organization, administration, and discipline of the schools under its jurisdiction. This system of dual control does not apply to special and technical schools, as these are under the direct jurisdiction of the provincial department.

Canadian education, influenced by loyalists from New England who carried with them the English tradition of local government, is more a local function than it is in Australia, especially in its financing. Although in recent years the provinces have assumed part of the financial burden, because of increasing stress on the necessity of "equalizing educational opportunity," local authorities, mainly by taxing local real estate, still provide about 80 percent of the funds required. The movement for consolidation of local schools into larger units has been growing in recent years.

Supervision of the local authorities is maintained by inspectors and superintendents of the provincial Department of Education. The provincial authorities exercise control over the school plants, courses of study, textbooks, teacher training, and legislative grants. The law also delegates authority to the local school boards elected in the local school areas. These boards exercise general control over their districts in such matters as engaging teachers, erecting and maintaining school buildings, procuring equipment, and raising money for educational purposes.

If, in Australia, the criticism has been made that the educational systems are too uniform and allow for insufficient variety, the criticism in Canada has been that more uniform curriculums and standards are needed in the English-speaking schools throughout the country. In the elementary grades of the English-speaking schools, a good deal of uniformity in subject matter has already been achieved. Emphasis is still upon the fundamental subjects, although the drill and recitation method is largely disappearing.

As in Australia, public education extends from kindergarten through the university, but in Canada few, in proportion to the population, attend either the kindergartens or the universities, and attendance in primary and secondary schools is also more limited than in Australia. Canada's population of 14 million is almost twice that of Australia; but Canada's school population is not nearly twice that of Australia.

Many of the school systems are divided into three categories: elementary, intermediate, and high school. The elementary schools, from grades one to six, teach the basic language and arithmetic skills, as well as social studies, health, literature, art and craft work, music, and nature study. In the intermediate schools (grades seven to nine), English, French, general mathematics and science, social studies, health and physical education, the arts, general shopwork, and home economics are taught. Provision is made for guidance and for some choice in curricular and extracurricular activities. The high schools are for grades ten to twelve. There are separate vocational and academic high schools in the large cities, but elsewhere the preferred type of high school is the composite or multilateral school, offering a choice of some of the following programs: academic, technical, commercial, agricultural, and homemaking.

In all the provinces except Quebec, the division between the elementary and secondary schools is at grade eight. Generally the prescribed secondary-school course, set by the provincial Departments of Education, extends over four years. The traditional secondary-school course is oriented toward the needs of those students preparing for university entrance. The final year is considered equivalent to the first year of the university, but most universities now require completion of secondary-school education as a prerequisite for honors or professional courses. Course prescription and textbooks, as well as the qualifications for teachers in the secondary schools, vary considerably, however, from province to province.

Technical institutes offering specialized practical training at the senior-high-school or higher level will probably prove to be more important in the future. They have largely been established by grants from the federal government, especially by the Vocational Schools Assistance Act of 1945.

In addition to the public school system there are private schools that do not, except in Quebec, receive financial aid from public sources. A high proportion of these schools are boarding schools. Most of them are Catholic schools, but some are Protestant, some nondenominational, and a very small percentage Jewish. The private schools are financed largely by fees, charity, religious orders, and legacies and endowments. Some are rather inexpensive, but in others the fees charged are as much as one thousand dollars per year. There are also a number of private "business colleges," which train their students for office and clerical positions.

The universities are not under the direct control of the provincial Departments of Education. Typically, however, they offer one-year training courses for graduates in arts, leading to professional certificates for high-school teaching.

Adult education on a non-university level is offered by a variety of institutions. With the illiteracy rate less than 3 percent, adult education rarely concerns itself with the rudimentary tools of learning. The chief centers for adult education in most of the provinces are the extension departments of the universities. Several provinces have recently established adult-education divisions within their respective Departments of Education. The Canadian Association for Adult Education, which was formed in 1935, coordinates the work of various agencies, conducts research, and has been a potent force in stimulating adult-education activities. A similar French institution, La Société Canadienne d'Enseignement Postscolaire, with headquarters at Laval University, Quebec, has awakened an active interest in the problems of adult education in the province of Quebec.

As in Australia, the national government in Canada has been forced to step in and take over some educational functions. The education of Indians (who are wards of the government) has always been a responsibility of the national government. The national government is also responsible for the education of those who reside in the territories (outside the provincial area) as well as of members of the armed forces. More recently the federal government has undertaken vocational and technical education.

About one sixth of the total Indian population of 125,000 is enrolled in schools. Half of these schools are residential institutions operated by religious denominations but supported financially by the national government. In addition, schools in the northwest territories and the Yukon receive government assistance, although they are conducted chiefly by two religious groups, the Anglicans and the Roman Catholics. The Canadian Supreme Court in 1939 ruled that for administrative purposes the Eskimos in the territories are to be considered as Indians.

More directly the federal government, through the Department of National Defence, trains personnel of the air force, army, and navy. Special technical courses are given to meet the needs of the individual services. During World War II extensive use was made of the educational services of various civilian agencies. Canada's postwar rehabilitation and reconstruction program has included assistance to veterans for vocational and university training. Agricultural and technical education is also subsidized by the national government under legislation originally introduced in 1913 and 1919 and subsequently renewed. In 1949 there were thirty-seven publicly supported technical schools in Canada.

In addition to this direct control, some measure of liaison is maintained through the Canadian Education Association, which holds annual conventions, maintains an information service, and publishes the quarterly *Canadian Education*. The permanent and professional heads of the provincial Departments of Education are represented on the directing board of the Association.

NEW ZEALAND

New Zealand, in its early colonial days, accepted the then current English view of education as a private function for the benefit of a small minority. In addition, education was sometimes provided by the charitable well-to-do for the deserving poor in order to make them good workmen. Control over education was left to the churches, private enterprise, or local bodies. With the setting up of provinces in 1852, authority was assumed by the provincial councils. Since the provinces had been settled under the auspices of various organizations, many of them connected with a particular religious denomination, the provincial systems of education varied considerably and were independent of one another.

The groundwork for a unified system of education in New Zealand was laid by the Education Act of 1877, enacted one year after the abolition of the provinces. This act made elementary education compulsory, free, and secular. It established a central Department of Education, headed by a Cabinet Minister, who was provided with a very small staff. Control of the system was, however, left in the hands of twelve Education Boards which were virtually the same bodies as the old provincial Education Boards. The functions of the Central Department were at first limited mainly to distribution of grants and certification and classification of teachers, but gradually the Central Department took over more control. It now also supervises private schools to enforce required standards of building, equipment, staffing, and curriculum. The public primary and district high schools are at present administered jointly by the Department and nine Education Boards and local school committees, with the central government providing almost all the funds. In the field of postprimary education, the Department subsidizes schools and exercises general control in cooperation with the various Boards of Governors and Boards of Managers of the schools. Postprimary education is free until the age of nineteen to any pupil who meets the standards of the school he attends. The Department also subsidizes the four university colleges and the two agricultural colleges which comprise the University of New Zealand. Although the University Senate is the controlling body of the University of New Zealand, the Department has a voice in all matters affecting educational policy.

The official aim of New Zealand's system of education—and it is carried out to a large extent—is to offer every child, in whatever circumstances, the education for which he is best fitted. This opportunity is viewed as the child's birthright and the government's responsibility. The success of this policy may be gauged by the fact that the school population for 1952 is estimated at 300,000 in a total population of about 2 million.

Education is compulsory from the age of seven to the age of fifteen. A small minority of children begin their formal education at the age of three in kindergartens conducted by the Free Kindergarten Association, a private agency which is, however, heavily subsidized by the government. The government also subsidizes the New Zealand Federation of Nursery Play Centres Associations. Most children begin their education in a primary school at the age of five. At present 85 percent of children leaving primary schools continue with some formal postprimary education, as compared with only 37 percent in 1917. A number of these students will, after three or four years, pass the university entrance examination; for a smaller number, a further year of satisfactory secondary work will lead to free tuition at a university college.

There are relatively few private schools in New Zealand. A small number of fee-charging private primary and secondary schools are run by religious bodies or private individuals, but they must meet set standards and undergo state inspection in matters of buildings, equipment, staffing, and curriculum. The majority of these schools are conducted by the Roman Catholic church. Pupils in private schools are provided by the government with authorized arithmetic and English textbooks.

The mainstay of the primary program is the three R's; also included are geography, history, civics, some music, art and handiwork, nature study and elementary science, physical and health education, shopwork, and home economics. During the last two decades, the gospel of the "new education" has had a great influence, and John Dewey has provided much of the philosophical groundwork for teacher training. The nineteenth-century English devotion to examinations and rigidly uniform standards is now giving way to a greater emphasis on the individual. The influence of the American junior-high-school course is very apparent in the establishment of intermediate schools.

The English influence on secondary education has been under heavy attack for many years. The course of study in the English secondary schools, which was aimed at preparation for university work, continued to be the model in New Zealand secondary schools even after there had been a great influx of students who would never go on to the university. Social custom and prestige, however, as well as the demands of employers, forced the schools to prepare their pupils for the university entrance examinations, which were based largely on the nineteenth-century English secondary-school curriculum. The provision in 1934 for a School Leaving Certificate Examination of the same standard as the university entrance examination, but based on a broader curriculum, proved of no avail. The new curriculum was regarded as merely an inferior variant of the secondary education previously given to the academically minded few. The introduction in 1944 of a very liberal scheme of accrediting various courses for entrance to the university has had a greater effect. The emphasis is now on social studies and on the cultivation of individual capacities, practical, academic, or aesthetic. All pupils take the common core of studies—English, social studies, general science, elementary mathematics, music, art or a craft, and physical education, as well as a group of optional subjects. It is thus possible for any pupil to take the School Certificate Examination if he remains at school for not less than three years. There are also many schools providing short-term technical training for children. In these schools students get a general education in addition to specialized training in a particular industry.

Rural education in New Zealand ranks among the best in the world. The official policy has always been to give the children in rural areas the same educational opportunities as urban children, and the establishment of substantial equality has been hailed as New Zealand's greatest educational achievement. Remuneration for teaching is higher in country than in city schools for the same rank and every teacher must serve three years in the country schools in order to obtain promotion. Wherever possible, rural schools are consolidated. For children living in isolated places and for invalids there is a correspondence-school service, and radio instruction is also given.

The relationship between the white settlers and the aboriginal Maoris has been less idyllic than is sometimes pictured, but there is no doubt that the record of the white settlers has been, on the whole, very good. At present all state schools are open to Maori and white children alike, and about half of the Maori children receiving formal education attend these schools. There are also mission schools and native village schools with devoted and imaginative white teachers. The syllabus at the latter schools is almost the same as in the regular state schools, but with stress on oral English, as well as Maori arts and crafts, songs, legends, and history.

There are four main university colleges, one at each of the main centers of population, and also two agricultural colleges. These six colleges constitute the University of New Zealand. Each college offers the traditional arts and science subjects and, in addition, has one or more professional schools, such as law, medicine, and engineering. An increasingly large proportion of the population attends college. There are four training colleges at which students with four years of postprimary education take a two-year course in the theory and practice of teaching, which is followed by a probationary year on a school staff. A new departure in teacher training in New Zealand was the opening, in March 1948, of a coeducational and residential teachers' college. A one-year course is offered for university graduates, and a degree is required for teaching in the secondary schools.

The National Council for Adult Education and local advisory committees in the university centers help in the development of the adult-education program. The Workers' Educational Association, founded on the English model, is the principal agency for adult education. Books and materials are sent out for individual study, and assistance is provided by traveling tutors.

The New Zealand Council for Educational Research was established in 1935 with the aid of the Carnegie Corporation. The spirit and achievement of the education system in New Zealand has been widely acclaimed, but the citizens of this small country have no intention of resting on their laurels. As the Minister of Education emphasized in his report for the year 1948, the aim is "a flexible and many-sided educational system which can be adapted and developed constantly to meet the changing individual and community needs."

THE UNION OF SOUTH AFRICA

As is the case in most of the British Dominions, control over most of the public educational activities is not in the hands of the central government in the Union of South Africa. When the four former British colonies became constituent provinces of the Union of South Africa, the South Africa Act of 1909 expressly allocated certain powers and functions to the provincial councils, which now control the administrative machinery of the four provinces. These powers included control over primary and secondary education, or what is described as "education other than higher (university)." Power over university education was reserved to the Union government. Although all provincial powers may be revoked by the Union Parliament, and in actual practice the Union government subsidizes primary and secondary education to the extent of about 50 percent, the national government has not interfered with the provincial administration of education.

There are very grave and special problems in the Union of South Africa, notably those arising from the dominance of a white minority in a multiracial caste society, and further complicated by the bilingualism of the white minority. Of a total population of about 12 million, over 7 million are African, about one fifth are "European" (whites), about 1 million are "colored" (of mixed parentage), and about one fiftieth are Asiatic. Among the whites, or Europeans, the proportion of those speaking Afrikaans (the South African form of Dutch) to those speaking English is about three to two.

The schools for European and non-European children are always separated, and generally there are separate schools for the English- and the Afrikaans-speaking children. There are also separate schools, separately financed, for the other categories of children: colored, Indian, and native. None of these groups is a homogeneous unit in itself, although, on the whole, the tensions and conflicts which arise within each group are suppressed because of greater hostility toward the other groups. The white minority, in particular, despite serious differences between the Afrikaans- and English-speaking people, set off as it is, against a large majority of nonwhites, generally considers itself a group apart, homogeneous at least in the sense that it views itself as the aristocracy of the land.

The legislative and executive authority for primary and secondary education of the white children in each province is the provincial council, with its Administrator and Executive Committee. The chief officer is the Director or Superintendent of Education, who is the head of a staff of inspectors. Local district school boards deal with general administrative matters in their own districts. There is for each school a committee elected by parents, which, together with the district school board, selects teachers subject to the approval of the provincial Department of Education, which makes the final appointment. The local authorities, unlike those in Canada, have no power to tax for educational purposes.

In general, the organization of primary and secondary education follows the continuous ladder arrangement typical of the American system. Normally the child begins school at the age of six and a half and spends two years in what are called substandards, or grades below Standard One, which is the equivalent of the third grade in the United States. Primary education is completed with Standard Six (equivalent to the eighth grade in the United States). Subjects usually studied in the primary course are Afrikaans, English, arithmetic, history, geography, science or nature study, health and physical education, singing, and drawing. The boys receive instruction in manual training, and the girls in home economics. Nondenominational religious instruction (from which pupils are exempted at their parents' request) is also given. The Act of Union, which is the South African constitution, provides that both Afrikaans and English shall be the official languages and shall be treated as equal. In the application of this provision, a child is taught through the medium of his home language and also learns the other official language. Upon the satisfactory passing of an examination which stresses ability in spelling and arithmetic, the pupil receives a school-leaving certificate. His primary education is now complete and he may continue with his secondary schooling.

Another path which the pupil may choose is to take a public examination for the Junior (High School) Certificate. This examination is based on syllabuses and courses which are fundamentally the same in all provinces and is offered for those pupils who do not expect to complete high school. Those pupils who wish to receive a Senior Certificate, which is equivalent to high-school graduation in the United States, go on to high school through Standard Ten and then take an "external" examination conducted by the Joint Matriculation Board. Success in this examination is the qualifying test for entrance into a university, and is also very helpful in obtaining private or public employment. Because of its prestige and practical value, this examination is taken by students in all public and in nearly all private high schools. Candidates are examined on not less than five and not more than seven subjects of their choice, which they may select from a list of thirty-five. The subjects usually taken by the candidates are Afrikaans, English, mathematics, chemistry, Latin, history, and occasionally German.

Education for the whites is compulsory till the age of fifteen or sixteen and, except in a few isolated cases, is free during the compulsory period. Because of the very well-developed public school system, only about 5 percent of the white students attend private schools. The South African whites, coming from Dutch, English, French, and German stock—peoples of high cultural level—place a high value on education. Unfortunately for the non-European peoples of South Africa, the stress of the ruling European minority is on education for themselves. Believing in their own superiority, fearful of losing their position at the top of the pyramid, the Europeans seem determined to resist any attempts on the part of other groups to achieve equality. And since education is generally regarded as a liberating agency, the ruling European minority, in seeking to preserve a system which ensures power to itself, is opposed to providing equal educational opportunity for others.

No attempt is made, even in principle, to provide equal educational opportunities for the natives. As for the practice, the situation with respect to native education may be best summarized in terms of statistics. Less than one third of the natives ever attend school, and about $1\frac{1}{2}$ percent obtain secondary education. The amount spent on the education of the Africans on a per-capita basis is a small fraction of the amount spent on the education of white children. Most of the schools for natives are private schools, partly controlled and supported by missionary societies, with some financial assistance provided by the Union government. Administrative jurisdiction rests with the provincial Departments of Education.

The original purposes of educating the natives were to teach them the Bible and to teach them to work with their hands. The very first school established in South Africa was started in 1658 for West African slave children, in order to propagate the Christian religion. (Because of truancy, it was recommended that attendance be rewarded by a tot of rum and 3 inches of tobacco.) The point of view of many Europeans in South Africa has not changed very much since then. Education for the natives, in their opinion, is only for the purpose of providing docile workers. And the Europeans will do their utmost to see that the natives will not be able to use education as a means of contesting the existing structure of society in South Africa. A story, not apocryphal, may be cited to illustrate the attitude of many South African whites toward the natives. A white pupil was asked to discuss the principle of the lever. In order to demonstrate the practical application of these principles, he was asked to show how he would make use of a crowbar to move a rock on the roadside. After explaining how he would adjust the fulcrum to get adequate leverage, he added, "Then I would get a native at the other end of the bar to lift the rock." So long as this attitude persists and the Europeans retain their power, there is obviously little prospect of major reforms in education for the non-European groups.

Technical education is controlled by the Union. Fees are required, but are waived for able needy students. Although some attempts have been made to provide technical and vocational education for the natives, this specialized training exists mostly for the benefit of the whites. A state school was opened in 1948 to teach adult natives a limited number of technical skills. A much more comprehensive system of technical and vocational education in colleges and evening continuation classes exists for the whites. The government Miners' Training Schools were inaugurated in 1917; in addition, private enterprises, such as the famous Johannesburg School of Mines, provide technical and vocational training. Four agricultural colleges are under the jurisdiction of the Union Department of Agriculture.

The universities are aided and controlled by the Union government. Except for scholarships awarded to some, all students pay fees for university education, although the actual cost of running the universities is more than twice the sum collected through tuition fees. The total enrollment in the universities in 1947 was about 22,000. There are universities at Cape Town, Natal, Pretoria, Stellenbosch, and Witwatersrand. In addition, the University of South Africa, which is an examining body, consists of several university colleges located in various parts of South Africa. Stellenbosch, Pretoria, Potchefstroom University College, and Bloemfontein University College use Afrikaans as the medium of instruction; Cape Town, Witwatersrand, Natal University College, and Rhodes

University College use English, since they draw their students mainly from the English-speaking population. Medical and engineering schools are situated at Cape Town and Witwatersrand. A handful of Bantu, colored, and Indian students attend these universities, which are the only ones admitting students irrespective of race. The Huguenot College at Wellington is for white women only, and has both English- and Afrikaans-speaking students. In 1947 the student body numbered 122.

The universities confer degrees in arts and sciences and have the usual professional facilities in education, law, medicine, engineering, and other fields. They also offer courses for nonresident students. Most of the non-European (nonwhite) university students are educated at the South African Native College, at Fort Hare, in the Cape, which offers courses in the arts, sciences, theology, education, agriculture, hygiene, and medical aid. Scholarships are available to students of this college for medical training at the University of Witwatersrand. In 1947, the total registration at the South African Native College was 328. This total includes Indian students, who are limited to a quota of 15 percent in order to preserve the college's "African and Christian character," and Bantu students from the other countries of southern Africa.

Although there is practically no illiteracy among the adult white population, adult education is practically unknown. E. G. Malherbe, in the *Educational Yearbook*, in 1940, put it as follows: "To write about adult education in South Africa is almost tantamount to writing about snakes in Ireland." The tradition and spirit of the Workers' Educational Association, so active in Great Britain and in most of the other Dominions, is foreign to South Africa. Within the past few years, however, some steps have been taken in the direction of building up an adult-education program. In 1945 a committee on adult education, appointed by the Minister of Education, recommended a scheme estimated to cost the government a half million pounds a year. The National Council for Adult Education has also been set up and a Director of Adult Education has been appointed.

More serious and urgent, in the minds of many, is the problem of education for the natives. Like the other Dominions, the Union of South Africa speaks of "reconstructing" its educational system; but for the natives it is rather a problem of constructing an educational system which will meet their needs and demands. In South Africa, as everywhere else, the problems of educational reform reflect the problems of the society. No fundamental change can be made in the area of South African native education without changing the whole concept of social relationships in that country.

THE COLONIES

The term "British colonies" is used to include all the non-self-governing lands of the British Commonwealth. The word "colony" is an abbreviation of the official designation "colony not possessing responsible government" and includes all such colonies whether or not they possess an elective legislature. It is, thus, a loose expression which includes colonies, protectorates, protected states, and trust territories. More strictly, colonies (properly called "crown colonies") are overseas territories which have been annexed to the British crown. Some examples of crown colonies are the Barbados, Hong Kong, and Fiji.

Great Britain has by far the largest number of colonies of any country in the world. The total land area of the colonial empire is about 2 million square miles, over three fourths being in Africa. The total population is over 60 million in fifty territories. The English historian Sir John Seeley once asserted that the British colonies were acquired in a "fit of absence of mind." But even the British Colonial Office admits that, since the oldest colony dates from 1612 and the youngest from 1946, the British "must be chronically absent-minded."

No brief description can cover adequately the educational systems of the British colonial lands. Aside from the size of the colonial empire, the problem is complicated by the variety of territories included. No other colonial empire has so wide a cultural variety. Many of the inhabitants live in primitive agricultural and pastoral communities and have little contact with the outside world; others are almost wholly westernized. In some colonies, although there are university colleges run on European lines, the majority of inhabitants are rural and illiterate and remain untouched, if not unaffected, by the institutions of higher learning in their midst.

Great Britain, more so than those other two great colonial powers, France and Holland, has sought, in the past, to superimpose

European government upon the native. And, since education is an integral part of colonial administration and policy, the educational policies followed in Britain's colonial dependencies have differed from those followed in the Dutch and French colonies.

The Dutch have practiced a system of dualism. They have not tried to superimpose their culture upon native society, but have developed a kind of dual hierarchy of authority designed upon parallel lines—the European and the native. The same is true of their educational system. The Dutch have generally set up two separate and distinct educational systems in their colonies—one for the Europeans and the other for the natives. Yet their attitude is not quite one of "never the twain shall meet." For, although these two systems do not overlap, the Dutch permit almost perfect mobility to the natives, and consider as Europeans all persons of mixed blood and even natives who live as Europeans.

The French, on the other hand, think of their native subjects as potential French citizens and look forward to the time when they will be fully assimilated. Holding this point of view, the French can hardly be expected to be sympathetic to native nationalistic aspirations. To France, her dependencies are not separate countries, each to be considered by itself, working its own way to its own aspirations, its own economic, social, and political future; rather, they are all parts of the whole—the French Empire.

These varying attitudes have, of course, been reflected in the educational systems. In recent years the British have been changing their approach to the problems of native administration and education, and the objectives of British colonial education are now well defined (if not as well implemented, let alone achieved). They may be summarized briefly as follows:

1. To spread education as widely as possible among the peoples of the dependent empire in order to give them both the desire and the capacity for social, economic, and political progress and at the same time preserve the best elements of their original culture.

2. To train as many natives as possible for government service, the professions, and business, and as leaders in politics, local government, trade unions, and the cooperative movement.

3. To strengthen and develop cultural and other links between Western civilization and the dependent territories.

Although not quite enough to make a heaven on earth, these are the professed aims of the British government, seeking to establish the *Pax Britannica*. More recently, the emphasis has been on education for "self-government." The Secretary of State for the Colonies announced, in July 1943, that the aim was "to guide Colonial peoples along the road of self-government within the framework of the British Empire, to build up their social and economic institutions, and to develop their natural resources." His successor, in the Labour government, substantially repeated this credo, but omitted reference to "the framework of the British Empire." In July 1946 he pledged that the aim was "to develop the Colonies and all their resources so as to enable their peoples speedily and substantially to improve their economic and social conditions and, as soon as may be, to attain responsible self-government." The "test of our policy," he continued, "should not be British advantage, but the happiness, prosperity, and freedom of the colonial people themselves." This is all the more striking when it is contrasted with the "Dual Mandate" philosophy of Lord Lugard, one of the most famous of British African colonial administrators. For Lugard, Britain was a trustee for the colonies. The natives of Africa were to be protected and aided in their development, but at the same time the economic needs of the outside world were to be met insofar as Africa could meet them.

Article 73 of the United Nations Charter states that the "Colonial peoples" must be educated "for democracy." In any event, as an official committee appointed by the Secretary of State for the Colonies has pointed out, Western civilization has irrevocably impinged upon old social organizations, and former habits of life and conduct have been blurred beyond recognition. The question is no longer whether the native should be educated, but what type of education he should have. The native now demands it as a right. No coercion or cajolery is required. The school is the workshop supplying tools for building power. The native has learned that many European ways are superior; he sees European methods and education as giving control over the forces of nature and the circumstances of life. Only an insignificant minority of people are impressed by those who disparage Western standards and extol the indigenous culture.

In practically all of its dependencies, the British government at first ignored education, being concerned with the maintenance of law and order, defense from external attack, and economic development. Education was left to the Christian missions, the government usually giving them a free hand and rarely interfering with local and indigenous methods of education. Beginning in 1918, the Colonial Office began to concern itself with general educational problems. After 1923, educational policy in tropical Africa was developed by the Advisory Committee on Native Education. In 1929, this committee, reorganized as the Advisory Committee on Education in the Colonies, extended its operations beyond Africa.

As the demands for education have increased, the government has stepped in more and more—both by establishing its own schools and by making grants-in-aid to missionary establishments to enable them to enlarge the scope of their work. At present there are three types of primary and secondary schools in the colonies: government schools, state-aided schools which are required to meet certain standards, and private schools. Although reliable figures on school attendance and on literacy are not available, both literacy and school attendance have undoubtedly gone up sharply in recent years. Education is compulsory in only a very few of the colonies, and even here is rarely enforced. Fees are required in the colonies even where education is "compulsory." The education of females has lagged behind that of males, but here, too, advances have been made in recent years. This is especially important because in many areas of Africa women occupy a socially strong position.

In recent years emphasis has been placed on "mass education," which includes more than mass literacy. The term was defined, in 1948, by the Colonial Office as "a movement towards community betterment, carried on with the active participation, and if possible at the spontaneous initiative, of the community." It works toward all forms of betterment: in agriculture by proper soil conservation, improved farming methods, and better care of livestock; in health by improved sanitation and provision for infant and maternity welfare; in education by the improvement and extension of schools for both children and adults. Mass education embraces cooperative societies and is intimately bound up with the development of local government. The essence of mass education is the stimulation of initiative, and it is probable that the existing provincial and district administration, especially if imaginatively conceived, will provide the best coordinating machinery. The British government, under the Colonial Development and Welfare Acts of 1940 and 1945, has been making extensive grants for colonial development, including educational development.

An important question is what place should be given to native languages and to English in the educational scheme. The problems are not the same in all the territories. In some, the vernacular was long ago reduced to writing, and not only has become an important means of communication among people of the same generation but has enabled the culture to be handed down to successive generations. In other territories there is no one standard or consistent vernacular. In some territories, moreover, there has been a considerable influx of foreign elements.

Technical education has been seriously neglected in the past. The lack of it is perhaps the most important gap in the educational structure and is having a very damaging effect on the development of the dependent territories. Technical schools on primary and secondary levels are now being established, great impetus having been given during World War II by the necessity of training troops and after the war because of the educational demands of former servicemen. The machinery established for training veterans is now being converted to serve the rest of the civilian population.

Although the need for technical education is very great, its importance at the present time must not be overemphasized. The colonies are, and will remain in the near future, at least, primarily agricultural communities which will not be able to absorb large numbers of skilled manual or white-collar workers into their economy. Many native farmers fear the effects of education; they believe that education, at least as practiced in the schools at present, tends to discourage children from remaining on the land. A problem facing the educational authorities is to devise a curriculum which will meet the needs not only of the small minority who will engage in nonagricultural pursuits but of the bulk of the population, in order that they may be able to lead a better, richer life in a rural environment.

Within recent years higher education has been the subject of comprehensive study throughout the colonial empire. Implementation of plans for improvement has already begun. Universities are being developed or expanded in the Far East, in Africa, in the West Indies, and in other areas.

The process of organizing educational systems in the colonies is bound to be slow, no matter how rapid the progress has been, on a comparative scale, in recent years. The problems in the colonies are not problems of education alone. Economic, political, and social improvements, if they do not entirely precede, can certainly not lag far behind any system of education. The problems of finance are always present. The Committee on Higher Education in the Gold Coast Colony, for example, was very enthusiastic about educational advances, yet, in its report in 1946, it was unable to slur over the problem: "There is an impelling sense of urgency and a demand that political progress shall be swift and that the extension of education, which must accompany sound political advance, shall be limited only by the ability of the country to finance it and the capacity of the young people to assimilate it." Lack of money may not be the root of *all* evil, yet educational advance is hardly possible without adequate finances.

The official statement of policy on colonial development and welfare (1946) is more ambitious. It asserts that the history of colonial policy has already gone through two stages: first, that of ruthless exploitation, and second, that in which the policy followed was that each colony was to have only those services which could be maintained out of its own resources. Now, it states, the time is ripe for the third stage, in which the British taxpayer, as trustee for the well-being of the peoples of the colonial empire, must see to it that in each dependency, irrespective of its resources, there will be a full and balanced development in the administrative, technical, and social services.

BIBLIOGRAPHY

Official Government Publications

The official Yearbook of each Dominion, generally published annually, is a good starting point for any student interested in developments in these countries. Of course the books vary in quality, but each presents a comprehensive picture—statistical and descriptive—of the respective Dominion.

The Department of Education of each Dominion publishes, usually annually, a review of educational developments. Where education is also administered by states or provinces, each of these subdivisions also generally publishes an annual review of educational developments. For the colonies, the Annual Reports of the Director of Education in each colony are invaluable.

Of the many other official reports dealing with education in the colonies (all published by His Majesty's Stationery Office, London), the following are the most helpful:

Education for Citizenship in Africa

Mass Education in African Society

Report of the Commission on Higher Education in the Colonies

A Survey of Vocational Technical Education in the Colonial Empire

Oversea Education (London), a quarterly journal of educational experiment and research in tropical and subtropical areas, is a mine of information on educational developments in the colonial empire. It is the organ of the British Colonial Advisory Committee on Education in the Colonies.

The chief drawback to using the above-mentioned publications is that they necessarily reflect the official point of view and at times tend to present the picture in less than objective terms. Self-criticism does crop up sometimes, but often developments are described in overfavorable and self-congratulatory terms.

A SELECTED LIST OF NONOFFICIAL REFERENCES

BREBNER, JOHN BARTLET, "Canadian Education," in Rexford Guy Tugwell and L. H. Keyserling, eds., Redirecting Education, 2 vols. (New York: Columbia University Press, 1935), Vol. II, pp. 237-261. Canadian education in the context of Canadian social forces and history. Emphasizes that the dominant trend should be sought in North American rather than in English or French terms.

————, Scholarship for Canada (Ottawa: Canadian Social Science Research Council, 1945). An eloquent plea for providing Canadians with additional educational opportunities for the benefit of Canada.

BROWNE, G. S., ed., Education in Australia—A Comparative Study of the Educational System of the Six Australian States (London: Macmillan & Company, Ltd., 1927. The most detailed study of Australian education in one volume.

BUTCHERS, ARTHUR G., Young New Zealand (Dunedin: Coulls Somerville Wilkie, Ltd., 1929).

————, Education in New Zealand (Dunedin: Coulls Somerville Wilkie, Ltd., 1930). This volume and Young New Zealand comprise a historical survey of education in New Zealand up to 1929. The standard works on the history of European and Maori education in New Zealand.

CANADIAN YOUTH COMMISSION, *Youth Challenges the Educators* (Toronto: Ryerson Press, 1946). Mainly a summary of how a representative sample (1500) of young people regard the education which they received since about 1935. Also contains the result of a "Gallup poll" and briefs presented by organized groups such as churches and junior farm bureaus.

CLARKE, SIR FRED, *Quebec and South Africa, A Study in Cultural Adjustment* (London: Oxford University Press, 1934). No. 5 in the series of Studies and Reports of the London Institute of Education. A sympathetic, short discussion of the problems of cultural conflicts.

COLE, PERCIVAL E., ed., *The Education of the Adolescent in Australia* (Melbourne: Australian Council for Educational Research, 1935). In the words of the editor, this unofficial effort "strives to do for Australia what the Hadow Report on the Education of the Adolescent has done for England." The theme is that secondary education must be regarded as a continuation of primary education rather than as a preliminary to university education.

The Colonial Review (London). A quarterly digest of articles on colonial affairs. Contains articles relating to education in the colonies, selected from leading British, foreign, and colonial periodicals; includes a very comprehensive bibliography.

CUNNINGHAM, KENNETH S., *Primary Education by Correspondence* (Melbourne: Australian Council for Educational Research, 1931). An account of the methods and achievements of the Australian correspondence schools in instructing children living in isolated areas.

DRAKE, HOWARD, *A Bibliography of African Education South of the Sahara* (Aberdeen: University Press, 1942). A very comprehensive bibliography.

GARNETT, A. CAMPBELL, *Freedom and Planning in Australia* (Madison, 1949). The pages on education are clear, concise, and critical.

HAILEY, LORD, *An African Survey* (London: Oxford University Press, 1938). Despite the fact that it is somewhat dated by the pace of recent developments, this is still the best over-all picture of the African continent.

JACKSON, PATRICK M., ed., *Maori and Education* (Wellington: Ferguson & Osborn, Ltd., 1931). A detailed study of native education in New Zealand and its dependencies.

JOWITT, HAROLD, *Principles of Education for African Teachers in Training* (London: Longmans, Green & Company, 1932). A description of the aims and methods of "vital" as opposed to "formal" education; with a foreword by Arthur Mayhew.

KANDEL, I. L., ed., *Educational Yearbooks of the International Insti-*

tute (New York: Teachers College, Columbia University, 1921-1944). An annual review of education.

MAIR, L. P., *Welfare in the British Colonies* (London: The Royal Institute of International Affairs, 1944). Includes a discussion of education.

MALHERBE, ERNST GIDEON, *Education in South Africa, 1652-1922* (Cape Town: Juta & Co., Ltd., 1925). The best critical history, written by an outstanding authority.

————, *Education and the Poor White* (Stellenbosch, 1932). Volume III of a five-volume report of the Carnegie Commission on the Poor White Problem in South Africa. An important study of a neglected problem.

MASON, H. G. R., *Education Today and Tomorrow* (Wellington: E. C. Paul [government printer], 1945). A clear picture of education in New Zealand presented by the Minister of Education.

MAYHEW, ARTHUR, *Education in the Colonial Empire* (London: Longmans, Green & Company, 1938). An account of educational aims and methods by a recognized expert and public official.

MULES, MARY, and ARTHUR G. BUTCHERS, *Bibliography of New Zealand Education* (Auckland: New Zealand Council for Educational Research, 1936). An exhaustive bibliography of official and nonofficial publications on every aspect of education in New Zealand.

PELLS, E. G., *European, Coloured, and Native Education in South Africa, 1652-1938* (Cape Town: Juta & Co., Ltd., 1938). A popular presentation; useful because it brings the story sixteen years beyond Malherbe's account.

PORTUS, G. V., *Free, Compulsory, and Secular* (London: Oxford University Press, 1937). A brief, critical survey of Australian education.

PRICE, A. GRENFELL, *Australian Education in a Changing World* (Adelaide, 1943). A short, critical discussion.

SMUTS, ADRIAAN J., *The Education of Adolescents in South Africa* (Cape Town: Juta & Co., Ltd., 1938). A discussion by a graduate of Teachers College, Columbia University. Reflects the influence of American progressive educational theories.

WYNDHAM, H. A., *Native Education* (London: Oxford University Press, 1933). A useful, if dated, comparative and historical survey of educational practices in American, British, Dutch, French, Japanese, and Spanish possessions.

The Year Books of Education (London: Evans Brothers Ltd.). Published annually since 1932 (except during the war period). A picture of educational developments around the world.

7 · EDUCATION IN *France*

GEORGE F. KNELLER

France's area is approximately 213,000 square miles, and the population is over 41 million. The density of population is in the medium range, about 193 persons to the square mile, in contrast to the heavy densities of England, the Low Countries, and Germany. The urban and rural populations are almost evenly balanced. The country's farms are relatively small, averaging approximately 24 acres. The country has a very well-balanced economy; it is one of the few countries in Europe which can feed itself and, at the same time, produce a wide variety of industrial manufactures. The influence of France has been outstanding in all fields of human living, from government and economics to the arts and education. As one of the oldest unified nations in Europe, it has occupied a position of leadership for centuries. French became the language of diplomacy and government.

French education has traditionally followed an elite pattern; there has been an attempt to select and educate the few for positions of control in government, education, and other activities. French education has been in a process of flux ever since the Revolution. The conservatives attempted to hold to an elite type, and the liberals and radicals, from Condorcet in the eighteenth century to Langevin in the twentieth, worked for the extension of a universal system. The elite system did produce outstanding individuals, but not enough of them. In fact, a great deal of talent had no outlet. The apprenticeship system was the primary factor in maintaining the high level of French production and artistic endeavor. The present trend is in the direction of extension of the benefits of education so that there will be greater opportunity for the development of talent and so that all may realize their potential productivity as members of society. The rate of illiteracy is low, less than 4 percent, in contrast to Italy's 21 percent and Spain's 23 percent.

The analyses of French and Italian education which follow are characterized by a detailed investigation of the contemporary patterns with considerable quotation of source material which may prove useful to the student in gaining an intimate view of the texture of these particular patterns.

—A. H. M.

As short a time as a generation ago it would hardly have been necessary to examine the social, political, and economic situation in France in order to understand the country's educational system. Even taking into account the many theories that influenced the progress of elementary education along developmental and activity lines, there was little about education in France, public or private, that would have revealed dependence upon the demands of national life or upon the country's physical make-up. A leader in pedagogical thought and psychological experimentation, France was among the slowest to make use of the findings.

The reason for the detached position of education is not difficult to find. France became a nation over a thousand years ago, at a time when her neighbors had scarcely begun to plant the seeds of unity. First forged into a political entity by Charlemagne, France received early impetus toward formulating a national school system when in 789 A.D. the Emperor published his celebrated edict in favor of increased education. Education from the very first was defined and controlled by ecclesiastical authorities, and for centuries neither definition nor control was seriously questioned. This meant that for a thousand years the aims and accomplishments of French education responded almost exclusively to the ideals of the Catholic church. It meant that scholasticism determined content and method. Influences for educational emancipation came largely from within the church itself, first from the Jesuit order and then in turn from such groups as the Port-Royalists and the Christian Brothers. But the work of these orders was fairly well confined to intellectual progress within a program of better organization of traditional subject matter and improved teaching methods.

History reveals, however, no lack of progressive thought in lay circles. The philosophy of the Renaissance period, and particularly the writings of such men as Erasmus, Ramus, Budé (founder with Francis I of the Collège de France), Rabelais, Montaigne, and others protested against the formalism, the artificiality, and the insularity of education in the world of their time. As humanists, these men emphasized the worth of the human being, and accordingly they advocated the humanization of both curriculum and instruction.

Throughout French educational history, as Deming Hoyt observes, the prevailing obsession has been to acquire pure knowledge via the Aristotelian method.[1] The classics have always been of major importance. Students have been trained to talk politely and to use their language with polish and finesse. *"L'art de persuader"* has been highly developed, and subjects have been taught with the idea of molding the mind into an instrument of precision and brilliance. To France's educational philosophers, knowledge may have been subservient to intelligence, but in practice subject matter has reigned supreme and become important as a thing in itself. Education, indeed, has been almost exclusively an intellectual adornment, but it has consistently developed praiseworthy skill in the use of words and in self-expression—a realm of accomplishment in which the French have no peers.

The discipline, the unity, and the rigidity of early French education came to be reflected in the total organization and administration of the school system. Jesuit school structure was basic to Napoleon's policy of centralization. It is at the root of the pyramidal structure of bureaus so characteristic of the system today. Throughout the centuries the French have been overwhelmingly preoccupied with logical thought processes, with syllogistic thinking, with rationalism, and later with its logical consequent, positivism. And, as Hoyt pertinently concludes, with this type of national mind not a single detail is left untouched in the regulations of the Ministry of Education: "Courses, hours, texts, methods of teaching, incredibly long and detailed inventories of material down to the last pen point, are

[1] Deming N. Hoyt, "Educational Reform in France," *Harvard Educational Review*, Vol. XVIII (October 1948).

all treated in many thousands of pages which stagger the investigator. . . ."[2]

Educational conservatism has been attacked as much in France as elsewhere. The eighteenth century and the Revolutionary period produced the modern pedagogical ideas of the Encyclopedists, of Rousseau, La Chalotais, Roland, Condorcet, Sieyès, and Daunou (*écoles centrales*), all of whom considered education to be primarily training in civic virtues. Temporarily outlawed by Napoleon, the ideas of these progressivists nevertheless became the driving force toward reforms which were later advanced by such modernists as Edmond Desmoulins (Ecole des Roches), Freinet, Cousinet, and Decroly (a Belgian).

The influence of French education, long embedded in the relatively unbroken history of a talented people, spread to other nations in the forming and served as the classic example for planning their educational life. It may safely be said that no nation has had a greater influence than France on the founding of national school systems throughout the world. But, as these foreign systems have progressed, they have needed more and more to divest themselves of the rigid intellectualism, the monistic approach, and the classicism that characterized their French model.

The power of the church was seriously challenged by the Constitution of 1791, which declared elementary instruction to be legally free and compulsory. Later, under the Guizot Law of 1833, the state assumed control of elementary education. But a mere change of administrators meant little alteration in practice. Actually, French educational history during the first half of the nineteenth century clearly demonstrated that the influence of the church over the country's schools remained firm. Teachers who did not belong to religious orders were excluded from the schools. In fact, a strong case could be made to prove that public laws actually contributed to the conservatism of French schooling by codifying the very administrative procedures and curriculum content which had caused their enactment. Foreign observers could not help being impressed with the easy uniformity, the smooth operation, and the comparative educational smugness that prevailed in French schools up to the present century. Small wonder that the bastion of pure intellectualism falls hardest in the land of its builders! However,

[2] *Ibid.*

laicism (*l'école laïque*) finally emerged victorious in 1882. Since then French schools have been subject, legally at least, to lay or state authority.

EDUCATIONAL STRUCTURE TO WORLD WAR II

The attitude of leading French educators toward the purposes of their schools may have changed radically in the last two decades, but, as has been indicated, the present organization and to a large extent the administration of French schools differ little from the creations of the post-Revolutionary period. In 1806 Napoleon centralized all secondary education in one teaching body called the Université de France. In effect, he thus created a national monopoly over the secondary-school teaching corps of the nation. Thirty years later the operation and maintenance of elementary education were assigned to the local communes. But it was not until 1845 that the need for articulation brought about a division of the country into sixteen (now seventeen) *académies*. As an educational, political, and geographic unit, each *académie* had, and still has, its own university and its own rector, appointed by the Minister of Education. Assisting the rector are the prefect and the inspector general of each department (the nation's largest political subdivision) encompassed by the *académie*. The prefect might well be considered the educational administrator of the department. The inspector general, appointed formerly by the minister but in recent years by the rector, is responsible for the normal school and for all the elementary schools within his department. Each *arrondissement* (ward or district) within the department is headed by an elementary-school inspector.

The centralization of French education was stoutly but not effectively resisted by certain provincial and private groups—religious orders especially—which demanded legal provisos for increased individual educational enterprise and local community control. Outstanding among these groups was the liberalistic, progressive-minded Compagnons de l'Université. Organized as a result of the national failures exposed by World War I, the Compagnons sought to advance local educational effort in order to create a more representative national leadership. But public funds offered very strong competition. And when wealth was matched with educational edicts, notably those of 1882 and 1904, which limited private endeavor and finally forbade religious orders to educate children on the elementary level, there was little left for private initiative, except in the secondary schools. Today the state has virtually a complete monopoly on elementary education and controls over three fourths of the secondary schools. Recent legislation eliminating tuitions and increasing the school-leaving age to fifteen has added materially to the school population on the secondary level, and thus increased the number of students and schools dependent upon state aid.

Notable among the accomplishments of the Compagnons and basic to an understanding of contemporary French school reform was the conception of the *école unique*. The French educational system, it must be noted, developed downward rather than upward, unlike the American system. The secondary school was wont to reach down expressly to prepare its future entrants in the way best suited to the secondary-school ideal. The elementary school developed as a separate entity and remained a thing apart. It was a training in and of itself, representing little or no thought of sending the graduates to secondary school. In fact, post-elementary-school training (called the *cours supérieur*), was never conceived of as equivalent to secondary education, or even as competing with it. Parents had to decide early in a child's life whether to give him a secondary education with appropriate preparatory training, or an elementary training. Once the decision was made, it was difficult to change. The question of family prestige and ability to pay for secondary-school training constituted the chief determinant, of course, so that French secondary schools quickly gained the reputation of being "aristocratic" and "selective" and of catering to a dubious type of intellectual elite.

There thus existed in France an awkward parallelism of elementary and secondary education. To combat this, the *école unique* idealized a single educational ladder system, whereby elementary education was to be basic to all training for all the people. Secondary-preparatory schools were to be discouraged. All post-elementary schooling was to be termed secondary education, and this schooling would aim to satisfy the varying needs of the entrants, by means of both enriched curriculum offerings and different types of school buildings for different courses of study. Thus, under the concept of the *école unique*, French young people would pass through three levels (*degrés*), of education: (1) elementary, from age six to age twelve; (2) secondary, from age twelve to age eighteen; and (3) higher, from age eighteen up. In each case the length and type of schooling were to be scientifically determined for each pupil. Just how this ideal has been modified in recent practice is a matter for later discussion.

France remains among the most centralized nations, education-ally, in the world. Parliament controls every aspect of schooling—aims, methods, curriculums, procedures, examinations, teacher training, financing, and general administration and organization—both public and private, and on all levels. Although local autonomy is permitted in numerous minor matters, it remains a fact that the court of last resort, even in the instance of the rural school-teacher, is the Parliament sitting in Paris. The Minister of Education occupies a position of infinitely greater power and responsibil-ity than does the Commissioner of Education in the United States. Appointed by the Prime Minister, he is a Cabinet member and enjoys equal status with other Cabinet ministers. His duties are so comprehensive as to include the appointment, or the delegation of the appointment, of all the personnel in public secondary and higher educational institutions. He rules concerning examinations and the awarding of degrees. He may preside over university coun-cils, school boards, and other educational organizations, and must pass on the legality and feasibility of their recommendations. He also has general supervision of private schools.

Two committees assist the Minister of Education: the Upper Council of Public Education and the Consulting Committee on Public Education. The former advises on school procedures, the latter on school personnel. A plethora of councils and committees involving all three levels of education combine with bureaus of fine arts, museums, monuments, music, oratory, and technical educa-tion to form the Ministry of Education.

Especially in the field of elementary education the Ministry is aided materially by the recommendations of the local general coun-cils, elected by popular vote in each of France's ninety-three political departments. In fact, the local councils for primary educa-tion, chosen by the general councils, have become powerful and dependable bodies. Their prestige in handling the internal matters of the schools under their jurisdiction has increased so markedly that the Ministry has assigned to them not only greater responsibility for the management of the elementary schools but in certain instances responsibility for the management of the secondary schools within their respective districts. Finally, a system of school inspectors keeps the Ministry informed at all times on the status of personnel, equipment, and general progress of every last school in the Republic, public or private, kindergarten through secondary.

Changes in organization and administration in the period immediately preceding the outbreak of World War II may be summarized as follows: (1) In 1930 secondary education was declared tuition-free. The change was gradual, beginning with the first year of the secondary school and extending by 1937 to the last. (2) Under the Reform of 1937 the school-leaving age was raised to fourteen and new types of vocational training were introduced to satisfy the educational needs of the additional pupils. (3) Private preparatory schools were abolished, along with the parallelism of secondary and post-elementary education, and a program of increased articulation was initiated among all schools. (4) Beginnings were made with the *année d'orientation* (orientation year) and the *sixième nouvelle* (the "new sixth") toward providing a secondary education that would take into greater account the individual needs of students. (These innovations will be discussed below.)

The progress of these reforms suffered during the war. For one thing, under Pétain tuition fees were restored in the secondary schools. For another, the secondary-education program reverted to the traditional disciplinary approach. But with reforms begun in 1944, the spirit and the trajectory of the innovations mentioned above were carried forward with renewed vigor.

THE ROOTS OF REFORM

Although at the time of the German occupation and for some months thereafter the general demoralization that set into French life was the predominant theme of most of the literature, and although some regrettable alterations were made in school discipline and in the ranks of the teachers in charge, an objective appraisal of the actual damage done by the Germans to French schools shows that it was limited for the most part to the destruction of buildings and equipment. William C. Bagley, in *School and Society* (September 23, 1944), editorializes: "The 'reforms' dictated by Nazi influence seldom got below the surface . . . the teachers . . . seem to have honored the new programs and regulations largely in the breach." In other words, "Plus ça change," as the Frenchman says, "plus c'est la même chose" ("The more it changes, the more it is the same thing"). Referring especially to the secondary schools, George J. Kabat, of the United States Office of Education, resignedly observes that the "classical nature" of the French school "could not be for or against anything in this modern and chaotic world."[3] Four hours per week of physical education were added to the curriculum, along with provision for religious instruction (not particularly Nazi-inspired), and of course the German language gained in popularity over English. But the internal life of the schools was otherwise little affected.

The consequences of the material destruction have, of course, been far-reaching. Not the least of them is the present overcrowding in the schools. Certainly, also, one would agree that educational progress was postponed for a decade. But the spirit of educational reform remained largely undisturbed. The deficiencies of the French nation were laid bare by military defeat, which actually served to drive the Fourth Republic to an early satisfaction of educational needs that had existed long before the war. France's educators, swept along with their compatriots in the current of political turmoil and economic instability that followed the war, and caught in the spiral of inflation and commodity scarcity, nevertheless shook off immediate tribulations and resolutely accepted the responsibility of providing a type of education that would do credit to French national progress. The educational system was to be based on the peculiar needs and demands of the country and its people. It was not only to spring from French political, economic, and social life but was to become an intrinsic part of it. It was to reflect France's responsibility in a world of nations.

Oddly enough for a nation with such strong centralized controls, for a nation that has been politically united throughout most of the history of Western civilization, for a nation that has had to band together many times to repel invasion, and for a nation whose spiritual life has been guided for so long by one religion, the French

[3] George J. Kabat, "Postwar Secondary-School Reforms in France," *Journal of the National Education Association*, Vol. XXXV (May 1946).

people demonstrate an unusual amount of individualistic preference. This is evident not only in their philosophic writings and
artistic creativity but even more pertinently in their purely political
history. Between 1870 and 1940, for example, internal political dis-
unity and indecision created 142 different governments, each with an
average life of only six months. From the liberation until 1950
France had at least twelve governments; and it actually became a
matter of universal astonishment that M. Queille's party managed
to remain in power for just over a year. Not only this, but every
Parliament has been studded with a galaxy of political parties that
have become notorious for their lack of form and organization, and
the more so for their ever-changing moods. The spectacle of such
wanton political instability and license has promoted many Frenchmen to advocate the restoration of the monarchy, that there might
be some fixed and guiding force, or to recommend a limit of two or
three parties, to press for more *types communs* (average persons)
as national leaders, or in extreme cases to demand a dictatorship.
The more realistic prefer changes in the Constitution which would
reduce the number of ministerial crises and give the country
straighter lines of political behavior.[4] For their part, however, most
French educators are alert to the need for establishing national
political unity and progress through suitable school training. They
put their faith in an education which frankly recognizes and exposes
the frailties of French political behavior and all the indecisions
and corruption that go with it.

But political deficiency is not the sole source of France's troubles.
Her economy has been too often disrupted, and this in a land which
of all lands of Europe is in a favorable position to provide for the
material wants of its people. In normal times France is in large

---

[4] André Philip, chairman of the Committee for the Constitution of the
Fourth Republic, warns against exaggerating France's political instability,
and maintains that the more cabinets rise and fall the more they stay the
same. Continuity, according to Philip, exists in foreign policy, international
economic policy, and personnel: "In almost all posts the same men have
been in power since 1946." However, Philip's convictions quickly fade
as he dilates on the causes of French political instability and ends his
article with proposals on how to remedy the situation: "There will be no
stability in French politics until the day when the democratic constitutional
parties control an adequate majority. . . ." (*New York Times Magazine,*
November 27, 1949.)

measure self-subsistent. Her soil has a high level of fertility. Her subsoil yields large amounts of coal (Anzin, Valenciennes, Escaut), iron ore (Bassin de Briey), potash, talcum, corindon bauxite, and other products. In normal times France has actually exported her surplus agricultural produce—fresh fruit, vegetables, preserves, tinned goods.

In light and heavy industry the volume of output is not impressive, but the lack of quantity is compensated by the quality and deftness of French workmanship. Manufactured products consist of porcelain, pottery, and stoneware, along with leather and textiles, especially silk, rayon, and lace. The fact that Paris maintains her position as the fashion center of the world indicates to what extent French inspiration and invention are utilized to guide world trade. French educational leaders know that to retain the country's position as one of the world's outstanding purveyors of fine merchandise, French vivacity, creativity, and individuality must be cultivated and cherished among all her people. Of necessity France must now concentrate on the reconstruction and extension of those material as well as spiritual attributes which will ensure national wealth and contentment. The training for this must commence early in the schools. It must be free and easily accessible to every individual in accordance with his own bent. It must be closely linked with French natural productivity.

In view of the historically high level of French accomplishment and individuality, what criticism, one may ask, can be raised against the school which has presumably engendered such qualities? France's long line of writers, philosophers, musicians, artists, and savants would seem to justify the continuance of the kind of education that produced them. But the answer is that this greatness, this brilliance, was too often confined to intellectual, legal, and artistic pursuits on lofty levels. History shows that the cost of French brilliance has had to be reckoned in terms of reduced national vitality, of restricted opportunity, of an inordinate selectivity in the educational progress of the individual. What may be said of the political life of the French nation may also be said of the educational life—namely, that national life advanced beyond the grasp and comprehension of the school system. It is to be expected that schools so solidly and so sensitively grounded in intellectualism, philosophy, literature, and art would by their very nature produce men of distinction within these realms. But, as the nineteenth-century pedagogues warned, schools had other great purposes, and these involved the total life of the individual and the nation.

A second doubt arises from a consideration of French handicraft, which is among the finest and most delicate in the world. How were the French educated to this level of perfection if not in the schools? The answer is that most of the trades were learned "on location," through the apprenticeship system. They were not learned in school. Traditionally, the French school has been no place to learn a trade or even to study the fundamentals of a vocation. This deficiency was somewhat alleviated in the 1920's with reforms promoted by Léon Blum and again with the reforms of 1936-1937. But such reforms remained largely on paper. A mere statement of aims and desires, even if enacted into law, is abortive unless the material and the personnel are concomitantly provided. In France especially, technical training and vocational education have too long remained on the periphery of educational respectability.

The lag in vocational education becomes a minor matter when compared with the deplorable vacuum that has existed in the training of French youth in civic responsibility. D. W. Brogan, one of the world's most capable commentators on French life, joins Alexander Werth in noting that the fertility, the talent, and the primacy in artistic achievement that were traditional in France suffered no loss as a result of foreign invasion. Accomplishment in science remained firm; moral life, too, was relatively unaffected, and indeed showed signs of a healthy renewal. But in politics the dualism of people and state became even more marked. The state, in fact the whole political organization of the country, instead of rising to new political heights following liberation actually disintegrated before an apathetic, irresponsible voting populace. The authority of the executive was reduced, and power fell into the hands of scores of separatist groups, represented in turn by hundreds of independently minded senators, deputies, and lesser politicos. Stunted as always by a defective, insecure electoral system and with badly organized political parties that seemed to stand for themselves rather than for the progress of France as a nation, the growth of the French state fell behind the growth of the nation as a cultural unit. It was painfully evident that the Frenchman had not learned to govern himself and his country. He had not measured his obligations to his countrymen. He had not acquired a proper sense of political responsibility. It was therefore up to educators to point the way toward a solution through the proper type of schooling. Training in democratic citizenship had to be basic to school reform.

Political pluralism is of course interdependent with a social configuration that in France has a double aspect. The *égalité* enacted into law with the Revolution eliminates discrimination in any form, whether based on social class, wealth, religion, or race. And it follows, legally at least, that equality of educational opportunity for all French children is guaranteed. In practice, however, a very different condition has prevailed, some mention of which has been made above with regard to the type of secondary-school enrollments. A study of the social origin of France's leaders by Henri Laugier, rector of the University of Algiers, reveals some very pertinent data: (1) There is a very powerful tendency toward the hereditary transmission of professional activities, especially in the army, the navy, the magistracy, and law. (2) The nation's leaders are not representative of the diverse social groups; in fact, the representation in the case of a number of these groups is extraordinarily low. (3) There is a marked absence of the sons of farmers, laborers, factory workers, and small artisans in the higher cadres. Dr. Laugier concludes, and with a great deal of justification, that France's leaders neither represent nor speak for the rank and file of the people, and that the caste system was one of the outstanding causes of the decline of national feeling after 1940.[5] He might also have stated that, since the avenues toward leadership were closed to the lower classes, there seemed to be little point in the latter's exerting themselves to achieve much more than the minimum for success within their social stratum. If people are traditionally excluded from participation in national destiny it is unlikely that many of them will accept the responsibility for it.

One would imagine that social inequality would have given cause for greater concern in a country as advanced culturally as France.

[5] Henri Laugier, "France," in I. L. Kandel, ed., *Postwar Educational Reconstruction in the United Nations, 21st Educational Yearbook of the International Institute* (New York: Teachers College, Columbia University, 1944).

The fact is that what one inherits one tends to accept. The immediate victims of inequality, unless they are suffering mentally and physically, are very often unmindful of, or indifferent to, their lower status. Amid the normally pleasant conditions of French life, particularly in rural areas, there has traditionally been a contentment, complaisance, and self-sufficiency that would be disturbed only by interference from the outside. It has rarely occurred to the son of a French worker or farmer that he might some day become a national leader, simply because he knew that he was not born in the right milieu.[6] The significant thing about this, as Dr. Laugier observes, is that the realization has hardly embittered him. Prospects of fame have remained so remote and so unrealizable that they have aroused in him little desire to claim his equal right as a French citizen and to seek a higher place in political and social spheres.

France's educational leaders have thus been faced with the necessity of providing educational measures to remedy the social inequality in their national life, first by ensuring the education of every citizen to his full capacity regardless of economic and social status, and secondly by a strong program of mass education propagandizing the need to draw more and more leaders from the bosom of the people. The details of this program as recently enacted by the French Parliament follow, under the appropriate headings.

PHILOSOPHY AND STRUCTURE OF CONTEMPORARY EDUCATION

Paris was liberated in August 1944. In that year Britain presented for Parliamentary approval her Education Bill, the product of many years of study and preparation. In that year, too, the French Parliament entrusted to Paul Langevin, professor at the College de France, the formidable task of reorganizing the entire French educational system. Langevin appointed a distinguished group of educators (called the Commission Ministérielle d'Etude) to assist him, among them the eminent child psychologist Henri Wallon, who was a colleague of his at the Collège de France and president of the French Pedagogical Society. Wallon succeeded Langevin on the latter's untimely death in 1946.

The findings of the Commission are contained in a report pub-

[6] Daladier and Laval were among the more notable exceptions.

lished under the title *La Réforme de l'enseignement*. Submitted to
the government in 1947, parts of it have already been enacted
into law. The opening sentences of the early paragraphs take immediate cognizance of France's educational dilemma and indicate
the nature of the reforms needed:

> French education for a long time has been known and re-
> spected throughout the world for its superior quality and cultural
> value. . . .
> However, even before the War it became evident that our
> education had to be reorganized. . . .
> The structure of our education must in fact be adapted to our
> social structure. . . . For half a century there has been no pro-
> found change in our education. The country's social structure,
> on the other hand, has undergone a rapid evolution with changes
> of a very fundamental nature.
> Our elementary, secondary, and higher studies are too often
> on the margin of reality. The school seems to be a closed milieu,
> unpenetrated by the world of experience. . . .
> Resting on the margin of life, education has not profited from
> scientific progress. . . .
> . . . the training of youth in civic affairs is one of the funda-
> mental tasks of a democratic state.

Finally,

> All these reasons justify a profound reform of all our educa-
> tional institutions, which, if in the past they have successfully
> fulfilled their mission, must transform and adapt themselves to
> present economic and social conditions in order to maintain
> their enviable reputation.

The principles underlying the Reform are then set forth; the
most outstanding of them may be summarized as follows:

> 1. "Educational justice" requires that all children be entitled
> to the maximum development of their personality. The democ-
> ratization of education means that the good of all is best served
> when individual aptitudes define the course of education. The
> distribution of social tasks is dependent not on social position
> but upon the capacity to fulfill them.
> 2. Educational equality recognizes that all social tasks must be
> accorded equal status. Manual labor, practical intelligence, and

vocational education are every bit as dignified as the more traditional types of training.

3. Education must be founded on the latest psychological knowledge of how people best learn. This involves provision for the instruction of abnormal children. It means that all education should take place under hygienic conditions and amid circumstances that are conducive to learning.

4. The principle of educational orientation is basic to a discovery of individual aptitudes as they relate to social needs.

5. The formation of the man as a worker must not harm the formation of the man as an individual. Indeed, the education of the individual as a member of the human race must not be lost in the development of purely personal power.

6. A general education unites men, whereas specialized education tends to separate them. "In a democratic state, where every worker is a citizen, specialization must not become an obstacle in the way of understanding broader problems; a wide and well-grounded cultural training frees man from the narrow limitations of the technician."

7. The school must therefore become a center for the dissemination of general culture, modified, of course, by the needs of the locality in which education takes place. "As the depository of thought, of art, of a past civilization, the school must transmit these acquisitions at the same time that it is the active agent of progress and modernization. It must be the point of meeting, the cohesive element which ensures the continuity of the past with the future."

These principles carry with them several implications for educational organization and administration; the Reform goes on to state, in essence:

1. Education must be organized on the basis of simplicity, unity, and coherence. There are too many types of schools, most of which are interested in their own development rather than in the young people who attend them. Progress from one level of education to the other and transfer from one type of training to another involve too many difficulties that will have to be overcome.

2. Schools must be organized in such a way as to respond to the level of development of the students and to an appraisal of their aptitudes. Schools must be established and administered in

accordance with student needs rather than on the basis of rigidly preconceived curriculums.

3. The various levels of education must follow a single, unified plan, each segment of education working in conjunction with the others.

4. If schooling is to be obligatory and if young people are to be allowed every opportunity for education, it follows that all education must be free. Not only this, but financial aid must be provided wherever necessary both to the student and to his family. The student is thus considered a potentially productive member of society and must be assisted in fulfilling his potentialities.

5. Teacher education and professionalization must be further improved and dignified. Teachers must be accorded the necessary material and spiritual rewards which go hand in hand with their "eminent position in national life." The number of teachers must be increased and their training intensified.

6. A tremendous number of buildings will have to be enlarged and remodeled and thousands of new buildings will have to be constructed. The "material reconstruction" of the school, involving laboratories and equipment, is a necessary counterpart to the extension of the school's role in the civic, economic, and social life of the nation. These buildings must be constructed in such a way as to respond to the demands of a new education.

The organizational provisos of the Reform call for two main levels of education that follow a single, unified pattern. The first level is called the *premier degré*. It embodies what formerly constituted *enseignement primaire, secondaire,* and *technique,* and consists of three cycles. The first cycle enrolls children between the ages of seven and eleven; the second, ages eleven to fifteen; and the third, ages fifteen to eighteen. In time, education is expected to be compulsory from age seven to age eighteen.

The first cycle (ages seven to eleven) features an education that will be common to all children, although the content and method will be adapted to individual differences. In addition to teaching fundamental subject matter, the first cycle puts increased emphasis on the development of personality and on adjustment to civic and social life. During this time the child masters those basic skills and knowledges which will "enable him to understand and be understood." The final year of the elementary school merges with the first year of the secondary to form a preparatory year to secondary training within the secondary school proper.

The second stage (ages eleven to fifteen), called the *cycle d'orientation*, aims to arouse in the young adolescent a feeling of individual and group responsibility. The student is to orient himself vocationally and professionally. The first two years are to be devoted to exploring interests and abilities, the last two offering a wide range of subject-matter choice, with greater concentration on one's speciality. Elective courses are grouped under the following heads: scientific, literary, technical, and artistic. (The Ministry of Education rightfully claims that in general students are not equipped to make choices or come to intelligent decisions regarding their future until they are at least thirteen.)

The third stage (ages fifteen to eighteen, called the *cycle de détermination*), is subdivided into three sections. The student may choose the *section pratique*, which involves training in manual arts in trade schools; the *section professionnelle*, which provides vocational training in commercial, industrial, agricultural, and artistic pursuits; and the *section théorique*, which encompasses training in the humanities, the classics, and the sciences.

The student advances from one cycle to the next with a minimum of administrative or educational difficulty. No formal examinations are to be given before the end of the *premier degré*, and promotion from class to class is dependent upon the judgment of a teaching council (*conseil de maîtres*). Examinations are to be given, however, at the end of the *premier degré*. Successful candidates in the *section pratique* are to receive a *certificat d'aptitude*; vocational students are to be awarded the *brevet d'enseignement professionnelle*; and students in the *section théorique* will still be granted the *baccalauréat* ("university matriculation," not a "bachelor's degree"!).

Under the Reform, higher education commences with the program of the *deuxième degré*, or second level. During the first two years students are expected to prepare for their higher professional studies in schools dedicated primarily to that purpose. The following two years are to be devoted to a preparation for the *licence*, which is the qualifying certificate, and the *concours*, a competitive examination for entrance into higher training. (Little change is contemplated, therefore, in the traditional postbaccalaureate program, which has for many years been preparatory to university entrance and the *grandes écoles*.)

The four-year preprofessional training necessitates changes in the organization of higher education with the special aim of penetrating the traditional autonomy of university faculties and the *grandes écoles* (the higher schools) and effecting a greater cohesion of interests and activities. This action is primarily a result of the schism which has always existed between technical and theoretical studies. In the words of the reform, "In order to avoid the dispersion (*éparpillement*) of studies among and across the various institutes and faculties of the same university and to combat their present tendency to be either exclusively technical or exclusively thoretical, a coordination among them must be effected." Extending this idea, the Reform proposes that studies of a complementary nature be organized into centers of study (officially termed *instituts d'université*). The example is used of the Institute of Psychology of the University of Paris, which at present controls all the teaching of psychology and all the laboratories and equipment that go along with it. This institute would serve as a model to an Institute of Physiology, the Reform suggests, which would embody all the instruction in physiology now given separately in the university faculties of science, medicine, etc., at the Collège de France and at the National Museum. Likewise, courses in economics now given separately in faculties of law, science, and letters would be concentrated in a study center for economics. Specially organized faculty councils would coordinate the courses of study and the work of individual students. Otherwise, the various university faculties and institutes would retain their present organization and method of operation.

As for *grandes écoles*, which are in reality vocational institutions of higher education, their theoretical courses and studies in general education, "now scattered among them at needless expense and duplication of effort," will either be entrusted entirely to university faculties or at least controlled by examinations set by the university. As a consequence, each *grande école* will be left to concentrate more on its speciality—public works, mines, agriculture, etc.—leaving general education to agencies better able to handle it. (The enactment of this segment of reorganization naturally remains dependent upon agreement with such ministries as those of agriculture and public works.)

Acknowledging the inferior quality of some of the provincial universities and the deficiency of their programs, the Reform advocates a regrouping of higher educational facilities and offerings. In the Ministry's attitude, all universities should not feel obligated to teach all subjects, but rather concentrate on those fields which they are best equipped to handle. This means, of course, that higher educational personnel would also be regrouped; professors in the same or related fields would be brought together under the same roof, and would thus be in a better position to pool their knowledge for more intensive effort and more productive achievement. The example is given of the University of Besançon, one of the smallest universities in France, which would "do well to cease giving all courses necessary for the *licence* and concentrate on its specialities, chronometry and geology," for which, with added personnel and equipment, it would become "even more renowned."

Far more radically, the Reform advocates that universities offer their facilities to worth-while social and cultural groups in what might well be termed extension courses. This extension work, similar in aim to that given in England by such organizations as the worker's institutes and by a government-supported program of adult education, would demand no extensive background of academic preparation and aspire to no credits, certificates, or degrees. Thus it is hoped that throughout the entire Republic knowledge will be disseminated which will contribute significantly to public enlightenment in every realm of human endeavor.

Needless to add, the proposals for reform in higher education have been among the slowest to take hold. It will take considerable time for university faculties to accede to the kind of mobility and shift of academic emphasis implied in such recommendations, or to accommodate themselves to a better undergraduate program. Government legislation will, of course, go far in supplying the necessary impetus. Such legislation will no doubt be enacted as students now in the secondary school advance to higher levels.

ELEMENTARY EDUCATION

Elementary education (*l'école primaire*) was declared free and compulsory in 1880-1881. Originally embracing ages six to thirteen, it has been expanded to include those levels of education which in the United States are termed preschool or nursery, kindergarten, primary, and elementary.

Education below the first primary grade is voluntary. Originally called *salles d'asile*, preschools became known as *écoles maternelles* in 1881. With time the *école maternelle* developed exclusively as an independent kindergarten admitting children from two to five years of age. A second institution branched off and took the name of *classe enfantine*, admitting children from three to six in subclasses attached to an elementary school.

Under the present system, preschool education is divided into two age groups. Youngsters below the age of three may attend *crèches* ("cradles"), or *maisons d'enfance*, which are supported by the Red Cross, and those from three to six are enrolled in *écoles maternelles*. Although the Ministry accepts no responsibility for the support of preschool education, it reserves the right of supervision, and indeed in many instances stretches out a helping hand to facilitate the work of private groups. About half of France's preschool population attend some form of educational institution below the primary school.

The most arresting difference between a French *école maternelle* and an American kindergarten lies in the fact that the French respect the derivation of the word "kindergarten" by providing actual gardens (*jardins d'enfants*) for the locale of training. The French kindergartens, like kindergartens in other educational systems influenced by the French, are apt to be communities of their own; they concentrate on outdoor activity in their gardens. They are rarely appendages to elementary schools.

The French elementary school after World War II offered a six-year training divided into three sections: the *cours élémentaire* (ages seven to nine), the *cours moyen* (ages nine to eleven), and the *cours supérieur* (ages eleven to thirteen or fourteen). Additional training beyond the fourteenth birthday was provided in continuation schools. Such a division came about largely as a result of France's difficulty in inducing farmers and underprivileged workers to send their children to school. Despite legislation enforcing school attendance, there has been a tendency on the part of too many parents to send their children to work. By providing breaks in elementary schooling, a harried administrative and teaching personnel could at least point to some educational goal, some sort of terminal training, to which the hapless youngster might aspire. However, with the further implementation of the *école unique* idea and the single ladder system, with a better program of publicity, and with increased pressure on parents, a complete education up to age fifteen is now becoming accepted very much as a matter of course for all French children.

Elementary education is now considered to be a four-year basic training for all French children from age seven to age eleven. Recent reforms have affected the internal behavior of the elementary school least of all; but, as Roger Gal emphasizes, the very fact that elementary education is no longer terminal results in a program of preparation for further training that formerly was of minor concern.[7] It means that subject matter need no longer be taught prematurely, and certain subjects which formerly the elementary teacher felt obliged to handle may be postponed for treatment at the secondary stage. In other words, a greater concentration is possible on the basic knowledges and skills. The curriculum proper remains little changed, and contains an array of subjects similar to those taught in the elementary schools of other lands. Methods stress the faculties of observation and expression in drawing, music, and plastic arts, and a greater adaptation of both teaching and subject matter to regional demands. Prevocational preparation is provided, student guidance arising from a closer attention to individual differences; but the program is very much in embryo, the one dramatic exception being preparation for the *classes nouvelles* experiment, which is discussed below.

In religious matters the state has adopted a policy of neutrality, so that religion is not taught in any public school. To most religious bodies the advocacy of such a policy is tantamount to practicing godlessness in the schools, or at least agnosticism. The Ministry replies that the only morality which can safely be taught is one which approximates the French concept of the *honnête homme* (the ethical man), a man imbued with the best that moral, if not theological, philosophy has produced. At any rate, denominationalism is anathema to modern French practice as regulated by governmental authorities, and it is restricted to private schools.

[7] Roger Gal, *La Réforme de l'enseignement, et les classes nouvelles* (Paris: Les Presses d'Ile de France, 1946).

SECONDARY EDUCATION

The most radical changes have occurred in the secondary schools
—changes that have not sprung up overnight but have been the
outcome of educational planning promulgated by the reforms of
1936-1937.

General secondary education is imparted in either a *lycée* or a
collège (not "college"!); it has been historically highly selective,
especially in the *lycée*. In fact, the restricted aims of these two types
of schools have been such that only members of the privileged classes
or those who were expressly destined for university careers could
possibly have received the type of academic preparation that was
pertinent to their life goal. The charge that secondary education
was "aristocratic" does not mean that only the "upper crust" were
privileged to enjoy it. But it does betray the fact that its purposes
were strictly limited to the education of an elite, of a ruling class,
on a narrow, intellectualized basis. And when that purpose was
combined with the necessity of paying for the instruction, the clien-
tele remained as exclusive as the curriculum. Examinations have
traditionally been difficult, and the work required during the year
has been of such unreasonable proportions as to create an alarming
number of psychological and pathological cases among secondary
students. So competitive did secondary education become that examination periods were dreaded by students and parents alike, who
were painfully aware that despite long hours of "cramming" there
was at best only an even chance of success.

The *lycée* is world-renowned for the intellectual achievement of
its graduates; it has long been the educational symbol of French
culture. The *collège*, established and controlled in largest part by
provincial and municipal authorities, originally was intended to
expand the narrow subject-matter concepts of the *lycée* into a curriculum of a more general, more practical, and more experiential
nature, based on local demands. But the idea never really took hold,
and the *collège* grew to be just another *lycée*, except that the teachers were not as well prepared and academic standards were generally
lower. Directors of the *collèges* quickly learned that if they did not
lend the same weight to traditional subject matter as did the *lycée*,
and establish the same linguistic emphasis in all method, their
schools would soon lose academic respectability. After all, there re-

mained the very practical problem of having to compete with the *lycée* in producing students intellectually equipped to handle university work. Far too many French educators, particularly on the higher educational level, placed their undying trust in examinations as the omnipotent proof of educational achievement. There was little left for the *collèges* to do, therefore, but to give their students the brand of information and the type of approach that would guarantee the proper results on examinations.

A first invasion into the exclusive precincts of the secondary school was launched with the awarding of scholarships and state aid to meritorious students regardless of social status. This was followed by provisions for easier transfer from the elementary-school ladder to that of the secondary school. (In practice, however, only those who had won scholarships succeeded at first in effecting such transfers.) A third inroad was created when classes of the elementary *cours supérieur* joined with the same or similar classes of the secondary school in communities where educational thrift became a factor. Fortunately enough, this fusion of classes was all the more successful because of the uniformity of curriculum content and method so characteristic of the French system. Finally, the complete abolition of tuition fees and the raising of the school-leaving age to fourteen, decreed first in 1930 and ultimately achieved in 1937, cleared the way for the acceptance of the *école unique* idea. The recent reform bill has administered the *coup de grâce*, thereby not only solidifying the single ladder system but establishing a wider choice of secondary educational programs in more varied school structures.

Secondary training, as exemplified by the *lycée* and the *collège*, is seven years in length, the last of which is devoted to a preparation for the second part of the *baccalauréat* and for university examinations. Majors, confined to the final year of study, were formerly restricted to mathematics and philosophy, subjects which were considered to be the best "trainers of the mind." But they now include the physical sciences. With a good knowledge of these fields the student is considered to be sufficiently well equipped to tackle anything. Oddly enough, the classics as majors fell by the wayside. Some effort was made in 1937 to effect changes which would allow modern languages and the classics to form a major field, but, despite the fact that learned tracts were written illustrating how languages, too, could train the mind, the schools remained unconvinced, or at least were not convinced sufficiently to put the idea into practice. Nevertheless it must serve as a source of consolation to classics teachers that by law they are now being assured of the preservation of their subject matter, especially at a time when devastating assaults are being made on it in other school systems of the world. Indeed, under new rulings the teachers of Latin and Greek can depend upon a small but steady flow of students and, in Kabat's mischievous terms, "will be able to teach sentence parsing, word juggling, and mental calisthenics to the true lover of semantics." On the other hand, the Reform sees to it that students may learn their classical civilization and ancient cultures by studying ancient history and literature. "They will not need to conjugate irregular verbs by lamplight," Kabat consoles.[8]

Students begin their secondary training at age eleven or twelve. For this stage the French have initiated an experimental program that for sheer progressivism and educational awareness has few equals. The first year of the secondary school is termed the *classe de sixième,* or the "sixth class," the French counting their secondary years in reverse up to the "first class." The experiment was launched in its instructional phases in 1945 and was known the first year as the *"sixième nouvelle,"* the "new sixth." As students of the new sixth moved up they entered the *cinquième nouvelle* ("new fifth"), then the *quatrième nouvelle,* and so on until all six classes were completed.

The greatest innovation with respect to the *classes nouvelles* lies not so much in subject matter proper, most of which at heart remains basic to all secondary schooling, but in the way in which youngsters are tested for various aptitudes, both in the field of abstractions and in the expressive arts. Personal character, qualities of leadership, depth of curiosity, and extent of energy all enter into the planning of the child's school life. The new classes are small, consisting of twenty-five to thirty students, and are usually conducted by three teachers acting in cooperation. The morning program is devoted to such basic subjects as French, history, literature, geography, a modern language, natural science (stressing the "science of observation"), and mathematics. The afternoon is given over to such elective subjects as drawing, painting, modeling, music, etc.,

[8] George J. Kabat, *op. cit.*

which contribute to a field of concentration in practical and applied arts. Sports, physical education, health classes, and a new subject called *étude du milieu* (study of the environment) are all compulsory in the afternoon session.

The *sixième nouvelle* is most challenging in its psychological and guidance aspects. Julienne Farenc justifies the experiment on this ground alone, if not on any other:

> Modern psychology has effected a revolution in understanding child growth—a revolution which has not yet penetrated our secondary schools. For the child between 10 and 12 . . . we must provide new types of instruction which respond to his nature, his needs, and his interests, thus releasing a spontaneous and total activity which in its very essence is intense and fecund.[9]

Instructors are specially trained in guidance as well as in subject matter and are chosen because they are more vitally interested in all-round student growth than in subject-matter acquisition. A comprehensive program of tests and measurements followed by weekly personal conferences and periodic check-ups of student progress enables instructors to adapt programs and educational activity to needs, abilities, and changes in attitude. Whereas under the old system large numbers of students failed or were forced to leave school, with only negligible attempts made to get at the root of their educational dilemma, the new program unites all aspects of student development on the principle of the old trinity of head, heart, and hand. The school is no longer an institution where students simply study. It becomes instead a community where they live, work, and play in a broader, more sympathetic, and more meaningful environment, and where the relationship of teacher and student is based on friendliness and cooperation.

One of the leaders in the execution of the *sixième nouvelle* experiment, Madame A. M. de Saint-Blanquat, director of the Lycée Balzac, at Tours, relates her personal experiences in part as follows:

> . . . pupils and staff volunteered. . . . Parents must have been interested by the prospect of active, individualized methods for their children, as more applications were made than wanted. We were able to choose. We picked out children 11 years old as an

[9] Julienne Farenc, "Le Stage de la sixième nouvelle," *Revue Universitaire,* Vol. I (January 1946).

average rather than taking the older ones, as we thought they would better adapt themselves to methods very different from what they had been accustomed to.

We also thought it would be interesting to have a class as representative as possible of a good average in intelligence as well as in social standing. We took all the children's records and chose excellent pupils, good ones, middling ones, and very ordinary ones. We also made a point of having them come from very different homes; we wanted our new classes to be true to a diversity of characters, attainments, and origins, so as to be able to judge rightly of the result.

We started off our "adventure" with great interest. One of the three teachers was head of the team—an important item in the new pedagogical structure. She . . . was to plan out the work with the other members, studying and comparing methods and results in classes, meetings held once a week. She also acted as counselor to the pupils and their parents. The head of the team taught French as well as history, and tutored the children in civics. . . . Apart from the principal teachers, we had one for arts, one for music, one for handicrafts, and naturally one for physical education. Drawing, modeling, and music were assigned longer hours than before. The pupils tried each subject in turn with a view toward future option. Handicrafts were made compulsory.[10]

The most outstanding characteristics and motivating principles of the *classes nouvelles* may be summarized as follows:

1. Improved guidance procedures, encompassing a wider range of tests and measurement, enable the student to pursue a wiser and more suitable course of study.

2. Education loses much of its rigidity and restricted bookish quality and becomes a more generalized training for life. With fewer required subjects and more electives, education becomes more productive for the individual student.

3. Handicrafts and artistic activities assume a more important place, the attitude being that these subjects divert students and teachers from the overintellectualized spirit of French education. They also allow a greater opportunity for ascertaining the tastes and abilities of young people.

4. The experiment is expected to discover technical talent and produce a greater number of technicians, of which France has greater need than ever before.

[10] A. M. de Saint-Blanquat, "Educational Reform in France," *Educational Forum*, Vol. XII (November 1947).

5. A better choice of studies, made on the basis of capability, will result in fewer failures, hence less psychological strain and greater educational efficiency.

6. The increased cooperation of parents, teachers, and students creates a healthier basis for educational progress. A warmer student-teacher rapport enhances and harmonizes learning.

7. Self-government and individual responsibility for one's success replace the old idea of teacher-controlled discipline. This contributes to character formation and a more open-minded personality, based on an understanding of what it takes to work with one's fellow man rather than compete against him, and resulting in a more delicate feeling for human relations.

8. The creative power of students is challenged and native energy aroused as a result of intelligent motivation.

9. Specialization once considered possible around age eleven or twelve is now postponed to around age fourteen or fifteen.

10. Although the content of basic courses remains much the same, the method now includes "centers of interest." There is consequently a greater play of subject-matter integration, so that a course in history, for example, includes a study of the literature, the architecture, the clothing, the manner of living, the art, and the general culture of the period, even at the expense of a slower rate of progress.

Sponsors of the new secondary education are not unaware of the criticisms. In the first place, many a French teacher claims, and justifiably so, that the vicarious, restricted quality of his teaching has been due in large part to a demand for economy. With increased appropriations and with sufficient laboratories, workshops, playgrounds, and equipment, more could have been done in the way of "modernizing" educational procedures long before the reform of 1947 appeared. Also, the more traditional type of educator joins with many a parent in observing that the new methods tend to make the student lazier; they create a path of least resistance; they do not force him to do those unpleasant yet necessary things he will be faced with later in life. Parents in particular are still puzzled as to how learning can be achieved without homework. Finally, there is fear lest the humanities suffer and students ultimately acquire little but contempt for pure learning.

One of these criticisms has been answered by a French wit, who observed that "formerly pupils slept during school hours and

worked at home, but today they sleep at home and work at school."
In response to a fear lest the humanities be dehumanized, the reformer replies that in actuality their warmth and vitality will be
inculcated in students, and in any case no student will be deprived
of an opportunity to elect whatever course of study he wishes, provided he gives promise of being able to handle it. Thus it is hoped,
for example, that, although the number of students taking Greek
and Latin will be reduced, the quality of the student will be raised.
With greater talent concentrated in fewer enrollments in the humanities the result should be one of greater and more abiding satisfaction to all who participate. Finally, with regard to the lack of
wherewithal and matériel, Madame Blanquat inserts a pertinent
comment: "Just to show how difficult the task was from a material
standpoint, we had to use soft paper for sewing. Still the children
made lovely things." In fact, as one observes the genius and resourcefulness of the teachers who have participated in the experiment, one
is forced to conclude that material obstacles are being overcome by
love of the task. In any case, the educational atmosphere in France
today clearly indicates that the new education has taken hold. Official directives, enacted into legislation, and published reports of
teachers in service are concrete evidence of this fact. (See *Classes
nouvelles* in the Bibliography.)

Any sort of comprehensive report on the secondary-school curriculum would be a study in itself. Indeed, the Ministry of Education
has issued a good-sized volume containing nothing but syllabuses,
and another publication devoted to course content and method. Let
it suffice for present purposes to mention certain outstanding pecu-
liarities that exist in the French system as contrasted with the
American.

In the first place, the actual school day tends to be longer, averaging about six hours, five days per week. Thursday, instead of Saturday, is a free day, although outdoor activities are scheduled for some
part of the day, especially in the higher classes. According to the
typically French letter of the law, "The school week is five days in
length for the first cycle, Thursday being entirely free. In the second
cycle classes may be held Thursday morning. There will be no classes
on Thursday in the first cycle and as far as possible in the second
cycle." A half-day per week, usually Saturday, is devoted to outdoor
physical activity or indoor sports in case of inclement weather. The

school year is also longer, averaging about forty-two weeks, or at least a month longer than the average in the United States.

The number of subjects studied simultaneously is more than double the number that would be offered in an American high school, although the variety of subjects studied over a period of years is similar. The American educator would raise a question as to the advisability of holding certain types of classes only once a week, or once in two weeks, and would seek to show the greater value of concentrating such subjects in one or two years of study. Teaching a modern language only two or three days per week, for example, does not as a rule produce desirable results, since by its very nature language study demands drill and habit formation over concentrated rather than scattered class periods.

Another difference lies in the amount of concentration in, and the general attitude toward, such subjects as economics, sociology, and current events. Granted that much of the subject matter is covered in courses already being taught, the French educator has not yet deemed it of sufficient importance to devote much of his teaching time to the social studies per se. He assumes, furthermore, that since the background of interpretation is obtained in basic courses, along with the intellectual curiosity that this background "automatically" brings, the student will of his own accord keep abreast of world events. He will voluntarily make an intelligent selection of reading matter from France's plethora of newspapers and periodicals. Whereas American educators in many instances may have gone too far in fostering class discussion on contemporary problems without the proper background of study, the French educator has gone to the opposite extreme. For nothing is more certain than that students need considerable guidance in their selection of contemporary reading matter and as they interpret the issues of the day. Especially in a world as chaotic and confused as that of the mid-twentieth century there is great need for applying knowledge expertly and resolutely to the contemporary scene. Students cannot be expected to effect this transfer unaided.

The atmosphere of a French secondary school is likewise some-what different. The lecture method is used more than it is in American high school, and students accustom themselves to large amounts of note taking from dictation by the teachers. In fact, notebook compilation is central to classroom behavior, there being relatively few textbooks, study aids, and works of reference at ready disposal. There are no libraries worthy of the name in the French *lycée* or *collège*. This deficiency tends to make the French student rely too much on handbooks and on his notes, and leaves him untrained in the use of original documents and supplementary source materials. The American teacher would be adversely impressed by the lack of educational *realia* and audio-visual materials, although he would have to admire the individual artistic production of students where the teacher displayed an active interest in fostering such worthy effort.

Finally, mention must be made of the peculiar boarding-school features of the secondary school, especially of the *lycée*. Fully half the students are boarders. Living in dormitories which contain as many as fifty beds, they are subjected to a regimen which is quasi-military. Their lives are strongly regimented. They are not allowed to smoke, and they may not leave the school grounds except at specified times. They walk two by two, under the supervision of a *surveillant* (proctor) and are rarely granted the blessings of privacy. Deprived of intercourse with the outside world, unable to benefit from part-time jobs, rarely privileged to attend movies, concerts, and other cultural attractions, the secondary-school boarder suffers under the ascetic severity of a school experience which has been handed down almost unchanged from the days of Napoleon. It is not difficult to imagine the maladjustment that occurs when boarding-school graduates experience for the first time the unlimited freedom of university life.

Thus little imagination is needed by the individual French teacher in the way of constructing or organizing curriculum, syllabuses, or day-by-day class activity. The Ministry of Education tends to eschew regulations as to methods, but prescribes the amount and kind of subject-matter content to be taught. The teacher who wanders too far astray will be found out at examination time. Still, such uniformity tends to keep teaching standards and educational accomplishment up to an acceptable level of achievement. Teachers at least know where they are going and what they are expected to do. Uniformity also works well in the case of student transfers from one school to another, in that educational status is not lost and learning can readily be continued in the new school where it was left off in the old.

Under these circumstances—a longer school day and a longer school year, a greater selectivity of students for general education and university preparatory courses, a more rigid system of examinations, a greater concentration on pure subject matter, a more unified and direct approach to learning, and less time for extracurricular activities—small wonder that the French secondary student outstrips the average American high-school student in pure intellectual achievement. He may not be so advanced and so mature in his social behavior, and he may not have had sufficient opportunity to explore his leadership qualities in clubs and societies, but intellectually he is at least one year ahead of his American counterpart at the same age.

HIGHER EDUCATION

In France higher education (*enseignement supérieur* or *troisième degré*) is almost entirely public and ordinarily begins after the student has completed six or seven years of secondary school. At that time he is usually eighteen or nineteen years old and scholastically would be on a par with the American student commencing his sophomore or junior year in college. The *baccalauréat* or its equivalent is necessary for university matriculation. For candidacy to the doctorate in law, letters, or sciences, the corresponding *licence* is obligatory.

The whole field of advanced training is undergoing considerable revision similar to that taking place in secondary education; the external features of the change have already been mentioned. The present section will concern itself with higher education as it exists currently and will give a brief estimate of needed progress.

In all, there are seventeen universities in France, strategically situated throughout the Republic in the principal locality of each of the seventeen *académies*. The faculties of the various universities differ in number and kind, from the Universities of Besançon and Clermont, with science and letters only, to the University of Strasbourg, which offers all the faculties: letters, science, law, medicine, pharmacy, arts, and theology. The University of Paris, with 50,000 students, is the largest. In those academic districts which have no faculties of medicine the first five years of training are offered in the *écoles de plein exercice*.

Each university maintains a galaxy of *instituts* dedicated to special and regional studies. At present there is an imposing total of about 150 *instituts* of every possible description connected with the universities. As in other countries, the French *institut* is in reality a research center.

All universities support libraries, archives, museums, and observatories. Libraries tend to be organized in separate units according to faculties or subject matter, rather than under one roof with a centralized administration. The University of Paris, for example, lists a dozen principal libraries with what the authorities term "a large number of subsidiaries," a complete presentation of which, they add, would be too long to include in the catalogue. (Approximately one hundred are mentioned.)

Upon conclusion of university studies, state certificates and diplomas (*grades et diplômes d'état*) and university titles and diplomas (*titres et diplômes d'université*) are awarded, the former on the basis of successful completion of a program which may be pursued in more than one university but within the same faculty, and the latter on successful completion of studies taken in one university. Unlike academic decorations conferred in many other countries, the French degree is tied to the faculty in which it is awarded. The result is that there are scores of different types of degrees, depending not only on the length and quality of one's educational accomplishment but also on the particular field. In general, the *grades et diplômes d'état* include in order of attainment the *certificat de capacité*, the *baccalauréat*, the *licence*, the *diplôme d'études supérieures*, and finally the *doctorat*. One example of a variation of this titular hierarchy may be drawn from the field of science, which rewards its students as follows: the *certificat d'études physiques, chimiques, biologiques* (called the "PCB"), the *certificat d'études supérieures*, the *licence*, the *diplôme d'études supérieures*, the *doctorat-ès-sciences*, and the *titre scientifique d'ingénieur-docteur*.

The degrees conferred by the individual universities are even greater in number and kind, and tend to reflect the historical and educational make-up of the university. Except in medicine and pharmacology, for which the courses of study set by the state are the same as those set by the universities, state degrees are considered to be of higher quality, or at least of greater importance, than corresponding ones of the university. The *doctorat d'université* is

usually sought by foreign students who have completed the requirements for the *diplôme d'études supérieures* and have presented an
acceptable thesis. On the other hand, it is difficult for the foreign
student to win a state doctoral degree without a French *baccalauréat*,
especially in law and medicine, although of course he may aspire
to the university doctorate in either field.

The school year extends from November 2 (following All Souls'
Day) through June 30. It is divided into two *semestres* and subdivided into four *trimestres*, the latter about two months in length.
The length of the university school year is therefore about thirty-
two weeks, which is roughly the average in other countries.

In 1945-1946 there were some 80,000 students enrolled in the universities proper, of whom by far the greatest number were in law
(25,000). Faculties of letters and medicine were about equal, with
15,000 each, and science and pharmacy had around 7,000 each. It is
difficult, of course, to compare these enrollments with those of
higher education in other countries, since the span of years involved
is at variance, and since higher education is given in institutions
other than universities. It is safe to conclude that in comparison
with other countries of Europe except Italy, France's university
enrollments are high.

If the methods in secondary-school teaching have been pedantic
and verbal, they have had their peer in the lofty circles of higher
education. It is a fact that in the past the teaching and the accomplishments of the French university in medicine, science, literature,
and law have served as a guide to many a foreign system, and that
French research and writings have been inspirational to learning in
lands thousands of miles removed. But it is equally true that this
great influence has been on the wane in the last thirty years. Part
of the explanation lies in archaic research methods and in instructional procedures which fail to relate what is taught to social progress. Even more important is the general indifference on the part
of most professors to the phenomenal development of science and
technology abroad. The French medical textbook, once a leading
depository of information, remains a thing of beauty and a joy to
read—but only for its tasteful presentation. As for laboratories,
Professor Laugier, himself a physicist, gives a concrete example of
the inadequacy of existing equipment:

At the Sorbonne the physiological laboratory, established about half a century ago . . . was intended as a laboratory for research and could accommodate 20 researches and 20 students at the maximum. Although physiology in the course of the last fifty years has had a remarkable expansion and has become the keystone of medicine . . . yet the same laboratory has been attended between 1930 and 1940 by an annual average of 200 students without any change in its premises.[11]

For the rest, the stereotyped quality of instruction and scientific experimentation has led, as it always does, to stereotyped results. Reform in French higher education comes, indeed, thirty years too late.

Non-university higher education takes place in the *grandes écoles*, in normal and higher-normal schools, in schools of arts and trades, and in technical institutes.

The *grandes écoles* are deeply embedded in France's traditional education for an elite. National leaders other than those in purely academic or professional fields have in nearly all cases emerged from the "great schools." Requirements for entrance usually include the *baccalauréat*, either in letters or in science, two years of preparatory training (waived in certain cases), and a very rigid examination. As a rule the student is twenty years old when he begins his first year. Courses of study extend from two to four years in length and cover the widest variety of fields: technical education, commerce and industry, physics and chemistry, mines, teacher training, agriculture, agronomy, veterinary surgery, fine arts, architecture, music, foreign affairs, etc., plus military training in the three institutes for air, land, and sea, respectively. The schools of agriculture, fine arts, and in some instances technical education maintain their own preparatory divisions, which enroll students around age fourteen or fifteen. The military preparatory schools and the schools for maritime apprenticeship (including the more advanced schools for navigation) prepare candidates for entrance into the three higher military institutions.

Since the *grandes écoles* have carried selectivity in admission of students to an even greater degree than have the secondary schools, it follows that the schools have become cut off from the main stream of French life. They have become detached communities, sufficient

[11] Henri Laugier, *op. cit.*

unto themselves and averse to sullying their reputations by admitting the full impact of social change. Granted that eminent leaders have emerged from these institutions, the fact remains that enrollments are not sufficiently representative of the people, and the training received is far too narrow in view of the broader concepts that are needed for success in a wider world of work. More specifically, there is great need, so the Ministry submits, for the *grandes écoles* to unify their work with that of the universities, particularly on theoretical levels, where a depth of concentration and a level of accomplishment will tend to increase and liberalize educational attainment. The Ministry of Education laments the fact that university faculties "ignore each other." But even worse, "the *grandes écoles* and *instituts* not only ignore each other but ignore the faculties."

Radical reformers go so far as to suggest that the *grandes écoles* be gradually eliminated and their work absorbed by the universities. In this way, technical and liberal education would, it is hoped, become more productive. It must be submitted, however, that the purely physical obstacles that confront such a union would at this time be insurmountable, especially in view of the more urgent changes that have to be made in France's educational structure. For the present, the *grandes écoles* would probably do best to concentrate on a wider and more intelligent recruitment of students and on the production of national leaders more aware of their professional and democratic responsibilities to their countrymen. In any case, the "great schools" have little to fear, since their continued life is assured in recent plans issued by the Ministry of Education.

Deserving of special mention in a consideration of reform in higher education is the establishment of the *Ecole Nationale d'Administration* for the training of national administrators. Guy Desgranges, in fact, calls it "the only really great accomplishment [*réalisation*] in higher education, [since] it seems to express to a marvelous degree the general spirit which animates the Reform."[12] Desgranges refers, of course, to the need for a systematic training for the higher echelons of public life that will be less concerned with brilliance and bookishness and more with the realities of the job. France has tended even more than England to appoint to high

[12] Guy Desgranges, "Les Grandes lignes de la réforme de l'enseignement en France," *French Review*, Vol. XX (May 1947).

places men who have not been trained specifically for their office. Knowledge of the classics or of basic subject matter has always been deemed sufficient to enable any "good man" to cope with the intricacies of diplomacy and public administration. Admission to the National School for Administrators will be by competitive examination. Candidates must be twenty-six years of age at least, and must present either a diploma of higher education or five years of successful public service. The course of study is three years in length, all of it pursued in the field rather than in any one central educational institution. Courses of study include cultural, economic, and political foundations, specialized subject matter in one's major field, foreign languages and customs, commercial studies of an elementary nature (such as typewriting), and physical education. The first year is usually spent abroad and the second and third years practicing in the various ministries and government agencies in the capital. It is hoped that the new appointments will consist of men who have had a wide experience in the field; they will have had personal contact with the diverse social groups in France and in her colonies; they will have familiarized themselves with rural and city workers, with their unions, and with their material and spiritual needs. This training thus becomes truly a "human and social formation of the future public servant," who will at the same time be a trained expert in his field.

Mention has already been made of the provisions for higher education contained in the Reform Bill. The directional lines of contemporary thought and organization may be summarized as follows:

1. There is need for a better articulation between courses of study in secondary and higher education, including a more pertinent preparation for specialized fields of interest.

2. Following the first stages of accomplishment, as represented by the *licence,* greater opportunities for research, experimentation, and advanced studies need to be provided.

3. The faculties of science and technology especially need increased government support so as to be in a better position to produce men and findings which are fundamental to French industrial progress. Scientific research must be made to recover from its present moribundity.

4. Creative thinking needs to be encouraged, intensified and supported. Antiquated teaching procedures need to give way to newer pedagogical approaches which will free both instructor and teacher for a greater display of individual talent and genius.

5. More chairs need to be created for the study of current developments in all fields. Concomitantly, places need to be made for visiting foreign scholars and teachers who are specialists in their field.

6. Conversely, French scholars and professors need to be afforded the means for travel and study in other lands. (In this respect the country has been inexcusably deficient.)

7. There is great need for new buildings and completely new university cities, or centers, that would be located in the country or in the suburbs of large communities, thus removing students from the noise and congestion of downtown areas and affording more suitable conditions for outdoor activity.

It will take decades before French institutions of higher education open their doors to as great a number of aspirants as crowd into colleges in the United States. A partial explanation lies in the fact that many students are absorbed by the secondary schools and complete their education with the *baccalauréat*. (This accomplishment would balance that of the American junior college.) Another explanation lies in such physical limitations as lack of buildings. But perhaps the greatest determinant is the firm and respectable attitude of the French educator that careful selectivity needs to be exercised beyond age eighteen. At any rate, it will be seen in the following sections on teacher training and technical education that the winds of liberal educational doctrine have blown through the stuffy confines of French higher education to produce programs that are far more vital and far more purposeful.

TEACHERS AND TEACHER TRAINING

The training of elementary- and secondary-school teachers in France has traditionally been separated. Academically, the elementary-school teacher has not been expected to know as much as his secondary-school confrere and therefore has not been compelled to undergo the same length and intensity of training. Since in any case the education of secondary-school teachers in France has been inordinately severe, what with the multifarious types of examinations the aspirant has had to undergo, the consequent disparity of professional training has resulted in a marked cleavage between members of the same profession. This cleavage has been aggravated by the higher social position and the higher salary accorded the secondary-school teacher. Even in the ranks of the elementary school proper, differentiations have always been made between the training of teachers of the *cours élémentaire* and the *cours supérieur*. In any case, the demand for elementary-school teachers has been so urgent that the basis for selection has had to become more liberal than that for secondary-school candidates.

Training institutions for elementary-school teachers are located in and are controlled chiefly by the political departments, although the central government contributes the lion's share of the expense. Ordinarily these schools are boarding schools. Most of the students receive their training at government expense and in return are required to serve for ten years after graduation; in case of withdrawal they must reimburse the government. The program is three years in length, the subject matter covering a wide range of professional and academic material. If a student enters at the customary age of sixteen, he is eligible for the teaching certificate at age nineteen.

An outstanding characteristic of the French teacher-training institution is the practice school that is always a part of it. The close proximity of pupil material and the locale wherein training and experimentation can take place is favorably matched by the relatively large amount of time, usually about fifty half-days a year, that is devoted to practical teaching. On successful completion of his course the student is awarded the *brevet supérieur*. He must, however, win his *certificat d'aptitude pédagogique* as evidence of successful practice teaching before he becomes a recognized teacher.

Advanced training for posts as teachers in normal schools, in secondary schools, and in the upper grades of the elementary schools takes place in the higher normal schools (*écoles normales supérieures*), of which there are two: Saint-Cloud for men and Fontenay-aux-Roses for women. The minimum age for entrance is nineteen, and, as is usual with entrance into all types of French schools on the upper level, the selection is made primarily through examinations. Required also are the *baccalauréat* (the secondary-school certificate), the *brevet supérieur,* or the higher certificate of elementary instruction (usually requiring a fourth year of training in the lower normal school). Instruction and maintenance continue to be borne by the state. The minimum course is two years in length, with a common core of psychological and pedagogical studies and two main academic branches: letters (French language and literature, geography and history) and science (mathematics, physics, chemistry, and natural science). Graduates are awarded a *certificat de l'école normale supérieure*.

Training for secondary-school teaching also takes place in the *grandes écoles normales supérieures* (Rue d'Ulm, Paris, for men and Sèvres for women), and within the universities proper. Strangely enough, the caliber of candidates is usually not so high in the universities as in the scholarship-providing higher normal schools, although in recent years there has been a reversal of the trend. The *licence* is granted after two years of training, the *diplôme d'études supérieures* after the third year, and the *agrégation* after the fourth year (called the "*stage pédagogique*"). The *agrégation* is properly a state certificate, not an academic degree. It is awarded after the successful hurdling of state-imposed competitive examinations, but only to those who have met governmental requirements for secondary-school teaching. Even then, the number of *agrégés* is limited to the number of positions available. Thus the *agrégation* becomes practically a guarantee by the government of a teaching position.

Since only one tenth of the aspirants to training in the higher normal schools are admitted, since the instruction takes place in small groups under close supervision, and since the enrollment is pegged to the demand, the purely educational achievement of the students tends to become a superior one indeed. So difficult of entrance and so exacting in requirements is this institution that it has earned for itself a position without peer in French pedagogical circles. Pertinently enough, it was at the girls' branch in Sèvres that the teachers of the *classes nouvelles* were originally trained.

In France as in most other European nations the social and professional status of the teacher is guaranteed and protected by lengthy and comprehensive legislation. As civil employees, teachers are paid directly from the general budget in accordance with the particular category in which their training and experience place them. All teachers must be licensed by the state, and salaries, pensions, leaves, sick benefits, and other emoluments are favorable and are highly uniform throughout the Republic. Men and women enjoy the same salary schedule, although additional compensation is paid to those with large families.

The new reform devotes considerable attention to the problem of teacher training and welfare. An attack is being made, first of all, on the traditional discrimination between teachers on the elementary level and those on the secondary level. The stress henceforth is to be laid on two types of teachers: the one who elects to teach basic studies (*matières communes*) and the one who prefers to specialize. The teaching of basic subject matter is restricted to the elementary school, and the teaching of a speciality is reserved for advanced secondary education. Teachers of youngsters between eleven and fifteen years of age may be either general practitioners or specialists.

Regardless of their preference, all teachers pursue their training in common up to age eighteen, or to the *baccalauréat* in their major field. They then continue for two years in the normal school, where candidates whose primary interests lie in youngsters—their physical, emotional, and psychological growth—may concentrate on that field, and those whose tastes lie more in subject matter may devote themselves to letters and science. Successful pursuit of the course of study leads to the *licence*. There then follows a year of interneship and the ubiquitous final examination, mostly on teaching aptitude, preparatory to the awarding of the state certificate. Aspirants to the *agrégation* are aided materially by the state, provided they have demonstrated outstanding fitness for instruction on higher levels. Future *agrégés* will, however, have to spend some time in service rather than move directly from the *licence* to further education.

Training beyond the *licence* is also given in the higher normal schools, but again is divided into accentuation on (1) pedagogy, psychology, and such educational matter as administration and organization and (2) subject matter of the more academic type. Training for the former, that is, for administrators and professors of education, is to be centered in the two higher normal schools at Saint-Cloud and Fontenay, whereas the institutions on the Rue d'Ulm and at Sèvres will concentrate on preparation for teaching and research in higher education. The higher normal school for technical education and the higher normal school for physical education will unite the pedagogical and the academic in cases where educational administrators are to be prepared specifically in the field of technical endeavor or in physical education. No definite limits are prescribed for the length of the course, the number of years being dependent upon the speciality. Educational magnanimity is extended even further by the proviso that reports and final papers should take the place of examinations. Progress indeed!

Although much of this new pedagogical training has considerable merit, especially as it caters to individual taste in teaching, great danger will probably lie in the tendency of the two branches to become mutually exclusive. More and more educators are coming to realize that the good teacher must unite good educational practice, involving such matters as student guidance and classroom administration, with his subject-matter speciality. There is considerable controversy everywhere, of course, as to the extent to which every teacher should be a guidance teacher. No doubt both types of French normal-school training will unite the pedagogical with the academic, but care will everlastingly have to be exercised lest another dualism of respectability split the ranks of the teaching profession into two more camps.

VOCATIONAL AND TECHNICAL EDUCATION

Scattered throughout this essay are a number of statements regarding the course of vocational or technical schooling as this branch of educational endeavor responds to the changes that are effected in other branches of educational progress. With the passing of time, and as the reforms now promulgated by the Ministry become actual school practice, the tendency for vocational education to be separated from the more traditional type of schooling will be restrained. A concrete example of this trend occurred in 1947, when the Directory of Technical Instruction (Direction de l'Enseignement Technique) was transferred almost bodily to the Ministry's main division of general instruction.

As in most countries, technical education has been historically the stepchild of traditional schooling. The point need not be labored here, but the very fact that French vocational educators in a fit of desperation have sought to unite their studies with those of the humanities under the general heading of "technical humanities" gives merely one indication of the inferiority complex that has constantly afflicted technical education. Happily, under recent reforms vocational educators may show their faces in respectable pedagogical circles. In fact, as the recognition grows that technical prowess is indispensable for the very existence of the French Republic, they are becoming favored in the Ministry's educational planning.

Job training has been handled by state authorities in a particularly
gauche manner. The government was enlightened enough at the
turn of the present century to pass laws against juvenile labor, yet
it failed to provide schooling for the apprentices who were thereby
thrown out of work. This essay cannot enter into the field of
French labor problems, but one may well imagine the job dilemma
that faced young people and those who depended on them for
support. The consequent forced importation of foreign labor further
intensified the problem, especially among youngsters who could
neither work nor attend a suitable school.

World War I led to a showdown on the issue, culminating in the
law of 1919 which provided for government support of technical
training. The lack of funds to implement this support was evident
at the very outset, but little was done until 1925, when an apprenticeship tax was passed. Under the terms of this law, industrial
and commercial establishments were obliged to help finance the
cost of technical education, either in the nation's schools or in the
establishments themselves. Although to the casual observer this
type of educational legislation would appear to be highhanded and
discriminatory, it has, as Henry Lester Smith indicates, turned out
to be a boon to private initiative in the matter of training future
workers. In fact, the administration of the program, Smith continues, "is so organized as to bring home the responsibility to the
local districts for self-administration. Special councils have been
established in every district. . . . They control the tax and allocate
scholarships and subventions."[13] Where small businesses have been
unable to support the program, government subsidies have been
provided. Today the central government bears the brunt of the
costs, although the local communes and departments contribute a
sizable share of the expense of building construction, equipment,
and scholarships.

In general, the Ministry of Education maintains control of vocational instruction, although other ministries share the responsibility
in certain national schools. Upon completing elementary school the
student enrolls in a preparatory vocational school for a basic two-
or three-year training. This may take place in a practical school of
commerce and industry, household arts, or agriculture, or in a trade
school. Most of these vocational schools are administered by local

[13] Henry Lester Smith, *Comparative Education* (Bloomington, Ind.: Educational Publications, 1941).

communes or departments. However, in accordance with the vocational-education tax procedure, trade schools are supported mostly by trade associations and chambers of commerce.

The second phase of vocational training takes place in the national vocational schools (*écoles nationales professionnelles*). The length of the course varies from three to four years, and depends on the particular trade or the desire for further education. The *brevet d'engénieur* is awarded on conclusion of this stage of training; the student is then ready for advanced work in special institutes of higher vocational education. As a result of government interest, manifested in the (Code of Technical Instruction) (Code de l'Enseignement Technique, 1947), enrollments have increased tremendously. Over 100,000 students are currently registered in the early stage of technical education (*centres d'apprentissage*), and 115,000 in other technical schools.

In 1947 the five normal schools of technical education enrolled one thousand future teachers. In the same year, 2200 candidates took examinations for the new technical *baccalauréat-ès-sciences*— of whom, alas, only 40 percent passed. (Characteristically enough, French educators report greatest satisfaction with this achievement of the new *baccalauréat*, and point with pride to the success of the 40 percent who managed to get through.) Although these numbers may not be very impressive at first glance, they are strong proof of the great fermentation that has taken place in the entire realm of technical training.

Not that vocational education will become the order of the day in the new progressivism. Henri Wallon warns against any idea of advocating a narrow technical education that leads to overspecialization: "The development of technology renders necessary the formation of an élite that is not only specialized but is well-rounded culturally." In Adolph Meyer's terms, the whole idea resolves itself into an effort at placing the various types of youth training in their proper perspective: "To bridge the gap between their modern industrial order and the school, the French have undertaken to reduce the latter's top-heavy intellectualism, and to put all curricula—manual, technical, artistic, and intellectual—on an equal footing."[14] Referring especially to agricultural education in rural areas the Ministry makes its position clear: "It must not be

[14] Adolph E. Meyer, "The Langevin Plan for the Reform of Education in France," *School and Society,* Vol. LXVIII (July 10, 1948).

exclusively agricultural. . . . All technical education should be given in schools that have many specialities."[15]

SPECIAL TYPES OF EDUCATION

The ramifications of the French educational system are, as in most countries, many and varied. Two types deserve special mention in an exposition of this kind, namely, education for defective children and adult education.

Special Education for Defective Children. Schools for the feeble-minded—that is, for children who are considered educable but incapable of assimilating the subject matter taught in regular schools—were first provided by the law of 1909. In France 8 percent of the school population participate in this type of training. French experience has shown that, although individual tasks may be allotted to dull children with a commendable degree of success, their educational experience should preferably be a common one. To prevent a natural tendency toward isolation, these children should be taught in groups and should learn the elements of acceptable social behavior. Drill and repetition cannot be too greatly emphasized, but the teacher must always be alert to capitalize on any tendency of his charges to think clearly and originally. It goes without saying that instruction should be in the concrete rather than the abstract, but even instruction in the concrete does not excuse the teacher from relating learning to practical behavior, or, as the French prefer

[15] Frederic Lilge's reflections on the course of vocational education are mature and reliable: "The importance of the technical *baccalauréat* lies in encouraging a larger number of intelligent young men to go into responsible positions in French commerce and industry where they are needed. It should be pointed out, however, that the chief purpose of the technical schools is not to prepare all students for the *baccalauréat*. On the contrary, the majority attend only for three, and in some cases for four, years. . . . The real purpose of these technical schools is to create that large middle stratum of technicians, foremen, and shop managers in which France has thus far been deficient." Referring to the *centres d'apprentissage*, Lilge states: "Their main purpose is to create a larger reservoir of skilled workers for French industry. The work done by the centers is supplemented by vocational schools organized by private and commercial firms and by vocational courses obligatory for all young people employed in industry or commerce below the age of 18." ("French School Reforms," *School and Society,* Vol. LXX [December 3, 1949].)

to state it, to *savoir-faire*. Vocational training (*préapprentissage*) should be commenced earlier than with children of average intelligence and wherever possible should be continued to age eighteen. It does not follow that because a youngster is a slow learner or is feeble-minded his schooling should be cut short. In fact, so long as he remains educable he is probably better off in school, sharpening what few dull talents he has, than entering the labor market an inept worker.

The equality of opportunity that characterizes modern French education thus becomes all the more evident in the firm resolution to provide mentally deficient children with the same opportunity for a full and profitable educational experience as is enjoyed by others. The French educator is only too acutely aware that idleness and loafing are often the result of occupational as well as social maladjustment. Increased effort in the field of special education is a great social obligation.

Education for handicapped children—for the deaf, dumb, blind, and crippled—has been haphazard and without form. Education for the blind got off to an auspicious start in 1784, when Valentin Houy founded the Institution Nationale des Jeunes Aveugles, the first school for the blind in the world. Additional work was carried on by Louis Braille, who in 1825 invented the point alphabet. The first school for the deaf was opened in Paris in 1760 by Abbé de l'Epée, inventor of the sign language. This school became a government charge in 1791. But as these and other institutions developed, their administration was in too many instances relegated to agencies, private and public, whose methods and accomplishments were seriously open to question. Under the new reform all institutions for the physically defective will be coordinated and placed under direct government supervision. This means that purposes, programs, and methods will come from a central authority and will be uniform for the entire Republic. The Ministry is most firm in its published statements that future plans will lay especial stress on the training of the educably defective.

Conceived as an extension of these services, the education of children whose behavior consistently clashes with the norm will take place in special rehabilitation centers. Young people who constantly run afoul of the law will be examined psychologically and, if pronounced educable, will be enrolled in suitable training centers under the responsibility of the Ministry of Education. The chief tasks in the education of the "irregular child," as the French call him, will be to eliminate any feeling of personal rancor toward or hatred of society and to provide an education that will turn misguided energy into productive good. The Ministry is careful not to put itself in the position of compelling any irregular youngster to prepare for a "concrete" type of employment. It would defeat the very purposes of education to give irregular children any cause for concluding that their independent, mutinous nature condemns them to manual labor. The child must feel that he is free to make his own choice of future employment. The central task is to enable each individual to make his own best contribution to social welfare, and to understand that it is only through society that he can realize personal success. Even more so than in the case of other types of defective children, the education of "irregulars" must be organized on the basis of a close personal relationship between student and teacher. Also, constant effort should be made to prepare irregular children for early transfer to regular schools.

The French are intensifying their program for the education of transient children. Migratory families, not particularly numerous in France, consist largely of seagoing peoples, harvesters, and refugees who have taken to the road. It is difficult to give transient children any sort of continuous education. Consequently, most of them seem condemned to inherit the same kind of life as that of their parents. Special boarding schools have been provided for the education of migrant children, but parents have been markedly reluctant to give up their young. Especially in the case of seagoing people, observes the Ministry, "the families form like cells, as it were, which are difficult to break up. . . . We shall have to render this separation indispensable and as acceptable as possible by providing a system of boarding schools that will be as flexible as possible." (The literary style of official French educational publications is not always as choice as it might be. In fact, in too many instances it belies the reputation of the French language for clarity and punctiliousness of expression.)

In all these instances of special education, teacher training looms as the most formidable task. As may readily be concluded from the customary French attitude toward education, teaching faculties are dreadfully understaffed and incentives to future candidates for this type of work will have to be improved. Recent increases in juvenile delinquency will combine with a greater awareness of social responsibility and a greater availability of future teachers to do much toward advancing the cause and the achievement of special education.

Adult and Popular Education. France has been slower than some of her neighbors to provide for the continued education of those who have left school, and in particular of those who have passed their eighteenth birthday. In fact, no legislation has been enacted with regard to the "further education of adults," as the British call it, although some commendable activity has taken place on an informal scale in public elementary schools, in social clubs, and occasionally within the precincts of the universities. Traditionally, the state has delegated the responsibility for adult education to private groups. Increasingly, however, it is beginning to recognize its responsibility, especially in view of the danger that besets national progress when the education of the voter is left entirely to agencies that are in reality self-centered pressure groups. At present, adult education takes place chiefly in labor colleges, the equivalent of British workers' institutes. Indeed, labor organizations sponsor a strong program of radio broadcasting, popular lectures, and advice on holiday and leisure-time pursuits.

Contemporary French reformers prefer to call this segment of training "popular education." The Ministry is careful to state that popular education is not an "education for all," but an opportunity afforded to all to pursue their training after giving up their formal schooling. It is based on the very pertinent realization that times and customs change, and that not only new gadgets but new ideas control the world's progress. The effects of these changes must constantly be imparted to people if the people wish to remain enlightened. "Popular education," in the words of the Reform, "must not be a simple continuation of schooling, with scholarly methods aimed solely at completing a program previously unfinished or judged insufficient. Of particular interest to adults, it must originate with their present interests and utilize adult aptitudes." It demands a special type of instructor; an adult educator must be a specialist in his field, not a person simply transferred from educating young people in formal schools. Popular education calls on all educational and cultural agencies to cooperate in lending their facilities to adult enlightenment. Finally, "popular education will incorporate intellectual, technical, and aesthetic progress, not only for individual purposes but for the collective good [*collectivité*]." To date, however, progress is mostly on paper, and it will inevitably remain there until funds are provided.

The Radio.   Audio-visual aids are still in the exploratory and experimental stage. French prowess in this field is unexcelled, but again the lack of funds has interfered with any sort of adequate utilization of varied teaching aids. The Ministry of Education has been on record since World War II as advocating radio programs to meet existing needs in both general and vocational fields, and has instituted training especially in the higher normal schools for teachers who are interested in disseminating knowledge via radio. For their part, radio authorities have instituted a series of educational programs which are similar to those in England in that they are composed on three levels: for children, for adolescents, and for adults. Here is an effort, at least, to appeal to the varied intellectual achievement of a radio audience instead of adulterating programs so as to reach the lowest levels. In this way, too, education by correspondence has a valuable adjunct—one that is well known to French authorities but that must await further accomplishments. As for the development of a more discriminating radio audience, perhaps France can afford to wait; the need for improvement is by no means so marked as it is, for example, in the United States.

ENVOI

Despite the finer elements of progress that have recently been displayed by the French school system, there are glaring physical deficiencies yet to be corrected. They were revealed for example, when school opened in 1949. Some 5 million youngsters between the ages of six and fourteen returned to public school buildings that were more inadequate and crowded than ever. A good 10 percent of this enrollment had to be housed in annexes, barns, and other such structures, with only minor regard for hygienic facilities. The Ministry of Education revealed that between seven hundred and eight hundred classes had fifty pupils and more; in some instances there were as many as eighty. Not that the French school population had increased in numbers. Actually, as a result of the drop in France's birth rate, which reached a peak in the late thirties, there were some 500,000 fewer children of school age in 1949 than there were ten years before. (After 1945, however, the birth rate began to rise.) Nor can the blame be laid entirely to the war's destruction of school buildings, since at the most only 10 percent were lost. The difficulty lies with the whole program of school building and maintenance, which is now exhibiting the inevitable result of years of neglect. The Republic is thus faced with the necessity of making up for this neglect by financing a school building program that absorbs over 12 percent of the total budget for national education.

The enrollment situation is even worse in the secondary schools, where totals swelled from 315,000 in 1938 to 442,000 in 1949 without a corresponding growth in housing facilities. If it had not been for an intensification of the entrance examinations, which eliminated more than half the applicants, the *lycées* and *collèges* would have collapsed under the load. (One practical benefit of an examination system!) This increase in enrollment does not, however, properly reveal the extent of the crisis. The greatest deprivation is found in girls' schools. In Paris alone there are eighteen *lycées* for boys and twelve for girls, yet there are at least as many female as male candidates for entrance. In one instance, the Lycée Hélène Boucher received as many as 450 applications for only 150 places but admitted 300. Many of the unsuccessful found their way to private schools, of course, but others were either forced into the labor market earlier than their time or were obliged to accept further instruction where it could be found.

The Ministry reveals that in five years a building program will have been completed that will accommodate the secondary-school population of that time. Concerning the ultimate future, when France's currently increased birth rate swells the secondary-school population, the Ministry says little, in the knowledge that little more can be done than to cope with present emergencies. Specifically, on the elementary-school level it is expected that at least one thousand new classrooms will be constructed every year for the next six or seven years. At present there are one million youngsters in private elementary schools and another half million in other types of private schools. If the government presses for public education of these students, as it has occasionally indicated it will do, the present building program will be abortive. In fact, it may very well be concluded that had it not been for private endeavor the French school system would have been in an impossible situation from the point of view of providing a seat for each child. The increased enrollments in the secondary schools will demand the construction of at least one thousand more schools within the next few years. The chances of achieving them are anything but hopeful. The total cost of the Ministry's five-year plan for school building amounts to 755 million dollars, of which one third is earmarked for war-damage repairs. In 1948 M. Yvon Delbos, Minister of Education, was able to collect scarcely 2 million dollars from the government. All these facts combine to convince the most inept mathematician that, unless budget allotments are tremendously increased in the next few years, French children will still be attending school in tents and barns.

Such is the complexity of the educational scene in France today. Yet in contrast to the pathetic amount of confusion, restiveness, and vacillation of contemporary French life, the course of the schools is fairly even-keeled. Perhaps in no other major component of French life is there a more resolute plan of progress than that being realized in education. As in England, provisions for educational advancement have been debated with measured antagonism among opposing parties. This is, of course, a welcome sign for education in an era when all values are under critical reassessment. The historic struggle continues between the French left and Catholicism on the problem of religious instruction in the schools. Political parties representing both sides naturally consider the problem to be more than pedagogical, or even moral. The church today is fighting for its life and for its fundamental influence on education, and it will naturally not only resist all efforts to bar religious training from the schools but will seek constantly to expand its own endeavors. As Professor Kandel brings out, supporters of denominationalism in France have always fought for state subsidy of private education.[16] No doubt they will continue the fight.

But the educational life of a country extends beyond its schools. Of the intellectual ferment within France today, of the intellectual café life of the "Boul' Mich'" and Montparnasse, of the deep

[16] I. L. Kandel, "Proposals for the Reform of Education in France," *Educational Forum,* Vol. X (March 1946).

moral schism between the Catholic and the atheistic existentialist, and of the depressed frame of mind of the patriotic Frenchman as he sees his glorious country reduced to a second- or third-rate power, little mention has perforce been made. Nor has it been possible to deal fully with the implications for education of France's tenuous, midway position between communism and capitalism; or of a national reconstruction program that persistently fails for lack of men, supplies, and leaders; or of the narrow margin of reserves in wealth and physical assets on which all progress depends. The present disgruntled, underpaid worker and the entrenched, apathetic bureaucrat combine to dispirit the most enthusiastic and the most capable. Everywhere in France today pessimism prevails. And this pessimism cannot fail to enter the life of a school system. It creates skeptical, doubting, hypertense youngsters who have seen life at its lowest moral ebb. But it also poses a challenge to the schools to give youth something to live for and something to achieve. There is no lack of understanding among youth as to the cause of their country's wretched decline, and even in adversity there is no lack of determination to make the best of their lives. This is a hopeful sign. For within the ever-flowing tide of new life that surges annually into their schools French teachers know that a new nation can be born. If schools *can* build a social order, then certainly French schools have their opportunity. More than any other single social agency, the schools can lay the foundation of a new national existence, based firmly on France's intrinsic material and spiritual attributes and geared to her already proved potential.

BIBLIOGRAPHY

Annuaire international de l'éducation et de l'enseignement (Geneva: Bureau International d'Education, 1948), pp. 95-103. The section on France reviews facts and events of recent years in French educational life.

BARKER, JOSEPH, "Impressions of France, 1946: Cultural Exchanges, Reorganization of Secondary Schools," *French Review*, Vol. XX (February 1947), pp. 284-291. An interesting estimate from personal experience of educational reform amid conditions of economic deprivation. "France lacks many things," concludes Barker, "but certainly does not lack intellectual activity."

BROGAN, D. W., *France under the Republic* (New York: Harper & Brothers, 1940). The classic volume in this field, by a master craftsman.

Classes nouvelles (Paris: Association Nationale des Educateurs des Classes Nouvelles de l'Enseignement du Second Degré, 1948). An analysis of progress made to date in the new classes, with suggestions as to further procedures. See especially the April and July editions, 1948.

DESGRANGES, GUY, "Les Grandes lignes de la réforme de l'enseignement en France," *French Review,* Vol. XX (May 1947), pp. 445-453. An excellent, comprehensive, and sympathetic statement of the trends of modern French educational reform. (For a reply to Desgranges see Pierre Girard, below.)

————, "Défense de la réforme de l'enseignement en France," *French Review,* Vol. XXI (May 1948), pp. 467-470. A pointed reply to Pierre Girard (*q.v.*), in which Roger Gal's educational findings are given special commendation. (See Roger Gal, below.)

Les Etudes dans les universités (Paris: Ministère des Affaires Etrangères, January 1, 1947). An official publication answering questions usually asked by foreign students wishing to enter French universities.

FARENC, JULIENNE, "Le Stage de la sixième nouvelle," *Revue Universitaire,* Vol. I (January 1946), pp. 1-8. An adequate, warmhearted defense of the new sixth class, based mostly on the latest psychological research on how children grow.

GAL, ROGER, "L'Education a la croisée des chemins," *Education Nationale,* January 1, 1948, pp. 11-12. An important article by one of the leaders of educational reform, demonstrating how education has fallen behind cultural progress in France and advocating that education be creative rather than imitative.

————, *La Réforme de l'enseignement, et les classes nouvelles* (Paris: Les Presses d'Ile de France, 1946). As a member of the Langevin Commission, Professor Gal philosophizes on the Reform and ably explains its relation to modern pedagogical theory.

GIRARD, PIERRE, "Controverse sur la réforme de l'enseignement en France," *French Review,* Vol. XXI (May 1948), pp. 461-466. A reply to Guy Desgranges (*q.v.*), warning against the adoption in France of certain principles of modern education which, according to Girard, do injustice to the disciplinary qualities of education proper.

HOYT, DEMING N., "Educational Reform in France," *Harvard Educational Review,* Vol. XVIII (October 1948), pp. 220-227. A useful commentary which considers the reform in its historical setting.

Instructions du 30 Septembre, 1938, fixant les programmes de l'enseignement du second degré (Paris: Librairie Vuibert, 1939). Official directives concerning the application of educational laws and programs for secondary education as of 1938.

KABAT, GEORGE J., "Postwar Secondary-School Reforms in France," *Journal of the National Education Association,* Vol. XXXV (May 1946), pp. 248-249. A brief but breezy account of changes at the secondary level, with implications for the rest of the French school system. Kabat gives ample evidence of intimacy with the French school system.

KANDEL, I. L., "Proposals for the Reform of Education in France," *Educational Forum,* Vol. X (March 1946), pp. 303-315. An objective appraisal of recent development by a master hand, acknowledging the need for change, yet pointing up the obstructions in true Kandelian manner.

LAUGIER, HENRI, "France," in I. L. Kandel, ed., *Postwar Educational Reconstruction in the United Nations* (New York: Teachers College, Columbia University, 1944). The twenty-first educational yearbook of the International Institute of Teachers College. A useful and highly profitable survey of needs at the close of World War II, containing suggestions as to how they may be met.

LILGE, FREDERIC, "French School Reforms," *School and Society,* Vol. LXX (December 3, 1949), pp. 353-356. Professor Lilge, of California, brings up to date the progress of the Langevin and other reforms, setting these reforms in the country's changed social and economic structure and strengthening his findings with personal experience in French schools.

Livret de l'étudiant, 1948-49, Université de Paris (Paris: Presse Universitaire, 1948). A lengthy information bulletin on the University of Paris which, although called a student's handbook, resembles a catalogue of a large American university.

MEYER, ADOLPH E., "The Langevin Plan for the Reform of Education in France," *School and Society,* Vol. LXVIII (July 10, 1948), pp. 17-20. An expert and sympathetic analysis of the original reform, with especial reference to the needs of French national life.

Nouveaux horaires et programmes de l'enseignement du second degré, 1948-49 (Paris: Librairie Vuibert, 1948). New schedules, programs, and course content as prescribed for secondary schools by the Ministry of Education.

Les Quatrièmes nouvelles: Résumé des stages et des entretiens de l'année, 1947-48 (Paris: Ministère de l'Education Nationale, Imprimerie Nationale, 1948). An inventory of the progress made in the new fourth classes, containing advice on how to improve conditions.

La Réforme de l'enseignement: Projet soumis a M. le Ministre de l'Education Nationale par la Commission Ministerielle d'Etude (Paris: Ministère de l'Education Nationale, 1947). The original text of the Langevin Reform.

SAINT-BLANQUAT, A. M. DE, "Educational Reform in France," *Educational Forum,* Vol. XII (November 1947), pp. 75-84. Perhaps the best account of the *sixième nouvelle,* since it profits from the personal experience of the author, who is headmistress of the Lycée de Balzac, at Tours, one of the schools participating in the *classes nouvelles* experiment.

SMITH, HENRY LESTER, *Comparative Education* (Bloomington, Ind.: Educational Publications, 1941). The chapter on France, although worth while, is a bit unseasoned and lacking in its comparative aspects.

The Year Book of Education, 1948 (London: Evans Brothers Ltd., 1948), pp. 215-251. A useful description of educational progress to date, in France.

8 · EDUCATION IN *Italy*

GEORGE F. KNELLER

The long peninsula of Italy projects southeastward from the southern shores of Europe into the Mediterranean. Its area is about half that of France, approximately 116,000 square miles, and its population is slightly larger than that of France, amounting to 46 million. Italy's population density is therefore twice that of France, or almost 400 persons per square mile. Although agriculture is the chief industry, Italy cannot feed herself, since the amount of cultivable soil is limited by the very rugged and mountainous character of the land. The only large river valley, that of the Po, is in the north. Italy is very short of critical mineral deposits, such as coal, iron, and oil, but she produces much sulphur. Italy has compensated in part for lack of coal by developing a huge number of hydroelectric installations (approximately 20 billion kilowatts of electricity are produced in normal times). The manufacturing and industrial area is concentrated in the north, in the Po River valley. Textiles are the chief product, and they are followed by chemicals, automobiles, heavy machinery, and electrical goods. There is a great contrast between the standard of living of northern Italy and that of southern Italy, related directly to industrialization, urbanization, and soil conditions.

The Mediterranean climate, with winter rains, little snow except in the mountains, and much sunshine, is favorable in terms of health and agriculture. Italy's outstanding problem is that of poverty, since it is one of the most densely populated states in Europe and lacks the industrial development to assist in carrying this chiefly rural population. The population is approximately 6o percent rural and 40 percent urban. Italy's present population is actually an amalgam of a great number of Latin, Teutonic, and other peoples who have entered this corridor area by land or sea during Italy's long past. Italy has a great capacity in terms of physical strength and intellectual and artistic ability, but the population has suffered from poverty, frequent war, and lack of opportunities for social mobility.

Italy's educational pattern is "two-track" traditionally, but there has been a very strong, continued effort to move in the direction of a universal form of education. There are a number of reasons why it is essential that education be extended. Among them are the high incidence of illiteracy, about 21 percent, and the tendency toward myth and superstition, especially in the rural areas toward the south. If Italy is to meet some of the major challenges resulting from overpopulation, lack of resources, and effects of war, it is essential that the pattern of education be made more efficient, so that the people may learn a better technology, both in the field and in the factory, and may take advantage of their very fine potentialities.

—A. H. M.

When the first Italian national parliament met in 1860 it was confronted by a country lamentably backward in practically every aspect of life except the more external forms of culture. In art, literature, and music Italy had preserved her traditional leadership, but in many parts of the nation, especially, south of Rome, feudalism prevailed with only slight modifications as it had for centuries. Socially, there was a huge gulf between the Italians of the north and their brethren to the south, a gulf that has not to this day been closed. Social classes were marked and distinct, from the indigent peasant through the middle classes and the clergy to the aristocracy. Politically, the common people were almost totally indifferent to the problems of state; they were never very concerned over the extent of their civic responsibility. Politically, too, the people idolized the city-state, so that the locality of one's origin rather than the wider political unit determined the limit of personal loyalty and patriotism. The only important unifying elements were the church, which opposed unification, and the language, although it can hardly be said that Italian was spoken so as to be understood everywhere. Even today the dialects of the south are unintelligible to the Italians of the north. Finally, and most crucially, some 30 million people were being ruled not by themselves but, as one critic euphemistically puts it, "by 3,000 for the benefit of 3,000." Although the figures are not quite correct, they do reveal the unalterable fact that political and economic tyranny and intimidation had been the lot of the Italian people as long as they could remember. There was consequently no reason to suppose that the larger political entity would necessarily bring emancipation and prosperity.

The Italian educational system was well enough conceived from the administrative point of view. Centralization received its early impetus from the expulsion of the Jesuits in 1771 and the establishment in Sardinia of a state system resembling that of Frederick II in Germany. So attractive was this system that Napoleon extended it throughout the land and used it as the basis for education for nationhood. The work of Napoleon was destroyed with ensuing invasions of Jesuits, Austrians, and Bourbons, but the fabric remained. Piedmont founded a ministry of education in 1847 and, under the leadership of that state, educational centralization as the principle of organization was adopted throughout the new kingdom.

The rock on which modern Italian education is built is the Casati Law of 1859, which organized the school system on approximately the same basis as the system of France. The administration of elementary schools was delegated to the communes, but because of mismanagement the privilege was taken away in 1911 from all except the larger municipalities and transferred to a provincial school council appointed by the Central Ministry. The church was excluded from educational control, but religious instruction was preserved in the schools. Private institutions were allowed to function only on condition that they met state requirements. An attempt was made to articulate elementary with secondary education, but the old idea of a double ladder never succumbed. Even if educators had decreed its end, Italy's peculiar cultural influences would have obstructed their efforts. In the field of vocational education Italy stepped forward with a secondary school for technical training (*scuola tecnica*) and its higher division (the *instituto tecnico*), establishments which were rather advanced for their time.

The curriculums of these institutions revealed a strong preference for studies which would contribute to the country's material advancement. So useful did these schools become that ultimately a downward extension of vocational training into the elementary schools was effected in response to the wave of educational realism which struck Italy in the 1890's. The Casati Law also established bases for elementary-teacher training in the three-year *scuola normale*, an institution of about secondary-school rank. Finally, and most disastrously, the law dictated higher educational organization in such a way that Italian universities for all practical purposes became organs of the state and suffered a type of control and uniformity that stifled creativity and crippled any sort of healthy growth.

The foundation may have been firm, but the structure built thereon was deficient in many ways, and not entirely through any fault of the builders. If money has been lacking in any European school system, it certainly has failed to come forth in anywhere near the amount necessary to support Italian schools. The allotment for education has never exceeded 5 percent of the total budget. Even then the figure is flattering, since a lion's share has gone to institutions of higher learning. The situation has been aggravated by the fecundity of the Italian people. Italy has one of the highest birth rates in the world, and the Central Ministry, let alone the communes, has been totally unable to cope with the ever-swelling numbers of children that annually flock into the schools. Before World War I especially, compulsory education was a mockery in Italy, since the government had not the classrooms, the teachers, or the money to provide for much more than half the population. The communes went bankrupt educationally in 1911. World War I led to social and economic collapse in Italy and, as in all national fiascoes, the educational system was held for its fair share of the blame. The assessors could point to little in the way of educational gains but the general extension of the school system to wider areas and to larger segments of the people, notably in the urban and industrial north. The illiteracy rate had of course been reduced, and the way had been paved for further educational progress. But the surface of democratization had only been scratched. Indeed the events of the 1920's underscored that depressing fact.

What has been said of the detached, monolithic quality of French education as it continued through the ages might well be repeated of its Italian counterpart. Complaints that Italian schools were not only refusing to contribute to national unity but were actually defeating its very purposes by restricting cultural and political life to a chosen few reached a climax with the turn of the present century, when vocational emphases began to appear. Even in recent years Lewis Bilancio is able to report little progress: "[The curriculum] is not consonant with life needs. Education offers to the average Italian hardly any tools with which to grapple his many and burdensome daily problems; and what is worse, it often leaves his thinking less free than before."[1] In similar vein, Professor Vincenzo Arangio-Ruiz, of the University of Naples, applies typical Italian verbal pyrotechnics in his authentic pronouncement that "the plethora of polyglot facts, far beyond the range of the tender intelligences of 'teen-age pupils, begins in the primary schools, gathers momentum in the secondary schools, goes crashing into its climax in the senior year."[2] One thing that the Fascists did not inherit was a model school system.

IDEALISM AND THE FASCIST INTERLUDE

On October 28, 1922, Benito Mussolini, blacksmith's son, reporter, and former schoolteacher, "marched" with his Black Shirts on Rome. Hailed by some members of the clergy as one sent by Providence to put an end to anarchism and bolshevism, *il Duce* set about the task of restoring public order and national dignity on the basis of Italy's great and glorious Roman past. Out of the depths of chaos and anarchy Benito's words came forth in the manner of a prophet's and savior's as he expounded the principles of Fascism, the "only hope" for Italy:

> Peoples which are rising, or rising again after a period of decadence, are always imperialist; any renunciation is a sign of decay and death. Fascism is the doctrine best adapted to represent the tendencies and the aspirations of a people, like the people of Italy, who are rising again after many centuries of abasement and foreign servitude.

[1] L. A. Bilancio, "Italian Education as of Now," *Progressive Education,* Vol. XXIV (November 1946).

[2] V. Arangio-Ruiz, "Liberal Orientations: Problems of the School." *School and Society,* Vol. LXI (January 20, 1945).

But the acceptance of this doctrine meant the acceptance of the state as all-supreme:

> In every class, among all citizens, nothing is done against the state, nothing is done outside the state. Many have finally opened their eyes to this serene and severe truth; the Italians feel themselves of one fraternity in a great work of justice. The sense of duty, the necessity of action, the manner of civil life mark now an intense reawakening. In Fascism politics is fused into a living moral reality; it is a fate. It is one of those spiritual forces which renovate the history of great enduring peoples.

And finally the usual personal appeal for sublime loyalty and undying devotion:

> I am near to the heart of the masses and listen to its beats. I read its aspiration and interests. I know the virtue of the race . . . I feel that all Italians understand and love me. . . .

Fascism quickly stifled the opposition and gained early recognition from abroad for having restored peace and quiet. At the same time it squelched certain types of educational progress which extolled the ideology of trade unions and workers' organizations, both rural and urban. As Dr. Umberto Borghi writes:

> The old state, appanage of the higher strata of the Italian people, gave full support to the Fascisti, who systematically destroyed cooperatives . . . burned the labor chambers, the "houses of the people," suppressed the newspapers of the progressive parties, and closed popular universities. . . . In 1922 the results of two decades of peaceful and devoted sacrifices of the working classes were almost completely cancelled.

Fascism was a deliberately exclusive and selective coalition of the army, the monarchy, and the Italian liberal, Catholic, and middle-class parties. It won in a death struggle with parties of the left, which otherwise might have established a dictatorship of the proletariat, Italian style. The consequences in any case were catastrophic, not only for Italy but for the rest of the world.

The coalition of the more conservative political parties of the right and center and the early desire of Mussolini to lend dignity to his movement gave rise to his appointment of the renowned Giovanni Gentile as Minister of Education. Educational philosopher par excellence, follower of Hegelian idealism, opponent of leftish democracy, exponent of nationalism and authoritarianism, Gentile provided the ideas that served as inspiration for Italian education throughout the entire Fascist interlude. Aided by the equally renowned Benedetto Croce, who a few years later had a change in heart, Gentile did his best to shake Italy out of the "doze of naturalism and positivism" that had affected national development. He wanted to root national progress in an idealistic nationalistic philosophy, in which schools would be "animated and vivified by the spiritual breath of the fatherland." Gentile's reflections, contained in his *Reform of Education*, have become classic. For that reason it is well to outline their substance, with special stress on implications for education.

Gentile's philosophy is the logical descendant of philosophies of idealism and monism that had their nearest exponents in Fichte and Hegel. Under idealism and monism the mind and the spirit are one. The mind is the all-embracing reality. It is identical with behavior and experience. All experiences have their source and become unified in the individual. The purpose of education, therefore, is to produce the well-rounded, harmoniously developed personality, which in turn seeks to come ever closer to perfection. This perfection must, however, go hand in hand with a higher type of perfection, which is the state. Individual good, in other words, is one with the good of the state. The individual does not participate democratically in government; he reaps the benefits of his allegiance and of the higher good that the state is in best position to dispense.

The moral conscience of the child also must be developed, says Gentile, within the framework of the ideals of the state, since the state is perforce the higher expression of the common conscience and the common will. The common conscience and common will are best evoked through training in common language, history, culture, religion, and art. The ultimate purpose, then, is to train the child not as a private personality but as an individual who, since he must live and function within the framework of the state, automatically becomes one with it, and hence devotes his life to the state's inevitable perpetuation. The state demands this sacrifice not only because it is identical with all the individuals and societies within it but because it is the only link that joins generations of individuals and societies.

As a highly subjective philosophy, Gentile's idealism leaned heavily on insight, on autoconsciousness, and on the recognition of one's proper place in the universe. This was especially pertinent in the matter of religious instruction, which, according to Gentile, should emphasize not so much a certain truth but a certainty of knowing truth through a personal examination of the facts and through a type of rationalization that was based on personal judgment and evaluation. Man is, indeed, his own destiny: "Man is unworthy of education unless he is master of himself, capable of initiating his own acts, responsible for his acts, able to discern and assimilate the ideas which he accepts and professes, affirms, and propagates, so that whatever he says, thinks, or does, really comes from him." Gentile would teach the dogmas of the Catholic church, despite the fact that he considered them the "mythical wrappings of a spiritual reality." He was aware that Catholicism was a peculiarly Italian institution; it was a storehouse of Italian tradition. Religion was the basis of a universal faith, whereas Gentile's idealism was rooted in a national faith: "The school is never the form and instrument of the uplifting of the conscience. . . . The school must be human in its adherence to a universal faith, but it must also and always be Italian, because of its trust in a national faith."

The teacher, in Gentile's system, becomes the embodiment of the student's autoconsciousness, as he helps his charges through his own example to assimilate bodies of knowledge within their own interpretive selves. The teacher thus becomes the spiritual parent of the student. He is advised by Gentile as follows:

> As long as the freshness of our vocation lasts, as long as we can remain free from mechanical routine and from impositions of fixed habits, as long as we are able to consider every new pupil with renewed interest, discover in him a different soul, unlike that of any other . . . so long as it is still possible for us to enter the classroom thrilled and throbbing in the anticipation of new truths to reveal . . . so long shall we really live and love the teacher's life. . . . Our children are said to be properly raised when they give evidence of being able to take care of themselves without the help of our guidance and advice. . . . He [the teacher] must . . . transfuse the pupil with something of himself, and out of his own spiritual substance create elements of the pupil's character, mind, and will.

The teacher, we see, must be a great personality indeed!

Gentile's teachings were essentially a reaction to the materialism, the objectivism, and the positivism that had beset Italian educational life following national unification. The new Minister of Education demanded a restoration of those spiritual qualities of the past that had made Italy a distinctive national configuration. Alien importations were to be scrutinized and eliminated if they conflicted with Italy's intrinsic destiny, and all efforts toward internationalism were to be secondary to national prowess. The specific implications for education were obvious:

1. Elementary education was to afford a broad training in rudimentary matters, with preparation for secondary training for the few who could qualify.

2. Secondary education, "aristocratic by its very nature," was reserved for the *pauci electi*, the "chosen few" who would do the governing.

3. Teacher training was to stress individual development within the confines of national consciousness. Formalized methods in classroom instruction were to give way to the training of happy workers.

4. The universities were to be coordinated and brought under direct control of the Ministry, even in minor administrative matters. The door to higher education was to be a "small one," open to all, but "not big enough to let the crowds in."

5. Fees were to be continued and even raised where necessary in those institutions which catered to selective education.

6. Emphasis in curricular study was to be on the history of the Italian people—their contribution to the world in the field of discovery and invention and in literary, artistic, and musical life. The grandeur and beauty of things Italian and the influence of Italians in other parts of the world were to constitute compulsory basic information.

Like other educational reformers, Gentile had his day. His idealism proved far too sublime for the ideological trappings and militaristic ambitions of the Fascist party. He was consequently released after a two-year term. After his discharge, the Opera Nazionale Balilla, the official Italian youth movement, usurped many of the prerogatives of the school and, under the aegis of the Ministries of War and Education, enlisted youth in direct service to "a great military and warlike nation," as Minister of Education Rocco characterized it.

Local school autonomy—what little remained—was abolished in favor of centralized controls. Private schools were rendered less attractive, so that by 1938 official directives had actually become intimidating. Minister of Education Giuseppe Bottai decided: "The private schools have not, except in limited degree, met the expectations of legislative and public need." Finally, academic confines were invaded by loyalty oaths, which compelled obedient teachers and professors to educate "honest citizens loyal to the country and to the Fascist regime." The slogan of Fascist education was, in short, "Believe, Obey, Fight!"

The vicissitudes of Fascist educational endeavor cannot be of concern here except for the final product, the Bottai Reform of 1939, which codified the educational thinking of nearly two decades. The chief provisos of this reform were as follows:

1. The kindergarten was compulsory for children from four to six years of age.

2. Elementary schooling, a three-year training from ages six to nine, was divided into urban and rural types. This was followed by a "school of work" for children between nine and eleven which featured curricular experiences related to practical work. The "school of skilled labor" completed compulsory education at age fourteen, and incorporated a modicum of cultural training.

3. The middle school, for pupils aged eleven to fourteen, was preparatory to secondary-school training of the more strictly classical type. The vocational school, running concurrently with the middle school, prepared pupils for semiskilled work. The technical and art schools were complementary to the middle schools and gave training in industry, commerce, agriculture, and the arts.

4. The secondary school, consisting of the classical and scientific *licei* and the technical, commercial, agricultural, and art institutes, contributed a five-year program preparatory to entrance into higher education.

5. Teacher training began after the middle school. For prospective elementary-school teachers this training was five years in length, commencing at about age fourteen.

6. The schools, faculties, and institutes of the universities were redefined and reorganized.

7. Numerous other educational establishments were created or revised, among them schools and institutes of art, agriculture, industry, land surveying, and navigation. The women's institute

provided a three-year training in household duties, predicated, no doubt, on Fascist wisdom as to the proper place of women in a man's world. For the intransigent, however, transfer to the teacher-training institutes was facilitated.

The Bottai Reform is important for its insistence on a coordination of the school with activities in the Fascist state, especially as regards work training and political indoctrination. All youth organizations were to work together, with Italian industrial, agricultural, commercial, cultural, and national aspirations as the basis of their work, to provide for the total moral, political, and physical growth of the youth. With respect to school organization, the ideals of the *scuola unica*, which corresponded to the French *école unique*, were to be partly realized in the newly created middle schools, which took the place of the lower secondary schools. Articulation was to be effected between the elementary school and the middle school, upon completion of which the student branched off to the higher secondary school of his choice. Thus, occupational decisions were to be postponed from age eleven to age fourteen—decidedly a step forward.

Although the Bottai Reform gave a more stable organization to education on the earlier levels and provided Italy with the basis for a more vital educational system, the consequences were, in the minds of opponents of the Reform, deleterious to social progress. Especially critical is Professor Borghi, who writes:

The lower classes would be frozen, with compulsory methods which remind one of the provisions enforced by Diocletian at the beginning of the 4th century in order to prevent the Roman Empire from crumbling. . . . Fascism proclaimed that it would give free instruction to some of the children of the poor rural and urban classes in order to allow them to continue their studies, and would, in this way, "put the people in a position to be represented by its best elements in the ruling class of the country" (Bottai). But in fact was this education given free to the poor classes? First, it was reserved for those who had "special aptitude." Second, it had to assume "a distinctly military and fascist character." As a consequence, those very few members of the lower classes who would be allowed to continue their studies would be kept under the strictest control of the state . . . would become its watchdogs and instruments, and would offer fascism a pretext for asserting that all the strata of the Italian people were being called on to form the ruling class in the corporate state.

Perhaps the wisest pronouncement, however, was made by Mussolini himself, who demonstrated remarkable intuition in his prediction that the Bottai Reform would take "considerable time" before it could be put into operation!

FOUNDATIONS OF A NEW SYSTEM

For all its deleterious effects Fascism did more to turn the minds of Italians to the power of education and the proper place of schools in national life than any other development in Italian history. Granted that before 1922 the masses had made great strides on their own toward formulating a better school system, the fact remained that truancy was rampant, schools were grossly inadequate, huge segments of the population had little respect for learning, and local effort was pathetically weak.

Fascist education although erected on a peculiarly subjectivistic conception of Italian culture, was a creation engendered in the very physical contours of the Italian peninsula and in the historical exigencies of the Italian people. As T. V. Smith observes, Italian national spirit was neither exhausted by Fascism nor invented by it: "It [this spirit] is the heaviest single fact because [it is] the oldest and the deepest which education must reckon with in Italy." This is another way of stating that the very same inequalities of land, people, and privilege which have historically produced gross inequalities in educational opportunity prevailed under Fascism and prevail today. With a population of 46 million crowded into a territory about the size of Idaho, two thirds of which is mountainous, Italy is physically a poor country. Over half the population consists of peasants who live in almost squalid conditions; their income is barely enough to provide their daily bread. Wealth has been dissipated, poverty has afflicted the city dwellers, and all this has combined with the country's precarious economic status to prevent the rise of a healthy and effective middle class. The illiteracy rate has always been high in Italy as compared with other Western countries, simply because the education of the masses has not meant enough to those in a position to provide the necessary help. The democratization of Italy, as Americans and British interpret the expression, and the democratization of Italian education have rarely been considered essential to school agenda. The class system was strong and secure even before Fascism; morally, at least, it persists to this day. This system has historically resisted educational opportunity, equality, and democracy.

The dilemmas of Italian life today are not the direct consequence of Fascism and war alone. They are the culmination of a long history of causes that were only momentarily affected by the Mussolini interval. Fascism, as Professor Kandel puts it, was never more than skin deep. As early as 1942, when Fascism was still in power, Professor Howard Marraro, of Columbia University, after studying Italian textbooks concluded that the temper and extreme individualism of Italians "make it extremely improbable that fascist educators and leaders will succeed in inculcating these ideas in the minds of Italian children." The proof of this, asserted Marraro, was to be found in the fact that after two decades the Fascist school had failed to produce the kind of Italian that Fascist leaders had hoped to create. The majority of Italians were ready to embrace Fascism because it gave them, among other things, promise of economic security; when promises were unfulfilled they were resolute in destroying the leaders. There was nothing, in short, that was endemically Italian about Fascism, except, perhaps, the origin of the word in Latin and the gap that perennially exists between an Italian's fine aspirations and his physical capacity to fulfill them.

After World War II, housing, food, and work were lacking to millions. Amid the rapid succession of Fascism, occupation, resistance, and liberation, all within a scant five years, moral and political standards became confused. The remnants of the leftist groups and even the more conservative socialists united with the communists to reassert themselves after twenty-three years of suppression and create a political situation that caused the Western democracies dire concern lest Italy be abandoned to Russian influence. The threat was effectively met, or at least forestalled, by financial assistance from the United States and by the national election of 1948. The result was that the conservative Christian Democratic party, with 307 seats and 48 percent of the national vote, emerged as the largest political group in power. The opposition consisted of four socialist and communist groups with 182 seats and 30 percent of the vote. The Socialist party won a total of thirty-three seats. The nationalist bloc of liberals and southern rightists boasted eighteen votes for the *scuola laica* (the lay school); the monarchists and republicans followed with fourteen and eight seats respectively. Combining on many issues with the nationalist bloc was the Italian movement known as M.I.S., which consists of young reform rightists with six votes in their control. Several smaller groups, more or less ephemeral in nature, completed the multifaced political configuration that guided Italian destinies to 1950.

The Italian Christian Democratic party corresponds broadly to the Christian Democratic party in Germany and Belgium and to the M.R.P. in France. It supports the policy of the Catholic church in its desire to unite political with religious life. The religious urge is therefore a powerful determinant of the party's social and political aims. In Italy the Christian Democrats assume an even more important role, because of the strength of the Church's position in national life and the historical struggle of the Vatican against communism and atheism. Primarily conservative in attitude, but with a strong sense of the need for social and agrarian reform, Premier de Gasperi's party sponsors a school program that preserves religion and the more traditional subject matter. But the necessity for coalition with other parties is so great that many of the conservative preferences of the party frequently have to be compromised.

The substitution of a democratic philosophy for one of Fascism was no problem. The Allies received warmest cooperation in this regard. The main task of the liberating forces, especially those of the United States, was to provide the material wherewithal for the reconstruction of thousands of school buildings neglected through the years or destroyed during the war.[3] As Lawrence Battistini

[3] T. V. Smith records the following theme in his inimitable "Swan-song from the Ex-Director of the Education Subcommission, Allied Control Commission": "The campaign had blighted Italy from end to end, devastating school buildings, with all other buildings, impoverishing the people, unrooting families, ruining transportation, lowering morale, and adding hope. The best that can be said for our success against such difficulties— and it is enough to say—is that with unwonted speed it was brought about in every area as liberated that no child remained divested of educational opportunities through any acts of our omission nor was subjected to wrong school influences through any acts of our commission. Our monthly reports make clear successively what we did, who did it, and how much was done,

writes, school supplies such as desks, benches, and blackboards were
(and still are) needed. Well may Battistini record:

> Hygienic services have been practically completely disrupted.
> In many schools drinking water needs to be made available.
> Electricity needs to be provided. All kinds of teaching and
> scientific material is needed for the classroom. Zoological and
> botanical collections, scientific apparatus for laboratories, . . .
> model machines, and measuring instruments are needed. Student
> needs are appalling, from elementary grade pupils to university
> students. Requests in this direction have already been presented
> to the Allied Sub-Commission for such things as notebooks, paper,
> drawing paper, pens and penpoints, pencils, erasers, chalk, oil
> colors, paints, solvents, etc.[4]

In a country shorn of wealth and material possessions, and among
a people desperately in need of food, clothing, and housing, little
time and energy were left for the niceties of democratic pedagogy.
Late in 1945 Battistini pertinently concluded: "The future of democratic education will naturally depend on how soon a semblance of
economic prosperity is restored to Italy."

The Allied commission for the re-education of Italy immediately
set to work to prepare a "basic program" for the elementary
schools, consisting of certain suggested and compulsory courses of
study and principles of elementary-school instruction that were
essentially American in flavor. The aim was not to saddle the
teacher with a particular syllabus or method but to allow freedom
of instruction wherever posible. The new school could not, however, wholly divest itself of Fascist influence. Reporting on the
work of recent Italian reformers, Professor Marraro brings out the
continuity of many principles which were endorsed by Fascism:

> Teachers are warned that the new programs will oblige them
> to renew constantly their own culture by drawing their informa-
> tion not from the little manuals in which are gathered the

to restore such normal educational opportunities as war to the North
permitted. They make clear also what we did, who did it, and how much
was done, to guarantee, by revision of texts and purging of teachers, that
the wrong things would not be taught." (*Educational Record,* Vol. XXIX
[January 1947], p. 334.)

[4] L. H. Battistini, "Italy's Educational Crisis," *Educational Forum,* Vol.
X (March 1946), pp. 317-325.

crumbs of knowledge, but from the living fountains of national culture of the Italian people. These fountains are to be found in the popular traditions and in Italy's great literature. Teachers are told that the new programs avoid the commonplace beliefs and notions which have for so long dulled the Italian elementary school. Rather, these programs require sincere poetry, candid search for truth, investigation of the popular spirit, restless and never satisfied, the contemplation of works which are brought back to life and almost made present through the words of the teacher. The teacher is warned not to be "a pedantic repeater," for in this manner he will end the spiritual life of the school, causing the child to become restless and distracted. These advices and admonitions are essentially the same as those that were given to fascist teachers.

If to this is added the latest concepts of learning by doing, advocated by Fascism within its own limited purposes, educational continuity becomes even more enhanced.

CONTEMPORARY EDUCATIONAL STRUCTURE

It has already been pointed out that Italy's educational structure has remained much the same since its inception in the early stages of national unification. Supreme over all educational endeavor is the Minister of Education, who has an educational cabinet of his own. Assisting him are an undersecretary for education and eight director generals. The latter are in charge of general affairs and personnel; elementary education; classical, scientific, and normal education; technical education; university and higher education; antiquity and fine arts; academies and libraries; cultural relations and border areas. Other offices include an inspectorate for non-government schools, a bureau concerned with appointment of secondary-school teachers, and an accounting division.[5]

[5] Other advisory bodies include (1) the *consiglio superiore della pubblica istruzione*, a council on higher education consisting of forty-six members, some of whom are elected by university faculties, and divided into three sections to correspond with the three types of higher educational institutions; (2) the *consiglio superiore delle antichità e belle arte*, consisting of twenty-five members who handle matters involving the study of archeology, paleontology, ethnography, medieval and modern art, monuments, town planning, national beautification, contemporary art, music, and the theater; (3) the *consiglio superiore delle academie e biblioteche*, consisting of

Within the provinces the highest state school authority is the *provveditore agli studi*, the chief inspector of studies, who is directly responsible for all matters concerning elementary education, including teacher appointments. He is also charged with the supervision of secondary schools. The *provveditore* is assisted by a corps of local school inspectors and educational directors, who perform the actual task of school visitation, inspection, and supervision. The power of the *provveditore* is traditionally somewhat greater than that of district inspectors in other countries, attested in part by the privilege granted him in the appointment of a provincial school council (*consiglio scolastico provinciale*). This council consists of an expert in elementary education (appointed by the Minister), a professor, a teacher, a head state physician, and the chief engineer of the government engineering office. The council not only provides the *provveditore* with the expert technical advice that he needs but under his chairmanship also handles questions regarding school organization and operation, including finance and personnel.

Italian education today is in the throes of another reform, based on the recently published *Conclusioni dell' inchiesta nazionale per la riforma della scuola* (see the Bibliography), a gigantic and pretentious three-columned recital of needs and proposals as submitted by numerous educational commissions and subcommissions assembled from every part of the country. (More will be said concerning these conclusions later in this essay.) Meantime, the school system continues to function on the basis of an organization originally approved by the Allied authorities and now controlled solely by the Italian Ministry of Education.

The present government prefers to call the first eight years of schooling *istruzione elementare*, including the kindergarten (*scuola materna*); it divides these eight years of instruction into three levels (*gradi*): preparatory (ages three to six); lower (ages six to nine); and upper (ages nine to eleven). Certificates are presented on completion of lower and upper elementary schooling. Post-elementary education is available up to age fourteen, which is now legally, although not actually, the school-leaving age.

---

twelve members concerned with books, libraries, and publications; (4) the *consiglio di amministrazione,* an agency which advises on school administration; (5) a disciplinary commission, concerned mostly with matters regarding personnel.

There are three kinds of lower secondary schools: the middle school (*scuola media*), lower technical, or "work," school (*scuola secondaria di avvimiento professionale*), and the lower normal school (*magistrale inferiore*). The middle school approximates the American junior high school or the British secondary modern school and provides a three-year training for entrance into either the *ginnasio superiore* or the lower *liceo scientifico*. The lower technical school prepares either for the *liceo scientifico* or for the *instituto tecnico*. The lower normal school is four years in length and precedes the *magistrale superiore*.

The upper secondary institutions comprise (1) the *ginnasio superiore*, a two-year classical training, and the *liceo classico*, which follows it; (2) the lower and upper levels of the *liceo scientifico*; and (3) the technical institutes. All three divisions afford an upper secondary training five years in length and preparatory to university or higher-technical-school entrance.

The Italian student usually enters a school or faculty of the university, or one of the higher technical schools, at age nineteen after he has completed eight years of secondary school. (Entrance into the higher normal school or teaching college—*scuola normale*—takes place one year earlier.) The university schools and faculties are varied in length. Law or letters usually takes four years, and engineering and medicine require five and six years respectively. Courses in the higher technical school last from four to five years. Training in the *instituto di magistero* is likewise four or five years in length.

In sum, then, compulsory education begins at age six; the child spends five years in the elementary school, and eight years in the secondary school; higher education varies from four to six years in length.

Unlike the French and British reforms, which have effected considerable revision in school organization, the Italian reform now under discussion advocates no great changes, with the exception of proposals for decentralizing controls. The decree of August 30, 1946, for example, increased the power of local head school inspectors (*provveditori agli studi*) and opened the way for increased local initiative. The essential framework remains the same; the internal organization, however, and in particular the curriculum, is to be modified in accordance with contemporary national demands.

With regard to general internal reorganization, the tendency is to do away with the rigidity of student programming and of compelling youngsters to lie forever in their academic bed once they have made it. Instead the plan is to adopt a liberal procedure of course changing where changes are obviously to the advantage of the student. Transfers within the schools are to be made easier, along with transfers from one school to another, provided there is evidence that such transfers will be beneficial. Increased educational articulation is to be counterbalanced by an insistence that all schools remain closer to their speciality and that the technical schools reduce the amount of general education available beyond the lower secondary school. Finally, all education above the lower secondary stage is to become more selective, more intense, and increasingly difficult to obtain. Italy takes account of her need for younger specialists of a semiskilled nature by providing types of education which will tend more and more to terminate with higher secondary training. It is hoped that a saving will thus be made in costs of higher education and a reduction effected in the number of university graduates. Further effects of this reform will be treated in the appropriate sections below.

ELEMENTARY EDUCATION

As with French elementary education, the concept "elementary" is meant to include preschool, primary, and elementary training. Under the Bottai Reform of 1939, nursery schools were voluntary but the kindergarten (*scuola materna*) was compulsory from age four to age six. It was considered not as a separate realm of education but as an integral part of the elementary-school system.

The development of kindergartens until World War II was little different from that in other countries. Some amount of free instruction was afforded by the state, but in general both the support and the management of kindergartens were left to private groups licensed by the state. The result was that approximately twice the number of kindergartens were administered by religious groups as by lay authorities, and only one third of Italy's kindergarten population ever received instruction on that level.

The modern official concept of the purpose and function of the kindergarten is contained in a decree issued on May 24, 1945, and published under the title *Programmi didattici per le scuole elementari e materne* (see the Bibliography). Here the state emphasizes that the natural educator of the child is the mother: "The *scuola materna* cannot be a substitute for the family and for the mother, but can integrate growth and introduce the child to a richer world of experience." In doing so, the program "must be spontaneous and free of scholastic rigidity, but conserving of a warm family atmosphere, so that the child will not feel lost and strange." The teacher must realize that she is not training scholars but developing personalities: "The entire life of the *scuola materna* should be so organized that the child is able to give full expression to activity and word; he should not remain a passive onlooker, but should be induced to productive effort on his own and in collaboration with his companions." Of especial significance, and certainly Italian in motif, is the official attitude toward religion: "In religious instruction the behavior of the child during daily prayers must receive special attention. Essential religious ideas must be imparted with short stories on the life of Jesus, thus illustrating the infinite love of the Great Creator for all things created." Finally, education is to be essentially a "fusion" of the best in moral and physical personal attributes.

The program proper of the *scuola materna* is divided into five fields: religion, moral and physical education, work and play, the Italian language, and drawing and singing. Aside from suggested directional lines of the subject matter to be taught, the details of the program are left to the individual teacher, whose qualifications are clearly defined: "Everything taught presupposes that the teacher have a fondness for children, be endowed with spiritual freshness (*freschezza spirituale*) and proper cultural bearing. She must have a fervid imagination, a faculty for telling stories in a natural and suggestive fashion, a firm and kindly patience, at once calm and understanding, no matter what occurs. All these attributes, not always possible in mothers, are sometimes indispensable in the teacher." In the hands of so accomplished a *maestra* printed programs are superfluous indeed!

When the Allies entered Italy, elementary education was already free and compulsory up to the fifth year, at least according to the law. Under the Bottai Reform, progress had been made toward dividing the elementary school into a three-year primary training followed by a two-year work school (*scuola di lavoro*). Guido de Ruggiero, former Minister of Education, assessing the situation at the opening of schools in September 1946, reports that students could be compelled to attend school for the prescribed period only in those larger communities in which buildings and teachers were adequate; "but in the country, partly because of insufficient means and personnel and partly because of the demands of their duties on the farms, it was difficult for children to reach the fourth class."[6]

The problem of the length of elementary training has been argued with especial reference to national demands. Those advocating the four-year elementary school held that that period represented a "truly elementary cycle," as Battistini words it. A fifth year served only to delay the entrance of the student into further training, a delay which many Italian families are unable financially to afford. Students generally complete the fourth grade when they are ten years old. At this age they are considered mature enough for higher studies. As of 1949, the advocates of the five-year elementary school prevailed.

The aims and functions of the elementary school are clearly defined by the decree of May 24, 1945, revised in 1947 and published under the title *Ordinamento della pubblica istruzione*. The elementary school, states the Ministry, "must not limit itself to combating illiteracy, since far more dangerous than verbal illiteracy is spiritual ignorance manifested in civic immaturity, unfitness for political life, impracticality of work attitudes, and insensibility with

[6] Guido de Ruggiero, "Problems of Italian Education," *School and Society*, Vol. LXIV (September 14, 1946). Lewis Bilancio, of the University of Chicago, goes further than Ruggiero in deploring the poverty of the content of elementary education, as he relates from his personal experience: "The most serious weakness is a grossly inadequate elementary school system. The elementary school consists of only the first four grades; yet vast numbers of children never finish this school, and the great majority never advance beyond it. There were in 1939 over five million pupils in the elementary schools, as against less than one million in the rest of the public schools and universities combined. (Data is from the *Annuario Statistico Italiano: 1939*, Rome, 1939, p. 302) . . . Children throughout Italy are afraid of the school. Possibly nowhere in Italy can one find a single child who has regretted his liberation from elementary school during this war. This fear tells the educator more than books of the unhealthy educational methods, of the oppressive inculcation of authoritarian conformity, of the mortification of the mind through disciplines." (*Op. cit.*)

regard to social problems in general." Education should "combat
such forms of ignorance and create in the child the man and the
citizen." Other provisos may be outlined as follows:

1. The old distinction between rural and urban schools must
be abolished, since the new education proposes a curriculum of
basic training in citizenship that all Italians should have. Local
cultural influences and demands must not be ignored: "Every
school must draw from its immediate environment the cultural
and practical motives which constitute its very life."

2. The elementary school should feature a training in human
brotherhood which transcends the bounds of nationalism. It
should create a "serene desire for work and service to the fatherland with honesty of purpose." It should be imbued with a clear
knowledge of ethical principles, especially in courses in religion;
moral, civic, and physical education; history and geography; and
vocational education.

3. All instruction should be unified and integrated under the
following nine suggested heads: religion; moral, civic, and physical education; work; the Italian language; history and geography;
arithmetic and geometry; science and hygiene; drawing and
belles-lettres; singing.

Formerly religion and the arts were central to the Italian curriculum. Religion's new handmaid is moral, civic, and physical
education taught as a unit. With these two subject realms as the
core, lower elementary education is expected to impart "fundamental knowledge" (*prime nozioni del sapere*) and the upper grades
to "develop, intensify, and complete the work of the lower grades."
Religious instruction still conforms to the general terms of the
Lateran Treaty of 1929 between Italy and the Vatican. The program
is one based frankly on the tenets of the Roman Catholic church
and consists of daily prayer, religious music, formal instruction in
the history and precepts of the church, the Bible, the life of Christ,
and the lives of the saints as they are intimately connected with
Italian history and as they point the way toward better individual
and social behavior.

The course in moral, civic, and physical training in the elementary
school is considered of especial importance because at this stage the
child's character is in the process of formation. This formation
should take place, according to the *Programmi didattici*, "in

[Italy's] climate of justice and liberty," and should prepare citizens of the new Italy not only in the classroom by lesson recitation but by the personal example of the teacher and by outdoor activity. This publication then goes on to relate the various attributes which enter into the formation of the new citizen: a sense of individual responsibility, a desire for social discipline, and a striving for mutual respect and reciprocal helpfulness. It advocates democracy in school procedures: student self-direction, student government, student control of minor discipline, student-centered classroom procedures, the practice of initiative and of referendum, and countless other democratic procedures obviously influenced by American specialists on educational rehabilitation.[7] The guiding force in all this training is religion: "Character education finds its crowning achievement and significance in the application of the principles of religious precepts, which form the essential and universal content of the human conscience."

Reporting on changes in the textbooks to conform to new political ideas, Marraro finds that Fascist ideology and teachings for the most part have been eliminated, but the content of the textbooks remains the same. He indicates some of the specific changes:

A page deleted in the textbook of the first grade, used by children six years of age, showed a group of Balilla boys bearing guns and flags, answering the call: "To Rome! To Rome!" In its place the new textbook has a picture of the monument of Victor Emmanuel II in Rome, bearing the words: "Rome . . . Love . . ." Statements such as the following have been omitted: "Long live the King . . . the soldier King . . . the victorious King . . . all Italy loves him." Other statements that were omitted in the new text encouraged boys to be "daring young sailors of Italy," described airplanes as "the wings of Italy

[7] This does not imply any lack of originality on the part of the Italians. Walter Ganzaroli's *Scuola democratica* offers specific methods and ingenious suggestions as to the democratic way of teaching elementary education. *Il Metodo di insegnamento nelle scuole elementari d'Italia,* by Aristide Gabelli, presents the fundamental differences between the demands of Italian elementary education as compared with those of other countries. These are but two of the outstanding educational texts that illustrate the thinking of Italian pedagogues and that could have been written only by Italians.

returning from distant lands," and ended with the words: "Long live our aviators! No one has ever conquered you! Carry our flag always higher and to more and distant places."

On the other hand, an illustration showing a large Italian flag with the shield of Savoy and the following legend have been retained in the new text: "Flag, our flag, flag of Italy, always wave victoriously in the sun. Repeat to the world: 'Italy! Rome! The fatherland is where the flag stands. The flag must be honored, one must defend it to death, one must never abandon it!' "

New emphases on self-expression through drawing and painting and on moral, patriotic, and religious sentiment through music (folk tunes and regional lyrics) combine with modern interpretations in history and geography to produce an elementary program which, in Marraro's judgment and that of others, harmonizes with the spirit and character of the Italian people. Although he wrote a few months in advance of the appearance of the new programs Marraro's intuition remains sound as he concludes:

> If the educational principles and morals which govern the new Italian elementary school succeed, we may expect the young generation of Italians to be imbued with a fervent religious spirit; to value and appreciate democracy and democratic institutions; to be well acquainted with the great contributions Italy has made in the course of many centuries to world civilization and culture; to take sincere and just pride in the glorious achievements of Italy in the arts and sciences; to have a better understanding of and love for other peoples of the world; and to appreciate the importance of developing and fostering better cultural and commercial relations with other countries.[8]

[8] Howard R. Marraro, "Democratization of the Italian Elementary School," *School and Society,* Vol. LXI (June 23, 1945), p. 404. With regard to the teaching of history and geography Marraro's delineation still holds: "Italian educators have introduced drastic changes in the scope and object of the teaching of geography and history, because it is primarily through these subjects that they hope to defascistize the minds of Italian children and teach them democracy and the benefits of democratic institutions. . . . The teacher is advised to place in clear light the fact that the division of labor constitutes a fundamental and useful law, not only in the domestic relations of a country, but also in international commerce. Thus the

Work (*lavoro*) as subject matter is important in the Italian school. The term is not to be interpreted narrowly in the sense of manual labor; it involves all types of honorable productive activity. Because, in the terms of the Ministry, "work is the fountain of moral living and an economic provider, it must have a place of adequate importance in education." Work is considered to be of three types: "artisan," "agricultural," and "feminine." In all three instances, children are expected to acquire theoretical groundwork in the school proper and then to visit and actually work "on location." Practical activities in the school include the construction or repair of useful objects and the cultivation of plants, in place of "meaningless exercises with cardboard, wood, or wire." The teacher is instructed to inform the child that Italy is "essentially a rural country" and that Italians should therefore develop a love of land and soil, farm and field. Urban schools are urged to cultivate plots of land, so that young people who otherwise would never have an opportunity to realize the benefits of gardening and planting might actually find their lifework in agriculture. "Feminine" work (*lavoro femminile*) is not to be interpreted strictly as confining women to domestic life. The woman is not only in charge of the household but is also the most important spender and consumer. She is to be well informed concerning domestic economy and trained in those delicate matters that are essential to family well-being and happiness.

The work syllabus recommends for both boys and girls, in addition to planting and harvesting, a wide variety of elementary technical skills, such as book repairing, laundering, poultry raising, leatherwork, poster making, and the rudiments of electricity for household purposes. The school is the laboratory, and the children find ample opportunity to be of service in a real and constructive way. Thus it is evident that if Italian education can offer anything at all to other national systems it is the program of integrating work

---

teacher may well point out to his pupils that the region of Campania in southern Italy may intensify the cultivation of hemp, fruit, and food preserves, and receive in exchange cotton, coffee, industrial and other products. The new programs insist on the treatment of great scientific discoveries of such men as Columbus, Galileo, Volta, Galvani, Pacinotti, Ferraris, Marconi, who contributed much more to civil progress than have many warriors who have bathed Europe in blood, often without leaving any traces of their deeds." (Pp. 402-403.)

activities with the school curriculum. Italian labor is demanded the world over. The Italian government has a very definite and well-defined stake in training it.

Recommendations for elementary-school reform as proposed in the *Conclusioni* advocate little change in the curriculum; rather, they aim toward bringing more and more children into the schools. The mortality rate is high in Italian elementary schools. For every three children who enroll in the first grade only one enters the fifth grade. The problem centers, then, on how to increase enrollments and provide adequate housing and personnel for a simple program of expansion. In the face of a law which requires school attendance up to age fourteen, even greater difficulties arise at the post-elementary level. Somehow, in the next few years, the Ministry must provide schooling for nearly 3 million youngsters between the ages of eleven and fourteen who do not enter the secondary schools and who require a training of a semiskilled nature. Marraro is optimistic, reminding the reader that if the present rate of construction—10,000 new classrooms per year—continues, there will soon be more than enough classrooms for Italy's elementary-school population. Finding the teachers is no problem; in fact, Italy is perhaps the only country of any size today in which there is considerable unemployment in the teaching profession. The chief difficulty is one of finding enough money to pay for more teachers. If the present pupil-teacher ratio of over 40 to 1 were reduced adequately, the unemployment problem would be solved.

SECONDARY EDUCATION

The Italian secondary school, it will be remembered, is divided into an upper and a lower division, the lower academic division having been termed in 1940 the *scuola media*. The purpose of the *scuola media* is to provide a more specialized training preparatory to higher study than would be possible in a post-elementary school. The latter institution is preserved for individuals whose prime object is to fulfill the requirements of the school-leaving age. The courses of study are as follows: religion, Italian, Latin (a highly favored subject in Italy), history, geography, mathematics, foreign language, drawing, physical education, work (*lavoro*), music and

singing. At the conclusion of the three-year course a license examination (*esame di licenza*) is taken as a requisite for entrance into
higher secondary schools.

The modern *scuola media*, hardly a decade old, is still in the
experimental stage. Although frankly an improved means of meeting the need for a more humanistic type of training than could be
afforded at the post-elementary level, the school is not so rigidly
academic in attitude as the traditional secondary school; hence it
attracts a wider cross section of youth. The *scuola media* has at least
three further advantages: (1) it postpones definite choice of vocation
or profession for two or three years; (2) it gives students as well as
teachers additional opportunity to assess interest and abilities, and
therefore provides a better, more mature type of guidance; and (3)
it provides a terminal education with an academic bias.[9]

Higher secondary education in the more classical sense is divided
into two sections: the two-year *ginnasio* followed by the three-year
liceo classico. In actuality, the courses of both schools are unified
and form a five-year training for university entrance. However,
examinations are given upon completion of the *ginnasio*, and the
mortality rate is almost as high as it is in French secondary schools.
A *diploma di maturità classica* is awarded on completion of the
liceo and success in examinations, and the student is then ready for
the university. According to the ministry, instruction in the *liceo*
classico is "essentially humanistic and formative." The courses of
study for the two schools are as follows:[10]

[9] Of the *scuola media*, Guido de Ruggiero has this to say: "During the
last years of fascism there was in progress a reform which sought to unify
the first three years of middle-school education and only from the fourth
year to begin the various specialized forms of the humanistic classical
lyceums, of the technical institutes, including industrial, agricultural, and
commercial types of schools, and of the normal school, which trained
elementary-school teachers. This reform was motivated by the desire to
postpone until a more mature age the choice of a career on the part of
the students. Under the old regulations it was possible to begin specialization, and therefore to make the choice, in the first year of the lower middle
school. . . ." ("Problems of Italian Education," *School and Society*, Vol.
LXIV [September 14, 1946], p. 179.)

[10] For a description of course content see Howard R. Marraro, "The
Secondary School in Liberated Italy," *Educational Forum*, Vol. X (November 1945), pp. 75-91.

	Hours in ginnasio		Hours in liceo classico			
	1st year	2nd year	3rd year	4th year	5th year	Total hours
Italian language and literature	5	5	4	4	4	22
Latin language and literature	5	5	4	4	4	22
Greek language and literature	4	4	3	3	3	17
Foreign language and literature	4	4	..	..	..	8
History	2	2	3	3	3	13
Geography	2	2	..	..	..	4
Philosophy	..	..	3	3	3	9
Natural science, chemistry, geography	..	..	4	3	2	9
Mathematics	2	2	3	2	2	11
Physics	..	..	..	2	3	5
History of art	..	..	1	1	2	4
Religion	1	1	1	1	1	5
Physical education	2	2	2	2	2	10
Total hours	27	27	28	28	29	139

The *liceo classico* enjoys all the exclusiveness and privilege that most of the classical secondary schools of the world have inherited through the years. It is the secondary school par excellence, the institution to which all students go whose intellectual attainment has been proved by extensive examinations. Although science is relegated to a minor position, graduates of the classical *liceo* are privileged to enter any faculty or institution of higher education they choose, except the faculty of pedagogy. (Indeed, higher schools of science and engineering give every evidence of favoring the classical graduate over his scientifically oriented confrere.) Although progressive inroads have been made into the rigid academic preferences of the *liceo classico*, the heavy hand of tradition still preserves such educational attributes as compulsory Latin and Greek for all who wish to study the humanities.

The *liceo scientifico*, also established in two divisions, is in reality a complete five-year secondary school. (Until 1945 the course was four years in length.) The purpose of the *liceo scientifico* is to "develop and intensify the education of students who aspire to university studies in medicine and science, with particular emphasis on scientific culture." Thus the law of 1923 which founded this *liceo* remains intact, and the anomaly persists that the *liceo scientifico*, because of its scientific bias, is not considered of sufficient educational excellence to equip students for entrance into all the university faculties. The anomaly seems even more pronounced when one compares the total hours of instruction in the subjects comprising the two curriculums:

	Hours in classical ginnasio-liceo (5 years)	Hours in scientific liceo (5 years)
Italian language and literature	22	19
Latin language and literature	22	20
Greek language and literature	17	..
Foreign language and literature	8	17
History	13	12
Geography	4	2
Philosophy	9	8
Natural science, chemistry, geography	9	10
Mathematics	11	18
Physics	5	8
History of art	4	..
Drawing	..	10
Religion	5	5
Physical education	10	10
Total hours	139	139

Actually, the chief differences between the curriculums of the two *licei* lie in such areas as Greek, modern language (studied throughout the entire scientific course), and history of art (replaced in the *liceo scientifico* by science and drawing), and, of course, in emphasis on scientific studies. No doubt the general I.Q. caliber of the students of the *liceo classico* is considerably higher than that of their scientific comrades, and no doubt greater selectivity prevails; but the I.Q. is more a measure of verbal than of scientific attainment; hence it is a reliable measure only to that extent. The essentially theoretical, verbal type of examination, typical in Italy, combines with this fact to create an artificial measurement of intellectual prowess. Nor does it help, of course, for the reformers to suggest that Latin no longer be compulsory in the *liceo scientifico*, since such an omission vulgarizes the academic program of the latter and creates an even greater difference in scholarly respectability. At any rate, the student receives on successful completion of the *liceo scientifico* a *diploma di maturità scientifica*, which entitles him to en-

trance in corresponding university schools, with the exception of
law, letters, philosophy, and education.[11]

Despite the benefits accruing from the traditional disciplinary
quality of Italian secondary-school training, epitomized by the *liceo
classico*, Lewis Bilancio expresses the antipathy of its critics by
referring especially to the ineffective methods of teaching the classics
and the humanistic studies, to the strict compartmentalization of
subject matter, and to the failure to relate what is learned to life's
actualities:

> The classics are taught in the original as linguistic exercises.
> Humanism as taught in the secondary schools seems calculated to
> bring not a rebirth but intellectual stagnation. The student re-
> ceives with his *laurea* not a greater mastery of his natural and
> social environment, or a key to sublime vistas of classical lore, but
> only the confidence that he can confute his less learned hearers.
> . . . After only four years of common education [now five], the
> pupils separate into what roughly corresponds to their social
> strata. . . . Should they wish to transfer to another course later,
> they may do so only at considerable sacrifice of time and money.
> . . . There is great lack of continuity among the separate courses.
> Occasionally a subject course is not only independent of life past,
> present and future, but it is also independent of every other
> course.[12]

In an effort to remedy these and other deficiencies Italian reformers have applied themselves to the internal organization of the
upper and lower divisions of the secondary school. With regard to

[11] Assessing and comparing Italian and American secondary education,
Howard Marraro considers the Italian training to be "satisfactory" and
"most adequate" in all fields but natural sciences, where instruction is
"deficient . . . the knowledge imparted is largely theoretical, since there
is little or no equipment for laboratory work. . . . The quality of instruction [otherwise] compares favorably with, and in some subjects is superior
to that which obtains in many of our American liberal arts colleges.
Although it is difficult to make comparisons . . . it is fair to state that a
graduate from an Italian secondary school . . . has approximately the
equivalent education of an American student who has finished his sophomore year in a liberal arts college." The chief defect, as many writers
have indicated, is in social education—it is "all but ignored." ("The
Secondary School in Liberated Italy," p. 9.)
[12] Lewis Bilancio, *op. cit.*, p. 78.

the *scuola media* and lower secondary schooling in general, the National Investigation Commission for School Reform (see under *Conclusioni* in the Bibliography) in 1949 made the following proposals:

1. Lower secondary education should be offered to youngsters between the ages of eleven and fourteen in two branches: (a) a post-elementary school integrated with the present five-year elementary program; and (b) a regular lower secondary school.

2. Transfer from the post-elementary school to regular secondary training should be permitted and facilitated.

3. The lower secondary school should be organized in such a way as to permit students to enter any of the higher secondary educational institutes. (This is another way of stating that transfers from one type of schooling to another should be facilitated; no student should be barred from a higher training of his own choosing if he proves his ability to handle the subject matter.)

4. Examinations for entrance into institutions of higher secondary education should be preserved.

5. Changes in course elections should be granted wherever students demonstrate their aptitude or where interests change, provided they remain commensurate with abilities.

6. The possibility exists of separating the *scuola media* into two divisions: a classical division, with compulsory Latin, and a scientific division, without Latin. (This procedure would eliminate the *scuola di avviamento professionale.*)

In the field of higher secondary education, the Commission works its way through the fantastic total of some 300,000 proposals to come out approximately as follows:

1. The present distinction between the classical and the scientific *licei* should be maintained; the specific features of the two institutions should be more clearly delineated.

2. "The possibility that the classical *liceo* and the scientific *liceo* might function as separate entities of a single establishment shall not be excluded."

3. Technical institutes should have preference over the *licei* in the school building program; in fact, no *liceo* is to be constructed except where technical institutes already exist.

4. Study programs should be reduced in scope. Observes Minister Gonella: "Too much food is being badly digested." Quality should take the place of quantity.

5. Preparation for entrance into the universities should be intensified, and examinations made more comprehensive and more difficult.

6. The terminal features of the various secondary institutes should be stressed; courses of study should lead to professional or vocational diplomas that equip students for immediate entrance into their lifework. The purpose in part is to reduce the excessive number of students who enroll in the universities.

7. The two sections, or cycles, into which higher secondary education is now divided should be preserved, the first a two-year course, the second a three-year course. Qualifications for promotion from one level of training to the next should be intensified. Selection should be more rigid.

In consideration of Italy's national needs these proposals and recommendations for secondary education will doubtless be disappointing to the progressive educator. The *Conclusioni* are heavily weighted with acknowledgments of the social and economic demands that are currently being made on the school system, and they dwell at length on the dire necessity for reforming education in accordance with latest psychological findings on individual growth and the learning process. Yet the reader is confronted with a final set of principles that at heart preserves old administrative structures. The reform is to be commended for many innovations, among them an educational reorientation which places proper value on the personal initiative and spontaneity of the child, and a desire to bring the schools into closer relationship with other social developments. But doubts will be raised as to whether Italian educators are going far enough and whether they seriously believe that fundamental changes are necessary. All this is a simple reminder that there is a great deal of cultural nostalgia residual in Italian national leaders, and that an unusually large segment of educators prefer to remain unreconstructed. When the ranks of these educators are swelled by others in a strong position to determine national progress, as is the case in Italy today, obstructionism becomes a formidable foe indeed.[13]

[13] Two cases in point are (1) a recent pronouncement from Benedetto Croce's Liberal party: "The task of the schools is twofold: first, the diffusion of elementary education throughout all the classes of the population, and second, the preparation of the ruling class"; and (2) a statement by former Minister of Education Arangio-Ruiz: "Education depends on

VOCATIONAL AND TECHNICAL EDUCATION

Contrary to what has happened in most of the school systems of the world, vocational and technical education have enjoyed comparatively favorable though by no means adequate treatment at the hands of the Italian government. The Casati Law of 1859 provided for a six-year technical training to follow the elementary school. This was to be obtained in a three-year *scuola tecnica* and a three-year *istituto tecnico*. As was to be expected, these schools were largely theoretical in approach. Even as they advanced, they never quite achieved the more practical purposes demanded by technical training in its stricter sense. Nevertheless, this early start provided a sound basis for the burst of interest in technical training that occurred in the 1890's, so that, except for a brief interval during the years of Fascism, schools of vocational education have enjoyed a relatively greater progress in both enrollment and school building than their classical counterparts.

Gentile's aversion to pure vocational education was transcended in the 1930's by the establishment of new types of technical schools, the purpose of which was to contribute to a much-needed development of national economy. But the direct route to vocational education, interpreted in its strictest sense, was to be the higher division of the elementary school. Minister of Education Giuseppe Bottai as late as 1938 was taking no chances on corrupting secondary education with technical curriculums. For some reason, Fascist educators preferred to associate education in the trades with popular education. To their mind, young people with intellectual acumen of the more traditionally academic type would become the real leaders of the new nation, and would not be found in technical pursuits. The education of this elite was not to be contaminated by the toiling of fellow students in manual arts under the same roof. This attitude did not extend down to the elementary school, however, where serious efforts were made, despite their Fascistic orientation, to introduce work programs of sound educational value. Much was done in the field of practical activities, and Battistini reports that

---

surplus wealth . . . that is, the wealth that is left over after people have provided themselves with the basic necessities of life." Such symptoms of sociological reactionism make it difficult for Italy's friends to be optimistic about her immediate educational future.

"almost every institution had acquired or built up a considerable amount of property and tools necessary for this endeavor."[14]

Concessions to the classical schools were made by vocational educators in Italy as well as in France. Henry Lester Smith brings out very pertinently the fact that cultural subjects were given undue deference in an effort to enhance the respectability of technical training.[15] In other words, the technical schools were laden with academic requirements that created an unresolvable dualism of aims. Actually, the *scuola tecnica* became just another junior high school which differed from the classical *ginnasio* chiefly in that it offered science and omitted Latin. The *istituto tecnico* was a bit more independent, since students of greater maturity and greater talent naturally tend to demand material of a more specialized type.

According to the letter of the law (*Ordinamento della pubblica istruzione,* 1945), technical education "aims to furnish youth with the preparation necessary for those practical vocations [*professioni*] which are needed in the economic life of the nation. It is offered in technical schools, in independently organized courses for vocational education, in vocational schools for girls, in teacher-training institutes for women, and in technical institutes." Substantially, this is but a repetition of the laws of 1931 and 1932, although the political implications are decidedly different.

Post-elementary technical training is obtainable in the three-year "work school" (*scuola di avviamento professionale*), which features the following course divisions: agriculture, industry, commerce, and nautical science. There are subdivisions for each of these categories. In the case of nautical science, for example, such subdivisions are listed as navigation, mechanics, and construction. Information on cultural backgrounds forms part of the study and is composed of the same subject matter as that of the *scuola media*, although naturally less intense in nature.

Many technical schools restrict their efforts to one speciality. The agricultural technical school, for example, has a program involving general cultural studies (Italian, history, and geography), mathematics, physics, natural science, vegetal pathology, agricultural chemistry, economics, rural economy, industrial agriculture, agricultural mathematics, drawing, zootechnics, rural legislation, re-

[14] L. H. Battistini, *op. cit.*

[15] Henry Lester Smith, *Comparative Education* (Bloomington, Ind.: Educational Publications, 1941).

ligion, and physical education. Technical schools of industry and commerce offer a similar program of studies within their speciality. The commercial course is particularly interesting in that two foreign languages are required. In England and in the United States foreign languages are rarely considered essential to commercial courses; in fact, one of the chief attractions of these courses is their freedom from subjects of just such an academic nature. The usual examination (*esame di licenza*), given at the end of the course, entitles the student to a technician's, agricultural agent's, or accountant's diploma (*diploma di tecnico, di agente rurale,* or *di computista*), depending on the course pursued.

The vocational school for girls (*scuola professionale femminile*) provides a three-year course with the same entrance and terminal requirements as the *scuola media*. Its purpose is preparation for female occupations and good home management, for which it provides the following program: general cultural studies, mathematics, elementary accounting, natural sciences, drawing, history and fundamentals of art, domestic economy, hygiene, female occupations, foreign language, religion, and physical education. One peculiarity of this school resides in the fact that it not only prepares for entrance into the teacher-training institutes but also features a program for the preparation of kindergarten teachers.

The *istituto tecnico* offers a composite five-year training which, when followed by an examination, permits entrance to university technical studies. The technical institutes usually combine their specialities in one establishment, exceptions being noted in the case of commercial and engineering institutes, which customarily are separate entities. In any case, all branches of technical education must feature a common core of basic knowledge: religion, Italian, history, foreign language, mathematics, physics, natural science, and physical education. As a rule, students begin the course of study at age fourteen and complete it at age nineteen.

Successful completion of the *istituto tecnico* entitles the graduate to a diploma in his speciality. Diplomas are entitled: *di perito agrario, di perito industriale capo tecnico, di ragioniere e perito commerciale, di geometra,* and, in the nautical division, *di aspirante*. This type of diploma is necessary for entrance into the university schools, institutes, and faculties of economics and commerce (without examination), agronomy, science, and engineering (with a supplementary

examination proving intellectual ability—mostly in cultural matters
—equal to that of the graduate of the *liceo scientifico*).

Trends and needs in vocational education are illustrated by the
proposals for reform submitted in 1949:

1. More types of technical schools must be constructed, with
structures fitting the demands of the particular localities in which
they are built.

2. More technical schools for girls are needed, especially schools
concentrating on family education.

3. No change is contemplated in the program of the technical
institutes, except for increased concentration on an education
suited to the demands of national economy.

4. Concentration in the technical institutes will be on the
finished product—on the graduate ready to take his place in
national life—rather than on university preparation. On the other
hand, students who give promise of being able to handle advanced
work with profit are to be encouraged to continue their study, and
the way is to be made easier for them to enroll in whatever institution of higher learning they choose.

5. Vocational schools are to be given preference in the school
building program over other institutions of secondary rank, specifically the *licei*.

Finally, Professor Arangio-Ruiz sees in vocational education an
increased opportunity for elementary-school graduates who, despair-
ing of their literary-linguistic abilities, prefer to abandon the school
together:

We do not propose that the less-endowed sons of the "have-not"
families should be abandoned to their own devices upon the completion of their primary examinations. There is a branch of
instruction which up to the present has had only a half-hearted
development in Italy. I mean, of course, the technical training of
the future specialists, artisans, and agriculturists of our country.[16]

HIGHER EDUCATION

No branch of Italian education has encountered sharper criticism
than has higher education. Strapped by the Casati Law, which made
them subject to the Ministry of Education, Italian universities in
the present century have generally found small audience for educational enterprise or for the findings of the intellectually alert.

[16] V. Arangio-Ruiz, *op. cit.*

Before unification, independent progress had been evident within each of the states supporting institutions of higher learning, and there was a healthy competition which resulted in the production of valuable research. But in 1860 the assumption by the central government of responsibility for the control and the maintenance of all state universities was met by an almost complete forfeiture of responsibility by the individual states. The result was that the central government found itself with too many universities to support; it dared not close the doors of any single institution, yet it could not find the material means to keep them flourishing. The administration of Gentile sought to remedy the difficulty by granting national status to a select group, leaving the remainder to be supported in part, or closed down, by the local communities. Being of no mind to curtail the blessings of higher education and the prestige that such training brought to the communities fostering it, local authorities preserved their institutions, but only at the expense of impoverishing them. Since the number of institutions of higher learning has actually increased since Gentile's day, Italy now finds herself with a top-heavy school system.

The status of university education is clearly defined by the *Ordinamento* of 1945. The Ministry lists twenty-two national universities, five free universities, two polytechnical schools (in Milan and Turin), two national university institutes of architecture and one of economics and commerce (in Venice), three higher normal schools (Naples, Rome, and Pisa), and seven other institutions of higher learning.[17] All these institutions are governed by the Ministry of Education through its council for higher education, except the institutes of commerce, agriculture, and forestry, which are in the charge of the Ministry of Agriculture, and the Catholic University of the Sacred Heart, in Milan, which is administered by the Vatican. Although legally the Ministry still controls all higher learning, much of this control has been relaxed and in many cases has become merely nominal. Internal administrative matters are being handled increasingly by the institutions themselves.

Different from the universities of the United States and England, but similar to those of France, Italian universities and university in-

[17] Among the national universities supported almost entirely by the Ministry of Education are Bologna (founded 1088), Genoa, Palermo, and Rome (largest in Italy). The universities of Bari, Florence, Modena, and Perugia are among those maintained by both local and central authorities.

stitutes are organized in faculties and schools, each of which is virtually autonomous in the administration of affairs within its own confines. The rector of the university is appointed for a three-year term by the university council (all the full professors of the various faculties), subject to approval by the Minister of Education. Academic matters are managed by an academic council, consisting of the rector, the deans of the faculties, and the directors of the university schools and institutes.

Higher education in Italy is constructed on a subject-matter program essentially classical in orientation, culminating in the doctorate (*laurea* or *dottore*). There is no less advanced degree, so that, as Bilancio well observes, doctor's degrees have become nearly as common in Italy as bachelor's degrees in the United States. (The Italian doctorate is, however, more nearly the equivalent of the M.A.) Ordinarily the doctorate represents the completion of four or five years of professional study, together with a successful public defense of the dissertation. But this degree does not permit the holder to practice in his field. As in other countries, state licenses are required for admission to practice, and examinations for these licenses usually require months of additional study. For comparative purposes, the analysis of the late Dr. C. D. Ebaugh, of the U. S. Office of Education, is reliable:

> The Italian laurea thus represents completion of at least 4 years of highly specialized professional study, averaging 30 semester hours a year over and above the one year of the United States college credit included in the work for the maturity diploma required for university admission. This places the graduate of the 4-year Italian university course at a point of training approximately one year beyond the U. S. bachelor's degree. . . . As in other foreign countries, higher education in Italy is entirely at the professional level. A broad cultural background of liberal arts and science is developed in the ginnasio-liceo, roughly equivalent to one year of college in the U. S.; therefore, specialization is begun in the first year of university study.[18]

[18] C. D. Ebaugh, "Higher Education in Italy," *Higher Education*, Vol. V (March 1, 1949), p. 153. Ebaugh also provides an example of the course of study leading to the *laurea* in letters:

First year: (1) Two of the basic subjects common to all students: Italian literature, Latin literature, Roman history, geography, philosophy. (2) Two specialized subjects. (For the major in modern letters the choice is among romance philology, medieval history, modern history, history of medieval

As stated in the section on secondary education, admission to the university is ordinarily by way of the diploma of classical maturity or scientific maturity obtained in the *licei,* although the faculties of agriculture, economics, and commerce admit students who have successfully completed the requirements for the diploma of the technical institute. The various faculties with appropriate statistics as gathered by Ebaugh are listed as follows:

HIGHER EDUCATION IN ITALY, 1945-1946

Faculty	Number of faculties	Length of course (years)	Enroll- ment	Graduates
Medicine and surgery	21	6	34,399	2,117
Economics and commerce	11	4	30,139	1,933
Engineering	11	5	24,417	1,167
Law	26	4	23,820	5,240
Letters and philosophy	16	4	21,569	3,870
Sciences	19	4	15,276	1,559
Education	7	4	12,131	1,972
Pharmacy	22	4	8,315	952
Agriculture	10	4	3,447	485
Veterinary medicine	10	4	3,127	304
Architecture	5	5	2,719	116
Political science	5	4	1,926	263
Industrial chemistry	2	5	452	54
Naval Institute	1	5	1,161	80
Statistics, demography, and actuarial sciences	2	2	236	29
Totals	168		183,134*	20,141

* Of the total enrollment, 47,632 were women students.

---

art, history of modern art.) (3) Two electives from a large number of so-called "complementary subjects."

Second year: Continuation of two subjects from the first year, two basic subjects common to all, two specialized (major) subjects, one elective.

Third year: Continuation of one of the new subjects taken in the second year, the remaining subjects required in the major field, two electives.

Fourth year: Three electives.

This arrangement is fairly general in all courses in arts and letters. Programs in faculties of science and technical education are, as elsewhere, more rigid and more highly specialized.

The perennial failure of Italian higher education to live a corporate life with that of the nation has turned the attention of many educators to the dire need for reform. The most disturbing factor has been that of excessive enrollment. The average Italian university today accommodates nearly three times the number of students it did a decade ago. This enrollment inflation has been accompanied, in Ruggiero's good judgment, by a "precipitous decline" in the quality of university training, brought about by a "deterioration of teaching personnel and by the impoverishment of financial resources." Answering the question of what remedies may be proposed, the former Minister of Education suggests:

> There are only indirect means, such as reducing the excess of students by a more vigorous selective middle school; by making the university more selective through careful examinations and expulsions at the end of the first two years; by giving greater impetus to technical, vocational, and teacher training, thus enhancing the educational quality of such schools; and by introducing as an extreme measure an entrance examination to the particular university faculties.

Ruggiero is wary of modifying university education by means of external regulations, especially if they involve more examinations; he makes other proposals, such as that specialized faculties be reorganized to effect a better distribution (some universities have only one or two faculties!) and that existing establishments be coordinated to provide education more economically—processes now under consideration, by the way, in France.

Ruggiero's criticisms are mild, however, when compared with those of Professor Arangio-Ruiz (formerly Minister of Justice in the Badoglio Cabinet). It is interesting to note the tang of his expression, purely Neapolitan, as he raps the very essence of Italian higher education:

> We may as well admit . . . that youths capable of making a tangible contribution to the liberal arts represent a very small percentage, closer perhaps to one out of every thousand than to one out of every hundred, in these prevailing conditions of intellectual inflation. To pretend that this conglomerate of graduates can be dignified by an educational pedigree (the illusory pomposity of the epithet "doctor") is to blow molehills into mountains. More important, it denies to the majority the vocational

training of which the nation has such great need. . . . Whosoever has been in contact with educational systems abroad knows by experience that the highly specialized Italian student when confronted with problems of cultural perspective is unable to compete with his foreign colleagues. Indeed, college or even high-school graduates (because of their more comprehensive curricula) of other countries are far better prepared than the overwhelming majority of our "doctors."[19]

Although Arangio-Ruiz is perhaps unduly hard on his countrymen, since, as will be pointed out later, there is considerable current production in Italian art and letters, the essence of his indictment is incontestable. Ebaugh correctly concludes that in most respects higher education in Italy remains little changed by the events of the 1930's and 1940's. Reform has indeed been long in coming to Italian university life. The negative job has been done by eliminating the nepotism and the political extremism of Fascism, but more positive action needs to be taken to resolve some of the conflicts, brought out above, which have nettled university authorities for at least a generation. In this connection, Marraro, in his characteristically charitable fashion, reports that the recent decrease of 10,000 students will combine with greater selectivity and more intensified specialization to raise university standards.

As for further provisions of the reform of 1949, the following revised procedures are suggested: (1) A comprehensive examination should take the place of the dissertation. (2) This examination would eliminate the need for state license examinations. (3) The *laurea* should be awarded after two years of study beyond the doctor's diploma. (4) Tuitions should be raised and additional scholarships provided. If these reforms, together with others mentioned above, are energetically enacted and followed through, they should do much to remedy existing deficiencies in higher learning in Italy today.

THE TEACHER

Italy's program of teacher training tends to parallel that of France; it is another example of a type of preparation, characteristic of all countries influenced by France, which features early specializa-

[19] V. Arangio-Ruiz, *op. cit.*

tion. The original *scuola normale*, established by the Casati Law of 1859, was exceptional, however, in that specialization did not take place until after the lower secondary school. The candidate had to be sixteen years of age before he was allowed to enter, and he was enrolled for a three-year course. The product was far from satisfactory, largely because teacher training tended to attract only those whose capabilities were insufficient to warrant success in other types of secondary or higher education. Further, the demand for teachers was so great, and the rewards so low, that all kinds of concessions had to be made in the training program. It was not very long, for example, before teachers were being licensed for instruction in the elementary grades after only two years of preparation. The requirements for elementary-school teaching were stiffened in 1890 to include the successful completion of three years in the lower secondary school plus three years in the *scuola normale*. The need for further preparation was met by the universities, which in 1906 established a two-year advanced course for those desiring to teach in the upper elementary school.

Summarizing the reforms to the rise of Fascism Henry Lester Smith observes that they attempted to show two forces at work: one emphasizing the cultural training of teachers and another stressing the professional. Although confusing idealism and positivism, Smith is nevertheless correct in concluding: "The professional in its opposition to the cultural tended to become mechanistic, to crush rather than to mold teachers into intelligent and integrated personalities. Teaching became dogmatic and narrow. . . ."[20]

Before the Bottai Reform of 1939 the lower secondary school was combined with the normal school to form a seven-year *istituto magistrale*, of which the first four years served as a lower division. Under Bottai, the normal school reverted to type and became a five-year institution following the middle, or lower secondary, school. Today the *istituto magistrale* has again become a seven-year course, divided into lower and upper divisions of four and three years respectively. Higher normal training is available in the *scuola normale superiore*, a teachers' college or higher normal school offering a four-year course which prepares instructors for secondary schools.

[20] Henry Lester Smith, *op. cit.*

According to the *Ordinamento* of 1945, the humanistic emphasis which had characterized teacher training under Gentile and his followers is being substituted for greater concentration on professional studies. Practice teaching, once limited to the last year of training, is now extended to the last two years. The core of academic preparation is Italian, Latin, history, and geography, all taught as a unit. Other academic subjects are mathematics and physics, natural sciences, chemistry, drawing, history of art, foreign language, choral singing, and physical education. Professional studies center on pedagogy, philosophy, and psychology. History is to be integrated with Italian literature, and geography with natural science and chemistry. Graduates must, of course, pass the final examination (*esame di abilitazione magistrale*) and, since all teachers in Italy are public servants, they must be licensed by the state.

The current reform movement proposes a teacher-training institute which will have a lower two-year and an upper three-year division following lower-secondary-school (*scuola media*), preparation. This adds one year more to the training of elementary-school teachers, making a total of eight years after completion of elementary school. The new institution will feature humanistic-scientific studies (with the teaching of Latin dependent upon the aims of the school) organized around the science of education and relevant to the demands of Italian culture. It will be a "popular school," emphasizing professional pedagogical studies and practice teaching increasingly as the student progresses. Henceforth all normal schools are to possess elementary-school annexes, wherein practice teaching can be done under the best master teachers available. The new teacher's certificate will serve the dual purpose of entitling the holder to a teaching position, when he has been licensed by the state, and of providing the necessary authorization for entrance into the *istituto magistrale superiore*. For their part, the teachers' colleges will continue to prepare students for positions in the secondary and normal school and will award degrees in the science of education. Considerable stress is laid in recent recommendations on the need for teacher freedom and the extension of opportunities for teacher initiative and enterprise. Teachers are urged to establish a greater rapport with parents in order to ensure adequate educational and social guidance.

Needless to append, the present government is endeavoring to attract more capable people to the teaching profession by increasing the material as well as the spiritual rewards. The salaries of teachers in Italy are at a minimum existence level and, although provisions for retirement, pensions, and sick leave are not particularly backward in relation to corresponding programs elsewhere, the purchasing power of the salary check is limited indeed. As stated previously, there is no shortage of teachers in Italy. Rather, the problem of teacher unemployment is acute—and it can be resolved, at least in part, only by reducing the present pupil-teacher ratio. This procedure will require far greater budgetary allotments than are now requested by the Ministry.

SPECIAL TYPES OF EDUCATION

Eliminating Illiteracy. By far the most plaguing educational problem in Italy is that of illiteracy. The visitor to Italy, if he wanders away from tourist centers, cannot fail to note the appalling number of persons of all ages who must rely on others to do their reading and writing. Lewis Bilancio reports that when an Allied proclamation was posted on the walls, natives of the village would gather in small groups and gape at it until the mayor, the pharmacist, or the priest would come and explain it to them: "Often the whole correspondence from a village would come in one handwriting. It was the priest or pharmacist who wrote for the whole village."[21]

Nation-wide statistics on illiteracy are old and unreliable, but it is a safe guess that at least 20 percent of the population can neither read nor write. If this deficiency were spread evenly across the face of the country, the remedy would be easier of attainment. The regions of Sicily, Lucania, and Calabria are the most formidable bastions, with rates of over 40 percent. Such large-scale illiteracy is closely bound up, of course, with the retarded economic and social progress of the south. As the author and artist Carlo Levi analyzes it, illiteracy is born of poverty and breeds poverty in its turn. Arnaldo Cortesi, correspondent of the *New York Times,* links illiteracy and ignorance to inequitable land distribution: "The most depressed areas in Italy are those where ownership of the land is highly concentrated in relatively few hands. This is true in terms of

[21] Lewis Bilancio, *op. cit.*

illiteracy, sanitation, infant mortality, housing conditions and food."[22]

But the cause is not entirely economic. There are political and spiritual implications which are intrinsic to the structure of the Italian state and the substance of its culture. Then, too, since schools in many cases are remote from homes, since parents lack the money to buy books, and since means of transportation are insufficient and expensive, parents can do no other than keep their children at home performing chores. Levi's description of these difficulties is most graphic:

> The hard life of the peasants does not leave much time for that miracle of communication, the written word. . . . Poverty and illiteracy fall into a vicious circle. The illiterate peasant is hampered in any attempt to better his lot; he is condemned to stay on the land without any possibility of migrating or raising his social status. And so it is that he hands down the state of servitude into which he was born.[23]

To widespread poverty and self-perpetuating class distinction must be added the very personal preference of the peasants for their way of life. A pathetic inertia and a peculiar blissfulness in ignorance characterize the Italian rural dweller, particularly in the south. His entire enlightenment seems to consist of unquestioned devotion to magic, miracles, superstition, fetishes, and spiritual quackery. His humanistic orientation is limited to memorized adages, doggerels, and proverbs. He lives in an immobile, timeless world, circumscribed by age-old rites and customs, and his daily tasks change only as the seasons change. His culture consists of legends, folk tales, popular dramas, and songs that have been handed down without benefit of the written word. Yet the peasant has adopted a method of expression and communication that serves him well. Indeed, at times the poetic fancy and literary images he conjures from his imagination have actually fertilized Italian artistic and literary production. And so the peasant sees no need for change. He cannot be sure that benefits are to be derived from becoming literate.[24]

[22] *New York Times,* November 20, 1949.
[23] *New York Times Magazine,* November 6, 1949.
[24] "For centuries," writes Levi, "the peasants have been acquainted with this privileged art [literacy] only through periodic proclamations of mili-

The problem of eliminating illiteracy, then, is not one merely of financial appropriations, or of the enthusiasm of educators, but of overcoming deep-rooted psychological and subjectivistic inhibitions in the peasants themselves and of conquering the obstacles to social and economic progress that have been preserved by a neofeudalistic way of life. The primary need, of course, is for government leadership in providing the necessary teachers and teaching aids. Meantime, much has been done by private agencies in teaching people to read and write by person-to-person contact, such as was initiated in Mexico and China. Loudspeakers have helped in spreading information concerning the formation of literacy classes, and door-to-door campaigns by persons near to the hearts of the peasants have resulted in overflowing classrooms. In the province of Basilicata, for example, 291 adult courses were opened in 1948 to 10,000 persons. There is no lack of enthusiasm among the people in general for learning the blessings of the written word when the proper approach is used. When these blessings are accompanied by the promise of a greater say in political and legislative processes, the benefits become tangible indeed. Italians are learning that literacy is obligatory in the practice of democracy. It is essential in understanding scientific procedures which lead to greater productivity and better use of the land. Finally, it is intrinsic in the extension of human progress that has been too long denied the isolated Italian rural dweller.

Adult and Popular Education. Aside from the attention given to illiteracy and to provisions for adult education in the regular school system, adult education in the usual sense is not considered to be a state affair. Certain vocational and technical courses have been set up in areas where schools are not available, and adults may profit from attendance at lectures. But popular education is left largely to trade unions, cooperatives, and labor and agricultural organizations of a private nature. This type of education achieved moderate success before the Fascist regime, but the hostility of

tary mobilization, which meant that they must give up their lives beneath some foreign sky; through announcements of new taxes imposed on their scanty harvest, or summonses to appear in court and answer for some crime of which they had no understanding. . . . The written word is for them a symbol of the remoteness and indifference of the central government . . . in short, the expression of a hostile civilization. . . . They react by defending their own ignorance, as if by so doing they could protect ancient values from corruption and shield themselves from a hostile world."

Fascism to labor organizations virtually obliterated what precious progress had been made. The new reform makes no mention of adult and popular education as a government affair, partly because it will be a long time before the more common levels of education receive anywhere near the assistance adequate to their needs. For that purpose alone the state is having great difficulty mustering enough support.

Schools of the Arts. Outstanding in artistic achievements, the Italians have dedicated a number of schools to that special purpose, among them the *scuola d'arte* (three years), the *istituto d'arte* (three or four years), the *liceo d'arte* (four years), and the *accademia di belle arti* (four years). These four art schools correspond to the four levels of regular education, commencing with the middle school. Other institutions are the *conservatorio di musica*, the *corsi musicali di perfezionamento*, schools of the dance and the drama, and schools for curators of art and administrative and teaching personnel. Licenses, degrees, and diplomas correspond to those given in regular schools of similar rank. Care should be taken, however, in translating and interpreting properly the meaning of these diplomas. The *diploma di maestro d'arte*, for example, is not a master of arts degree, but rather a certificate of "master artist," awarded on successful completion of the *istituto d'arte*, an institution of secondary-school rank.

Contemporary Cultural Life. Authorities are agreed that of all countries overrun by war Italy is the first to give evidence of a cultural reawakening. The country teems with a wide variety of books, pamphlets, journals, and periodicals, from the scholarly and erudite to saucy imitations of American weeklies. In art there is every indication of renewed strength, vitality, and creativity. Museums and art galleries have been reopened, and exhibitions are now being held in every leading cultural center in the country. Artistic expression is a temperamental necessity for the Italians, and it exhibits itself not only in art but in music. The opera programs of Milan (La Scala) and Rome have added new titles to their lists; local concert ensembles have increased in number and are much in demand. Influenced by the need for tourist trade, the country is showing itself more enterprising than ever in such projects as the film festival in Venice and the university summer schools. Finally, in the field of literature, Professor T. G. Bergin, of Yale University, cites meritorious achievement:

> Such writers as Moravia, Alvaro and Palazzeschi, who were well known before the war, have continued to write and with renewed energy and perception, while there are a good half-dozen very promising newcomers, some of whom, such as Carlo Levi and Buzzati, are already well known in translation. There are literally hundreds of younger authors trying their hand and many of them with unusual skill and penetration; out of all these I think three or four really great writers may easily emerge. Of course there is a voracious interest in foreign literatures—this was true even under Fascism, but now that Italy is back in the community of nations this interest has been intensified.[25]

Education and Society.   When the academic year opened in 1949 the schools found themselves closer than ever to the communities in which they had been established. Educators and the people were slowly becoming aware of the mutual dependence of school and society. However, it was becoming increasingly evident that educational reformers would have to look further afield than the horizons of pedagogy and educational idealism to effect school reforms in a society that was badly out of balance. It is true that the forms of democratic government are present in Italy, and to the extent that democracy exists in Italian life progress continues. The country is not wanting in such external democratic attributes as freedom of speech and expression. In fact, no nation is fundamentally more tolerant of ideas and peoples than Italy. The mere fact that communism is condoned illustrates the extent to which political freedom prevails. Thought uncensored and unrestricted takes to the four winds in countless newspapers and periodicals that express every possible ray of opinion. Finally, personal intimidation is rare, and witch hunts are alien to the Italian scene.

Socially and economically, however, the need for reform is critical. Arnaldo Cortesi, centering his criticism on land distribution, terms recent reforms "too little and too late."[26] Basic to the country's

[25] T. G. Bergin, "Italy Is the Bright Spot in Europe," New Haven: *Yale University News Bureau*, March 27, 1949.
[26] Cortesi elaborates his argument as follows: "What infuriates the peasant is that large estates are often allowed to lie completely idle. . . . There is not enough land in Italy to satisfy everyone and the choice seems

prosperity, land has actually been seized and possessed illegally by hungry peasants, who had little hope of acquiring property in any other way because landowners normally do not sell. The new desire for social and economic emancipation which now fills the air in Italy is marked by a decided political turn to the left. In southern Italy especially, organized groups are taking the law into their own hands. Not so serious as in the months immediately following World War II, this political shift is nevertheless fraught with foreboding; it must be met with intelligent, conservative democratic orientations and a concomitant program of deeds, not words, to remove economic and social inequalities that are intolerable in any modern society.

The effects of this emancipation are being experienced in the schools, from which Italians are now demanding a more practical type of training, not only in the more restricted forms of liberal education but in those learnings that develop the free man. The real need is for a truly popular school—one open more widely to all social classes. However, recent proposals for reform, assembled and published by the Ministry of Education, seem unrealistic. They are overloaded with pedagogical idealism and replete with verbalisms that give little indication of how the recommendations are to be implemented. That is to say, the operational significance of the reform of 1949 remains undefined. The explanation lies, we repeat, in the defective cultural, social, political, and economic configuration in which the schools must operate. Until some of the basic ingredients of democracy—a thriving middle class, an adequate system of social services, a more equitable distribution of land and wealth, a wider extension of individual opportunity and responsi-

---

to lie between giving each peasant a little, thus condemning them all to semi-starvation, or dividing up only the large estates, which can provide enough land to meet only a part of the demand. It would be bad policy to split economically sound farms into a large number of tiny, inefficient holdings. . . . It has been said repeatedly that less than one-half of one per cent of the landowners possess more than one-third of the total area held as private property. This statement is correct but misleading. It gives the impression that large estates are the general rule. . . . The misconception concerning the prevalence of large estates is caused by an enormous number of tiny land holdings—holdings so small that they are well below the minimum required for a self-contained farm. . . . The amount of land available for redistribution is considerably smaller than would appear at first." (*New York Times*, November 20, 1949.)

bility, a fairer and more effective method of tax collections—form
the substance of national life, progress in the schools will remain
only nominal.

The implications for the course of Italian education are therefore
clear:

1. Schools must become better adapted to Italy's diverse economic
and social environment; they must be flexible enough to respond
to regional and local as well as national needs.

2. New programs must be oriented toward the development of
personality and a sense of collective, social responsibility. They must
help pupils to acquire a greater sense of unity between school and
life and a warmer, more spontaneous feeling of cooperation leading
to a more wholesome national solidarity.

3. An intense campaign is needed to put all Italy's children in
school. For this purpose an additional 30,000 classrooms must be
constructed, thus increasing the present holding power of the elementary school by at least 25 percent—which represents the total
number of school-age children not in attendance today.

4. New vocational, technical, and agricultural schools must be
built throughout the land and increased attention given to training
students who give evidence of potential vocational leadership. This
branch of education needs to come into its own as an educational
experience as respectable as that of the classical schools.

5. Extraschool educative agencies such as the radio, the press,
motion pictures, libraries, and correspondence courses need to be
drawn on to a greater extent, not only to enrich existing school experiences but to provide education where organized schools are
lacking.

6. Better articulation of the various levels of education must be
achieved. Within subject matter proper a greater integration of the
various fields studied should take the place of the present sovereignty
professed by every subject in the curriculum.

7. Higher education needs not only a complete external reorganization to provide a more economical and a better-distributed set of
offerings but also a revision of antiquated teaching methods and
outdated preferences. Too many littérateurs, classicists, and academic
humanists are being prepared at the expense of physicians, dentists,
opticians, psychiatrists, sociologists, and specialists in education, of
which the nation is in direst need.

8. A complete reorientation is necessary among many educational leaders who still consider schools to be second in importance to the preservation of social and cultural tradition.

9. New textbooks need to be prepared, especially in scientific fields, to dispel popular notions derived from superstition, black magic, witchcraft, astrology, and dream books rather than from rational thinking.

10. The country's countless dialects should either be played down or instruction provided in them so that Italy's people can learn to understand each other.

11. Increased financial aid must be provided by those in a position to pay. This means that tax collections must be put on a sounder basis; taxes will have to be raised and resolute efforts made to collect what is due the state.

12. Education and the schools must increasingly be considered part and parcel of Italy's entire national life, not separate entities. Educational and social progress must go hand in hand, one dependent on the other and neither seeking to thwart the progress of the other.

If the Italian people can roll up their sleeves and tackle their educational problems with the same commendable forthrightness, resolution, skill, and precision with which they tackle road building, works projects, and machine construction; if at the same time they can model their accomplishment on the cultural attributes and wisdom of living that have made the country world-renowned; and if all this can be accomplished within a framework of enlightened social, economic, and political progress, too long delayed, then the future of Italian education cannot fail to be an excellent one indeed.

BIBLIOGRAPHY

Arangio-Ruiz, V., "Liberal Orientations: Problems of the School," *School and Society*, Vol. LXI (January 20, 1945), pp. 33-35. Written by a former Minister of Justice, this article, characteristically Italian in flavor, is an impassioned recital of the evils and deficiencies which have brought Italian education to its present impasse. Contains spirited suggestions as to how to remedy the evils.

Battistini, L. H., "Italy's Educational Crisis," *Educational Forum*, Vol. X (March 1946), pp. 317-325. Battistini expertly and sympathetically surveys the major segments of Italy's school system, singling out specific areas where reform has already begun and where further revision is necessary.

La Bilancia italiana dei pagamenti, 1948-1949, (Rome: Istituto Poligrafico dello Stato, 1949). A valuable, concise, artistic, statistical presentation of Italy's economic needs, especially in terms of exports and imports.

BILANCIO, L. A., "Italian Education as of Now," *Progressive Education*, Vol. XXIV (November 1946), pp. 52 ff. A fast-moving and highly absorbing account by a member of the Library School of Chicago University who was on the scene during the liberation. Bilancio is sharply critical of Italian educational accomplishment, and he does not let his opinions remain undocumented.

Conclusioni dell' inchiesta nazionale per la riforma della scuola: La Reforma della scuola, 1947-1949 (Rome: Ministry of Education, 1949). As a result of polls, investigations, and professional recommendations, the Ministry of Education issued this tremendous compendium of proposals and conclusions regarding the proper course of educational reform. The actual conclusions in the final pages give little indication of the very vital desires and expressions embodied in the volume, which had come from Italy's diverse population groups. (For a brief review of these conclusions see Marraro, "Italian School Reform under the Republic.")

EBAUGH, C. D., "Higher Education in Italy," *Higher Education*, Vol. V (March 1, 1949), pp. 151-155. A businesslike exposition of the facts of Italy's higher educational scene. The late Dr. Ebaugh, who was fully aware of education's cultural determinants, can always be relied on for soundness and sincerity in his publications.

FERRETTI, GIOVANNI, "Italie, le mouvement éducatif en 1946-7," *Annuaire international de l'éducation et de l'enseignement, 1947* (Geneva: Bureau International d'Education, 1947), pp. 139-144. A useful but bare-boned presentation of educational events.

GABELLI, A., *Il Metodo di insegnamento nelle scuole elementari d'Italia* (Florence: Vallecchi Editore, 1945). A presentation by a private professional educator indicating the role of the elementary school in imparting the spiritual interpretations which have been reawakened by the Allied liberation.

LEVI, CARLO, "Italy Fights the Battle of Illiteracy," *New York Times Magazine*, November 6, 1949, pp. 14 ff. An extremely readable account, by a master craftsman, of the social and economic forces behind Italy's literacy problem.

MARRARO, HOWARD R., "Democratization of the Italian Elementary School," *School and Society*, Vol. LXI (June 23, 1945), pp. 401-

404. A well-reasoned article by an expert in the field. Professor Marraro, of Columbia University, gives the facts on methods by which Italy hopes to democratize her elementary schools in accordance with progressive practices elsewhere, yet wholly mindful of local and national needs.

————, "Italian School Reform under the Republic," *School and Society*, Vol. LXX (November 12, 1949), pp. 308-309. Marraro is mild and uncritical in his brief summary and appraisal of the recent educational reform. His estimate of Italy's educational future is optimistic.

————, "The Secondary School in Liberated Italy," *Educational Forum*, Vol. X (November 1945), pp. 75-91. A most useful exposition, with tables, of the status of all schools on the secondary level as of 1945, with a few recommendations on methods of improvement. Marraro is characteristically conservative, sympathetic, and reliable in this article.

Orari e programmi d'insegnamento per gli istuti tecnici per geometri (Rome: Libreria dello Stato, 1947). An official government publication outlining course schedules, content, and methods for the engineering institutes.

PRATT, W. E., "Fascists Can Teach Us a Thing or Two," *School and Society*, Vol. LXV (April 26, 1947), pp. 308-310. Pratt pertinently argues that there is much in Fascism which could be useful in training American youth to become strong and active exponents of the democratic way of life.

Programmi didattici per le scuole elementari e materne (Rome: Libreria dello Stato, May 24, 1945). An official government publication listing the programs, content, and methods recommended by the Ministry of Education for use in kindergartens and elementary schools.

Riordinamento dell' istruzione media tecnica (Istituto Poligrafico dello Stato Libreria, 1947). Regulations, programs, content, and method officially prescribed for practice in the middle technical schools.

RUGGIERO, GUIDO DE, "Italy under Fascism," *Year Book of Education, 1948* (London: Evans Brothers Ltd., 1948), pp. 566-577. Somewhat dated despite its recent publication, but valuable for the personal experience of the author and indispensable for its splendid and sympathetic analysis of the work of Giovanni Gentile.

————, "Problems of Italian Education," *School and Society*, Vol. LXIV (September 14, 1946), pp. 177-180. A valuable presentation by a former Minister of Education listing the various reforms needed in the major branches of Italian education. Few see the

difficulties as clearly as Ruggiero and at the same time emerge
with helpful, constructive suggestions.

SMITH, HENRY LESTER, *Comparative Education* (Bloomington, Ind.:
Educational Publications, 1941). The chapter on Italy is a useful,
comprehensive account.

SMITH, T. V., "Personal Impressions of Current Education in Italy,
Germany, and Japan," *Educational Record,* Vol. XXIX (January 1947), pp. 21-32. Although there is little information on
special problems of Italian education, this work is cited for its
comparative approach and for reader interest in T. V. Smith's
very personal reactions.

————, "Swan-song from the Ex-Director of the Education Subcommission, Allied Control Commission," *Educational Forum,* Vol.
XI (March 1947), pp. 339-357. Reflections in multicolored prose
on Colonel Smith's educational adventure in Italy with the Allied
Military Government. Highly personal for the most part, this account is none the less valuable for its factual data.

VESSEO, A., "Italy under Allied Military Government," *Year Book of
Education, 1948* (London: Evans Brothers Ltd., 1948), pp. 578-592.
A detailed and colorful account of education under Allied occupation.

WASHBURNE, C. W., "Education under the Allied Military Government in Italy," *Educational Record,* Vol. XXVI (October 1945),
pp. 261-272. A recital of events which took place during the first
months of the Allied invasion. Colonel Washburne was in charge
of educational rehabilitation.

————, "New Schools for Italy," *Survey Graphic,* Vol. XXXV (November 1946), pp. 380-386. A companion piece to "Education
under the Allied Military Government." The value of Washburne's exposition lies chiefly in his treatment of the details of
administration, although he is fully aware of the circumstances
which control Italian educational progress.

9 · EDUCATION IN *Germany*

ARTHUR HENRY MOEHLMAN

Germany is the central power of Europe in terms of geographical, strategic, technological, and cultural position. Owing to the fortunes of war, Germany's area has been decreased to some 143,000 square miles; the country is now not a great deal larger than France. The population is still close to 68 million, which means that its density is approximately 475 persons to the square mile and is exceeded only by that of the Low Countries and England. Germany is one of the most heavily industrialized areas in the world, with an urbanized population of almost 80 percent as against a rural population of about 20 percent. Germany cannot feed herself and must depend upon trade and manufacture to redress the balance. Furthermore, Germany is handicapped with regard to natural resources. Although she has large amounts of coal, lignite, potash, and salt, her supplies of iron and petroleum are very limited indeed. The results of World War II were very unfavorable for Germany. She not only lost most of her merchant marine but lost some 25 percent of her industrial installations and suffered heavy damage with regard to housing and transportation. The division of Germany into zones and the conflict between the Communists in the eastern zone and the democracies in the western zone increase difficulties. When some of the country's richest agricultural land was given to Poland and the population was extensively displaced westward, enormous housing and employment problems were created.

Germany's historical development was one of conflict between force and freedom in all aspects of life, from political to educational. An elite which believed in a "blood and iron" policy has been in control since the beginning of the Reich as a modern power (1871), with only the brief interlude of the Weimar Republic. Germany has had a marked class system against which liberals and a great middle class struggled without noteworthy result. The population has been one of the most literate in Europe and also one of the most skilled in every field of human activity, whether it be industry, agriculture, or the arts; but these factors have not prevented Germany's involvement in a succession of wars.

The German educational system has been not only "two-track" but also greatly specialized. An elite of leaders in government, military pursuits, manufacturing, business, and education were trained in a separate advanced system of education. The great majority were trained to be first-class factory workers, farmers, and soldiers in another system extending approximately through the twelfth year. Many, of course, went on to specialized training schools for agriculture, business, and manufacturing. The number of specialized secondary schools was striking, but the old style *Gymnasium*, or classical school, was the major road to preferment. The Weimar Republic made a very strong drive toward universal education, but the gains were largely eliminated by the Nazis. In fact, the Nazis did serious damage to the educational system.

One of the great present-day world problems is whether the extremely capable population of Germany can overcome the traditional appeal of force and, at the same time, deal with some very critical problems in government, economics, and social life. Germany remains a key factor in Europe.

This analysis of educational development in Germany is compact, emphasizing major outlines. Otherwise it would become lost in the maze of special elements which exist in German education.

—A. H. M.

A culture seeks an answer to its problems of survival and progress in a manner based upon its indigenous pattern of land and people and living. The action undertaken depends upon the culture's value systems or theories concerning the nature of man and the world, and what constitutes good and evil.[1] The Germans have been con-

---

[1] Bertrand Russell, *A History of Western Philosophy* (New York: Simon & Schuster, Inc., 1945), p. xiv.

tinuously faced with a conflict between value systems resting upon force and upon freedom. Their culture pattern was in many ways a resultant, and the educational instrument which they evolved mirrored the phases of this continuing conflict.

The Germans built up a myth centered in the manifest destiny of their national culture to lead Europe through disciplined and ordered force. They understood that the modern myth could sway a great nation—myth being defined, as Georges Sorel defined it in his *Reflections on Violence*, as "a body of mental images capable of evoking sentiment instinctively." Sorel popularized his theory that myths have been a great force in history and that every great social movement has been a pursuit of a myth. Bismarck and others before him constructed the "blood and iron" myth of state supremacy by force and implemented it with a "two-track" school system that produced an elite corps leading a disciplined mass of workers, soldiers, and technicians. Broken only by the short interim of freedom in the Weimar Republic, this myth of force continued to grow, as demonstrated in Hitler's *Mein Kampf* and Alfred Rosenberg's book with the revealing title *The Myth of the Twentieth Century*. The Nazis understood that a myth did not need to be true. All that matters is that the people be made to believe in it, accept it, and make it come true. Education in its broadest sense was the instrument, in Hitler's words, to "say it simply, say it often, make it burn." Education above all could make the myth an interpretation of history determining the future. The Germans realized that people live in a symbolic universe which they themselves create through linguistic forms, educational patterns, and mythical symbols.[2]

THE CONFLICT BETWEEN FORCE AND FREEDOM

A gifted Swiss historian, Jakob Burckhardt, saw this conflict of force and freedom clearly from his ancient university in Basel on the Rhine. He was able to analyze the chaos present in Germany without the rigidity of Hegel. He had a historical consciousness of the main points of difference between civilized man and the barbarian. Burckhardt foresaw the twentieth-century political-military juggernauts. He saw the terrible simplifiers of our own century being born of an enormous will to power, of a criminal clique fol-

[2] Ernst Cassirer, *An Essay on Man* (New Haven: Yale University Press, 1944), pp. 25 ff.

lowing the myth of force. He was particularly concerned about Germany and visualized it as a country in which there was warfare between the spirit of freedom in religion, art, and research on the one hand and the spirit of force typified by bureaucracy, the army, and cartels on the other.[3]

Even greater than the conflict between the people and the land, as visualized in the second part of Goethe's *Faust,* has been the conflict between the thinker and the *Junker.* The idea of force had deep roots in Germany. The history of the land and the people is one of battle between opposing groups in which the appeal was primarily to force. The German knightly power was used to fight in a frontier moving eastward against the wilderness and the Slavs. A combination of Teutonic knights, monastic orders, and the Hansa pressed forward, trained in the rule of force and extreme discipline. Hence the regard for valor, loyalty (*Treue*), discipline, and order. Serfdom was of long duration in Germany and feudal traditions died hard, especially toward the east. There was a feeling that possession of land and training as a soldier provided the highest nobility of character. This ideology contributed later to the growth of Prussia and to the formation of the instrument of control known as the Great General Staff (the high command of the army and its general staff divisions), to the doctrine of total war, and to the various interpretations of the "superman." Jahn, a physical-education expert, and Fichte and Hegel, the philosophers, were direct designers of the blueprint for Hitler, together with Prince Bismarck, the *Junker* diplomat, and the Krupps, an industrial dynasty. Fichte believed that "certainty of knowledge depends upon teaching a single system of philosophy." Hegel emphasized the absolute state above the individual. The idea of force had many sires in Germany, judging by the historical record—some wearing knightly armor, some writing estimates on the General Staff, and some lecturing in the university or conducting business in great industries.

The German struggle for freedom has ranged from the peasant revolts and the work of educators such as Melanchthon through the period of the German Renaissance to modern times. Goethe, with his idea of the complete life, his unending curiosity, and his research

[3] Jakob Burckhardt, *Weltgeschichtliche Betrachtungen* (Basel, 1929). Translation by James Hastings Nichols entitled *Force and Freedom* (New York: Pantheon Books, Inc., 1943), pp. 24, 40, 41, 43.

balancing creative writing, was one of the greatest German representatives of the search for freedom. With him must be mentioned
Schiller and the critic of art and religion Lessing.

In the nineteenth century the German university, which stood for
Lehrfreiheit (freedom in teaching) and *Lernfreiheit* (freedom in
learning), the union of research and the classroom, of the laboratory
and the seminar, was a bright light in civilization's search for knowledge and freedom. Among its leaders were the naturalist von Humboldt and the historian von Harnack. Constantly fighting against
this trend, however, was the drive toward power, represented by
Fichte's plan for a university: "The intellectual and political unity
of the nation requires but a single central university for the education of its elite—the natural state must secure its survival by any
means and is not bound by common laws and treaties." In the two
world wars and the intervening depression, the idea of force won
repeatedly in its battles with the idea of freedom. The tragedy of
the decline and fall of German education and learning occurred.
Professor Ebbinghaus at the reopening of Marburg University after
World War II said:

> One fact remains, unfortunately, all too true. The German
> universities failed while there was still time to oppose publicly,
> with all their power, the destruction of *Wissenschaft* [science] and
> of the democratic state. They failed to keep the beacon of freedom
> and right burning during the night of tyranny so that it could be
> seen by the entire world.[4]

Even a brief study of the conflict of force and freedom in German
education is of vital significance to students of comparative
education.

THE GERMAN PEOPLE AND THE GERMAN LANDS

Germany has been the central power (*das Reich der Mitte*) within
the framework of Europe. It has also been a corridor and conflict
zone with connections and tensions linked to the cultural trends of
the entire continent. The pathology of encirclement has always
been present—encirclement by the British across the North Sea, the

[4] Frederic Lilge, *The Abuse of Learning* (New York: The Macmillan
Company, 1948), p. 170.

French on the western plain, the Russians on the eastern plain, and the Balkan Slavs along the Danube. The country has accurately been referred to as the "German Lands," since it was divided into many principalities until the last quarter of the nineteenth century. In a sense there was an atomization of the country growing out of the varied character of its inhabitants, the many landscape regions and compartments, the religious conflict, and the language conflict. The German Lands have been compared to small and large ice floes colliding, freezing together, and splitting apart.[5] The German people have increasingly sought for unity by force in the last hundred years, whether through the growth of Prussia, the Second Reich, or the Third Reich. The German drive toward unity of people and land, toward a national culture and education, toward a leading role in Europe and the world is a continuing challenge on this planet. The German Lands after World War II were split into zones of occupation and the people were shifted and displaced. However, the old conflict between force and freedom in the search for a pattern of unity continued.

Germany consists of three major physical regions: the new folded Alpine ranges (*Alpen*) in the south; the intermediate old, worn-down mountain lands (*Mittelgebirge*); and the great north-German lowland or plain (*Tiefland*) on the coast of the North Sea. The greater part of Germany is in the intermediate mountain and lowland area which is part of the great European plain. This plain or corridor stretches from eastern England across France, the Netherlands, and Germany into Russia. The soil ranges from sandy heath to rich alluvial and loess deposits. Along the shores of the islands of old rocks in the middle mountain area are great coal fields extending from the Ruhr on the west to Silesia on the east; these provide the industrial base for Germany. Other mineral deposits include light metals, salts, heavy metals, and fertilizer; but there are great resource gaps in oil and iron.

Warm and cold fronts of air masses pass across Germany moving from the milder, temperate marine climate of western Europe and from the harsher climate of Russia and Asia. One of the results is the eternally changing cloudscape or cloud cover which is as characteristic of the German landscape as the predominant clarity is of

[5] Eugen Diesel, *Germany and the Germans* (New York: The Macmillan Company, 1931), pp. 8-9.

the Mediterranean lands. In general the rainfall is sufficient and favorable for agriculture. Germany is a middle area, a corridor land, in climate as in other things.

When one traverses Germany, he sees the historical forces very clearly in the human features of the landscape. The contrast between modern industrial technology and the feudal agricultural past is expressed in the cultural landmarks. The great aristocratic estates, the ecclesiastical cloisters, the fortified medieval towns on the streams symbolize the early agricultural and feudal phase. The structure of the modern power age is superimposed upon this ancient landscape and includes such features as the railroad net, the modern motor roads, and above all the growth of metropolises with their industrial quarters, rental barracks (*Mietskasernen*), and seas of houses (*Häusermeer*). The scars of World War II remain apparent across this landscape in the overwhelming destruction in most urban areas. Within this German landscape an educational pattern has evolved and continues to evolve. What were its major stages of development?

FORMATIVE PHASES OF GERMAN EDUCATION

The pattern of education in Germany mirrors the change in the German culture pattern as it moves through time and space. The historical study of phases of cultural and educational change is essential to an understanding of the walking museum of the past which is Germany's education today. The Reformation and its aftermath was a period in which the land was laid waste and the people decimated. Furthermore, the country was divided into two religious and philosophical camps—the Protestant north and the Catholic south. Each area had many provincial divisions known as *Länder*. Each had a different political background. In many ways the story of the succeeding years was the story of the rise of Prussia to control of this patchwork of states. The period before 1800 was in the main in the dawn of technology; it was characterized by agrarian villages, small cities, and slow tempo of life.

After 1850 the social and educational revolution began to hit Germany with terrific force. Philosophically the romantic idealists, ranging from Goethe to Kant, gave place to realists, ranging from Bismarck to Helmholtz. The country changed from an agrarian to an industrial state and from a patchwork of provinces to a powerful empire which reached out for land and business around the world. Through it all stratification of the various social classes continued —the old farmers and landed nobility, the new middle class of the growing cities, and the government bureaucracy and army. Above all, there was the conflict between force and freedom, and Germany turned in the direction of force, breaking with the common human heritage of the Western world. In the nineteenth century, however, despite the control by reactionaries, there were trends toward democracy and liberalism, shifts to power machines, religious liberty, public education, and world peace. As Croce put it, "Mankind went through one of those moments in which it is completely filled with a happy confidence in itself and its future." In fact, a World Peace Conference convened at Geneva in 1867. But Bismarck and Prussia began to move in the direction of reliance on power. The "blood and iron" philosophy of history was born and the Franco-Prussian War destroyed hopes of peace in Europe and helped begin the vicious alternation between actual war and cold war which has endured through the present.[6]

GENESIS OF PRESENT EDUCATION

The growth of education in Germany reflected the stress of Germany's change from an agglomeration of farming provinces to an empire based upon industry and trade, a strong ruling group, and an efficient armed force. At the beginning of the nineteenth century there was great hope for a trend toward freedom in living and education, despite the fact that Germany's tradition had been education for the few and indoctrination of the masses in obedience. There was great pressure toward progress in education. In Prussia, Frederick William III (1770-1840), after the defeat of the country by Napoleon, listened to liberal ideas expressed by such men as von Humboldt and Süvern, who believed in education as a means of building up Prussia. They spoke for a unified system of education of the democratic ladder type. Each child would have equal opportunity to climb as far as his talents permitted. Thus talent would come to the fore and class distinctions would be wiped out. Progress

[6] Conrad Henry Moehlman, *Understanding the Contemporary World Crisis* (Rochester, N. Y.: Smith, 1941), p. 46.

GERMANY

in education paralleled social reforms of 1807 to 1811. Towns were released from the old feudal control, and peasants began to own land when serfdom was abolished. Prussian schoolmasters studied under the pioneer Pestalozzi in Switzerland and returned to head educational reform. The new elementary education in Prussia gave promise of being the most advanced in the world but was weak within. Horace Mann, who first studied it in operation, admired its efficiency but criticized its narrowness. He pointed out that the mass of people left the schools well before the age of fourteen—too early. They had no school libraries and newspapers were under rigid censorship. Education had no real interest in the "responsibilities of citizenship." It was not practical in that it did not prepare the individual for responsibility. "Government steps in to take care of the subject much as the subject takes care of his cattle."[7]

Mann's searching analysis was an accurate survey of the short life of liberal trends in German education. The Prussian king ordered a shift back to religious and aristocratic control of education aimed at achieving discipline and military obedience; the change was supposed to make the masses happy in their lot and loyal to the monarch. By 1830 the Germans had made the great decision in education which was in many ways to determine their future. The German rulers chose a dual, or "two-track," system of education. The common people went to elementary schools (*Volksschulen*) from the sixth to the fourteenth year. That is, for 90 percent of the population education ceased at fourteen. The upper class, consisting of less than 10 percent, went on to the secondary schools. Furthermore, the choice of those who would go to upper schools was made in the fourth grade, when the child was ten years of age; this procedure has not yet been changed materially.

DICHOTOMY THROUGH EDUCATION

The Germans increasingly worshiped at the shrine of efficiency, order, obedience, practical preparation, and national destiny. The "two-track" system of education produced masses of efficient, skillful laborers, clerks, and technicians who were disciplined and obedient to command; and, at the same time, an elite minority conscious of

[7] Horace Mann, *Annual Reports, 7th Report, 1843* (Boston: Lee and Shepard, 1891), p. 375.

its right and competency to command. Germany became, in spite of its few voices for freedom, a vast and inhuman machine whose power was force. Education helped to create a dichotomy, or division into two parts, an elite and a mass. Such splitting up of human groups assisted reactionary forces in halting Europe's nineteenth-century strugglers for freedom of the individual, of science, and of education, to whom humanity was the measure of all things. The Revolution of 1848 in Germany was supposed to bring freedom in education. But it was suppressed immediately after the Revolution and some of its most able proponents migrated to the United States and contributed to the progress of universal education. The dichotomy went on. The new expansion of Germany was based upon specialization which impoverished the life of the individual in order to advance the destiny of the state. Helmholtz, one of the great German scientists, believed that each student must be satisfied with specializing and with contributing something to the over-all fund of knowledge; that is, he had to give up his general interest in humanity. As Sir Patrick Geddes, the Scottish biologist and city planner, noted, German education produced Philistines in the workshop and pedants in the universities.

In the first part of the nineteenth century, romantic idealism exerted a tremendous influence upon education; it emphasized increased instruction in the German language and history together with insistence upon physical health and vigor. With the coming of the Industrial Revolution and the rise of Prussia, the pressure was headed in the direction of training competent craftsmen, soldiers, and businessmen. The growing empire was concerned with *Realien*, or practical realities. This pressure produced, above all, changes in the secondary schools and in the universities. In the secondary schools two new types of nine-year schools were gradually added to the humanistic *Gymnasium*. The first, the *Realgymnasium*, emphasized the natural sciences and modern foreign languages together with Latin; the second, called the *Realschule*, emphasized natural sciences and modern foreign languages, without the Latin. However, the old *Gymnasium*, with its emphasis upon Greek and Latin, was still the preferred channel to the university and to positions of control in government, the army, and the university. The universities became efficient research and teaching machines with ex-

panding laboratories and seminars for graduate study. Bismarck
emphasized education as an instrument to unify the many and
varied elements in the new empire as William I became emperor
of the new Second Reich in 1871. He tried in 1872 to remove
clerical and religious controls from the schools but failed. The law
of 1872 emphasized vocational and continuation schools, which became very popular in German cities; their purpose was to train
skilled workers for the industrialization of Germany. Education
became highly centralized, with a chain of command like that of
an army. Germans were organized by their educational pattern into
a patriotic and efficient mass accustomed to command by an aristocratic elite.[8]

Until the catastrophe of World War I shattered the German
Empire, German education remained a "two-track" system, controlled from the top by an aristocracy composed of the nobility, the
army officers, the Protestant and Catholic churches, and big business.
At the age of six, children were divided into two groups. The
upper-class children went to the *Vorschule*, which gave them three
years of preparation for entering one of the secondary schools. Of the
secondary schools the *Gymnasium* remained the best channel to
superior station in German life. In order to enter the university
one had to pass a leaving examination called the *Abitur* at the
end of the secondary school. The lower-class children were sent
to the *Volksschule*, which they attended from the sixth to the fourteenth year. This compulsory education from six to fourteen
separated not only the classes but, wherever possible, the sexes as
well. Despite the strong pressure for school reform that followed
the 1890 School Conference in Berlin, very little was accomplished.
Religious control of education, Protestant in the north and Catholic
in the south, continued to be very strong. A few changes were
made by the Prussian government in the direction of sectarian
public schools controlled by the Central Ministry of Education;
but in the main the schools were an instrument for training
efficient workers and soldiers and a commanding elite, and were
used to combat social progress. The Germans sold out to great

[8] O. Boelitz, "Schulreform," in Hermann Gunkel and Leopold Zscharnack,
eds., *Die Religion in Geschichte und Gegenwart* (Tübingen: J. C. B. Mohr,
1931), Vol. V, pp. 298 ff.

armies, colonies, and materialism. The cultural tragedy led to the school tragedy.[9]

THE GERMAN REPUBLIC'S STRUGGLE FOR UNIVERSAL EDUCATION

In the aftermath of World War I there was, at first, great optimism that the Weimar Republic would found a democracy supported by a universal school system. Article 146 of the Constitution of Weimar (1919) attempted to democratize the schools through a new system of common elementary schools. The plan was to give all children a common educational background and to unify social classes. There was to be a revision in the dual system of education, which, together with service in the army as schooling for the people, had supported resort to force rather than belief in freedom. Furthermore, the reform postponed separation of the secondary from the elementary schools until the children were ten years old. At this division point, the new school reform attempted to give the competent children of the lower classes opportunity to move into the secondary schools and eventually into the university by means of free tuition and scholarships. As an important part of the *Einheitsschule* (universal school system), the *Aufbauschule* (progressive or constructive school) was created. This new institution was a four-year secondary school for gifted pupils which was to provide a transition from the eight-year *Volksschule*, or common elementary school, to the university. The less favored classes were at last to have their opportunity for secondary and higher education.

Another attack was made on the dual system in Article 143 of the constitution, which said that elementary-school teachers should be prepared "according to the principles which apply generally to higher education." Article 144 curtailed control of the clergy over clerical elementary-school teachers by providing for full-time professionally trained officials for supervision of schools. In addition, Article 147 attempted to cut down the number of private schools for the aristocratic elite.

The reform attempts of the German Republic were greeted with great optimism. Many German teachers were enthusiastic about

[9] Fritz Kellermann, *The Effect of the World War upon European Education* (Cambridge, Mass.: Harvard University Press, 1928), p. 9.

progressive methods of teaching, expansion of the curriculum, and outdoor activities and projects. However, careful analysis of the situation at the time and later events demonstrated that the idea of universal education in Germany faced serious difficulties. The powerful forces of Germany's past—the *Junker*, the army, the cartels, and the upper social classes—did not intend to release their control. The carrying out of the new reforms in education was left to the provinces, where reactionary pressures in general won out, so that by the 1930's the trend was largely reversed. Nevertheless, in spite of many obstacles, the Social Democrats of the German Republic had accomplished much for all Germans through education. School had been made a more interesting and vital place. In the significant Youth Movement, young people were given an opportunity to know the outdoors and music as a part of life. The place of women in society was materially improved. The Weimar School Reform made a deep impress upon German education and culture which Kellermann summarizes very lucidly:

1. It [the Reform] has created unity and clearness in the school system [*Einheitsschule* experiment].

2. It has diminished caste feeling, by abolishing the private preparatory schools; by substituting the Gymnasia and graduate university work for the elementary teachers' training schools; by placing the different types of Gymnasia on the same standing; by decreasing school fees and increasing stipends for the poor.

3. It has strengthened community spirit, by organizing student self-government, parents' advisory councils, and teachers' study groups; by instituting monthly excursions for all schools; by establishing social school activities, such as exhibitions, concerts, lectures, festivals, sports; by introducing civics as a subject in all schools; and by increasing and deepening the study of German, history, geography.

4. By establishing the four—if the *Realgymnasium alten Stils* is included, five—types of Gymnasia, the Reform has assigned one definite, restricted sphere of culture to each school, thus replacing the superficial, disconnected smattering of knowledge by mastery and depth in one field, and making the courses of each type, not ends, but means, of education.

5. By establishing the *Deutsche Oberschule*, it has founded at last one type of school which devotes itself to a thorough pene-

tration of the finest German culture, the heritage of Luther, Dürer, Goethe, Fichte, Beethoven, Kant, and Humboldt.

6. By establishing the *Aufbauschule*, it has given an opportunity for secondary and higher education, after completion of the elementary school, to exceptionally endowed children of the poorer classes, this quite apart from the fact that the children of the poor now have the same chance with all others to pass on from the Grundschule to the Gymnasium.

7. By establishing a compulsory three-year vocational course for all elementary school graduates, the Reform has offered to all members of the people a free vocational training and an insight into the ethical aspect of vocational work.

8. It has worked out, in the curricula, good illustrations of correlation of subjects for each class and adaptation of subjects to the natural development of the students.[10]

The German Republic's creative contributions to education and general culture were choked off by the growing reversion to force that culminated in seizure of control by Hitler and the National Socialists in 1933. The Nazis proceeded with evil genius to bring about, according to a well-organized plan, a "pathology" in German education and culture.

THE NAZI "PATHOLOGY" IN EDUCATION

The term "pathology" is used advisedly to define the diseased condition of education created in the Nazi phase. The Nazi policy betrayed the true mission of German education and culture, consigning such great German spokesmen for the freedom of humanity as Goethe, Kant, Mann, and Einstein to the shadows. A major migration of German talent and genius, both Gentile and Jewish, was set in motion by the planned persecutions of the Hitler regime. The refugees were catalysts for free Western educational and cultural progress. Meanwhile the Nazis elevated puny interpreters of the demoniac aspects of the German mind: war, race hatred, force. The combined effects of the Nazi policy reduced school life to a sham of military and party routines and utilized all channels of educational communication to brutalize the individual into an obedient slave of a power-mad state.

[10] Fritz Kellermann, *op. cit.*, p. 55.

The German philosophy of education during the Nazi period is clearly set forth in Adolf Hitler's *Mein Kampf*. These memoirs of the *Führer* not only outlined the general Nazi plan of attack but presented the educational theory which was to be utilized therein. Hitler visualized the aims of education in three parts—first, the building up of healthy, pure-blooded German bodies; second, the process of character growth, which included responsibility and loyal obedience to those in authority; third, the giving out of so-called useful practical instruction.[11] Hitler outlined policy and left details to such men as Goebbels, Ley, Rust, and Rosenberg.

The Nazis believed that intellectualism was the reason Germany lost World War I. They felt that education, in producing officials, scientists, writers, and, worst of all, professors, had been weakening the stamina of the Teutons. They felt, furthermore, that the education of boys and girls for the roles of men and women should be quite different and that coeducation weakened the fiber of the race. Above all they emphasized the necessity of obedience to a chain of command which intellectualism, with its belief in freedom, would oppose. As regards instruction, the great emphasis was upon information which would be of direct benefit to the community through its practicality. Instruction in biology and race hygiene was primary. Stress was laid upon the common good of the country, upon unity of the folk above profession or class, and upon all the past history of Germany as a means of teaching narrow racial patriotism and pride.

In actuality the Nazis engaged in a simplification of education which was to give everyone a general training in the National Socialist philosophy through a unified elementary school. A member of the German Ministry of Education in 1936 made clear the method of infiltrating youth in the following statement: "We use teachers of physical education who are closest to boys and girls to drive home the fundamental ideas of National Socialism." The secondary school and the university were de-emphasized except to a select Nazi elite. The paramilitary educational organizations began on the elementary level with the *Pimpf* groups for boys and the *Jungmädel* for girls. The *Hitler Jugend*, or HJ, for boys and its companion, the *Bund Deutscher Mädel*, or BDM, took

[11] Adolf Hitler, *Mein Kampf* (Munich: Verlag Franz Eher, 1933), pp. 452 ff.

over the direction of education for German adolescents of the
secondary-school level. They were educational leagues—one preparing the boys to be good soldiers and citizens and the other
preparing the girls for fields of work peculiar to women. One
leader in the BDM was annoyed by the charge that a girl's education
was based on the "four K's"—*Kinder, Küche, Kleider, Kirche*
(children, kitchen, clothes, and church) and emphasized the broad
preparation of girls for all aspects of future living. After the training in the HJ and BDM came further periods of work identifying
young men and women with the German state. As members of the
Reich Labor Service, the RAD (*Reichs arbeits Dienst*), young men
gave their labor free to the state for two years and were in the
meantime toughened for their army duty. At the same time, the
Women's Labor Service, the FAD (*Frauen arbeits Dienst*), attempted
to bring girls in close contact with rural and domestic pursuits
by means of participation in farm life for some six months, with
labor in the home and fields. The statements of Robert Ley, who
directed the over-all control of all the widespread activities of the
Labor Front, showed that the Nazi party intended to control the
education of the German people virtually from the cradle to
the grave.[12]

Specifically, this meant that the Nazis took over the unified
common elementary school (*Grundschule*) instituted by the Republic. At the close of elementary education—that is, at the tenth
year—the girls' schooling was separated from the boys'. The
secondary-school system was simplified in the Education Act of
1938. The Hitler government abolished all of the sixteen types of
secondary schools existing under the Republic but three: the *Gymnasium*, the *Oberschule*, and the *Aufbauschule*. In addition it set
up a separate system of "Adolf Hitler schools," for selected members of the HJ. These boarding schools admitted members of the HJ
irrespective of financial or social status when they had reached a
certain rank in the HJ. The schools concentrated upon developing
National Socialist leaders; major emphasis was placed on national
political education, physical education, and military subjects. In
other words, in the elementary field the National Socialists moved
in the direction of the universal school to build up proper party-

[12] Gregor Ziemer. *Education for Death* (New York: Oxford University
Press, 1941).

line ideas concerning health, obedience, race, and soil; then they moved toward an elite system to train Nazi leaders in the secondary schools and the university; at the same time, they provided in governmental organizations such as the HJ and BDM a continuation schooling to produce soldiers, workers, housewives, and mothers. Intellectualism was de-emphasized. The Nazis propagandized the doctrine that the mass of people were better off with a carefully planned postschool program, living prescribed lives in secure niches of work, motherhood, and service for the national state. Above all, they concentrated upon the German *Volk*, or nation, as the ultimate ideal, not recognizing the value of other culture patterns. They did not understand that the ideals of all humanity are more significant than that of a particular *Volk*.[13] Nevertheless, the Nazis emerged with an educational instrument that seemed efficient and satisfying, with its so-called common-sense pattern of a healthy body, loyal character, practical instruction for government-planned careers, and security.

THE ZONAL PHASE IN GERMAN EDUCATION

The joint efforts of the Nazi Central Ministry of Education and of the paramilitary educational organizations of the Nazi party had created a ponderous and distorted instrument of education which disintegrated in the course of World War II and left a type of educational vacuum. The military forces of the United States, Great Britain, and France completed the last stages of Operation Eclipse and met the Russians on the Elbe line in the spring of 1945. The occupation of Germany and the zonal phase in German education got under way. The new arrangement included the Russian zone, in eastern Germany; the British zone, in the northwest; the American zone, comprising central and southern Germany and the Bremen enclave; and the French zone, in the lower Rhine area. In addition, the Berlin area was divided into four miniature occupation sectors isolated in the midst of the Russian area. The zonal powers stated their educational policy in the Potsdam agreement of 1945: "German education shall be so controlled as to eliminate completely National-Socialist and Militarist doctrines

[13] George F. Kneller, *The Educational Philosophy of National Socialism* (New Haven: Yale University Press, 1941).

and to make possible the successful development of democratic ideas" (Section III, Par. 7). The "re-education" of some 70 million Germans was projected.

The tremendous task encountered serious obstacles which may be summarized as follows. Germany was now a country occupied by four different military governments splitting it into zones separating agricultural from industrial areas and superimposing four governmental systems. German children and adults faced a group of conquerors with power and privilege—scarcely a situation to help win them over to democracy. Furthermore, all zones included both German refugees overcrowding limited local housing and displaced persons segregated in camps. German children heard their parents talk about "those loafers from the east," or "those Polish swine," and the old ideas about inferior races were hardly dispelled thereby. Moreover, some one third of the German children in the beginning years of school were without fathers and will grow up without fathers. Added to this was the mass destruction of housing, nearly one half of the dwellings in the larger cities being uninhabitable, and a broken rail and road system which threatened famine in many urban areas.

The educational system itself was in chaos. The loss of teachers had been high through liquidation by the Nazis and war casualties; some teachers are still being held as prisoners of war. The students had been scattered by the thrusts of war, evacuation, and economic conditions unsuitable for any type of education. The German school plant had been destroyed or requisitioned for military purposes; the textbooks heavily infected with the Nazi "pathology" had to be pulped. The denazification program led to dismissal of approximately half the former teachers.

The occupying powers as early as July 1945 began to reopen schools, each utilizing the blueprints of its own planners. In spite of emergency measures the teacher-pupil ratio in the American zone alone was one teacher to eighty pupils. The "shift system" made maximum use of the limited school plant. Textbooks were produced by reprinting those used during the Weimar Republic. School lunches were instituted to combat the general malnutrition of children. The opening of elementary schools progressed through 1945. The secondary schools and universities were opened in the winter of 1945-1946.

Meanwhile long-range school reform was being discussed. In 1947 the four powers agreed on a directive which may be summarized as follows:

1. There should be equal educational opportunity for all.

2. Tuition, textbooks, and other necessary scholastic materials should be provided free of charge in all educational institutions; in addition, maintenance grants should be made to those who need aid.

3. Compulsory full-time school attendance should be required for all children between the ages of six and at least fifteen; thereafter, for those pupils not enrolled in full-time educational institutions, part-time attendance should be compulsory up to the age of eighteen.

4. Schools for the compulsory period should form a comprehensive educational system. The terms "elementary education" and "secondary education" should mean two consecutive levels of instruction, not two types or qualities of instruction which overlap.

5. All schools should lay emphasis upon education for civic responsibility and a democratic way of life, by means of the content of the curriculum, textbooks and other materials of instruction, and organization of the school itself.

6. School curriculums should aim to promote understanding of and respect for other nations, and to this end attention should be given to the study of modern languages, without prejudice to any.

7. Educational and vocational guidance should be provided for all students.

8. Health supervision and health education should be provided for all students. In addition, instruction should be given in hygiene.

9. All teacher education should take place in a university or in a pedagogical institution of university rank.

10. Full provision should be made for effective participation of the people in the reform and organization, as well as in the administration, of the educational system.

However, the four-power directive was implemented in very different fashion in the eastern and western zones. The available data seems to indicate that the Soviet zone has used the directive to set up a unified school system intended to assist materially in indoctrinating Germans in the Communist way of life. By September

1945 the Russian zone had set up a central administration for education with its seat in Berlin. The Russians were very direct in their program to promote educational reform. The central administrative group in Berlin, composed of Germans trusted by the Russians, drew up a tentative school law which the Soviet military authorities approved and which was carried out. The new Soviet-zone school system was described as follows:

1. Education in schools was exclusively the responsibility of the state.

2. Religious teaching was the responsibility of religious corporations; details were to be regulated by directives.

3. The form of public education, which was the same for boys and girls, was an organically articulated (*organisch gegliedertes*) democratic school system—the democratic *Einheitsschule*.

Further directives issued in July 1946 stated in addition to (1) that the responsibility of the state was not merely supervisory. They explicitly forbade private schools of any kind, even private kindergartens or vocational schools. The Soviet zone claimed to have instituted a democratic system of unified schools. At one stroke the Soviet zone barred state-supported schools which were staffed and supervised by church authorities; this was quite in contrast to the policy of the western zones.

In the Soviet zone the system included a primary school (*Grundstufe*) for children from six to fourteen. The last two years were really a middle school in which languages and sciences were taught. The next stage was organized into four types of schools: (1) the upper school (*Oberschule*), providing four years of preparation for the university, (2) continuation schools (*Berufsschulen*), designed for the part-time education of young workers, (3) trade schools (*Fachschulen*), for full-time general and vocational education, and (4) folk high schools and evening schools, for adult education.

When closely scrutinized the Soviet system reveals the continental tendency toward specialization in the secondary schools. It also includes the payment of school fees. In actuality the Russians installed an elite, or "two-track," system, which favored followers of the party line. Furthermore, a reversion was made to the supercentralization which the Nazis introduced in their first Central Ministry of Education in 1934. The Central Administration for National Education (*Zentralverwaltung für Volksbildung*), in Berlin, was empowered to use the closely controlled Soviet-zone school system for re-educating the German people under a new label in the old tradition, which had already brought tragedy to Germany.

The western zones wished to have the Germans participate democratically in the long-range school reform envisaged to provide equal educational opportunity. The British, French, and American zones encouraged the Germans to take responsibility for the transition to the next phase in educational development. A central ministry for education was not set up and given a directive to follow, as in the eastern zone. The tendency of the Germans was to resist school reform and revert to their "two-track" system with a supposed elite going on to the secondary school and university. The Germans argued that funds were never sufficient to permit large numbers of children to stay in school beyond the age of fourteen years. Security and stability of social structure were supported by the specialized secondary schools. The Germans felt that the standards of secondary-school work would suffer if students of various abilities were mixed together. They stated that all "gifted" children could be detected by subjective examination at the age of ten and assisted to enter secondary schools.

Furthermore the traditional control of the Lutheran and Catholic churches in the school system was to a large degree reinstated. The German Empire and the Weimar Republic—the latter under protest—had permitted the separate states to determine the organization of elementary schools on a confessional basis. The Third Reich had finally eliminated the confessional schools during the war. The western zones in 1946 agreed to the re-establishment of confessional or denominational schools where they had existed before 1933 and where the parents of a sufficient number of children desired them. Predominantly Roman Catholic areas in Westphalia, the Rhineland, and Bavaria revealed a strong demand for confessional schools. The German local authorities had restored religious instruction to its pre-Nazi position in the curriculum without prompting.

The general pattern of education in the western zones of Germany was not altered drastically and had a regional character ranging from the liberal tradition of the Hansa city of Hamburg to the relatively conservative tradition of Bavaria. The pre-Nazi practice of beginning the school year after the Easter holidays was put in force again. The crucial point in the "two-track" educational system was retained—separation of a small elite class of fee-paying students at ten years of age to enter upon specialized secondary and higher education. Four years in the primary section (*Grundschule*) of the elementary school (*Volksschule*) was compulsory for all children between the ages of six and ten. At this point there was a three-way division according to social and economic class. About 90 percent of all children continued until the age of fourteen in the second half, or senior section, of the elementary school. Then they entered into apprenticeship and attended a part-time vocational school (*Fachschule*), before taking jobs in the various trades or commerce.

The pupils from the lower middle class at the age of ten entered the six-year intermediate school (*Mittelschule*), which prepared them for lower civil-service positions, trade, industry, and commerce. A few of the abler students went on and prepared for the university at an *Aufbauschule*, a boarding school with low fees. Approximately the same number of students enrolled in the intermediate as in the secondary schools.

The upper middle class and upper class attended one of the two basic secondary schools of Germany—the *Gymnasium* and the *Oberschule*. The students were selected partly on the basis of a subjective examination and the ability to pay fees. The *Oberschule* and the *Gymnasium* differed in their emphasis upon languages. In both, German, history, mathematics, physics, chemistry, biology, art, geography, and religion were taught. Biology and physical education have been reduced to minor subjects since 1945. Under the act of 1938 they were major subjects, physical education being devoted to improvement of the German youth, and a racial biology (*Rassenkunde*) to the philosophy that the German race is supreme. In the *Gymnasium*, English, Latin, and Greek were the major foreign languages. The *Oberschule* had two divisions—one for those majoring in natural sciences and one for those majoring in foreign languages. In these two divisions the curriculum for the first four years was identical. Four years of English and two years of Latin were required. After the first four years those students wishing to major in languages had to take French as an additional foreign language, and those majoring in natural sciences discontinued the study of languages entirely.

For example, a student completing the *Gymnasium* had a total of eight years of English, six years of Latin, and four years of Greek. A student completing the *Oberschule* with a foreign-language major had a total of eight years of English, six years of Latin, and four years of French. A student completing the *Oberschule* with a natural-science major had a total of four years of English and two years of Latin.

After the completion of eight years of secondary school the pupil was required to pass an examination (*Reifeprüfung*) before receiving his final degree (*Abitur*). Only the holder of this degree could be admitted to a university.

Some simplification occurred, but the secondary schools were still specialized educational instruments limited to certain social classes. Some areas in the north de-emphasized the *Gymnasium* and built up the role of the *Oberschule*. In fact it was even contemplated that the *Gymnasium* should be eliminated entirely and that the *Oberschule* should become a tuition-free continuation of the elementary school. In Bavaria the "two-track" system persisted very strongly, with only some 6.4 percent of the children advancing to the special schools. The *Gymnasium* was strongly entrenched as the traditional route to high position for the elite.

The universities in all the western zones were overcrowded and had meager staffs and facilities, but showed a recrudescence of the true spirit of German higher education before its failure. The rector of the newly reopened University of Mainz, which was located in the French zone, after criticizing "Prussianism as the precursor of Nazism," discussed the role of the new university: "a University is conceived in the classic spirit, which teaches and tests knowledge in the widest sense of the word, and which, going far beyond mere specialization, introduces the student to the important general tasks and the vital questions of our time, and which exerts itself to preserve and develop social progress, human liberty, and the increase of material well-being." But university faculties were also concerned over the desire of students to prepare for a good job—and to avoid politics and a social consciousness.

The western zones gave the Germans freedom of choice and responsibility in their educational future. There has been evidence of distinct resistance to school reform and educational progress, but there have been marked gains which can be laid to the people and their own struggle for freedom. A new generation of elementary- and secondary-school teachers is being trained upon a basis of equality. Progress has been made in changing the four-year elementary school into a six-year unit, thereby raising the time of selection of students for secondary school from the tenth year to the twelfth year. The educational profession has been revitalized by regional meetings in which ideas and plans can be discussed freely. The German heritage of freedom has reappeared in the reprinting of books banned by Hitler, in the new radio programs, in the revived press and periodicals as channels of communication. The folk high school, the people's universities, and other instruments of informal education have opened up new vistas for the long isolated German mind. Perhaps most important are the interchanges of teachers and administrators on all levels between Germany and the occupying powers, including youth leaders, professors, and teachers in all fields.

The peaceful future of Europe cannot be achieved unless Germany moves toward a new freedom based upon equal opportunity in education. All of the occupying powers struggled for freedom in education—Britain from 1870 to the Education Act of 1944; France from Condorcet's blueprint of universal education to the *école unique* and the Langevin Plan of 1947; the United States from before the Revolution to the twentieth-century stages of universal education; and Russia from the decrees of 1782 which called for free secular education for both sexes to the post-1917 preliminary advances in education and the subsequent regression. Germany had her own tradition of freedom in education in the nineteenth-century liberals and the twentieth-century Social Democrats. Fundamentally those who struggled for educational freedom were all part of a common culture with common educational problems which they all participated in solving. The manner in which education is manipulated in Germany during this zonal stage, and the choices that are made between force and freedom, may be the index to Germany's future and even to that of the rest of the world.

A realistic estimate of the educational situation in the German Lands must always include mention of certain pressures. The democracies of the western zones and the dictatorship of the eastern zone have engaged in a great ideological and cultural struggle between freedom and force—a struggle which extends around the strategic rim of Eurasia. In the course of this conflict the advocates of force may find their opportunity to burst forth again: the imperialists, the officer corps, the General Staffs, the cartels, the Fascists, and the Communists. The development of German education mirrors the course of the continuing conflict between force and freedom.

BIBLIOGRAPHY

BARON, SALO WITTMAYER, *Modern Nationalism and Religion* (New York: Harper & Brothers, 1947). An analysis of the interaction of state and religion and of its many implications for indigenous educational development. Baron's studies provide excellent source data in relation to German education.

BURCKHARDT, JAKOB, *Weltgeschichtliche Betrachtungen* (Basel, 1929). Also a translation by James Hastings Nichols entitled *Force and Freedom* (New York: Pantheon Books, Inc., 1943) with an excellent biographical introduction.

BUTTS, FREEMAN, *A Cultural History of Education* (New York: McGraw-Hill Book Company, Inc., 1947). A useful general reference on German education in its cultural setting.

CASSIRER, ERNST, *An Essay on Man* (New Haven: Yale University Press, 1944). A valuable investigation into a possible philosophy of human culture based upon the symbol as the clue to the nature of man. Since education is a major social instrument for giving people control of the common human symbols, this book, by a great refugee German philosopher, is of fundamental significance.

DIESEL, EUGEN, *Germany and the Germans* (New York: The Macmillan Company, 1931). A thoughtful analysis of German cultural growth.

————, *Land der Deutschen* (Berlin: Bibliographisches Institut, 1933). A remarkable summary of the German landscape, illustrated with aerial photographs.

GUNKEL, HERMANN, and LEOPOLD ZSCHARNACK, eds., *Die Religion in Geschichte und Gegenwart* (Tübingen: J. C. B. Mohr, 1931),

5 vols. This encyclopedia of religion, known by German scholars as the RGG, was one of the last flowerings of German scholarship before the deluge of modern barbarism. It contains invaluable source material on German education.

HITLER, ADOLF, *Mein Kampf* (Munich: Verlag Franz Eher, 1933). The memoirs and blueprints of the Nazi *Führer*, which provide the source statements on Nazi educational policy.

KANDEL, I. L., *Comparative Education* (Boston: Houghton Mifflin Company, 1933). A classic contribution to the field.

KELLERMANN, FRITZ, *The Effect of the World War on European Education* (Cambridge, Mass.: Harvard University Press, 1928). Contains a detailed analysis of and a broad philosophic insight into postwar German education.

KNELLER, GEORGE F., *The Educational Philosophy of National Socialism* (New Haven: Yale University Press, 1941). An outstanding analysis of the Nazi period in education.

LILGE, FREDERIC, *The Abuse of Learning* (New York: The Macmillan Company, 1948). A fine study of the failure of the German university as an integral part of the breakdown of German education and culture.

RUSSELL, BERTRAND, *A History of Western Philosophy* (New York: Simon & Schuster, Inc., 1945). A unique historical and structural analysis of the relationship of philosophy, education, and culture.

SEYDLITZ'SCHE, E. VON, ed., *Geographie Deutschland* (Breslau: Ferdinand Hirt, 1925). A useful reference compiled by a group of able German geographers.

U. S. DEPARTMENT OF STATE, *Report of the United States Education Mission to Germany* (Washington, D. C.: U. S. Government Printing Office, 1946).

The Year Book of Education, 1948 (London: Evans Brothers Ltd., 1948). Excellent monographs on educational developments in the four zones.

ZIEMER, GREGOR, *Education for Death* (New York: Oxford University Press, 1941). An illuminating account of education's role in making Nazis; based on considerable field study.

10 · EDUCATION IN Scandinavia

HERBERT SCHUELER

Despite its small population, Scandinavia constitutes an important area in Europe. Their high level of education, technology, and culture has enabled the Scandinavians to make the best possible use of their resources in building up a very advanced standard of living and culture. Scandinavia may be defined as including the countries of Denmark, Sweden, and Norway and the adjacent islands.

Denmark has an area of about 16,575 square miles and a population of over 4,230,000. It is in the main a peninsula made up of associated islands thrusting out into the North Sea from the central-European area. The low, rolling plains have sandy soil and very little in the way of mineral resources. However, by an amazing combination of education and technology the Danes have built up a world-famous dairy industry and agricultural system. The fishing industry and maritime trade are major sources of income. The Danes led in the establishment of cooperatives, especially for handling dairy products. They also pioneered in the setting up of folk high schools to educate young people beyond the elementary school in the history and culture of their country as well as in improved agricultural procedures. Grundtvig was the Danes' great pioneer in education. Not only Scandinavia but all of Europe benefited from his work in establishing the folk high schools in the nineteenth century.

Sweden is the largest of the Scandinavian countries, with an area of 173,426 square miles and a population of close to 7 million; it comprises the eastern half of the Scandinavian peninsula. The country is mountainous and forested but has a large amount of low land in the south and more good productive land in valleys of the peninsula. The Swedes are characterized by a very high level of education and technology, which they have utilized to build up an unusually fine standard of living. Sweden has a highly developed agricultural system and is noted for fine forestry and associated industries. Manufactures are extensive, including textiles, paper, and iron. Sweden's mineral resources are excellent; she has the world's best supply of almost pure iron. The Swedes have also developed hydroelectric power to a high degree of efficiency. Economically speaking, they have pioneered in a combination of capitalism and cooperatives which has brought them unusual stability and a fine distribution of income. Educationally speaking, the Swedes are outstanding; emphasis has traditionally been upon education of the very highest quality.

Norway occupies the western part of the Scandinavian peninsula. The area of the country is over 124,500 square miles and the population approximately 3,250,000. Norway may be described as an essentially maritime country with only a limited amount of land available for cultivation because of the rugged nature of the country. Norway has utilized its forest resources and hydroelectric power very intelligently and extensively. The farm economy is combined with fishing and forestry. For her size Norway has always had one of the richest merchant fleets in the world and has played an important role in the world's cod, herring, and whale fishing. Mining—especially nickel mining—is important. As in the rest of Scandinavia, there is almost no illiteracy and the educational system is well developed in the direction of a universal type. The folk high school has also been valuable here.

—A. H. M.

The countries of Scandinavia have long exercised an influence on civilization out of all proportion to their size. The combined population of the three countries is less than 15 million, the usable land area relatively small, and the density of population, in Norway and Sweden at least, far below the European average. Although the fluctuations of European and world economy in the twentieth century have not failed to affect them, the countries of Scandinavia have managed to maintain a standard of living significantly above that of their neighbors to the south, with a gap between the rich and the poor much smaller than in most other countries. The reasons for this relative economic comfort of the Scandinavians are within the realm of controversy. The Scandinavians themselves tend to give major credit to the advanced social-welfare program in which the countries of Scandinavia have long pioneered. Another major contributory factor has undoubtedly been their ability to remain aloof from most of the violent international political upheavals of the last one hundred years. To be sure, both Norway and Denmark suffered occupation by the Germans during the last war, but only Norway was seriously impaired thereby, and Sweden managed to maintain her neutrality.

Politically the countries of Scandinavia are constitutional monarchies in which the function of the monarch is analogous to that of the king of England. The controlling power of government is vested in the people, who elect parliamentary bodies through systems of universal suffrage. The dissemination of culture is wide and the participation of all classes of people in community and national affairs is high. The literacy rate is among the highest in the world —probably as near to 100 percent as it is possible to get. (In the United States the literacy rate is about 2½ percent lower.)

In their application of political, social, and economic principles, the Scandinavian countries have been called the countries of the "middle way"; they have steered a course midway between the extremes of state monopoly and private monopoly. That they have been able to do so in the face of the violent international upheavals of the last hundred years, helped by geographical factors, to be sure, is due in fundamental part to a sane and practical idealism that pervades the social thinking of the people. Their interest is not so much in theory and dogma as in life and what makes it better, and in the process of discovering and applying ways to make life better they have become a notable example of a people who have acted with a degree of reason and reasonableness that is unique in the modern world.

In no other country is social collectivism and private capitalism as coextensive as in the Scandinavian countries. In Sweden, for example, public utilities are owned and operated by local governments; the majority of urban housing units are state financed and under either municipal or cooperative control; 80 percent of the railroads and 50 percent of the airlines are state owned and operated. On the other hand, 95 percent of all industrial workers are privately employed, and all the arable land is privately tilled. Almost all of the farmers, however, are members of the processing and marketing cooperatives.[1] The same theme of coextensive state and private collectivism and private capitalism is true, with variations, of Denmark and Norway.

Whatever one's opinion may be regarding the so-called "welfare state" as a means of achieving economic and social stability, it must be recognized that the Scandinavian countries have been providing a social laboratory of public-welfare practices for the last half century. As early as 1892 Denmark had old-age pensions and health insurance. By now virtually every person in Scandinavia is protected, either through private cooperatives or through the state, from loss of security due to illness, disability, age, unemployment, low income, and even additions to the family. Although the people of all three countries are united behind the ideal of social welfare, it is typical of them that they achieve the ideal in different ways. In Denmark, for example, where virtually every person is covered by social insurance, the basis for social insurance is largely private and voluntary, whereas in Sweden the state plays a larger part and the trend is toward a greater proportion of compulsory features. (Beginning in 1951, health insurance, for example, is to be compulsory.)

The collectivism of Scandinavia is to a high degree voluntary and not imposed. The imperative is of the first person, not the second: not "Work together!" but "Let us work together!" That education must take its proper share of the responsibility and the credit for this widespread and voluntary acceptance of the philosophical and material advantages of cooperative effort is evident, and it makes a study of the education of Scandinavian countries particularly pertinent for educators in other lands.

WAR AND POSTWAR PROBLEMS IN EDUCATION

The late war affected the three Scandinavian countries differently. The occupation in Denmark was quite unlike the occupation in

[1] A thorough and most readable account of the Scandinavian way of using the advantages of both collectivism and private initiative is Marquis W. Childs, *Sweden, the Middle Way* (New Haven: Yale University Press, 1939).

Norway. In Denmark, there was little attempt on the part of the German occupation authorities to effect changes in the social and cultural life of the people. The schools were left remarkably free of molestation, especially in what they taught; the advanced social legislation was left intact and operative, and the physical damage to the country was small. In Norway, on the other hand, the Nazis not only attempted to effect the tactical advantages of military occupation but tried with dramatic lack of success to make over the cultural, social, political, and educational life to conform to their own pattern. The resistance was bitter and the consequences were immediately tragic, but ultimately the invaders failed abjectly. Particularly inspiring in the Norwegian resistance was the stand taken by the teachers. As one step in the attempted nazification of the schools, a central association of teachers was established, patterned after the corresponding organization in Germany to which all teachers had to belong. On April 9, 1942, the great majority of teachers in Norway signed a letter of resignation from the *Norges Laerersamband,* which included the following eloquent pledge to their pupils:

We have been entrusted with the task of giving you children that knowledge and training in thorough work which is necessary if you are to receive full and many-sided development as human beings, so that each one of you can take his or her place in the community for the benefit of himself and others. We have been given this calling by the Norwegian people, and the Norwegian people can call us to account for it. We also know that the sum total of knowledge and labor capacity which a country disposes of is the greatest and most durable of all its sources of wealth. It is our duty to protect those values. We should be untrue to our vocation if we did not devote all our energies to the service of this task, especially in this period of affliction through which we are now living. Every restriction on the activity of the school undermines the foundation on which our people's future must be built.

The teacher's vocation, however, is not only to give the children knowledge. He must also teach the children to believe in and desire that which is true and just. He is therefore unable to teach anything which is in conflict with his conscience without betraying his calling. Anyone who does so is committing a wrong both against the pupils whom he should lead and against himself.

That, I promise you, I will never do. I will never ask you to do anything which I consider to be wrong, nor will I teach you anything which in my opinion is not in accordance with the truth. As hitherto, I will let my conscience be my guide, and I believe that I shall then be in agreement with the great majority of the people who have entrusted me with my educational duties.[2]

As a result of such resistance many schools were closed and teachers put into prison and concentration camps. At one time the entire student body and faculty of the institutions of higher education in Oslo were arrested. Very few teachers turned Quisling. Many teachers without schools went underground and carried on their educational work in private homes. As a consequence, the immediate postwar period found the Norwegian people with educational problems which were mainly physical. There was little need to denazify Norwegian teachers, but schools had to be rebuilt and re-established. In addition, the reforms in education embodied into law between 1935 and 1940, the application of which had been interrupted by the war, had to be carried out. These reforms established the "unity school principle," called for common schooling in elementary schools up to the age of fourteen for all children (see the discussion below, under "Elementary Education"), and provided for a considerable expansion of school facilities. The postwar problems in education in Norway are therefore mainly problems of rebuilding and expansion.

Sweden's educational system has been in the process of fundamental re-examination since 1940, when the first of a series of school commissions was established to make a thorough examination of the aims and the organization of Swedish education. Definite proposals for fundamental changes were submitted in 1948 and are still under study.[3] The changes proposed envision an educational ladder very much like the one established under the new

[2] Quoted in Nils Hjelmtveit, *Education in Norway* (London: Hodder and Stoughton, Ltd., 1946), p. 16. The complete text of the letter is quoted in I. L. Kandel, ed., *Educational Yearbook of the International Institute, 1944* (New York: Teachers College, Columbia University, 1944), pp. 265-266.

[3] *Statens Offentliga Utredningar: 1946 ars skolkommissions betänkande 1948* (Official State Investigation: Proceedings for 1948 of the 1946 School Commission) (Stockholm, 1948).

English system; secondary as well as elementary education would be made available to all, and economic barriers to equal educational opportunity would be removed by the abolition or lowering of fees and the extension of scholarships and loans. In addition, Sweden, like England and the United States, must face the problems of an increased birth rate and a serious undersupply of teachers and school buildings.

GENERAL ORGANIZATION AND ADMINISTRATION

Extent of Education. Even though education in Scandinavia is compulsory only from age seven to age fourteen, significantly large numbers of the population receive education beyond the compulsory limit. In Norway, for example, over 70 percent of the school population attends full-time school beyond the age of fourteen. In addition, the extensive use of adult education by all levels of the adult population in Scandinavia is unmatched in any other part of the world. (In Sweden, it is estimated that 50 percent of the adult population makes use of some form of organized adult education.)

Elementary and secondary education are usually public, and many of the small number of private schools that do exist receive public financial support and are subject to inspection. In fact, it is rather at the adult level than at the elementary and secondary levels that private education is at all a factor (see the discussion below, under "Adult Education"). In Norway, which has the fewest private schools, 99.5 percent of all children to the age of fourteen go to public school; in Denmark and Sweden the figure is nearer 90 percent.

The tradition of public education in Scandinavia goes back as far as the sixteenth century, when it arose as a part of the urge toward popular enlightenment ushered in by the Reformation; it was not really until the beginning of the nineteenth century, however, that the ideal was realized to any significant extent. (A royal decree of 1739 required that parish schools be established in Norway and Denmark for elementary instruction in Christian knowledge and the three R's, but it was only partially applied.) The first real steps toward the establishment of a system of public education were taken in 1814 in Norway and Denmark and in

1842 in Sweden. From that time to the present the participation
of the public, in both local and national bodies, in the administration and support of education has steadily increased. All three countries now have a comprehensive system of essentially free education,
comprising all levels, supported by public funds, and open to all
with the required age and aptitude qualifications.

Administration of Education. Administration and control of
education are vested in both local and national bodies. All three
countries have national ministries of education whose powers of
inspection, certification, and examination, although considerable
and calculated to maintain standards of achievement, are tempered
by direct controls exercised by local bodies.

Local bodies vary somewhat in their composition and responsibilities. Denmark has a system of local education committees appointed by local government councils. In urban districts these
committees are appointed by municipal or town councils; in rural
districts they are appointed by parish councils. In rural districts
there is, in addition, a higher body, the county board, appointed
by the county council, to which the local parish committees are
responsible. Both the county boards and the municipal boards are
responsible to the Ministry. In addition, parents' councils may be
established for each school if the parents so desire. These parents'
councils have the power of school inspection and may assist the
boards of education in the selection of teachers.

In Norway and Sweden there is a similar system of local bodies
subject both to local government councils and the Ministry. In
Norway the composition of the local boards is unique in some
features. Not only must the local boards be representative of the
community at large, but the teachers elect one of their number
and the bishop of the state church appoints a clergyman to membership. The latter feature is all that remains of the once considerable
control over the schools exercised by the state church.

In all three countries there is more local control at the elementary
level than there is at the secondary level. At the secondary level
many state schools are administered nationally, especially in Sweden,
where secondary education is largely a national administrative
responsibility. In Norway each state secondary school is administered
by a board with membership from both the local board of education and the Ministry. In Denmark there are both locally and

nationally administered schools above the elementary level. In general, however, despite some differences among the three countries and within each country, one can say that the administration of elementary education and the administration of secondary education are largely the responsibility of different boards of control. This feature is in marked contrast to the practice in the United States of administering all public schools through the secondary level by means of one common system of control.

Financing Education. Local and national governments share in the support of education. The proportion of the total assumed by each varies with the financial ability of the local authorities and with the type of school. In general the amount of state support is proportionately larger in the higher levels. A characteristic pattern of support is the following: For elementary schools the local community assumes the cost of the school premises and their upkeep and as much of the teachers' salaries as it is able, and the state contributes the equipment, the supplies, part of the teachers' salaries, and whatever welfare services are offered—dental care, transportation, etc. In Norway the total expenditure for education is divided about equally between the community and the state. In 1936-1937 the state contributed 54 million kroner (approximately 11 million dollars) and the local governments 53 million (10¾ million dollars); these amounts represented 14.7 and 20.8 percent of the total budget expenditures respectively. The percentage of total state and local government expenditures devoted to education amounted to 17.2. The figures for Denmark and Sweden are comparable.

Characteristic of Scandinavia is the practice of giving state grants to educational endeavors that are under private or semipublic auspices and control. This is especially true of the many programs of adult education. In Denmark, for example, the work of the folk high schools and the Workers' Educational Union, although essentially private and free of government control, is in part subsidized by the state (see the section below called "Adult Education"). In addition, all three governments have long made a practice of offering grants to students at the secondary and higher levels of education, to enable them to continue their studies. In 1946, to cite an example, Sweden introduced a grant system for students in

secondary schools who must live away from home in order to attend
state schools. Grants range from 500 kronor ($100) to over 1000
kronor per student annually, depending on the need.

ELEMENTARY EDUCATION

Each of the three countries has a common elementary school
which all children (with comparatively few exceptions in separate
private schools) attend at the beginning of their school careers.
However, the number of years of common elementary schooling
is at present different in each country.

Norway. The longest common schooling is embodied in the
Norwegian elementary or "people's" school, which extends from
the age of six or seven to the age of fourteen and forms the basis
for all further schooling. It is attended by 99.5 percent of all children in the appropriate age brackets. Attendance is compulsory and
tuition is free. In remote areas where daily transportation is feasible,
pupils are transported to and from central schools at public expense, and where transportation is not feasible boarding schools
are provided and the children are boarded at public expense.

The curriculum of the Norwegian people's school is comprehensive. It includes religious instruction, the Norwegian language,
arithmetic, drawing, singing, geography, history, natural science,
physical training, and handicrafts. English has been introduced
recently in the upper years, and domestic science is compulsory in
the larger town schools. Fixed standards are set by the Ministry
for each subject; textbooks must be chosen from an approved list
published by the Ministry.

In all urban and in many rural districts medical and dental
service is available to school children free of charge. At most
schools the children are served a free meal (the "Oslo breakfast").
In addition, all textbooks and supplies for both academic and handicraft instruction are provided free of charge.

For those who do not enter secondary or trade schools, many
local education authorities have established continuation schools,
open to all and frequently compulsory for the first year. In some
districts these continuation schools have had the effect of raising
the compulsory schooling age to fifteen and even beyond. They are
of two types: academic and vocational. The academic type usually

gives instruction in mathematics, Norwegian, hygiene, history, and citizenship. A movement is gathering momentum to make continuation school compulsory for all who do not take advantage of secondary or vocational education.

Denmark. In Denmark, common schooling extends only to the eleventh year. From eleven to fifteen (the so-called "middle school" years), students are placed either in an academic school or division which makes them eligible, when they have passed a uniform leaving examination, for academic secondary schools, or in a general or extended elementary school which is usually terminal but may lead to trade and technical schools or free continuation schools. In the extended elementary school there is no uniform leaving examination. In the practice of establishing at the eleventh year a twofold division of students—(1) those who will be prepared for secondary and higher education and (2) those who will receive terminal elementary or trade education—Denmark follows the traditional European dual pattern, from which England divorced itself in 1944, which American educational advisors are trying to induce educators in Germany to abandon, and which Sweden will in all probability abandon in the near future. As in Norway, the trend is toward the amalgamation of small rural schools into central schools. Bus service is provided; where that is not possible, children are furnished with bicycles.

The curriculum is set by law. It includes religious instruction, reading, writing, arithmetic, history, geography, nature study, physical training and manual subjects (woodwork for boys, and sewing and home economics for girls). The requirements in physical education are elaborate and include hygiene and health instruction, gymnastics and games, and compulsory baths. Academic subjects are required to be taught with applications to present-day interests: history must include sociology, nature study must include emphasis on hygiene and physics, and in general the work of especially the senior classes is to be geared to the occupational and social life of the environment.[4] As in Norway, medical and dental care are available universally, at least in municipal and town schools, and free school meals are given widely.

Sweden. In Sweden the educational ladder is not uniform at the

___

[4] *Social Denmark, A Survey of the Danish Social Legislation* (Copenhagen: Socialt Tidsskrift, 1947), p. 351.

present time but will probably develop, insofar as the relationship between elementary and secondary education is concerned, into a system comparable to the British and the Norwegian. The period of common schooling is usually up to the age of eleven, as in Denmark, after which several patterns of separation are applied. Children who show promise early may leave for a secondary school after the fourth grade (at eleven); others may transfer after the sixth grade (at thirteen). Those who are left behind remain in the elementary school another year and attend continuation school for a year after that, or stay in the elementary school two more years. There are also trade elementary schools, which can be entered after the seventh or eighth grade, and so-called higher elementary schools, which can be entered after the sixth grade. In sum, therefore, elementary education may comprise four, six, seven, eight, or even ten years, depending on how the selective process is applied and on what pattern of schools is available in each locality. Present recommendations for change seek to achieve greater uniformity and above all greater equality of opportunity and a longer period of common schooling. A nine-year period of common schooling (the "citizen's school") is proposed, in which the final two years would be preparatory for further secondary schooling for some of the students, and preparatory for vocations for the rest, who will terminate formal schooling at fifteen or sixteen.[5]

The curriculum of the Swedish elementary schools is similar to that of the other Scandinavian countries. Special attention is given to handicrafts (*sloyd*), in which the Swedish schools have long pioneered, and gymnastics and sports. English instruction is rapidly being introduced into all schools, and is to be made obligatory as soon as enough trained teachers are available.

As in Norway, free board is supplied for students in outlying areas, and where central schools are feasible, free transportation is provided.

SECONDARY EDUCATION

Norway. Secondary education in Norway was greatly simplified in 1935. There are now two types of secondary school: the

[5] *Statens Offentliga Utredningar: 1946 ars skolkommissions betänkande 1948.*

gymnasium and the "modern" school (*realskole*). The curriculum of the two schools is the same for the first two years, so that transfers are possible. The "modern" school is usually of three years' duration and the *gymnasium* of five; both schools take students directly from the elementary schools. For rural areas there are also two-year "modern" schools and three-year *gymnasia* for students coming from the continuation schools. These are state boarding schools designed for youths from outlying districts to whom secondary education would otherwise be denied.

The "modern" schools provide a general education and the *gymnasia* provide a general education plus specialization in various fields. The general curriculum includes religious instruction, Norwegian with Old Norse, English, German, French, history, citizenship, geography, biology, mathematics, art, gymnastics, needlework for girls, and woodwork for boys. Five areas of specialization in the *gymnasium* are offered: Latin, English, mathematics and physics, Old Norse, natural science (biology).

Both schools culminate in a uniform final examination prepared by a special national Council of Secondary Education, members of which are appointed for five years by the king. The *realskoleexamen* is usually taken at seventeen, and the *examen artium*, or university matriculation examination, is usually taken at nineteen or twenty.

More than half the graduates of the elementary schools attend one of these two types of secondary school. In 1939 about 45 percent entered the *gymnasium* and about 13 percent entered the *realskole*. There is a tuition fee, but government scholarships are available.

Denmark.   In Denmark, with its divided system after the age of eleven, only about 15 percent of the children attend schools which can be classified as "secondary," the larger proportion attending the upper grades of the elementary schools instead.

The student leaving the elementary school who has been chosen to enter the secondary ladder first attends a middle school to the age of fifteen. He then takes a state leaving examination; if he passes he may either stay for another year and qualify for the state *realeksamen*, or he may enter the *gymnasium* and qualify after three years for the *studentereksamen*, or matriculation examination.

The middle school offers a general education, whereas the *gymnasium* has three lines of study—classical languages, modern languages, and mathematical and natural sciences. Tuition is free for the great majority of students, but for those with wealthier parents (about 10 percent of the whole) tuition is fixed in proportion to income.

Sweden. About 29 percent of the appropriate age groups transfer to secondary schools after either the fourth or sixth elementary-school year; the rest continue in elementary school. Like the system of elementary schools, the secondary system is not uniform at present, but the following is the prevailing pattern: (1) a four- or five-year lower secondary school (*realskola*) culminating in the state *realexamen* and (2) a three- or four-year upper secondary school (*gymnasium*) culminating in the *studentexamen*. The variation in years is conditioned by the student's leaving the elementary school after either the fourth or sixth year. The projected school reform proposes to do away with this variation and to amalgamate the elementary and secondary schools into one school type through the *realskola* level. Tuition has recently been made free in all state and municipal secondary schools. In addition to the *realskola* and *gymnasium*, there are special seven-year girls' schools normally run by local authorities. (Other secondary schools are predominantly state schools.) Students are normally admitted after the fourth year of the elementary school.

The lower secondary school and the special girls' secondary schools have the usual general-education curriculum, with emphasis on foreign languages and science. The *gymnasia* offer two main lines of study: the classical and the scientific. Common to both lines and to the curriculum of the *realskola* is the study of modern foreign languages. It is especially necessary for students preparing for university matriculation, since most of the references in higher levels of study are in English, German, or French. Normally, therefore, the student begins his English at the fifth school year (age eleven), German two years later, and, if he is preparing for the *gymnasium*, French three years later. Thus the student who stands before his matriculation examinations has had eight years of English, six years of German, five years of French, several years of Latin, perhaps Greek if he chose the classical line of the *gymnasium*, and in some cases a fourth modern foreign language. Add to that the usual work in Swedish language and literature, and the many other secondary-school subjects, and you have a curriculum which in its demands on the students finds few parallels except in Norway and Denmark, where the secondary schools are of a similar character.

Common Characteristics. It can be seen from the foregoing that the secondary schools of Scandinavia have several common characteristics. First and foremost there is the state examination system, which not only provides the main force behind the maintenance of uniform standards but determines to a marked extent the academic nature of the curriculum. Similarly, the possession of either of the two or both academic certificates enables the possessor to become eligible for positions in the civil service and for further training in the professions and at the universities. Possession of the matriculation certificate is a mark of intellectual distinction that is highly regarded.

Characteristic too is the selective character of secondary education, especially in Denmark and Sweden, where the selective process begins at the age of eleven. Even in the proposed school reform in Sweden, the selective character is to be maintained in the upper division of the proposed citizens' school. Educators in Scandinavia have always preferred a selective system of secondary education to the comprehensive system as practiced in American junior and senior high schools. Although they favor equality of opportunity for all, they emphasize the training of the intellectual elite.

Curriculums are most exacting and, since so much of Scandinavian cultural, economic, and social contact is with nations outside Scandinavia, especially Britain, France, and Germany, the number of subjects to be mastered is much greater than in larger, less dependent countries. As a result, most of the work within a given line of study is prescribed, and the student has a wealth of material and skills to master. That a system fulfilling requirements so exacting and multitudinous will resist change in traditional methodology and curriculum is to be expected.

VOCATIONAL AND TECHNICAL EDUCATION

The Scandinavian countries have well-developed systems of vocational and technical education, largely state-sponsored and controlled, but usually working in close relationship with the various

trades and industries. The traditional high standard of craftsmanship of the skilled Scandinavian worker is recognized everywhere;
it is in large measure due to rich and varied training programs,
both of a preservice and in-service nature. In all three countries
much attention has been given in recent years to the development
of vocational training that will not only be even further sharpened
but will rank in the public mind as comparable in prestige to
academic training.

Vocational education and technical education are provided at
all levels from the last years of elementary school through the
university. Much of it is administered jointly by public authorities
and representatives of the trades and industries concerned. In the
Norwegian technical schools, for example, half of the board of
control must consist of representatives, both workers and employers,
of the industries concerned. In Denmark many technical schools
are still owned by societies of artisans and technical societies,
although they are under state supervision and receive substantial
state grants. Technical training, other than commercial training, is
usually tied up with work experience and apprenticeship.   In
Norway, for example, there are schools which provide instruction
before apprenticeship (workshop schools), during apprenticeship
(apprenticeship schools), and after apprenticeship (schools for foremen, technological institutes, and schools of various kinds for
skilled workmen, journeymen, and masters). The programs of these
schools range from evening part-time to full-time courses of as long
as four years' duration.

The regulations governing the relationship between technical
schooling and apprenticeship are set by law and place obligations
upon school, apprentice, and employer. For example, the Danish
Apprenticeship Act of 1937, embracing handicrafts industries, office
work, retail and wholesale trade, restaurant operation, gardening,
etc., provides conditions of contract between apprentice and employer which include regulation of hours and conditions of work,
the qualifications of both apprentice and master, the duty of the
employer to provide and pay for complementary training of the
apprentice at a technical school, and the standards of the journey-
man's test to be passed by the "graduating" apprentice. Even a
court of arbitration is provided for, to settle disputes between
apprentices and masters. The Act is an attempt to bring together

the best features of the realistic on-the-job training that is an inheritance of the old guild system and the modern professionalized school
training that is an outgrowth of technological development in the
twentieth century.

In all three countries, the ideal toward which vocational education is working is to provide training of many varieties and at all
possible levels, so that it will be possible for a young person to
work himself up to the highest technical level, no matter how early
he has had to enter employment. The effort is made to give the
unskilled as well as the skilled worker ample opportunity to acquire
as much additional training as his aptitude and interest allow him.
All the levels of the school system, public and private, the various
artisan organizations, labor unions, industrial associations, and
cooperatives work with the government in this endeavor. One has
the distinct impression, therefore, that the student who, for whatever reason, does not enter academic secondary training is at least
as well provided for in being helped to find his proper niche in
the world of work as is his more academically minded counterpart.

HIGHER EDUCATION

There are at the present time seven universities in Scandinavia:
Copenhagen and Aarhus in Denmark, Oslo in Norway, and Uppsala,
Lund, Stockholm, and Gothenburg in Sweden. All but Stockholm
and Gothenburg are state universities. There are in addition many
institutes and colleges of university grade. No tuition fees are
charged in the Danish and Norwegian universities; in Sweden
tuition is charged at present, but the government is considering
proposals to abolish all fees, to extend additional scholarships and
subsistence grants, and to provide students with government housing, canteens, medical and dental care, and free transportation.

The administration of the state universities is characterized by
the old European tradition of faculty self-determination; although
these universities are state financed they have virtually complete
autonomy and freedom of teaching. In several of the universities
the students not only have a high degree of student self-government
but also participate in university administration. In Oslo, for
example, the students elect a student council which meets with the

Collegium (consisting of the deans of the faculties and the rector) on affairs in which the students are directly concerned. The student council recommends candidates for scholarships and loans, is consulted on questions involving examinations and alterations of curriculum, and in general acts as the channel for making student opinion known to the university authorities.

To achieve matriculated status in the universities one must pass the state matriculation examination (*studentexamen* or *examen artium*) at the end of the *gymnasium*; at this time one is nineteen or twenty. Degrees follow the pattern that prevails in other European universities—*Candidatus, Magister,* and *Doctor*—and in some of the older institutions (some date back to the fifteenth century) they involve such traditional degree-earning conventions as the public disputation and defense of the thesis. Professors, although appointed and salaried by the government (in all but the two private Swedish universities), enjoy a high measure of academic freedom. The degree of such accustomed freedom is attested by the previously mentioned resistance of the entire student and professorial body of the University of Oslo to dictation by the Quisling government during the Nazi occupation.

The universities and the many colleges and institutes of university grade are the centers for the training of the upper bracket of civil servants, for training for the higher professions, and for scientific scholarship and research. In addition, they are, in a sense, cultural centers for the community at large, since several of them, notably Copenhagen and Oslo, keep their "ordinary" or regular lectures open to the public; anyone may attend regardless of previous education.

Because of the system of free higher education and the assistance given to students in the form of grants and loans for living expenses, books, transportation, housing, etc., equality of opportunity for higher education for students who are academically qualified is as near to being achieved as it is anywhere in the world, and is perhaps nearer than it is in the United States. The basic limitation, however, is the state matriculation examination, which by its very nature restricts entrance to the university to those students who have successfully graduated from the *gymnasium*, with its largely prescribed and very rigid curriculum.

THE TRAINING AND STATUS OF TEACHERS

Training. Elementary-school teachers are usually trained in institutions similar to the American teachers' colleges. A student enters such a teachers' school at about the age of seventeen (usually having passed the lower certificate examination) and continues his training for four years in a curriculum that includes the usual upper-secondary-school subjects plus psychology, professional courses, and work at a related demonstration school. If he has passed the matriculation examination for the higher certificate, he enters the training college at about nineteen and stays but two years. At about the age of twenty-one he takes the state teachers' examinations and is ready for appointment. There is usually no tuition and the student may receive subsistence grants from the government.

Teachers in secondary schools are university graduates who have had additional pedagogical training at the university. In Norway, for example, future secondary-school teachers follow a university course of from four to seven years' duration. They must earn university degrees in at least three subjects, attend a postgraduate pedagogical seminary for one semester, and do apprentice teaching at the secondary schools in Oslo. There are opportunities for both elementary and secondary teachers for further study in teachers' colleges and in the universities, by means of which they can receive further specialized training in order to improve their status in the profession.

Teacher Status. Both local and central educational authorities participate in the appointment of teachers. In Denmark, for example, when a position is vacant in a community school, the vacancy is advertised and candidates send their applications to the local school board. The school board and the parents' council decide on a slate of three candidates and submit their names to the county board. The county board then makes the final selection.[6]

In Norway the local school boards appoint the teachers, but the choice must be approved by the School Director (one of seven in the nation), the representative of the Ministry.

Teachers enjoy the security of tenure and after a period of

[6] "Education in Denmark," in Harry N. Rivlin and Herbert Schueler, eds., *The Encyclopedia of Modern Education* (New York: Philosophical Library, Inc., 1943), p. 224.

probationary service may not be removed without serious cause. Their hours of service and their minimum salaries are fixed by law, and they are protected by contributory pensions.

In general, teachers in Scandinavia are noted for their participation in local and national affairs, and they hold a place of high regard in the community. During the Nazi occupation of Norway they were in the forefront of the resistance, and nothing so stirred the people as their wholesale arrest and imprisonment.

Teacher Supply. Like the United States and Britain, and most other countries directly or indirectly affected by the late war, Scandinavia needs an increased supply of young teachers to take care of expanded enrollments which have resulted from the postwar increase in birth rate and the postwar plans for expanded school systems. Particularly hard hit in this respect is Sweden. The Ministry estimates that by 1956 the country's elementary schools will need at least nine thousand more teachers (an increase of one third) to cover increased enrollments. The situation in the secondary schools is comparable. Sweden has therefore embarked on a recruitment and emergency-training program. In 1946 alone 1727 candidates entered the teachers' colleges, as compared with the normal prewar annual figure of four hundred. Every encouragement is given promising young people to enter upon training for the teaching profession. In Norway, even though there are no tuition fees in teachers' colleges, most students receive subsistence grants.

ADULT EDUCATION

In no other part of the world is there so much widespread participation in adult education as in the countries of Scandinavia. In Sweden alone it is estimated that about half the population is active in some form of organized adult education. It is characteristic of Scandinavia that much of this activity is initiated by the people themselves, not merely handed to them as a form of educational philanthropy.[7] This adult education takes many forms, the most

[7] P. G. Stensland, "Adult Education, a Force in Swedish Democracy," *American Scandinavian Review*, Vol. XXXIII (June 1945), pp. 118-128. A. Kildal, "Light Again on the Land; Adult Education Comes Back in Norway." *Adult Education Journal*, Vol. V (October 1946), pp. 167-170. *Social Denmark, A Survey of Danish Social Legislation*, pp. 360-372.

notable of which is the folk high school, far and away the most significant Scandinavian contribution to the development of education.

The Folk High Schools: Background.   The folk high schools are boarding schools for young adults. They originated in Denmark and owe their original conception to Bishop Nicolai Grundtvig (1783-1872), who is revered by the Danes as one of their greatest national and cultural leaders. The idea of the folk high school grew out of Grundtvig's conviction that a universal, life-centered education for all was essential to the building of a true democratic community. He reacted strongly against the prevailing classical character of secondary and higher education of his time and the class feeling that it engendered, calling the classical schools "scholastic reformatories" and "schools of death." Living at a time when Denmark was under the cultural and political domination of its non-Norse neighbors, he sought to find ways to bring his people back to the consciousness of their own cultural identity. His translations of the classics of Norse mythology into the vernacular, and his championing of vernacular literature, earned for him a place in Danish culture similar to that of Martin Luther in Germany. But his crowning achievement was the idea of the folk high school, which he envisioned as an instrument to bring to the common people a means for their mental and spiritual growth and to contribute to the development of a culture indigenous to the common people.

From the beginning the folk high schools were unlike other schools. They attracted students, usually from eighteen to about thirty-three years of age, interested in self-improvement not in a narrow vocational or professional sense but in a broad liberal and humanistic sense. This is all the more remarkable in that the first schools were established for the peasants, and to this day these schools attract many more students from rural than from urban areas. There were usually no examinations—Grundtvig hated the examination system and its implication that students learned not for self-improvement but for the competitive status that good examination marks gave them. Instead of the usual subjects of the traditional classical school (Latin and Greek taught in the prevailing formalistic Ciceronian tradition) the folk schools emphasized Danish history, language, and literature, current social problems, and religion. In keeping with Grundtvig's conviction that the living, spoken word was the best means of communicating culture, the folk high schools have always favored the lecture and discussion as the predominant method of instruction. The most favored of the folk-school instructors were invariably brilliant lecturers, with the skill to communicate the most profound and erudite matters in terms of everyday experience. This does not mean that the work of the teachers was "popularization" in the conventional sense. Firsthand accounts of the folk schools invariably point with surprise and admiration to the way in which the most profound matters of philosophy, history, and morality were brought to the understanding of the simple people with as little as a bare elementary education. It was Grundtvig's hope in naming the schools "high schools" that they would bring the common people into contact with "high" thought, and assist them to aspire to the highest ideals of character and community feeling.

One of the most successful of the early leaders in the high-school movement was Christen Kold (1816-1870), who more than any other typified the spirit of the movement. Kold was a shoemaker's son whose early disillusionment with formalistic teaching turned him away from teaching as a career; but when he met Grundtvig he became his most ardent disciple. His school at Ryslinge, an exceedingly small place with Spartan accommodations for the teacher, his family, and twenty students, was the first of a series of progressively larger and more popular schools which he founded and ran in his lifetime. He was so inspiring a lecturer that people came from far to hear him and to study with him. He seemed to make the most progress with adult farm workers, since he spoke their language and was able to use it to bring home to them historical, religious, and moral subjects on a level that heretofore had been the exclusive province of the cultured classes of urban society.

From the beginning the folk-school movement, which was basically privately supported, was able to obtain some financial support from public authorities, even though there was much suspicion of its work in highly placed governmental and church circles because of the well-founded fear that it would tend to undermine the blind acceptance of class authority. Subsistence grants were at first quite meager, and sometimes disappeared altogether when the work of the schools was out of official favor; but by 1892 a pattern of quite liberal state support was established, and since then the Danish

folk school and its students have enjoyed ever-increasing government support. By the regulation of 1892 each school received a
fixed grant of 300 kroner and a further grant of 10 kroner for each
yearly student, payment of up to one third of the teachers' and
principal's salaries, and teaching materials. In addition, needy
students received a subsistence grant. When one considers the low
state of public assistance to education in other lands at this time,
this support of schools that were essentially private (though subject
to public inspection), that stood outside the official school system,
and that catered to adults beyond the traditional ages of schooling is
a remarkable proof of community devotion to self-improvement.

The influence of the folk high schools soon extended into other
community activities. It was inevitable that former students would
create a demand for public lectures and discussions open to the
public at large. In many schools these programs were so greatly in
demand that they outgrew the limited accommodations of the
schools proper and led to the building of village halls and community centers. These centers, following in the wake of the folk
schools, and initiated and supported in the main by former students,
became the best proof of the lasting effectiveness of the work of the
folk schools. They became truly cultural and social centers, offering debates, lectures, public readings, singing, folk dancing, and
gymnastics, as well as meeting places for the conduct of practical
community affairs.

The idea of the folk school soon spread to other Scandinavian
countries. In Norway the first such school was established near
Hamar in 1864, and in the next thirty years thirty-three more were
founded; but because of opposition from the government and
from conservative religious bodies, their number soon declined,
until by 1904 only four were left. But the growth of a national
youth movement, as a result of the rebirth of a Norwegian cultural
consciousness coincident with the separation from Sweden, soon
created a new demand for folk schools. In 1918 an act of Parliament
provided the folk schools with financial support which included
payment of teachers' salaries. The Norwegian folk schools developed
along Grundtvigian lines, although they never managed to gain
as influential a place in popular adult education as they did in
Denmark.

In Sweden, folk schools found quick favor and did not seem to have provoked the same degree or kind of opposition as in Norway. They soon developed their own distinct character. They have always been more successful than both their Danish and Norwegian counterparts in attracting a more representative body of students from various social, environmental, and occupational groups. They soon veered away from individual private ownership to ownership by associations and even by local government. Their emphasis has always been more on study groups than on lectures, and their curriculum has included more emphasis on social, scientific, and practical subjects than have the curriculums of the Danish and Norwegian folk schools.

Present Status of the Folk High Schools: Denmark. Approximately sixty folk high schools exist in Denmark today, with their seven thousand students distributed among all classes of society but with the rural farmers and smallholders still predominant. In 1940 it was estimated that 43 percent were farmers, 14 percent smallholders, 12 percent craftsmen, 8 percent unskilled workers, and the remaining 23 percent from other groups, including the professions.[8] It has been estimated that in the past forty years about a fourth of the young men and women in the rural districts have attended a folk high school. The average age of the students has continued to rise, attesting to the fact that these are indeed adult schools. At the present time about 80-90 percent of the students are between eighteen and twenty-five. In the last decades, the ownership and primary control of the schools, while still private, have developed away from individuals to trust bodies. The High School Act of 1942 has assured the schools considerable support from public funds and has given a measure of security to the teachers. Although subject to government inspection, the schools are largely autonomous in their work and have wide freedom to determine their own curriculums and practices. The cost to the students for tuition, board, and lodging has been fixed relatively low, and many students receive government grants to assist them in meeting these costs. In 1940 about 57 percent of the students received subsistence grants from the government.

The great majority of the folk high schools are residence schools; indeed, one of their greatest contributions is the community life of

[8] Fridlev Skrubbeltrang, *The Danish Folk High Schools* (Copenhagen: Det Danske Selskab, 1947), pp. 61-70.

teachers and students. Both men and women attend, but in separate sessions; the women usually attend a three-month summer session, and the men attend the five-month winter course.

In the years between the world wars, the movement for adult education extended more and more into the centers of population, especially among the organized working classes. That such a movement would have its own unique characteristics is self-evident, but a meeting of the folk-high-school idea and the ideals of workers' adult education was effected in the establishment of two successful labor folk high schools. One of these is partly owned by the Workers' Educational Union.

The effect of the folk high schools through the years has been in the main liberal and democratic. Their influence on the extension of popular adult education cannot be overestimated. Although in the early years of their development they had a strong national-cultural slant, and although their emphasis has always been on fostering knowledge of and pride in the literary, cultural, and spiritual heritage of the Danes, their work in the twentieth century can with confidence be said to be broadly humanitarian and democratic.[9] In fact, one of the most promising experiments in international education is being carried on in the International Folk High School at Elsinore, in which students from England, Germany, and other countries join the students from Scandinavia in exploring ways of furthering international cooperation and understanding.[10]

For reasons that have never been properly explained, the German occupation during World War II allowed the folk high school to carry on its work largely undisturbed. What restrictions were imposed were physical in nature; for example, some school buildings were requisitioned for other purposes. In fact, some Danish leaders professed themselves to be quite humiliated by the lack of interest on the part of occupation authorities in what was being said at

[9] A. H. Hollman, "The Folk High School," in *Democracy in Denmark*, (Washington, D. C.: National Home Library Foundation, 1936), pp. 142-155. Olive Dame Campbell, *The Danish Folk School* (New York: The Macmillan Company, 1928), pp. 297-336. Fridlev Skrubbeltrang, *op. cit.*, pp. 71-75. Agnes Rothery, *Denmark, Kingdom of Reason* (New York: The Viking Press, 1937), pp. 55-63.
[10] Holger Begtrup, Hans Lund, Peter Manniche, *The Folk High Schools of Denmark and the Development of a Farming Community* (London: Oxford University Press, 1949), pp. 147-159.

meeting halls and from high-school platforms. Indeed, since the Germans censored the press of Denmark, the high schools became more popular than ever during the occupation, providing as they did oases of free thought and discussion.

Present Status of the Folk High Schools: Norway.   In Norway three types of so-called "youth schools" have grown out of the original Grundtvigian idea. The early folk high schools became, as in Denmark, centers of liberal thought, and they engendered much opposition among political conservatives and religious groups. As a consequence, private youth schools with a more pronounced religious cast, county schools, and state schools more conservative in nature were formed, and for a time there was much friction among these three types. However, their differences have become less marked in recent years and, although they maintain distinct characteristics, they work with much the same ultimate goal—to give the youth of the nation, particularly the youth from rural districts, further education after the elementary school. They cater to youth between the ages of seventeen and twenty and serve as preparatory schools for further training in higher vocational schools and teachers' colleges, in marked contrast with Danish folk schools, which have a more liberal program and independent status. The Norwegian folk schools are supported by the state in much the same way as in the other Scandinavian countries and are subject to state supervision. Since they are practically the only schools that offer dormitory facilities, they are alone in providing the advantages of community living and social life that such schools can best offer. Before the war there were ninety-three such schools with a registration of upwards of six thousand students. During the German occupation they suffered as all schools in Norway suffered, and they are now working up to their former position.

Present Status of the Folk High Schools: Sweden.   The Swedish folk high schools are associated to a greater extent than the Danish and Norwegian with specific movements, such as labor, sports, religious, and temperance movements, and they are usually not owned by individuals but by their sponsoring associations and in some cases by local governments. The teachers and principals are appointed by the education authorities, but public control is limited to control over finances and administration and does not extend to teaching activities, in which the schools have a free hand. The Swedish folk high schools differ, too, from those in Denmark in being more institutional in character; most of them give examinations and grades to students, for example. They also attract a more representative student body from urban and industrial areas as well as from rural farm areas. In methodology they place less emphasis on oral instruction and more on study circles centering in books. Their curriculum, while including many liberal-humanistic courses, places more emphasis on social, scientific, and practical subjects. At present there are about seventy such schools in Sweden.

International Effects of the Folk-high-school Movement. The folk high schools have received almost universal praise from educators in other countries and, although they have nowhere attained anything approaching the popularity they enjoy in Scandinavia, they have had some measurable effect.[11] In the United States and Canada, some folk high schools were established in the Middle West in the nineteenth and twentieth centuries in centers of Danish immigration, and a few of these are still active. In Germany during the Weimar Republic, many schools of the folk-school type were established in towns for industrial workers and in rural areas for farmers. But the work of these schools was interrupted by the Nazis, although in their typical culturally parasitic fashion they attempted to find a foreshadowing of Nazi ideas in Grundtvig, "the prophet of the North." In Switzerland, a Swiss High School Association was founded in 1925, with which are now associated three Swiss folk schools. The Danish folk schools maintain close relations with the Swiss schools. Other folk high schools have been maintained in Holland, Poland, Austria, Hungary, and other European countries, and great interest was shown in them in both China and Japan before the last war.

Although there is little evidence that the folk-high-school idea has been applied to any significant degree in the founding of many such institutions outside of Scandinavia, the idea has maintained its attraction for educators in other lands. There exists a strong feeling, especially among the leaders of the Danish folk high schools, that a true appreciation of their ideas and the widespread institutional application of these ideas could be an important factor in postwar spiritual and cultural reconstruction.[12]

Other Types of Adult Education. Many private organizations are active in sponsoring adult-education activities. Notable among them

[11] Fridlev Skrubbeltrang, *op. cit.*, pp. 76-85.
[12] *Ibid.*, p. 85.

are the Workers' Educational Associations and the various Cooperative Unions. The Workers' Educational Union of Denmark can be cited as an example typical of the three countries. The Union's educational activities take many forms. Lectures and courses are given in towns and country communities either in regularly organized evening schools or in libraries and other suitable public buildings. Study circles (an importation from Sweden) with specially trained leaders and carefully selected and arranged books, materials, and study guides are established wherever there is a demand. The Union has even gone into the publishing business through its "Book Circle," which has published a fiction and a popular science series. It helps to arrange theater evenings, visits to art galleries and industrial plants, etc. It establishes and runs holiday homes, where the program includes short courses of interest to the various groups attending—trade-union delegates, members of communal councils, participants in cooperative stores, youth leaders, housewives, etc. On a more formal basis, the Union runs two workers' high schools and many evening schools for civic education and for special vocational education. The participants in these activities run into many thousands each year; in 1947, study circles attracted about 10,000, evening schools 16,000 to 18,000, summer courses 2500, lectures in rural communities 35,000 to 40,000, lectures in towns 75,000 to 100,000.[13] The lecturers, teachers, and study-circle leaders are by no means recruited solely from the ranks of the Union but come from all social and cultural groups—the press, the high schools, the regular school system, the universities, political life, trade, and many groups and organizations. This widespread activity is financed by the members of the trade unions and the Labor party. In addition, the Educational Union receives an annual grant from the state.

In Norway and Sweden, where distances in outlying, northern districts are great, correspondence courses have found great favor. In Sweden, for example, an estimated 400,000 persons were studying by correspondence in 1948.[14] Almost any kind of course may be taken—technical, commercial, social, general, of many lengths and grades of difficulty. In fact, it is possible to earn eligibility to take the same state examinations given in the regular secondary, tech-

[13] *Social Denmark*, pp. 368-371.
[14] *Education in Sweden* (Stockholm: The Swedish Institute, 1949), pp. 14-15.

nical, or commercial schools. The Robertsfors Schools are a special type. These 140 schools offer studies by correspondence culminating in a final coaching at the school proper in preparation for the regular state examinations.

A particularly significant feature of the adult-education movement in Scandinavia is the large number of public libraries and the large percentage of the population that makes use of them. They are supported by communities with the assistance of state grants, and are found in all the towns and in a great many of the rural communities. Indicative of the use made of the libraries are the lending figures for Denmark: in 1944, 1166 libraries lent a total of 15 million books in a nation of approximately 4 million people.

SOME CONCLUDING GENERALIZATIONS AND COMPARISONS

In general, education in Scandinavia occupies a leading position in comparison with education in the other major countries of western Europe. The quality of academic education is high, and the participation of Scandinavia's adult population in education, both formal and informal, is unsurpassed. However, the challenge of greater equalization of opportunity is stimulating efforts in Scandinavia, as it has in England, in France, and in Germany, to increase the years of common schooling before differentiation into academic and vocational education begins, to bring higher education within the reach of more who deserve it, and in general to make formal education more and more the right of the many rather than the privileged few.

The concept of academic education for the intellectual elite, as opposed to the American ideal of general education for all, at least through the high-school years, is strongly entrenched in Scandinavia, even in such liberalizing proposals as the common citizens' school in Sweden. It is doubtful that current proposals for greater equalization of opportunity will ever completely lose sight of that dominant concept.

The philosophy underlying adult education, however, is quite the opposite, emphasizing as it does the advisability of widespread public participation in cultural activities. Thus this philosophy acts as an effective supplement to the more restrictive one of formal public education at the elementary, secondary, and higher levels.

In this duality of educational philosophy, the countries of Scandinavia are unique, and the complementary action of the two concepts has kept the Norse peoples in the first rank in literacy and in the extent of popular participation in cultural and social affairs.

In contrast to the pattern in the United States, but consistent with the western-European pattern, religion is a standard part of the formal school instruction. (This is not at all surprising, considering the homogeneity of religious affiliation and the existence of an official state church.) Control of education is largely secular, however, with religious control confined largely to the content of religious instruction.

The relationship between local and national control of education is a rather even one, with some preponderance of power on the national side. This is in contrast to the state and local domination of education in the United States, on the one hand, and the continental-European tradition of national domination, on the other.

In two areas of education, Scandinavia has pioneered: (1) in the development of handcrafts, gymnastics, and physical culture as a major part of the common curriculum and (2) in the development of a rich and diversified program of formal and informal adult education. The first accomplishment has had many concrete effects on the curriculums of schools in other lands; the second, although universally admired, has not achieved as great an influence in education in other countries.

Outstanding, and in keeping with the high standard of craftsmanship traditional to Scandinavia, is the high level of technical and crafts education. Virtually unique to Scandinavia is the widespread cooperation of management, labor, and government in the support and administration of technical education.

As an exponent of the "middle way" between the extremes of state monopoly and private enterprise, Scandinavia has combined what it considers the best features of public and private sponsorship and support of education. Its educational problems in the decade following World War II involve not only the physical expansion that a rising birth rate requires but also problems of restudy and reassessment of fundamental aims and their consequences. Scandinavia has been more fortunate than her continental neighbors and England in not having so great a problem of postwar reconstruction.

BIBLIOGRAPHY

Adult Education in the Struggle for Peace. Written by Teachers, Students and Friends of the International People's College, Elsinore. (Copenhagen: G. E. C. Gad.) A forthcoming book on the most significant Scandinavian experiment in international education.

Adult Education in Sweden (Stockholm: The Swedish Institute, 1949).

BEGTRUP, HOLGER, HANS LUND, and PETER MANNICHE, *The Folk High Schools of Denmark and the Development of a Farming Community* (London: Oxford University Press, 1949). Written by three veterans of the high-school movement, this book shows the part the folk high schools have played in furthering the cultural, social, and even economic development of the rural population in Denmark.

BOJE, ANDREAS, ERNST J. BORUP, and HOLGER RUTZEBECK, *Education in Denmark* (London: Oxford University Press, 1932). Although this book is most useful as a description of the status before 1932, much of it, especially as it concerns fundamental principles and structure, is still true today.

BOYESEN, E., "Norway's Educational System," in Norway (Norwegian Travel Association, 1948), pp. 79-97. An up-to-date, summary account of the present state of education in Norway, written by the present Director of the Board of Education.

CAMPBELL, OLIVE DAME, *The Danish Folk School* (New York: The Macmillan Company, 1928). A rhapsodic account of personal contact with the folk schools by an American who attempted to found similar schools in the United States.

CURTIS, H. S., "Sweden Trains for Democracy," *Educational Forum,* Vol. X (January 1946), pp. 173-177.

Education under Enemy Occupation (Washington, D. C.: U. S. Office of Education, Bulletin 1945, No. 3).

Education and Service Conditions of Teachers in Scandinavia, the Netherlands, and Finland (Washington, D. C.: U. S. Office of Education, Bulletin 1940, No. 9).

Education in Sweden (Stockholm: The Swedish Institute, 1949). A rather sketchy account, but valuable because it summarizes the proposals for fundamental educational reform that are now before the Swedish people.

HARRIS, W. J. A., "Denmark During the War: Effects on Adult

Education," *London Times Educational Supplement,* December 14, 1946, p. 616.

HJELMTVEIT, NILS, *Education in Norway* (London: Hodder & Stoughton, Ltd., 1946). A short but comprehensive survey of education in Norway by the former Minister of Church and Education. It is considered by Norwegian authorities to be authoritative.

HOLLMAN, A. H., "The Folk High School," Part II of *Democracy in Denmark* (Washington, D. C.: National Home Library Foundation, 1936). A translation from the Danish of an early (1909) but classic description of the folk high schools in their first fifty years of existence. The chapter "Methods of Instruction" brings one right into the classroom.

KANDEL, I. L., ed., *Educational Yearbooks of the International Institute* (New York: Teachers College, Columbia University). Denmark: 1935, 1936. Norway: 1924, 1932, 1935, 1936, 1944. Sweden: 1926, 1930, 1932, 1935, 1936.

KILDAL, A., "Light Again on the Land; Adult Education Comes Back in Norway," *Adult Education Journal,* Vol. V (October 1946), pp. 167-170.

KNIGHT, EDGAR W., *Among the Danes* (Chapel Hill: University of North Carolina Press, 1927). A readable and engrossing account of an educational odyssey, written by a prominent American educator.

MANNICHE, PETER, *Denmark, a Social Laboratory* (London: Oxford University Press, 1939). A discussion by the veteran folk-high-school leader of the various movements that make Denmark a social laboratory: cooperatives, folk high schools, and social legislation.

RIVLIN, HARRY N., and HERBERT SCHUELER, eds., *The Encyclopedia of Modern Education* (New York: Philosophical Library, Inc., 1943). The articles "Education in Denmark," "Education in Norway," and "Education in Sweden" give a concise summary of basic features of education in the Scandinavian countries up to 1942.

SANDBERG, F., and B. KNOS, *Education and Scientific Research in Sweden* (Copenhagen: A. Bonnier, 1938). Useful as an account of the status before 1938.

SANDWEN, J., "Norwegian School System; General Structure and Main Working Principles," *New Era,* Vol. XXVIII (April 1947), pp. 92-94.

SEIP, D. A., "School Problems in Norway," *American Scandinavian Review,* Vol. XXXIV (June 1946), pp. 120-122.

Social Denmark, A Survey of the Danish Social Legislation (Copenhagen: Socialt Tidsskrift, 1947). A well-conceived and comprehensive account of social legislation in Denmark. The chapter "Education and Popular Enlightenment" gives a particularly thorough account of apprenticeship, technical, and professional education.

STENSLAND, P. G., "Adult Education, a Force in Swedish Democracy," *American Scandinavian Review*, Vol. XXXIII (June 1945), pp. 118-128.

11 · EDUCATION IN *Czechoslovakia*

JOSEPH S. ROUCEK

Czechoslovakia is a national island, so to speak, in the middle of Europe; it connects the Teutonic and Slavic areas. Its area is approximately 50,000 square miles and its population is estimated at close to 13 million. This landlocked country lying across the heart of Europe is encircled by mountains. Czechoslovakia is very rich in natural resources and industrial development. About 40 percent of the population is agricultural, growing most cool-weather crops on a system of small farms since the Land Reform Bill of 1924. Industry is exceedingly well developed, from heavy industry and munitions (the Skoda plants) to light industry such as glass, textile, chemical, and shoe manufacture. The mineral wealth, which includes uranium deposits, is extensive; only petroleum resources are lacking.

Czechoslovakia was one of the great liberal democratic republics until the 1948 seizure of power by the Communists. Educationally speaking, Czechoslovakia has an outstanding tradition centered in Comenius, the Moravian bishop who did so much for the progress of education in the seventeenth century. Before the Communist coup the new Czechoslovakian republic had been moving in the direction of universal democratic education and had developed some very progressive experimental schools. Illiteracy in Czechoslovakia was very low—only about 4 percent.

—A. H. M.

The development of Czechoslovakia's educational system shows four sharply defined stages. The first was inaugurated after 1918, when the newly formed Republic of Czechoslovakia arose from the ashes of the defunct Austro-Hungarian Empire and began to build up its educational system under the influence of the democratic ideals of President Thomas G. Masaryk. Many of the educational theories and practices of the Republic received world-wide acclaim for their democratic features, which were rooted in the theories of one of the greatest educators of modern times, Johann Amos Comenius, and in the willingness of the government and peoples of Czechoslovakia to accept the best that modern educational experiment and theories—particularly those from America—had to offer. Masaryk's and Beneš' governments, during the postwar decades, followed an aggressive and constructive educational policy. Astonishing progress in all branches of formal and informal education was made during the twenty years of Czechoslovakia's independence.

The second period was inaugurated with the tragedy of Munich, when, under the heel of Hitler's legions, Czechoslovakia was dismembered and the educational system was made to reflect the Nazi aims and goals. But this was only a transition period; although it left irreparable damages, it ended just as suddenly as it had appeared. The disappearance of the Nazi hordes from the country in 1945 marks the beginning of the third period. It was then that Beneš' government returned to Prague and tried to reconstitute, in general, the prewar democratic system of education.

But this short breathing period ended in 1948, when Czechoslovakia had to inaugurate the fourth—that is, the present—period. characterized by the imposition of the Russian system on the recalcitrant and resistant Czechoslovakians.

These changes—particularly the contemporary pro-Soviet tendencies—make Czechoslovakia a very good subject for study in the field of comparative education. The country is a typical example of the "satellite" whose education is now forcibly adapted to the desires and needs of Soviet Russia rather than to the wishes of most of the inhabitants. A survey of these changes should indicate the tendencies that are being developed in all the countries living today under the shadow of either direct or indirect domination of Russia.

CZECHOSLOVAKIA'S HISTORICAL TRADITIONS

The Republic of Czechoslovakia, although created in 1918, was not a new country. The roots of this state went back to the fifth century, when the Czechs and Slovaks (Slavic tribes) settled in the regions that they now occupy. The invasion of Europe by the Magyars (903-907), a Turian race, akin to the Finns and the Turks, divided the Czechoslovaks from the southern, or "Yugo," Slavs. Slovakia was cut off from the Czechs for more than ten centuries and hence developed its peculiar type of culture under the domination of Hungary—a fact which, as we shall see, was of considerable importance to the educational problems in Czechoslovakia after 1918.

The Czechs meanwhile had developed their own state of Bohemia. Charles IV (1316-1378), Bohemia's king and a Holy Roman Emperor, made Prague the political and cultural capital of central Europe. In 1348 he founded the famed Charles University in Prague, the oldest institution of higher education in central Europe.

Bohemia's history has always reflected its geographical background. Situated in the very heart of Europe, the country was the scene of the collision of races, cultures, and ideas. Here was part of the northern frontier of the Roman Empire; migrating tribes of Gauls, Germans, and Slavs passed over this area. Here the incursions of Turks and Tartars were halted. In the fifteenth century, violent Czech reaction against the influence of the Germans in the country was fused with the Protestant movement of John Hus, rector of Charles University, who became the champion of the Czech people. The Hussite wars did not, however, check the increasing strength of the Germans, and eventually, in 1618, the revolt against the Hapsburg ruler began. The Czechs, weakly supported by their Protestant allies, were defeated at the battle of the White Mountain (1620); terrible reprisals followed. The Czech people were left without leaders, and the Czech language was spoken only by the "hewers of wood and draughters of water."

Comenius. From the standpoint of the history of education it is important to note that at that time a great educator left Bohemia: Johann Amos Comenius, or Komenský (1592-1670). Born in Moravia (a province of Bohemia), he was brought up in the Union of Brethren, of which he later became a priest and bishop. The

Brethren, and Comenius with them, were scattered in exile after 1620. The rest of Comenius' life was spent in Poland, England, Sweden, Prussia, Hungary, and Holland. (Unfortunately, he did not accept the invitation to become president of Harvard College.) He died in Amsterdam in 1670.

Without going into Comenius' voluminous and disorderly philosophy (called "Pansophism"), we must credit him with giving the world an immense mass of pedagogical literature. Therein he outlined a plan for the "mother school," vernacular school, classical school, and university. He laid the basis of modern language teaching in his textbooks, which propounded the principle that the pupil shall acquire a foreign tongue by exercise in words and phrases which are themselves informative and interesting. He wanted schools "which would be provided with good books and sound methods, so that the study of science, morality, and piety would be stimulated." His views on universal education were summed up in the *Great Didactic* (1632), or "science as to how everybody could learn everything." Schools ought to become "the workshop of humanity." Comenius also believed that education was the only means to the greater political well-being and prosperity of nations and of humanity in general. He planned an international academy of savants (to be located in London), a universal language, and universal peace—and worked out a system which, although not generally known, resulted in the formation of Freemasonry.

In short, Comenius' educational ideas have been of considerable importance in the history of comparative education. Still timely are his notions of universal and popular education and coeducation. His influence on education in general and on such educators as Francke, Rousseau, and Pestalozzi has never been questioned. And "the progressive state school systems of Germany, France, Holland, Norway, Sweden, Denmark, England, the United States and Japan were conceived and worked out in their most important particulars by him nearly three hundred years ago."[1]

National Revival. The Czechs were subordinated to the Germans in the Austrian (and after 1867 in the Austro-Hungarian) Empire. But the memory of a distinct national existence lingered, and its preservation was no doubt aided by the fact that the division be-

---

[1] Will S. Monroe, *The Spell of Bohemia* (Boston: L. C. Page and Co., 1910), p. 234.

tween upper and lower classes largely coincided with the division
between German and Czech. The national revival began at the end
of the nineteenth century, when a Czech middle class slowly
emerged.

The Slovaks, however, were not so well prepared for their liberation as the Czechs.[2] Under the Magyar regime the 2 million Slovaks
had no more than 276 elementary schools, not a single secondary
school, and only three political journals.

The Formation of the Republic of Czechoslovakia.   The Czechs
and Slovaks were liberated by the influence of Dr. Thomas Gar-
rigue Masaryk, Dr. Eduard Beneš, and a handful of conspirators
who grasped the opportunity of World War I to awaken interest in
Czech independence. They journeyed through the United States and
Europe, proclaiming that the Czechoslovaks had a right to independence and that this independence was essential to the much-
needed reconstruction of Europe.

Masaryk and His Ideas.   The son of a coachman, Masaryk represented both tribal wings of the Republic he helped to create. His
father was Slovak, his mother Moravian. Through his marriage to
an American and through later contacts with the United States
he was exposed to the democratic philosophy which came to dominate his thought.

Before World War I, Bohemia was under Austro-Hungarian
domination, and Masaryk was interested in directing the nation's
energies to the strengthening of its goals. Everything in the field
of national endeavor was to be measured by the standard of
national utility. His basic thesis was that politics, law, morality,
art, and science all result in part from underlying social developments and economic conditions. He also regarded psychological,
emotional, and particularly religious factors as of great importance
in the determination of these various aspects of social and ideological life. Masaryk stood up against empty or false patriotism and
insisted that history should be looked upon in a realistic spirit.

Masaryk's concept of realism took the form of an effort to search
for greater truth and deeper morality in life. He believed that the
world and mankind are ruled by certain principles and laws of

[2] For a convenient survey of the history of the Czech and Slovak peoples,
see Joseph S. Roucek, *Central Eastern Europe* (New York: Prentice-Hall,
Inc., 1946), Chapters 3 and 17.

absolute truth; that man is the living expression of these principles of God or Providence, and has to live up to these laws. All individuals, as well as nations, have an equal right to freedom. In application, history should teach the nation to seek a better educational, intellectual, moral, artistic, political, and, especially, realistic outlook on life by conceiving things as they actually are and not as they appear to be.

On this ideological framework, Masaryk worked out his political and educational principles as follows: Czechoslovakia's main theme of history can be found in the ideas and struggles of the Hussites and of the Czech Reformation; Masaryk viewed the aims of Comenius and the Hussites as being the precursors of the world-wide aims of democracy. To Masaryk the Czech question was, therefore, a universal question, since the ideas of the Czech Hussites were also the ideas which formed the basis for the rise of modern Europe and for the French Revolution. Hence, the struggle against Germany and Austria-Hungary was also the struggle for democracy—a struggle for a better world and for more human relations among all people.

In view of the claims of the pro-Soviet regime in Czechoslovakia since 1948 that Czechoslovakia has always had ideological tendencies to unite itself under the aegis of "Slavic" Russia, it is interesting to note Masaryk's clear-cut view on this point. Masaryk did not like the czarist regime, and even less did he like Lenin's revolution and bolshevism.[3] For Masaryk, individual initiative and the right to think for oneself were the indispensable foundations of political and intellectual life. He wished to strengthen European democracy among the Czechs and he desired the Europeanization of Russia.

At any rate, in line with his convictions, Masaryk led the Czecho-slovak revolutionary movement against Austria-Hungary during World War I and exerted his influence on the course of political events in Czechoslovakia as its first president. His program was adopted *in toto* by his foreign minister, and later his successor as president, Eduard Beneš. Both saw in the West the salvation of world problems, since the West was the depository of all democratic dynamics.

[3] See Hans Kohn, "The Heritage of Masaryk," *Annals of the American Academy of Political and Social Science*, Vol. CCLVIII (July 1948), pp. 70-73.

In accordance with the ideological framework built by Masaryk, the temporary Constitution of November 1918 created a democratic Republic of Czechoslovakia and abolished the privileges of birth and class. The "permanent" Constitution, ratified by the National Assembly on February 29, 1920, was to be the only document of its kind in central Europe which survived for two decades. Modeled partly on the American Constitution, it was redolent of Jeffersonian ideals of democracy and government by the consent of the governed, but contained a strong dash of nationalism and socialism. It created a centralized, not a federative, state. Legislative power was vested in a bicameral Parliament, consisting of a House of Deputies whose members were elected for a term of six years, on the basis of numerical electoral representation, and a Senate elected for eight years. The president was chosen by both houses, sitting in joint session, for a term of seven years. The Constitution permitted only two terms, but the first president, Masaryk, was allowed to hold office for seventeen years. The Constitution guaranteed racial and religious rights and in general incorporated the provisions of the international treaties for the protection of minorities.

EDUCATION UNDER MASARYK AND BENES

Under the prosperous Republic of Masaryk, and then of Beneš, education from kindergarten to university was free for all citizens, and scholarships were provided for the poor but gifted. In line with Masaryk's unceasing emphasis on universal education as the basis of democracy, the Republic made secondary and higher education available to the Slovaks, whereas before 1918 such education was practically nonexistent. Special schools were also established for minorities. Thus 96.2 percent of German, 94 percent of Hungarian, and 92.5 percent of Polish children received instruction in their native tongue. German polytechnical schools in Prague and Brno were supported by the state—as were all other minority schools. Two new universities, Masaryk University at Brno and Comenius University at Bratislava, were established.[4]

[4] See Francis H. Stuerm, "Education in a Democracy," pp. 302-315, and Joseph S. Roucek, "Czechoslovakia and Her Minorities," pp. 171-192, in R. J. Kerner, ed., *Czechoslovakia: Twenty Years of Independence* (Berkeley: University of California Press, 1940). Joseph S. Roucek, "Some

In line with Masaryk's and Beneš' reasoning, rooted in the ideas of John Hus and Comenius, adult education received tremendous impetus with the setting up of educational committees in every community to conduct lectures and adult courses and operate libraries under the supervision of the Masaryk Institute of Adult Education.[5] As a result of these efforts, illiteracy was lower in Czechoslovakia (7.5 percent in 1921 and 3.25 percent in 1930) than in any country in central-eastern Europe. A lot of commendable work was also accomplished by the famed *Sokols*. The Czech *Sokol* was founded in 1862, the name, meaning falcon, being the traditional symbol of folk heroes. During the years of Hapsburg domination, *Sokol* groups served to keep Czech nationalism alive, by means of systematic adult educational work, composed of class and gymnastic work. When World War I broke out, members filtered into Allied armies, formed *Sokol* legions, and fought their old masters. One out of every twenty persons in Czechoslovakia belonged to a *Sokol*; the flashing uniforms—red shirts, gray jackets slung from the left shoulder, and little round caps with falcon feathers—never failed to rouse national enthusiasm.[6]

But the process of extending educational activities was not advancing without considerable difficulties. At the beginning of the Republic, Masaryk's Czech legionnaires and governmental functionaries, flushed with the achievement of independence, came to Slovakia and in several instances indulged in deeds which gave offense to the churchgoing Slovaks, especially the Catholics, and in other ways manifested a hostility to Slovak clericalism which was

Phases of Development of the Czechoslovak Educational System," *School and Society*, Vol. XXXV (June 11, 1932), pp. 802-804; "The Education of Gypsies in Czechoslovakia," *School and Society*, Vol. XLV (April 17, 1937), pp. 548-549; and "Concept of Education in Czechoslovakia," *Review of Educational Research*, Vol. IX (October 1939), pp. 377-380 and 432-433.

[5] Joseph S. Roucek, "Adult Education in Czechoslovakia," *School and Society*, Vol. XXXV (January 2, 1932), pp. 19-21; Vol. XLIII (January 25, 1936), pp. 125-127. S. D. Turosienski, *Education in Czechoslovakia* (Washington, D. C.: Bureau of Education Bulletin, 1935, No. 11) is a valuable, systematic survey of Czechoslovakia's education under Masaryk.

[6] The *Sokols* soon spread and were imitated in other Slav countries. For an account of the work of the *Sokols* among American-born Slavs, see Joseph S. Roucek, "Czechoslovak Americans," and the chapters concerning the other Slavs, in Francis J. Brown and Joseph S. Roucek, *One America* (New York: Prentice-Hall, Inc., 1948).

used by the Hungarians to promote their nationalistic policies. Many of the Czech officials coming to Slovakia after 1918 were either Protestants or freethinkers and thus they offended the religious feelings of the Slovak peasantry. This, in turn, promoted the strength of the Slovak Clerical party (the Autonomists), which preferred "Slovak" to "Czechoslovak" patriotism, and which eventually, after Munich (1938), was used by Hitler to promote the artificial rise of Slovakia's Quislings to power and the separation of Slovakia from Czechoslovakia.

The influences of American ideas and practices were more than evident in the Republic of Masaryk and Beneš and were reflected especially in the work of Jan Uher (1891-1942) and Václav Příhoda (1899-   ).[7] Uher's acceptance of Masaryk's humanitarianism and democratic ideals led him to believe more in John Dewey than in Thorndike and Watson; but his independent reasoning led him to criticize Příhoda's overemphasis on the mechanistic and quantitative aspects of his educational reforms and to demand a philosophical and particularly idealistic Christian orientation of Příhoda. Příhoda, on the other hand, a proponent of economic determinism and Thorndike psychology, favored especially the use of tests, *Gestalt* psychology, and the formation of a unified school. His ideas were, in fact, tried in five experimental junior high schools. The moral problem of education interested Otakar Machotka (1899-   ), a sociologist trained in America, who insisted that all educational experiments and ideas must be supported by extensive case studies carried on according to definite scientific research methods.

CZECHOSLOVAKIA UNDER NAZISM

When the shadow of Hitler's aggressive policies began to threaten Czechoslovakia, Masaryk, who had resigned the presidency, was already on his deathbed and Beneš had assumed the presidency. The country was confronted with the growing demands of Konrad Henlein, Hitler's "unofficial" representative among Czechoslovakia's Germans. Although the German minorities had been, from the be-

[7] See Joseph S. Roucek, "Educational Theory, Czechoslovakia," in Joseph S. Roucek, ed., *Slavonic Encyclopedia* (New York: Philosophical Library, Inc., 1949), pp. 280-282.

ginning, treated more generously in Czechoslovakia than in any other country, Nazism appealed to many of them, since Hitler offered the Sudeten Germans a possibility of regaining their dominant, pre-World-War-I, position. The economic crisis of Czechoslovakia after 1929 gave a powerful impetus to the movement. The use of fifth columns in Czechoslovakia had become a serious problem by 1938, and the government took steps to halt the growing danger which began to be reflected in the educational system, especially after the dismemberment of Czechoslovakia at Munich.[8]

Under the Nazi dictates, both the Protectorate of Bohemia-Moravia and Slovakia had to inaugurate an educational system resembling that of the Nazis. Most of the spokesmen of Masaryk and Beneš had to escape abroad, were killed, were deported, or were placed in concentration camps. In fact, the destruction of Czech cultural and intellectual life and extermination of the Czech intelligentsia were carried out with deliberate thoroughness. Czech universities were closed and faculties disbanded; the students who tried to resist were shot, imprisoned, or otherwise disposed of. Czech elementary and high schools were closed during the winter, but the German schools were encouraged to remain open. The Czech cultural courses were prohibited in the schools, but the study of the German language was made compulsory. Nearly all Jews of the region were exterminated.

Meanwhile, however, Beneš had been active abroad on behalf of his lost democracy. After visiting London and serving as professor at the University of Chicago, he eventually succeeded in organizing a Czechoslovak government in London. Recognized by the Allies, it eventually took control of Czechoslovakia when the country was liberated in May 1945 by the joint military action of the Soviet and United States military forces.

While fighting was still in progress, a postwar Czechoslovak government of the National Front of Czechs and Slovaks was formed at Košice (Slovakia). Of the twenty-five members of the government, sixteen were Czechs and nine Slovaks. One of the most outstanding

[8] Joseph S. Roucek, "Militarization of Czechoslovak Education," *School and Society*, Vol. XLVII (March 5, 1938), pp. 413-415; "The Extension of Education for Defense in Czechoslovakia," Vol. XLIX (February 18, 1939), pp. 214-215; and "Educational Reforms of the Protectorate of Bohemia-Moravia," Vol. L (October 14, 1939), pp. 503-504.

members was Jan Masaryk, the late President Masaryk's well-known son, famed especially in England and the United States. The Košice program promised to re-establish all public life upon a broad democratic basis, guaranteed full constitutional liberties, including freedom of speech, assembly, and religious allegiance, and strictly prohibited discrimination on racial grounds. Czechoslovakia was to unite the Czech and Slovak nations with equal rights for both. The foreign policy program of Košice stressed the intensification of Slavonic amity and friendship among the democratic countries of the West.

Of importance from the standpoint of subsequent events was the appointment of a number of Communists to the first (Košice) coalition as well as the appointment of Klement Gottwald (the leader of the Communist party, who remained in Moscow during World War II) to the premiership in May 1946.

But the hopes of President Beneš that his agreement with Stalin of December 12, 1943, which guaranteed that Czechoslovakia's independence would be kept by Stalin, were doomed to terrible disappointment. By a cleverly maneuvered *coup d'état*, Gottwald's Communists, under the supervision of Soviet Russia's Deputy Foreign Minister Zorin, succeeded in February of 1948 in eliminating all the opposition from the government and Parliament and replaced Beneš with Gottwald as president. Jan Masaryk, although remaining foreign minister under Gottwald, either committed suicide or was murdered a few days later. As events worked out, Masaryk's and Beneš' beloved Czechoslovakia began to live under a yoke infinitely heavier than Francis Joseph's.

CHANGES UNDER COMMUNISM

That Czechoslovakia's educational system of 1945 would never be the replica of that developed under Masaryk and Beneš was something to be expected; the horrible damage and destruction inflicted upon it by the Nazis had changed its basic character. However, the new government of Gottwald soon put measures into effect which at first mirrored the post-World-War-II changes in the country but then became full expressions of the Communist-party mentality. Most of the Germans were expelled and their schools and universities abolished; a similar attempt was made in regard to the

Hungarian minority, although schools of the other minorities were retained. The practices of Soviet Russia—and of the Nazis, for that matter—began to be imitated as early as August 1946, when the government began compulsory harvest labor for youths between the ages of eighteen and nineteen. At that time several political parties classified as Fascist had already been dissolved and their adult-education work integrated with the state educational set-up. The government had considerable difficulties with Slovakia's Catholics, who opposed its Communist tendencies.

The Communist regime passed a new Constitution to replace that of 1920, and it was to go into effect on June 10, 1948. It was but an imitation of the Soviet Constitution, granting all democratic rights and privileges to the citizen in theory, but denying them in actual practice. Beneš refused to sign the document, which, further-more, lacked an adequate division of powers, and resigned one day before the deadline for the presidential signature. Gottwald, who replaced him, signed promptly. In general, Gottwald's govern-ment used the standard formula of the Russian and satellite elec-tions: the government presented a single list of candidates, "the National Front," and the only opportunity afforded the voters for expressing disapproval of the single slate, or any part of it, was to turn in a white ballot—thus exposing himself to reprisals. The totalitarian regime began operating mainly for the advantages of Soviet Russia. After 1948, in fact, Czechoslovakia was thoroughly subjugated to the policies and to the ideology of Soviet Russia, as it had been to those of the Third Reich between 1939 and 1945. It is true that Moscow's intervention in Czechoslovakia's internal affairs was not nearly as overt and brutal as Hitler's had been, yet the final result was practically the same.

The changes in the educational structure and ideology under Communism reflect the great drama of Czechoslovakia, the process in which a free people rooted in the spirit of democratic traditions has been gradually humbled by a satellite government. After the new government had organized elections with a single list of can-didates (in May 1948), nobody in Czechoslovakia had any political illusions left. It was evident that there was only one political power in the state: the Communist party. The intellectuals, the professors, and the students soon learned that they had to submit to this power or at least keep silent in order to remain alive. The Protestants and the Jews issued official proclamations for their churches in favor of the Communist policy. The Catholic bishops tried to resist at first, but eventually the government used physical force to silence them. It had been hoped, up to 1948, that Czechoslovakia could serve the world as a laboratory to test whether Communism and democracy could govern together in the same state; but the result of the experiment was the destruction of democracy.

Changes in education took place immediately after the Communist conquest of power, when the educators considered dangerous by the Communists were dismissed. But the educational system itself underwent a gradual but systematic reorganization between 1948 and 1950.

Immediately after the liberation of Czechoslovakia from the Nazis in 1945, Czechoslovak educators and politicians began to work on the blueprints for a sweeping school reform. Czech experts used the precedent and experience of other countries while deliberating their own needs. They studied the mass-education concept of the United States and of the Soviet Union, as well as the more recent reform projects in Britain and the Scandinavian countries. By 1947, the principle of the school reform seemed to have been accepted in most educational and political circles.[9] The remaining points of disagreement concerned technical details only, and it appeared certain that the reform would have been supported by all the major parties. However, the educational reform[10] was never voted into existence by the political parties which had collaborated in the planning. The parties themselves were decreed out of existence, and the Communists reserved for themselves the sole power to determine educational and political policy.

Nevertheless, the progressive, all-party school program was adopted by the Communist regime. Shortly after the *coup d'état* of February 1948, an official announcement charged that "reactionary elements" had obstructed the reform and that it had therefore become the duty of the new government to put the plan into effect. In fact, the "people's democracy" treated the blueprint as its own work and thereby paid an unwilling compliment to one of the last efforts of the real Czech democracy before its death. The Education Act

[9] Fred M. Hechinger, "Reds Seek Full Rule of Czech Schools," *New York Herald Tribune*, April 3, 1949.

[10] See *School Reform in Czechoslovakia* (Prague: Orbis, 1948).

embodying the program was passed on April 21, 1948, and went into effect on September 1; it did not apply to schools of university status, to military schools, and to theological institutes of learning.

The basis of the new Czechoslovak educational system is the uniform school, both compulsory and free for all children regardless of social, financial, religious, and racial background. Children attend nursery schools from the age of three to the age of six, national schools of the first grade from the age of six to the age of eleven, schools of the second grade from eleven to fifteen, and then schools of the third grade. The schools ensure "the universal, intellectual, emotional, moral, and physical development of pupils." In fact,

> . . . they shall educate youth in the spirit of the progressive national traditions and of the ideals of humanity; they shall aim toward independent thought, purposeful action, creative work, and harmonious cooperation, and shall evoke in youth the desire for self-education and progress. They shall cultivate a sense of social community, being the community of the family, the community of the nation, the community of the Slav peoples, and the community of humanity. They shall bring up socially and nationally conscious citizens of the people's democratic state, courageous defenders of their country, and devoted workers in the cause of the working people and of socialism.

All schools are state schools, and the supreme direction of all schools is vested in the Ministry of Education (since October 1948, named the Ministry of Education, Sciences and Arts). In view of the difficulties that the Roman Catholic church had with the government in 1949, it is interesting to note the following legal provisions:

> The school shall be liable to care for the religious instruction of children in accordance with their religious faith, save for cases where parents or legal guardians countermand such instruction. Religious instruction and the supervision thereof shall be the function of the organs of the church or of religious bodies, without prejudice to the right of the Ministry of Education of supreme direction and supervision. Teachers of religion, organs of the church and of religious bodies, shall observe the regulations issued in pursuance of the law by the education authorities.

First-grade and Second-grade Schools.   Schools of the first grade have five successive terms of one year each; they teach social sciences, languages, arithmetic, technical subjects, aesthetics, and health and physical culture. Schools of the second grade provide a general education in four successive terms of one year each; they teach social subjects, languages (Czech or Slovak and Russian), mathematics, natural sciences, technical subjects, aesthetics, and health and physical training. "Pupils of the final consecutive term shall be liable to undertake manual work for a period of not less than four weeks in some sector of the economy."

Third-grade Schools. Schools of the third grade are composed of (1) compulsory, basic technical schools; (2) selective technical schools, providing less than four years of study; and (3) selective higher technical schools and gymnasiums (advanced grammar schools, which prepare for the study of nontechnical faculties of university rank), with a course of study not less than four years in length. Then there are special kinds of compulsory and selective technical schools (agriculture, industry, trades, commerce, transport, women's professions, arts and crafts, social and health services, nutrition, etc.). All pupils of a higher selective school or gymnasium have to take a final examination and receive an official certificate. The Ministry of Education established central advisory councils as auxiliary organs for compulsory and selective technical schools, and local advisory councils for individual schools.

Basic technical schools usually have four consecutive terms of one year each; attendance is compulsory for all pupils not attending another school of the third grade. The school provides basic technical training and extends general education.

Technical schools provide specialized training for specific professions and extend general education; they have, as a rule, two or three consecutive terms of one year each.

Higher technical schools provide advanced specialized training, as well as general education, to such an extent as to enable pupils to proceed to study at schools of university rank. They have four consecutive terms of one year each. The general subjects covered are social sciences, languages (Czech or Slovak, Russian, Latin, and one other modern language), mathematics, natural sciences, philosophy, technical subjects, aesthetic subjects, and health and physical culture.

Schools for Children Requiring Special Care. Special schools have been established for those with physical and mental defects.

General Provisions. Schools are, as a rule, coeducational and expenses are defrayed by the state. The state establishes youth hostels and clubs which serve social and educational purposes. All textbooks have to be approved by the state, and (save those books which are used for religious education) are published by the State Publishing House. "Textbooks for religious instruction shall be approved by the respective religious bodies; these textbooks may be used at schools with the approval of the Ministry of Education, provided that they are suitable in respect of the requirements of civil and religious tolerance." Each school is administered by a director.

Institutions of Higher Learning. In order to complete the picture of Czechoslovakia's educational set-up, let us include here a short survey of the institutions of higher learning.[11] All such institutions are maintained by the state. In 1945 there were four universities—three Czechoslovak (in Brno, Prague, and Bratislava) and one German (in Prague) which was later abolished—and four polytechnical schools—two Czechoslovak and two German. Later a school of commerce was added to the Czech polytechnical school in Prague. There were nine independent colleges (two theological faculties and the following colleges: agriculture, veterinary medicine, mining, an academy of arts, and three schools of higher studies for Russian and Ukrainian *émigrés*). A complete Czechoslovak university had five faculties: theology, law, medicine, philosophy, and natural history. The director of the university is called the rector, and a dean heads each college; both are elected for one year by the faculties. The polytechnical schools have similar organization; their faculties, however, are called sections. After World War II, independent faculties of medicine were instituted at Pilzen and Hradec Králové. In addition to the "pedagogical colleges" at Pilzen and Prague, eight were started in 1947.

The schools of higher education are open to graduates of secondary schools as well as to graduates of professional schools.

REFORMS CLAIMED BY THE COMMUNISTS

The Communist government of Czechoslovakia has been stressing the "democratic character" of the educational scheme. The traditional distinction between elementary- and secondary-school teach-

[11] For more details see "Education, Czechoslovakia," in Joseph S. Roucek, ed., *Slavonic Encyclopedia*, pp. 261-266.

ers, with its attending professional "class struggle" between the "instructor" of the one and the "professor" of the other, has been abolished. At present all Czechoslovak teachers are trained in the pedagogical faculty of the universities.

Many equalitarian features of the American system have been adopted and blended with the more selective tradition of western Europe. Under the new system, all children must attend elementary schools from the sixth through the tenth year and a common secondary school up to the age of fifteen. Then, however, one may choose the "classical" gymnasium, technical education for engineering and the allied professions, commercial training, or vocational schooling (which combines practical apprenticeship with part-time general studies). All graduates except those from vocational schools are qualified to enter the free state universities.

The Czechoslovak government stresses a number of educational innovations as Communist achievements. Student government is extended to all schools, student newspapers and magazines are encouraged and financed by the local school authorities, and "open house" days are held to bring parents into closer contact with the school and its teachers. (It is particularly interesting that all these features, advertised as victories for the Communist state, are long-standing traditions of American education.)

Czechoslovakia plans a long-range building program to accompany the structural reform plan. Within forty years (after 1949) an estimated 50 billion crowns (about 1¾ billion dollars) will be spent to build 3500 new schools. Work on 375 of them was already being done in 1949 and, despite shortages of material, a number of them were being completed at that time.

COMMUNIST INDOCTRINATION

To discuss the Czechoslovak school reform without considering the problem of ideological pressure and indoctrination would be entirely misleading. A partial explanation of that aspect comes from an official Czech proclamation in connection with the school reform: "The contents of textbooks are being revised so that there are no discrepancies with the present state of the people's democracy."

In line with this reasoning, a campaign was begun in Prague in

February 1949 to propagate Michurin biology and the work of Trofim D. Lysenko, Soviet scientist and exponent of the Michurin theories. This campaign was conducted on a higher level in Czechoslovakia than in another Soviet satellite state, Bulgaria. There Michurin biology was propounded in conformity with the Soviet practice: the Communist party decreed that leading Bulgarian agronomists promptly repudiate the "anti-Marxist" biological views of Mendel, Weismann, and Morgan. The approach in Czechoslovakia appeared to be based on an effort to persuade by reason rather than by allegations that Western scientists who disagreed with the Michurin and Lysenko doctrines were warmongers and Fascists.[12]

The Communist regime did not stop, however, with the ideological drive. In 1949, 50 percent of all school children belonged to the Czech Youth League, which had branches in 95 percent of the schools. In March 1948 the government had already passed a bill requiring all youths from the age of seventeen to the age of nineteen to enter national military service (this also applied to persons up to the age of fifty-one who had hitherto been exempt). On October 25, 1948, the Czechoslovak Parliament had legalized compulsory labor camps, some of which had already been established in Karlový Vary, Pardubice, and Kladno for "work shirkers" and "disrupters." So ill-defined were the terms "work shirkers" and "disrupters," and so sweeping were the provisions of the law, that it appeared as though it could be applied to anyone whose political and economic character was not acceptable to the government. (The law could also be used for the purpose of directing older workers to jobs not covered by the law of October 1, 1945, which provided for compulsory work assignments for men of sixteen to fifty-five and women of eighteen to forty-five.) The law provided that labor camps were to be created "to educate for work as a civic duty" for the following categories of able-bodied persons between the ages of eighteen and sixty: (1) those who "shirk work or threaten the building of the people's democratic system of economic life, particularly

[12] Mr. Herčík and Professor Antonín Klička, of the Agriculture School in Prague, gave special lectures on Michurin biology at Prague's Socialist Academy; Klička emphasized the importance of the Lysenko methods for progress in agriculture; Herčík confined himself to chiding "conservative scientists" in the West who "try to stop what cannot be stopped."

the supply sector"; (2) those convicted for violating laws relating to the protection of the Czechoslovak Republic, the prohibition of black-marketing, the carrying out of the Two-year Plan, and the protection of state-controlled industry; and (3) those guilty of an administrative offense carrying a penalty of more than three months in a workhouse. Detention periods in labor camps ranged from three months to two years, depending on the nature of the offense. Regional three-men commissions had the power to commit to labor camps offenders convicted by the courts.

Further steps were taken in 1949 to promote the pro-Soviet attitude. In February of 1949, Czechoslovakia's sports organizations were asked to conduct all correspondence with athletic groups in other "people's democracies" in the Russian language and were instructed to support the acceptance of Russian as an official language in all international organizations in which Slav countries were to be represented.

COMMUNIST DIRECTIVES

While Czechoslovakia's school children were vacationing in the summer of 1949, their teachers were attending political courses. The courses were designed to train the teachers to apply new directives in accordance with the declaration of the Minister of Education, Zdeněk Nejedlý, that "the goal of the schools is the same as that to which all our efforts are directed—socialism." The directives were intended to eliminate all influence at variance with this objective. Emphasis was placed on collective work and play. Efforts were scheduled to be made to enroll all five- and six-year-olds in nursery schools and eventually to bring about compulsory attendance of all infants over three in these schools, where, according to Nejedlý, "it will be necessary to bring particularly children of rich parents who have thus far evaded the general basic collective and socialist education."[13]

Primary schools, beginning with those in the villages, were to receive the first basic textbooks written to support the Soviet line; hitherto the paper shortage had forced the Communist regime to rely mainly on the First Republic's textbooks. Pupils who failed to

[13] Dana Schmidt, "Regime Modifying Czech Schooling," *New York Times*, July 25, 1949.

show "positive attitudes" were not allowed to go on to secondary schools. Those who qualified were to be introduced, starting September 1, 1949, to a new subject called "the study of society," based on "reliable scientific foundations" and embracing history, geography, civics, and philosophy. More attention was devoted to physics, chemistry, and biology, including the theories of T. D. Lysenko on the inheritance of acquired characteristics. The total number of hours of attendance for secondary schools was to be reduced from thirty-three to thirty a week, and compulsory subjects were to be confined to mornings in order to give pupils more time for activities in the state youth organization. A law prohibiting private lessons by any except state-licensed teachers was put into effect. (This law applied even to driving lessons.) Parents, too, were to be educated along the new lines by means of "parents' committees." Instead of being allowed to influence the schools according to the traditional pattern, parents had to learn that "it was best to bring up children at home along the lines laid down at school."

Important developments in education and re-education in a people's democracy took place in July 1949. The first class of army officers recruited from the ranks of workers and farmers was graduated. Czechoslovak scientists were accused of being "politically naïve," and the Ministry of Education arranged a series of fourteen courses for them, to cover political economy and ideology; the program was to include "singing in the morning" and "organized swimming parties."[14]

In line with these developments the government ordered the school children of Czechoslovakia not to read about fairy-tale princesses. Instead, they were to read about Communist leader Klement Gottwald, president of the country.[15] The purging of the princesses and the elevation of Gottwald to the role of a school-book hero was announced by Bohumir Kujal, chairman of the government's Editorial Committee. The Committee's job was to prepare new textbooks to speed Czechoslovakia's educational system along the road to Communism. "Our children shall no longer find their examples in the princes of fairy tales, but in the shock

[14] Dana Schmidt, "Prague Arranges Political Instructions to Train the Nation's 'Naive' Scientists," New York Times, July 28, 1949.
[15] "Gottwald Is Now 'Prince' in New Czech Fairy Tales," New York Times, August 25, 1949.

workers [above-quota producers] and heroes of work," said Kujal.
"The first duty of the teachers is to deepen and intensify the education of our youth toward socialism."[16]

THE STRUGGLE WITH THE CATHOLIC CHURCH

In 1949, Czechoslovakia was repeating the common pattern being
followed by the Communists from Vladivostok to the farthest
western point of the Czechoslovak frontier Alps in regard to
religious questions. The regime, prepared to go to any length to
have the country follow the Communist model both in thought and
action, passed in October 1948 a law for "the protection of the
People's Democratic Republic," which contained pages after pages
of punishable offenses against the regime.

Thereafter the press assailed the Vatican repeatedly as the center
of "reaction," and there was a series of trials of priests and monks
on various sedition charges. In 1949 the Communist assault on
Archbishop Beran and the Catholic church reached a climax. The
first step was not to destroy the church or separate it from the
state; on the contrary, it was to establish state-controlled churches,
run by the Communist-indoctrinated Action Committees (in the
same way that they run all non-Communist organizations which
are permitted to exist). The government soon succeeded in making
two churches fully subservient to its rule—the small Orthodox
church, which was placed under the jurisdiction of the Orthodox
church in Moscow, and the National Czechoslovak church, which
had broken away from Rome after World War I. The Roman
Catholic church, under the leadership of the able and extremely
popular Archbishop Beran, refused, however, to listen to cajoling

[16] For the documentary material available on the educational changes
in Czechoslovakia, see The Central Committee of the Youth of the Czechoslovak Republic, *The Youth of Czechoslovakia* (Prague: Orbis, 1947).
Ministry of Information and Public Culture, *Czechoslovakia on the Road
to Socialism* (Prague: Orbis, 1949), is one of the first "revisionist" textbooks of the Communist government. See especially pp. 5-35, where it is
proclaimed that "in the years after 1929 the bourgeoisie endeavored to
strengthen and stabilise its ruling position in the country," that "Hitler's
rise to power was a stimulant for Czechoslovak fascists," and that Beneš'
government-in-exile, during World War II, was "led by the 'progressive'
bourgeois politicians, who . . . relied on a speedy defeat of the U.S.S.R."

and threats and became a subject of severe persecution. The Archbishop was under house arrest and his followers everywhere were
threatened; in Slovakia the faithful reacted with open defiance:
with pitchforks, clubs, and scythes they guarded their priests, and
in several villages they fought bloodily with the Communist police.

The struggle brought to mind the martyrdom in February 1949
of Hungary's Joseph Cardinal Mindszenty. In Czechoslovakia, however, the Communist overlords pitted themselves against a people
who had a tradition of political and religious freedom, symbolized
in the great names of John Hus, Comenius, and Masaryk. But the
state nearly won the struggle; the church's hands were tied, and it
was gagged. Its schools were being nationalized and its press had been
suppressed; its bishops were forbidden by law to meet, except with
government permission, or to issue pastoral letters or instructions
to the clergy except through government channels.

The impossibility of agreement between the church and the
government became clear at the meeting of church and state
representatives on February 15, 1949, when the state made a pledge
of loyalty by the bishops its principal demand. In return, the state
offered many concessions: full compensation for nationalized church
property, increase of state financial support of the church, revoca-
tion of limitations on church schools, press, and other spheres of
activity. In a series of pastoral letters and letters to the clergy the
bishops asserted that negotiations could not be continued because
microphones planted by police had been found in the bishop's
conference room, and because the announcement by the Minister of
Education that the state reserved the right to administer the entire
educational apparatus in the spirit of Marxism made further talks
useless. Finally, however, the bishops declared that they stood by the
oath of loyalty to the Republic which they had taken when they
assumed office and that any further oaths were therefore superfluous.
In a wider sense the bishops declined to take the oath demanded
by the government because it would have to be a pledge of loyalty
not simply to the Republic but to the present government, the
"people's democratic" regime.

It was while this stalemate persisted that the government deprived
the church of most of its remaining outside activities. It progressively nationalized church schools and introduced political
instructors to priests' seminaries; it controlled Catholic publishing

houses through national administrators and censorship; it controlled all Catholic organizations such as *Charitas* through national administrators and by interference with Catholic assemblies and with pilgrimages.

Czechoslovakia and other "people's democracies" have not indulged in the "religion-is-the-opium-of-the-people" phase that the Soviet Union went through. But they have attempted to convert the Roman Catholic church, together with its powerful and extensive educational resources, into an instrument of the state.

By the fall of 1949 it was evident that Czechoslavakia had been chosen to prove the Kremlin's thesis that the religious issue had to be settled the Communist way. The steps taken showed that Czechoslovakia's Communist rulers wanted to nationalize heaven but had no objections to letting God stay on as general manager provided He would take orders from the Communist government. The Church Bill, which was enacted on October 14, 1949, and which went into effect on November 1, 1949, made the Roman Catholic church a legal adjunct of the Communist state. The protests of the bishops of Czechoslovakia were of no avail, and their attempts to authorize a "conditional" pledge of loyalty to the Communist government did not satisfy the determination of the Communists to allow no reservations. On November 10, 1949, the government placed all religious publications and educational, financial, and charitable activities under the thumb of its new Ministry of Church Affairs. In addition, the Ministry will decide what can be taught in seminaries and theological schools, what textbooks can be used, and how much is to be spent for the upkeep or restoration of religious institutions.

CULTURAL CHANGES UNDER COMMUNISM

By the end of 1949 the destruction of the cultural standards and a complete ideological somersault had emerged as the U.S.S.R.'s pattern for Czechoslovakia as one of the satellite countries. When the Czechoslovaks celebrated the thirty-first anniversary of the founding of the Republic, on October 28, 1949, the portraits of the nation's two founders, former Presidents Thomas G. Masaryk and Eduard Beneš, were noticeably absent from the decorations that covered Prague's streets and buildings. Pictures of the two founders on the postage stamps were also to disappear as of November 1,

1949. Soviet Premier Stalin and Czechoslovakia's President Gottwald were the only two men whose pictures were displayed in this
nation-wide celebration. A kind of rearrangement of tradition took
place. For Stalin's seventieth birthday a 118-foot memorial was
erected in Prague between Hradcany Hill and the Moldau River.[17]
An intensive campaign was launched to sovietize all aspects of life.
Russian-language courses were instituted in schools, factories, and
clubs. The first volume of the collected works of Stalin was published in Prague in a first edition of 200,000 copies—enormous for
Czechoslovakia's conditions. Lawyers, doctors, and engineers were
warned that their professions would be affected if they did not
learn Russian. The government's new revised textbooks were
beginning to make their way into the school system of Czechoslovakia. In preparation for more than a year, they followed the
Communist line on all social, historical, and scientific matters.
They extolled the virtues of the Soviet state. The part played by
the Western armies in the liberation of Czechoslovakia was ignored.
The books described in great detail the "evils" of life before the
Communists came into power in February 1948. Educational reforms were, in turn, geared to the general plans of the government
for achieving "socialism"; thus, in the spring of 1949, a law was
passed abolishing private publishing, lest any disapproved writing
get into print. The Ministry of Information set up an annual book-
publishing plan and supervised its execution by the authorized
publishers and distributors—political parties represented in Parliament, government-sponsored economic, social, and cultural organizations, and the like.

The Czechoslovak example shows clearly how, through totalitarian methods, the schools and other educational and cultural apparatus can be used to undermine and destroy a liberal and
democratic form of life.

BIBLIOGRAPHY

CHALUPECKÝ, VÁCLAV, The Caroline University of Prague: Its Foundation, Character and Development in the Fourteenth Century

[17] When the sculptors protested that the monument would be too high,
Minister of Education Zdeněk Nejedlý replied, "Stalin's memorial must
not be in Prague, but over Prague."

(Prague: Orbis, 1948). A valuable contribution to the field of comparative education.

Constitution of the Czechoslovak Republic (Prague: Czechoslovak Ministry of Information, 1948). An official text of the Czechoslovak Constitution of June 9, 1948.

DRUCE, GERALD, *Czechoslovakia, Past and Present* (Prague: Orbis, 1947). Contains two valuable chapters, "Czech and Slovak Culture," pp. 153-168, and "The Sokol and Sport," pp. 169-174, both covering Czechoslovakia's developments under Masaryk and Beneš.

KERNER, R. J., ed., *Czechoslovakia: Twenty Years of Independence* (Berkeley: University of California Press, 1940). The best systematic survey of Czechoslovakia under Masaryk and Beneš. See Chapter 9, "Czechoslovakia and Her Minorities," pp. 171-192, by Joseph S. Roucek; Chapter 15, "The Religious Situation in Czechoslovakia," pp. 284-301, by Matthew Spinka; Chapter 16, "Education in a Democracy," pp. 302-315, by F. H. Stuerm, and bibliographies at the end of Chapter 16.

ODLOŽILÍK, OTAKAR, *The Caroline University, 1348-1948* (Prague: Orbis, 1948). A valuable survey of the development of Charles University, Prague, written, fortunately, without Communist supervision.

ROUCEK, JOSEPH S., "Adult Education in Czechoslovakia," *School and Society*, Vol. XLIII (January 25, 1936), pp. 125-127.

————, "Concept of Education in Czechoslovakia," *Review of Educational Research*, Vol. IX (October 1939), pp. 377-380; Bibliography, pp. 432-433.

————, "Educational Changes in Slovakia," *School and Society*, Vol. L (August 19, 1939), pp. 249-250.

————, "Educational Reforms of the Protectorate of Bohemia-Moravia," *School and Society*, Vol. L (October 14, 1939), pp. 503-504.

————, "Educational Trends in the 'Second' Czechoslovakia," *School and Society*, Vol. XLIX (March 18, 1939), pp. 349-350.

————, "Recent Reforms and Progress in the Czechoslovak Educational System," *School and Society*, Vol. XXXVIII (December 23, 1933), pp. 837-839.

————, "Some Phases of Development of the Czechoslovak Educational System," *School and Society*, Vol. XXV (June 11, 1932), pp. 802-804.

————, ed., *Slavonic Encyclopedia* (New York: Philosophical Library, Inc., 1949). Contains numerous references to educational problems; see especially "Education" and "Educational Theory."

School Reform in Czechoslovakia (Prague: Orbis, 1948). An indispensable booklet, containing the Education Act of April 21, 1948, Dr. Zděnek Nejedlý's exposition of its ideological justification, and Jeroslav Paur's glorification of the act.

SKERPAN, ALFRED A., "Liberalism and Eastern Europe," *Bulletin of the American Association of University Professors*, Vol. XXXIV (Winter 1948), pp. 719-731. Surveys the struggle between the liberal and Communist forces in central-eastern Europe.

SKILLING, H. G., "The Partition of the University of Prague," *Slavonic and East European Review*, Vol. XXVII (May 1949), pp. 430-449. A scholarly survey.

THELENOVÁ-HAVLIČKOVÁ, SYLVIA, *Czechoslovak Women To-Day* (Prague: Orbis, 1948). Contains several sections dealing with the educational changes in Czechoslovakia in respect to women.

TUROSIENSKI, D. D., *Education in Czechoslovakia* (Washington, D. C.: Bureau of Education Bulletin, 1935, No. 11, U. S. Government Printing Office, 1936). A systematic, formal survey.

The Youth of Czechoslovakia (Prague: Orbis, 1947). An official presentation of the "auxiliary" aspects of Czechoslovakia's education by the Central Committee of the Youth of the Czechoslovak Republic.

Soviet Union

WILLIAM H. E. JOHNSON

Russia is one of the great powers of the world, with an area of about 8½ million square miles and a population estimated at over 193 million. Its area is twice that of Brazil or the United States, but a huge amount of it is rendered relatively unusable by climate conditions (for example, the tundras of northern Siberia and the mountainous areas on the south border of European and Asiatic Russia). Russia's technology is only now in the process of modern change and advance. Her natural resources include nearly all of those used by man. The known coal deposits are second only to those of the United States, the petroleum deposits are among the richest in the world, and the lumber and water supplies amount to about one third of the world's totals. Russia is in a phase of change from an agricultural to an industrial economy.

The governmental system constitutes the first large-scale experiment in state socialism and has involved the use of national plans known as the Five-year Plans. Russia is characterized by a very aggressive foreign policy based upon military, economic, and propaganda pressures. This is a trend directly out of the past, since czarist Russia was a great propagandist of force and imperial expansion. To many observers Russia has merely changed masters and is still engaged in state control of the individual, police surveillance of private life, and imperial expansion facilitated by all of the newer developments in technology and education. The Russians have used psychological warfare extensively, especially around the outer edge of Eurasia, that is, "the strategic rim." In the thirty years following 1917 the Soviet Union turned out some 11 billion books of 830 titles. Joseph Stalin's *Short Course in the History of the Communist Party* was the biggest item. Over 34 million copies of this book were sold in some sixty-two different languages. The Russians are experts at talking to people in their respective languages about the new world religion of Communism as interpreted by Stalin and key members of the Communist party. The Russians have made marked progress in reducing national illiteracy, although no firm figures are obtainable, and they have extended compulsory education from four years to seven, presumably, in urban areas. There is a heavy emphasis upon education in the new technology. There is also a very high degree of selectivity in education beyond the elementary level; in fact, it would seem that a new elite is being built up by well-organized educational techniques. In general the Russians have a "two-track" system of education in which the masses are trained, obedient, productive units in the Soviet system of production and expansion and in which the few are trained to be leaders enforcing the party line.

A. H. M.

When the Bolsheviks came to power in Russia, in November 1917, that nation had long been dedicated to a trinity of concepts best expressed in the phrase "Orthodoxy, Autocracy, and Nationalism." Russia had been officially Orthodox since the conversion of St. Vladimir, in 988; uninterruptedly autocratic since the coronation of Ivan the Great, in 1462; and strongly nationalistic since the founding of the Romanov dynasty, in 1613.[1] But the roots of these forces go back even deeper into Slavic tradition.

The folk notes of the ancient *Rus* settlements in northeastern Europe during the ninth century contain many references to the "principle of unanimity" which prevailed, whereby citizens of a community were severely punished if they failed to conform com-

[1] Frederick L. Schuman, *Soviet Politics at Home and Abroad* (New York: Alfred A. Knopf, Inc., 1946), pp. 99-113.

pletely to the majority decisions of local assemblies.[2] It appears that autocracy, however, was a policy learned by Russian rulers during the Mongol occupation in the thirteenth and fourteenth centuries. The same Mongols, by mingling their stock with that of the original inhabitants, created a wide diversity of semi-Oriental languages and cultures which, because of their dogged persistence, later incited the more militant Russian nationalism to assume a frequently violent and nearly always oppressive character. In the words of one historian, "Everything of enduring import in the early development of Russia is encompassed in the migration of Asiatic tribes westward toward Europe along the steppe road, and in the flow of Scandinavian and Slavic peoples southward toward Byzantium along the water road."[3] Borrowing practices at one time from the East, at another time from the West, and then fashioning these practices to fit existing Slavic institutions—thus did the Russian Empire create and mold its religion, its government, and the attitudes of its people even before the seventeenth century.

During the course of the next three hundred years, several new forces made their lasting imprints upon the Russian national character and social institutions. Through the activities of the various church brotherhoods, schools and academies arose in the southwestern section of the country, and in subsequent years they exerted a profound influence on Russian culture. Peter I brought in Western practices in industry and trade and laid the foundations for state control of the church, which has continued to the present day. Catherine II, at first as Western-minded as Peter, shaped Russian manners and literary expression in a European mold and created an educational system of which the objectives, if not the structure, exist today in modified form in the Soviet Union. Alexander II exerted a wide influence on the legal and administrative apparatus, and the early years of his reign brought these institutions, too, closer to Western forms. Although through no design on his part, it was under Alexander also that one of the really great forces in recent world history first planted its seeds in Russia: the doctrines of Marxism.

[2] M. M. Kovalevsky, *Modern Customs and Ancient Laws of Russia* (London: D. Nutt, 1891), pp. 121-123.
[3] Frederick L. Schuman, *op. cit.*, p. 93.

The Marxist system of thought found fertile and receptive ground in the country of the Czars. Even though serfdom was nominally abolished in 1861, many of its remnants remained to plague the government up to, and even beyond, the Revolution of November 1917. Also, the late but rapid growth of industry created a small but very self-conscious proletariat whose leaders were particularly adept at capitalizing upon every weakness in the complex social structure. Finally, a group of well-educated and courageous intellectuals constantly called for reforms which a comparison with the West showed to be long overdue, but which seemed impossible to wring from the entrenched autocracy.

Under such conditions, revolution was inevitable. It now appears that this revolution brought a new orthodoxy of a political rather than a religious nature, a new autocracy which is even more jealous and powerful than the old, and a new nationalism which is as ambitious as that which had for so long dominated the policies of the Empire.[4]

SOCIAL AND EDUCATIONAL HERITAGE

Although the Soviet Union is undoubtedly following many of the traditions inherited from the past, it must not be assumed that these traditions have not also been remolded during the brief but violent history of the current regime. The Russia of today has erected a new economic system, a new political administration, and a new ethical philosophy, and all these innovations have strongly influenced the present educational program. Later pages of this chapter will reveal the greatly increased governmental concern with education at all levels, and the enormous quantitative and qualitative progress experienced during the past three decades. Since each level and phase will be considered individually, some indication should be given here of the composite system of educational administration, which appears to combine some features of the old with many elements of the new.

The Constitution of the U.S.S.R. defines the nation as "a federal state" consisting of sixteen constituent republics. Some administra-

[4] William H. E. Johnson, *Russia's Educational Heritage* (Pittsburgh: Carnegie Press, 1950), Chapter 12.

tive activities are nation-wide in scope and stem directly from a central ministry in Moscow; others are combinations of centralized and decentralized control with centers both in Moscow and in the capital of each constituent republic; still others have no common central authority and are directed only from the capital of each republic. Examples of the first type are foreign trade, communications, and most of the large-scale industries; among the second group are the several food industries, domestic trade, justice, public health, and higher education; in the third category are such activities as local industry, municipal economy, and general education.

It is not difficult to understand why, in a nation as ethnologically complex as the Soviet Union, general education on a native-language basis would require a high degree of formal decentralization. The pages to follow will indicate many instances of decentralization, particularly at the higher educational level, and it appears that certain aspects of these practices are due as much to traditional Empire procedure as to the pressure of current requirements. Under the czarist system, some elementary schools were governed by the state, some by the church, some by local communities, and others by private individuals. Secondary schools also were under the jurisdiction of private as well as public authorities, and establishments of higher learning were frequently attached to industrial or agricultural organizations outside the old Ministry of Public Education itself.[5]

One very significant difference between the old and new educational systems must constantly be borne in mind, however. Whereas under the Empire the decentralization frequently permitted wide variations in educational philosophy and methods, the Soviet Union countenances no such autonomy. By means of rigid control of all important offices through the only existing political party, students in Central Asia learn the same things in the same way as do children in Moscow and Leningrad, even though many languages may serve as media of communication. Thus the varied systems of administration and organization and the diverse languages themselves become the very means by which a fundamental homogeneity in thought and action is acquired by the citizens of the Soviet Union.

[5] *Ibid.*, Chapters 9-12.

PRESCHOOL EDUCATION

Soviet leaders have long been aware of the power and value of an indoctrination which begins early in the life of the citizen. "Train up a child in the way he should go, and when he is old he will not depart from it" is an ancient maxim, and many societies have used it as a guide in their educational processes. But none has done so more thoroughly and effectively than the Soviet Union. Less than a week after the Revolution of November 1917, the new People's Commissariat of Education of the Russian Socialist Federated Soviet Republic created a Department of Preschool Education which has functioned ever since, and at the same time went on record as considering this level of training one of the most important in the entire system. The following year an Institute of Preschool Education was established to train teachers in this field, and during the next few years several nation-wide conferences were held to discuss problems peculiar to preschool institutions.

The three decades since the Revolution have brought about many changes in the aims, organization, and methodology of preschool education in the Soviet Union. The level has now been subdivided into two distinct phases: the *creche*, or nursery school, now caters to children up to the age of three years, and the *detskii sad*, or kindergarten, is devoted to children from three to seven. Each phase includes a large number of playgrounds which are operated in connection with the more institutionalized aspects of the work. Since the care of the younger group is largely a physical matter, the nursery schools are under the jurisdiction of the Ministry of Health, but the kindergartens remain a responsibility of the Department of Preschool Education in the various Ministries of Education.

The basic principles of the preschool institutions have found their latest complete expression in the "Rules for Kindergartens" adopted by all the proper educational agencies in December 1944. These rules declare that, although the fundamental purpose of the Soviet kindergarten is to achieve the all-around development of children between the ages of three and seven years, such agencies should also be recognized as a means of providing mothers of young children with the opportunity to participate more actively in the complex "productive, governmental, cultural, and sociopolitical life" of the nation.[6]

In addition to these general functions, the rules state that Soviet kindergartens must pursue the following specific aims: (1) the protection of the physical health of the child; (2) the development of "the intellectual capacities, the speech, the will and the character of the child," at the same time providing him with artistic appreciation and a knowledge of the world and of people; (3) the creation of habits of independence and cleanliness, as well as correct habits of work and an understanding of the proper use and care of one's possessions; (4) the instillation of the proper attitudes toward adults and other children, and "of respect for elders and love for parents"; and finally, (5) "the cultivation of love for the Soviet Motherland, its people and its leaders, its Soviet Army, its wealth of natural resources, the creative genius of its people."[7]

Under Soviet law, no preschool institution can be operated privately, although many of them charge fees ranging from small amounts to sums far beyond the reach of the average family income. However, any public agency—such as a factory, a trade union, a cooperative enterprise, or a collective farm—can establish a nursery school or kindergarten provided the school is placed under the supervision of the proper educational body and conforms to all the regulations set up by that body. Contrary to the practice followed in the early years of the Soviet regime, committees of parents are now encouraged to work closely with members of the kindergarten staff.

Since the kindergarten remains a one-grade institution despite the wide range of age among the children, the latter are usually divided into age groups (three to four, four to five, etc.) of about twenty-five members. Methods vary, of course, according to the age group, but the daily schedule of nine to twelve hours always includes periods devoted to play, sleep or rest, eating, and some form of learning activity. Excursions, walks, games, examination of children's books, and conversations with the teacher play a major role in kindergarten methods. Upon completion of the final year, the child should be able to

[6] E. N. Medynsky, *Narodnoe obrazovanie USSR* (Public Education in the U.S.S.R.) (Moscow, 1947), p. 31.

[7] *Ibid.*, pp. 31-32.

. . . count up to 20 or 30, recognize and compare figures, add and subtract numbers of one digit, use simple units of measurement such as kilogram and meter, name the days of the week, and tell time by the clock at least in terms of hours. He must be able to express what he means through an adequate vocabulary of words, correctly arranged in sentences which are coherent and understandable to others. In addition, he should be able to retell short stories, give an account of some of his experiences, and recite from memory several poems.[8]

The child is then considered ready to enter elementary school.

ELEMENTARY EDUCATION

The system of general education in the U.S.S.R. comprises three main types of schools: (1) the elementary school of four grades; (2) the "incomplete secondary" school, which provides the four grades of the elementary school and an additional three grades; and (3) the "complete secondary" school, which provides the seven grades of the "incomplete secondary" school and an additional three grades. This 4-3-3 structure has existed since 1934, and corresponds roughly to the 6-3-3 system of elementary, junior high, and senior high school in the United States. Because the school year in the U.S.S.R. consists of thirty-three weeks of six days each with four to six forty-five-minute classes daily, Soviet educators believe that their ten-year school is academically equivalent to the twelve-year course offered here and in other countries. Soviet schools open on September 1 and close on May 20 except for pupils in the graduating grades (the fourth, seventh, and tenth) in each type of school, who must take final examinations until June 5. Holidays are few: three days in early November, ten days in late December and early January, and six days in March. The number of elementary class hours per week ranges from twenty-four in the first grade to twenty-seven in the fourth grade.

Until September 1944, children entered Soviet schools at the age of eight, but now the elementary schools are concerned with children between the ages of seven and eleven years. Even before the Revolution of 1917, several unsuccessful attempts had been made to pass legislation on compulsory elementary education, and

[8] *Ibid.*, p. 38.

the new regime found it inadvisable to introduce so sweeping a measure until 1930. During the decade 1928-1938, elementary-school enrollment rose from 10 million to 21 million, and during these years laws were passed extending compulsory education to cover the incomplete secondary school in towns but leaving such extension of the rural term to local initiative. Perhaps the greatest educational achievement made by the Soviet Union at this level is the provision of elementary education for the many backward national minorities, which now claim approximately the same enrollment proportions as the European groups, or between 90 and 100 percent. All elementary grades in the Soviet Union are coeducational and free of any tuition charge.

The elementary-school curriculum consists of eight subjects: singing, drawing, physical training, geography, history of the U.S.S.R., nature study, arithmetic, and either Russian or the native language of the students, or the two in combination in the upper grades. There can be little doubt regarding the emphasis of the Soviet elementary school: more than half (51 percent) of the total course time is devoted to language, and more than a quarter (27 percent) to arithmetic; the six remaining subjects together occupy only 22 percent of the total of 3301 class hours spent in the four years of elementary school.

Since compulsory seven-year education is now in effect in all cities and towns of the U.S.S.R., these localities usually supplement the lower four grades with an additional three years to form an incomplete secondary school. The independent elementary school is therefore confined largely to the rural areas.

SECONDARY EDUCATION

The Incomplete Secondary School. As explained in the preceding section, the Soviet secondary schools are of two types, designated as "incomplete" or "complete." The incomplete secondary school has a seven-year course, the first four years of which correspond to the curriculum of the elementary school. Therefore, the child who has passed the final examinations of the fourth grade in either an elementary or incomplete secondary school may enter without entrance examinations the fifth grade of the latter institution.

The upper grades of the incomplete secondary school are similar in many aspects to the junior high school in the United States. In both countries this level evolved from the recognized need for a transitional period between the relative informality of elementary instruction and the more stringent discipline of secondary education. Moreover, since many children in both countries do not attend school beyond this level, this type of school offers some preparation for immediate occupational and civic responsibilities. But there are also important distinctions between the two national systems at this level. Whereas in the United States the scope of the junior high school is determined largely by local conditions, in the Soviet Union all incomplete secondary schools include the four elementary grades plus grades five, six, and seven. Thus the Soviet pupil always enters the intermediate level between the ages of eleven and twelve and leaves it between fourteen and fifteen. Whereas in the United States the great majority of pupils in the junior high schools are preparing to continue their education in senior high school, the Soviet incomplete secondary schools act more as "feeders" for the numerous vocational schools (which will be described in a later section of this article).

Another important difference is an outgrowth of a recent Soviet decree regarding segregation of the sexes. The Soviet regime had prided itself ever since its inception upon the complete lack of segregation at all levels in its system of education. Nevertheless, in 1943, an experiment was begun in the seventy-six most important cities and towns of the U.S.S.R. which was designed to test the value of separating boys from girls in the last three grades of general education. Each succeeding year the scope of segregation has been extended, and at present it is universal in grades eight, nine, and ten, and in effect in grades five, six, and seven in most of the cities. Incomplete secondary schools in towns, in villages, and in farm regions still adhere to the practice of coeducation, but Soviet officials apparently plan to extend segregation to these areas when more adequate physical facilities can be provided.

It should be pointed out that this separation of the sexes has not involved any differentiation in the course of study in the intermediate grades: both boys and girls follow the same curriculum at this level. The course in Russian and/or other native language continues in grade five, as do classes in arithmetic, geography, drawing, and physical training. Three new subjects (botany, ancient history, and foreign language) are offered in this grade, and in the next two years the student takes up algebra, geometry, zoology, physics, chemistry, medieval and modern history, drafting, and Constitution of the U.S.S.R. There are thirty-one class hours a week in grade five, and thirty-two in grades six and seven; a total of 3134 hours is devoted to the entire three-year course. Tuition is free throughout this intermediate level.

The Complete Secondary School. The complete secondary school is actually a ten-grade establishment combining the four elementary grades, the three intermediate grades, and the three final grades. Thus, although the structures of the Soviet and the American systems of general education are very similar, the organization is quite different in the two countries. As has been indicated before, the large network of metropolitan elementary schools, so common in the United States, is almost unknown in the U.S.S.R. In like manner, the large junior-senior high school which is a current favorite in American cities has no counterpart in the Soviet Union.

Admission to grade eight in the complete secondary school is permitted without entrance examination to those children aged fifteen to sixteen who have passed the final examinations of grade seven in either the incomplete or complete secondary school. Here again, as between the elementary and intermediate levels, an attempt is made to provide a smooth articulation in the course of study. In grade eight several of the subjects studied in the preceding grade are continued and only two new courses are added (anatomy and physiology), although the former concentration upon language study is now shifted to Russian and foreign literature. In the last two grades of this level, trigonometry and Darwinism are added to the curriculum, and history of the U.S.S.R. is taken up again after a three-year omission during the intermediate grades. There are thirty-two hours of classes a week in grades eight and nine, but only thirty and one half in the final year to allow the graduating students more time for work on individual projects. The entire three-year course consists of 3119 class hours. Added to the totals for the elementary (3301) and the intermediate (3134) grades, this means a grand total of 9554 class hours for all subjects in the ten-year program of general education.

Throughout the Soviet Union, as mentioned before, boys and girls attend separate classes in grades eight, nine and ten. However, the curriculum is the same for both sexes except in one particular: in the three-year course in physical training, the boys take military training while the girls divide their time between physical training and domestic science. Although until very recently all Soviet constitutions have guaranteed free education at all levels, small tuition fees were until recently charged annually in the last three grades of general education. It is reported that the better students receive stipends which more than cover this expense. Pupils usually are graduated from the complete secondary school at the age of seventeen or eighteen and are then qualified for admission to any of the various types of institutions of higher learning through competitive examinations. Graduates with marks of "excellent" in all subjects on the final examinations receive a diploma *cum laude*, which entitles them to admission to higher institutions without competitive examinations. Since applications to such institutions are usually more than double the number of vacancies, and since

APPORTIONMENT OF TIME AMONG THE VARIOUS SUBJECTS IN THE SOVIET
TEN-YEAR PROGRAM OF GENERAL EDUCATION

Subject	1942-1943		1947-1948		Revision in hours	
	Hours	Percent	Hours	Percent	Increase	Decrease
Russian language and literature	2676	28	3003	31	327	
Mathematics	2092	22	2112	22	20	
Physics, chemistry, astronomy	848	9	857	9	9	
Natural sciences	523	6	462	5		61
Geography	570	6	545	6		25
History and Constitution of U.S.S.R.	797	8	776	8		21
Modern language	653	7	743	8	90	
Writing, drafting, singing	330	3	462	5	132	
Physical and military training	1048	11	594	6		454
Total	9537	(100)	9554	(100)	17	

all *cum laude* applicants are accepted before the competitive examinations are held, relatively few vacancies in the more popular higher institutions remain open to competitive examination.

The table above,[9] providing data for all subjects in the ten-year

[9] Figures for 1942-1943 from Embassy of the U.S.S.R., Washington, D. C., *Information Bulletin*, Vol. V, No. 131 (December 27, 1945); figures for 1947-1948 compiled from E. N. Medynsky, *op. cit.*, pp. 51-81.

curriculum, indicates interesting trends. Although there has been only a slight change in the total number of hours, the time devoted to Russian and/or other native language and literature has increased by 13 percent and the time devoted to the skill subjects 40 percent, whereas the time allotted to physical and military training has been reduced by 43 percent. Slight increases in mathematics, physical sciences, and modern languages are accompanied by slight decreases in natural science, geography, and history.

INSTITUTIONS OF HIGHER LEARNING

There are three basic types of higher educational institutions in the U.S.S.R.—universities, institutes, and colleges. Unlike the schools in the three-level system of general education previously described, most Soviet higher institutions are governed by an all-Union administrative apparatus rather than by the educational ministries of each republic. In 1936 an All-Union Committee on Higher Schools was created and attached as a subcabinet agency to the Council of People's Commissars; ten years later this Committee was raised to full cabinet rank and renamed the Ministry of Higher Education of the U.S.S.R.

Although the powers of this Ministry are broad, its jurisdiction extends to fewer than half of Soviet higher institutions. All thirty-one universities are included in its authority, along with about 280 institutes devoted to such fields as technology, agriculture, forestry, veterinary sciences, economics, and law. The remaining five hundred higher institutions—such as institutes of transport, medicine, art, physical culture, and pedagogy—are assigned to the ministry most concerned with the field of study. Pedagogical institutes, numbering 325, are governed by the ministries of education in each republic, since there is no all-Union ministry for this field.

Each university has a rector, and each institute and college a director, who is the chief administrative officer of the institution and is responsible directly to the appropriate ministry. There are no boards of trustees such as are almost required adjuncts in the United States, and there are no privately operated higher institutions of a recognized character. Each institution is divided into several faculties or departments which are administered by department heads, and several of the more important department heads constitute a "senate" to advise the rector or director and assist in carrying out policy decisions.

Higher education in the Soviet Union is extremely specialized in character and completely professional in purpose. Except for the thirty-one universities which provide training for teaching and research in such broad subjects as mathematics, language, the social and physical sciences (and, occasionally, law) and the nineteen polytechnical and industrial colleges which offer a rather general education along technological lines, all establishments of higher learning are called "institutes" and are devoted to specific fields such as machine building, aviation, metallurgy, and food production. Contrary to American practice, there are no "colleges" of medicine or engineering or liberal arts as integral parts of large universities; medical institutes are separate agencies, the field of engineering is covered not by one but by several types of specialized institutes, and the universities themselves are the closest approximation to what the United States knows as the college of liberal arts.

The U.S.S.R. does not permit the growth of very large student bodies in any one higher institution. Possessing about half as many such establishments (808 in 1949) as the United States, the Soviet Union has a total of much fewer than half as many students (734,000 in residence and 298,000 in correspondence courses in 1949, an increase of 26 percent over the prewar years). Enrollment in the institutes usually ranges from seven hundred to one thousand, although a few of the larger cities have five-year institutes with four, five, and even six times that number. The universities, all of which offer a five-year course, have student bodies of two thousand to five thousand; only the University of Moscow, with an unbroken history of nearly two hundred years, has as many as seven thousand students.

Tuition fees were until recently charged in all universities and most institutes, but Soviet officials claim that the majority of the students obtained either individual exemption or a stipend which more than covered the fee. All higher institutions are coeducational, with the proportion of women students ranging from 28 percent in industrial studies to about 50 percent in pedagogical courses and nearly 70 percent in institutes of public health.[10] In 1948, Soviet establishments of higher learning graduated 122,000 men and women, an increase of about 20 percent over the best prewar years. The degree granted upon completion of the four- or five-year undergraduate course is called the *diplom*, and is equivalent to the bachelor of science degree in the United States.

Many of these institutions are also qualified to prepare students for the two graduate degrees, candidate of science and doctor of science. The former degree may be awarded by certain of the institutes themselves, and is usually gained after a three-year period of study and work beyond the *diplom*. In most cases this period is divided about equally among academic courses, practical employment in the chosen field, and preparation of a thesis or project. Few Soviet students attain this degree before the age of twenty-five, since it requires a total of at least seven years of higher education. The degree of doctor of science is awarded not by the institutes but by a special examining commission attached to the Ministry of Higher Education of the U.S.S.R. There is no definite time requirement for the course of study leading to the doctorate, but the recipient must already possess the candidate degree, must have demonstrated complete mastery of his field in practical work, and must make, in his final thesis, a contribution to knowledge which is deemed both original and significant by the examining commission in Moscow. Only in rare cases is the degree awarded to persons under thirty years of age. It is estimated that in 1949-1950 about 15,000 persons were engaged in graduate work in Soviet universities and institutes.

ADULT EDUCATION

In the early years of the Soviet regime (1917-1926), the major task of adult education was the reduction of the appalling degree of illiteracy bequeathed by the Empire. The only complete census of population ever taken by the czarist government revealed that, in 1897, 78.9 percent of the 126 million inhabitants were unable to read or write in any language. Even among children of school age, three fourths were illiterate, and the literacy rate of females in this age group was only a little better than half that of the males. The situation was particularly acute among the national minorities of

[10] E. N. Medynsky, *op. cit.*, p. 169.

central Asia, where only a small proportion of the native youth went to school at all.[11]

The conditions described above were not improved to any great extent during the final twenty years of the czarist regime: a consensus of estimates indicates that in November 1917 the literacy rate in Russia as a whole was 25-30 percent. The new Soviet government was unable to do much about the problem during its first two years in power. But in December 1919, a decree was issued requiring all citizens between the ages of eight and fifty years to learn to read and write either in Russian or in the native language. To implement this decree a nation-wide campaign to "liquidate illiteracy" was organized. All school children with illiterate relatives were required to teach the latter to read and write, all types of schools were opened in the evenings to provide free assistance to those who wished to learn, and kiosks were set up in parks, on farms, and even on street corners, in order to provide facilities for instruction in reading and writing. Although no accurate figures could be kept under such conditions, it is estimated that, between 1920 and 1940, 50 million persons took advantage of these informal centers to become literate. By 1926, literacy had risen above 50 percent in the western republics and to about 20 percent among the more backward peoples;[12] the Soviet census of 1939 states that in that year the rate for those aged eight to fifty among the 170 million inhabitants of the Soviet Union was 81.2 percent. No official figures have been published during the last ten years, but several recent Soviet sources claim that 85-90 percent of this age group is now literate.

After the introduction of the First Five-year Plan, in 1928, the Soviet government turned its attention from the dissemination of mere literacy to the more complicated task of providing its citizens, both young and old, with the rudiments of technical knowledge and skill. A vast network of technical schools for adults was established, and millions of workers were given on-the-job training to prepare them for study in such schools. By the middle of 1935, Stalin was able to declare that the elementary stage of technical education had

[11] V. Ivanovich (Charnolusskii), "Iz itogov pervoi russkoi vceobscchei perepisi" (From Summaries of the First Russian General Census), *Vestnik Vospitaniia* (Educational Herald), Vol. XVII (January 1906), pp. 38-55.

[12] Embassy of the U.S.S.R., Washington, D. C., *Information Bulletin*, Vol. V, No. 131 (December 27, 1945), p. 3.

been passed for the mass of Soviet workers and that all citizens should proceed immediately toward the complete *mastery* of technique, including its proper application to improving the conditions of life in general.[13]

Thus, adult education was given the same prestige and the same fundamental principles as general education. Even during the recent war, adult schools were continually being reorganized to provide citizens aged eighteen to sixty with a really sound education beyond mere literacy and simple techniques. In 1943-1944, two new types of school were created: a day school for youths aged fourteen to twenty-five who were working in industry, and a night school for farm workers. The first type parallels grades five to ten of general education, and the second is at the elementary-grades level with extensions up through grade seven. Both types of school offer curriculums almost identical with those of the general-education schools, but the hours of study are arranged differently, all classes are co-educational, and individual consultations permit an accelerated progress toward completion.[14] In the 1949-1950 academic year, these schools for young adults alone registered more than three fourths of a million students in regular attendance, and many more adults attended other types of schools or enrolled in correspondence courses. With such a wealth of opportunity provided for almost everyone to attend school, there is certainly some basis for the Soviet claim that one fifth of its entire population of 200 million is now engaged in some form of institutionalized study.

CHARACTER EDUCATION

In the early years of the Soviet regime the official attitude toward character education was rather iconoclastic and nihilistic. The aim seemed to be to tear down the old concepts of morality, patriotism, and discipline and to allow the "free growth" of new humanistic virtues. In pursuance of this aim, marriage codes were abolished, church attendance severely discouraged, militarism frowned upon, and manners and courtesy made the butt of rude jokes. Standards of dress and personal hygiene were lowered to such a degree that

[13] J. Stalin, Address to the Graduates of the Red Army Academies, Moscow, May 4, 1935.

[14] E. N. Medynsky, *op. cit.*, p. 116.

neatness and cleanliness were despised and dishevelment and mal-
odorousness became revered symbols of honest toil.

Certain changes in this attitude began to appear during the First
Five-year Plan, and by 1936 marked revisions could be noted. The
demands of the national economy made greater labor discipline a
vital necessity, and the rising standard of living permitted better
clothes, more food and entertainment, and a generally elevated
plane of social relationships. The prospect of approaching war
probably had a great deal to do with the Soviet decision to outlaw
voluntary abortions, erect stricter marriage and divorce laws, and
encourage an increased birth rate. When war came in 1941 it provided a supreme test of Soviet endurance, and the lessons learned
from it brought about greatly increased discipline in all walks
of life.

Today the expressed aims of Soviet education include new aspects
of character and citizenship, as indicated by the "Rules for Kindergartens" previously described and the "Rules for School Children"
adopted in 1943.[15] The late Andrei Zhdanov, a member of the Communist Politburo who was responsible for many of the recent shifts
in educational policy, declared that

> ... the Soviet younger generation must be taught to be staunch
> and courageous, fearful of no obstacle, but able to meet obstacles
> halfway and overcome them. Our people must be well educated,
> must possess the highest ideals and culture, the highest morality
> and aesthetic tastes. In order to have such people we must nurture
> our youth in the spirit of supreme fidelity to the Soviet regime
> and supreme service to the interests of the people.[16]

In a Soviet pedagogical textbook of the same period, the following
attributes are listed as essential "volitional qualities" of character:
purposefulness, resolution, persistence, initiative, courage, and endurance.[17]

It must be emphasized that character education in the Soviet
Union has never been the responsibility of the school alone but has
also been carried on by several types of outside agencies. Chief

---

[15] George S. Counts and Nucia P. Lodge, *I Want to Be Like Stalin*
(New York: The John Day Company, 1947), pp. 149-150.
[16] E. N. Medynsky, *op. cit.*, p. 11.
[17] George S. Counts and Nucia P. Lodge, *op. cit.*, pp. 125-130.

among them are those organizations, created and directly controlled
by the Communist party, which parallel the educational system: the
Octobrists, for children of preschool age; the Pioneers, for elemen-
tary- and intermediate-grade pupils; and the Komsomol, for young
people aged fifteen to twenty-five. A decree of the eleventh Komsomol Congress in 1949 stated that the primary task of the organization is "to educate Soviet youth in the spirit of Soviet patriotism."
Since Soviet trade unions and cooperatives include in their combined memberships at least 90 percent of all gainfully employed
citizens, the extensive educational activities of these agencies play
a major role in shaping the ideals, outlooks, opinions, and behavior
of many millions of people. The military forces also cannot be
disregarded in this connection, for a significant portion of military
service is devoted to character education in addition to instruction
in the more formal subjects. The scope of this training can be
better understood if we realize that the Soviet army of 4 million to
5 million men is constantly being fed with new personnel
through a system of compulsory military training for nearly all male
youths. Finally, many clubs and societies based upon sports, hobby
interests, travel tours, and even academic or professional pursuits
arrange their programs so as to include some form of character
training. This wide diversity of organizations, however, should not
lead one to doubt the monolithic nature of the training program
as a whole. Regardless of their particular structure or specific purpose, all these agencies cooperate in molding the character of Soviet
citizens in the pattern designed by the leadership of the Communist
party.

MORAL AND RELIGIOUS EDUCATION

In many countries of the world, moral and religious education
would be considered almost as one and could be dealt with as such.
In the Soviet Union, however, they are not only divergent but definitely antagonistic. Since its inception, bolshevism has been extremely hostile to religion, and even though the Soviet government
now permits the church wider latitude than before, the Communist party carries on the struggle against any kind of religious
belief. Whereas "God's Law" was a required subject in the Czarist
school system, the Communists insist that "Darwinism" be taught as

a separate subject and that all science study have an antireligious emphasis. A few seminaries for the training of priests have recently been permitted to open in the Soviet Union, but only graduates of the ten-year state school system can enter these institutions. No type of religious instruction may be given children under twelve, and then only individually and by the parents.

In view of the undeniably antireligious character of Soviet education, one might ask whether any moral education can exist. The Communists answer that it can, and point to many of the articles on this subject by Lenin, Stalin, Kalinin, Molotov, Zhdanov, and other Soviet leaders. According to these authorities, true morality consists in complete devotion to the Soviet system of society, unquestioned obedience to its leaders, willingness to make any personal sacrifice to advance its purposes, undying hatred for all its enemies, and the determination to devote all one's efforts toward extending this system throughout the world.[18]

As we have already pointed out, all educational activity in the U.S.S.R. is directed toward instilling such principles as these into each citizen, regardless of age; these qualities can be considered as indicating the basic tenets of Soviet character education. Little analysis is required to reveal the wide gulf between these aims and those which are representative of democratic philosophies of education. The difference is not merely one of piety as against atheism, nor even of a religious morality in contrast to an ethic based upon political doctrines. In the last analysis the question becomes one of the fundamental relationships between the individual and his society, between the citizen and his state. Despite many official declarations to the contrary, the Soviet creed sees the person as an instrument of the nation, and Soviet institutions are created and maintained largely to keep him in this capacity through benefits, persuasion, or force. Under this system, loyalty replaces devotion, morality bows before duty, and education—in the image of the society itself—becomes totalitarian in that it prescribes one system of thought for all.

Countless instances of rigid control of educational thought by Soviet political officials could be cited, but a few critical examples must suffice. In 1934 three members of the Politburo itself took

[18] George Fischer, "My Soviet School Days," *The Reporter,* Vol. I, No. 9 (August 16, 1949), pp. 4-6.

time out to decree a new methodology for all Soviet history teachers to follow. Two years later the famous "pedology" controversy resulted in the castigation and disgrace of several prominent Soviet educators who refused to recant their honest opinions on the subjects of child psychology and psychometrics.[19] Just a year after the end of World War II the Central Committee of the Communist party directed the schools to reshape the aims of education along lines better adapted to the indoctrination of accepted political concepts.[20]

But the most flagrant example of political domination of education and research occurred in 1948 and concerned the physical rather than the social sciences. The hypothesis that acquired characteristics are inherited had been advanced by T. D. Lysenko as early as 1932, but the Communist party did not grant his ideas complete approval until August 1948. It was at this time that all Lysenko's opponents were ordered to choose between acceptance of this hypothesis and removal from scientific work. Despite the fact that Lysenko offered only the most biased evidence in support of his theories, whereas a large body of experimental findings existed to prove the contrary, his views coincided with the dogma demanded by the political leaders and therefore his doctrines became the new law of Soviet genetics.[21]

Thus, as one field of learning after another is invaded by the tide of political orthodoxy, true research is stifled and education becomes an instrument of oppression rather than a ladder to freedom. The question here is not which group of scientists is considered right and which wrong, but the privilege of both groups to carry on research and express opinions.

RURAL EDUCATION

Under the unified system of general education, pupils in elementary, incomplete secondary, and complete secondary schools follow the same curriculum in the rural as in the urban areas. Certain minor differences in the internal organization exist at the elementary level, largely because nearly 90 percent of urban schools

[19] Maurice J. Shore, *Soviet Education* (Philosophical Library, Inc., 1947), pp. 176-179 and 223-224.

[20] George S. Counts and Nucia Lodge, *The Country of the Blind* (Boston: Houghton Mifflin Company, 1949), p. 268.

[21] *Ibid.*, pp. 193-232.

have three or more teachers whereas only 46 percent of rural schools have sufficient enrollment to require that many. (The usual basis is forty pupils per teacher.) Moreover, 26 percent of rural schools have only one teacher; the corresponding figure in cities and towns is less than 5 percent.[22]

Recent Soviet newspapers have spoken often of a growing effort to extend compulsory seven-year schooling to include villages and farms and thus to abolish the independent four-year school as an institution. Even before the war, the total enrollment of 9 million in grades five to seven included nearly 6 million rural children, and the number has undoubtedly grown in the last decade, perhaps to such a degree as to make this extension feasible. In the same year, however, the number of rural children in grades eight to ten constituted only a little more than one third the total enrollment at this level.

Perhaps the greatest advance in rural education in the past ten years has been the creation of special elementary schools and evening incomplete secondary schools for farm youth, as mentioned in an earlier section of this article. These schools offer an accelerated course without interruption of work, and they have been a boon particularly to rural teen-agers whose schooling was suspended during the war. Enrollment in these schools has risen from 200,000 in 1947 to nearly 600,000 in 1950.[23]

HEALTH EDUCATION

In all complete statements of the aims of Soviet education the health of the pupil is mentioned, and usually with emphasis. But the school itself is only one factor in the long-term education for health and sanitation. Since the illness of a worker in any productive activity can delay progress toward the planned goal, one's health ceases to be an individual matter and becomes the concern of the nation as a whole. Therefore, educational campaigns are constantly being carried on by medical and health agencies, schools of all types, the party organizations for youth (Octobrists, Pioneers, and Komsomol), and by factories, farms, and administrative offices. The most intensive indoctrination comes at the preschool level, when

[22] E. N. Medynsky, *op. cit.*, p. 54.
[23] *Ibid.*, p. 121.

THE SOVIET UNION

children are imbued with what are considered to be the proper habits of health, sanitation, and diet. Physical training is a required subject throughout the ten-year program of general education, and in many of the specialized schools as well. For older children and adults, trade unions and other agencies organize lectures, exhibits, and discussion groups, and many theaters and motion-picture houses give performances illustrating health hazards and proper care of the sick or injured. Because it is a mass affair based upon principles of good citizenship, health education permeates all aspects of Soviet life.

INDUSTRIAL EDUCATION

At present the three most prevalent agencies of vocational education in the Soviet Union are technical schools, railway schools, and factory schools. Their major task is to train skilled workers in trade, transport, and industry and thus to close the wide gap which has long existed between the institute-trained specialists and the semi-skilled workers. All such institutions are under the authority of the appropriate industrial ministry rather than an educational ministry. The types of curriculum are numerous and varied, since these institutions, too, are highly specialized. The courses are usually two years in length and are taken by boys and girls who have completed an elementary education. The training is conducted along lines approximating actual factory conditions, and many of these schools are able to sell their products. There are also factory-apprentice schools which offer six-month courses on an in-service basis for those workers whose skill does not warrant a more advanced training. Recent Soviet estimates place the enrollment in these schools at about one million.

INTERNATIONAL EDUCATION

It would seem natural that a nation founded upon the precepts of Karl Marx should espouse internationalism wholeheartedly, and of course the Soviet Union does favor a world-wide social system of a certain type. Soviet interpretations of internationalism have changed several times, however, since the Revolution of 1917, and the methods and content of international education have been revised accordingly. In the period 1917-1933, for example, Soviet children were taught that all foreign governments were equally inimical to the Soviet regime but that all the common people of the world were brothers and friends. With the rise of Hitler in Germany, Soviet propaganda began to discriminate between actively hostile governments and governments which cooperated to some extent with the Soviet Union. The approach of World War II brought several marked shifts in these attitudes, but the war itself found the U.S.S.R. allied with several democratic nations against the more aggressive dictatorships. As a result, from June 1941 until the autumn of 1945 the Soviet people were permitted to feel a modicum of confidence in certain of the other Allied governments.

Since the end of the war Soviet propaganda has re-erected the distinctions among foreign powers, but this time the standard of good and evil appears to be based not only upon cooperation with, but upon outright subservience to, the government of the U.S.S.R. Even certain Communist-dominated nations are suspect, and all other types of governments are reviled. In the case of the United States, the accusations extend also to our citizenry.[24] Thus, an active and bitter campaign is being waged all over the Soviet Union to eradicate the last vestige of friendliness which the citizens, young and old, might retain for forms of society other than their own.

LIBRARY SERVICES

At present there are about 60,000 libraries of all kinds in the Soviet Union and these house more than 132 million volumes. Libraries range in size from the huge Lenin Library in Moscow, with more than 5 million volumes, to small traveling libraries, which constitute about a third of the total number. Newspapers number 7200 and have a total circulation of 31 million; the total number of copies of all issues of the two thousand periodicals printed annually is about 300 million. Published books and pamphlets (mostly the latter) numbered 40,000 titles in 1948 and were issued in over 600 million copies. Publishing of all these types is carried on in a total

[24] William Nelson, ed., *Out of the Crocodile's Mouth* (Washington, D. C.: Public Affairs Press, 1949), *passim.*

of 119 languages.[25] Like all other agents of communication, publishing firms and libraries are controlled by some branch of the government or the party.

MOTION PICTURES AND EDUCATION

Since there has long been a shortage of all types of optical equipment in the Soviet Union, few schools have their own projection apparatus. However, local motion-picture houses and clubs cooperate with the schools in showing educational films, and most Soviet motion pictures can be classified broadly under this heading. Mobile units bring films to isolated districts. The current Five-year Plan aimed at providing sufficient projectors in 1950 to bring the total for the entire nation to 46,700.[26]

TEACHER EDUCATION AND ASSOCIATIONS

Unlike many other countries, the Soviet Union maintains entirely separate training institutions for teachers in the various types of schools, but the great majority of these institutions are under the jurisdiction of an educational ministry. Standards for appointment of nursery-school workers are established by the Ministry of Health in each republic; the same agency operates the training schools for such workers, but the Department of Preschool Education in each Ministry of Education has control over the training and appointment of all kindergarten teachers. Directors of even small kindergartens (about twenty-five children) are required to possess the equivalent of at least a secondary professional education, and the directors of the larger institutions must have had special pedagogical instruction at the college level. Even the group leaders must give evidence of some training for preschool work.

Elementary-school teachers must have had at least an incomplete secondary education (seven years) and in addition must have been graduated from a "pedagogical school" in a three- or four-year professional course. Most of the pedagogical schools offer a curriculum similar to that of the "normal school" of the United States, but

---

[25] Bernard L. Koten, The U.S.S.R.—Basic Facts (New York: American Russian Institute, January 1950), p. 5.

[26] Ibid., p. 5.

many of these schools are centered in specialized study in physical education, fine arts, or foreign languages, and graduates of such institutions find positions as teachers of these specialities in the larger elementary schools. Without further training, however, they cannot be certified to teach above the fourth grade.

The requirements for teaching in grades five, six, and seven are somewhat higher than those for teaching in the elementary grades, and a different type of training institution is utilized to prepare teachers for this level. Prospective intermediate teachers must follow one of three preparational courses: (1) completion of the seven-year school, attendance for two years at a pedagogical school, and graduation from a two-year teachers' institute; (2) completion of the seven-year school, graduation from a three-year pedagogical school, and an additional year at and graduation from a two-year teachers' institute; or (3) graduation from a ten-year school and from a two-year teachers' institute.

Teachers in grades eight, nine, and ten must have graduated from a four-year pedagogical institute, which is very similar to an American teachers' college. In the Soviet Union, access to such institutes is obtained by graduation from either the complete secondary school or a pedagogical school, or by taking special courses at a teachers' institute. Thus, the Soviet teacher can transfer from the elementary school to either of the higher levels of general education by increasing his or her qualifications through further study. Evening and correspondence courses offer additional opportunities in this direction.

As described earlier in this chapter, the road to the two graduate degrees is long and arduous. However, much motivation toward attaining them is provided by an arrangement which guarantees higher status and larger salaries to their possessors. In the teaching profession, for example, the holder of a *diplom* is certified for the rank of instructor or assistant, a candidate of science demands the rank of docent (equivalent to associate professor in the United States), and a doctor of science guarantees a full professorship. Each rise in rank is automatically accompanied by a salary increase of 50-60 percent, in addition to such other advantages as greater prestige and authority, more convenient hours of work, and admission to more exclusive social and professional organizations. The present distribution of such ranks is about as follows: professors, 6000; docents, 15,000; instructors and assistants, 35,000.

The most important teachers' associations in the Soviet Union are the educational trade unions, which, somewhat like the training institutions, are organized according to the level of teaching service. Nearly all the 1,300,000 teachers belong to one or another trade union, which provides them with sick-leave pay, vacation pay, and pensions after retirement. Many college teachers with higher degrees belong to the House of Scientists, a semisocial professional club which is restricted to persons who have engaged in some form of scientific research. In addition to these organizations, there are many teacher groups of a local or special-interest character. All Soviet teachers are encouraged to participate in as many of these societies as possible.

Institutions for the training of teachers stress the same values and indoctrinate the same attitudes as do the schools of general education, with even greater emphasis upon subjects of a political or ideological nature. Since the Russian teacher is steadily gaining more authority both in the classroom and in the community, it is increasingly important that he or she follow the dictates of the party, even though relatively few teachers are party members. "As is the teacher, so is the child" is a seventeenth-century Russian maxim which is now given much credence in Soviet education, and several recent newspaper editorials have warned teachers that the official attitudes on such topics as religion, patriotism, morality, and international affairs must govern all teaching in Soviet schools, as well as the personal behavior of the teacher. The nature of the official attitudes on these subjects has already been indicated.

BIBLIOGRAPHY

BERNSTEIN, MIKHAIL, "Higher Education in the U.S.S.R. During and After the War," *Educational Forum,* Vol. XII, No. 2 (January 1948), pp. 209-212. A brief account of recent developments, including those in postgraduate work.

CHAMBERS, M. M., ed., *Universities of the World Outside U.S.A.* (Washington, D. C.: American Council on Education, 1950). Contains a chapter on Soviet institutions of higher learning which includes the latest information available.

COUNTS, GEORGE S., and NUCIA LODGE, *The Country of the Blind*

(Boston: Houghton Mifflin Company, 1949). Subtitled "The Soviet System of Mind Control," this volume reviews important cases of political domination in several areas of art, science, and education.

—— and ——, *I Want to Be Like Stalin* (New York: The John Day Company, 1947). A translation of selected chapters from a 1946 official Soviet text on pedagogy. Contains the famous "Rules for School Children" as well as descriptions of education in morality, ethics, patriotism, and discipline.

DARLINGTON, THOMAS, *Education in Russia* (London: Wyman & Sons, 1909). An intensive analysis of Russian education up to the final decade of the czarist regime.

DUGGAN, STEPHEN, "Contrasting Social Systems: Russian and American," *Educational Record*, Vol. XXIX, No. 1, Supp. 17 (January 1948), pp. 41-54. Comparisons of the school, state, family, church, etc. in the two nations, by an outstanding authority on international education.

Education in the U.S.S.R. and in Imperial Russia—Selected References (Washington, D. C.: U. S. Office of Education, 1940). Contains the titles of the most important books and articles in English up to the date of publication.

FISCHER, GEORGE, "My Soviet School Days," *The Reporter*, Vol. I, No. 9 (August 16, 1949), pp. 4-6. An American boy describes briefly but vividly his impressions of his early education in the U.S.S.R.

GOODFRIEND, ARTHUR, *If You Were Born in Russia* (Farrar, Straus & Co., Inc., 1950). A well-organized and copiously illustrated account of Soviet life from cradle to cremation, with much material on the educational processes.

GRAHAM, MRS. MALBONE, "Picture of Russia for Russia's Children," *New York Times Magazine*, February 8, 1948. Brief description of limited themes and intensity of purpose in the field of Soviet children's literature. See also subsequent exchange of letters, "On Russian Books," *New York Times Magazine*, April 4, 1948, in which Mrs. Graham's point of view is attacked and defended.

HANS, NICHOLAS, *History of Russian Educational Policy 1701-1917* (London: P. S. King and Sons, 1931). The most readable and comprehensive study of czarist educational history.

——, "Recent Trends in Soviet Education," *Annals of the American Academy of Political and Social Science*, Vol. CCLXIII (May 1949), pp. 114-122. A brief article reviewing the major wartime and postwar changes in Soviet education. The author is an outstanding British scholar in the field.

HARPER, SAMUEL N., *Civic Training in Soviet Russia* (Chicago: University of Chicago Press, 1929). Although not up to date, this volume indicates the huge scope and intensity of Soviet out-of-school educational activities.

JOHNSON, WILLIAM H. E., "General Aims of Soviet Education," *American Quarterly on the Soviet Union*, Vol. I, No. 2 (July 1938). An analysis of Soviet educational objectives by a person who spent three years teaching in Soviet institutions.

——, *Russia's Educational Heritage* (Pittsburgh: Carnegie Press, 1950). A study of education in czarist Russia, 1600-1917, with especial emphasis upon the training of teachers during that period.

KING, BEATRICE, *Russia Goes to School* (London: William Heinemann, Ltd., 1948). The best account of Soviet education in English since the war, even though it is much more superficial than the same author's earlier work in the field.

KOURNAKOFF, SERGEI, "The Soviet Curriculum," *Education Digest*, Vol. XII, No. 4 (December 1947), pp. 53-55. Brief descriptions of the content of the major courses in Soviet secondary schools.

LEGISLATIVE REFERENCE SERVICE OF THE LIBRARY OF CONGRESS, *Communism in Action* (Washington, D. C.: Library of Congress, 1946), pp. 110-116. A comprehensive study of the U.S.S.R. Includes a brief but informative analysis of several important aspects of Soviet education.

LEVIN, DEANA, *Children in Soviet Russia* (London: Faber & Faber, Ltd., 1942). A firsthand report by an Englishwoman who spent several years teaching in Soviet schools.

MEDYNSKY, EUGENE, "Schools and Education in the U.S.S.R.," *American Sociological Review*, Vol. IX, No. 3 (June 1944), pp. 287-295. An informative article by the most prominent Soviet educational historian.

PINKEVICH, ALBERT P., *Science and Education in the U.S.S.R.* (London: Victor Gollancz, Ltd., 1934). One of the few authoritative works by Soviet educators which have been translated into English. Although no longer reliable for the aims of Soviet education, it provides a unique insight into actual practices of the early 1930's.

RUBINSHTEIN, S. L., "Psychological Science and Education," *Harvard Educational Review*, Vol. XVIII, No. 3 (Summer 1948). A description of how nineteenth-century Russian educators, particularly K. D. Ushinskii, have influenced Soviet educational principles. Translation of an original Soviet article.

SHORE, MAURICE J., *Soviet Education* (New York: International

Publishers Co., Inc., 1947). A mistitled and sometimes confusing analysis of the philosophical foundations of Marxist educational theories, but still a valuable contribution for the more advanced student. Makes use of a large number of original sources.

Woody, Thomas, *New Minds, New Men* (New York: The Macmillan Company, 1932). One of the most enlightening studies ever made of Soviet education. Despite its early date, its author foresaw many of the recent changes in educational policies and practices.

Zirkle, Conway, *Death of a Science in Russia* (Philadelphia: University of Pennsylvania Press, 1949). The most thoroughgoing study of the Soviet genetics controversy yet published in English.

13 · EDUCATION IN *Africa*

M. M. CHAMBERS

Africa as a continent includes an area of over 11,500,000 square miles and has a population of approximately 185 million. The African continent is a separate land mass which can be circumnavigated and yet is closely connected to Europe and Asia along the Mediterranean and Red Seas for about a third of its circumference. This giant land mass has no real peninsulas and is about three times as large as Europe. The great open spaces of Africa have important geographic consequences which are reinforced by the location of mountains on the outer edges. This means that the rivers developed to a remarkable length. Furthermore, Africa has very few harbors and near-by islands. The climate ranges from the Mediterranean type, through the Sahara Desert type, to the tropical-forest type, south to another desert type, and finally to a temperate variety.

The population density shows great variation. Desert areas have less than one person per square mile. The Nile valley, the lower-Niger-valley sections of the Atlas coast, the northwest shore of Lake Victoria, and the Cape of Good Hope area have populations of fifty to two hundred persons per square mile. The racial variation is also extensive, ranging from the white Berbers and Semites of the north to the Negro races that cover the greater part of the continent. The Negro groups vary greatly among themselves as to color, height, and build. Researchers have distinguished more than 514 separate languages and, in the native languages, 319 dialects. The major language groups include the Semitic (chiefly Arabic), the Somali,

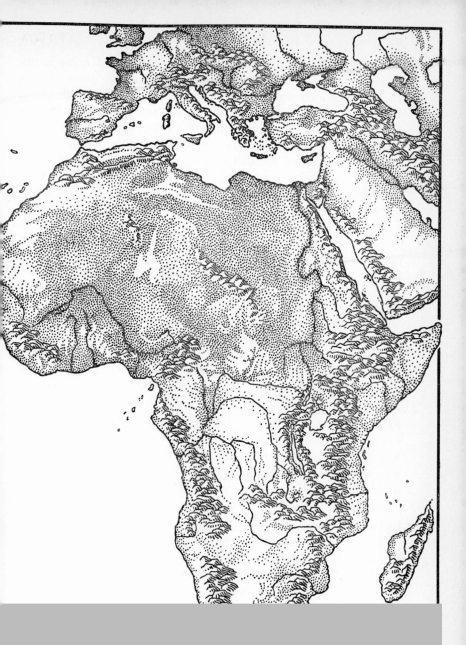

AFRICA

Sudanese, Bantu, and Zulu. Africa is a continent of many native tribes, and the tribal system and customs must be considered as basic in any long-range educational programs. Africa's soil, forest, and mineral resources are extensive, but the continent is heavily handicapped by either too much or too little rain and by inaccessibility of resources and poor transportation conditions. The mineral resources range from great deposits of copper and iron to precious minerals, especially uranium, gold, platinum, and diamonds. Coal is in short supply or inaccessible, and water power is largely undeveloped. Africa is primarily an agricultural continent; only small areas are devoted to industry, chiefly in South Africa.

In the main the educational pattern of each colony parallels that of the European power in control of the colony. In the case of independent or semi-independent territories, with the exception of some of the Arabic-speaking areas, the pattern is an amalgam of European educational practice. The great problem in Africa is one of achieving acculturation in which the values of the indigenous, tribal education may be conserved and, at the same time, the technology, the scientific method, and the literature of the Europeans may be gradually and intelligently introduced. Since there is so large a range of native languages, some of which have no written equivalent, the problem is extensive. It is further complicated by the foreign policies of the various colonial governments. Interracial and intercultural cooperation is a paramount problem, as is the very low level of literacy in this mainly rural population. The illiteracy rate varies with the age group, since the older population has had relatively little opportunity for education and youth is obtaining greater advantages. The over-all rate is about 95 percent among the native populations. The literate population consists, in the main, of the white groups. Illiteracy, poverty, and superstition are the major problems facing the educator in this extensive area. The relatively rapid cultural changes with regard to industrialization, agriculture, and trade have broken up much of the traditional tribal and family settings, with resultant destructive social effects.

Analysis of education in Africa presents a very difficult task, since one is dealing with a continental mass characterized by a tremendous range of regional, not to say tribal, variations in education. The analyst has necessarily laid considerable emphasis upon the great variation in the indigenous systems of education and the problems of contact with advanced Western technological education.

—A. H. M.

———————

This chapter speaks of the entire African continent, but excludes discussion of education in the northern and southern extremities and confines itself to certain great groups of colonial territories: British East Africa (plus the Anglo-Egyptian Sudan and British Somaliland), British Central and South Africa, British West Africa, French West Africa and French Equatorial Africa, and the Belgian Congo. The focus is on problems and progress in the education of the native peoples, and in order to avoid too great a complexity of detail, only occasional and incidental mention is made of the provisions for the schooling of the relatively small European and Asiatic populations.

Even within the scope as thus restricted, generalizations are difficult and nearly always subject to many qualifications and exceptions; but it is important that a broad concept be brought into view of the status, role, and future possibilities of education among more than 100 million indigenous human beings in this continent of which the resources are on the whole underdeveloped.

A number of background factors are preliminary to any consideration of education on the African continent. Among these are population, climate, material resources and the extent to which they are developed, and the political conditions under which the peoples of the continent have lived and live today.

THE AFRICAN SETTING

The total population of Africa is estimated at some 185 milion. Members of the Negro race predominate heavily, but there is a considerable Arab population in North Africa and in some other parts of the continent. Dutch and British settlers are largely concentrated in the Union of South Africa. There are small proportions of British, French, Italian, Spanish, and Portuguese colonists and administrators, and there is an infusion of East Indian immigrants along the east coast and in South Africa; but all these constitute only negligible fractions of the continental aggregate.

The total population is small in comparison with that of the other continents of the Eastern Hemisphere; it is only about half as large as that of Europe, which is much smaller in area, and it is less than half as large as that of either China or India. The population of Africa is more nearly comparable in numbers with that of either of the American continents.

Climate and topography play a large part in conditioning both the numbers and characteristics of the people. Vast parts of the northern half of the continent are arid and incapable of supporting more than a scanty population. A great part of the continent lies in the tropical zone on both sides of the equator. Consequently the low coastal regions generally have a climate excessively hot and humid, predisposing to disease and depressing to vitality. Some of the tropical interior, however, consists of high plateaus and mountains, some of which are snow-capped although near the equator. It is well to remember that tropical Africa is by no means all swampy jungle. There is a great variety of topography and climate, the characteristics of which are relatively little known because of the absence of systematic and continued scientific weather observations and of other investigations which would determine the potentialities of soil and weather. The only part of the continent where climatic conditions approximate those of the temperate zones are relatively small areas in the northern and southern extremities. It is in these relatively small areas that the bulk of the non-Negro population is found.

Malaria is prevalent in much of tropical Africa; it causes enormous losses of human vitality, as does the disease known as "sleeping sickness," which is carried by the tsetse fly. Methods of controlling these diseases are known to science, but have not as yet been successfully applied in large parts of Africa owing to the low status of economic and educational conditions. The relations among health conditions, economic conditions, and educational conditions are often said to constitute a vicious circle, because each operates to depress the others, or at least to retard progress. Educational facilities can be provided only when the people are economically productive, and children are educable in the best sense only when they are healthy and well nourished. Disease can be conquered, vitality increased, and economic progress accomplished only as a result of education.

The Negro peoples of Africa are by no means homogeneous; on the contrary, they exhibit great variations in physical characteristics and much diversity in types and levels of contemporary culture. Although in general the cultures are primitive, and the task of teaching the peoples to master their environment and lift themselves to higher levels of living is indeed enormous, there is now a world-wide consensus among scientists in fields related to human capacities and development that any supposedly inherent racial inferiority is not actually a factor in the situation. This concept, only lately coming into wide recognition and not yet universally accepted, is of the utmost significance for the future development of the African peoples.

A hasty survey of the political situation will afford additional background for present educational conditions in Africa. A very large part of the continent still consists of dependencies, possessions, protectorates, and mandates under the jurisdiction of European powers. At least 75 million people, nearly half the continental total, are in British Africa, including the Union of South Africa, the various British colonies and protectorates in East Africa which extend contiguously northward to the Anglo-Egyptian Sudan, and the several British possessions on the west coast, the most populous of which, Nigeria, has an estimated 24 million people.

Second in point of population are the French possessions in Africa, with an aggregate of more than 30 million people in Algeria, Tunisia, Morocco, West Africa, French Equatorial Africa, and Madagascar.

Belgian possessions are third, with an estimated 11 million people in the Belgian Congo. The Portuguese possessions in East and West Africa have an estimated population of some 10 million. The former Italian colonies of Libya, Eritrea, and Italian Somaliland have an aggregate of about 3 million. Territories under Spanish jurisdiction in northwestern Africa have perhaps 1 million people. If we disregard for the moment the former Italian colonies, which appear to be in process of being given nominal political independence, it is apparent that only about 28 million of Africa's population, or less than one sixth of the total, live in countries not under European suzerainty. These include 19 million in Egypt, 8 million in Ethi-

opia, and 1½ million in Liberia. The status of the Union of South
Africa as a self-governing British dominion would permit the addition of its 12 million people to this category; but its native African
people have no large voice in its government.

With Africa having been almost wholly absorbed within the orbit
of nineteenth-century European imperialism, then, a vast majority
of the peoples of the continent remain in colonial status, politically
dominated by foreign powers and economically dominated by foreign enterprisers. Thus it is that educational conditions of today
must be at least in some part ascribed to the policies of the European
colonial powers; and probably the best way to obtain a quick and
comprehensive view of the continental picture is to look at the educational policies and accomplishments in the African possessions of
those several powers.

EDUCATIONAL THEORIES AND PRACTICES

First of all it must be observed that the unvarnished theory of
imperialism so avidly espoused by European national powers during
the past two centuries—the theory which in practice meant the
forcible seizure of political control over primitive peoples and the
exploitation of their undeveloped material resources for the ag-
grandizement of rival colonial empires—is now in disrepute and far
on the way to oblivion. This situation has come about not wholly
as a result of saner and more humane views of world progress but
in large part as an inescapable sequence in the stern logic of events.
After World War I Germany disappeared from the scene as
an African colonial power, and Italy is apparently on the same
path. World War II has so profoundly altered the situations of
Britain and France in world affairs that their policies toward their
respective African territories will undoubtedly undergo evolution
in new directions, diverging from nationalistic imperialism toward
concepts in which the tutelage of primitive peoples is less a national
prerogative and more an obligation of all humanity, increasingly
shared by the colonial peoples themselves as active participants.

Meantime some distinctions, subject to many qualifications, can
be noted among the African educational policies of the principal
European powers in relatively recent years. Colonial educational
policy can choose between (1) emphasis upon the nurture of the

best elements in the native culture and the development of the native economy as an indigenous growth and (2) stress upon European-type education and the assimilation of the native peoples politically, economically, and culturally into a unit in which the European tutor-power is the nucleus. Neither choice can be absolute; but insofar as differences in emphasis are apparent, it seems that British policy in Africa has tended toward the former choice and French and Belgian policies have tended toward the latter.

Generally in African territories under British control, efforts are made to use the local vernacular as the medium of instruction in the early years of the primary schools and in the adult schools. The French attitude, on the other hand, is expressed in the statement that "the French school, at least by definition and organization, does not allow the use of local languages except for additional instruction for temporary or local experiments."

There is something to be said for each of the foregoing policies regarding the languages. The fact that there are hundreds of local dialects, some used only by tribes numerically small, and that there is a general absence of any written language necessitates great and time-consuming labor in reducing the many dialects to writing and in producing a minimum of elementary textbooks in each. The scene is complicated by the existence of a language such as Swahili, which is used as a trade language and means of intertribal communication in much of East Africa and parts of the Belgian Congo, but which is itself a foreign language for many of the diverse tribes, who are thus confronted with a trilingual situation in which their tribal dialect, an intertribal language, and a European language all appear. The crucial question which ought to influence the matter, and on which there is as yet a dearth of evidence, is whether a child speaking only an agglutinative local language from infancy encounters too great a psychological barrier if he is expected to acquire an inflected European language in his early school years, or whether this barrier is not sufficiently serious to outweigh the advantages to be had from early mastery of one of the great world languages, such as English or French.

There are other factors which constitute essential parts of the background sketch. In virtually every part of the continent such beginnings as have been made in the provision of schools for the native Negro populations have some of their roots in the efforts of

Christian missionaries of the several denominations. In many instances mission schools preceded all other educational institutions in point of time, and even though in general they have not been able to extend their services to reach more than tiny fractions of the people in any given territory, in many places even now they provide a great part of the total available facilities. Such systems of "government" schools as now exist have been developed more recently; and as the European colonial powers devote gradually more resources to the extension and improvement of these systems, problems arise related to the mutually advantageous correlation of the multiple education enterprises in a given territory.

This correlation in many instances has taken the form of the extension of government financial aid to the missionary schools. In the four provinces of the Union of South Africa this trend is most advanced. Most of the schools for natives are missionary enterprises, and government schools and nondenominational community schools are in the minority. But government aid to missionary schools now amounts to virtually full support, with the government funds coming not from the provincial governments but from the Union government. Allocation of funds is in the hands of the Union Advisory Board on Native Education. Each of the provinces has, however, a provincial advisory board representing the missions.

In other parts of the continent the relations between missions and secular government vary greatly, as do the relative roles of these agencies in the total educational scene; but from the generalized continental point of view the pioneering role of the missions continues to be important, not only in primary and adult education but also in the germinating of secondary and vocational schools and in the selection of small numbers of native Africans who pursue higher liberal and professional education in European and American universities. In fact, it appears that in all French West Africa and French Equatorial Africa considered collectively, at least half the pupils now attending schools of any kind are in private schools; and in the Belgian Congo the proportion is much greater.

In many parts of the continent where the Mohammedan influence is locally strong, there are considerable numbers of Koran schools in which the principal activity is memorizing the Koran. In localities where the Arab influence is predominant, there is often strong local opposition to the introduction of any written

European language, on account of the suspicion that such teaching would be a surreptitious method of undermining the Mohammedan faith. In the British territories the Koran schools, when recognized, are usually classified as offering instruction at a level equivalent to that of the substandards or of Standard I. In British Somaliland, where the people are virtually all Moslems, the Koran schools receive some small financial assistance from the government.

Wherever European or other foreign commercial or industrial enterprises are engaged on a large scale in exploiting African resources, there is found another type of school: the "company school" for native employees or prospective employees and their children.

SALIENT FEATURES OF AFRICAN EDUCATION

This complexity and variety might easily lead one to the impression that educational enterprises in Africa are numerous and large in proportion to the numbers and needs of the population. Any such impression would be gravely in error. In fact, only from 3 percent to 5 percent of the entire population of colonial Africa is able to read or write in any language. Scarcely more than 10 percent to 15 percent of children of school age ever attend a school of any sort. In comparison with European and American standards, attendance is extremely brief and irregular. The great bulk of all instruction is at the level of the lower elementary or primary grades, and the number of pupils who complete a primary-school course is extremely small. Secondary schools are very rare and far apart, and in some large territories they do not now exist at all.

Various local undertakings have been instituted with a view to developing mechanical, industrial, or vocational training of types and levels well suited to conditions in the native communities; but as yet most of these experiments are relatively small in scope and many of them appear to be having only indifferent success. Compulsory school attendance for children of specified ages has not been attempted in colonial Africa except in a few places where it has recently been instituted as a local experiment.

Higher education for native Africans often takes the form of the selection of a few hundred native scholarship holders who are enabled to go to Britain, France, or elsewhere in Europe or America as students in universities or professional or technical schools. Britain and France, however, have both encouraged the development of a few local institutions in their respective territories which offer training above the secondary-school level and which show promise of eventually becoming full-fledged universities. Among these are Gordon Memorial College, at Khartoum, Anglo-Egyptian Sudan; Makerere College, in Uganda, intended to serve the three provinces of British East Africa—Uganda, Kenya, and Tanganyika; Achimota College (now designated the University College of West Africa), at Accra, British West Africa; and a medical school at Dakar, in French West Africa. In many places various missionary or government schools of secondary or vocational grade bear the name of "college" but this is in accord with the nomenclature widely used in most of the non-English-speaking world, where a "college" is not an institution of university level. The foregoing mention of institutions of higher education excludes the ten universities and university colleges of the Union of South Africa, the universities of Egypt, and the French University of Algiers, because the purview of the present discussion is confined to the parts of the continent where the native population is in huge majority and where neither political independence nor a high degree of colonial autonomy has as yet been developed.

A characteristic of practically all the territories is the fact that the number of girls attending schools at the various levels is very much smaller than the number of boys. This is true especially in localities where the Moslem influence is prevalent, but even there some slight tendencies toward beginnings of formal educational opportunities for girls have been noted in recent years. A few exceptions to the general neglect of schooling for girls as compared with boys occur in some pastoral localities in South Africa, where the herds of cattle are tended by boys exclusively, and this nomadic occupation prevents their attendance at school. In a few such localities the number of girls reported as registered in the schools exceeds the number of boys; but this is a highly exceptional phenomenon in Africa.

In many places attempts to make the schools a factor in the improvement of the economic productivity of the immediate region by introducing practical instruction and demonstration in agricultural practices suited to the locality have met with considerable apathy; this is because the natives generally regard the tillage of the soil and the raising of food crops as the work of women, and the men of the tribes give only occasional assistance in the heavier tasks. Thus agricultural education for boys is often not appreciated. In common with the people of many other undeveloped areas in the world, native Africans tend to attach a very low prestige value to instruction in agriculture or other rural industrial activities and to prefer instead the types of academic or literary instruction which seem to be pathways to clerical or other work connected with territorial administration and politics.

Unfortunately, in the past the European colonial administrators have often perpetuated this attitude by actually limiting the facilities for higher primary and secondary education to such as would supply the number of clerks and other functionaries needed as employees of the colonial government. Although many evidences of this practice can still be found, it is now at least theoretically in disrepute among the colonial administrators in most of the territories, and there is a widespread and increasing feeling that native education needs to be intimately adjusted to the development of local material resources and the growth of economic productivity in each locality. This means, of course, that there must be experiments and demonstrations in practical agriculture, that mechanical and building trades must be established which are suited to the use of local materials, that marketing practices must be improved, and that much attention must be given to the control of disease, the improvement of nutrition, and the eradication of pests and parasites which attack plants, animals, and man.

The continent is so large and local geographic, climatic, demographic, and political conditions vary so enormously that no satisfactory comprehension of current educational conditions and prospects can be had from a series of generalizations applicable to the whole. Although there is a dearth of data regarding local conditions, and although it is extremely difficult to assess accurately the results of many local efforts which have been reported only in part, it is deemed advisable to mention briefly in turn five regions of the continent, each of which has some few elements of homogeneity but also exhibits tremendous diversity within itself.

BRITISH EAST AFRICA

The three territories commonly comprehended within the term British East Africa are Uganda, Kenya, and Tanganyika. North of these territories is the Anglo-Egyptian Sudan, a condominium administered by Egypt and Great Britain. East of the independent kingdom of Ethiopia is British Somaliland, a protectorate not contiguous with any of the lands already mentioned. All these areas considered collectively have a total African population of some 20 million. Probably 5 million are of school age, but no more than 550,000 receive instruction in schools.

Uganda. The protectorate of Uganda is the most advanced agriculturally and educationally in British East Africa. About one third of the children of school age are estimated to be registered in some kind of school, but two thirds of these are in "elementary non-aided and subgrade schools" which generally consist of little more than "catechistical classes." The total attendance is estimated at 300,000 out of a school-age population of 900,000 and a total population of 4½ million, almost all Negro. In 1943, 8 percent of the school-age population was in primary schools, and there were five postprimary vocational schools in the territory, located respectively at Kampala, Elgon, Kisubi, Arua, and Masindi; the last three were mission schools. There were also twelve training centers for primary-school teachers and twenty-three centers for vernacular teachers. All centers of both types enrolled a total of about one thousand pupils, of whom one third were women, and actually turned out about four hundred graduates.

Makerere College, originally a trade school, has been in transition toward university status, as a university college, since 1937. It not only serves Uganda but receives students from the neighboring territories of Kenya and Tanganyika, and it is intended to become a university of East Africa. In 1939 it had 182 students. In December 1948 the enrollment was 218, of whom thirteen were women. It has faculties of medicine, veterinary science, agriculture, science, and arts, and it also offers a special art course and a special adult-education course.

Kenya. The territory of Kenya is unique in that it has a compact European-settler community of some 21,000 people, occupying an elevated region of good climate and fertility. Although constituting much less than 1 percent of the total population of 5 million, the European element exercises a large degree of political control, and there is consequently a more evident tendency toward racial segregation and economic discrimination against natives than in the neighboring territories. The emphasis in education is largely on the training of farm labor, industrial workers, artisans, and clerks who can provide services needed by the European-controlled community. Less than one fifth of the children of school age attend any school, and nearly half of these are in some 1200 unaided schools, of which many are missionary schools but a few are nondenominational community schools maintained locally. Notable examples of native initiative are two local associations—the Kikuyu Independent Association and the Karinga Schools Association—which together maintain from fifty to sixty schools with some seven thousand pupils.

Twenty years ago an interesting effort was begun, centered in a school at Kapengurier in the West Suk district of Kenya, looking toward the improvement of agriculture and the conservation of forests and water resources. One early and successful feature of the effort was the introduction of potatoes as a crop and an article of diet. This involved not only instruction and demonstration in the suitable methods of planting and cultivation but also the growing and distribution of seed and demonstration of the methods of cooking the product, previously unknown to the natives.

Tanganyika. The territory of Tanganyika, with perhaps 7 million Africans, is more populous than either of its neighbors. Its European population is smaller and less homogeneous than that of Kenya and there are in general fewer practices of discrimination and repression. There has been less alienation of land; natives have not been restricted to reserves but have generally been free to cultivate their own land or work for an employer, with the exception of some conscription of labor during the war years.

As nearly as can be ascertained, about 200,000 children attend noncertified mission schools, and there are also some two thousand Koran schools, non-aided. The Education Department reported in 1942 that the enrollment in "government, native administration and assisted schools" had increased to 40,000 from 35,000 three years earlier. Probably about one fourth of all children of school age are in some sort of school, and the Education Department notes that within fifteen years the problem has largely changed from that of persuading parents and chiefs to send children to school to that of providing sufficient teachers and school plants to serve those who wish to attend. Recently there were only three secondary

schools in the territory, with only one offering the full six-year
course, and the total of all secondary-school students was only a
few hundred.

The Anglo-Egyptian Sudan. The Anglo-Egyptian Sudan consists
of two markedly different parts. The northern Sudan consists of
desert and semi-arid plateau. Its 4 million people are part of the
Moslem world. It is accessible by a railroad, and it has potentialities of local wealth, chiefly from the production of cotton. A
huge irrigation project, known as the Gezira Scheme, affects 5 million acres of productive land. The southern Sudan is forested and
has ample rainfall, but is accessible only by river. Its 2½ million
people are part of Negro Africa. It is one of the least developed
spots on the continent.

The northern Sudan has some 1500 Koran schools, or *Khalwas,*
some of which, in addition to teaching the Koran, provide a little
instruction in reading, writing, and arithmetic. These schools serve
about 60,000 boys, approximately one fourth of the male population
aged six to twelve. The government makes small salary grants for
some of the teachers who consent to take short training courses.

There are some mission stations in the southern Sudan, maintaining "bush schools" of varying quality, numbering from two
hundred to three hundred in all. Attendance is reported to have
risen from 7500 in 1932 to 10,000 in 1940, out of a school-age population of 400,000. The Sudan as a whole had in 1940 about 3200
pupils in standard primary schools, a small percentage of the population of school age. There are two postprimary technical schools,
one at Omdurman and the other at Atbara. One teacher-training
center at Bakht er Ruda has functioned since 1932. It turns out
about twenty-five elementary-school teachers per year, and it hopes
to double this output.

Up to 1945 the only secondary school was Gordon Memorial
College. In that year this institution was incorporated as a university college and most of the secondary instruction was transferred
to a rural site outside Omdurman. In 1948 the enrollment at
Gordon Memorial College was 228, of whom three were women.
The school has faculties of arts, science, administration and law,
engineering, agriculture, design, and veterinary science. The Kitch-
ener School of Medicine, in Khartoum, is independent of the

college but will probably become affiliated with it, if and when the institution acquires the status of a full-fledged university.

An experiment in rural community development was begun in 1944 at Um Gerr, involving 12,000 people in four villages on a 10,000-acre irrigated cotton- and durra-growing site. Emphasis is on training in public health and sanitation for selected villagers who subsequently act as advisers in their respective districts. Fortnightly meetings of women in each of the villages have been instituted for the purpose of disseminating instruction in sanitation and health, and other methods of reaching all families are in progress.

British Somaliland. The people in British Somaliland are largely nomadic and of a somewhat restless and unsettled tendency. Accordingly education is very little developed. As recently as 1937 there were no government schools, and less than £500 was expended annually for grants-in-aid to Koran schools. A Director of Education was first appointed in 1938. The territory was under Italian military occupation in 1940-1941. In 1943 three elementary schools were opened, and there are now about 550 boys in government schools, as well as six hundred boys in grant-aided Koran schools. Twelve boys have been sent on scholarships to secondary schools or teacher-training schools in the Sudan. Two small Koran schools for girls were opened in 1946, and in 1948 a small experimental government school for girls was begun, at which the Koran, Arabic, arithmetic, and oral English are taught but emphasis is put on sewing, knitting, dressmaking, and laundering. The Colonial Development and Welfare Program has allocated £35,000 for the period 1949-1955 for a girls' school. There is now one boarding primary school, and immediate plans envision the provision of a second one and, by about 1952, the possible introduction of secondary education. It is also hoped to extend the elementary-school course from three years to four and to complete the provision of elementary schools at eight places. It is reported that the nomadic mode of life and the prevalence of intertribal feuds make impracticable any immediate undertaking of mass education until further progress has been achieved in the extension of facilities of communication.

British Central and South Africa. Nyasaland, Northern Rhodesia, Southern Rhodesia, Bechuanaland, Basutoland, Swaziland, and Southwest Africa have an aggregate population of approximately

7 million. The bulk of these people are in the three territories of Nyasaland, Northern Rhodesia, and Southern Rhodesia, each of which has in the neighborhood of 1½-2 million. Density of population per square mile ranges from approximately one person in Bechuanaland and Southwest Africa to between forty and fifty persons in Basutoland and Nyasaland. The European inhabitants in the whole region comprise only about 2 percent of the population; they range from about 0.1 percent in Nyasaland to about 4 percent in Southern Rhodesia and 10 percent in Southwest Africa. The percentage of Asiatics is everywhere smaller than that of Europeans except in Bechuanaland, where it is about 1.5 (double the percentage of Europeans). There are similarities in the many languages spoken by the Africans, most of whom are called Bantu. They are Negro and Hamitic peoples of many physical types, who originally came from farther north in a series of migrations.

Cattle raising is a prevalent occupation, and wealth is reckoned locally by the size of the herds. A certain religious significance attaching to cattle also is responsible for the tendency of the people to overstock these animals, with resulting depletion of forage and erosion of soil. Destruction of soil resources also comes in part from the practice of shifting cultivation, under which land is used for the production of crops for a short time and then allowed to return to bush while new areas are cultivated. For the most part the people live in small villages. Bechuanaland has a few towns of considerable size, among which is Serowe, with some 25,000 inhabitants. Landmarks of progress which have been achieved within the past century include the total extinction of the Arab slave trade, the ending of intertribal wars, and the establishment of fairly stable administration in which native authorities play important roles.

The proportion of children attending schools ranges from less than 10 percent to over 50 percent. For many, however, the period of attendance lasts no longer than two years, and many do not become permanently literate even after longer attendance at some of the less efficient schools. Ninety percent of all children in school are in mission schools, but some government schools and some native-authority schools have been started, and some grants-in-aid are given to mission schools meeting required standards. Consolidated reports of the territories (not including Southwest Africa) as of about 1944 show some five thousand "government, native authority, and aided missionary schools," with a total enrollment of about

500,000 pupils, of whom about 190,000 were girls. In addition there were some 4700 "unaided schools" enrolling a total of about 92,000 pupils. Emphasis is being placed on the importance of education in the control and prevention of disease. Sleeping sickness, malaria, and internal parasitic diseases take a heavy toll, and leprosy is prevalent in some areas. There is a great deal of malnutrition, owing to ignorance or the lack of the necessary foodstuffs.

In certain localities compulsory education for all children has been begun. The movement of native families into concentrations in mining areas breaks up the traditional family setting and tends toward neglect of children and their moral degeneration unless adequate provisions are made to provide them with appropriate educational and recreational facilities. To meet a situation of this kind an experiment in compulsory schooling for children aged twelve to sixteen was begun in 1942 in the Broken Hill industrial area in Northern Rhodesia. Several new school buildings were erected on sites provided by the mining company. The necessary capital came in part from the Colonial Welfare and Development Fund. The experiment is reported to be successful and not as expensive or difficult as anticipated. Moreover, the beginning of compulsory education in the concentrated industrial area is reported to have stimulated interest in education among the people of surrounding rural regions. Success is also reported in requiring four years of school attendance for all children in a distinctly rural locality, among the pastoral Ila people of Nanwala, in Northern Rhodesia.

A technique of achieving mass literacy, drawn largely from the experience of Dr. Frank C. Laubach, the American missionary who developed his methods while in the Philippine Islands, was experimentally introduced in Mindolo, in Northern Rhodesia, in 1943.[1] The effort was first directed at women in an African Women's Institute locally organized and locally supported. Although it is not possible to report whether this type of activity can be spread rapidly and successfully over large territories, some such effort may be able to speed up the progress of education.

Goals for education in British Central and South Africa have

[1] Dr. Laubach constructs alphabets in Roman characters for a spoken native language. The alphabet characters are then drawn pictorially to resemble everyday objects or activities of the natives. Thus the characters can be identified and remembered easily. Drill in writing follows.

been stated as follows: the eventual establishment of universal schooling for children of school age; the increasing of adult literacy and of library facilities; and the rooting of mass education in the communities as a local enterprise, coordinated with plans for health and welfare to constitute a balanced program of progress.

BRITISH WEST AFRICA

British West Africa embraces four noncontiguous territories, with an estimated aggregate population of 30 million; they are Nigeria (with some 24 million), the Gold Coast (with 4 million), Sierra Leone (with 1,800,000), and Gambia (with about 250,000). Mission schools entered the field early, and they now play a large part in the picture. For example, in Nigeria 90 percent of all children in school are in mission schools. Government support generally began with financial aid to mission schools that met accepted standards, and this policy continues. Some observers believe that this system of cooperation achieves maximum results from the limited funds thus far available.

Nigeria. An estimated 350,000 children attend school in Nigeria. The coverage is very spotty, being concentrated mostly in areas where successful work was begun by the early missions and has been continued. One such area is in the province of Eastern Nigeria, in a densely populated district which has been served for a century by the Church of Scotland. Here there is a school in almost every village and a teacher-training center at Calabar. In contrast, Northern Nigeria is mainly Moslem, and Christian missions have had little success; less than 2 percent of the children in the area are in school.

In Anchau, in Northern Nigeria, a health project to stamp out sleeping sickness was instituted a number of years ago and, largely because of the great progress that resulted in both health and agriculture, the people have set up local village schools for children and adults. This is cited as an instance wherein the cooperation of several departments of the government, together with local initiative, has produced demonstrably good results.

There is also a farm school at Oyo, in Southwestern Nigeria, as yet small in scope but promising as to prospects. Small numbers of boys, chosen from village schools, attend for two years, beginning at about age fifteen. They learn mixed farming, cattle breeding, and the production and care of small livestock. During the second year each boy has a plot for cultivation as a project of his own; this method is believed to be a most effective way of teaching agriculture.

In all Nigeria there are estimated to be some 12,000 teachers at work in the schools, and there is a Nigerian Union of Teachers with a membership of three thousand and a full-time secretary. This organization works to improve salaries and tenure and to hasten the employment of teachers in villages not yet having schools. It supports the government's ten-year plan for education, a feature of which is the estimate that 80,000 teachers will be required. Government expenditures for education have recently been £500,000 annually, expended chiefly for grants-in-aid to inspected and approved mission schools. There are, however, some government secondary schools supported wholly out of these funds. A government secondary school for boys was established at Lagos in 1909, and a similar school for girls was begun at the same place in 1927.

Government training schools for teachers were established in 1929 at Ibadan and Umuahia. An institution was opened in 1934 at Yaba to provide selected pupils from mission and government schools with training in medical sciences and engineering. Subsequently teacher training and agricultural education were included, but during World War II the institution was taken over for military purposes and the students transferred elsewhere, largely to Achimota, in the Gold Coast. After the war the institution at Yaba was reopened, but it seems destined to be an engineering and technical school while the development of a university college at Ibadan, the largest town in Nigeria, is in progress.

The University College of Nigeria, with two hundred students, was functioning in 1948 in the wooden huts of a wartime military hospital at Ibadan. A spacious site of 5 square miles of wooded upland near the city had been allotted in 1947 and is being prepared for a new physical plant. Plans are under way for an institution having three faculties (arts and sciences, medicine, and agriculture), a teaching hospital, and a model village for the service staff.

Another notable experiment in fitting Nigerian schools to the condition and needs of the people was begun in 1938, centered at the Anglican Diocesan teacher-training institute at Awka, in Southeast Nigeria. This experiment developed into a cooperative regional undertaking in which the three major Protestant missions in the area participated, and to which the government contributed some financial aid and technical advice. The focus of the effort is on developing a so-called "rural bias" in the schools of the region, so that they will make a maximum contribution to the improvement of agriculture and the conditions of rural living.

The Gold Coast. The Gold Coast has a somewhat higher income per capita than most African regions, owing to the development of cocoa growing for export by large numbers of small farmers. There is also a small export trade in diamonds, timber, and copra. In general the people are somewhat more advanced educationally and economically than most of their neighbors, but the picture is not without shadows. It is reported that the farmers in some areas are so preoccupied with the attractions of the export trade in cocoa that they do not grow enough food for their local needs. Moreover, the cocoa-growing industry is menaced by a prevalent disease of the cocoa plant; the disease seems to be susceptible of control, but it is difficult to achieve universal application of the necessary control practices because relatively few of the growers can read in any language. In 1944 only about 15 percent of the children of the main part of the territory were attending school, and fewer than 1 percent of the children in the Northern Territories were in school. These percentages appear to have shown only slight increases in recent years.

About 14 percent of the children now in school attend Roman Catholic mission schools; about 64 percent attend schools maintained by four Protestant mission groups, and about 22 percent attend government, native-administration, and other schools. Government grants to mission schools constitute somewhat more than two thirds of the total of public funds spent annually on education. Some critics of the present situation note that in many schools too heavy an emphasis is placed upon a curriculum and instruction nearly identical with that of the corresponding grades in Great Britain, but there is some tendency to introduce indigenous arts and crafts and practical agricultural and industrial training. Efforts of this kind are under way at the Bunsu Plantation and at a central government school at Tamale.

Some critics also assert that at the local level there is jealous competition among some of the mission schools, which in some instances attempt to discredit the schools of other denominations and entice pupils from one church to another. There are more than two thousand "non-assisted" schools, many of which are said to have appeared locally without aid from either the churches or the native authorities. Five hundred such schools were reported to have been begun during 1946. The native authorities sponsor a growing number of "bush schools," and the proportion of their revenues expended on education rose considerably throughout the 1940's. In 1947 nearly one fourth of the total revenue accruing to the native authorities of Ashanti was thus expended.

Since 1944 the government has made annual supplemental grants of £25,000 to assist local schools which are unable to meet the higher salaries agreed upon for teachers. The native authorities designate about one third of their schools on an average as having first priority in the receipt of this aid. The government appointed an officer of the Education Department in 1947 who was to concern himself especially with the promotion of mass education. Steps were taken to obtain a visit by Dr. Frank C. Laubach and to institute a trial of his methods of expanding adult literacy rapidly.

The largest center of population is Accra, with some 120,000 people. Near this city is Achimota College, which is the principal institution of higher education in West Africa. Founded in 1925, its original plant cost £600,000 and has had substantial additions. In 1948 it was given the name of University College of the Gold Coast. In the spring of 1949 it had an enrollment of ninety-two students at the university level, of whom two were women. It has faculties of art, pure science, economics, theology, African studies, and extramural studies and an institute of education.

Sierra Leone. In the late eighteenth century a few thousand freedmen from North America were settled in Sierra Leone, and their descendants now comprise a considerable part of the population of the capital, Freetown, and of the coastal region. They speak English as their mother tongue. The interior of the territory, on the other hand, has several tribal groups speaking a number of languages; the Moslem influence is present in the northern region. Several Protestant missions operate schools with some financial assistance from the government, as in other British West African territories. A union of the Protestant missions maintains a secondary school at Bunumbu. An effort at emphasizing agricultural education is exemplified in a school and experiment station at N'Jala and at some other centers. An institution known as Fourah Bay College has existed since 1827 at Freetown, under British missionary auspices. During World War II the college plant was used by the British navy, and the college was housed in temporary quarters at Mabang. It has been concerned principally with liberal and theological education and has had much influence upon education in the territory.

FRENCH EQUATORIAL AFRICA AND FRENCH WEST AFRICA

French Equatorial Africa and French West Africa have a combined population estimated at more than 23 million, of whom some 7 million are in the equatorial regions and some 16 million in French West Africa. The Federation of French Equatorial Africa has a population of about 3½ million people in the four territories of Chad, Ubangi-Shari, the Middle Congo, and Gabun. Near by are the French mandated territories of Cameroon, with about 2,700,000 people, and Togoland, with slightly less than a million. French West Africa consists of the seven territories of Mauretania, Senegal, French Guinea, Ivory Coast, Upper Volta, Dahomey, and Niger Colony.

Within the total area four hundred oral languages are spoken, but there is virtually no written language other than French. Primary schools are free and instruction is in the French language. The total of all children in school is estimated at 300,000, only a tiny percentage of the children of school age. There is in progress a ten-year plan for African education which envisions the establishment of many more primary schools, of teacher-training centers, and of secondary schools. One aim of the plan is to have 50 percent of the children in school at the end of the period. The plan involves substantial credits to the territories by the governmental agency known as FIDES (Fonds d'Investissement pour le Développement Economique et Social des Territoires d'Outre-mer), aggregating 6½ billion francs.

There are small academic secondary schools in the towns of Saint-Louis, Dakar, Abidjan, and Brazzaville and at other places. The most recent report showed a total of thirty secondary schools in French West Africa, with a total of 2215 pupils; and a total of

twenty secondary schools in French Equatorial Africa, with a total
of about two thousand pupils. About four hundred African pupils
are studying in secondary and technical schools in France; and an
equal number are in that country attending universities.

In French Equatorial Africa the aggregate of sums appropriated
for education rose from 5 million francs in 1941 to more than 28
million francs in 1945. The number of pupils in state-supported
schools also increased greatly during that period, although the
number is still very small in proportion to the population. In
1945 over 14,000 pupils were in state-supported primary schools,
about 350 were in secondary schools, and about 300 were in vocational training. At the same time more than 15,000 pupils were
attending Catholic and Protestant mission schools. Since 1941 mission schools which satisfy certain requirements concerning the curriculum have received financial aid from the state. The total of this
aid amounted to 5 million francs in 1945. In considering the foregoing numbers of pupils and sums of money, it must be remembered
that there are an estimated 500,000 children of school age in French
Equatorial Africa alone.

Delegates from all the French African territories held a conference in Brazzaville in 1944 and formulated a number of recommendations regarding education, most of which were subsequently
adopted by the French government. The gist of the recommended
program is as follows: (1) Schooling should be extended to the
masses, including girls as well as boys, and designed both to improve
the local community life and to provide means of selecting Africans
capable of leadership. (2) A school should be provided for every
village having as many as fifty boys and girls of school age. (3) Advanced primary schools, vocational schools, and satisfactory higher
educational facilities must be made widely available. (4) Scholarships enabling selected Africans to continue their studies in France
should be given on a larger scale as a means of hastening the foregoing processes.

The current plan for the Federation of French Equatorial Africa
extends over a period of forty years; it is divided into four ten-year
plans, the first of which terminates in 1954. During this first
decade the goals include the establishment of five normal schools
for the training of primary teachers, a sufficient number of addi-

tional primary schools to serve 100,000 children, ten new schools offering the second stage of primary education, and six vocational and technical schools. It is estimated that this program will require the expenditure in 1954 of 50 million francs for buildings and 100 million francs for personnel expenses. Although the budgets of the French Equatorial territories have increased greatly in recent years, it is almost certain that the successive 10-year plans for education will require financial aid from France. There is a likelihood that such aid may be forthcoming from the French Union General Fund. According to one long-range estimate, annual expenditures for education in French Equatorial Africa from local sources should amount to 280 million francs by the year 1984.

At a conference on education held in 1944 at Dakar, the consensus was that a period of thirty years would be necessary to implement the extension of school facilities to all children in French West Africa. In that year there were 2½ million children aged seven to thirteen in the territory, and it was estimated that 16,500 schools would be necessary to accommodate them; at that time there were in existence only two thousand schools with approximately 100,000 pupils.

There are five teacher-training centers now functioning, one of which specializes in the training of women teachers and one of which emphasizes agricultural and forestry education. The School of African Medicine was opened at Dakar in 1945, where students from all French African territories may pursue studies in medical and related fields.

A considerable amount of practical adult education is accomplished in the French African territories by numerous local associations organized by African farmers for joint economic action and mutual benefit. These associations are generally known as *sociétés de prévoyance*. They finance themselves by small yearly membership dues and are eligible to borrow from the Agricultural Credit Bank. Some of them employ agricultural experts and many of them accomplish a wide variety of measures of local benefit to farmers, such as cooperative purchase of tools, machinery, and seeds. It is said that these organizations tend to reconcile old personal and tribal disputes, and that their various activities are in large part practical vehicles of adult education.

THE BELGIAN CONGO

Statistics for the year 1943 indicate that somewhat more than 7 percent of the total African population of the Belgian Congo were undergoing some type of formal instruction. The number of pupils attending school was reported as exceeding three quarters of a million. A very large percentage of these went no further than "the first degree" of primary instruction, involving only two years of attendance. Most of the schools for this type of instruction are under African teachers working with some supervision from a mission station. There are some five hundred higher primary schools located at the mission stations, offering "the second degree," which requires three additional years of attendance.

Schools financed entirely by the government, and known as "official" schools, are only a handful in number, and the total enrollment consists of only a few thousand pupils. Although they are government schools, most of them are administered by members of Catholic orders.

The great majority of all schools in the Congo are mission schools. Under a somewhat confusing system of nomenclature, Catholic missions are recognized as "national missions," and missions of all other denominations are designated as "foreign missions." Educational subsidies from the government go only to "national missions," with few exceptions. In order to qualify for a subsidy, a "foreign mission" must show that two thirds of its administering body are Belgians and must meet a number of other requirements. The net result is that Protestant missions are virtually excluded from government aid. Catholic missionaries are heavily in the majority, constituting somewhat more than three thousand of the total of approximately four thousand Christian missionaries in the Congo. Catholic missions function in about 350 local centers, and Protestant missions of numerous denominations work in a total of about two hundred local centers. The Protestant missions have established the Congo Protestant Council, which employs a full-time educational secretary.

In addition to having a large majority of the mission schools, the Belgian Catholic orders administer most of the schools maintained by private industrial companies, as well as most of the relatively few "official" schools. Government subsidies are granted to a majority of the schools of the "national missions," but not to all. Statistics of a recent year showed about 300,000 pupils in about 5500 "national mission" schools receiving subsidies, and about 185,000 pupils in such schools which were nonsubsidized. In addition there were some 282,000 pupils in "foreign mission" schools, virtually all of which were nonsubsidized.

Above the level of the primary schools, there are relatively few institutions, and the number of students is small. Included are thirty-seven normal schools with an aggregate of about two thousand pupils; seven vocational schools for technical and clerical training, with a total of three to four hundred pupils; twenty-three schools of domestic economy enrolling a total of six to seven hundred girls; and nine middle schools with an aggregate of five to six hundred students. The middle schools are at a level similar to that of an American junior high school.

Although the enrollment in primary schools in the Congo appears to be comparatively large, observers have reported that the content and quality of the instruction are such as to make the schools relatively ineffective, so that the general educational level of the native population is as low as anywhere on the continent. As elsewhere, the task of the schools is complicated by the existence of several hundred native languages. In various places a number of related dialects have been considered together and one language chosen for literary use. The vernacular is used as the medium of instruction in the rural schools, but as soon as a pupil completes "the first degree" and enters upon higher primary education he begins to learn French, which is thereafter used at least in part as a language of instruction.

Because the Christian missions play so large a part in the whole school system in the Congo, it is necessary to note that considerable antagonism has been reported between Catholic and Protestant missions. This is thought to be especially unfortunate, because, as an automatic result of his attending one or another type of school, the African pupil is projected into a controversy which is not of his own making and from which he is almost certain to derive detriment rather than benefit. There is, however, some tendency toward developing instruction with less emphasis upon religious doctrinal differences and with more attention to the elements of native life and customs which are worthy of encouragement and preservation.

Most recent observers appear to agree that there is very great need for more effective cooperation among the government, the missions, the industrial companies, and the native Africans aimed at attaining a type of education that will achieve practical results in such fields as nutrition, public sanitation, housing, the improvement of agriculture, and the conservation of resources of soil, timber, and water. It is felt that the government should take the lead in preparing and adapting the main outlines of such educational effort and should take measures to demonstrate its plans in numerous places and to encourage its diffusion throughout the territory.

GENERAL AND COMPARATIVE ASPECTS OF AFRICAN EDUCATION

Having noted in some detail the conditions prevailing in several of the great colonial areas in which most native Africans now live, we may now list a number of principal problems which are common to all, or nearly all, of those areas. To be sure, the common problems exist in varying degrees and in varying superficial forms, and for that reason it is again necessary to insert a caution that generalizations are subject to exceptions and qualifications.

The existence of multiple native languages and dialects, differing greatly from European languages in their structure and underlying thought patterns, keeps alive the unsolved question of whether the interests of Africans will ultimately be better served by the use of a European language as a medium of instruction in the elementary and primary schools, or by the reduction of selected indigenous languages to written form, the production of textbooks and other literature therefrom, and the use of these native tongues as the medium of instruction in the schools. It has already been noted that the first of these alternatives is largely emphasized in the French African territories, whereas the second has received somewhat more attention in some of the territories under British administration.

The problem has not been finally solved. Several practical considerations, including the labor and expense involved in producing books and literature in numerous African languages and the evidence that many natives desire to study and use a European language, favor the French practice. On the other hand, some psychologists raise the question of whether elementary or primary education carried on in a European language can actually promote to best advantage the development of African children, and whether education so conducted can ever escape from the tangles of a futile verbalism which tends to prevent it from directly affecting the everyday lives and welfare of the pupils and their families.

Whatever may be the ultimate solution of the language dilemma, there is wide agreement that, in a population which is approximately 95 percent illiterate, attention and trial should be given to methods of achieving mass adult literacy which are more rapid than the passage of successive generations of children through the schools. Experimental efforts along that line, now being actively encouraged by the United Nations Educational, Scientific and Cultural Organization, constitute a promising possibility of more rapid progress than any preceding generation has known.

It is to be noted at once that the concept of "fundamental education" as now envisioned by UNESCO and by other agencies and persons is by no means confined to the matter of mere functional literacy, although that is regarded as an important element in it. Fundamental education embraces in addition the concept of imparting to individuals, whether through the medium of a written language or otherwise, a knowledge and understanding of such practices as will tend immediately to lift their standards of living through the conservation and development of the economic resources of their land as well as through the improvement of conditions of health, nutrition, sanitation, and other facets of general well-being. The local efforts being made in various African territories to operate schools and adjust the content of instruction in such a manner as to make schools and instruction immediately effective in bettering local living conditions are in harmony with the concept of fundamental education.

Although facilities for elementary education are as yet only fragmentary and pitifully inadequate for the native population, schools designed expressly to offer training in skilled mechanical or technical occupations—schools for vocational education suited to the needs of the people—are far more rare, and at present they are capable of serving only the most infinitesimal fraction of the school population. Moreover, in some places this type of school is heavily dominated by the idea of preparation for clerical and related careers in the civil service; although this aim is commendable enough as a means of gradually increasing the proportion of natives engaged in carrying on the work of the various governmental departments, it should not dominate vocational education to the near-exclusion of other types, as it does at present in some African colonies.

An idea of great importance which is growing among persons concerned with education in Africa is that there must eventually be more effective relations among the several authorities now administering more or less separate school systems in many of the territories. Normally there are no fewer than four school systems: mission schools (which themselves constitute several systems, because of the division among the Catholic and the various Protestant denominations), government schools (wholly controlled by the territorial government and wholly supported by governmental funds), native-authority schools (initiated in small local political units and supported wholly or in part by revenues collected by native chiefs), and local school systems maintained by European industrial and commercial firms on their own premises. To all these may be added the Koran schools, which exist in many communities where there is substantial Moslem influence. It has been noted that the territorial governments very often subsidize the mission schools, or at least such of them as meet standards prescribed by the government; and that in some instances these subsidies have come to amount almost to full support, so that the government is virtually supporting a system of schools which are administered and controlled by the missions as its agents.

The logic of history seems to indicate that the needed articulation and coalescence of the several school systems in a given territory will probably be achieved if a statesmanlike leadership is assumed and maintained progressively by the territorial governments. Current tendencies seem to include the extension of greater financial support to worthy mission schools, and there are indications that many of these schools are likely eventually to become government schools with the full consent of their denominational founders. Thus, as the educational system develops, government schools will probably play progressively larger roles; but this does not by any means necessarily presage the extinction of mission schools or, indeed, any reduction in the total volume of missionary efforts.

The territorial governments can also strongly influence the character and quality of schooling throughout the territories by establishing progressively higher standards for both government schools and subsidized mission schools; by fostering the extension of systems of native-authority schools wherever they show themselves to be capable of maintaining high standards; by increasing the requirements laid upon industrial employers regarding the maintenance of schools for their employees and the children of their employees; and by devising and conducting many and varied local experiments and demonstrations by which the way may be pointed to closer ties between the schools and the present needs of the people.

Although the sums of money involved are not large in comparison with the school populations and school needs of the several territories, it is encouraging that the principal European governments concerned are taking steps to provide some long-term financial aid to education in the African territories. Examples of this trend already noted are the enactment of the British Colonial Welfare and Development Act of 1940, under which certain allocations for the support of education in eligible British African localities have been made, and the setting up of the French governmental credit agency bearing the initials FIDES, with a schedule of contemplated loans to French African territories for educational purposes.

It is also heartening to observe that both the British and French governments regard the development of education in Africa as a long-term undertaking which can, nevertheless, be scheduled by years and by decades, for each of which definite goals can be established and probably attained. Among such goals which are at present regarded as appropriate for the measurable future are the provision of primary schools for half of all children of school age, and the achievement of universal compulsory school attendance as soon as school facilities can be sufficiently extended. Many other goals are implicit in the accounts in earlier parts of this chapter and need not be explicitly recapitulated here.

Secondary schools in Africa are rare and small in enrollment. No consideration of the future should omit the necessity of extending opportunities for secondary education to substantial proportions of the children of secondary-school age. This task will be difficult enough from the standpoint of financial reasons alone, although it is very probable that in the long run the necessary outlays will repay themselves many times over in the form of the accomplishments of an African leadership developed in such schools. Most certainly the task of extending secondary education should not be hamstrung by obstructionists among the Europeans in Africa who may be motivated by race prejudice or economic greed. There is much evidence that these unworthy motives are coming to be outweighed by the newer concept that educational opportunity is not merely a rare advantage to be granted to a privileged few but a human right which appertains to every child according to his potentialities and which must not be affected by discrimination based on his race or economic status.

BIBLIOGRAPHY

BARTELS, F. L., "The Gold Coast: Educational Problems," in *The Year Book of Education, 1949* (London: Evans Brothers Ltd., 1949), pp. 348-358. A discerning description and critique of progress in the Gold Coast, a colony which is in some respects more advanced educationally than most of the African territories.

BELL, C. R. V., "Somaliland: Educational Development," in *The Year Book of Education, 1949* (London: Evans Brothers Ltd., 1949), pp. 342-347. Candid annals of the very recent and very scanty provisions for education in the British Somaliland protectorate.

BROWN, P. P., "West Africa: Learning a European Language," in *The Year Book of Education, 1949* (London: Evans Brothers Ltd., 1949), pp. 338-341. A thorough examination of some of the characteristics of the Akan languages, spoken by some 3 million tribesmen of the Guinea Coast.

CHARTON, ALBERT, "French Overseas Territories," in *Fundamental Education: Common Ground for All Peoples* (New York: The Macmillan Company, 1947), pp. 45-63. A statement of French colonial educational policy by the Inspector General of Public Instruction, in the Ministry of Overseas France.

———, "French Tropical and Equatorial Africa: the Birth of African-French Culture," in *The Year Book of Education, 1949* (London: Evans Brothers Ltd., 1949), pp. 366-379. An exposition of French policy and a statistical summary of education in each of the territories for 1947.

COMMITTEE ON AFRICA, *The War, and Peace Aims: Africa* (New York: Committee on Africa, 1942). A report by the Committee called "The Atlantic Charter and Africa from an American Standpoint" and a supplement, "Events in African History," compiled by Edwin H. Smith.

DAVIS, JACKSON, "Education in British West Africa," *Journal of Negro Education,* Vol. XV (Summer 1946), pp. 358-369. A penetrating and superbly organized discourse on the historical aspects, present status, and future trends in education in the four territories of British West Africa.

EISELIEN, W. W. M., "South Africa: Education for Non-Europeans," in *The Year Book of Education, 1949* (London: Evans Brothers Ltd., 1949), pp. 222-234. Treats education for the European, Indian, mixed-blood, and native elements of the South African population. Advocates "full opportunities for the Natives in their own spheres of life."

FYFE, SIR WILLIAM HAMILTON, "Higher Education in the British Colonies," *Higher Education,* Vol. VI (December 1, 1949), pp. 75-76. Brief firsthand account by a member of the British Inter-University Council for Higher Education in the Colonies.

GRAY, WILLIAM S., "Education in Egypt," *Elementary School Journal,* Vol. XLIX (May 1949), pp. 485-495. An excellent sketch of progress since 1922, present-day obstacles and needs, and future prospects.

HARRIS, J. S., "Education in the Belgian Congo," *Journal of Negro Education,* Vol. XV (Summer 1946), pp. 410-426. An account of the current roles of missions, government, and companies engaged in industry and transport, and of the "disjointed" situation and the need for coordination.

HELLMAN, ELLEN, and QUINTIN WHYTE, "Union of South Africa," in *Fundamental Education: Common Ground for All Peoples* (New York: The Macmillan Company, 1947), pp. 63-80. A description of the current status and problems of education by an officer and a staff member of the South African Institute of Race Relations.

JANDY, E. C., "New Ethiopia and Socioeducational Problems," *Sociology and Social Research,* Vol. XXXIII (November 1948), pp. 113-124. Observations of a member of the United Nations Relief and Rehabilitation Administration Mission to Ethiopia, 1945-1946.

LA ROCHE, JEAN DE, "Education in French Equatorial and French West Africa," *Journal of Negro Education,* Vol. XV (Summer 1946), pp. 396-409. Includes the recommendations of the Brazzaville Conference of 1944, subsequently largely adopted by the French government.

LEWIS, L. J., "Africa: Social and Economic Background," in *The Year Book of Education, 1949* (London: Evans Brothers Ltd.,

1949), pp. 312-337. Discusses the influence of World War II; mentions some experiments in rural community development in various British territories; cites trends in other aspects of education in Africa, including the French, Belgian, and Portuguese colonies.

MALINOWSKI, B., "The Pan-African Problem of Culture Contact," *American Journal of Sociology*, Vol. XLVIII (1943). A discussion of the techniques needed "to make a branch of humanity jump across centuries of development."

PLUMMER, GLADYS, "Training of Women Teachers in Nigeria," *Educational Record*, Vol. XXIX (January 1948), pp. 50-55. A vivid description of the variety of native peoples and cultures, and a firsthand narrative of progress in the education of girls.

SIEGEL, MORRIS, "Educational Opportunity in Dependent Territories in Africa," *Journal of Negro Education*, Vol. XV (Summer 1946), pp. 552-563. A critique of the colonial policies of Great Britain, France, and Belgium and a pessimistic view of the prospects of educational advance.

STOKES, ANSON PHELPS, THOMAS JESSE JONES, J. D. RHEINALT JONES, and L. A. ROY, *Progress in Negro Status and Race Relations: The Thirty-five Year Report of the Phelps-Stokes Fund* (New York: Phelps-Stokes Fund, 1948). Includes a paper on the racial situation in Africa and numerous brief statements concerning the activities of the Phelps-Stokes Fund in promoting education in Liberia.

VAN DEYCK, C., "The Belgian Congo: European Education and Tribal Communities," in *The Year Book of Education, 1949* (London: Evans Brothers Ltd., 1949), pp. 359-365. Contains comparative statistics for seven types of schools for 1939 and 1944, a description of current conditions, and recommendations for future developments and adaptations.

WIESCHOFF, H. A., "Education in the Anglo-Egyptian Sudan and British East Africa," *Journal of Negro Education*, Vol. XV (Summer 1946), pp. 382-395. A realistic view of the situation, with strong recommendation of allocation of larger sums of money for the development of African education.

WRONG, MARGARET, "Education in British Central and South Africa," *Journal of Negro Education*, Vol. XV (Summer 1946), pp. 370-381. A systematic presentation of conditions in each of the territories and a fourfold recommendation for improvement.

less than one per square mile in the desert and mountain areas. Illiteracy is very high—from 65 to 95 percent. Modern technology is just beginning to penetrate in a few areas in connection with the extraction of oil, transportation, and trade.

Educators face the very difficult problems of widespread poverty, illiteracy, and the opposition of traditional religion. Nevertheless, noteworthy advances have been made, especially in Turkey, Iraq, Syria, Lebanon, Israel, and, to a smaller extent, Egypt. The reforms of Kemal in Turkey as regards both use of Roman letters and extension of universal education constituted great gains. In the Arabic-speaking areas the retention of the old classical script and printing constitutes a major obstacle, since the everyday speech is quite different.

Israel should constitute a special study in itself, since it is an enclave with a population made up of immigrants from the more advanced cultures of the Old and New Worlds. From the Arab point of view, Israel represents an intrusion of another religion and culture into a fundamentally Mohammedan area. The government and people of Israel have a firm, effective external policy, but within the country there are distinct conflicts between the orthodox religious and the liberal, modern elements, and there is a wide range in economic and political belief.

Today it is of the essence that Westerners become acquainted with the East—the Near East as well as the Far East. It has been said that our own education has been not only male and aristocratic but also exclusively Western and has not had broad enough contact with and understanding of the cultures of the East. In the chapters which follow, we have tried to achieve balance by devoting adequate space to the world of Islam and to the great cultural and educational areas of the Far East. The nature of these cultural areas places definite limitations upon the type of analysis used in each case.

—A. H. M.

There is a twofold revolt going on today in the Arab countries of the Near East: a revolt against the West and against the status quo. Dr. Charles Malik, Minister from the Republic of Lebanon to the United States of America and one of the Near East's most penetrating and articulate spokesmen, describes the new situation thus:

Asia today is on the threshold of a great dawn—a dawn that is characterized both by an awakening and by a revolt. The awakening is as to Asia's own actualities and possibilities. The revolt is at once against the West, at whose hands Asia has known much humiliation, division and exploitation, and against the more sordid conditions under which Asiatic life has been running its course for centuries.[1]

The patterns of education are beginning to reflect, with less than the customary lag, the dominant political, social, and economic needs of these states. The modern Arab educational systems, with their comparatively short history, are as yet an agglomeration of curriculums and methods largely imported from the West and either superimposed upon or substituted for the inadequate traditional education. These national systems of education are still in the planning stage, a variety of unintegrated systems reacting to high-tension currents both from within and from outside these countries.[2]

It has been said that an ideal nation should have the five essential factors of racial, religious, linguistic, and territorial unity and political sovereignty. As sovereign states these countries are all young. Iraq, with its minorities, lacks racial unity, and Lebanon, with a Christian majority, is unique; the others are predominantly Moslem. All possess linguistic and territorial unity.

The geographical position of these Arab states is of vital importance in their cultural development. They lie at the crossroads of three continents and for several millenniums have been the battlegrounds of conquerors who would hold this strategic link. Today the discovery of vast mineral wealth in Iraq and the Arabian Peninsula makes this region even more strategic for world economy and places these countries under powerful political and economic pressures.

Nationalism is a predominant political and social force in all the

[1] Charles Malik, "The Problem of Asia," p. 8. Speech delivered in the Political Committee of the General Assembly of the United Nations, December 11, 1951.

[2] The problems and trends to be discussed in this chapter are those of Egypt, Iraq, Syria, Lebanon, and Jordan (Transjordan became the Hashimite Kingdom of Jordan in December 1948). Estimated populations for 1950 are: Egypt, 19½ million; Iraq, 4½ million; Syria, 3½ million; Lebanon, 1½ million; Jordan, one half million.

bargain in the bazaar. He, and not the doctor, heals every disease, or He sends death in spite of the doctor.

Allah's name is breathed into the ear of every newborn infant and is the last word on the lips of the graybeard as Azrael takes his soul. And in all the intervening years, Allah's name is uttered every waking hour and is muttered in every dream. And all this, not simply out of habit, but because Allah is a great and, indeed, desperate reality which the Arab cannot escape. Be he saint or sinner, monarch or minion, prince or pauper, to an Arab Allah is always right there.[6]

Professor Hitti, of Princeton University, the leading authority on Arab history, states that from Mohammed came "the greatest phrase in the Arabic language," the cry "la ilaha illa-'llah!" ("There is no god but Allah!"), which drove the Arabs to conquer and spread their civilization to most of the known world.

The beliefs concerning the origin and nature of the Koran are of utmost importance in the understanding of Moslem peoples. For them the Koran was not written by Mohammed. Allah through Gabriel spoke to His prophet and the messages were transcribed on the ribs of palms, tablets of white stone, and shoulder blades of sheep. The Koran for the true Moslem is the word of Allah, and every letter of it is sacred and divinely inspired. The Koran is the basis of all theology and law; it is the one supreme standard for literary excellence in classical Arabic; and at the Al Azhar University, in Cairo, its study is a major part of the curriculum.

The Koran is thought to be the most widely read book in the world, because the Moslems, even though they are only half as numerous as the Christians in the world, use it not only as their Bible but also as the textbook from which virtually every Moslem who can read Arabic has learned to do so.[7]

In dealing with the content of the Moslem's religion as well as the practices of Islam, one must mention the so-called "five pillars of Islam."[8]

1. The first pillar is profession of faith. One expresses his faith

[6] John Van Ess, *Meet the Arab* (New York: The John Day Company, 1943), p. 29.
[7] Philip K. Hitti, *The Arabs: A Short History for Americans* (Princeton, N. J.: Princeton University Press, 1949), p. 34.
[8] The description given here of the five pillars of Islam is condensed from the account given by Philip K. Hitti in *The Arabs*, pp. 40-43.

in the inclusive formula "There is no god but Allah: Mohammed is the messenger of Allah." This phrase is in the call to prayer and no other phrase is more often repeated by the Moslem.

2. The second pillar is prayer. Five times each day the Moslem is supposed to turn his face toward Mecca and recite his prescribed prayer: at dawn, midday, midafternoon, sunset, and nightfall.

3. The third pillar is almsgiving. It is considered an act of piety and is left largely to the individual Moslem's conscience.

4. The fourth pillar is fasting. The major fast takes place during the ninth month of the Moslem calendar, Ramadan, when the pious Moslem abstains from all food and drink from sunrise to sundown. This fast is a particular strain on those engaged in outdoor work when Ramadan ("which means the hot month") comes in a warm or hot season. (Because the Mohammedan calendar is a lunar calendar, Ramadan does not always fall in the same season.)

5. The fifth pillar is the pilgrimage. Once in a lifetime, all Moslems of both sexes are supposed to make the holy visit to Mecca if they can afford it. (The average number of pilgrims annually between World Wars I and II was 172,000.)

The current revival of Islam as a force in the Near East is viewed by some more as the result of nationalism than as a truly religious revival. However, Islam with or without nationalism influences deeply the lives of most of the people and thus is a major factor in their education.

The influences of the French, British, and American curriculums and examination systems are quite evident in the educational systems of the Near East. The mélange of curriculums and methods indicates that none of the nations we are considering has yet achieved what might be called an indigenous educational pattern. The vestiges of cultural imperialism are very prominent in most of the countries. In Lebanon much of the education is still carried on by foreign and private schools, the latter largely after foreign models. Although the Arab people are growing increasingly suspicious of foreign influences, they still look to the West in education. One of the critical problems in their cultural advance is how much they should take from the West and how much of their own culture they should revive.

In general the Near East is in a state of political and cultural ferment. Old values are losing their weight as the radio, press, returned students, the theater, world airlines, and foreign oil companies inject ultramodern ideas into the stream of life and thinking of the Arab peoples.

Against this background the following educational problems will be presented briefly: illiteracy and compulsory education, curriculum revision in public education, the education of girls and women, teacher training and supply, nationalism and education policy, and, finally, special problems. In considering these topics it is well to guard against evaluating standards in terms of the West. Real progress is evident only when these problems are viewed in the light of the recent history of these Arab countries.

ILLITERACY AND COMPULSORY EDUCATION

In the cities and government offices of Cairo, Alexandria, Beirut, Damascus, and Baghdad, one finds not a few highly educated young men and women possessing one or more university degrees. This intelligentsia is in striking contrast to the masses of fellaheen (peasants of the river valleys) and Bedouins, who, although far from being ignorant, are for the most part illiterate.

To be literate in Arabic requires some knowledge of the classical written language as presented in the Koran. This language is quite different from the colloquial dialects and can be acquired only through systematic study. One author, speaking of Egypt, describes the problem in this way:

> We have our own particular problems with the teaching of Arabic as the mother tongue. Our mother tongue is not so simple to impart as, say, English in England. The divergency between the spoken and written language in Egypt is so great that most of our children speak and think in one way, whilst they read and write in almost another. The two channels of language, the colloquial and the classical, may meet in most vocabularies, but even so the grammatical rules governing the construction of the written tongue necessitates so many inflexions and inversions when spoken as to make classical Arabic almost incomprehensible to an Egyptian ten-year-old.[9]

Egypt's Committee for the Simplification of Grammar was well

[9] Ahmad Khaki, "The Teaching of Arabic," *Bulletin of the Egyptian Education Bureau*, Cairo, May 1947, p. 46.

aware of the problem involved in teaching a classical language as a basic tool when it reported:

> So long as colloquial Arabic is the tongue spoken in the home and so long as it is a medium by which a majority of the subjects in the school curriculum are taught, it will always be the principal living language. Correct classical Arabic will stand alone as an unwanted luxury. Our young people will not take to such a luxury unless it is forced upon them, and will not care whether they acquire mastery over it or not.[10]

Yet the educational systems are committed to classical Arabic.

The ancient and traditional way of learning Arabic was in the ungraded Moslem school known as the *kuttab*. Here the child memorized the Koran and also acquired the elements of the three R's. Only Egypt has attempted to keep and reorganize this native school, making it the standard, graded elementary school (*maktab*) for the country.

The official attack on illiteracy, which is estimated to be as high as 70 percent in Egypt and as low as 25 percent in Lebanon, is seen in the legislation for compulsory education in those localities where adequate primary-school facilities exist. Article 19 of the Egyptian Constitution, adopted in 1923, made education compulsory for Egyptian boys and girls and free in all public elementary schools.[11] Egypt first tried half-day compulsory elementary schools, with boys attending in the morning and girls in the afternoon. This plan is gradually being replaced by a full-day elementary school with no fees and with lunch provided. In 1945 there were more than 600,000 pupils in attendance at schools of this type.[12] In Syria, primary education is free in public schools and is supposed to be compulsory. The law requires compulsory education in places decided upon by the Ministry of Education. In general the laws for compulsory education exceed the facilities available, making full enforcement impossible. Syria and Iraq have the special problem of providing elementary education for the children of nomadic Bedouin tribes which are normally on the move. Lebanon leads in elementary and

[10] *Ibid.,* p. 48.

[11] R. D. Mathews and Matta Akrawi, *Education in Arab Countries of the Near East* (Washington, D. C.: American Council on Education, 1949), p. 21.

[12] *Ibid.,* p. 41.

primary education, if we judge on the basis of percentage of school-
age children attending school. However, Lebanon still depends
heavily on private and foreign schools. The figures in the following
table reveal the quantitative nature of the problem for the respective countries:

PERCENTAGE OF CHILDREN IN SCHOOL IN SIX ARAB COUNTRIES, 1942-1945*
(The number preceding the country indicates its respective rank)

Country	Estimated population (1942-1945)	Estimated population of elementary-school age	Number attending elementary school	Percentage of appropriate age group in school
(3) Egypt	18,000,000	2,870,000	1,360,000	47.4
(6) Iraq	4,500,000	675,000	135,000	20.0
(4) Syria	3,000,000	375,000	148,000	39.4
(1) Lebanon	1,100,000	165,000	120,000	72.7
(5) Jordan	400,000	50,000	14,000	28.0
(2) Palestine (Arab)	1,250,000	207,000	107,000	51.6

* R. D. Mathews and Matta Akrawi, *Education in Arab Countries of the Near
East* (Washington, D. C.: American Council on Education, 1949), p. 544.

Estimates of the elementary-school-age population for all countries are based
upon the age-distribution tables of the 1937 census for Egypt. Similar distribution figures were not available for the other countries. The estimates make allowance for a six-year range for Egypt, Iraq, and Lebanon, a five-year range in
Syria and Jordan, and a seven-year range in Palestine.

In some areas there is such dire poverty among the peasants that
their children are not able to take full advantage of educational
opportunities even when they are available. This report of conditions in Southern Iraq could be duplicated in Egypt, Syria and
Jordan:

> The majority of farmers in Southern Iraq dwell in reed or mud
> huts . . . a large number of farmers find it difficult to supply their
> children at school with even paper and pencil. In some years the
> farmer may not get enough to feed even his own family, much less
> to buy the simplest linen clothes.[13]

Although compulsory education can wipe out illiteracy for the
rising generation, the governments of Arab countries recognize the
importance of attacking illiteracy in the present adult population.
Egypt, in its Five Year Education Plan started in 1947, includes an
anti-illiteracy campaign. This campaign requires that all large firms

[13] Matta Akrawi, *Curriculum Construction in the Public Schools of Iraq*
(New York: Teachers College, Columbia University, 1942), p. 57.

provide literacy instruction for those employees who need it. In 1944 a law was passed in Egypt making attendance compulsory in evening classes for illiterates of both sexes and requiring big land-owners as well as employers to provide literacy instruction for their employees. It is estimated that about 200,000 people are receiving instruction in Arabic under this law.[14]

Iraq is combating illiteracy by conducting evening courses under the direction of primary-school teachers. During the summer volunteer secondary-school students carry on the campaign. In 1946-1947 the Ministry of Education supplied books and facilities for adults in 158 centers and adult attendance totaled about six thousand.[15]

We can see that both illiteracy and the lack of facilities for compulsory education are major problems in these Arab countries. School facilities are inadequate, except perhaps in Lebanon, which relies heavily on both foreign and private schools. The problem is complicated by the fact that all the countries are committed to teaching classical Arabic. Nevertheless, progress is being made through anti-illiteracy campaigns sponsored by the governments in Egypt and Iraq, where the need is greatest. Pupils are being supplied with free lunches in some of the Egyptian elementary schools, and there is a strong trend toward making elementary education free. Elementary-school facilities are being gradually increased as the budgets permit and financial assistance is being given to private schools as encouragement.

CURRICULUM REVISION IN PUBLIC EDUCATION

A key question to ask concerning national systems of education is: Do the curriculums of the elementary and secondary schools meet the real needs of the majority of the school population and of the nation? Formerly the elementary curriculum in Arab schools consisted largely of reading and memorizing the Koran. Pupils sat in a circle around the master and were taught by the oral method. Learning to read and to memorize the Koran were considered the

[14] Ismail el-Kabbani, *A Hundred Years of Education in Egypt*, Pamphlet No. 1 (Washington, D. C.: Egyptian Ministry of Education, no date), p. 14.
[15] M. Hassan Aldujaili, "Irak—Le Mouvement éducatif en 1946-1947" (Geneva: Bureau International d'Education, 1948), p. 135.

greatest achievements possible in the school.[16] Under the modern plan in the Arab countries of the Near East, the curriculums are prescribed in detail by the Ministries of Education. For the most part these curriculums have not evolved in response to real needs but have been transplanted and imposed; they are largely copies from the French, the British, and to a smaller extent the American systems. There has not yet been enough time for the development of native curriculums.[17]

One exception to the following of Western patterns is the emphasis upon religious instruction. Instruction in the Koran, except in Lebanon, is a required feature of all the elementary curriculums. The elementary curriculum now in force in Iraq, shown in the table below, is rather typical of all the countries.

PRIMARY-SCHOOL PROGRAM OF STUDIES, IRAQ, 1945-1946*

	Periods per week					
Subject	1st Grade	2nd Grade	3rd Grade	4th Grade	5th Grade	6th Grade
Religion and Koran	4	4	3	3	2	2
Arabic language and penmanship	11	12	10	10	6	6
English	..	..	..	..	6	6
Arithmetic and mensuration	6	6	6	6	5	5
Object lessons and hygiene	2	2	2	2	2	2
Geography and history	..	..	4	4	4	4
Moral and civic duties	..	..	..	1	1	1
Drawing and manual arts	3	3	4	4	4	4
Physical education and singing	4	3	3	2	2	2
Total	30	30	32	32	32	32

* R. D. Mathews and Matta Akrawi, *Education in Arab Countries of the Near East* (Washington, D. C.: American Council on Education, 1949), p. 149.

The courses are set forth in complete, rigid syllabuses to which the teacher must adhere closely. Promotion and certification for graduation are entirely dependent upon official examinations. Thus the passing of examinations, in some cases both written and oral, is the climactic objective of instruction. An example of the importance attached to the examination and of how mechanical the system may become is seen in this description of a new secondary plan for Syria:

[16] A. Kh. Kinany, "Muslim Educational Ideals," in *The Year Book of Education, 1949* (London: Evans Brothers Ltd., 1949), p. 421.
[17] Cf. R. D. Mathews and Matta Akrawi, *op. cit.*, p. 541.

A new plan for school examinations provides for three kinds: daily oral or written quizzes, midyear, and final examinations. The midyear examination papers are to be corrected by the class teacher, but final examination papers are to be read by a committee of which the class teacher is a member. All midyear and final examinations are written except those in languages, which are oral as well. Marks are on the scale of 100. The results of quizzes for the first and second terms are averaged separately, added to the results of the midyear examination, and divided by three. The resulting mark is added to that of the final examination and divided by two.[18]

Shades of Western academism are certainly evident here!

According to a recent survey, the most important change in the elementary curriculum of Iraq has been the shift from world history and geography to Arab history and national geography. This trend has also been followed in other Arab countries. Although it is considered a sound principle of learning to begin with the child's more immediate environment, this shift is very likely due to the demands of the nationalists. The same influence is seen in the practice of restricting the school singing in Iraq almost entirely to national songs.

There is ample evidence that the elementary schools, particularly in the rural areas, are failing to meet the pupils' needs; in fact in some localities the schools are hardly accepted as community institutions, as this description by an Egyptian educational leader indicates:

The rural school in Egypt, like all other types of government schools in the country, has very little to do with the community. It is a government establishment, and like any government department, it considers itself head and shoulders above everything else in the village. It does not condescend to penetrate into the life of the people. It does not descend to their level; it hardly acknowledges itself as part of them. Even the parents of pupils are often denied an interview with the teacher or headmaster, and if the latter meets with the parents he does so in a condescending attitude. The school is a government department and therefore it must stand aloof from the fellaheen in order to keep its "dignified" position as such. Its function does not extend beyond the

[18] *Ibid.*, p. 365.

doors of the classroom. Once they "cover the ground" of the syllabus their task (the teachers') is done.[19]

In contrast to this account, it must be stated that the Egyptian authorities are aware of their needs in rural education and are acting to meet them. In 1943 a special type of rural elementary school was begun to provide instruction in agriculture and related subjects for rural children. The following year seventy-eight schools of this type were opened. The entire curriculum is geared to agriculture and rural life. Skills in pottery, rugmaking, and matmaking are developed for use in times when farm work is slack. One of the best schools of this type is reported at Kom Ombo, in southern Egypt. The specially designed school building there will serve also as a community center and will include a medical center, a community kitchen, a library, and shops in addition to regular classrooms.[20]

Since 1933 both the American University and the American Junior College for Women (now the Beirut College for Women) at Beirut, Lebanon, have been conducting a Village Welfare Service program. Students volunteer to devote their summer vacations to teaching reading, writing, and the fundamentals of health. One of the slogans used was "Have a patriotic vacation with the Village Welfare Service."

Vocational education presents peculiar problems in the Arab countries. In Iraq, for example, there are four-year technical schools (trade schools), located at Baghdad, Mosul, and Kirkuk. They have adequate facilities, and full expenses, including board, clothing, and laundry, are paid by the government. Yet the enrollment regularly falls below capacity. One obvious deterrent to the development of vocational education in Iraq is the requirement that those who enroll for it must do two years of military service as privates, whereas the graduates of regular secondary schools may enter the reserve officer training course, which takes only nine months. Despite various inducements, the technical school at Mosul, Iraq, graduated only eighty-four students in twelve years.[21]

Vocational education is thus far relatively unsuccessful in the

---

[19] Amir Boktor, *Schools and Society in the Valley of the Nile* (Cairo: Elias Modern Press, 1936), p. 163.

[20] R. D. Mathews and Matta Akrawi, *op. cit.*, p. 46.

[21] *Ibid.*, pp. 175-176.

Arab countries. Some of the explanations for this are that the apprenticeship system is still in vogue; industrial development is still in its infancy; and most important, perhaps, the regular secondary certificate leads to government white-collar positions of security and prestige. There is still a stigma attached to manual labor in these countries, and this prejudice is a basic psychological hindrance to the development of a functional vocational education that will attract youth. The current in-service training programs of Aramco (Arabian-American Oil Company) and other oil companies may help to modify this attitude toward vocational education.

The excessive school mortality in all the countries, together with the high percentages of over-age children in the schools, particularly in the village or rural schools, is convincing proof that the elementary curriculums are not adapted to the pupils' needs. In Egypt, for example, hundreds of thousands were registered in the lower compulsory schools, but only a few thousand were found in the fifth grade.[22] In Iraq, Jordan, and Syria, no more than 5 to 10 percent of the elementary pupils continued in the upper grades.

Egypt is making efforts to remedy this situation in one field by tying education in with industrial development. The Misr Textile Company at Mehalla Kubra is an outstanding example of this experiment. The managing director, Mr. Hamada, writes thus in describing the firm's educational program:

Education is one of the important features of the social program of the Misr Textile Company and it is provided for the workmen and their children. There is a school for the workers to teach those who do not read and write, and there is also a cultural center for those who show interest in music, photography, etc. The children of the workers are given free education in the schools which the company has built in its first "Workers City." There are at present two schools, one for boys and the second for girls, and the company is preparing the building of two similar schools. Each school has 12 classrooms, a music room, and a playground, besides the necessary accommodations for teachers and meals. There are at present about 300 pupils in each school and they are all children of the company's workers. Education in these schools is administered by the Egyptian Ministry of Education and in order to facilitate general education and culture for the parents, evening classes are given in reading and writing and in needlework for the wives of the labourers.

[22] *Ibid.*, p. 547.

It is a very expensive program but the results are, so far, encouraging. There is better production and contentment.[23]

And, we might add, there is better education.

This experiment at Mehalla Kubra may well be the pilot model for an educational program that will reach the workers of Egypt, so far largely by-passed by the present system.

The extension movement in Egypt known as the "people's university" is another noteworthy development in curriculum improvement for those not reached by the regular system. It was begun in 1945 on the initiative of Dr. Ahmad Amin, Mr. A. N. Hashim, and Professor A. M. Mosharrafa, who had observed the success of similar programs in London. The people's university may start in any center where the university has a branch, provided at least twenty-five people request a course. In 1947 there were about sixteen branches stretching from Alexandria and Cairo to Asyut. The people's university is broad and flexible in scope and thus far includes courses ranging from stenography, salesmanship, and clerical work to literature, art, and aeronautics. There is a nominal tuition fee of 5 piasters (about 12 cents). The teaching staff is largely composed of university faculty. The whole program is directly under the Ministry of Education. This leisure-time education for adults is a sort of university without degrees. It is meeting with increasing response, particularly in the larger urban centers.

Some constructive suggestions for general curriculum revision in public education for Arab countries are found in a study by Dr. Matta Akrawi. These were presented as tentative objectives for primary education in Iraq in 1942, and they reflect progressive thinking on real needs. There is not space for all these suggestions to be listed here, but the following indicate basic social and economic problems:

SOME EDUCATIONAL OBJECTIVES FOR PRIMARY EDUCATION IN IRAQ

Under the Objective of Health and Physical Well-being

To fight superstitious conceptions with regard to the origin of diseases and superstitious methods of curing them.

Teach the germ theory of disease.

[23] Letter to the author, November 3, 1949, from Mr. Hamada, managing director of the Misr Textile Company at Mehalla Kubra, Egypt.

Create the attitude of mind of calling a doctor or of visiting a hospital or clinic in case of illness.

Make the people appreciate the importance of a pure water supply and spread some of the simpler methods of purifying water.

Educate the people to appreciate the importance of registering births and deaths.

Spread scientific knowledge about the physical care of children in order to reduce the large rate of infant mortality.

Break gradually the prejudice against calling physicians for the care of pregnant women.

Combat the attitude of fatalism toward disease.

Under the Objective of National and Political Ideals

Bring up a generation of united citizens who will owe allegiance to and willingly work for the state, subordinating or broadening all other allegiances, such as: narrow religious intolerance; racial allegiance, family allegiance, tribal allegiance.

To help the mass of the people to understand and appreciate the principle of democratic government and life and to practice its application.

Under the Objective of Religious Ideals

Spread a dynamic modern view of one's own religion so that it will be a factor for progress rather than against it.

Spread the ideal of religious tolerance.

Under Civic and Personal Ideals

Inculcate in the children the ideal of social service.

Develop a good moral character and standard of honesty and truthfulness.

Counteract the extreme individualistic tendency of the Arab by educating him in cooperation.

Develop some personal character traits which are of use both to the individual and the community, some of which are rather lacking in the average Iraqui: initiative and creativeness; willingness to assume responsibility, resourcefulness, habits of work and application, particularly careful planning and thoroughness; accuracy in thought and expression.

Under the Objective of Social Ideals

Raise the standard of home life through the general education of men and women and the spirit of fellowship and love among members of a family by bringing women up to the intellectual, spiritual and social level of men.

Cultivate the notion that woman, to be a useful member of society, must gradually attain her freedom and independence.

Check the great amount of foul language in use in ordinary conversations among the mass of people.

Help the people in adopting a selective and critical attitude towards foreign institutions and devices.

Under the Objective of Economic Life

Cultivate a feeling of respect for work and a desire and zeal for the development of natural resources.

Stem the tide of office-seeking and direct attention of the younger generation into more productive and independent fields.

Cultivate habits of thrift and careful budgeting in order not to fall disastrously into debt.

Combat habits of laziness and inactivity.

In farming communities:

Increase the income of the farmer by increasing the quantity and variety of his produce and improving its quality.

Introduce better methods in farming, particularly the use of simple and efficient tools and the use of fertilizers.

Teach methods of fighting plant and animal pests.

Improve the breeds of animals and the strains of products.

Introduce the simple knowledge of drying and canning vegetables and fruits.

Introduce ideas of grading and marketing produce, perhaps ultimately cooperative marketing.

Encourage the development of village crafts such as weaving, rug making, mat making, etc., and improve their quality particularly on the artistic side.

Encourage the doing of one's own menial work (in the cities).

Under the Objective of Culture and the Use of Leisure Time

Encourage the use of sports, particularly such sporting activities as are more in the nature of Arab life, e.g., horse riding, camping, scouting, pathfinding and finding one's direction by the stars.

Encourage appreciation of the beautiful and artistic through: amateur handicrafts and industrial arts activities; cultivation of musical talents and appreciation of music, especially Arabic music.

Cultivate habits of reading.

Under the Objective of Understanding the Environment

Understand man's geographical habitat, particularly as applied to Iraq.

Study one's own immediate environment including: the natural environment, the economic resources, the historical sites and buildings; types of life whether tribal, rural or urban; customs, traditions, dress, etc.

Under the Objective of Language

Attain the mastery of a foreign language as far as is possible in order to establish better social, commercial and political intercourse with the West, to promote better understanding of Western Civilization and to help in increasing one's knowledge of modern science, inventions and methods developed in the West.[24]

Since the author of these suggestions, Dr. Akrawi, is now in a position of authority and influence as Director General of Higher Education in Iraq, there is a real possibility of seeing some of these ideas realized. This discussion of curriculum revision in public education has been restricted almost entirely to elementary education and adult extracurricular education. The general problem of creative adaptation at these two levels is much the same as for secondary and higher education. The hope of realistic curriculum revision and reorganization rests with enlightened leaders, such as Dr. Akrawi and those who started the new type of rural elementary school and the people's universities in Egypt.

THE EDUCATION OF GIRLS AND WOMEN

Equality of educational opportunity for girls and women in the Arab countries of the Near East is an expressed but far from realized ideal. The attitudes of Arab men on this matter have undergone a radical change in the past generation and opportunities are increasing for girls to obtain an education. Even coeducation is now practiced to a limited extent in these countries where the veiling and segregation of women are still the custom in many places.

[24] Matta Akrawi, *Curriculum Construction in the Public Schools of Iraq*, pp. 217 ff.

The Inspector of Public Schools in Syria, writing of Moslem educational ideals, has this to say about the Moslem attitude toward women: "The chosen place for women in Muslim society is the home. However, there is no religious rule forbidding them to take any fitting occupation if they obtain the consent of their husband. They are allowed to be judges and to teach even adult males. Ibn Asakir, a great reporter of *Hadith*, was proud of having women among his teachers."[25]

This is the traditional point of view. The more progressive view is expressed thus by one of the leaders in the Arab National Movement: "In all these rights and duties (political, economic, social) the woman must be equal to the man, so that she may share in the formation of this new Arab society."[26]

This positive statement of women's equal rights is a comparatively new doctrine and has not yet been fully implemented in terms of equal educational opportunity.

An Egyptian educator presents this significant description of the women of Egypt: "An aristocracy of highly cultured women who have had European governesses in their childhood and who have studied in European colleges and travelled extensively abroad, a small minority of middle class women who had a fair and modest share of education, and a vast majority of illiterate female masses who had no education at all, are the sum total of the female population of Egypt."[27] These "illiterate female masses" remain a primary problem for education in the Arab countries.

There is still a traditional prejudice against and a lack of experience in coeducation. In Egypt, however, the compulsory elementary schools have changed from the half-day schedule, with boys and girls attending alternately, to the full-day elementary school, and authorities have found the new plan to be more satisfactory. This step toward coeducation was partly the result of the limited school facilities. In 1945 Egypt had well over a half million children in the compulsory elementary schools, almost equally divided as to sex. At the secondary level coeducation is still unacceptable in the Near Eastern Arab countries, but at the

[25] A. Kh. Kinany, *op. cit.*, p. 416.

[26] Musa Alami, "The Lesson of Palestine," *Middle East Journal,* October 1949, p. 399.

[27] Amir Boktor. *op. cit.*, p. 74.

college or university level the prejudice against it seems to be diminishing. Enrollment statistics of Fuad I University for 1945-1946 show women students in all faculties except that of veterinary medicine. Even though their numbers are small (less than 10 percent of the total), the significant fact is that they are represented.[28]

Much credit must be given to foreign missionaries for their efforts in setting the pattern for the education of girls in Arab countries. The Sidon Girls' School under the American Mission in Sidon, Lebanon, is a fine example of one type of pioneer work, education in homemaking. One of the graduates of this school, who later took her M.A. degree in home economics at an American university and has prepared a home economics textbook in Arabic, writes the following about her alma mater:

> Sidon Girls' School is outstanding among all the schools, foreign and national, in the country in the fact that it devotes a large part of its time to homemaking education. The girls begin their formal home economics training in the seventh grade and continue throughout high school. By the time a girl graduates from this school she would have had the following courses in homemaking: family relationships, the family budget, home furnishing and decoration, home and community, home nursing, food planning and preparation, dietetics, textiles, clothing selection and construction, prenatal care, child care, clothing and feeding the infant and the young child, and child development.[29]

The girls at this school live in cottages, each of which is equipped and furnished like an average home in Syria or Lebanon. The twelve girls in each cottage are selected from various age groups, so that each group is like a family. The seniors act as the housemother's assistants. The total enrollment is limited to seventy-five girls. The school is definitely a new type for the Near East. The education it provides in homemaking is slowly winning male support but is not yet widely duplicated in public educational systems.

[28] These figures are from *A Statement about Fuad I University,* a pamphlet (in Arabic) published on the occasion of the visit of King Ibn Sa'ud, January 1946.

[29] Sophie Wakim Karayusuf, "Preparation of High School Girls for Homemaking and Marriage," *The Cedar Bough* (Beirut: American Press), Autumn Number, 1949, pp. 9-10.

The cost, even though moderate, is prohibitive for those of the lower socioeconomic classes. Yet the school is a successful model and will undoubtedly make its impress on educational planning for girls. Egypt has something like it in the so-called "feminine culture schools," and for girls of the upper social classes there are in Egypt two girls' "colleges" that aim at social training on a high level. The American Junior College for Women (now the Beirut College for Women) founded at Beirut, Lebanon, in 1924, is another fine example of higher education for women, but it is both private and under foreign auspices, as are many of the other better schools in Lebanon.

The Hamilton Wright film "It's a Woman's World" shows Egyptian women active in many walks of Egyptian life. One scene shows a woman doctor performing an appendectomy. It is true that in some of the larger cities of the Near East one can find many well-educated Arab women among the upper social and economic groups, but the problem of the "illiterate female masses" in Arab countries is still unsolved.

TEACHER SUPPLY AND TEACHER TRAINING

No national system of education can ever rise above the quality of its professional teachers. No nation has ever developed a strong educational system without first developing an effective system of teacher recruitment, selection, and professional training.

The Arab countries of the Near East do not have an adequate supply of trained teachers and they are particularly lacking in teachers for rural schools. Only two countries in the Near East (Egypt and Iraq) are even approaching the point of providing enough teachers for their elementary and secondary schools. Even these two would be far from having an adequate supply of trained teachers if they increased the number of schools to take care of all school-age children.

There is little agreement on what constitutes adequate professional teacher training. The courses now range from two to four years and in many cases provide no more than what is offered as secondary education. Among the better types of teacher-training institutions is the Higher Teachers College of Baghdad, Iraq, which has had a four-year course since 1939. Egypt has institutes of education for men and for women which offer a two-year post-graduate course to holders of the bachelor's degree. These institutes are devoted entirely to teacher training. Egypt also has seventeen training schools for elementary teachers.

The general practice in the government-supported teacher-training institutions is for the government to pay all fees for the candidates and in some cases to provide board, room, clothing, medical care, and even travel expenses. In return the potential teacher is required to sign a contract to teach one year for each year of study or refund the equivalent of $100 for each year of training received.

Teacher candidates are selected primarily on the basis of their academic records and examinations. According to modern standards of selection, this basis is too narrow. Candidates are also required to pass physical examinations. Their home province is also considered in selection, since there is considerable pressure by teachers to be assigned to teach in their home towns. Attracting girls into the teaching profession presents special difficulties. According to one authority, "In upper Egypt, to be a school teacher is the last resort for any girl who is not the daughter of a pauper or a coachman."[30]

A practice that increases the problems of rural education is the assignment of teachers with poorer qualifications to the rural schools, which tend to become a dumping ground for misfits. Since one of the most urgent needs is the development of rural life, this practice is most deplorable. Iraq, recognizing the need for the special training of rural teachers, in 1948 opened five normal schools for them exclusively; the graduates are to staff the new rural schools to be opened during the following five years.[31]

Another source for trained teachers is the so-called Educational Mission, a plan under which students are sent abroad at government expense. The majority of these foreign-educated students used to go either into teaching or into the Ministries of Education. They now serve in all branches of the governments. Egypt has had the longest experience in sending students abroad; the first one was sent in 1813 by the great Mohammed Ali. The first students went to Italy, then some went to France, and later some went to England.

[30] Amir Boktor, op. cit., p. 75.
[31] Abdul Hamid Kadham, "Irak: Le Mouvement éducatif en 1947-48," in Annuaire international de l'éducation et de l'enseignement (Geneva: Bureau International d'Education, 1948), p. 186.

In recent years the preference has shifted to England and America. In 1946, there were 522 Egyptian students abroad under the Educational Mission, distributed as follows: in Great Britain, 244; in the United States, 187; in France, 53; in Switzerland, 35; and in Italy, 3.[32] (In addition there were 50 students from Egypt studying at their own expense in America.) The Egyptian government pays the expense of these students, including a monthly allowance for living, and assigns them to study in certain fields. In return the student must complete his studies in the specified period and serve for seven years in that ministry which sent him.

Iraq began sending students abroad in 1921, and more than seven hundred have been sent since that date. The Educational Missions were practically suspended during World War II but have grown rapidly in the postwar years. Now there are students abroad assigned to virtually every field of study, with especial emphasis on science, technology, and agriculture, as well as military science.

Professionally competent educational staffs are a critical need for the teacher-training institutions of the Near East. Although the returned students are well educated in their subject fields, their special training has been in a foreign language as well as in a foreign land. They are sometimes "denationalized" in their academic orientation and require considerable adjustment before they can be of practical value in their native lands. The current need is for teachers who are well grounded in modern psychology and modern methods of curriculum organization and instruction, as well as in modern philosophies of education. There is also a need for teachers of special subjects such as agriculture, industrial arts, home economics, health and physical education, and reading.

In-service training of teachers is comparatively undeveloped. Limited efforts are made to offer courses to teachers during the summer vacation. Syria is attempting to train village primary-school teachers in agriculture during the vacation period.[33] Iraq is offering special courses for English teachers and kindergarten teachers in service.[34] These efforts are sporadic and as yet there is

---

[32] R. D. Mathews and Matta Akrawi, op. cit., p. 91.
[33] Ministry of Public Instruction, Syria, "Syrie: Le Mouvement éducatif," in Annuaire international de l'éducation et de l'enseignement (Geneva: Bureau International d'Education, 1948), p. 283.
[34] Abdul Hamid Kadham, op. cit., p. 186.

no national program in these countries for the upgrading and in-service training of teachers. School inspection is too often a matter of bureaucratic routine rather than an opportunity for discovering the real problems of the teachers at work.

It is reported that the educational officials holding the top posts in the Ministries of Education and those serving as inspectors and principals are often not properly trained for their professional assignments in education. They are for the most part well educated, but often without reference to their particular responsibilities. According to one of them, they "have had little acquaintance with educational methods and curriculum construction, and the various problems of educational administration and organization."[35] Consequently only an amateur performance in education service can be expected, even when there is serious purpose and conscientious effort.

NATIONALISM AND A PHILOSOPHY OF EDUCATION

Arab nationalism as distinguished from the separate nationalism of the Arab countries has achieved a semblance of political reality in the creation of the Arab League. The seven states of Egypt, Iraq, Syria, Lebanon, Transjordan (now Jordan), Saudi Arabia, and Yemen signed the Pact of the Arab League in 1947. The Pact is the culmination of a nationalist movement that aimed at freedom from Ottoman rule, and then, from 1918-1946, at freedom from the French and British, who had ruled during the period of the mandates. The mandate powers failed to train adequate native leadership for the functions of self-government. Thus, with the achievement of political freedom in 1946, the Arab states were not fully prepared to deal with the problems of government. Nevertheless, when seeking the philosophy that sets the goals and values for education, we find that Arab nationalism is today the most dynamic force directing the educational programs of these countries.

The final relationship of Islam to Arab nationalism is one of the most crucial problems in the Arab countries of the Near East today. Islam will be a major force in any program of reform, but whether this force will work for liberalism or reactionary nationalism still

[35] R. D. Mathews and Matta Akrawi, *op. cit.*, p. 541.

remains in question. As one student of the problem sees it, the outlook is not too hopeful:

> Totalitarian Islamic nationalism manifests itself in a variety of forms: in the attempt to control education at all levels and hold in check all means of forming public opinion whether by the press, the platform, or the radio; in the use of the wireless for continuous Koranic readings; in the insistence on the provision of Islamic teaching and places of prayer to Moslem pupils in all schools, Moslem or non-Moslem; in the testing of legislation by its conformity to Moslem law; in the movement for replacing modern legislative codes by that of the *Sharia* [ancient Moslem law] in the renewed emphasis on the importance of Mecca and the pilgrimage; and in frequent references at official ceremonies to Islam and its past and present glory. . . . The new enthusiasm for Moslem orthodoxy finds popular expression in youth organizations. . . . Once nationalism and Islam are identified in men's thoughts, there is no hesitation in looking to the state to protect Islam both from supposed betrayal from within and from corrosion from without.[36]

The creation of the new state of Israel in Arab Palestine is considered by the Arabs as both an "invasion" and a direct threat against the aspirations of the Arab national movement. The common goal of Arab nationalism is the stemming of Zionist expansion. Political Zionism has thus become the target for nationalistic animosity in place of the old Ottoman rule and the mandate powers. Reactionary Arab nationalists gained strength as the result of the refusal of the United Nations to recognize the validity of the Arab case for Palestine.

One of the characteristic aspects of Arab nationalism is the faith in education as a road to national strength. The political leaders, many of whom are far from liberal, seem in agreement on the point that a strong program of public education will strengthen the state, although there are different opinions of what this program should be. Evidence of efforts to nationalize education is seen in the strong emphasis upon national subjects, such as history, geography, and literature, and upon physical education and military training; in the laws that bring all foreign schools under the direct control and supervision of the Ministries of Education; in the

[36] S. A. Morrison, "Arab Nationalism and Islam," *Middle East Journal*, April 1948, p. 156.

prescription of uniform curriculums, and in the charges that foreign schools are denationalizing the students.[37]

The goals of Arab nationalism have been expressed as follows by a prominent nationalist leader: "The Arab nation has a deep desire to revive, to lift itself up, to recover its place in history, to be counted as a great nation with a glorious past."[38] Describing the possible role of national education, the same author writes:

Experiments performed by a number of modern states have shown that any political regime which aims at the realization of speedy and total reforms and the creation of a new life demands an educational system to spread its principles and beliefs among the people. . . . Each one of the educational systems adopted by such modern states has been derived from a complete political and social philosophy. It is up to our thinkers at this moment to propound such a national philosophy on which an educational program may be built.[39]

Thus far no such national philosophy for Arab education has been explicitly defined. More surprising still, Professor H. A. R. Gibb, a profound and sympathetic student of Arab culture, has stated, "I have not seen any book written in Arabic for Arabs themselves which has clearly analyzed what Arabic culture means for the Arabs."[40]

Dr. Zurayk, former Syrian Minister to Washington and now head of the Syrian University in Damascus, published in October 1949 a little book in Arabic under the title *The Meaning of Disaster*, in which he deals with the tragedy of a divided Palestine. In this critical analysis he shows the current trend of liberals toward self-examination and self-criticism and sets forth what he considers are the essentials for social progress. He writes:

The Jews are living in the present and the future, while we still dream of the past. . . . There must be a new society involving a real revolution in the Arab way of thinking and acting. This society must be popular, united, and progressive. To achieve it, the following are necessary:

Separation of the state and religion
Discipline in the practical and experimental sciences

[37] Cf. R. D. Mathews and Matta Akrawi, *op. cit.*, pp. 565 ff.
[38] Musa Alami, *op. cit.*, p. 388.
[39] *Ibid.*, p. 400.
[40] P. W. Ireland, ed., *The Near East, Problems and Prospects* (Chicago: University of Chicago Press), 1942, p. 60.

Openmindedness toward the best spiritual and intellectual values in other civilizations[41]

Dr. Zurayk's point of view is representative of the best liberal thought among the leaders in Arab education today. It is from this group that a modern Arab national philosophy of education will most likely come, and fortunately some of these men are in positions where they can give such a philosophy practical expression when it is formulated.[42]

SOME SPECIAL PROBLEMS FOR ARAB EDUCATION

The problem of the Arab refugees from Palestine has created exceedingly heavy burdens for all the Arab countries of the Near East. Unemployment, poverty, and disease have made for appalling conditions in the refugee camps, which contain a destitute population of over a half million persons. Teachers and education must also be provided for the children of these refugees. The United Nations mission under Gordon Clapp has recommended a subsidized work and relief program, but this is an emergency measure which cannot be a final solution of the tragic problem.[43]

The financing of Arab public educational systems for these new states constitutes a heavy drain on their limited resources. There is virtually no financial support for education at the local level (except for private and foreign schools), so that the expenses of public education must come from the national budget. For these states to attempt to carry out the educational programs needed for universal compulsory education would require an estimated 30-60 percent of their current national budgets. Thus the adequate financing of public education must await increased national income plus the development of support at the local level.[44]

[41] Quoted in Cecil Howrani's review of *The Meaning of Disaster, Middle East Journal,* October 1949, pp. 469-470.

[42] Cf. Charles Malik, *op. cit.*

[43] Cf. Bayard Dodge, "The Problem of the Palestine Refugees," *Yale Review,* Autumn 1939.

[44] Current appropriations for the Ministries of Education range from 8 percent of the national budget in Iraq (1947) to 17 percent in Syria (1949), with the other countries ranging in between. Egypt spends the largest amount of money on public education, with a budget appropriation of more than 19 million Egyptian pounds (about 54½ million dollars) for 1949-1950. (Figures supplied by R. D. Sethian, Near East Section of the U. S. Department of State.)

The possibility that oil will bring in money for education is a hope for the future. The Arabian-American Oil Company is build ing a pipe line from Saudi Arabia to the Lebanon coast. With it will come new opportunities for employment as well as new royal- ties. King Ibn Sa'ud will then receive more than 40 million dollars a year in royalties. However, the oil may not flow in volume until real peace comes to the Near East, and there may be more urgent uses for oil royalties than in education.

The threat of Communism in the Near East is growing as un- employment, frustration, and poverty increase. It is reported that even in the conservative mission schools of Lebanon reorganization was necessary in the summer of 1949, because it was found that nine staff members were teaching Communism in the classroom.[45] Students are a potent force in Near Eastern political life, especially when minority parties are in power. Drastic action has been taken by the governments and police against Communist agitators and agents when they can be apprehended. The Communist party is officially outlawed in all the Arab countries.

It is of interest to note a recent report that

> The students [at the American University, Beirut] had decided to keep clear of political agitation. Instead of blaming the foreigner for everything that was going wrong, they were inter- ested in self-criticism. With real humility they were trying to find out how they could make their newly won independence less of a disappointment and more of a success.[46]

Nevertheless the dangerously top-heavy social and economic struc- ture is a choice target for Communist agents. Not only is Russia interested in winning the Arab people but, more important, she wants Arabian oil.

Education in these Arab countries, from elementary school to university, has shown a phenomenal growth despite handicaps of limited national finances, mass poverty, the crises of wars, and political instability. The question now is whether or not Arab education will become the tool of a narrow, reactionary, and embittered nationalism or will be permitted the freedom to grow into an integrated, native, democratic system such as the liberals and the progressive "young effendi" would have it.

[45] Bayard Dodge, *op. cit.*, p. 71.
[46] *Ibid.*, p. 74.

BIBLIOGRAPHY

AKRAWI, MATTA, "The Arab World: Nationalism and Education," in *The Year Book of Education, 1949* (London: Evans Brothers Ltd., 1949). A pointed discussion of the impact of Arab nationalism on Arab education, including a statement of the problem of cultural change by the Director General of Higher Education in Iraq.

———, *Curriculum Construction in the Public Schools of Iraq* (New York: Teachers College, Columbia University, 1942). A progressive critique of curriculum construction for Iraq, including a comprehensive listing of desirable objectives by one who is an authority on Iraq's educational problems.

ALAMI, MUSA, "The Lesson of Palestine" (translated and condensed from the book *Ibrat Falastin*, Beirut, 1949), *Middle East Journal,* October 1949. A patriotic and realistic appeal for the reformation of Arab society, presenting both problems and guiding principles for their solution, by a distinguished veteran of the Arab national movement.

ALDUJAILI, M. HASSAN, "Irak—Le Mouvement éducatif en 1946-1947," in *Annuaire international de l'éducation et de l'enseignement, 1947* (Geneva: Bureau International d'Education, 1948). A brief, official, factual summary of some recent educational developments in Iraq.

ANTONIUS, GEORGE, *The Arab Awakening* (New York: G. P. Putnam's Sons, 1946). An authoritative account of the historical development of Arab nationalism by one who had access to many of the previously unused Arab source materials. The author traces the development of nationalism from the middle of the nineteenth century to the mandate period.

BOKTOR, AMIR, *Schools and Society in the Valley of the Nile* (Cairo: Elias Modern Press, 1936). Egyptian educational problems as seen against the background of Egyptian society, with a frank appraisal of both. The author is now Director of the Faculty of Education at the American University, Cairo.

COON, CARLETON S., "Point Four and the Middle East," *Annals of the American Academy of Political and Social Science,* July 1950, pp. 83-94. The author specialized for twenty-five years in Middle East studies. He is a cultural anthropologist and presents in this article descriptions of city, village, and desert life in Middle Eastern culture, along with suggestions for the implementation of Point Four in that region.

DODGE, BAYARD, "The Problem of the Palestine Refugees," *Yale Review*, Autumn 1949. An informative and sympathetic discussion of the plight of the Arab refugees, based on a recent personal survey of the situation. The author served as professor and president of the American University at Beirut, Lebanon, for thirty-five years.

DORMAN, HARRY GAYLORD, JR., *Toward Understanding Islam*, (New York: Teachers College, Columbia University, 1948). A discussion of the contemporary apologetic of Islam and its relation to Christian missionary policy, by an American who is now teaching in the Near East School of Theology, Beirut, Lebanon.

GIBB, H. A. R., *Mohammedanism* (London: Oxford University Press, 1949). A concise historical survey of Mohammedanism by an authority on Arab culture and religion. Chapter 10, "Islam in the Modern World," is particularly relevant for those who would understand the psychological climate of Arab countries.

HANS, NICHOLAS, *Comparative Education* (London: Routledge and Kegan Paul Ltd., 1949). Discusses such factors as race, religion, language, geography, and nationalism in relation to educational development. The author is lecturer in comparative education at London University.

HITTI, PHILIP K., *The Arabs: A Short History for Americans* (Princeton, N. J.: Princeton University Press, 1949). The author is professor of Semitic Literature at Princeton University. His *History of the Arabs*, 4th ed. (New York: The Macmillan Company, 1949), is the standard work in English on this subject. *The Arabs* is a shorter interpretation for the general reader in America.

HOWRANI, CECIL, review of *The Meaning of Disaster* (in Arabic), by C. Zurayk, *Middle East Journal*, October 1949. A penetrating and critical appraisal of what Arabs can learn from the tragedy of Palestine as lessons for future growth. Dr. Zurayk is president of the Syrian University in Damascus.

EL HUSSRI, SATI, "Syria: Post Mandatory Developments," in *The Year Book of Education, 1949* (London: Evans Brothers Ltd., 1949). A brief summary of recent educational changes in Syria, by the Cultural Adviser to the Arab League. Outlines reforms based on the educational laws of 1944.

JAMALI, MOHAMMED FADHEL, *The New Iraq: Its Problem of Bedouin Education* (New York: Teachers College, Columbia University, 1934). A description of Iraq's special problems in trying to pro-

vide education for her tribal groups. The author subsequently
served as Minister of Education for Iraq.

EL-KABBANI, ISMAIL, *A Hundred Years of Education in Egypt*,
Pamphlet No. I (Washington, D. C.: Egyptian Ministry of Education, no date). A concise summary of Egypt's educational
progress by one of Egypt's outstanding educational pioneers.

KADHAM, ABDUL HAMID, "Irak: Le Mouvement éducatif en 1947-48,"
Annuaire international de l'éducation et de l'enseignement, 1948
(Geneva: Bureau International d'Education, 1948). An official,
factual account, in brief, of recent educational developments in
Iraq, for the Office of International Education.

KARAYUSUF, SOPHIE WAKIM, "Preparation of High School Girls for
Homemaking and Marriage," *The Cedar Bough* (Beirut: American Press), Autumn Number, 1949. A general description of the
curriculum organization and purpose of the Sidon Girls' School,
Lebanon, by one of the distinguished alumnae.

KHAKI, AHMAD, "The Teaching of Arabic," *Bulletin of the Egyptian
Education Bureau*, Cairo, May 1947. Presents some of the special
problems involved in teaching classical Arabic in the public
schools.

KINANY, A. KH., "Muslim Educational Ideals," *The Year Book of
Education, 1949* (London: Evans Brothers Ltd., 1949). The Inspector of Syrian Public Schools summarizes the traditional
Moslem ideals for education and reveals the scope of Islam as a
way of life.

KIRK, GEORGE E., *A Short History of the Middle East* (Washington,
D. C.: Public Affairs Press, 1949). A concise analysis of the
political and social development of the Near East from A.D. 600
through World War II, including a chapter on Russia and the
Middle East.

KURANI, HABIB AMIN, "Lebanon: Educational Reform," in *The
Year Book of Education, 1949* (London: Evans Brothers Ltd.,
1949). A summary account of educational reform and changes in
Lebanon from the period of the mandate, including a discussion
of educational legislation, by a professor of education at the
American University of Beirut, Lebanon.

MALIK, CHARLES, "The Problem of Asia." Speech delivered by
Charles Malik, Minister of the Republic of Lebanon to the
United States of America, in the Political Committee of the
General Assembly of the United Nations, at Lake Success, Decem-
ber 11, 1950. (Mimeographed copies available from the Lebanese
Legation, Washington, D. C.) A political and philosophical an-

alysis of the factors that are retarding the self-development of the nations and peoples of both the Near and Far East, and the changes necessary in thinking and international relations before these nations can find their rightful place.

MATHEWS, R. D., and MATTA AKRAWI, *Education in Arab Countries of the Near East* (Washington, D. C.: American Council on Education, 1949). A recent survey of educational organization, administration, and curriculums based on a study of 471 schools in six Arab countries. An invaluable descriptive reference, but without evaluation. The last chapter interprets the problems of cultural change in the Arab world.

MORRISON, S. A., "Arab Nationalism and Islam," *Middle East Journal*, April 1948, pp. 147-160. The author served as Secretary of the Committee of Liaison for non-Moslem communities in Egypt and is also Secretary of the Church Missionary Society of Egypt.

SASSANI, ABDUL H., "American Institutions of Higher Learning in the Near East," *Bulletin of Higher Education*, September 15, 1949. A factual but brief account of all American institutions of higher education in the Near East by a specialist in the United States Office of Education.

VAN ESS, JOHN, *Meet the Arab* (New York: The John Day Company, 1943). The author lived among the Arabs for forty years and founded some of the first schools for Arabs in Iraq. He is the author of two standard Arabic grammars. This book is a very human and illuminating interpretation of Arab life, including some of the educational problems and achievements.

15 · EDUCATION IN *Turkey*

DOUGLAS RUGH

The Republic of Turkey occupies territory in both Europe and Asia, and as a frontier power at the gateway to the Middle East she has consciously identified herself with the culture of the West. Turkey's geostrategic position with relation to the Middle East and as the power controlling the Straits has made her a perennial target of power politics.

A great central plateau of dry steppes, turbulent rivers, and treeless hills stretches to the east, bordered on the west by a narrow but fertile coastal plain. Four fifths of the population derive their income from agriculture. The main products include tobacco, cereals, olives and olive oil, wool, silk, cotton, figs, nuts, and fruits of many varieties. There are large mineral resources as yet undeveloped, including petroleum. As late as 1916 the Turkish Empire comprised about 700,000 square miles. The Republic is less than half this large, with 300,000 square miles and a population of about 20 million. The Republic has renounced the idea of empire and has no territorial ambitions.

The Turkish racial type is sometimes called "Hittite"; it is a composite of strains from the early Greek and Roman conquests and basic traits from the Seljuks, Tartars, and Osmanlis. The present population is 85 percent Turkish, the largest minority group being about one million Kurds, who live in the border country near Iran and Iraq. The Kurds are Moslem and to some degree nomadic.

Kemal Atatürk, who died in 1938, laid down the pattern for the Republic of Turkey and set in motion the dynamic forces that characterize it. The West may think of Atatürk as a dictator, but he is considered by his own people as their savior (*Gazi*). First as a revolutionary leader and then as president of the Republic for its first fifteen years, he gave to the Republic the political ideology known as "Kemalism."

The ideology of "Kemalism," stated in one sentence, asserts that "the Turkish State is republican, nationalist, populist, étatist, laique and reformist."[1] Some of these principles require further explanation if one is to understand the cultural climate in which Turkish education is carried on.

Nationalism. The *Türcülük* (Turkism) movement has gone back to pre-Ottoman times to tap the wellsprings of Turkish history for a positive nationalism; it has succeeded in making the Turks conscious and proud of their heritage. Despite Turkey's strong military tradition, her nationalism contains no elements of hatred or animosity toward other nations or ethnic groups but concentrates on a vigorous development of Turkish potentialities. The spirit of Turkish nationalism is sensed in the watchword of the popular poet Mehmet Emin: "I am a Turk. My race and language are great." And in the words of Ziya Gökalp, inspired sociologist and theoretician of the movement: "I do not read about the glorious deeds of my ancestors from the dead and faded and dusty pages of history books, but in my own bloodstream and in my own heart."

Populism. The principle of populism aims to provide all Turkish citizens with equal social, economic, and judicial rights and calls for a democratic exercise of suffrage rights by both men and women (women have had equal suffrage since 1935) in local elections. Derived in part from Islam, populism aims also at a classless society in which no privileges depend upon family, occupation, economic status, or place of residence.[2]

Etatism. Turkish étatism denotes neither Fascism nor National Socialism but is primarily an insistence upon the interest and responsibility of the state in matters, particularly economic, which concern the welfare of the nation. Private enterprise is in no way discounted when it can so function as to serve the national needs. The government of Celal Bayar (Democratic party), elected in a free election,

[1] Donald E. Webster, *The Turkey of Ataturk* (Philadelphia: American Academy of Political and Social Science, 1939), Chapter 11.
[2] *Ibid.*, p. 166.

May 14, 1950, with 89 percent of the eligible voters at the polls, favors turning state-owned factories over to private industry.

Laicism. Laicism is the secularization of political life but does not denote the "liquidation" of religion. To separate Islam completely from the civic life of the community, after centuries when the Holy Law (*Seriat*) was dominant, was one of Atatürk's most radical proposals. The caliphate, office of spiritual leadership over all Islam which the Sultan combined with his secular powers, was abolished in 1924, shortly after the abolition of the sultanate. This broke Turkey's official link with the world of Islam.[3] The new constitution (1924) contained an article proclaiming Islam the official religion of the Turkish state, but this provision was later eliminated by amendment. Turkey has chosen to follow, in place of the religious dogmatism of Islam, the new Western doctrine of scientific positivism. This is shown in the following statement by the editor of the Turkish edition of the *Encyclopedia of Islam*:

> The Republic has never ceased to declare itself the citadel of scientific positivism. . . . The entire mechanism of the state, by common accord, has been trying to put into its different institutions the positivist formula—the Good, the Beautiful, and the True—as a new doctrine. Within the past twenty years the vast majority of Turkish youth has been brought up without any official religious teaching. Western positivism is being imposed on it just as Islamic dogmas had been in the past.[4]

The new government of Celal Bayar, however, has again recognized Islam as the source of Turkish religious faith and has encouraged religious teaching in the schools (1951).

Reformism. The sixth principle of "Kemalism" is both a policy and a method. It means change and improvement of customs and institutions by law.[5] An example of reformism in action was the decision of Atatürk to reform the alphabet. Until 1928 the Turks wrote in Arabic script, which was a link with Turkey's Islamic and

[3] Barbara Ward, *Turkey* (London: Oxford University Press, 1942), pp. 62 ff.

[4] A. A. Adivar, "Islamic and Western Thought in Turkey," *Middle East Journal*, July 1947, p. 279.

[5] An interesting account of how and why the Turks accepted these reforms by edict is presented in Selma Ekrem's book *Turkey: Old and New* (New York: Charles Scribner's Sons, 1947), pp. 45-67.

imperial past. Both as an aid in combating illiteracy and as a means of breaking this link with the past, Atatürk achieved the official adoption of the Roman alphabet in November 1928. By autumn of 1929, teaching in the public schools was begun in the new script. Among adults the learning of the new alphabet was facilitated by the "folk houses."[6] Within a decade the new alphabet was rather well assimilated and all newspapers, books, and notices were printed only in the Roman alphabet.

THE NATIONAL EDUCATION PROGRAM

Since 1923, education has been assigned a dominant role in the life and development of the nation. Public education is compulsory, free, and secular; owing to the inadequate supply of school buildings and teachers, however, compulsory education cannot be enforced in all localities. In 1926 the Ministry of Public Instruction invited the American educational philosopher John Dewey to come to Turkey, and many of his suggestions were adopted in the new system, particularly those concerned with method. The official program of the People's Party of the Republic, as adopted in May 1935, sets forth in specific form the main aims and guiding principles for national educational development. These continue in effect at the present time with slight modification. For this reason the twelve articles of Part V of the program, "National Education and Instruction," are presented herewith in full and should be carefully studied by any one who would grasp the spirit and intent of Turkish education.

Article 41. Our main principles for national education and instruction are as follows:

(*a*) The cornerstone of our cultural policy is the suppression of ignorance. In the field of public instruction a policy of teaching and training more children and citizens every day shall be followed.

(*b*) The training of strongly republican, nationalist, populist,

---

[6] The Republican-People's Party opened in almost every city *Halk Evis* (people's or folk houses), in which Turkish youth and adults could obtain, along with instruction in party program and ideology, a kind of popular education. The houses were centers for lectures, sports, and dramatics and also had departments for language, history, and literature. In all there were about five thousand.

étatist, and secular citizens must be fostered in every stage of education.

To respect, and make others respect the Turkish nation, the Grand National Assembly of Turkey, and the Turkish State must be taught as a duty to which every one must be very sensitive.

(*c*) It is our great desire to attach importance to intellectual as well as physical development, and especially to elevate the character to the high level inspired by our great national history.

(*d*) The method followed in education and instruction is to render Learning an instrument in the hands of citizens for guaranteeing success in material life.

(*e*) Education must be high, national, patriotic, and free from all sorts of superstition and foreign ideas.

(*f*) We are convinced that it is important to treat the students in all institutions of education and instruction tactfully, in order not to hinder their capacity for enterprise. On the other hand, it is important to accustom them to serious discipline and order, and to a sincere conception of morals, in order to prevent their being faulty in life.

(*g*) Our Party lays an extraordinary importance upon the citizens' knowing our great history. This learning is the sacred essence that nourishes the indestructible resistance of the Turk against all currents that may prejudice the national existence, his capacity and power, and his sentiments of self-confidence.

(*h*) We shall continue our serious work in rendering the Turkish language a perfect and ordered national language.

Article 42. Our main ideas about the schools are the following:

(*a*) The normal primary education consists of five years. The number of primary schools in cities, villages, or groups of villages shall be increased according to a regular program of application, and according to the needs. In the village schools ideas on hygiene, better living, agriculture and industry that have a bearing upon the region in question shall be taught.

(*b*) Village schools of three or four terms shall be opened to give the village children, in a short time, the essential learning required in practical life. A plan shall be made to establish such schools and to increase their number.

These schools shall be of a separate type from those which propose to prepare the children for higher education. It is necessary to begin the education in these village schools at a maturer age, to continue it without interruption, and to have it controlled by the State in the same manner as the military service duty.

(c) The professional and trade schools, as well as the night trade schools, shall be increased to cope with the needs of the country, and necessary new courses shall be instituted.

(d) We are convinced of the necessity of having secondary schools in capitals of Vilayets and in the regions of kazas wherever it is necessary, following the principle of spreading secondary education throughout the country.[7] We shall endeavor to create organizations to provide boarding facilities which shall enable the children of the country to benefit from these schools in peace and security.

(e) We shall strengthen and complete our Lycées in every way, so that they may prepare students fully qualified for higher education.

(f) The University and our schools for higher education shall be brought to a state of perfection where they can give the results expected of them. We are thinking of increasing the number of Universities.

Article 43. Boarding facilities of a practical nature for the ordinary primary schools for the children of several thickly populated villages, as well as for the special type village schools, shall be established and protected.

Article 44. The fine arts, and especially music, shall be given an importance in accordance with the high expression of our Revolution.

Article 45. Importance shall be attached to collecting historical objects in order to enrich our Museums. For this purpose, we shall undertake excavations, classify the works of antiquity, and preserve them where they stand, if necessary.

Article 46. Matters in connection with books, publications and libraries are important for the Party. We want to establish and increase the number of libraries in cities and villages.

Article 47. Our Public Instruction policy shall be organized after a plan taking into consideration the present and future requirements of education. After this plan, all the degrees of education shall be reformed according to the needs of professions and trades.

Article 48. We consider it important to give the masses a continuous adult education, outside the classical school education, in harmony with the advancement of new Turkey. The State shall protect with all possible means the People's Houses which are working to this end.

[7] A *vilayet* is roughly the equivalent of a state; a *kaza,* of a county.

Article 49. The Party shall found a Museum of the Revolution. We consider this an effective means of instilling the revolutionary culture in the people.

Article 50. The Turkish youth shall be organized in a national organization so as to bring them together in clean ethics and a high love of Fatherland and Revolution. They shall be given a physical education that will foster their joy, health, and their belief in themselves and in the nation. The youth shall be brought up with the conviction of considering the defense of the Revolution and of the Fatherland with all its requisites of independence, the highest duty of youth. They shall be taught to be ready to sacrifice everything in order to fulfill this duty.

In order that this fundamental education shall attain its full results, high qualities requisite for success, such as thinking, making decisions and taking the initiative shall be developed in the Turkish youth. In the meantime, they shall be required to work under strict discipline, which is the sole means of accomplishing every difficult task.

The sports organizations in Turkey shall be established and furthered in accordance with these principles. The connection and cooperation of the ideals of the new youth organization with the University, the Schools and Institutes, People's Houses, the factories and establishments, employing a number of workers together, shall be organized.

Uniformity in physical and revolutionary education, as well as in matters relating to sports in the country, shall be considered.

It shall be made obligatory for everybody in schools, government institutions, in private establishments, and factories to take part in physical education according to their age. The sport fields and organizations necessary for physical education shall be established. In securing the sport fields, the municipalities and local administrations shall be led to take a special interest.

Article 51. The Party considers the radio to be one of the most valuable instruments for the political and cultural education of the nation. We shall erect powerful broadcasting stations, and shall provide for the easy purchase of cheap receiving sets. We shall consider it our task to render the moving pictures in the country useful to the nation.

Article 52. The national opera and the national theater are among our important tasks.[8]

---

[8] Donald E. Webster, *op. cit.*, pp. 313 ff. (Official translation, published by the People's Party, Ankara, 1935.)

ADMINISTRATION OF EDUCATION

The affairs of education and instruction are administered by the Ministry of Public Instruction, which includes:[9]

1. The Minister of Public Instruction, selected from the deputies of the National Assembly by the Prime Minister. He is responsible to the Grand National Assembly.

2. The General Education Board, which plans and modifies programs and school regulations, organizes courses for teachers, selects themes for graduation compositions, and is concerned exclusively with education matters.

3. The Office of Inspection, which is composed of a president and general inspectors whose duty it is to inspect schools from the administrative and educational points of view and report to the Ministry.

4. The Head Office of Higher Instruction, which was in charge of affairs concerning the universities and higher education. (The universities have recently become autonomous and independent of the Ministry of Education.)

5. The Division of Secondary Education, which has charge of the affairs of junior high, senior high, and primary normal schools.

6. The Division of Primary Instruction, which has charge of matters concerning primary schools supported out of local funds.

7. The Division of Technical and Vocational Education, which has charge of schools of art, trade, and handicraft and of junior and senior high schools of commerce. This category includes all evening and vocational schools.

Other divisions include the Division of Fine Arts, the Division of Private Schools (which supervises all private schools), the Personnel Bureau, the Bureau of Museums, the Office of the National Library, the Office of Physical Education, the Office of Financial Affairs, the Office of School Museums and Instructional Material, and the Office of Publications (which supervises a number of state printing presses). There is also a Committee on Discipline, consisting of the Council of Inspection, which meets under the chairmanship of the Under-Secretary of State to consider disciplinary

[9] Kazim Nami Duru, "Turkey," in I. L. Kandel, ed., *Educational Yearbook of the International Institute, 1937* (New York: Teachers College, Columbia University, 1938), pp. 458-473.

cases of teachers and educational officials. Decisions are not put into effect until the person concerned has had an opportunity to appeal.

In addition to the central organization there is in each department of administration (*vilayet*) a director of public instruction who represents the Ministry. In the subdistricts (*kazas*), one of the instructors in the primary schools represents the director of the *vilayet*. Turkey has thus set up a highly centralized system of education with respect to administration and supervisory authority.

We shall now turn to the organization of education at the various levels.

ELEMENTARY EDUCATION

Elementary education in Turkey is compulsory for children of both sexes between the ages of seven and twelve. There are about 2½ million children of elementary-school age, and the most recent statistics[10] show that 1½ million of these children attended school during 1947-1948. Of this number 1 million were boys and 500,000 girls. Elementary-school attendance has risen rapidly in the past decade but there are still many school-age children not in school, as the following figures[11] indicate.

PERCENTAGES OF SCHOOL-AGE CHILDREN NOT IN SCHOOL

	*1941-1942**		*1948-1949**	
	Boys	Girls	Boys	Girls
In villages	67.5	83.2	29.4	46.7
In cities	26.1	56.1	25.0	43.0

* The 1941-1942 percentages are for all villages; the 1948-1949 percentages are for villages having schools.

Providing school buildings for all her school-age children and providing an adequate supply of properly trained teachers for a total of some 34,000 villages are major problems which Turkey must face.

In an effort to meet the need for rural teachers, the "village institutes" were established in 1938. From the village boys and girls

[10] *Education in the New Turkey* (New York: Turkish Information Office, 1948), p. 3.

[11] From *Millî Eğitim—Istatistik Ozetleri*, 1932-1949, pp. 4-5.

who had completed their elementary education, the best candidates were selected by competitive examination for further training in these institutes. The institute is a boarding school in a rural community. It offers a five-year training program divided into a curriculum that is half study and half practical work such as carpentry, masonry, plumbing, agriculture and, in the coastal villages, fishing. For the girls there is instruction in the domestic arts, hygiene, and child care. After successful completion of the course, the teachers are sent back to their native villages not only to teach but to devote half time to the improvement of their village and land. Thus the rural teacher is prepared to be a leader in the rural community in raising the standard of living as well as to teach the academic curriculum. In 1948 there were 15,000 students enrolled in twenty-one institutes. There were 9400 graduates on active duty. In addition the village institutes trained through special courses nine hundred village health officers and nearly eight thousand *egitmen,* a special type of rural teacher for village children.[12]

The elementary school consists of two cycles, of three and two years respectively. The method of integrated education is employed. In the first cycle the course includes Turkish (reading, grammar, dictation, memorizing of poetry, calligraphy, and composition), arithmetic, drawing, singing, manual work, and physical education. All lessons are related to "life orientation." Life orientation is achieved through field trips and observations, with emphasis upon individualized work and socialization. Teachers are required to make out weekly lesson plans that are submitted to the headmaster. In the second cycle of the elementary school the curriculum includes the Turkish language, history, geography, civics, arithmetic, geometry, natural sciences, manual work, and physical education. Silent reading is stressed and the content is explained and analyzed by the French *expliquée* method. In all instruction the psychology of interest is given an important place.

SECONDARY EDUCATION

The secondary system includes both state-supported and locally supported schools. Secondary schools are divided into two stages:

[12] *Ibid.,* p. 4.

the middle school for grades six to eight, comparable to the American junior high school, and the lyceum for grades nine to eleven, which goes beyond the curriculum of the American senior high school, providing advanced instruction in mathematics, science, history, the social sciences, literature, and music. The middle schools are open to pupils with a primary-school diploma. Upon graduation from the middle school the student is awarded a certificate entitling him to continue his studies in either a lyceum or a vocational school. Coeducation is practiced at this level as well as all other levels of education. Students who finish the lyceum and pass the baccalaureate examinations may enter the university or other institutions of higher education.

Enrollment in secondary schools has increased thirteenfold in the past quarter century: in 1923 there were seventy-two middle schools and twenty-three lyceums, enrolling 7146 students; in 1946 there were 252 middle schools and eighty-eight lyceums, with 91,193 students.[13]

VOCATIONAL EDUCATION

Vocational and craft schools for both boys and girls have been given increasing support by the government and have shown a rapid development since 1923. The craft schools for boys offer four main subjects: electricity, woodworking, drafting, and metalwork. The girls' schools offer home crafts. The statistics of growth in this field are significant: in 1923 there were nine craft schools for boys and three for girls; in 1946-1947 there were seventy-six for boys (with 29,191 students) and forty-four for girls (with nine thousand students), as well as eighty-one evening schools offering classes in crafts (with an attendance of 22,000 girls and women).[14]

To teach crafts to boys and girls in rural districts, there are itinerant or extension courses. For boys there is instruction in brick work, plastering, and roughcasting. For girls, the itinerant institutes offer instruction in child care, dietetics, dressmaking, and light domestic crafts. During 1947-1948, there were seven hundred boys attending construction institutes and seven thousand women and girls in attendance at the "traveling courses."

[13] *Ibid.,* pp. 7 and 8.
[14] *Ibid.*

HIGHER EDUCATION

Formerly higher education in Turkey was restricted to a small and privileged group. Today it is open to all who can pass the matriculation examinations. There are scholarships for those who contract to enter the public services in health, law, and medicine upon graduation. The following figures[15] show recent enrollments in some of the leading universities:

Name	Number of faculty members	Number of students
University of Ankara (Reorganized 1946)	298	6,830
Istanbul University (Reorganized 1896, 1927, 1933)	147	13,645
Technical University, Istanbul (Founded 1933)	48	1,600
Istanbul School of Economics and Commercial Science (Founded 1883)	34	1,350
Robert College, Istanbul (Founded 1863)	91	914
		24,339

As a general rule no one may teach unless he has satisfactorily completed academic work one level above that which he is to teach: college teachers must be university graduates and so on down the educational ladder. Those who wish to teach in universities first become assistants, and later, after they have passed aptitude tests, are appointed assistant professors. The Ministry of Education fixes the salary scales for teachers; if their service is satisfactory, they receive an increment every three years, as do the other civil servants.

The Ministry of Education administers the following teachers' colleges: the Istanbul Higher Teachers' Training College, the Ankara Teachers' Training College and Gazi Pedagogical Institute, the Balikesir Teachers' Training School and Necati Pedagogical Institute, and the Istanbul Physical Education Teachers' Training

[15] *Europa* (London: Europa Publications Ltd., 1950), p. 24.

School. In 1946 there were eleven normal schools and twenty-one village institutes training teachers. Yet the teacher-school ratio was not high: in 15,000 schools there were only 38,000 teachers (27,000 men and 11,000 women).[16]

TURKISH STUDENTS ABROAD

An increasing number of Turkish students are being sent abroad for specialized study by the government. These students are under the supervision of the Ministry of Education, which operates through three educational inspectors—one in Berne, one in London, and one in New York. The inspectors supervise both scholarship students and those studying at their own expense in Europe and America. Since the outbreak of World War II, in 1939, the number of Turkish students in Great Britain and the United States has increased in relation to the number in other countries. The figures for 1948, from the Turkish Information Office in New York City, show the following distribution: 676 (not including military students) in the United States, 320 in Switzerland, and 168 in Britain.

The main branches of study pursued by the Turkish students in the United States are mechanical, electrical, chemical, and civil engineering, architecture, mining, telecommunications, petroleum, metallurgy, specialized fields of medical science, commerce, economics, agriculture, journalism, and textile engineering.

In addition to this government program, which has been in operation for some years, there is the new Fulbright Act Agreement between Turkey and the United States, which was signed on December 27, 1949. It provides for the exchange of students and professors and for other cultural relations on an exchange basis.

FINANCING EDUCATION

The percentage of the national budget allocated to public education is a good index of the importance which a nation attaches to education. For Turkey this percentage has increased steadily since 1928. In that year it was 3.17; in 1948 it was 13.00. Of the funds appropriated for education in 1948, 61 percent was spent on elemen-

[16] Cf. *Education in the New Turkey*, p. 18.

tary education, 15 percent on secondary education, 13 percent on technical education, and 3 percent on university education.[17]

It should be added that military training is compulsory in Turkey and that this training might also be considered a part of public education, even though it comes under a different ministry and budget.

SUMMARY AND CONCLUSION

The major educational developments in Turkey during the past decade may be summarized as follows:

1. The increased number of public school buildings.

2. The growth and success of the village institutes in training rural teachers. (It has recently been reported that reactionary politicians have brought about the abolition of some of these institutes.)

3. The growth of vocational and technical education and the development of extension courses and traveling institutes.

4. The law establishing the autonomy of the universities which were formerly under the direct control and supervision of the Ministry of Education.

5. The reinstitution of religious instruction in the schools and the establishment of a faculty of theology at the University of Ankara.

6. The liberation of the folk houses from close political party control, thereby strengthening their function for nonpartisan citizenship education and enlightened public opinion.

7. The increase in the number of students studying abroad on government scholarships, in military institutions, and in the two-way cultural exchange now possible through the Fulbright Act Agreement.

8. Increased financial support for public education from the state, reaching an all-time high of 13 percent of the national budget.

9. The incorporation of the venerable and efficient Civil Service Training School as a faculty of the University of Ankara, which is now independent of the Ministry of Education.

10. A growth in the media of mass communication. (In 1949

[17] Figures from the Turkish Information Office and from Donald E. Webster, *op. cit.*, p. 219.

there were 248,179 radio receiving sets and fourteen broadcasting stations. American and other firms have offered to build and equip television stations at Istanbul and Ankara.)

11. Reduction of illiteracy from 90 percent in 1923 to less than 50 percent at the present time.

Some of the most urgent needs in Turkish education are: more teachers, more school buildings, more facilities for training technical experts to serve industry and develop the nation's resources, and, finally, more money to finance a vigorously expanding program.

These problems of public education in Turkey can and probably will be solved if Turkey can continue to carry on her program undisturbed. Former President Ismet Inönü expressed the primary Turkish objective, one which directly involves education, thus: "We have no other political objective than to become one of the most civilized nations of the world so that Turkey ascends to the ranks of a useful and hardworking member of the family of world nations."[18]

Turkey has become a pioneer leader in educational reform and development among the nations of the Middle East. In the past quarter century the progress she has made in education has surpassed all normal expectations.

BIBLIOGRAPHY

ADIVAR, ABDULHAK ADNAN, "Islamic and Western Thought in Turkey," *Middle East Journal*, July 1947, pp. 270-280. The author is the editor of the Turkish edition of the *Encyclopedia of Islam*. This article is based on a paper delivered by him at the Near East Conference held at Princeton University in March 1947.

ALLEN, HENRY E., *The Turkish Transformation* (Chicago: University of Chicago Press, 1935). A study in Turkey's social and religious development under the Republic. Chapter 9, "Missionary Education in the Light of Nationalism," is of especial interest.

BISBEE, ELEANOR, *The New Turks* (Philadelphia: University of Pennsylvania Press, 1951). The author was professor of philosophy at Istanbul American College from 1936-1942. Since returning to the United States she has lectured extensively on Middle Eastern and particularly Turkish affairs.

[18] Ismet Inönü, *Vital Speeches of the Day*, December 15, 1945, p. 160.

————, "Test of Democracy in Turkey," *Middle East Journal,* April 1950, pp. 170-183.

DURU, KAZIM NAMI, "Turkey," in I. L. Kandel, ed., *Educational Yearbook of the International Institute, 1937* (New York: Teachers College, Columbia University, 1938), pp. 458-473. The author was a member of the Turkish Ministry of Education. Although there have been some changes in Turkey's national system since this article was written, in the main it holds true.

EKREM, SELMA, *Turkey: Old and New* (New York: Charles Scribner's Sons, 1947). The author is a granddaughter of the Turkish poet and patriot Namik Kamal. Her father was governor of Jerusalem and the Aegean Islands. Her book on Turkey is excellently illustrated with photographs of Turkish life.

GUNTEKIN, RESAT NURI, *The Autobiography of a Turkish Girl* (London: George Allen & Unwin, Ltd., 1950). Considered one of the best books on Turkish family life and the position of women in modern Turkey. Translated from the Turkish.

JACKH, ERNEST, *The Rising Crescent* (New York: Farrar & Rinehart, Inc., 1944).

JURKAT, E., and L. K. KISER, "The Peoples of the Mohammedan World," *Annals of the American Academy of Political and Social Science,* January 1945, pp. 97-101. Presents considerable demographic material on three contrasting countries of the Middle East: Turkey, Palestine, and Egypt.

ORGA, IRFAN, *A Portrait of a Turkish Family* (New York: The Macmillan Company, 1950). A vivid and graphic account of a Turkish family's history through three generations.

TOMLIN, E. W. F., *Life in Modern Turkey* (London: Thomas Nelson and Sons, Ltd., 1946).

WARD, BARBARA, *Turkey* (London: Oxford University Press, 1942). A concise, general history of modern Turkey with good chapters on the social revolution, the village, and building an industrial system.

WEBSTER, DONALD E., *The Turkey of Atatürk* (Philadelphia: American Academy of Political and Social Science, 1939). The standard work on Turkey under Kemal Atatürk.

"What Should Be Turkey's Role Between the East and West?" Bulletin of America's Town Meeting of the Air, Vol. XV, No. 16, (August 16, 1949). Can be obtained from the Turkish Information Office, 444 East 52nd St., New York 22, N. Y.

WRIGHT, WALTER LIVINGSTON, "Truths About Turkey," *Foreign Af-*

fairs, January 1948, pp. 349-359. The author was president of Robert College, Istanbul.

The following publications are available free of charge from the Turkish Information Office, 444 East 52nd St., New York, N. Y. They are informative and factual, with emphasis on the positive achievements of the Republic.

"Facts on Turkey"
"Education in the New Turkey"
"Women in Modern Turkey"
"Turkey, Key to the Near East"
"Self-Government in Turkey"
"Modern Turkish Literature"
"The Turkish Constitution"
"Modern Turkey" (film strip)

16 · EDUCATION IN *India*

ARTHUR HENRY MOEHLMAN

The Republic of India occupies an area of about 1¼ million square miles and has a population of over 342 million. It occupies the larger part of the great subcontinent which stretches from the Himalayas southward into the Indian Ocean. The three major areas of India are the almost unbroken high mountain ranges of the north, the river-valley plains (the Indus and Ganges), and the table-land of the Deccan, south of the Satpura mountain range. The climate varies from the mountain climate of the Himalayas through the semidesert climate to that of the great tropical forest of central and south India. But in general it is that of the monsoon lands: a dry season in the winter and spring and a rainy season in the summer and fall.

The population of India has one of the heaviest densities in the world—over 290 persons per square mile in the lower Ganges area and in large cities such as Calcutta, Bombay, and Madras. But the land is primarily agricultural; 70 percent of the people depend upon farming for their living. The population is dense even in the agricultural areas, where it is settled in villages. India has begun a vast program of industrial development which includes a dozen great hydroelectric systems. Chief products are textiles, steel, cement, and jute; steel production ranks seventh in the world and jute mills process over 90 percent of the world's production. India is rich in mineral resources, including coal, iron, manganese, precious stones, and uranium-bearing sands. There is a well-organized transportation system. Despite its many assets, India is faced with

the serious problem of a rapidly increasing population and a consequent worsening of the already unfavorable ratio between the
number of people and the amount of arable land. At present there
is less than one acre per person, whereas there should be 2.5 or over.
The situation is similar to that of the densely populated industrial
areas of Europe. The Republic of India has recently had under
investigation the problems of birth control and improved agronomy.

The story of Indian education is that of a series of great intrusions
and following syntheses. These intrusions included the Indo-European, after which Hindu education was developed and, subsequently, affected by the coming of Buddhism. (Asoka, the great
Buddhist king of the third century B.C., is memorialized in a twenty-
four-spoke wheel in the center of the present-day flag of the Republic of India.) The Mohammedan intrusion of about 800 A.D. brought
another educational pattern and language. Then, in the eighteenth
century, the English elite system of education and European technology began making their impact felt. By the twentieth century
India was moving in the direction of a new synthesis of education;
unlike the older patterns, the new one was to make education universal. The great problems to be faced were illiteracy (more than
88 percent), conflict with neighbors such as Pakistan and China, the
poverty of the Indian villager, the traditional types of religion, and
the range of language.

—A. H. M.

Education in India today is of primary significance in the global
pattern of education, not only because of the country's huge size
and population but because it is an enormous laboratory for the
intrusion and synthesis of a number of educational systems. In
India there exists, to a major degree, the conflict between the hand
and the mind, between the masses and the elite, which is prevalent
throughout the world today and which education must help to solve.
One of India's important philosophers, Humayun Kabir, visualizes
the problem vividly:

Thus we have on the one hand the masses that lack the power
of initiative or expression but are possessed of a primeval strength
derived from the soil. We have on the other hand an intelligent-

sia that is restless, eager and inquisitive. Like flotsam it floats on the surface of Indian life but has no roots in the life of the people. . . . Community between the masses and the intelligentsia would enable each to compensate its weakness by the other's strength. Instead of strengthening, the modern system of education tends to break the bond of that community.[1]

Education in India poses the problem of achieving a balanced and lucid educational philosophy based on a clear picture of long-range values and of the methods necessary to achieve them. In India's past there have been many philosophies of education, from the ancient time of the Upanishads (the ethical teachings of early Indo-Europeans, c. 600 B.C.), when the student lived to acquire intellectual and spiritual training from his teacher, to those of modern times. Various philosophies of education have been put forward by such leaders of the Indian Renaissance as Raja Ram Mohan Roy and, later, Tagore and Gandhi. At the present time the philosophy which will form the basis of a new synthesis of Indian education is still in the making. The famous Report of the Advisory Board of Education of the Government of India, published in January 1944, unfortunately does not provide a comprehensive picture of the purposes of Indian education. It is true, however, that this plan, sometimes called the Sargent plan, asserts that the new system of education must be "essentially Indian," and that it must recognize "the importance of fostering in the rising generation such attributes as physical fitness, intelligence and integrity of character." Furthermore, it states that "at all stages of education the training of the intellect and the training of character must proceed side by side."[2]

Above all, education in India today faces the problem of synthesizing the many past intrusions of educational systems. The Indo-Europeans invaded India from the northwest and forced the original Indian inhabitants south of the Satpura line. The problem of

[1] Kabir, H., *Our Heritage* (Bombay: National Information and Publications Ltd., 1946), pp. 93-94. Ranjana Sidhanta has contributed to this chapter on Indian education from her own Ph.D. thesis, *A Study of Basic Concepts Relating to India* (Iowa City: State University of Iowa, 1950), and from her experience as a participant in Indian education.

[2] *Post-War Educational Development in India* (New Delhi: Government of India Press, 1944), pp. 1-2.

synthesizing education from these two cultures has continued from 2000 B.C. to the present. By 800 A.D. a new intrusion of Islam had appeared, and it was reinforced by the Mughal-Persian intrusion of the sixteenth century. A synthesis was again achieved. The British industrial, imperial intrusion was the most recent and in some ways the most important for the contemporary scene. The British brought their educational system with them and imposed it upon the previous syntheses of Indian education. The English, under Macaulay's influence, superimposed a thin veneer of the English elite system of education upon India.

In today's confused educational scene there are three indigenous educational institutions and philosophies each of which will contribute something to the future. (1) Tagore's Shantiniketan at Bolepur, near Calcutta, with its University and rural reconstruction department, is one of the outstanding educational institutions of the world. Built originally as a retreat, it has become a school and college where the love of nature has been combined with the fine arts, the usual academic disciplines, vocational education, village uplift, and internationalism. Rousseauesque methods coexist with modern approaches. The institution ranks as one of the greatest monuments of Tagore's versatile genius. (2) Gandhi's educational program is directed toward a solution of the rural needs of India. The villager is to be educated through his profession of cotton farming, cattle herding, or whatever it may be. (3) The Jamia Milia, at New Delhi, founded by nationalist Moslems as opposed to the communalists or those desiring separation, stands as the most progressive among Indian primary and secondary schools. It is a pioneer in the latest educational techniques. All instruction, as in the other two institutions, is carried on in the mother tongue. A fourth philosophy, that of an improved technology, may be the most essential philosophy for Indian education.

India, although it appears to be separated from the rest of the world by very high mountain ranges and the sea, has actually been in almost continuous contact with other culture areas from 3000 B.C. to the present day. Cultural influence penetrated the mountain passes, and the sea in actuality has been no barrier. Early voyagers from Egypt, Mesopotamia, Greece, and Rome as well as from Cathay touched the shores of India, and Indian envoys were seen at the courts of these countries. With the caravans and ships from the outer world came not only goods and people but ideas. At the same

time, Indian philosophy and mathematics, as well as tangible products such as muslin and incense, graced the then civilized world.
India has continued making contributions to civilization until the
present; they include the metaphysics of Hinduism, the poetry and
philosophy of Tagore, and the ethical politics of Gandhi.

Education in India must face numerous major challenges. Some
88 percent of the Indians are illiterate. Others have been educated
to serve as clerks and cipherers. Too few have been trained to deal
with the primary problems of improving the use of the land, building up the new industry, and coping with contemporary issues. Let
us examine the major characteristics of the Indian people, land, and
culture pattern—the characteristics which must be understood and
met by educators.

THE PEOPLE AND THE LAND

India today is a geographical unity but a political dichotomy
consisting of the Republic of India and the Dominion of Pakistan.
India is a subcontinent projecting from the southern edge of mountain-hearted Asia. It is almost as large as all Europe, if one excludes
Russia. Its population is almost one fifth of the world total. In
relief and climate its presents great variations and regional differences, because of its extensive area.

The three outstanding social institutions until the last few decades
were the caste system, the joint family (a system under which many
relatives live together in one compound), and the self-supporting
village, each having advantages and limitations. Today each is dis-
integrating under the impact of industrialization and its concomitants, urbanization and railway and bus travel. Caste has been
further weakened by social reform and legislation, so that untouch-
ability does not exist according to the new Indian constitution.
Nevertheless, caste is still a source of conflict and waste. The
break-up of the joint family and autonomous village means new
problems with which education will have to cope. Moreover, effective channels of informal education are being weakened. On the
other hand, villages are being infused with fresh vigor by the resus-
citation of self-governing institutions on the model of the old village
council (*panchayat*) of a headman advised by five elders; the current
versions are, of course, based on a broader franchise.

Although urban India is becoming increasingly secular, religion

is still a focal point in village life. Religion has been the supposed
cause of recent conflict between Hindus and Moslems, but actually
economic and political grievances of the two communities must be
considered the more crucial factors. After the division into Pakistan
and India, many Moslems migrated to Pakistan; however, there is
still a substantial minority of Mohammedans in India. Religion,
despite its hold on the ceremonial life of the people, has been relegated to a subordinate role in the ideologies arising in the new
India, so that education along classical lines is out of the question.
Moral education and metaphysical abstractions are nevertheless
considered essential by some Indian spokesmen, who want to incorporate them into the curriculums.

Although there are a great many languages in India—about
eleven major linguistic systems—the Census and other reports have
grossly exaggerated the number. The usual two hundred include
several dialects spoken by perhaps two or three members of a hill
tribe. Some authorities feel that the real educational problem lies
not in the number of languages which an Indian will have to learn
but in educating the millions who are illiterate as well as providing
for the generations that are unborn. Hindi has been adopted as the
basic language of India, and Urdu is that of Pakistan. The two
languages have a core of common words and a fairly homogeneous
grammatical structure but different scripts. Besides Hindi, every
Indian is going to be taught his mother tongue, be it Tamil, Ben-
gali, or Marathi. English is going to be one of several foreign languages to be learned by those who need them for professional or
academic pursuits. Large appropriations are being set aside for
translation purposes. The trail has been blazed and pioneer work
done in coining scientific and other terminology at the Osmania
University, in Hyderabad, where the medium of instruction has
been Urdu for several decades. However, some students of the
language problem are pessimistic concerning the practicality of this
multiple-language approach.

Political problems have been somewhat stabilized since August
1947, when India was divided. Both Pakistan and India have the
legal status of Dominions within the British Commonwealth of Nations. The constitution adopted January 26, 1950, by India is that
of a republic with a federal form of government. The former
princely states have been abolished by law. The smaller principali-

ties have merged, and the former British provinces have combined with the newly consolidated states to form a federation. The British parliamentary pattern is followed: there is a Cabinet responsible to the legislature. Both India and Pakistan have sworn allegiance to the democratic way of government. There is a universal franchise, so that the new education will have to prepare for civic duties and obligations. Political affairs, always of keen interest to Indian students, will determine much of the content of Indian education from the lowest rung.

Other crucial problems face Indian education: chief among them are bitter poverty and rapid population increase. India has one of the lowest agrarian incomes in the world, and it is primarily a land of farmers. Some 2.5 acres of arable land per person are needed to provide adequate food, shelter, and health, according to a reliable estimate. India has less than one acre of arable land per person. The combination of improved health and sanitation measures and religious obstacles to birth control has contributed to a dangerous acceleration in population growth. The absence of a broad middle class (related to the lag in industrialization) makes an adequate tax base for education problematic. An improved technology, both industrial and agricultural, is basic to any solution of India's greatest problem—poverty.

A HISTORICAL PERSPECTIVE[3]

Indian education today is a synthesis of various educational systems brought by a succession of invaders. Indian education may be divided into the following major periods: the ancient Hindu, the Mohammedan, and the British. Each intrusion brought a new pattern of symbols and an educational system for communicating them.

Ancient Hindu Education. Indian culture before the coming of the Aryans was already well organized. The excavations in the Indus valley have uncovered evidence of organized city life from 3000 years before Christ.[4] These Mohenjo-daro and Harappa exca-

[3] This section draws upon the Ph.D. dissertation of Aubrey A. J. Zellner, *A History of Education in the Lower Ganges River Area of India from 1858 to 1948* (Iowa City: College of Education, State University of Iowa, 1949).

[4] J. Marshall, *Mohenjo-daro and the Indus Civilization* (London: A. Probsthain, 1931).

vations show a highly developed architecture with baths and drainage systems built to a plan. There was probably some connection between this architecture and the early cultures of the Tigris and Euphrates valley civilizations. The education of these urban areas by 2000 B.C. may have been relatively advanced, since a recent Sumerian excavation shows that in that period schoolboys were studying geometry which anticipated Euclid by a long interval of time. In this area they used no clay tablets; writing was on easily destroyed leaves and parchment.

Dravidian culture was equally advanced, so that there was fairly facile assimilation with the Aryans culturally. Hindu education was based upon religious teaching which formuated the whole pattern of living. To about the age of five, the home was the school for children and the mother was their teacher. Then a professional teacher taught the children word study, reading, writing, arithmetic, prayers, and psalms. Between the eighth and the sixteenth year boys were initiated into the study of the *Vedas*, as the holy books were called. (In the Vedic period both boys and girls were so educated, but later segregation of the sexes was carried out.[5]) The teacher, or *guru*, was a kind of second father; he was in charge of the initiation, which included a strict discipline, a ritual, a special garment and staff, a new name, and investment with the sacred girdle. Brahmanical educational supremacy was based on the Brahman's extensive knowledge of the sacred books and records, although there were scholars among the other castes. The students usually lived with their teachers for a good many years, often from the age of seven until the age of twenty-one. Memorization was necessary, but education was primarily a matter of dialectics—the Socratic method. Great schools and universities were developed, including the Nalanda, Taxila, and Amravati international centers.

The indigenous ancient Hindu schools had many values. The schools stressed ethical training; there was a fine personal relationship between teacher and pupil; students assumed teaching responsibility, acting as monitors; and definite advance was made not only in literature but in art, science, and mathematics. The secular and practical aspects of the early *gurukuls* (ancient Hindu schools)

[5] S. K. Das, *The Educational System of the Ancient Hindus* (Calcutta: The Author, 1930).

should not be overlooked. On the other hand, education was certainly not democratic by twentieth-century standards; it was not in any part of the ancient world. Its greatest weakness, however, was its inability to maintain its initial eclecticism and breadth of view. It became increasingly rigid, and creative thinking degenerated into dogma, although periodic renaissances were inevitable. One of the earliest renaissances was the Buddhist.

Buddhism had its roots deep in the philosophic thought of Hinduism but differed in certain important details. Gautama, the Buddha, brought a highly ethical pattern of living which was open to all and was very much welcomed by influential merchants and rulers—for example, Asoka, in the third century B.C.—who did much to advance it. The Buddhist schools were connected, in the main, with the Buddhist monasteries. The pupils and their masters had a well-organized routine of learning, work, and worship. The curriculum included much emphasis upon Sanskrit language and grammar as a basis for the study of philosophy and literature. The students included not only those who wished to become monks but also those undertaking a wide range of secular occupations. A system of popular education in connection with Buddhist monasteries gave a more universal texture to Indian education and helped broaden its base.

The Mohammedan Intrusion in Education. The Mohammedan intrusion brought vigorous new peoples ranging from Arabs to Persians and Afghans. Each of these groups brought languages and educational patterns with them. Above all, the Mohammedan intrusion brought new art forms, a new democracy, and renewed internationalism.

The Moslems exerted a profound influence upon all of India despite their relatively small numbers. Initially a warrior group which forced its new religion upon many, the Moslems became assimilated, like previous invaders, and by peaceful means brought others into the religious fold. Their greatest rulers, such as Akbar, encouraged intermarriage and religious tolerance to stabilize the empire.

Moslem education brought an emphasis upon the Koran as a basic educational reference. It brought, too, primary schools administered by Moslem teachers known as *maulvis*. The upper schools were called *madrassahs*. Moslem education emphasized the training of the males and increased the tendency to restrict the activities of women. No real contribution was made toward the general increase of literacy, but popular education was effective through clerics and royal patronage. Persian culture in combination with the Sanskrit language came to comprise the education of the aristocrats and cultivated gentlemen. The rise of the vernaculars, including Urdu, together with populist-reformist movements, kept the masses fairly alert. But India, like Europe, had no organized public education.

The English Intrusion in Education. At first the invading British were concerned primarily with political and economic control of India. They were fighting the colonial powers of France and, to a smaller extent, the Netherlands. They had just lost a struggle with the United States. However, they soon saw the need for controlling the educational pattern in India. They began their experiments in Bengal, which was the governmental capital until 1912. Missionaries were pioneers in the idea that it was the duty of the English to communicate their intellectual and moral concepts through the channel of education, especially in southern India and the Ganges valley. The Indian government thought of education, at first, in terms of creating clerks and bureaucrats useful in their own administration and also in terms of dividing their opposition. For example, Warren Hastings in 1781 as governor-general founded the Calcutta Madrassah, or Moslem College, "to qualify the sons of Mohammedan gentlemen for responsible and lucrative offices in the State, even at that date largely monopolized by the Hindus." Jonathan Duncan in 1792 founded the Benares Sanskrit College for the purpose of training Hindus for public posts. Sir John Shore, who in 1798 succeeded Cornwallis as governor-general in Bengal, wrote that the British should establish schools and steadily encourage those that already existed. However, a major conflict in educational philosophy rapidly arose. One point of view, that of the Anglicists, was that English must be the medium of instruction in Indian schools which imparted secular education. This stand was supported by the missionary party and by certain government administrators. The opposing point of view, that of the Orientalists, was that the Indians should retain their own language or vernacular and that modern education should be *grafted* onto it. In 1813 the first grant for education in India, about $35,000, to "be used for the revival and improvement of literature and to promote knowledge of the sciences," began a real controversy over the meaning of "sciences." Did it mean the new Occidental experimental type or did it mean Oriental classical scholarship?

While the government remained relatively inactive, many private personages—Indian and European—began to work for promotion of education. One of the greatest was Raja Ram Mohan Roy. He helped to push education at all levels—primary, secondary, and college. An Englishman, Rev. William Adam, was much influenced by Roy and pioneered in the survey of the educational situation. He spoke for the training of native Indian teachers and the centering of schools in villages. He believed the Indians should be helped through allotment of land and through grants-in-aid. The following statement by Adam is worth recording: "It is impossible to fully express my confirmed conviction of the impracticability of the view of anyone who thinks that English should be the sole or even chief medium of conveying knowledge to the natives." Adam's plan and suggestions were voted down by government officials. However, he did a great deal to bring about the appreciation of indigenous and vernacular education.

The plan for Anglicizing the education of India won out against the ideas of the Orientalists and vernacularists. "Macaulay's Minute" in education appeared on February 2, 1835, and was confirmed as law the next month. The major aim of the British government's education policy should be the promotion of European literature and science among Indians, Macaulay wrote; the medium to be used should be English and the Education Fund should be employed on English education alone; furthermore, grants-in-aid for Oriental colleges should be stopped. The importance of this document has been overemphasized, but it was a formulation of a trend that had been under way for some time. "Macaulay's Minute" was penned by an individual of considerable attainment in English education who knew little about Oriental culture and was not interested in it. His attitude toward Oriental learning was unfavorable and unwise:

> The question now before us is simply whether when it is in our power to teach this language (English) we shall teach languages in which by universal confession there are no books on any subject which deserve to be compared to our own; whether, when we can teach European science, we shall teach systems which by universal confession whenever they differ from those of Europe

differ for the worse; and whether, when we can patronize sound philosophy and true history, we shall countenance at the public expense medical doctrines which would disgrace an English far-rier, astronomy which would move laughter in girls at an English boarding-school, history abounding with kings thirty feet high and reigns 30,000 years long and geography made up of seas of treacle and seas of butter. . . .

In all fairness it should be noted that the English faced a tre-mendously important decision—one basic in their whole colonial policy: should they continue the existing, indigenous culture or should they strive to Europeanize the subject people and raise them to a technological level? They elected the latter course, guided by many and somewhat conflicting motives; the result has been a nation which is probably far better suited to rule itself in today's world of realities than are those former colonies which were en-couraged to continue in their ancient ways.

It also should be underlined that Macaulay believed in educating an elite, the so-called higher ranks of society. In addition to disdain-ing the indigenous culture of India, he had the idea of diffusing education from the top downward—the "filtration theory"; but instead of returning to the villages the ever-increasing "English"-educated graduates turned their backs on the past, aspiring to bureaucratic heights.

> We do not at present aim at giving education directly to the lower classes of the people of this country. We aim at raising up an educated class who will hereafter, as we hope, be the means of diffusing among their countrymen some portion of the knowledge we have imparted to them. . . . If we can raise up a class of edu-cated Bengalis, they will naturally, and without any violent change, displace by degrees the present incompetent teachers. . . .

This policy obtained until the appearance of the Education Dispatch of Wood in 1854 and continued in many respects up to the twen-tieth century.

From 1835 to 1854 the government spent all of the education budget on its *zilla* (district) schools, in which English was the main subject and other subjects were taught through the medium of Eng-lish. Young children began to learn the alphabet and to use foreign words along with their own mother tongue. There was a great de-

mand even for this artificial and stultifying education, because it
opened avenues of employment in government service. English
became the "language of good appointments." Increased demand
induced the government to open schools which became the prototypes of today's high schools. The correlation is obvious between
this increased demand and the proclamation of Lord Harding that
in the selection of candidates for public service preference would
be given to graduates of government schools.

On each occasion of the renewal of the East India Company's
charter, an educational report was produced. The Wood Dispatch
of 1854, named after Sir Charles Wood, was one of these reports.
Although eulogized as the Magna Charta of modern Indian education, it was but an ordinary document of instructions to the government of India, approving of the educational policies practiced and
suggesting a few means of improvement from the perspective of the
Company. The Wood Dispatch suggested (1) the establishment of
provincial departments of education with qualified directors and
inspectors; (2) the establishment of three presidency (administrative
district) universities "to provide the highest test and encouragement
of liberal education"; (3) use of the grant-in-aid system rather than
state education. It was followed by the Educational Dispatch of
1859, after the sudden change of control of India from the Company to the crown.

Among the problems discussed in these Dispatches one which
received inordinate attention was the grant-in-aid scheme, which
resulted from the careful investigation of mission schools with a
view to maintaining the government's policy of strict religious neutrality. Only those schools received grants which had severed their
educational and proselytizing departments. The Indian Mutiny,
interpreted as Indian opposition to Christianizing, and the rise of
scientific skepticism, which contributed to religious neutrality, led
to a rigorously secular education in all schools which received government grants. Between 1854 and 1880, arts and professional colleges increased, together with secondary schools—Anglo-vernacular
and vernacular—but the literacy rate of the masses remained static
and the vernaculars developed fitfully and *in spite of* the government in Bengal and elsewhere. Because of such an attitude the more
aggressive of Christian missionaries began a virulent campaign
against "Godless" governmental educational institutions. Partly as a

result of this agitation and partly because of the desire to obtain a comprehensive survey of government educational effort a commission, presided over by W. W. Hunter, was appointed during the viceroyalty of Lord Ripon. The Report of the Education Commission of 1882 has been considered the most influential in determining educational administration in the last fifty years.

The only important achievement of the Commission was to entrust primary education to the care of the newly created local bodies, such as district boards and municipalities. It urged an extension of mass elementary education, but suggested nothing constructive to attack the problem, which was far beyond the capacities of local governmental organs. With respect to secondary education, the Commission reiterated the principle of grants-in-aid and proposed a gradual transfer of government secondary schools to local management. The policy of the government became clear: instead of undertaking the responsibility of educating the Indians, it was shifting that responsibility to private initiative and civic groups quite incapable of coping with the tremendous task. The curriculum remained as academically sterile as before. The course of general education suggested as an alternative to the college preparatory course was doomed to failure because of the absence of fruitful opportunity for training in industry or technology. Toward the close of the century, in the face of repeated criticisms of the curriculum of both schools and colleges and the demand for vocational education that would prepare young India for nonclerical jobs, the government of India published a memorandum suggesting the introduction of drawing and natural sciences in the school curriculum. Since Indian industry was undeveloped, the government saw no reason for the establishment of technical institutions.

If the government was not going to share the burden, nationalist India had to act in its place. As a concomitant of the gradual rise of nationalist and reformist movements sweeping India at the turn of the century, certain significant educational institutions were organized, the most famous being Tagore's Shantiniketan, the Arya Samaj *gurukuls* and colleges, Mrs. Besant's Central Hindu College at Benares, and Sir Syed Ahmad Khan's Anglo-Mohammedan College (later a university) at Aligarh. The correlations are many between the growth of nationalism and social reform in India and the championing of various kinds of private educational organizations. The founders of the Deccan Education Society, especially such men as Gokhale and Karve, did much to enrich education and to extend its influence.

The country was undergoing the most radical revolution when Lord Curzon became governor-general. Among his many activities to smash the rising nationalist movement was the appointment of the Universities Commission, in 1902. Conceived and evolved in secret, the Commission, supposedly created to improve the Indian universities, did not originally include a single Indian; the names of Dr. Gurudas Bannerjee and Syed Bilgrami were later added as an afterthought. The conclusions of the Commission were two-edged. On the one hand was the genuine desire of the Viceroy to improve the administration of Calcutta University and remedy such evils as low standards, cramming for examinations, and the wretched conditions of many of the students who obviously should not have been at a university. On the other hand, he and the committee, instead of tackling such basic ills as the state of education in village schools and the possibilities of high-school graduates' obtaining any kind of employment, chose to remedy the situation by administrative juggling toward greater authoritarianism by the government. Of the reformed senates of the Indian universities, 80 percent were to be nominated by the government.

Growing Movement for Indigenous Education. Lord Curzon could not, however, stop the rising tide of dissatisfaction among the intelligentsia or prevent nationalism from becoming more violent and determined. The partition of Bengal led to the Swadeshi movement. Government circulars prohibiting any student of a government institution from taking part in political activity led to the creation of the National Council of Education and the foundation of a national college with Sir Arobindo Ghosh as its first principal. The distinctive features of this college and subsequent national educational organizations were two—instruction in the mother tongue instead of English and inclusion of the national heritage in the curriculum instead of the history and culture of Britain. The failure of national education was similar and related to that of the nationalist movement in general. Not until after World War I did the emergence of Gandhi shake the country from dilettante reformism to outright revolution, although revolution conducted in a pacifist fashion.

In the prewar period the only significant move was the persistent effort of Gokhale to force the government to accept the responsibility of compulsory and free elementary education for boys between the ages of six and ten; he did not ask that this responsibility be extended to girls, thus proving the modesty of his demand. Although the bill was defeated in the Imperial Legislative Council with many arguments from official opposition against the need for public primary education, the government had a change of heart. In its Resolution on Indian Educational Policy of 1913, a grant of $17,000 was made for primary education. Moreover the decision to prevent universities from controlling recognition of high schools (and, consequently, from controlling high-school curriculums) spelled progress, if the transfer to local bodies could be made effective. Once again, however, much the greater portion of attention was devoted to reforms for university education. The latter, instead of being progressive, and embodying changes which would resuscitate creative scholarship, were directed toward establishing communalism in academic circles. It was stated that the government would give adequate financial aid to the Moslem University at Aligarh and the Hindu University at Benares and would found a university at Dacca in response to the claims of Moslems of East Bengal.

The year 1917 saw important pronouncements on Indian political development and education. Among them was the appointment of the Calcutta University Commission under the chairmanship of Dr. Michael Sadler and including the most outstanding Indian educationalist of his day, Sir Ashutosh Mookerjee. In spite of its being a landmark in the recent history of Indian education, the Commission was wholly concerned with collegiate education, especially with the improvement of Calcutta University. Secondary education was dealt with incidentally, although many trenchant comments were made on its status. The crux of the deficiencies in secondary education was said to be in the inadequate financial provisions for secondary education. No radical reform of the university system in Bengal was possible unless secondary education were overhauled. The most widely publicized aspect of the Commission's report—the need for teaching and unitary universities as opposed to the examining and federated bodies in existence—was the only one that saw concrete results. Eight new universities were established on the basis of the plan that was recommended by the Commission.

Attempts to Establish Compulsory Elementary Education. Elementary education became the concern of provincial governments and more particularly of the Ministers of Education created by the provisions of provincial dyarchy contained in the Constitutional Reforms of 1919. However, despite the fanfare of having transferred one of the nation-building fields to Indian control, finance of education remained under the control of the governor. Between 1920 and 1930 many attempts were made by Indian provincial legislatures to establish compulsory elementary education. Acts were passed, blueprints were produced prolifically, but progress was negligible. In the first place, owing to financial restrictions free education was not possible, and no Indian farmer can pay even the most meager fee for educating his child, a breadwinner. In the absence of incentive, financial sustenance, and practical advantages from the education imparted, compulsion could not be effective. Even if there had been any machinery for coercion, there would have been little success, because education does not thrive in an impoverished society. One of the earliest acts enforcing compulsion was passed in the Indian state of Baroda in 1906. In British India, legislation came by 1918. By 1927 in most major provinces legislation permitted the state to compel, but outside of the Punjab nothing was done. The statutes were "coaxing rather than coercive." In 1929 the cause of compulsion received the support of the Auxiliary (Hartog) Committee appointed to advise the Statutory Commission, but to no avail because of the deeper economic problems.

Public elementary education until 1946 was meager; there were many more private than public schools. The ills of elementary education in India as it exists in the village and urban areas are legion. The quality of instruction is poor, the physical facilities of school plants and accessories are nonexistent, and all modern innovations in method, curriculum, and administration are absent. The teachers are either untrained or so superficially educated as to be complete novices, and they are wretchedly paid. The salaries of an elementary-school teacher in India are so low and the working conditions so bad as to make one feel that the situation is virtually hopeless. There is nothing more important in India today than a sound financial base for teachers' salaries and school plants. Although sufficient money does not automatically spell good education, there can be few constructive measures in education or any other sphere without the free flow of appropriations.

With the tremendous changes which have taken place in the world since the cessation of World War II and the political advance in India, education has begun to feel the impact of new forces—national zeal to attack illiteracy and a spirit of social consciousness intent upon fostering constructive rather than destructive activities. The importance of education in the new Republic is seen in the inclusion of Article 36 in the Constitution; it says, "The state shall endeavour to provide, within a period of ten years, for free and compulsory education for all children until they complete the age of 14 years." In all nine provinces some degree of compulsory elementary education has been introduced. The United Provinces has opened the largest number of new schools—over 10,000. The goal is to provide at least one school within a radius of $1\frac{1}{2}$ miles of each village. Under the Assam Primary Education Act of 1947 no boy or girl should remain illiterate by 1958. Similar plans and programs are being launched in the country. Indeed the future looks more promising than it has looked heretofore.

CURRENT TRENDS IN INDIAN EDUCATION

Primary Education. Primary education in India requires, above all:

1. Expansion in sheer physical terms—new schoolhouses and other material concomitants of the aim of universal primary education.

2. The opening of new normal schools to train teachers, as well as other devices to meet the great need for trained personnel—for example, mobile training squads and training camps in villages.

3. Extension of vocational education, called "basic education" in India.

It is in elementary education that Indians expect to see the greatest changes in the immediate future, and emphasis is on this field. Like all other aspects of education, elementary education is a matter for the provinces rather than for the central government. Hence there are variations, with such poor provinces as Orissa and

West Bengal lagging behind the relatively less impoverished ones, such as the United Provinces and Bombay Presidency.

Although bills for compulsory universal and free elementary education have been introduced in most of the provincial legislatures, and although some of them have been enacted into law, the difficulty of enforcing them in the absence of most of the requisites of public education and in a very complex situation with innumerable problems is keenly felt by all. These are some of the problems:

1. There is little money available either for the provincial governments or the lesser local bodies, such as district boards and municipalities. Taxes cannot be imposed on the vast majority of the people as their incomes are meager. The middle and upper classes can be taxed, but the governments cannot levy or have not levied any of the special impositions. Furthermore, the excise revenue has been cut off because of Prohibition.

2. There are, in the eyes of the government, more pressing problems than education—for example, the refugee issue in such parts of the country as the United Provinces and West Bengal.

3. There is a lack of trained personnel willing to work for the scanty salaries offered. There are many very well qualified experts, trained in the best institutions both in India and abroad. But they cannot afford to devote their energy to the pedestrian but very necessary tasks of teaching villagers. This problem of living in the village and sacrificing one's career for nothing in the way of remuneration must be understood.

The obstacles which most foreign observers feel to be most serious, such as the great numbers of people and the many languages, are not really insuperable. If there can be a sound base for public education in a crucial proportion of the villages, human ingenuity can devise all kinds of plans for extending it in terms of mere quantity. Wartime provisions in China and Britain make this clear. The important thing is to get the machinery started in the best possible way.

The linguistic issue is not considered at all by most Indians, since Hindi has been accepted as the basic language and since it is felt that the Indian tradition for multilingualism will never disappear. Every Indian on approaching adulthood is expected to know at least his own mother tongue and Hindi. Those who wish to enter secondary and higher education will require an Occidental language as well. The situation is analogous to that faced by small European nations such as Holland, where every child has to learn several languages.

Secondary Education.   Secondary education in the last decades of the nineteenth century was in a deplorable state, suffering from inadequate finances and supervision. The aim was rigidly preparatory: the middle schools prepared for the high schools, the high schools prepared for the colleges, and the colleges prepared for the examinations of the universities and ultimately some white-collar job. Funds were not sufficient to provide for schools as they were, much less for schools introducing vocational education and having modern plants and equipment. Teachers were underqualified and underpaid and reflected the general inefficiency and aimlessness.

In the period 1854-1921, secondary education showed relatively rapid growth compared to either higher or elementary education. At the time of the Wood Dispatch, schools teaching English were just being established, and they had few pupils. With the demand by the middle class for an English education leading to lucrative employment in the government, new schools began to be opened both by official and unofficial agencies, the latter being chiefly missions, although by the beginning of provincial dyarchy private efforts, undertaken by Indians, were to dominate the field. However, it becomes evident that the increase in schools was not so great a contribution when we evaluate the kind of education imparted in the schools. The goal of college preparation dominated a narrowly academic curriculum, which, together with the instruction in English, laid the foundations for a sterile education that has few parallels in the modern world. Not only were there few subjects which were related to the life of the great majority of the students but the methods of instruction emphasized competition and success in examinations; consequently there was a premium on cramming, and the very spirit of the courses was crushed. By 1921 the two most pressing needs in secondary education were vocational training and instruction in the mother tongue of the students.

In the interbellum period, 1921-1939, there was progressive expansion of secondary schools and increasing experimentation with various philosophies of education. The rapid expansion of schools was due to several factors, including the new patriotism in rural India and extended philanthropic work in the nature of scholarships, reservation of seats for children of backward communities in government schools, and the establishment of special institutions. Whereas government secondary schools increased by about 150, the number of private schools rose by almost two thousand. Together with the nationalist upsurge that demanded more education came a fresh effort to substitute instruction in Indian languages for instruction in English at the secondary level. In 1925, for example the government of Madras issued orders permitting the use of modern Indian languages in the three highest grades of the secondary schools; by 1937 Indian languages had been adopted by over 50 percent of the high schools. Similar permissive regulations were passed by other provincial governments, so that answering examination in the mother tongue became increasingly popular.

Outstanding among innovations in the sphere of secondary education has been the improved status of secondary-school teachers through the expansion of training colleges and normal schools and especially through increased salaries and concomitant benefits. However, there are few features in Indian education more discouraging than the still miserable pittances of most secondary-school teachers, the unsatisfactory nature of their contracts, and their heavy teaching loads.

Finally, vocational education in the secondary school has been the most publicized educational issue of recent years. The Wood-Abbott Report on Vocational Education in India (1937) was the first definitive step toward constructive planning for technical and vocational training for the majority of students who would not go to college at the conclusion of their schooling but should be prepared for some employment. The tragic middle-class unemployment, the plans for industrializing India, and the nationalist schemes for vocational education forced the government to shift its traditional policy. The reorganized high schools as envisaged in the Sargent plan will be of two main types—academic high schools and technical high schools; there will be more complex plans at the elementary level to select students for the two kinds of secondary education. The question of vocational versus humanistic learning is tied in, but in India there is less talk about it than in the United States, since the humanists themselves are the chief advocates of vocational training. This is the cardinal feature of the contemporary scene in Indian education, that noted scholars in the humanities are working for a utilitarian education for Indian youth; the reasons are that they know better than any other group the stultifying results of a humanism unrelated to the basic needs of the students and that they are very sure of their own position. The latter point should not be overlooked. Indian thinkers are not sudden converts to the new technology or pragmatic materialism. They are aware of the needs of the hour and hence advocate technical training. But they are also deeply confident that the humanities will not collapse, because of the age-long veneration of these disciplines by the Indian people, because the universities are administered by humanists, and because the scientists are conscious of the value of these subjects. It is this feeling of security on the part of the champions of the liberal arts that accounts for the absence of any great controversy over general and specialized education.

If it can be said that trends exist in secondary education today, they are:

1. Inclusion of many kinds of curriculum—technical, scientific, etc.

2. Growth in the number of government schools; decrease in the importance of private schools.

3. Greater use of the mother tongue.

4. Greater emphasis on education for girls.

Higher Education. Hitherto, anyone who wanted a white-collar job had to go to the university. The question has been raised whether the highly academic secondary education can be diluted with more vocational courses, so that high-school graduates will be able to earn a livelihood. An even more vital question is *whether such vocational education will be given to all students or only to those who are economically less privileged.* The intentions of most thinkers are that financial considerations should not enter but that aptitudes and abilities should be the determinants. If a poor village boy shows marked academic talents, he will be permitted to go to the university. Further, it is proposed to raise university standards so that poor scholastic records but adequate finances will not provide entry into college. The universities have not been unanimous about the curtailment of their student body, but they all feel the need for high scholastic standards. That their power of controlling high schools will be diminished is accepted by the universities. They expect to play a very great role in the development of the nation; on every commission and committee for future and present improvements—whether it be for better defense or increased productivity—university teachers are in the vanguard.

Students of the problem feel that higher education should stimulate the following trends:

1. Greater emphasis on social service. This stands out as the most prominent landmark in Indian collegiate education. The gulf between the intelligentsia and the village is beginning to be crossed. Plans range all the way from proposed conscription of all prospective graduates for village-uplift work to required courses in social service.

2. Instruction in the mother tongue. This is not as daring as it sounds, for there is the helpful example of Osmania University, in Hyderabad, Deccan, which has been doing all its work in Urdu.

3. Greater emphasis on the training of scientists.

4. Increasing interest of university men in political and civic affairs. The premier philosopher of the country, Sir Radhakrishnan, is the ambassador to the Soviet Union, and one of the great historians is the head of the education department of the government of India.

Adult Education. Instruction of adults is India's most difficult educational problem and, from the standpoint of the country's progress, her most pressing. It is the field with more obstacles than any other, for the simple reason that mass illiteracy cannot be wiped out without state planning and grim determination. The only analogous situations are the Russian and the Chinese. The Russians used coercion and were successful in a very short space of time. The Chinese were aided by very high morale on the part of the population, both teachers and students. In India the desire to learn is present and is being stimulated every year. The flickering enthusiasm of the teachers is a great drawback.

Many difficulties face voluntary activity. This is one sphere in which philanthropy does not work, for education cannot be given to an illiterate in doses. It must be done all at once or the process must be started from scratch. Token gestures, such as instruction once a year, on Literacy Day, are useless.

Adult education in India is not something divorced from the

life of the people. It is tied in with the plowing, the indebtedness, and the sickness. In India education of the masses means education for health, sanitation, agrarian improvement, and rural reconstruction. As James Yen discovered in China, you cannot make a peasant read and write when doing so does not fill his stomach. Adult education in India, as in other countries, will be possible only when it brings results in the form of tangible benefits. That is why it must be introduced amid other activities, such as cooperatives.

This brief study of Indian education has reviewed the intrusions of the Indo-European, Moslem, and British educational patterns and the resultant syntheses. It seems clear that education in India may be a primary instrument for providing a common base of human experience which will have its roots in the indigenous culture pattern. India has made definite progress in meeting the challenge of more adequate education despite such obstacles as foreign intrusion, poverty, and the Great Division.

BIBLIOGRAPHY

ANDREWS, C. F., and G. MOOKERJEE, *The Rise and Growth of the Congress in India* (London: George Allen & Unwin, Ltd., 1938). Well-written, compact, impartial, but outdated account. Good for historical background.

ANSTEY, V., *The Economic Development of India*, rev. ed. (New York: Longmans, Green & Company, 1936). This book is the standard reference.

CHAND, T., *A Short History of the Indian People*, 2nd ed. (Calcutta: The Macmillan Company, 1944). A standard text.

CHANDRASEKHAR, S., *India's Population* (New York: The John Day Company, 1946). A slim, readable volume by one of the younger and brilliant economists.

COUPLAND, R., *The Indian Problem* (London: Oxford University Press, 1944). Constitutional problems of proposed division. Conservative but scholarly presentation of many issues.

Cultural Heritage of India, Vols. I-III (Calcutta: RamKrishna Centenary Publications, 1940). General reference work and compendium.

DAS, S. K., *The Educational System of the Ancient Hindus*. A useful analysis of early education in India.

DUTT, R. P., *India Today*, 2nd rev. ed. (Bombay: People's Publishing House, 1947). The best comprehensive treatment. Informative and interpretative.

EMERSON, G., *Voiceless India,* rev. ed. (New York: The John Day Company, 1944). An American woman's account of life in Indian villages. Written with knowledge and sympathy.

FORSTER, E. M., *A Passage to India* (New York: Modern Library, Inc., 1929). The best fictional account by an English writer on contemporary India.

GHURYE, G. S., *Caste* (New York: Alfred A. Knopf, Inc., 1932). A standard reference.

HUTTON, J. H., *Caste in India* (New York: The Macmillan Company, 1947). A relatively recent authoritative statement.

KABIR, H., *Our Heritage* (Bombay: National Information and Publications Ltd., 1946), pp. 93-94.

MITCHELL, K. L., *India Without Fable* (New York: Alfred A. Knopf, Inc., 1942). Taken largely from Dutt; however, one of the better books to be written on India. Very readable.

MOOKERJI, R. K., *Hindu Civilization* (New York: Longmans, Green & Company, 1936). An excellent study by an expert.

MORAES and STIMSON, *Introduction to India* (New York: Longmans, Green & Company). An outline survey of important features. Good for beginners.

NEHRU, J., *Autobiography,* rev. ed. (London: John Lane, 1942). The standard book for a psychological and semischolarly approach to nationalism in India. Beautiful style. Should be read by anyone interested in India.

————, *Discovery of India* (New York: The John Day Company, 1946). Semiphilosophical account of Indian history. Not academic but well written.

NURULLAH, S., and J. NAIK, *History of Education in India* (Bombay: The Macmillan Company, 1943).

Post-War Educational Development in India (New Delhi: Government of India Press, New Delhi, 1944). The text of the Sargent plan.

PRASAD, B., *India's Hindu Muslim Questions* (London: George Allen & Unwin, Ltd., 1946). An authoritative account of the communal-imperial tangle, written by one of the greatest professors of political science.

SMITH, W. C., *Modern Islam in India,* rev. ed. (London: Victor Gollancz, Ltd., 1946). A Canadian scholar's provocative analysis of Moslem position.

THOMPSON, E. J. and G. T. GARRATT, *Rise and Fulfilment of British Rule in India* (London: Macmillan & Company, Ltd., 1934).

17 · EDUCATION IN *China*

THEODORE HSI-EN CHEN

China has a population of approximately 470 million in a total area of about 3,760,000 square miles; the population density is about 125 persons per square mile. The land ranges in type from the plains of Mongolia and Manchuria on the north through the river valleys of the center to the high plateau of Tibet. The country is not much larger than the United States but has a population density more than twice as great. The population is, however, heavily rural. It is estimated that Chinese illiteracy exceeds 90 percent.

China is in the beginning phases of an industrial technology. Her transportation and communication facilities are extremely inadequate. The tradition of government has been a "god-king" type of absolute control—a tradition which remained unchanged until the revolution under Dr. Sun Yat-sen at the beginning of the twentieth century. Absolutist control returned with the disorder of the war with Japan and with the coming of the Communists.

China has had an elite educational system from the beginning; the country was ruled by a classically educated bureaucracy of mandarins until the Revolution of 1911. At that time, plans for universal education were instituted, but they were carried out only to a limited degree, because of poverty, war, and lack of stable governmental organization. Illiteracy was fought by the growth of the elementary schools and by the adult-education movement, but the odds against it were great, owing to the lack of an alphabet, the use of ideographs, and the many regional variants in the spoken language.

—A. H. M.

China in the twentieth century is characterized by change. Her social structure, her economic life, her political institutions, and her intellectual outlook are undergoing fundamental and rapid change. With old institutions and traditions challenged and discarded, China has been groping for new ways to enable her to solve her numerous problems. She has not yet settled down to a stable pattern of living; she is still in a period of transition marked by uncertainty of direction and of methods, by trial and error, by the adoption and rejection of one new way after another. All aspects of Chinese life are in a flux; education is no exception.

The Revolution of 1911. Dissatisfaction with the monarchy prompted the revolutionary leaders to found a republic in 1912. The ideas of republicanism and government by the people quickly gained wide popularity, but there remained the difficult task of devising practical machinery for implementing the ideas. It was soon found that a nation accustomed to many centuries of monarchial rule did not possess the traditions and the experience needed for a successful republican government. A civic consciousness on the part of the people was yet to be developed. Political parties had yet to learn the techniques of political participation. In the meantime, although the old institution of hereditary rule had been abandoned, no new machinery had yet been established for the selection of officeholders. Ambitious and adventurous persons engaged in a free-for-all scramble for power and position. The Republic of China was plunged into a period of chaos and instability when the country was overrun by war lords supported by their mercenary troops and motivated by the desire to reap the greatest personal gain in the shortest possible time.

Dr. Sun Yat-sen. Sickened by continual civil strife and the sad spectacle of selfish warlordism, Dr. Sun Yat-sen, the founder of the Republic, died a sorely disappointed man. The modern democratic state that he had dreamed about had not come into existence despite his own struggle and the efforts of his fellow revolutionaries. He had once considered Japan a friend, but he saw Japan turn into a dangerous aggressor. He had looked for the leadership of the Anglo-American democracies, but at the Paris Peace Conference at the end of World War I they seemed more eager to appease Japan than to support China's cause. Before he died, he was impressed by Soviet Russia's offer of friendly assistance to all oppressed peoples of the world and moved by Russia's readiness to treat China on a basis of equality, as shown by her voluntary relinquishment of extraterritoriality and special concessions in China. He gladly welcomed Russian advisers and accepted their counsel in a drastic reorganization of his party for stricter discipline and more effective action. He laid down plans for a second revolution, to be spearheaded by a newly formed military force starting in South China, and designed to clean the country of its war lords and unify it under one government guided by revolutionary concepts.

The Nationalist Revolution. Under the leadership of Chiang Kai-shek, the reorganized Kuomintang (Sun's political party) and its forces began the Northern Expedition to carry out the program of its deceased founder. Re-enforced by new recruits from the idealistic and patriotic student class and vitalized by a clearly formulated ideology propagated by methods taught by the Russian advisers, the Kuomintang did not find it too difficult to overthrow the war lords and establish a government exercising at least nominal control over all China. Although weakened by a split between the right and left wings of the party, the Nationalist government established in 1928 ushered in a new era of national life and raised the hopes of millions that unification would be followed by a constructive program of material development and educational growth.

One-party Government. The Nationalist government was controlled by the Kuomintang, which was to be the only political party. The idea of one-party government was borrowed from Soviet Russia. Dr. Sun Yat-sen had come to the conclusion that the Chinese nation needed considerable schooling in political participation and civic responsibility before a successful democracy could be realized. The idea of one-party government appealed to him as a feasible solution of the problems of a transitional period when the nation had yet to learn the ways of political democracy. According to the ideology formulated by him and adopted by the Kuomintang, one-party government was to provide for a period of political tutelage and would make way for genuine constitutional government as soon as the nation had learned the ways of modern democracy. It was not meant to be permanent; on the contrary, it was to prepare the way for constitutional government under which all political parties would enjoy equal rights. During the period of political tutelage, however, the people were not considered ready for the exercise of their sovereign rights and were to delegate their authority to the Kuomintang, which was pledged to terminate the stewardship and "return the power of government to the people" as soon as the nation was ready for constitutional government.

Progress and Reconstruction. After 1930, the Nationalist government had consolidated its position and was confident enough to proceed with long-range plans. During the next few years a program of constructive reform such as China had not seen for a long time was successfully executed.[1] Increased political stability served as encouragement for the development of industry, trade, and commerce. Nationalization of the currency further facilitated economic progress. Transportation and communication facilities were greatly improved. New railways were built, airways were developed, and motor roads began to connect isolated towns with one another. A program of public health was initiated and effort was made to control seasonal epidemics in selected areas. Scientific methods were employed for the improvement of agriculture and the promotion of home industries. The prestige of Chiang Kai-shek's government rose steadily and commanded the increasing support of various groups within the nation.

Effects of World War II. The undeclared war between China and Japan began on July 7, 1937. It was not long before all the coastal provinces were lost to the invader and with them the major portion of industries and the fresh fruits of national reconstruction. The center of national life now shifted into West China. In time, unoccupied China was completely cut off from the rest of the world except for the small amount of supplies that were flown over "the Hump." Wartime privations intensified the poverty and suffering of the people; but despite the long war, morale was surprisingly good, largely because the people felt that they were suffering for a cause and also because they bolstered their courage with beautiful dreams

[1] Owen and Eleanor Lattimore, *The Making of Modern China* (New York: W. W. Norton and Company, Inc., 1944), pp. 140 ff.

of the eventual day of victory, when they would be able to return to their homes and would live peacefully as proud citizens of a victorious and modernized nation.

Unfortunately, postwar conditions not only failed to fulfill the extravagant hopes of the peoples but imposed difficulties and privations which seemed less tolerable than those of the war years. The effects of a war-torn economy, the perplexing problems involved in returning to the coastal provinces, and the intensification of conflict and hostilities between the Kuomintang and the Communist party combined to create a postwar situation characterized by uncontrollable runaway inflation, more prevalent poverty and economic distress, widespread disillusionment and frustration, and violent reactions against the status quo. More and more people turned against the government, and the prestige of Chiang Kai-shek's party and government suffered a steady and rapid decline.

Somehow or other, the Kuomintang had lost much of the youthful vigor and revolutionary spirit which had enabled it to capture public imagination two decades earlier. It had become burdened with bureaucrats who seemed to be more interested in holding office and exercising power than in the promotion of public welfare. When these bureaucrats took advantage of the abnormal economic conditions of the postwar years for their selfish profit through speculation, black-market operations, and other irregularities, they became conspicuous targets of public attack and gave further impetus to the tendency to blame the government for all postwar evils. Thus a government which had once led the nation in positive reconstruction and progress became synonymous with incompetency and corruption, and the steady loss of public support spelled its doom.[2]

A New Chapter in China's History. The experiment of political tutelage by the Kuomintang failed to produce the results envisaged by Sun Yat-sen. Now the Communists are having their turn to see whether their program of modernizing and strengthening China will succeed. The People's Republic of China was proclaimed on October 1, 1949. It ushered in the "new democracy," a transitional stage between capitalism and socialism. It is a "democratic dictator-

[2] For a more detailed analysis of the collapse of the Kuomintang regime, the reader is referred to the author's article "Communist Victory in China," *World Affairs Interpreter*, Vol. XX, No. 4 (January 1950), pp. 369-389.

ship"—neither the outworn democracy of the West nor the proletariat dictatorship of the future but the "joint dictatorship" of revolutionary classes allied with the proletariat and political parties
allied with the Communist party. The governing principle of political and social organization is declared to be "democratic centralism":
democracy is expressed in popular elections and centralism in the
centralization of power and authority in the highest organs and the
chosen few acting in behalf of the many.

The economic policies are not the most revolutionary aspects of
the program inaugurated in the name of the new democracy. The
architects of the new order have set out to remake Chinese society.
They propose to replace individualism with collectivism, to place
loyalty to the state above other loyalties, to build up a dynamic
society, to step up the tempo of individual and social life, to exalt
labor and production, to glorify soldiery, to introduce new concepts
of marriage, of family life, and of womanhood. Not satisfied with
the passive acceptance characteristic of the Chinese people in the
past, they demand active, enthusiastic, and articulate support of
their program by the people at large. To achieve this support a vast
program of education and indoctrination has been launched.
Closely integrated with the political-social-economic revolution,
this educational program is indeed very different from the one followed in the past.

THE EDUCATIONAL HERITAGE

China has a long educational tradition and the Chinese are
known for their high respect for scholars. From early times it was
considered an important duty of government to provide the means
to teach the essentials of good living.[3] In the age of Confucius, there
were schools for the hamlets, for the villages, and for the feudal
states.[4]

Education and the Civil-service Examinations. A unique characteristic of traditional Chinese education is its intimate linkage with
a system of selecting public officials by means of competitive examinations. The practice of selecting men of ability for public
service by means of examinations dates back to the dynasties before

[3] P. W. Kuo, *The Chinese System of Public Education* (New York:
Teachers College, Columbia University, 1915), pp. 9 ff.
[4] *Ibid.*, p. 17.

the Christian era. As centuries went by, education became more and more closely related to preparation for the examinations that led to public service and official position, and the examinations came to be recognized as the natural climax of an educational career. Private as well as public schools of various types were evolved through the centuries, some at lower levels for children of the villages, and others with the specific purpose of preparing students for the official examinations. As the examinations assumed increasing importance, it became the primary motive of students to pass them; inevitably, because it was possible to prepare for examinations without school attendance, the examination system in time overshadowed the school system in importance.

The examination system underwent many changes through the centuries, both in content and in the degrees awarded. The system maintained before the adoption of modern schools provided for three academic degrees and four levels of examinations. Before presenting himself for the examination for the first degree, the ambitious scholar took a qualifying examination in his own district. Having survived this preliminary process of elimination, he was ready for the first official examination at the chief city of the county. Passing the examination admitted him to the first degree, the *Hsiu Ts'ai*, which may be compared with the bachelor's degree of modern education. The next level of competition was the examination held in the provincial capital, open to those who held the first degree. Successful candidates were awarded the *Chu-Jen* degree. The third and highest examination was held in the national capital and culminated in a palace examination in the presence of the emperor. The highest degree was called *Chin Shih*. Special honors were given to three top scholars, and the man who attained the highest honor was given the title of *Chuang Yuan* and was recognized as the foremost scholar of the land. Other *Chin Shih* of distinction were appointed members of the Han Lin Academy, a highly respected assembly of scholars supported by the state and established as early as the eighth century as an official advisory and editorial body.

On every level, the examinations eliminated the many and chose the few. "The competition was much more keen than any to which we are accustomed in the Occident."[5] The examinations were held

[5] Kenneth Scott Latourette, *The Chinese: Their History and Culture* (New York: The Macmillan Company, 1947), p. 531.

in specially constructed halls containing individual stalls in which the candidates were confined without any outside contacts until the completion of the examination. The examinations lasted more than a day and the candidates were not even permitted to leave at night. But once they passed the examinations, the scholars were entitled to privileges and immunities even before they received appointment as public officials.[6]

Before it became formalized and too narrow in scope, the system was not without merit. It was the foundation of China's "government by scholars" and her tradition of honoring scholars and civil authorities far more than warriors and military heroes. The examinations, known for difficulty, were administered with a remarkable degree of fairness. The temptation for cheating and bribery was great, but "even in the worst years of the dynasty only a small minority of the degrees were obtained fraudulently. . . . The competition was so exacting that as a rule success went only to men of more than average mental ability and capacity for concentrated application."[7]

The examinations were open to all. There was no requirement of minimum age or specified years of preparatory study; ability to pass the examinations was the sole criterion for awarding the degrees. Failure to pass an examination did not prevent further attempts. Grandfather, father, and son were known to have taken an examination at the same time. Theoretically, the examinations provided an open door to position and success for people of all classes; but in practice, long years of study required for preparation made it impossible for many of limited financial resources to make the attempt. Nevertheless, in the absence of any official discrimination, many a poor parent could and did cherish the fond dream of supporting a promising son in study and enabling him to rise to the top.

The prestige attached to membership in the class of scholars caused many to aspire to it—or caused families to aspire for them. Often one member of a family would be devoted to learning, as in other countries one child might be consecrated to the church. Such a fortunate individual would be supported by the

[6] Y. S. Han, "Molding Forces," in H. F. MacNair, ed., *China* (Berkeley: University of California Press, 1946), p. 11.

[7] Kenneth Scott Latourette, *op. cit.*, p. 532.

family, or sometimes by the village, if he were a promising student and his family could not afford to give him an education.[8]

Cultural Unity. One of the most important outcomes of this system of education and examinations was the cultural unity which it helped to produce and maintain. All over the length and breadth of the country, pupils and scholars were nurtured on the same intellectual diet on which the examinations were based. In spite of differences in dialects, but thanks to the existence of a common written language, the same primers, essays, and great books of the past constituted the common curriculum pursued by all who sought learning. Moreover, since public officials for all parts of the land were recruited from scholars who had followed the same path, they were governed by more or less the same concepts and ideals of government and morality. Thus, despite political upheavals and military conquests, China maintained a cultural unity and a continuity of history through the centuries.

Formalization. When the primary motive of learning was to prepare for the examinations, the nature of the examinations inevitably determined the content of education. In early times, public officials were selected on the basis of real ability and moral character and the content of education included music, archery, morals, and ethics.[9] In later centuries, the examinations were more concerned with a definite body of knowledge such as that embodied in the classics. A further process of narrowing came about when the Confucian school gained increasing dominance and the Confucian classics became the core of the examinations and of the learning process. At first, the Confucian scholars taught a "composite Confucianism" which incorporated ideas from other schools of thought, and the examinations covered a wide range of subjects, including "history, law, mathematics, poetry, calligraphy, and Taoist philosophy."[10] As the centuries went by, the content became more narrowly confined to the Confucian classics and to a narrow interpretation of them. Orthodoxy was enthroned and freedom of thought was severely limited.

In China as well as in Europe, a result of the study of the classics

[8] H. M. Vinacke, *A History of the Far East in Modern Times* (New York: F. S. Crofts and Co., 1942), p. 6.

[9] P. W. Kuo, *op. cit.*, pp. 12-13 and 28.

[10] Kenneth Scott Latourette, *op. cit.*, pp. 132-182.

was a gradual shift of emphasis from the creative ideas of classical thinkers to the style of classical writers. Just as the Renaissance humanism of Europe degenerated into Ciceronianism, so there grew up in China a worship of style and an emphasis on literary form which eventually killed the original spirit of classicism. So important did it become to conform to accepted style that it was often necessary to change ideas in order to fit the style. With painstaking meticulosity, scholars practiced writing the "eight-legged essay," a form of writing required in all the examinations. The classical style became, instead of a medium for the expression of ideas, an impediment to the development of thought. Moreover, historical and classical allusions were considered such important characteristics of good style that a premium was placed on the memorization of historical facts and classical sources. Verbatim memorization became the accepted method of study and learning. Originality of thought was not encouraged.

Other defects grew out of the identification of the scholar class with officialdom. Scholarship tended to become conservative and to resist the infusion of new ideas and new influences. This conservatism was exacerbated in the nineteenth century by the fear of rebellion on the part of alien rulers (the Manchus), who took careful measures to edit and standardize the classical texts and to expunge whatever might turn out to be unfavorable to the alien dynasty. Even before this conservatism became marked, there was already a strong tendency to identify education with literary skill and to divorce it from manual activities and practical but nonliterary studies. The educated man was to use his mind, not his hands; his concern was to develop the intellect, not his physical powers. The scholars not only failed to take interest in the study of nature and the practical problems of life but also cut themselves off from the activities and problems of the common people. Scholarship became sterile; science was neglected; scholars felt no challenge to apply their knowledge to the problems of the peasants and the toiling masses. Finally, since the chief concern of education was to prepare for official careers, popular education for the purpose of general enlightenment was neglected.

The Rise of Modern Schools. A succession of military defeats in the nineteenth century rudely shook China out of her complacency. Most astonishing and humiliating of all was the defeat by Japan, the small island empire which had borrowed extensively from Chinese culture and to which China had considered herself quite superior. The demand for reform included proposals for the adoption of a new educational program. In response to the protests of liberal leaders, the Manchu court issued an edict abolishing the "eight-legged essay" in 1901 and the entire system of examinations in 1905. It was not surprising that China's first modern school system, adopted in 1903, embodied characteristics of the system which Japan had recently established. With the birth of the Republic, in 1912, the nation felt the need of a school system more in harmony with the new ideals of the Republic, and a reorganization was thus made under which the major features of the American school system were adopted. When it became popular in the United States to divide the secondary school into two levels, China again followed the American example and adopted the 6-3-3 system: a six-year elementary school, a three-year junior middle school, a three-year senior middle school, and four-year college and university. The middle schools were paralleled by normal schools and vocational schools. This system has, with slight modifications, continued to the present day.

EDUCATION UNDER THE NATIONALIST GOVERNMENT

During the early years of the Republic there was a great increase of interest in modern educational theories and methods. New methodologies from abroad attracted study and experimentation. Dewey's educational philosophy, with its emphasis on pupil activity and release from traditional shackles, gained great popularity; the project method, the Dalton plan, the Montessori system, and other new proposals were tried with enthusiasm. World War I and the high ideals pronounced by Woodrow Wilson further released the energies and enthusiasm of a democratically inclined people. With self-determination and freedom as their watchwords, the students took a new interest in their own destiny and that of their nation and launched the significant Student Movement, which symbolized a new spirit for education as well as the beginning of student participation in patriotic and political activities on a large scale.

The Student Movement, dramatically launched on a nation-wide scale on May 4, 1919, in protest against the decision of the Paris

Peace Conference to sustain Japan's claims to former German holdings in China, was only one aspect of a broad movement of intellectual awakening and cultural advance which has now been
called the Chinese Renaissance. The difficult years of political confusion after the birth of the Republic were marked by a spectacular
release of intellectual energies and their expression in such movements as organized student participation in patriotic activities,
the efforts of scholars to simplify the written language and to produce a new literature more accessible in form and more appealing
in content to larger portions of the population, the enthusiasm for
new ideas from abroad, and a revaluation of China's traditional
culture in the light of modern conditions and modern needs.

An important part of the Renaissance was the Literary Revolution. The basis of the Literary Revolution was a language reform
known as the *pai-hua,* or vernacular, movement. There had existed
so great a difference between the spoken and the written language in
China that after each written word was learned it was necessary to
translate the written form into understandable speech. The difficulty
of the written language was undoubtedly one of the important
reasons why illiteracy was so high in China. It was necessary for the
learner to learn not only the pronunciation of each written character
but also its meaning in terms of the vernacular tongue. To overcome
this difficulty, the leaders of the Literary Revolution proposed to
eliminate the difference between the spoken and the written style
and to write according to the spoken language. This new style of
writing became known as the *pai-hua*—literally, "plain talk"—as
distinguished from the difficult classical style of writing. It obviated
the necessity of translating; once the written word was learned, its
meaning could immediately be comprehended. This style of writing had been used to some extent for some centuries, but scholars
had despised it as a crude contraption of the semiliterate. Some
cheap popular novels had been written in this style by anonymous
authors ashamed to reveal their identity, but the respected books,
essays, and letters had always been written in the classical style.

Now the scholars of the modern Chinese Renaissance boldly discarded the intricacies of the classical style and adopted the free and
easy style of the vernacular. The old vernacular novels were now
held up as examples of "live literature" and "literature of the
people." Untrammeled by the rules and requirements that made

the classical style stereotyped and formalistic, the new *pai-hua* style lent itself easily to the expression of all kinds of ideas and emotions. Moreover, it did not require the long, painstaking study that was necessary for the classical style. The new style would be readily intelligible to a much larger portion of the population.

The *pai-hua* movement opened up great possibilities for cultural advance. It made learning easier and consequently accessible to more people. It made possible a new type of literature, one that reflected contemporary life and expressed the hopes and fears, joys and disappointments of the people. It dethroned stylism and gave free play to ideas. The "New Literature Movement" was inaugurated, and a host of new writers produced novels, plays, essays, and poems dealing with various phases of contemporary life. Hu Shih, honored as one of the most influential founders of the movement, and others showed that it was possible to write poems in the *pai-hua*, without the rhyme and rhythm of classical poetry. There appeared a new type of poetry, which the ordinary literate person could enjoy; enjoyment of the classical poetry remained the exclusive privilege of the scholar.

The "New Thought Movement," as the Renaissance was called in China, was also expressed in an interest in ideas from abroad. China welcomed such world thinkers as Rabindranath Tagore, John Dewey, Bertrand Russell, and others. The *pai-hua* style made it easier to express new ideas and coin new terms. Translations were made in the *pai-hua* of the writings of Western thinkers, so that their ideas and philosophies could become a part of the new intellectual vistas being opened to students and scholars of the day. Even the students of the secondary schools began to read the translations of contemporary American and European thinkers. There was a mushroom growth of new publications, each contributing to the broadening of the intellectual horizon.

In education, freedom and initiative not only characterized the Student Movement but were also stressed in educational objectives and methodology. "Self-expression" and "creativity" became important words in the vocabulary of the teaching profession. But the classics were not thoughtlessly discarded. On the contrary, there was new interest in a critical examination of the cultural heritage of the past. Hu Shih's volume *The History of Chinese Philosophy*, written in *pai-hua*, provided an excellent example of the application of modern methods of research to the study of Chinese classics and a restatement of the ideas of classical thinkers in modern terms. The classics were now studied with a new and critical point of view very different from the formalism of the past. Underlying the entire Renaissance movement was a new skepticism, which refused to accept old traditions without question and which demanded a reevaluation of traditional ethics and values.

Nevertheless, educational progress in these years was seriously impeded by the unfavorable political conditions. The war lords who overran the country were too busy amassing personal wealth and engaging in political intrigue and internecine warfare to be bothered with education. Without political stability, there was no inducement for long-range plans in education. In the face of military expenditures and personal graft on the part of those in power, little money was left in the public treasury for education. Public schools suffered from pitifully inadequate funds and lagged far behind the private schools—particularly the mission schools—in equipment, in quality of instruction, and in general stability and respectability.

Education for Nationalism. The Nationalists came to power on the wave of a new national consciousness which they and the students had done much to create. They had learned from the Russian advisers and from the examples of Italy and Germany after World War I how education could be made a powerful force for national strength and solidarity. After establishing their government in Nanking, they lost no time in mapping out a positive program of education designed to create a new national consciousness and patriotism. For the first time since the adoption of modern education, the government now formulated a clear statement of educational aims:

> . . . to enrich the life of the people, to maintain and develop social life, to promote the livelihood of the citizens, and to continue to foster national life in accordance with the spirit of *San Min Chu I* ["Three People's Principles": nationalism, democracy, and livelihood], with a view to achieving the independence of the nation, the assertion of the people's rights, the development of the people's livelihood, and the realization of universal peace and brotherhood.

Education was now consciously used as an agency for the development of nationalism. Civics as a subject of the curriculum was given special attention. Schools all over the country, it was maintained, should fit into a national program of education, and private education must be governed by the same national aims as public education. The study of Chinese literature and Chinese culture assumed a new importance in this program; general courses on the history and culture of China received a new emphasis in the curriculum.

Language Unification.   An important feature of education for national unity was the effort to unify the spoken language of the country by the use of the *Kuo Yu*, or national tongue, in schools in all the provinces. It is not difficult to see why the diversity of dialects in China was an obstacle to national coherence. Fortunately, the dialects were more or less based on a common written language (there had never been more than one written language in China). Moreover, in many parts of the country the dialects were more or less related to the prevailing form used in North China—the language that used to be known as Mandarin. The *pai-hua* movement had been an important step toward the unification of the spoken language. Since the *pai-hua* was essentially the *Kuo Yu*, or Mandarin, the new literature had introduced the prevailing spoken tongue to the whole country. Even though they spoke their own dialects, the people in the southern provinces had learned to read and write in the *Kuo Yu*. Therefore the movement for the unification of the spoken langauge had already been given a good start by the Literary Revolution.

The Nationalist government now carried the movement one step further. It ruled that in schools of all grades in all parts of the country, the *Kuo Yu* should be used not only in the teaching of reading but also as the common medium of instruction. In areas notorious for diversity of dialects, pupils in kindergartens and primary schools were taught to sing, read, and converse in the *Kuo Yu*. In this campaign the school was greatly aided by the radio, which made national broadcasts in the *Kuo Yu* and gave lessons on how to change from a dialect to the *Kuo Yu* pronunciation, and by the rapid improvement of transportation facilities, which increased the mobility of the population and created a felt need for a generally understandable medium of oral communication. While the school population was learning to overcome dialect barriers, the adult population outside the schools was slowly being influenced, too. In the provinces of Kwangtung and Fukien, where dialects were most diverse, effort was made to conduct all public functions in the *Kuo Yu*. With more people arriving from other provinces, people in the cities of these two provinces learned to converse with "outsiders" in an improvised mixture of *Kuo Yu* and local dialects. On the whole, the movement for the national use of *Kuo Yu* was making great strides.

Educational Administration. To develop a national program of education, the Nationalist government introduced a highly centralized system of administration. The highest authority in education was the Minister of Education, an appointed member of the executive *Yuan*, or Cabinet. Exercising control over all branches of education, the Minister not only recommended the enactment of educational laws by the national government but also issued orders and regulations which must be obeyed throughout the nation. The Ministry of Education established departments to take charge of higher education, general education (elementary and secondary), social education, Mongolian and Tibetan education, and business matters: it also appointed special committees for medical education, compulsory education, translation and publication of textbooks, etc. Within each province the highest authority was the Department of Education. The Commissioner of Education, like other commissioners of the provincial government, was appointed by the national government and directly responsible to the Ministry of Education. In similar manner, educational officers in counties and municipalities were responsible to the Commissioner of Education.

This system of centralized control was considered necessary to carry out the reforms proposed for a country traditionally known for its provincialism and localism. Lack of planning and coordination had resulted in educational chaos in the early years of the Republic. To bring order out of chaos, the government now prescribed standards of curriculum, equipment, finance, and examinations to which all schools must conform. Standardized curriculums for all types of schools on all levels were set up by the Ministry of Education and enforced by the provincial and local authorities. Each semester, schools were required to report in detail the actual courses offered, students enrolled, and qualifications of the teaching personnel; before graduation, each student's record from semester to semester must be submitted to the authorities to be checked against the standard requirements. A uniform curriculum was thus established throughout the country. All textbooks were selected and approved by the Ministry of Education or provincial authorities. These requirements applied to private as well as public schools. All private schools had to apply for registration with the government and the application was granted only when the authorities were satisfied that all regulations regarding curriculum and other prescribed standards were complied with.

Missionary Education. There had been some private schools of very low educational standards. It was reasonable to require them to measure up to the prescribed standards or close their doors. But to many people, the application of this requirement to the mission schools seemed unreasonable. These schools had been the pioneers of modern education in China. They were the first to offer the new education to girls. They had been the foremost institutions of the country and had maintained a high educational standard. When the public schools had been victims of politics and warlordism, the missions schools had won respect as institutions of stability and efficiency. Their alumni occupied important positions of leadership and exercised an influence on national life much greater than one would expect from their small numbers. But, supported by foreign funds and administered by foreign personnel, they had been entirely free of public supervision or inspection.

There were several major issues involved in the question of requiring registration of mission schools and their submission to government regulations. One was the question of religion: government regulations did not permit compulsory religious instruction and compulsory chapel, which had been regular features of the mission schools.[11] Another concerned the administrative personnel: to assure the national character of the educational program, government regulations prescribed that the chief administrative officers of private schools must be Chinese citizens. Finally, the high wave of nationalism had produced a new sensitivity in regard to "cultural imperialism" and "cultural exploitation," and a mounting criticism of the denationalization of the mission schools, which had empha-

[11] Herman C. E. Liu, "China," in I. L. Kandel, ed., *Educational Yearbook of the International Institute, 1932* (New York: Teachers College, Columbia University, 1933), pp. 91-95.

sized foreign language and foreign culture to the neglect of Chinese studies. From 1926 to 1928, there was a movement for "the recovery of educational rights"; it was demanded that control of missionary schools be shifted from foreign to Chinese hands.

Responding to such challenges, the mission schools and colleges in time made the necessary adjustments. Important administrative posts were offered to Chinese Christian leaders for the first time; compulsory chapel and religious instruction were abolished; the schools were open to government inspection and followed government regulations in curricular requirements as well as organization. The school curriculum was reorganized to give more attention to the study of Chinese history and Chinese culture; the Chinese language gradually replaced the English language as the medium of instruction and for use in official documents. These adjustments were not made without hesitancy or protest. There were missionaries who feared that the Christian character of the schools would be lost; others objected to government interference with private education. Government spokesmen justified their policy on the grounds that (1) religion should be free and not compulsory and (2) private schools were an integral part of a national program of education and should be governed by the same fundamental objectives as public schools. On the whole, the missionary as well as the Chinese leaders of the Christian movement have not had much occasion to regret the major changes introduced at this time. By identifying themselves with the national cause, the Christian schools and colleges found themselves in an even stronger position for public service. They found ways and means other than compulsory religion to perpetuate the Christian atmosphere of their institutions. Most important of all, there emerged a strong Chinese leadership which enabled the entire Christian movement to increase in importance and in prestige.

Party Education.   In setting up a system of government controlled by a single political party, the Nationalists had been greatly influenced by their Russian advisers. It is not surprising, therefore, that the new regime seized upon education as a medium for propagating the ideology of the party, namely, the Kuomintang. Theoretically, the purpose of civic instruction at this stage of political tutelage (see p. 526) was to acquaint the people with the nature of the transitional stage of the revolution and to teach them the meaning of their democratic rights in order to prepare them for intelligent political participation and the acceptance of civic responsibilities under the constitutional government that was eventually to be evolved. Actually, the program required of the schools was one of indoctrination in the ideology of the Kuomintang. Dr. Sun Yat-sen had by this time been idealized as the founder of the party. Every Monday morning, schools all over the country were required to hold a memorial service, for which a standard ceremony was prescribed. The ceremony consisted of group homage to the portrait of Dr. Sun, salute of the national and the party flag, and public reading of the will of Dr. Sun. After this brief ceremony, the hour might be used for an address or announcements and conducted as an ordinary school convocation. This weekly ceremony was required of all schools from 1928 to 1947, when a relaxation of Kuomintang control was decided upon as a preliminary step to the actual inauguration of constitutional government.

The portrait of Dr. Sun Yat-sen was displayed in all school auditoriums. "Party Principles" was a required subject of the curriculum on all levels. The content of the course was drawn from the writings of Dr. Sun and commentaries on his ideology. All pupils were to become thoroughly familiar with *San Min Chu I* and with Dr. Sun's plans for the regeneration and modernization of China.

The Nationalists had risen to power with the help of the students, who responded with enthusiasm to the cause of nationalism, democracy, and livelihood. Organized student activities had paved the way for Nationalist victory and many young students applied for membership in the Kuomintang to become active workers for the revolutionary cause. In enforcing a program of party education, the Kuomintang had hoped to increase student support. Unfortunately, the indoctrination did not produce the desired results. Perhaps there is something in the Chinese temperament that reacts against indoctrination of this kind. At any rate, students who were compelled to study "Party Principles" in the elementary school, then again in the junior and senior middle schools, only to have to go through the same process in college, became sick and tired of the repetition. Many a young adolescent cautioned against Communism and Communist propaganda took to reading Karl Marx and related literature. Others attended the required classes without paying any attention to the lectures and the assigned readings. Even before the formal abandonment of Kuomintang control of the schools, the program of party education had become so dilute and its enforcement so lax that it had even ceased being a serious nuisance to students and school administrators.

Educational Planning. Until the advent of the Nationalist regime, political conditions were not conducive to the formulation of long-range plans for educational development. Owing to lack of planning, the provision of educational facilities had not been guided by the actual needs of the nation. Whereas many areas had hardly any schools and colleges, a few cities had so many institutions concentrated in one small area that there was much wasteful duplication and competition. There was no balanced development of the various types of schools needed by the nation, and there was great neglect of technical education and vocational education. In undertaking a study of national needs, the Nationalist government sought the advice of a mission of experts appointed by the International Committee on Intellectual Cooperation of the League of Nations. Originally composed of four educators,[12] the mission traveled and studied conditions in China in 1931; it then submitted a report[13] embodying important recommendations. The mission made specific proposals for a planned program of national education under the direction of the Ministry of Education, the authority of which was to be strengthened.[14] Deploring the "remarkable, not to say alarming, consequences of the excessive influence of the American model on Chinese education,"[15] the mission urged a more careful study of China's own needs and conditions. It recommended measures to bring about a more balanced development in the various areas of the country and among the various levels of schools.[16] In regard to teacher training, the mission again criticized the influence of the American example, declaring that there was an overemphasis on pedagogy, producing teachers "who

[12] Carl H. Becker, once Prussian Minister of Education; M. Falski, director of the Primary Education Department at the Polish Ministry of Education, Warsaw; P. Langevin, professor of the Collège de France, Paris; and R. H. Tawney, professor of the University of London.

[13] C. H. Becker and others, *The Reorganization of Education in China* (Paris: League of Nations Institute of Intellectual Cooperation, 1932).

[14] *Ibid.*, pp. 48-49.

[15] *Ibid.*, p. 25.

[16] *Ibid.*, p. 61.

know how to teach what they do not know themselves";[17] it recommended the European way of laying more stress on the subject matter to be taught. The report of the mission exerted a great influence on the policies of the Chinese government in the ensuing years. It may be noted that as need for national planning and a strong central authority to direct national education became increasingly evident, the Nationalist government turned increasingly to European countries for advice and guidance. Although the external features of the school system continued to be those of the American 6-3-3 plan, the spirit of administration and the organization of curriculums were moving more in the direction of the European model, particularly the French and the German.

Educational Progress under the Nationalist Government. The years preceding the outbreak of war in 1937 constituted an era of reconstruction and progress. Education made rapid advances. The Nationalist government supported education more generously than had any preceding government and for the first time the public schools were assured of financial support and even greater stability than some of the private schools. The national universities attracted faculties and students of the highest caliber, and their prestige was rising so fast that they were being recognized as among the best institutions of the land. Although centralized administration was not free of defects and was often abused in the hands of incompetent administrators, the national control of education did for the first time bring into being a national system of education guided by clear objectives and thoroughly imbued with a new national consciousness. Educational planning on a national scale was now possible and had actually been undertaken. Sizable funds were being appropriated by the government to aid and encourage private schools as well as public, and assured financial subsidies made it easy to inaugurate such plans as the literacy campaign, adult education, health education, audio-visual education, etc.

ORGANIZATION OF THE SCHOOL SYSTEM UNDER THE NATIONALIST GOVERNMENT

Compulsory Education. Although the principle of universal compulsory education had been accepted for many years, the realiza-

[17] *Ibid.,* p. 119.

tion of the ideal had been frustrated by political instability and financial limitations. The 1935 plan for achievement of universal education gave rise to more genuine hopes than the paper plans of the past, because there was for the first time a stable central government to carry out the plan and the government had set aside definite funds to subsidize provincial and local projects and also to conduct training classes for teachers and administrators. That the plan was really workable in the light of actual conditions was proved by the notable progress made in the first two years. Total enrollment in primary schools increased from 8,839,000 in 1928-1929 to 21,435,-353, which constituted approximately 43 percent of the school-age population, in 1937. If the progress had not been interrupted by the outbreak of war, the plan might have come close to meeting original expectations.

It must be pointed out that educational development was very uneven in the various parts of the country. Provinces less directly involved in civil wars of the past and provinces with larger financial resources advanced more rapidly in education. Shansi led the nation, with more than 75 percent of school-age children in primary schools, and such provinces as Kweichow and Hupeh lagged behind, with only 5-8 percent in school.

Elementary Education. Preschool education was given considerable attention in contemporary literature, but in actual practice it remained in an undeveloped stage. Kindergartens admitted children between four and six. There were private as well as public kindergartens, and there were kindergartens established by normal schools and universities for experimentation and demonstration; but the total number was relatively small. Nursery schools were even fewer.[18]

The basic laws provided for equal educational opportunity for boys and girls and for six years of basic education for children between six and twelve. Elementary education was supposed to be free, but financial needs often made it necessary to charge small fees. The first four years of elementary education were known as the lower primary school and the next two years as the higher primary. Four years of lower primary education were supposed to be compulsory. The elementary curriculum, fixed by centralized administration, consisted of civics, hygiene, physical education, Chinese

[18] Preschool education has been given more attention under the Communist regime.

language, social studies, nature studies, arithmetic, manual work, art, and music. Elementary-school teachers were poorly paid; their salaries averaged one fifth of those of secondary-school teachers and less than one tenth of those of university professors. Naturally, able men and women were not attracted by elementary teaching and the teachers were not well trained.

The curriculum and methodology of the elementary school were characterized by formalism. The acquisition of subject matter was given central emphasis. Bookishness dominated the entire system and the elementary school was no exception. There was far too little pupil activity in the classroom. Progressive methods and activity programs had no chance under this system of centralized administration. Very little of the educational theory taught in normal schools had been translated into practice in elementary teaching.

Elementary education was also handicapped by a scarcity of children's literature. Textbooks for the elementary school were very poorly written, abstract, and uninteresting. And on the whole, children who learned to read in school had very little reading material accessible to them other than their formal textbooks.

It must be noted that the teachers in many primary schools and village schools under private or semipublic auspices had had no normal training at all. The old type of tutor, common before the arrival of modern education, was by no means extinct. In the entire school system, primary education tended to be treated as a step-child and primary teachers were accorded little respect and little more than subsistence wages.

Secondary Education.   For children aged twelve to eighteen, there were three types of secondary school: the middle school, the normal school, and the vocational school. The junior middle school and the senior middle school, each offering a three-year course, were in some cases established separately, in others combined in one institution.[19] Separate schools for boys and girls were maintained wherever possible. Examinations for admission to the junior middle school were open to graduates of the elementary school or pupils of equal standing; likewise, graduates of the junior middle school or pupils

[19] Reducing the middle-school course from six to five years was proposed in recent years. See the *China Handbook, 1937-1945* (New York: The Macmillan Company, 1947), p. 327.

of equal standing were qualified to take entrance examinations for the senior school. Pupils paid tuition fees and library fees. The curriculum of the junior middle school consisted of civics, physical education, boy- or girl-scout training, hygiene, Chinese, English, mathematics, botany, zoology, chemistry, physics, history, geography, manual arts, drawing, and music. The senior middle school continued these studies, adding logic and substituting military training (for boys) or first-aid nursing (for girls) for scout work. The curriculum was determined by the Ministry of Education and allowed no electives. In recent years, efforts were made to stress the teaching of science. It is to be noted that English was a required subject through the entire middle-school course.

Although only a small number of the pupils actually went on to college, the middle school was very much dominated by the college or university. Not only was the curriculum determined by the requirements of college preparation but the teaching was influenced by college and university methods. The lecture method was commonly used; teachers prided themselves on the use of college notes and even college books. The result was an abstract and bookish type of education.

Elementary-school teachers were trained in the normal school, which admitted graduates of the junior middle school or pupils of equal standing for a three-year course. The curriculum was fixed by the Ministry of Education; pupils were admitted by entrance examination. Separate schools or separate classes for boys and girls were the rule. With few exceptions, all normal schools were established by the government. No tuition fees were charged; in many cases, free board was provided. After graduation, pupils were obligated to teach for at least three years before undertaking further study or taking up another occupation.

The subjects of the normal-school curriculum were civics, physical activities, hygiene, Chinese, mathematics, geography, history, biology, chemistry, physics, logic, manual arts, art, music, principles of education, educational psychology, teaching materials and methods in the elementary school, elementary-school administration, educational measurements and statistics, practice teaching, military training (for boys) or first-aid nursing (for girls).

There were two types of vocational schools: the junior vocational school, which offered a course of one year or three years to elementary-school graduates who passed the entrance examinations, and the senior vocational school, which provided either a three-year course for qualified graduates of the junior middle school or a six-year (sometimes a five-year) course for graduates of the elementary school. The main types of vocational schools were the agricultural, the industrial, the commercial, and the home-economics schools. In an attempt to counteract the traditional dependence on books and tendency toward empty verbalism, the regulations stipulated that vocational schools should strive to maintain a close tie with agriculture, industry, or commerce in order to facilitate arrangements whereby pupils might gain practical experience through actual participation and part-time work.

Vocational schools did not develop at the same rate as the middle schools. Retarded development of agriculture, industry, and commerce was a handicap. Another obstacle was the traditional preference for white-collar activities and for the more academic type of education. Much of the old concept of education as a gateway to a life relieved of all forms of manual labor remained and created a general preference for the more academic program of the middle school. Consequently, the growth of the middle schools far outdistanced the growth of the other types of secondary schools. In 1930, it was found that 70 percent of all the secondary schools were middle schools, 20 percent were normal schools, and only 10 percent were vocational schools. To offset this tendency, the Ministry set aside special funds for subsidizing vocational education and ordered in 1933 that the educational budget of provinces and municipalities must be so apportioned that 40 percent of the funds would be spent on middle schools, 25 percent on normal schools, and 35 percent on vocational schools.

Higher Education. There were three types of institutions of higher learning: the college, the university, and the technical or professional school. The college course consisted of four years, and a college might offer any of the courses recognized by the Ministry of Education, such as arts, science, law, education, etc. An institution comprising at least three recognized colleges was called a university, but one of the three had to be a college of science, agriculture, commerce, engineering, or medicine. The curriculum of each department, requirements for graduation, standards of admission, distribution of budget appropriations, qualifications of teachers, salaries and promotions, and the internal organization of committees and administrative officers were all prescribed by detailed regulations of the Ministry. The credit system was used, but the curriculums were much more specialized than those of the American undergraduate school. Departmentalization began in the first year and the freshman had to choose not only his college but also a specific department in the college. The required studies in a major subject added up to sixty to seventy credits, about half of the credit requirements for the bachelor's degree. Coeducation was the rule in colleges and universities.

Professional study of education was carried on in departments of education within colleges or in colleges of education in universities. In recent years the Ministry of Education favored the establishment of normal colleges for the preparation of secondary-school teachers. A normal college could be an independent institution or a part of a national university. It offers a five-year course providing for a balance between the study of subjects to be taught and the study of education and psychology. Given free tuition, board, and lodging, the students were obligated after graduation to teach for at least five years.

Like the college, the technical school admitted graduates of senior middle schools or students of equal standing by competitive entrance examinations. The course was two or three years in length. A school might offer one curriculum or more in engineering (such as electrical engineering, chemical engineering, surveying, etc.), agriculture, commerce, or some other field approved by the Ministry. Again, all details of curriculum, teaching, finance, and administration were prescribed.

The colleges and universities have exercised a great influence on Chinese life. The observation of the League of Nations Mission in this connection is worth noting.

In the last twenty years university education in China had advanced with extraordinary rapidity. The most superficial observer must be struck by the influence which it has exercised upon the life and thought of important strata of the population. Distinguished scholars have received part, or all, of their higher education in Chinese universities, and, in their turn, have taught in them; the personnel of the Civil Service, central and local, and of teachers in secondary schools—both key professions—is largely recruited from them. Their contribution to the advancement of knowledge has, in certain fields of study, been of genuine significance. It is not an exaggeration to say that modern China is, to a large and increasing extent, the creation of her universities.[20]

In pursuance of a policy recommended by the League Mission to stress quality rather than quantity, the Nationalist government took effective measures either to discontinue or to raise the standards of weak institutions, encouraged merging or close cooperation to avoid wasteful duplication, and set aside special funds to strengthen the private (including the mission) as well as the public institutions. Even with new requirements of minimum standards in finance, equipment, curriculum, etc., higher education continued to grow rapidly. At the end of World War II, China had a total of 145 institutions of higher learning of various types as compared with 108 in 1937 and seventy-four in 1928. Enrollment in these institutions increased from 41,922 in 1937 to 69,959 in 1945.[21] No doubt a good deal of this expansion was brought about at the expense of quality. Without libraries and laboratory facilities, refugee institutions in the interior barely managed to keep classwork going and to avoid a complete educational blackout. The economic poverty of teachers and students did not help to produce an intellectual atmosphere. There was therefore a noticeable let-down in academic standards. After the end of the war, the raising of standards was recognized as among the most pressing needs in higher education, but with continued political instability and increased economic chaos, it was not possible to bring about any real improvement in the quality of scholarship.

The promotion of science and technology was a major policy in higher education. Not only were the science colleges and departments given increased official encouragement and financial subsidies but specific administrative measures were adopted to restrict student enrollment in the nontechnical departments. The Ministry was averse to the establishment of new departments or colleges in the nontechnical fields; it set arbitrary limits to the number of new students to be admitted each year to such departments and colleges as were already in existence. Government scholarships for foreign

[20] C. H. Becker and others, *op. cit.*, p. 145.
[21] *China Handbook, 1937-1945,* pp. 328 and 329.

students were limited to students of science and technology. Increasing emphasis on science and technology brought about a growth of student interest in such subjects. The proportion of students enrolled in the technical departments of the colleges and universities rose rapidly from about one fourth in 1930 to one half of the total in 1940.

Approved universities could offer postgraduate courses in arts, science, law, education, commerce, agriculture, engineering, or medicine—the same fields approved for colleges. Each field was subdivided into departments. A full-fledged graduate school had to have departments in at least three fields. In 1944, the Ministry reported the existence of forty-nine graduate schools, forty-three of which were attached to universities and six to colleges. There were eighty-five departments in these schools; sixty-eight of them were in national universities or colleges and seventeen in private institutions.[22]

The establishment of research institutes was an important development in higher education. The most outstanding research body was the national academy of research established by the Ministry of Education in 1928 under the name Academia Sinica. Research fellows and associates carried on their pursuits under the various institutes maintained by the academy, such as institutes of physics, chemistry, engineering, geology, astronomy, meteorology, mathematics, psychology, history and philology, the social sciences.

Social Education.   Social education referred to a wide variety of forms of adult education and included not only schools and classes but museums, libraries, recreation centers, radio, educational films, and many other facilities for increasing literacy and the social intelligence of the masses. Although the first objective of this type of education was to combat illiteracy, it was also deeply concerned with civic education of the masses, improvement of social manners, betterment of home life, and intelligent solution of the practical problems of life. Since it embraced many kinds of informal education, its methods were not stereotyped: traveling libraries, dramatic troupes, mass singing, and many other new methods and facilities not yet used in school education were widely used in programs of social education. The use of phonetic symbols was urged as an aid to learning the characters of the Chinese language.

[22] *Ibid.*, p. 332.

The Mass Education Movement.   Perhaps the fundamental educational problem in China is that of illiteracy. It is estimated that 70-80 percent of the population is still illiterate. Among early experiments in the literacy movement, one of the best known outside of China began at the time of World War I, when James Y. C. Yen and other Y.M.C.A. secretaries organized literacy classes for Chinese laborers in France. The experiment was continued in China after the war under the auspices of the Y.M.C.A. until a National Association of Mass Education was organized in 1923. In the face of practically unlimited needs in a large country, it was considered advisable to choose small centers for experimental programs. One of the best organized programs was conducted in the district of Ting-Hsien, in Hupeh Province. Partly because some of the funds came from American sources, this project is better known in the United States than any other. With a staff of two hundred persons, many of whom were well-trained specialists, the project concerned itself not only with the literacy campaign but with the betterment of rural life in its varied aspects—with the introduction of modern methods of agricultural production, with the organization of cooperatives, with medical care and health education, and with practical problems of self-government. After the Japanese occupation in 1937, the project was transferred to selected areas in unoccupied China. A growing realization that mass education must be a part of a larger program of rural betterment led to the establishment in 1940 under government auspices of the National College of Rural Reconstruction for the purpose of training specialized personnel for the twin movement of mass education and rural reconstruction.

There were other important projects in mass education under the leadership of well-known pioneers. Deserving of special mention was the work of Tao Chih-Hsing, whose "relay teacher" and "little teacher" movement not only encouraged children and adult learners to pass on to others what they were learning but also produced a vital program of education closely integrated with life and the social environment.[23] Another important contribution to mass education was the work of educational psychologists who used scientific

[23] H. C. Tao, "China," in I. L. Kandel, ed., *Educational Yearbook of the International Institute, 1938* (New York: Teachers College, Columbia University, 1939), p. 116.

methods to determine the most commonly used characters of the Chinese language and compiled lists of everyday vocabulary which became the basis of simplified readers using no more than about one thousand characters. Finally, mass education was facilitated by the Literary Revolution, which unified the spoken and the written forms of the language and produced a literature much more accessible to the common man. Instead of the difficult literary style of the classics, the new schools in China, for children as well as for adults, began to teach the vernacular form known as the *paihua*, which makes is possible to communicate ideas by means of a simpler vocabulary.

Citizens' Schools. In 1940, the Ministry of Education formulated a comprehensive plan of adult education to be integrated with the program of universal education for children. The plan aimed to obliterate adult illiteracy within five years by graduated stages. In the first two years, a citizens' school was to be established for every three *pao*, which is a unit of local organization consisting of about one hundred families; the hope was to bring at least one year of schooling to 60 percent of the school-age children and 30 percent of the adult illiterate population. In the next two years, facilities were to be extended to provide a citizens' school for every two *pao* and schooling for 80 percent of the school-age children and 50 percent of the illiterate adults. It was hoped that by 1945 there would be a citizens' school for each *pao*, with schooling for 90 percent of the school-age children and 60 percent of the illiterate adults. Each citizens' school was to establish separate departments for children and for adults; no fees were to be charged. Again, the plan seemed excellent on paper, but fell short of actual achievement on account of unfortunate political and economic conditions. The Minister of Education reported optimistically in 1946 that "most provinces . . . [had] attained the goal of setting up one school in each *pao*," but he hastened to add that "the quality of the schools . . . is not quite up to standard" and that the Ministry was inaugurating a second five-year plan with particular attention to "those provinces and municipalities which have not fully carried out the first plan, which calls for the establishment of one school in each *pao*."[24]

[24] Chu Chia Hua, "Education," *The China Magazine* (New York: The Chinese News Service), Vol. XVI, No. 3-4, July-August 1946, p. 55.

EDUCATION IN THE PEOPLE'S REPUBLIC OF CHINA

The fundamental principles and policies of the People's Republic of China are stated in the Common Program, a document of sixty articles which serves the purpose of a constitution and is held up as the supreme law of the land, to which all must pledge wholehearted allegiance. Chapter V of the Common Program, entitled "Cultural and Educational Policy," contains the following articles:

Article 41. The culture and education of the People's Republic of China shall be New Democratic—national, scientific, and popular. The main tasks of the People's Government in cultural and educational work shall be the raising of the cultural level of the people, the training of personnel for national construction work, the eradicating of feudal, compradore, and fascist ideology, and the developing of the ideology of service to the people.

Article 42. Love of the fatherland, love of the people, love of labor, love of science, and care of public property shall be promoted as the public spirit of all nationals of the People's Republic of China.

Article 43. Efforts shall be made to develop the natural sciences in order to serve industrial, agricultural, and national defense construction. Scientific discoveries and inventions shall be encouraged and rewarded and scientific knowledge shall be disseminated among the people.

Article 44. The application of a scientific-historical viewpoint to the study and interpretation of history, economics, politics, culture, and international affairs shall be promoted. Outstanding works of social science shall be encouraged and rewarded.

Article 45. Literature and art shall be promoted to serve the people, to awaken their political consciousness, and to enhance their enthusiasm for labor. Outstanding works of literature and art shall be encouraged and rewarded. The people's drama and cinema shall be developed.

Article 46. The method of education of the People's Republic of China shall be the unification of theory and practice. The People's Government shall reform the old educational system, subject matter and teaching methods in a planned, systematic manner.

Article 47. In order to meet the extensive requirements of revolutionary and national construction work, universal education shall be carried out, secondary and higher education shall be strengthened, technical education shall be stressed, the education of workers during their spare time and that of cadres at their posts shall be strengthened, and revolutionary political education shall be accorded to both young- and old-type intellectuals. All this is to be done in a planned and systematic manner.

Article 48. National physical culture shall be promoted. Public health and medical work shall be expanded and attention shall be paid to the protection of the health of mothers, infants, and children.

Article 49. Freedom of reporting truthful news shall be safeguarded. The utilization of the press for slander, for undermining the interests of the state and the people, and for provoking world war shall be prohibited. The people's radio and publication work shall be developed. Attention shall be paid to publishing popular books and journals beneficial to the people.

Political Education. Education and politics are considered inseparable. The objectives of education are derived from the nature of the "new democracy." A primary duty of education, therefore, is to eradicate the old ideology and to implant the new. The old ideology is described as "feudal, compradore, and fascist"; the new, described as "the ideology of service to the people," is the Marxist-materialist system of thought and action as interpreted by Lenin and Stalin and applied to Chinese conditions. "Cleansing the mind" is a term frequently used to indicate the imperative need of inculcating the Marxist-Leninist ideology to produce ardent supporters of the new regime. In the schools, the process of "cleansing" consists of purging the curriculum of all content characteristic of Kuomintang rule, eliminating such subjects as the "Three People's Principles," forbidding such bourgeois-feudal organization as the boy scouts and girl scouts, and banishing such reactionary attitudes as skepticism regarding the friendliness and leadership of the Soviet Union. All students returning from study abroad must undergo such a process of "cleansing"; those returning from America are given especial attention to make sure that they cleanse their minds of the poisonous effects of living under the shadow of American imperialism.

Political education is of primary concern to the Communist leaders because they have always maintained that it is far better to win support by persuasion than by coercion. Coercion is not ruled out, but it is held in abeyance while persuasion is given a chance. The method of persuasion is the method of propaganda, of indoctrination, of education. In fact, education cannot be distinguished from indoctrination and propaganda. All over China today there is a vast "learning movement." The slogan is to "learn, learn, and again learn." To learn means to become familiar with the Common Program and related documents prescribing the organization of the People's Government on national, provincial, and local levels. To learn is to be unalterably opposed to the reactionary Kuomintang and to all "remaining vestiges of feudalism." To learn is to understand the policies of the new government and to support them with enthusiasm. To learn is to adopt the new vocabulary of the new democracy, to talk in terms of "democratic dictatorship" and "democratic centralism." To learn is to help in whatever tasks the government has set as the most important goal of the day: it may be to subscribe for victory bonds, it may be to enlist public support of the anti-inflation measures, it may be to make specific contributions to a public health campaign, it may be a study of the land-reform program. Above all, to learn is to accept the basic ideas of Marxism-Leninism, to realize the significance of the proletarian revolution, to appreciate the glory and the greatness of the Soviet Union, to cherish friendship and "brotherly love" for the Soviet Union and its people, and to "see through" the hypocrisy and aggressive design of American imperialism.

Changes in School Education. Two major tasks are to be performed by the school: political education and education for national reconstruction. Marxist materialism, the "scientific interpretation of history," the contributions of labor to civilization, the development of the class struggle—these are some of the recurrent topics of political education on all levels. The school, it is said, should make every effort to develop in the pupils the "five loves" mentioned in Article 42 of the Common Program, and the new school textbooks contain lessons specifically designed to inculcate "love of the fatherland, love of the people, love of labor, love of science, and love of public property."[25] A fond topic of political education is evolution,

[25] Theodore Hsi-En Chen, "New China: New Texts," *Current History,* Vol. XIX (December 1950), pp. 321-327. Also, by the same author, "Red Education in China," *Current History,* Vol. XIX (July 1950), pp. 14-20.

considered a key concept in Marxist materialism. In out-of-school indoctrination classes and "learning sessions" as well as in schools, instructors repeat again and again the story of man's evolution from the ape. This is considered an essential first step toward developing the "scientific point of view." Since most of the instructors are members of the Communist party more noted for party loyalty than for educational background, the story they tell must be simple and crude. Sometimes they are confronted with baffling questions as to how the transformation took place and why the monkeys in the zoo do not change into human beings, but in each case they religiously adhere to the stereotyped explanation that the ape became human because it descended from the tree and learned to walk with its legs and use its hands in labor; and the explanation always concludes with the moral that man became what he is through labor and therefore must continue to engage in labor.

About one tenth of the instructional hours in the secondary schools are devoted to political education. In the colleges and universities, the required subjects of the curriculum include "The New Democracy," "Dialectical Materialism," "The History of Social Development," and "Political Economy." Besides, students in all schools and colleges must take time out for special learning sessions on whatever political issue seems to demand public understanding and support. In the winter of 1950, regular class sessions were often suspended in order to hold sessions for the intensive study of American imperialism and discussion of specific ways to oppose American aggression and to extend aid to the people of Korea in their resistance against American aggression. In addition to such campus activities, students are asked to help in propaganda campaigns and to organize themselves as propaganda teams to carry the official message to the masses.

The second duty of the school is to train personnel for the tasks of national reconstruction. This means in the lower schools an emphasis on labor and production and in the higher schools especial attention to science and technical subjects which are likely to make direct contributions to the problems of national reconstruction. Efforts are made to encourage the study of science not only because of its practical value in production and reconstruction but also because it contributes to the materialistic view of the universe so fundamental to Marxism. The People's Government has conceived an ambitious program of production and industrialization. Whereas in the political field the slogan is to "learn, learn, and again learn," in the economic field it is to "produce, produce, and produce." The very organization of the State Administration Council of the Central People's Government testifies to the importance attached to production and industrialization. In addition to the Ministries of Finance, Trade, and Labor, separate ministries have been set up to control various aspects of national reconstruction: the Ministries of Heavy Industry, Fuel Industry, Textile Industry, Food Industry, Light Industry, Railways, Posts and Telecommunications, Communications, Agriculture, Water Conservancy, and Forestry and Land Reclamation. The school system is charged with the responsibility of producing trained personnel for each of these fields.

New methods of instruction are being introduced. Pupils are encouraged to engage in productive activities, from the raising of vegetable gardens on school grounds to working in factories. Classroom study, it is urged, must be closely linked with actual conditions and problems in Chinese society. Theory must always be integrated with practice. On July 28, 1950, after a national conference on higher education, the Ministry of Education promulgated the new regulations governing the establishment and management of institutions of higher learning. One of the most emphasized principles in the regulations is the unity of theory and practice. Communist thinking is extremely distrustful of theory which has no influence on practice and no direct bearing on action. Educators are being warned not to indulge in theories removed from actual practice. To keep in close touch with realities, teachers are urged to take their students on field trips to farms, factories, and various social institutions. Students and teachers in the technical subjects are encouraged to learn the use of tools and machinery. They should vitalize their classroom study by actual examples taken from factories, farms, and business enterprises. There is certainly no room for any form of "ivory tower" concept of education, for all students and teachers are constantly being reminded of their obligations to render concrete service to society and to the people.

Political education and education for national reconstruction can be and have been broadened to include education for national defense. Contributions of education to national defense were given increasing emphasis after the start of the Korean War, in 1950.

Students and teachers were asked not only to devote time to the study of American aggression and ways of combating it but also to participate in propaganda campaigns to arouse the public to enlist for service in the army. In the winter of 1950 a nation-wide drive was conducted to enlist students for the new military institutes and army cadre-training schools established to bolster national defense.

School Life. One of the most important innovations in school life is the emphasis on group participation in the name of democracy. School administration is "democratized" by the organization of administrative councils in which representatives of students and workmen are voting members on an equal plane with faculty representatives. In universities, janitors as well as students are thus given a voice in such major university policies as budget, curriculum, and personnel. The "democratic way" is also expressed in all kinds of meetings and discussion groups. The Communists have almost made a fetish of meetings and group effort. Students not only attend meetings to discuss political topics but are encouraged to study in groups. It is claimed that this practice in collective living will overcome the shortcomings of selfish individualism so marked in China of the past.

On the whole, the encouragement of meetings and discussion groups has yielded satisfying results to the leaders of the new regime. Their formula of "democratic centralism" is "discussion by the many, decision by the few." While the dictatorial power of the few remains undiminished, open discussion by many groups through the country serves to give a semblance of democracy. Moreover, in schools and out of schools, discussion meetings are under the watchful supervision of Communist-party members and cadres, who see to it that the party line and official policy are upheld by majority "vote." Thus is created a general climate in which dissenters are not likely to raise their voices to such a degree as to obstruct the official program. Thus is also created a form of "public opinion" in support of official policies.

Group meetings have also proved to be a good medium for a device of control known as "criticism and self-criticism." The Communists have for many years practiced this method as a means of enforcing discipline and now they have introduced it to the entire population. Meetings for criticism and self-criticism are held not only in schools but in government offices, factories, villages, and other places. At such a meeting, individuals are encouraged to criticize each other, to point out errors in thought and in action, to acknowledge mistakes and make public confessions. Among the most important mistakes criticized and confessed are the exploitation of fellow human beings, misguided distrust of the Communist party, subservience to the Kuomintang and imperialist America, and blind adherence to feudalistic practices. It is evident that such public criticisms and confessions exercise a powerful pressure on individuals. Once a person has confessed his past connections with reactionaries and imperialists and publicly declared his intention to serve the cause of the new democracy, he feels compelled by group pressure to guide his overt actions at least by his declarations. The watchful eyes of fellow men can at times be a more effective restraining influence than the secret police.

New Agencies. Anxious to get quick results, the new authorities have established several types of new schools to serve more directly the urgent needs of the People's Republic. The people's university, training schools for cadres, and special schools for peasants and workers are among the institutions established in 1950. In general, they may be divided into several broad categories: (1) schools with main emphasis on political indoctrination, to produce cadres and propagandists; (2) schools for specific purposes, such as training for work in the land-reform program; (3) schools specializing in the sciences and technical subjects, for the training of technicians, medical assistants, army doctors, etc.; (4) schools with especial emphasis on the study of the Russian language and culture; (5) schools for peasants and workers rich in revolutionary experience but deficient in formal schooling. Most of the new institutions offer short-term, abbreviated courses. Even the new "universities" graduate students after an intensive course of four to six months. In line with the policy of the Communist party to elevate the position of the proletariat, the regular colleges and universities have been ordered to increase the percentage of peasants and workers among their students.

Reference has been made to propaganda and indoctrination agencies outside the schools. Literature and art are coordinated with the political program and expected to draw their themes from the revolutionary activities of the day, such as the land reform, the fight against American imperialism, etc. The radio, the theater, the motion picture, cartoons, comic strips—these and many other media are being used to arouse public opinion, to explain government policies, and to enlist public support for various projects such as anti-epidemic campaigns, anti-inflation measures, new tax policies, and the purchase of government bonds. Informal education, or social education outside the schools, is given as much attention as formal education, if not more. The dance, group singing, mass meetings under direction, and other methods of "social education" testify to a new importance attached to adult education.

Since propaganda and indoctrination can be most effective among a literate population, the liquidation of illiteracy becomes imperative. People must be taught to read the posters, the banners, the handbills, and words on the cartoons. More and more people are being taught to read. Needless to say, instruction in reading is always accompanied by political education. With the pressing need of producing a literate population which can be more easily reached and influenced by propaganda and indoctrination, with increasing numbers of peasants and workers given instruction for more effective revolutionary work, with literacy stressed as a part of army training, with constant emphasis on arousing the masses and creating a favorable "public opinion," there is no doubt that greater effort than ever before is being made to reduce illiteracy and that the concerted effort of formal and informal agencies of education and propaganda is bringing the rudiments of reading and writing within the reach of many people heretofore denied such opportunities.

Private Education.   Private education is definitely on the decline. At the beginning of the new regime, it was emphasized that the government did not yet have the financial ability to provide all the needed educational facilities and would therefore encourage private individuals and groups to continue their institutions and programs. There never was any doubt that private education would be strictly controlled and that all private schools must assume the full responsibility of political education and ideological indoctrination. The new state controls all aspects of individual and group life, and education is no exception. Except for the source of financial support, there is to be no difference at all between private and public schools. Even the finance and budget are subject to government control, and all personnel must be officially approved. Democratic centralism in the People's Republic means that the part must be subordinate to the whole, the minority must yield to the majority, and lower levels of authority are subject to the control of higher levels, with the highest authority centralized in the national organs. With pressure toward conformity and uniformity, private education does not find itself in a healthful climate.

The most important private schools and colleges in China have been the Christian schools and colleges. The Christian educators were much more hopeful of a minimum of interference at the beginning of 1950 than at the end of the year. Theoretically the principle of religious freedom is recognized, but too often freedom means the freedom to attack religion as superstition and an "opiate of thought." At any rate, the Christian institutions were required to teach Marxist materialism and to take part in all officially sponsored propaganda campaigns and indoctrination programs. In the summer of 1950, Christian leaders were told by the highest authorities that they should try to wean themselves from the financial support and nurture of the foreign missions abroad. The government promised to aid in this movement, and it was generally understood that government subsidies would mean more rigid government control. From the beginning, relations between the new government and the Catholic church were more hostile than those with the Protestant groups. In October 1950 the Catholic Fu Jen University, in Peking, was placed under government control and turned into a government institution. The ultimate fate of the Protestant institutions arrived sooner than expected, hastened by the deterioration of political relations between the People's Republic of China and the United States. The Central People's Government issued an order on December 30,1950, to freeze American assets in China, in retaliation against an order of the American government to freeze the assets of Communist China in America. After this, events followed one another rapidly. In the ensuing weeks and months, the Christian schools and colleges, cut off from American financial support, became dependent on the government for subsidies. With the anti-American campaign being pushed feverishly all over the country, it was not difficult to create in the Christian institutions a vociferous demand to cut loose completely from American imperialism. Thus, in deference to "popular demand," the government moved to take over the Christian schools and colleges.

Summary. Although no proposal has yet been made to change the entire school system, fundamental changes have taken place in Chinese education. All education is firmly under the control of the state and closely coordinated with the ideology and the program of the state. Informal agencies of education are utilized to a greater extent than ever before and there is no difference in objectives between formal and informal education. Indoctrination and propaganda are prominent in both.

The new regime relies on education to inculcate the new ideology and to ensure popular support of the state. It considers universal education to be of first importance. Support of education will doubtless mean increasing appropriations from the state budget.

Emphasis on the development of a proletarian culture entails radical changes in the concept of education. The gap between the educated and the uneducated is being narrowed. The social prestige and privileges of the intellectual are decreasing just as the position of the working class is being elevated. The white-collared intellectual unable and unwilling to use his hands in labor is despised, and the academician is challenged to join the masses in tackling the pressing problems of the day. Education is expected to serve practical ends, to meet the needs of the state. Studies with immediate and direct application to the solution of practical problems are exalted and studies identified in the West with liberal education are being pushed aside as vague and unessential. The utilitarian trend in education will no doubt be strengthened. An interesting development growing out of the demand that education and culture be brought within the reach of the masses is a new campaign to simplify the written language. A new impetus has been given to the "Latinization movement" and to proposals to use phonetic symbols in place of characters. The *pai-hua* is used in official proclamations. In writing and in public addresses, a simple, direct style is favored. Since literature and art are instruments of propaganda and social education, the primary consideration must be to reach as many people as possible.

There is little prospect that the decline in academic standards that took place during World War II will be remedied in the near future. On the contrary, there are indications that educational standards may become even lower. For some time to come, major attention will be given to quantity rather than quality, to making education more nearly universal rather than making it more selective. To meet urgent needs, training courses are made as short as possible, so that personnel may be prepared within a few months for the tasks of political indoctrination and national reconstruction. The effort to bring more peasants and workers of revolutionary experience into institutions of higher learning has made it necessary to compromise with entrance requirements. Moreover, the frequent interruption of classes for propaganda campaigns and indoctrination sessions cannot be conducive to systematic study of regular subjects. Finally, in the new "democratic" atmosphere—in which students have a voice in school administration and the accusation of undemocratic practices by disgruntled individuals may bring very unfortunate consequences—teachers tend to avoid being strict and courting unpopularity by demanding too much of students.

Space permits only a passing mention of the growing influence of Soviet Russia on education and culture in the People's Republic of China. Soviet instructors and advisers arrive in increasing numbers. The Soviet techniques of farming, of industry, of engineering are taught as the most advanced techniques. Scholars are expected to accept the Soviet theories in psychology, biology, economics, and other fields. Soviet art and literature are being introduced in and out of schools. Soviet films are replacing American films. Students are beginning to study the Russian language increasingly; even the radio is used to broadcast lessons in the Russian language. More and more students will go to Russia to study. For decades American ideas and American examples have exerted a powerful influence on Chinese education, but today there is no doubt that the influence of Soviet Russia has become predominant and will grow in the immediate future.

BIBLIOGRAPHY

BECKER, C. H., and others, *The Reorganization of Education in China* (Paris: League of Nations Institute of Intellectual Cooperation, 1932). A good summary of the educational situation in China in 1932 and of the most important problems awaiting solution; emphasizes educational planning to suit national conditions.

BUCK, PEARL, *Tell the People* (New York: Institute of Pacific Relations, 1945). Tells the story of the Mass Education Movement and the work of James Y. C. Yen, based on interviews with the latter.

CHEN, THEODORE H. E., "The Educational Crisis in China," *Educational Administration and Supervision,* Vol. XXXIV, No. 8 (December 1948), pp. 468-478. Discusses concrete problems of postwar education and includes a section on Chinese students and politics.

Chia-o Yu Fa Ling (Educational Laws and Regulations) (Nanking: Ministry of Education, 1946).

DJUNG, L. D., *A History of Democratic Education in Modern China* (Shanghai: The Commercial Press, 1934). A comprehensive view of the school system, with emphasis on democratic trends.

FAIRBANK, JOHN KING, *The United States and China* (Cambridge: Harvard University Press, 1949). Chapters on old Chinese society contain a critical review of the old system of education; other parts of the book discuss modern intellectual currents and the relation of education to politics.

FENN, WILLIAM P., "Life, Liberty, and the Pursuit of Education in Chinese Universities," *Pacific Spectator,* Vol. II, No. 1 (Winter 1948), pp. 56-78. Discusses postwar problems of higher education: administration, curriculum, teachers, government control, etc.

FITZGERALD, C. P., *China, A Short Cultural History* (New York: D. Appleton-Century, Company, Inc., 1938). Excellent history of the growth of Chinese civilization, with emphasis on the cultural development of each period.

FREYN, HUBERT, *Chinese Education in the War* (Shanghai: Kelly and Walsh, 1940). A report on refugee institutions which moved from the coast to the interior.

HSIAO, THEODORE E., *The History of Modern Education in China* (Peking: Peking University Press, 1932). Historical survey of the growth of modern schools in China.

HSU, LEONARD, *Sun Yat-sen, His Political and Social Ideals* (Los Angeles: University of Southern California Press, 1933). An annotated source book of translated documents concerning the life and ideals of Dr. Sun Yat-sen and declarations of the Kuomintang.

HU SHIH, *The Chinese Renaissance* (Chicago: University of Chicago Press, 1934). Discusses new intellectual currents which provided a background for modern education.

Kuo, P. W., *The Chinese System of Public Education* (New York: Teachers College, Columbia University, 1915). A brief but clear history of public education in China from early times.

Latourette, Kenneth Scott, *The Chinese: Their History and Culture* (New York: The Macmillan Company, 1947). A good general reference on Chinese history and culture. The second volume contains sections on education in Chapters 14 and 19.

McNair, Harley Farnsworth, ed., *China* (Berkeley: University of California Press, 1946). A symposium on various elements of Chinese history and culture. Contains chapters on education, literature, thought, examinations, etc.

————, ed., *Voices from Occupied China* (Chicago: University of Chicago Press, 1944). A symposium on conditions in unoccupied China by a group of Chinese scholars. Contains a chapter on contemporary education.

Stuart, J. Leighton, "China," in I. L. Kandel, ed., *Educational Yearbook of the International Institute, 1933* (New York: Teachers College, Columbia University, 1934), pp. 301-350. An account of the growth and problems of missionary education in China.

Tao, H. C., "China," in I. L. Kandel, ed., *Educational Yearbook of the International Institute, 1938* (New York: Teachers College, Columbia University, 1939), pp. 103-118. Contains good sections on mass education and adult education.

Tong, Hollington K., ed., *China Handbook, 1937-1945* (New York: The Macmillan Company, 1947). Contains a good chapter on education and research, with a valuable section on higher education.

Winfield, Gerald F., *China: The Land and the People* (New York: William Sloane Associates, 1948). Good over-all view of China's basic problems and of constructive efforts to solve such problems. Contains two chapters on education specifically.

Zen, Sophia H. Chen, ed., *Symposium on Chinese Culture* (Shanghai: China Institute on Pacific Relations, 1931). Contains excellent chapters on philosophy, literature, education, social changes, etc.

18 · EDUCATION IN *Japan*

THEODORE HSI-EN CHEN

Japan at present consists of four major islands. Honshu is the main island; Hokkaido is to the north and Shikoku and Kyushu to the south. The total area amounts to only 148,000 square miles, and the population is approximately 83 million. The population density is extremely high—it averages over 560 persons per square mile. It should be remembered that the arable land is extremely limited, since the area is very mountainous; the ratio is approximately five persons per acre of arable land. The climate of Japan is in general a mild monsoon type, except on Hokkaido and on the Japan Sea slopes of the mountains, where snowfall is heavy. The deeply indented coast line provides many harbors. Situated in the center of an earthquake belt, Japan has experienced great disasters, such as that of 1923.

Japan uses over half of its agricultural land to produce rice, the chief food of the country; however, a variety of other crops, including barley, tea, and fruits, is also produced. Silk culture is also important for the farmers. Despite its agricultural past, Japan has become very heavily industrialized and has been the workshop of the Orient for textiles and all types of machinery. Up to the present Japan has been a feudal society with a large peasantry and with the control of great industrial enterprises concentrated in vast family trusts. Japan's mineral resources are extensive but are insufficient in terms of industrial needs. The transportation system is well organized. In fact, the country is characterized by a high degree of discipline and organization as regards government, religion, culture. industry, and education.

Before World War II the educational system was traditionally elite, and the illiteracy rate was under 10 percent. The aftermath of the war moved the country in the direction of democracy at least by statute, not only in government and economics but also in education. A major problem for the Japanese is the written language, with its thousands of characters; language reform is a very real necessity. The Japanese have shown great intellectual ability and vitality as well as a high degree of discipline—all of which they will need to overcome their difficult problems of lack of land, competition in the world market, and educational reform.

—A. H. M.

Japanese legends declare 660 B.C. to be the date of ascension of the Emperor Jimmu Tenno, the first human sovereign of the empire. Jimmu Tenno was revered as a direct descendant of the Sun Goddess and the first of an unbroken line of monarchs from early times to Hirohito, the present emperor. Although the legendary date of 660 B.C. was a "purely traditional date" questioned by historians, it became "officially considered to be the date of the foundation of the Empire of Japan and celebrated as such."[1] Repeated in school books and perpetuated by traditions, the legend of Jimmu Tenno and his divine descent exerted a powerful influence on Japanese thought and Japanese life.

Chinese Influences. In the development of her culture, Japan borrowed extensively from China. There was no written language in the country until the Chinese writing was introduced. In the fourth and fifth centuries A.D., Chinese culture flowed into Japan by way of Korea; Confucianism and Buddhism accompanied Chinese writing and the Confucianist classics came to be accepted as the main body of Japanese literature. Early Chinese legends were woven into accounts of Japanese history. In the seventh and eighth centuries, Japanese students studied in Chinese universities and brought back more Chinese ideas and influences. One author writes as follows:

[1] G. B. Sansom, *Japan: A Short Cultural History* (New York: Century Company, 1931), p. 27.

Throughout the seventh and eighth centuries, the influence of Chinese ideas, supplemented during the seventh century by those of Korea, was apparent in every phase of Japanese development . . . Chinese political institutions and Confucian philosophy were the guide and inspiration of the architects of the new social order. In matters of government and law, the dominance of Chinese ideas continued until the end of the eighth century. . . .

In non-political matters, Japan's debt to her continental neighbor was equally notable. From the days of Shotoku Taishi we find the imperial court patronizing architecture, sculpture, painting, and literature, in all of which continental models were followed. Similar encouragement was given to the development of ceramics, the casting of metals, and the various arts and crafts which the Chinese and the Koreans had introduced into the land. . . .

Even the name *Dai Nippon*, by which the empire is now known to its own people, and the western derivative *Japan* are of Chinese origin.[2]

Said Latourette: "The transformation of Japan by Chinese culture was one of the two greatest revolutions which that land has experienced. Indeed, it was more thoroughgoing than has been the second of the two, that produced by the impact of the occident in the nineteenth and twentieth centuries."[3] The Japanese, however, were not blind followers; they borrowed what suited their conditions and made adaptations to meet their own needs. In literature, in art, and in the crafts, they developed products which were distinctly Japanese and in many instances they improved upon the Chinese models. The Chinese written language was adapted to Japanese use by means of phonetic symbols to be used along with the Chinese characters. In government, many Chinese institutions were introduced, but the features of the Chinese system which were not in harmony with the aristocratic nature of Japanese society or the traditions of the imperial state were carefully excluded. "The imperial family had the continuation of the headship of the state as a permanent possession and not, as in China, on the basis of

[2] G. Nye Steiger, *A History of the Far East* (Boston: Ginn and Company, 1936), pp. 228 and 229.
[3] Kenneth Scott Latourette, *A Short History of the Far East* (New York: The Macmillan Company, 1946), p. 195.

its 'virtue.' "[4] The Chinese practice of civil-service examination was introduced, but, unlike the Chinese way of equal opportunity to all, the examinations were open to a limited few of the aristocratic class.

> In China, education aimed to train government officials and served at the same time as the basis of selection; in Japan, the old system of hereditary occupations was maintained and no official posts could be obtained simply on the basis of school records and examinations.[5]

Pre-Restoration Japan. Early Japanese life revolved around tribal clans ruled by patriarchal chiefs. By the beginning of the third century A.D., the Yamato clan had achieved dominance over the others; its chief was recognized as a direct descendant of the Sun Goddess and his suzerainty was recognized by most of the tribes in the central and southern islands of Japan. A centralized system of control was instituted in the seventh century; by this time an aristocratic society based on birth had been established and officialdom was definitely a prerogative of a small upper-class group. Although hereditary officialdom was abolished under the impetus of reforms based on Chinese examples, the examinations which led to public offices were not open to all classes and the imperial university was accessible only to sons of noble families. Already the tradition was established that the emperor was the titular head of the state but that the real power was exercised by officials who acted in the name of the emperor. The clans competed for this political power and the dominant clan monopolized political offices to the exclusion of other clans.

In the meantime, concentration of landownership in the hands of large holders brought about a feudal system in which the owners of estates were known as the *daimyo*. As feudal lords, the *daimyo* became virtually independent rulers; to protect their property and sustain their position, they retained armed guards who became a powerful force in Japanese society. Thus grew a warrior class, the *samurai*, who exalted "loyalty to the clan and the lord, physical

---

[4] *Ibid.*, p. 203.
[5] Kumaji Yoshida, "The Philosophy Underlying the National System of Education in Japan," in I. L. Kandel, ed., *Educational Yearbook of the International Institute, 1929* (New York: Teachers College, Columbia University, 1930), p. 436.

courage, and contempt of death. The sword became its badge and symbol."[6] When feuds among the *daimyo* led to armed conflict, the importance of the military class was enhanced.

In time, the military aristocracy reached out for political power. In 1192, the chieftain of the then dominant family of soldiers obtained for himself appointment by the emperor as a shogun, with authority over all the military forces of the empire. Thus began a succession of shogunates, with the substitution of military for civilian authority and with the emperor remaining in obscurity as the theoretical source of authority. When once the imperial family tried to curb the power of the shogunate, the military class exiled the emperor and put on the throne a descendant of the imperial family who would be content to remain a mere symbol and a tool of the military.

The shogunate was a lifetime office; moreover, the shogun was given authority to choose his own successor. The post was retained in the dominant family until the family was overthrown. The last of the shogunates, the Tokugawa shogunate, came to power early in the seventeenth century. Its eventual decline paved the way for the restoration of the emperor's power in 1868. Successful in eliminating opposition, the Tokugawa shoguns maintained more than two centuries of undisputed rule and internal peace. Internal stability was re-enforced by an entrenched class system, with the military class enjoying the highest prestige.[7] This was also a period of seclusion, when the only outside contact was a small amount of Dutch and Chinese trade at Nagasaki. The decline of the shogunate was due to the rise of powerful clans which challenged its power, and this decline was hastened by the forces unleashed by the opening of Japan to foreign trade and the new contacts that followed the expedition of Commodore Perry in 1853.

The Restoration. The Restoration ushered in the famous *Meiji* (the name of the period of Emperor Mutsuhito's reign), which was marked by outstanding success in the achievement of a strong national unity and in the modernization of Japan under capable leaders. The clans and the *daimyo* surrendered their power and their fiefs, and an effectual central authority was established in the

[6] Kenneth Scott Latourette, *op. cit.,* p. 213.

[7] J. F. Embree, *The Japanese Nation* (New York: Farrar & Rinehart, Inc., 1945), pp. 20 ff.

name of the emperor; to all intents and purposes, the emperor now became the greatest *daimyo* of the empire. A constitution was given to the nation by imperial decree; since it was a gift of the emperor, it carefully protected him and declared him "sacred and inviolable." As a matter of fact, the myth of divine descent was emphasized more than ever and deliberately used as a powerful force toward national unity. To re-enforce this myth, Shinto, Japan's primitive religion which grew before the introduction of Buddhism from China, was revived, strengthened, and exalted into a state cult stressing the worship of the imperial family and national heroes in national shrines. Along with the constitution was introduced the machinery of representative government cleverly integrated with the preserved traditions of the imperial state.

Modernization and the Rise to Power. Besides establishing a strong national government, the architects of the new state turned to two important steps in modernization: military reform to build an effective fighting force and material reconstruction to develop the industrial power of the nation. Japan achieved outstanding success in both. In a quarter of a century, she produced a modern army and navy which surprised the world by defeating China and Russia; and thanks to her newly developed military prowess, she was quickly recognized as one of the great powers in world politics. In material development, she showed remarkable aptitude and efficiency in the establishment of modern communication and transportation facilities and in building up light and heavy industries not only sufficient for the needs of a growing nation but successful in capturing foreign markets and providing formidable rivalry for the industrialized nations of the West. Unfortunately, three major wars —war with China in 1894, war with Russia in 1904, and World War I in 1914—gave impetus to the military and industrial expansion and continually elevated Japan's international position and prestige, with the result that military leaders arrived at the dangerous conclusion that war was a profitable business and the surest road to prosperity and greatness. With a pronounced military tradition and a recurrent dream of continental conquest, Japan did not hesitate long in embarking upon an ambitious program of imperialism and aggression.

The Social Structure. Despite the spectacular progress of the

Meiji reforms and the success of Japan's material reconstruction, much of the fundamental social structure remained unchanged. The class society of old was maintained, with members of the imperial family and the nobility enjoying the privileged position conferred by birth, and with certain commoners condemned to the lowest stratum of a virtual caste society.[8] "Every town and village has its own class hierarchy with its own upper-, middle-, and lower-class groups. . . . Families descended from the old warrior classes have high prestige even though today they may be very poor financially."[9] In politics, the emperor continued to be a figurehead and actual power rested with an oligarchy which commanded loyalty and obedience in the name of the emperor. A recent writer on postwar Japan writes as follows:

> Throughout its modern history, Japan had been ruled by a dictatorial oligarchy made up of five groups: the military-naval leaders, the financial-industrial combines (*Zaibatsu*), the top bureaucrats, the leaders of the political parties, and the big landlords. These several groups had often fought each other bitterly, as each sought its own power within the ruling coalition. But all five were thoroughly agreed on two basic objectives: to maintain their collective dictatorship over the Japanese people with the Emperor as their all-powerful spokesman, and to expand the power of the Japanese Empire by whatever means seemed most effective. Confronted with any challenge to either of these aims, they closed ranks, and in combination they formed a tough yet flexible authoritarian system.[10]

The Potsdam Proclamation and Postwar Reforms.   The terms of Japanese surrender in World War II were laid down by the Allied nations in the Potsdam Proclamation of July 26, 1945. The Allies demanded the elimination of militarism and militarists who had "deceived and misled the people of Japan"; they called for the "strengthening of democratic tendencies" and the establishment of "freedom of speech, of religion, and of thought, as well as respect for the fundamental human rights." On the basis of this important proclamation was formulated a statement of United States Initial Post-Surrender Policy for Japan, which was later amended and

[8] *Ibid.*, p. 122.

[9] *Ibid.*, p. 123.

[10] T. A. Bisson, *Prospects for Democracy in Japan* (New York: The Macmillan Company, 1949), pp. 3-4.

approved by other Allied nations and became the basic document defining the policies for the occupation and control of Japan after 1945. The policy statement specified the steps to be taken to bring about disarmament and demilitarization and to introduce democratic self-government. Among other things, it declared that "militarism and ultranationalism, in doctrine and practice, including para-military training, shall be eliminated from the education system," and that "exponents of militarism and ultranationalism shall be excluded from supervision and teaching positions." In pursuance of the objectives of demilitarization and democratization, a new constitution has been adopted in postwar Japan, equal suffrage and civil liberties have been introduced, the governmental system has been reconstructed, effort has been made to destroy the myth of the divinity of the emperor, the financial combines have been dissolved, a program of agrarian reform has abolished absentee landownership, and a new educational program has been inaugurated. But before we consider this new program of re-education, it behooves us to review briefly the education system that was abolished at the time of the Japanese surrender.

EDUCATION FOR NATIONALISM AND MILITARISM

Discipline. The Japanese people are known to be a well-organized and well-disciplined people. They obey authority and follow their leaders. They can endure much pain and hardship. They are intensely loyal to their emperor and their state and show great courage in self-sacrifice and self-abnegation for the cause they believe in. They are efficient in group action and conform to group standards. This national character is the result of a planned program of informal and formal education. The process of conditioning begins early in life.

The baby boy in Japan soon learns that there are set rules he must obey. The evening hot bath must not be touched until his father uses it. But all the women in the house must wait until he as the male child is through. All the men in the house are to be served first at meals, and women must wait until afterward. He discovers that his elder brother can order him about in the same way that his father orders him about. He himself can give orders to others in the same household as long as they are not older male relatives of his. To one who talks to him authoritatively, he replies submissively, and to those who speak submissively, he can talk authoritatively and get away with it.

As he grows older he realizes that even his father, who seemed the most important person in the world, has his own place in society. There are people to whom the father bows, and there are others who bow to him. Some speak to him with respect, and he speaks to others with authority.[11]

It has been suggested that rigid conformity and the denial of any real opportunity for self-expression create a continuing sense of frustration and a "dammed-up feeling" which at times breaks through the confines of polite behavior and is expressed in acts of violence and brutality such as Japanese soldiers were so often guilty of in World War II.[12]

Education for National Morality. Loyalty and conformity have been considered essential components of moral character. The development of moral character has been a central aim of education, and since moral character could not be divorced from national ideals, the entire program of education was thoroughly permeated with the national spirit. This emphasis is evident in the Imperial Rescript on Education issued by Emperor Mutsuhito in 1890, which remained the fundamental basis of Japanese education until the defeat of Japan in 1945. The text of the Rescript follows:

Know Ye, Our Subjects:

Our Imperial Ancestors have founded Our Empire on a basis broad and everlasting and have deeply and firmly implanted virtue; Our subjects ever united in loyalty and filial piety have from generation to generation illustrated the beauty thereof. This is the glory of the fundamental character of Our Empire, and herein also lies the source of Our education. Ye, Our subjects, be filial to your parents, affectionate to your brothers and sisters; as husbands and wives be harmonious, as friends be true; bear yourselves in modesty and moderation; extend your benevolence to all; pursue learning and cultivate arts, and thereby develop intellectual faculties and perfect moral powers; furthermore advance public good and promote common interests; always respect the Constitution and observe the laws; should emergency rise, offer

[11] Toru Matsumoto, "Japanese Are Human," *Asia and the Americas*, Vol. LXVI, No. 1 (January 1946), p. 9.
[12] *Ibid.*, p. 12.

yourselves courageously to the State; and thus guard and maintain the prosperity of Our Imperial Throne coeval with heaven and earth. So shall ye not only be Our good and faithful subjects, but render illustrious the best traditions of your forefathers.

The way here set forth is indeed the teaching bequeathed by Our Imperial Ancestors, to be observed alike by Their descendants and Their subjects, infallible for all ages and true in all places. It is Our wish to lay it to heart in all reverence, in common with you, Our subjects, that we may all thus attain to the same virtue.

The Rescript is quoted here in full because of its supreme importance in Japanese education. It constitutes an official statement of the basic philosophy of education in presurrender Japan.

A copy of this Rescript is given to every school in the Empire, and is read on the thirtieth of October of each year, as well as on other formal occasions, so that due reverence may be given to the Imperial Message. And throughout the whole field of education, whenever we need to clarify our fundamental educational policy, we regard this Rescript as the basic principle of education.[13]

Moral instruction in the school was inextricably tied up with nationalism, emperor worship, and State Shinto.[14] It must be noted that filial piety was considered closely related to national loyalty. "The idea of a great family with the emperor at the head has governed the mind of the Japanese people consciously and unconsciously."[15] Thus the cultivation of family virtues became an integral part of education for national loyalty and for service to the state and the imperial throne. "No other nation has developed such singleness of thought and purpose among the mass of the people as have the Japanese in the subordination of the individual to the will of the family and nation."[16]

The Emperor Cult. Since patriotism meant the worship of the

[13] K. Yoshida and T. Kaigo, *Japanese Education* (Tokyo: Board of Tourist Industry, Japanese Government Railways, 1937), p. 20.

[14] Robert King Hall, *Education for a New Japan* (New Haven: Yale University Press, 1949), pp. 176-186.

[15] Kumaji Yoshida, *op. cit.*, p. 449.

[16] J. F. Steiner, *Behind the Japanese Mask* (New York: The Macmillan Company, 1943), p. 106.

emperor and belief in his divine descent, it became the supreme duty of education to instill a deep reverence for the emperor. Imperial portraits in schools and universities were the most highly prized possessions, to be protected from damage at all costs, and many a teacher willingly sacrificed his life in attempting to save the imperial portrait from destruction in a burning school building. The portraits were given formal obeisance on important holidays. School directors were known to have committed suicide when the imperial portraits suffered damage in any way. Few intellectuals dared question the myth of divinity; most of them seemed quite ready to accept it without question. "The most dangerous thoughts in Japan are those that cast doubt upon the validity of the traditional structure of the state or seem to detract from the prestige of the Imperial Family."[17] Both for practical purposes of protection and in order to stress even more tangibly the importance of respect for the emperor, many schools built special fireproof buildings for the imperial portrait. Each day the pupils must bow toward this building to pay homage to the divine emperor. In the classroom and outside, the pupils were constantly being reminded that personal loyalty and service to the emperor constituted the cornerstone of national morality and patriotism. The emperor was not only the symbol of national unity; "he *was* the State, and the nation had no identity considered apart from him."[18]

Nationalism and Militarism. An educational program based on the philosophy stated in the Imperial Rescript meant a program thoroughly permeated with the spirit of nationalism and specifically directed toward the fulfillment of the needs of the state. With the passage of time, as the military came to dominate national policy increasingly, this nationalism was re-enforced by an aggressive militarism bent on the expansion of the empire. The "way of the warrior" was glorified and the soldierly virtues of obedience and sacrifice were exalted as the highest expressions of national morality. Military heroes were given a prominent place in national history. Into the minds of youth was instilled the idea that the Japanese were a superior race and had a mission to fulfill in bringing the

[17] *Ibid.*, p. 19.

[18] *Education in the New Japan* (Tokyo: Supreme Commander of the Allied Powers, General Headquarters, Civil Information and Education Section, 1948), Vol. I, p. 33.

Japanese way of life to other parts of the world. The military atmosphere of the schools was enhanced after 1925, when the Department of Education ordered that military instruction be given in all public schools by military officers on active duty. This militant nationalism was easily turned into a handmaid of aggression when, in later years, education was asked to contribute more directly to the "new order" of "Greater East Asia." It became the definite function of the school "to train the youth as citizens of a 'nation which destiny had made the leader of the East Asia Co-Prosperity Sphere.' "[19]

The ideology of militarism and ultranationalism was faithfully mirrored in the school curriculum of the immediately prewar and wartime period. This was especially true of courses in history, geography, morals, music, and physical education. History was exploited in two ways for the accomplishment of this purpose, by treating Japanese legends and mythology as if they were history, by interpreting the facts of history from an ultranationalistic point of view. The morals course, which had long been an important element of the curriculum, was aimed at indoctrinating the student with the principles of the ideology outlined above, of disciplined subordination to the state, and of the iconography of Japanese tradition. Geography, in its turn, became the study of geopolitics and the justification for overseas expansion. Likewise in the music courses songs were utilized skillfully. From 1941 on, approved music texts were avowedly militaristic, glorifying war and battle. Language, too, was made a study in tradition; the Japanese language was extolled as a medium through which the Imperial and national principles could be understood, a symbol of Japanese spirit and unity.

After 1925, military training had come to absorb more and more of the time devoted to physical education, until eventually that course was almost completely militarized. *Budo* (the military arts) comprised *kendo* (fencing), *judo* (jujitsu), and *naginata* (halberd practice). By the beginning of World War II, these had become actual training for war and sports had turned into military exercises. Students threw hand grenades instead of the shotput; they carried packs and practiced swimming carrying equipment and rifles.[20]

[19] Chitoshi Yanaga, *Japan Since Perry* (New York: McGraw-Hill Book Company, Inc., 1949), p. 549.
[20] *Education in the New Japan*, Vol. I, pp. 36-37.

State Shinto. Those who charted the course of national development after the *Meiji* Restoration fully appreciated the importance of education and the strategic role of the schools in the molding of a national mind. They were also astute enough to realize that education for national unity and loyalty would be more effective if it were vitalized by a powerful emotional drive and re-enforced by a religious force that could embrace people of all classes. They found their answer in Shinto, a primitive religion of early Japan which had been overshadowed by Buddhism and Confucianism. They not only revived the old religion, but built it up into a powerful state cult. As a matter of fact, Japan's statesmen actually constructed a new state religion on the foundation of the popular ideas of primitive Shinto. This new force was known as State Shinto.

Officially, State Shinto was not considered a religion. It was clearly differentiated from the sect Shinto, which, like other religions, was under the jurisdiction of the Bureau of Religions. State Shinto came under the jurisdiction of the Home Office. Since it was concerned directly with shrines and sacred places intimately related to national history and with the worship of ancestral spirits and the imperial family, State Shinto was declared to be not a religion but the expression of a national loyalty transcending sectarian religions. It was thus possible to teach State Shinto in the schools of the nation without violating the principle of religious freedom, a principle which forbade religious instruction in public schools.

The attitudes and beliefs of State Shinto were made an integral part of school instruction. Early myths in regard to the rule of the gods and the divine descent of the emperor were taught as authentic history.[21] Such instruction was designed to create in the youthful mind a strong sense of pride in the unique origin of the Japanese nation and the unbroken continuity of its history under one imperial dynasty directly descended from the Sun Goddess. The propagation of this state cult "provided the emotional and mystical basis for the fevered nationalism of the 1930's and 1940's with its fanatical conviction of the invincibility of Japan, of the superiority of the

---

[21] D. C. Holtom, *Modern Japan and Shinto Nationalism* (Chicago: University of Chicago Press, 1947), p. 60.

Japanese and their culture, and of the mission of Japan in Eastern Asia and the world as a whole."[22]

Participation in shrine worship was considered an important expression of patriotism and the prescribed rituals were taught in all schools. Group visits to shrines were an integral part of the school program. Shrines for the worship of the deities and the national heroes were supported by the state and were in charge of priests appointed by the government. Chief among the priests was the emperor. The rituals were prescribed by law. The dedication of a shrine to the souls of soldiers and sailors who had died for their country served to emphasize the militaristic flavor of Japanese nationalism.

The Control of Education. With education considered an instrument of the state for the development of national unity and national morality, it was logical that all phases of the educational program were closely supervised and strictly controlled. The highest organ of control of national education was the Department (later called the Ministry) of Education, headed by the Minister of Education. Local authorities were subordinate to the Minister. The extent of authority of the Department may be inferred from its various bureaus. In addition to separate bureaus for general education, higher education, technical education, and social education, there were the Bureau of Religions, the Bureau of School Textbooks, the Bureau of Thought Supervision, and the Bureau of Educational Research. Thus the Minister of Education exercised control over all matters relating to art, science, literature, and religion. He had jurisdiction over museums, art galleries, and literary and religious bodies, as well as schools of various levels. The Department of Education compiled all the elementary-school textbooks and approved all textbooks used in the higher schools. The organization of schools, their respective functions in the national system, their courses of study, the qualifications of teachers, equipment and finance—all these matters were prescribed by imperial ordinances. Strict control extended to all private as well as public schools. It was, of course, no mere accident that in the establishment of a national system of education Japan was greatly influenced by the examples of France and Germany.

Thought control was so important a part of educational adminis-

---

[22] Kenneth Scott Latourette, *op. cit.*, p. 407.

tration that the Department of Education established a Bureau of Thought Supervision under which were the Section of Thought Supervision and the Section of Investigation. The Bureau was charged with the duty not only of guiding and controlling student thought but also of investigating "dangerous thoughts" and of examining books for their thought content. The Section of Investigation was closely linked up with the secret police. As ultranationalism gained ascendancy, the "thought war" was directed against any trend not in harmony with the nationalistic ideology. The thinking of faculty as well as students was closely supervised and investigation was followed by arrests, imprisonment, and other punitive measures.[23] At the same time, student activities motivated by ultranationalism were encouraged by the Department of Education. In universities and higher schools, "coaching teachers" were assigned the duty of supervising the moral training of students, with each teacher in charge of twenty to thirty students.

It was the Bureau of Thought Supervision that sponsored the policy document published by the Department of Education in 1937, entitled "Cardinal Principles of the National Entity." This ultranationalistic document clearly defined the common role of government, education, and religious rites in the supreme task of supporting the imperial throne.[24]

THE SCHOOL SYSTEM

The main features of the school system underwent no significant change from 1871 to 1945. The system was well organized and guided by clearly conceived national aims to serve as "an instrument for the control of the populace by the state."[25] Although universal schooling was considered desirable and compulsory education was well enforced, the system provided one type of education for the common people and another type for the privileged few. Nationalism and utilitarianism constituted the guiding philosophy of the curriculum; the duty of the school was to produce loyal patriots who were equipped to offer their service to meet the practical and material needs of the state.

[23] Robert King Hall, *op. cit.*, pp. 15-17.
[24] *Ibid.*, pp. 168-176.
[25] *Education in the New Japan*, Vol. I, p. 25.

Elementary Education. Elementary education was free and required of all children between six and twelve years of age. The central purpose was to inculcate reverence to the emperor and the state. The elementary school was preceded by the kindergarten, which offered courses one to three years in length and was not compulsory. Compulsory education was well enforced; it was estimated that over 99.5 percent of school-age children were actually in school. The most important subjects of the elementary curriculum were morals, or ethics, and the Japanese language; morals was taught two hours each week through the entire elementary school, and the Japanese language occupied almost half of the school hours of each week in the first three years and about one third of the total time in the ensuing years. Other subjects of the curriculum were arithmetic, Japanese history, geography, science, drawing, singing, and gymnastics. Girls began sewing lessons in the fourth grade, and exercises in military arts began in the fifth grade for boys. All teaching materials must be approved by the government. Teachers were "told exactly what to teach and how to teach it."[26]

After completing elementary school, most pupils entered the higher elementary school for a terminal course of two or three years. The higher elementary curriculum continued the subjects of the elementary school and therefore could not be considered a part of secondary education. In 1941 the Department of Education issued the National School Plan, which converted the elementary schools into national schools and placed them under more direct centralized control. A part of the plan called for extension of compulsory education to eight years so as to include two years of higher elementary education, but this provision was not enforced. The National School Plan was supposed to emphasize a new philosophy of education; its aim was to develop a stronger national unity by a greater emphasis on the national spirit and the concept of the empire and more attention to concrete and practical education in keeping with national life.

Secondary Education. There were three types of secondary schools: the middle school for boys, the girls' high school, and the technical school. All curriculums and organizational details were prescribed and the most important aim of all schools was to con-

[26] *Report of the United States Education Mission to Japan* (Washington, D. C.: Department of State, 1946), p. 32.

tribute directly to national power by continued emphasis on national morality, loyalty to the imperial throne, and service to the state in concrete and practical capacities. Secondary education was not free and graduates of the six-year elementary school had to take entrance examinations to gain admission. Tuition fees made secondary education inaccessible to children from families of limited means, and entrance examinations further limited the opportunity.

The middle school for boys enjoyed the highest prestige. Its curriculum consisted of preparatory subjects for the university, although many of the pupils had no thought of further study. Morals, the Japanese language, and the Chinese classics were studied throughout the course. The middle-school course was five years in length, but pupils might take entrance examinations for the higher schools after the fourth year. Military training, in charge of officer instructors appointed by the War Department, was an integral part of the curriculum.

The girls' high school offered to selected girls a course which for the majority of them was terminal. Since there was not the pressure of preparing for higher studies, the program was more flexible than that of the middle school. The central emphasis was on national morality and womanly virtue. Some schools offered a three-year course for graduates of the higher elementary school. The scholastic standard of the girls' high school fell below that of the middle school, and the situation reflected the discriminatory attitude of educational authorities in regard to female education.

The technical schools provided vocational training for pupils who had completed the elementary or the higher elementary school. The courses varied in length in accordance with their nature. Technical courses were available for both boys and girls, but the schools were not coeducational. An interesting type of vocational preparation was provided by the training institutes of colonization, which attempted to give the necessary background for settling in Manchuria, Mongolia, or South America.[27] The courses in South Sea colonization also belong to this category.[28]

In addition to the full-time secondary schools already discussed, the youth schools may be mentioned in this connection, since they

[27] A General Survey of Education in Japan (Tokyo: Department of Education, 1937), p. 30.
[28] Ibid., p. 31.

fall within the same age level. These schools, established in 1935, provided part-time continuation education for those who had completed the elementary school. They were schools for the masses, which emphasized moral virtue and vocational training.

Higher Education. Although the middle school was a necessary prerequisite to higher education, its graduates could not enter the universities directly. To gain admission to a university it was necessary to attend a preparatory institution; one might choose the preparatory course of a university or the higher course of the *Koto Gakko* (higher school). Pupils who had completed the fourth year of the middle school would take a preparatory course of three years; those who had completed the fifth year would require only two years. The higher school consisted of a lower ordinary course of four years, followed by a higher course of three years. Although the ordinary course began on the same age level as the secondary school, the higher school was always classified under higher education, because it was the main gateway to the universities. It was the higher course that the boy from the middle school took to prepare for the university. It should be noted that the first year of university study was the fourteenth year of schooling and, therefore, the Japanese university was more like the European university than like the American college.

Only a few of the universities were open to women. The higher schools were for men only; selection was rigorous. One of the nine imperial universities was the most desired goal for the ambitious student, because the graduates of these institutions enjoyed a virtual monopoly over civil-service and teaching positions. Among the imperial universities, the law faculty of Tokyo Imperial University was the most productive of government bureaucrats.[29] There were also nonimperial government universities and private universities. A university might consist of one faculty or more; each faculty was required to provide a postgraduate course. The length of the university course was three or four years. The curriculum was specialized[30] and students were expected to do a great deal of "memorizing of undigested knowledge."[31]

Graduates of the middle school who did not enter the universities might apply for admission to the special or technical "college,"

[29] T. A. Bisson, *op. cit.*, p. 7.
[30] Hugh L. Keenleyside and A. F. Thomas, *op. cit.*, pp. 266-267.
[31] *Ibid.*, p. 275.

which provided a three-year course of occupational or semiprofessional nature to enable students to render service to the commercial, industrial, or agricultural life of the nation. Many of them were women's colleges, admitting graduates of the girls' high school for general collegiate education. The special and technical colleges enrolled three or four times as many students as the universities.[32]

Teacher-training Institutions. Elementary-school teachers were trained in the normal school, which provided a five-year course for graduates of the higher elementary school. Graduates of the middle school or the girls' high school were eligible for what was known as the second section of the normal school for a two-year course. Tuition, room, and board were free; after graduation, students were required to render teaching service for periods in proportion to the amount of public aid received. Normal-school students were required to live in dormitories under semimilitary discipline and in an atmosphere of nationalism.

Secondary-school teachers were trained in several types of institutions. The higher normal school offered a course of four years based on the completion of the normal school or middle school; its graduates were qualified to teach in normal schools and other secondary schools. The higher normal school for women accepted graduates of the girls' normal school or the girls' high school. In addition, there were special institutes for the training of teachers in specialized subjects and teachers for the technical schools and the youth schools.

THE RE-EDUCATION OF JAPAN

SCAP Directives. In conformity with the basic Allied policy of eliminating militarism and ultranationalism from Japanese education and encouraging the Japanese people to develop democratic institutions, the Supreme Commander of the Allied Powers (SCAP) early adopted measures to bring about the desired changes. On October 22, 1945, a memorandum was sent to the Japanese government laying down the basic educational policy of the occupation. It called for a critical examination of the content of instruction, an investigation and screening of teaching and administrative personnel with a view to removing the disciples of ultranationalism, and a revision of curriculums and textbooks to eliminate militarism

[32] *Education in the New Japan,* Vol. I, p. 97.

and ultranationalism and to establish practices "in harmony with representative government, international peace, the dignity of the individual, and fundamental human rights. . . ."[33] A directive of December 15, 1945, ordered the abolition of State Shinto, the prohibition of Shinto teaching in any public or semipublic schools, the discontinuation of visits to Shinto shrines under school auspices, and the elimination of such terms as the "Greater East Asia War" or "all other terms whose connotation in Japanese is inextricably connected with State Shinto, militarism, and ultranationalism." Courses in morals, Japanese history, and geography were suspended by a directive of December 31, 1945. When permission was later given to reopen courses in geography (June 29, 1946) and history (October 12, 1946), it was with the proviso that all textbooks be approved by SCAP. These SCAP directives became the basis of a series of orders by the Ministry of Education for the elimination of militarism and ultranationalism from the curriculum, for the removal of teachers judged unfit for the new program, for the abolition of glider training and the military arts in physical education, and like measures.

The United States Education Mission to Japan.   To help in constructive educational planning, SCAP requested the United States War Department to send to Japan a group of American educators to advise on educational reconstruction. Twenty-seven educators, under the chairmanship of George D. Stoddard, were asked to constitute an education mission; they went to Japan in March 1946. After about one month, during which time they were assisted by a committee of Japanese educators, the mission made a report[34] containing concrete proposals, which became an outline of the educational reforms recommended to SCAP and to the Japanese government. The mission condemned the uniformity and standardization of the old education and emphasized the importance of freedom and democratic participation. The mission recommended, instead of prescription by a central authority, teacher participation in curriculum making and in the preparation of textbooks. It suggested new aims and new methods for teaching morals, history, geography, and other subjects. "The over-all objectives should be the promotion of democratic Japanese education within a world society com-

[33] SCAP directives and other official documents may be found in the second volume of *Education in the New Japan.*
[34] *Report of the United States Education Mission to Japan.*

mitted to non-aggression and peace."[35] To facilitate learning, the mission advised language reform with a view to simplification and the elimination of the Chinese characters. In regard to the school system, it proposed a primary school of six years, to be followed by a three-year "lower secondary school," compulsory for all boys and girls, to be followed in turn by a three-year "upper secondary school," free of tuition and open to all without discrimination. Coeducation was recommended for all levels.

The New Education. A new constitution was passed by the Diet in October 1946 and promulgated by Emperor Hirohito on November 3, 1946, to go into effect six months later. It provided for equal educational opportunity, respect of individuals, freedom of thought and conscience, freedom of religion, academic freedom, and "the right of all people to maintain the minimum standards of wholesome and cultured living." These principles were incorporated into the Fundamental Law of Education passed by the Diet on March 31, 1947. The law reaffirmed equal opportunity in education and declared that the fundamental aim of education should be the full development of personality in order to produce individuals "sound in mind and body, who shall love truth and justice, esteem individual value, respect labor and have a deep sense of responsibility, and be imbued with the independent spirit, as builders of the peaceful state and society."

The School System. The old school system was discriminatory on the basis of sex, economic status, and social status. The majority of pupils had no opportunity to benefit from any form of secondary education. In order to provide equal opportunity and to give all children within the age limits of compulsory education some form of secondary education, the Japanese government, following the advice of the United States Education Mission, adopted a "ladder" type of organization, with schools on ascending levels available to all without discrimination. The School Education Law passed by the Diet on March 29, 1947, provided for a system more simplified than the old: a six-year elementary school, followed by a three-year secondary school (lower secondary) and a three-year high school (upper secondary), with a four-year university crowning the system. By the extension of compulsory education to nine years, all children would be given three years of secondary education. The law ex-

[35] *Ibid.,* p. 16.

tended free educational opportunities to the blind, the deaf, and the handicapped.

Educational Administration. The Bureau of Thought Supervision has been abolished. More important than any structural change is a new spirit of administration. Local boards are to have more responsibility and more authority. As its power of control becomes limited, the Ministry of Education is expected to assume more responsibility for professional advice and stimulus to promote educational growth in the nation. Teachers are given a new freedom not only in professional organizations free from state control but also in their professional activities in the schools.

Curriculum Revision. The elimination of militarism, ultranationalism, and State Shinto from the curriculum was meant to pave the way for the construction of new teaching materials. The production of stop-gap textbooks for immediate use was a first step. In July 1941, the Ministry of Education appointed a special committee to undertake the task of curriculum revision. By the following September, the committee had developed a new program of studies for the elementary and secondary schools. Among noteworthy characteristics of the new program are the elimination of special courses or special textbooks for girls, the adoption of the same basic courses and textbooks for various types of schools on the same age level, the introduction of an integrated course in social studies to take the place of separate courses in morals, geography, and history, and a change of emphasis from subject matter and knowledge to pupil interests and needs as the starting point of education. The study of Chinese classics and foreign languages was made elective for interested pupils. Provision was made for the adaptation of the curriculum to the local environment and the use of local resources by teachers working in cooperation with the pupils.

Teachers. The SCAP directive of October 31, 1945, in regard to the screening of teachers and educational officials demanded the removal of "all persons who are known to be militaristic, ultranationalistic, or antagonistic to the objectives and policies of the occupation." It instructed the Japanese Ministry of Education to establish the administrative machinery and procedures for the screening and to submit for SCAP approval the criteria for acceptability and certification. Before this official "purge" took effect, 115,778 Japanese teachers and administrators had already resigned or been dismissed by the Japanese authorities. In the year following the purge, 2643 persons were automatically disqualified on the basis of the official criteria, and 2268 others were found unacceptable after investigation by the screening committees.[36]

Obviously, the acceptable teachers were not completely free from the influences of the old system; even more questionable was their understanding of the new spirit and aims of education. A program of re-education or in-service orientation was therefore imperative. Among the methods used in this program were orientation lectures for teachers and administrators; a new teachers' manual pointing out the defects of the old system and explaining the new philosophy of education; a radio program known as "The Teachers' Hour"; teacher study groups and forums free from administrative control; short summer courses in normal schools with orientation in the new philosophy as their main purpose; conferences, workshops, and correspondence courses. In the normal schools, the regulations concerning the elimination of militarism and ultranationalism have been applied as in other schools. Effort has been made to put more emphasis on a broad general education as a background for professional study and to relax official control so as to allow normal schools greater freedom in administration and in the study of curriculum changes. Normal schools have been encouraged to establish experimental schools for trying out "democratically sound educational theories and practices."[37]

First steps have been taken toward the development of professional teachers' organizations. Whereas membership in the Greater Japan Education Association was required of all teachers before the war, teachers are now given freedom to form organizations of their choice. The Association, formerly controlled by the government, now maintains no official connections. As a matter of fact, its importance is overshadowed by that of the Japan Educational Personnel Union, which was born of the merging of rival unions that sprang up in the postwar years. Through aggressive collective bargaining, the union and its predecessors have achieved noteworthy success in demanding higher salaries and better working conditions for teachers.

Problems of Re-education. It is not easy to stamp out the influences of a long tradition; it is even more difficult to bring about a new program based on a new social philosophy which has yet to

[36] Robert King Hall, *op. cit.,* p. 439.
[37] *Education in the New Japan,* Vol. I, p. 291.

take root amid not too favorable conditions. The Japanese government has been promptly obedient in issuing orders and regulations in accordance with SCAP directives, but this very efficiency has caused some to wonder whether the reforms have touched more than the surface, whether the centralized administration that makes the quick changes possible may also be a potential danger, and whether reform by directives will really bring about a democratic system of education. It is also necessary to remember that there is a gap between paper plans and actual practice and that the encouraging reports submitted to SCAP authorities may be statements of intentions rather than descriptions of what has already been accomplished.

It is possible that the military dictatorship of the occupation has encouraged the continuation of absolute obedience in Japan and that the strict censorship and purging of undesirable teachers has not been conducive to independence or freedom from fear on the part of teachers. The Ministry of Education may have been strengthened through its administration of the screening and certification of teachers. Even in trying to learn democratic procedures in teaching, the teachers must follow Ministry orders and are afraid to exercise their own judgment. They "still received the detailed orders, the list of subjects, the teachers' manuals, and the official interpretations."[38] "When the threat of dismissal or purge is present in every class period, the teacher does not dare attempt any original interpretation."[39]

To raise such questions does not necessarily mean a lack of appreciation of the accomplishments of the SCAP and of the very complicated problems which have confronted it. From the beginning, the SCAP as well as the United States Education Mission has emphasized that the achievement of democracy is a task that must be undertaken by the Japanese people themselves and that the task will require much time. The most that the occupation can do is to help remove the obstacles to the growth of democratic institutions. It is still too early to know definitely to what extent Japanese education has been purged of militarism and ultranationalism. Whether or not the removal of past allegiances will create a psychological vacuum in which antidemocratic tendencies may have a chance to appear is another question that only the future can answer.

[38] Robert King Hall, *op. cit.,* p. 458.
[39] *Ibid.,* p. 447.

A fundamental problem concerns the general direction of political and economic development. Education is intimately related with political and economic conditions. Given the favorable environment of a political and an economic democracy, democratic tendencies in education will grow and increase in number. If, however, the political and economic scene continues to be dominated by the old bureaucrats and reactionary elements, it will be idle to expect paper plans for democratic education to produce concrete results. Early policies of the SCAP were guided by the principles laid down by the Potsdam Proclamation and designed to remove the obstacles to political and economic democracy in Japan. Some critics have questioned the wisdom of preserving the emperor system; they argue that as long as the emperor institution remains, it will be difficult to get rid of the attitudes formerly stressed by State Shinto and to change the basic social philosophy which considered the individual as subservient to the state. But if the retention of the emperor system were the only remaining obstacle to the democratization of Japan, the prospect for the future would not be so uncertain as it is today. In the first two years after the war, SCAP took important measures to emphasize the falsity of the myth of divine descent and to begin the break-up of the big financial interests and the old oligarchy. In 1948, however, there was a modification of the fundamental policy of the occupation. Owing partly to the financial burden of the occupation and partly to the international situation, the United States government decided to help speed up Japan's industrial recovery. This decision necessitated a revision of the original policy in regard to reparations and in regard to the dissolution of the financial, business, and political interests which constituted the old oligarchy. The possible consequence of this shift in policy has worried critics in the United States and other Allied nations. The opinion expressed below is representative of the grave concern of such critics.

My argument rests on two basic propositions. First, since 1945 there has been a far-reaching change in the attitude of the United States toward Japan. The hated enemy has become the coveted ally. Second, during the same period there has been no fundamental change in Japan's social structure or in the political outlook of her leaders. . . .

The Allies, in response to American persuasion, have greatly raised the levels of permitted production in secondary war-industries, such as steel, aluminum, magnesium, and shipbuilding. Washington has quietly put the brake on the 'democratization' program, particularly on the purge and dissolution of the *Zaibatsu*. . . . I have reiterated that the Japanese Government represents the most conservative forces in Japan, that its presurrender outlook is unchanged, despite its gestures of coopera-tion with SCAP authority. . . .

I believe there is . . . great danger . . . that in helping Japan rebuild her industrial strength and restore her foreign trade, the United States will enable Japan to establish an industrial and economic supremacy in East Asia which her leaders will once again exploit for political purposes. Economic penetration is the first step; political domination the second.[40]

Democratic education can grow in democratic society only. Unless there is a fundamental change in the presurrender political and economic structure, the future of democratic education in Japan will not be bright. Whether or not the re-education of Japan will be successful will depend to a large extent on whether or not Japan will, politically or economically, break away from her militaristic and feudalistic past and move in the direction of devotion to the welfare of the common man and to the peace of the world.

BIBLIOGRAPHY

BALL, W. MACMAHON, *Japan, Enemy or Ally?* (New York: The John Day Company, 1949). The author is an Australian who served as the British Commonwealth member of the Allied Council for Japan. His views are an example of the criticism and skep-ticism of America's Allies regarding occupational policy.

BISSON, T. A., *Prospects for Democracy in Japan* (New York: The Macmillan Company, 1949). A critical evaluation of the occupa-tion policy in Japan, with emphasis on the economic situation and on postwar politics.

Education in the New Japan, Vols. I and II (Tokyo: Supreme Com-mander of the Allied Powers, General Headquarters, Civil In-formation and Education Section, 1948). A brief survey of pre-occupation education followed by a comprehensive report on the reorganization of Japanese education through March 1948. The first volume contains the text, the second volume contains official documents of SCAP and of the Japanese government.

[40] W. MacMahon Ball, *Japan, Enemy or Ally?* (New York: The John Day Company, 1949), pp. 181-187 *et passim*.

EMBREE, JOHN F., *The Japanese Nation* (New York: Farrar & Rinehart, Inc., 1945). A social survey of Japanese life and society, with a chapter on education.

A General Survey of Education in Japan (Tokyo: Department of Education, 1937). An over-all view of the Japanese system of education, written to enable foreigners to obtain a general understanding of Japanese education.

HALL, ROBERT KING, *Education for a New Japan* (New Haven: Yale University Press, 1949). A critical study of Japanese education by a former education officer of SCAP, based on personal experience as well as an examination of official records and policies. Emphasizes a philosophical consideration of Japanese re-education.

KEENLEYSIDE, HUGH L., and A. F. THOMAS, *History of Japanese Education and Present Educational System* (Tokyo: The Hokuseido Press, 1937). A comprehensive volume dealing with types of schools, administrative machinery, and problems of educational reform.

MARTIN, EDWIN M., *The Allied Occupation of Japan* (Palo Alto, Calif.: Stanford University Press, 1948). A concise report on the major policies of the Allied occupation of Japan from 1945 to 1948; detailed analysis of the Presidential Policy Statement and the extent to which each phase has been carried out.

MYERS, ALONZO F. and LOUIS K., "The Japanese Take Their Education Seriously," *Journal of N. E. A.*, Vol. XXXII, No. 4 (April 1943), pp. 101-104. Important facts on the effectiveness of Japanese education, the high percentage of literacy, and the prevalence of nationalistic teaching.

Report of the United States Educational Mission to Japan (Washington, D. C.: U. S. Government Printing Office, 1946). Official report of the mission invited by SCAP to study Japanese education and make recommendations for its reorganization.

SANSOM, G. B., *Japan: A Cultural History* (New York: Century Company, 1931). A comprehensive and authoritative history of Japan from early times to 1868.

YANAGA, CHITOSHI, *Japan Since Perry* (New York: McGraw-Hill Book Company, Inc., 1949). A history of the growth of Japan in the last one hundred years, with chapters on education and cultural aspects of national development.

YOSHIDA, KUMAJI, "The Philosophy Underlying the National System of Education in Japan," in I. L. Kandel, ed., *Educational Yearbook of the International Institute, 1929* (New York: Teachers College, Columbia University, 1930), pp. 429-460. A clear statement of the social philosophy governing education in Japan.

Internationalism in Education

EMIL LENGYEL

The Roman orator Symmachus asked the basic question facing us in international education: "Why should we not live in peace and harmony? We look up at the same stars, we are fellow passengers on the same planet, and we dwell beneath the same sky. What matters it along which road each individual endeavors to find the ultimate truth? The riddle of existence is too great that there should be only one road leading to an answer." More than that, high-speed communication and transportation have broken through old boundary lines, making us all neighbors. Consequently we are faced with a very great challenge in international education, specifically, *acculturation*, or the exchange of elements of our various culture patterns.

We have been widening our horizons through the building up of new scientific knowledge and the attainment of universal systems of education. Humankind has progressed within the past few hundred years from belief in magic and slavery to science, freedom, and tolerance, although barriers to world understanding still exist. These barriers range from prejudices concerning race or possession of key resources to language and educational differences. It is increasingly apparent that the more than 2 billion human beings who inhabit our globe face common problems with regard to survival and progress. Each culture's system of education can be a great instrument in solving these problems if humanity is made the measure of all things and if each nation and culture pattern is willing to recognize the numerous educational solutions which are possible and the principle of relativism.

Above all, it is necessary to understand the need for bringing the basic data, the truth concerning ourselves and the universe, to everyone through the medium of universal education. As Albert Einstein has pointed out, "Restricting the body of knowledge to a small group deadens the philosophical spirit of a people and leads to spiritual poverty."

—A. H. M.

It was an international audience in the Cathedral School of Notre Dame de Paris that listened to the famous Pierre Abélard in the twelfth century expounding his stand on the controversy between realism and nominalism, the great issue of the age. It was also an international audience that sat at the feet of his antagonist, St. Bernard de Clairvaux, the "Thaumaturgus of the West," as he denounced Abélard's supposed rationalism as the rankest of heresies. At the renowned universities earnest seekers for truth converged from all over the Western world. "The universities were a single clerical system: one speech prevailed, and a single method of training was followed, in Oxford, and Paris, and Prague; and in education, as in other spheres, the Church was an international society."[1]

This was internationalism, indeed, but not as the term is used in modern times, when the nation is the human framework for concerted social work. Then social activity was guided by the church, which claimed to be catholic—that is, to encompass the world.

The international school was the goal of that early advocate of peace Pierre Dubois, Dante's contemporary; but here too internationalism in education was ancillary to church aims. *De recuperatione terrae sanctae*, written by Dubois, pointed the way to the Holy Land, which was to be wrested from pagan defilement. The princes of Europe were to be united in a common council and court, and the Christian children were to be saturated with this

[1] Ernest Barker, *National Character and the Factors in Its Formation* (New York: Harper & Brothers, 1937), p. 183.

all-important idea. Thus wars were to be eliminated among the followers of Christ, and the lamb would enjoy the company of the lion. The world was not told, however, what would happen after the holy shrines were safe. The lamb would be at peace with the lion—but outside of it, or inside?

On the eve of modern times, Johann Amos Comenius (or Komenský), a Moravian bishop and teacher, and author of the first picture book for children, also broached the idea of universal education. His plan was the "universal rededication of minds . . . not that external peace between rulers and peoples among themselves, but an internal peace of minds inspired by a system of ideas and feelings." In his *Pansophiae prodromus* he projected a Pansophic College in which scholars of all lands foregathered to arrange the elements of knowledge for mutual understanding among men.[2]

Two centuries passed before the idea moved from Europe's peripheries into its core. It was now Marc-Antoine Jullien (1775-1848), man of letters, Napoleon's diplomatic agent, Assistant Secretary of France's first Department of Education when he was only nineteen, who proposed a special commission to collect information on the educational system of the European nations. He believed that the harmonization of those systems could be accomplished and that the road to peace would thus be revealed.[3]

In the first decade of the twentieth century, internationalism in education as the road to peace was the guiding thought of a notable worker in the field of international law, Dr. Fannie Fern Andrews, of Boston, who deemed her contemporaries mature enough to heed the voice of reason. This was the age of the great optimism, when it was believed that wars were on the way out, along with wooden plows. Two international conferences had recently been held at The Hague and, even though they had produced little more than good will, Dr. Andrews believed that they pointed the way to peace. Teachers should be enlisted in that loftiest of all

[2] I. L. Kandel, "John Amos Comenius, Citizen of the World," *School and Society*, Vol. LV (April 11, 1942), pp. 401 ff.

[3] P. Rossello, *Les Précurseurs du Bureau d'International d'Education* (International Bureau of Education, 1943). Quoted by Adolph E. Meyer, *The Development of Education in the Twentieth Century*, 2nd ed. (New York: Prentice-Hall, Inc., 1949), pp. 569 ff.

causes, and therefore an international conference on education should be called.

Dr. Andrews pressed her point until she had the ears of the president of the United States, William Howard Taft, who set the State Department machinery into motion. The proposal was highly unorthodox and the diplomats could not put it in any pigeonhole. Since, however, President Taft himself displayed great interest in the project, the Foreign Offices had to react one way or another —until the Great War broke out.

When the armistice bugle sounded, the persistent Dr. Andrews was still around, and she resumed her pioneering work. Now that the League of Nations was in the making, it appeared logical to her that it should include an international office of education. But it did not appear logical to the assembled statesmen, whose minds were working in the grooves of powers and politics.

The League was already in existence when the idea sprouted again in a different form. This time it received more attention, because its sponsor was none other than former premier of France Léon Victor Auguste Bourgeois, head of the French delegations to the Hague conferences on peace, an author of the Covenant of the League, and the 1920 recipient of the Nobel Peace Prize. He saw that an important prop was missing from the structure of the League. A program must be drawn up in the fields of education and science. International education must be a keystone of the new postwar era—if it was really to be new and postwar. Acting upon his proposal, the League Council recommended to the Assembly that a commission be designated to study questions of intellectual cooperation and education.

The project traveled around the halls of the League and when it emerged into the open the word "education" had been deleted. Nor had there been much enthusiasm for intellectual cooperation. The Great War had shown again that modern wars were fought with modern weapons of which the laboratories were not the least important. Intellectual cooperation in such fields entailed certain risks which the leaders of the nations did not want to run. The pressure to do something about this problem was considerable, however, and in due time a solution was found. Education was left out, and intellectual cooperation was left in; it was to receive the quarantine treatment, however, to be isolated by the deep silence which is the fate of so many constructive ideas. A year after the death of Léon Bourgeois, which occurred in 1925, the Commission on Intellectual Cooperation came into existence, and it, in turn, gave birth to the Organization for Intellectual Cooperation.

Emasculated though it was, the Organization enlisted the ardent support of some of the greatest creative minds of the age: Albert Einstein, Marie Curie, the philosopher Henri Bergson, the classical scholar Gilbert Murray, and others. Nevertheless, the new body obtained no more than consultative powers at League headquarters.

The League could not overlook the problem of internationalism in education. Every nation considered itself superior to every other nation. *"Deutschland, Deutschland über Alles,"* the German sang, while his neighbor, the Frenchman, called his country *la grande nation*; Russia was holy; the British ruled the waves; and even a country as small as Hungary boasted: "If the earth is God's hat, Hungary is the bouquet on the hat." The League attempted to have history textbooks revised, so that they should show more understanding for other people and display less jingoistic spirit. It also launched a study of the remarkable new media of mass communication, which reached millions and could be turned to constructive use. Walls dividing the world's intellectual forces were to topple as universities, teachers, scholars, librarians, and researchers were to meet periodically under the auspices of the League.

Funds were inadequate, however, for the numerous activities projected, since intellectual cooperation appeared to be purely academic to practical politicians, who failed to realize that constructive politics was the lengthened shadow of constructive education. Nations were not prepared to spend a few millions on activities that might prevent wars, but they were more than prepared to spend billions on wars.

ATTEMPTS AT INTERNATIONALISM AFTER WORLD WAR I

International Education Associations. The thought occurred to many school people that if nations were to understand one another their young people should meet one another in classrooms. One of these teachers was a professor of political science at the College of the City of New York, Stephen Duggan, who conceived the idea that the exchange of students would help to foster international understanding. At first the number of the students might not be large, but the success of the plan would multiply the student exchanges and, besides, each student would be expected to become a powerhouse of international cooperation.

Dr. Duggan approached the Carnegie Endowment for International Peace with his plan and the sum necessary to launch the project was placed at his disposal. In the year 1919 the Institute of International Education was born.

The Institute began on a modest scale, but soon it became evident that it filled a gap. It helped to exchange students and also professors and lecturers. The number of student exchanges effected between the two wars alone amounted to more than five thousand.

The Institute of International Education also introduced the service known as Junior Year Abroad. Gifted young juniors were enabled to become acquainted with foreign countries by spending an academic year abroad. The Institute also set up a counseling service and in due course of time it became the principal clearing instrument between the United States and foreign lands in the educational field. Its integrity was so great and its efficiency so high that various governmental bodies were depending upon its services in a great many ways.

Other institutional contacts in the field of education were also introduced. Since the United States was not a member of the League of Nations, it was not linked with the league's educational work. However, American educators began to feel strongly that they would be remiss in the discharge of their obligations if they failed to coordinate some aspects of their work with teaching bodies abroad. It was in order to bring about this cooperation that the largest organization of its kind in this country, the National Education Association, called an international conference in 1922 to meet in the city of San Francisco. At that conference a large number of countries were represented by about six hundred delegates, who made the decision to launch the World Federation of Educational Associations with the object of implementing the new diplomacy of "open covenants openly arrived at." The Federation was to cultivate international good will by disseminating educational information and, generally, achieving international cooperation in the field of education.

The principal medium of this cooperation was to be a biennial conference. The first met in San Francisco; subsequently, others were held in Edinburgh, Toronto, Geneva, Denver, Dublin, and Oxford; the last one met in 1937 in Tokyo. These conferences were to compare the educational thoughts and teaching methods of the various countries, and the cause of mutual understanding and peace was to gain thereby. The World Federation published a bulletin about important events in the educational world. The Federation rose from the ashes of World War II with a new name: World Organization of the Teaching Profession.

The International Bureau of Education was conceived in 1925 by a group of teachers resident in Geneva, Switzerland. It was a private agency specializing in the publication of educational material throughout the world. It published a yearbook on the progress of international education, a bulletin, and a score of monographs on special topics. Some of the major countries, including Great Britain and the United States, never joined the Bureau. It was hinted that the United States kept out because the Bureau's place of birth was Geneva, home of the League of Nations, with which the United States was not then on speaking terms. Also, the materials produced by the Bureau appeared to be of problematic value, since they were based on suspect official Ministry of Education handouts and watered down so as not to offend any groups. The United States now supports the Bureau indirectly, however, through UNESCO.

International Education for Nationalism. The world was still nominally at peace, but local wars were exploding in China, Spain, and Ethiopia—admonitions of the great disaster soon to overwhelm man. Hitler was in power in Germany, preaching a racial internationalism of blood and iron. National boundaries should not separate people of identical blood, he screamed, since racial affinity took precedence over citizenship. In the south-German city of Stuttgart the *Auslandsorganisation*, "A.O.," was set up, to link the racial German *Volksdeutsche* to the fatherland. There was also the larger affinity of the Nordics, who were considered members of a superior race.

We may overlook the "internationalism" of Soviet education, which was an early phase, not fully developed, and which yielded to strong nationalism exalting the country's past with somewhat less critical sense than is the habit of most other nations. Soviet internationalism appeared to be more and more a foil for imperialism.

After the demise of Latin as an international tongue (which took place in some parts of Europe less than a century ago), one of its offspring, French, made a bid as a universal language. It came to be used as the basic language of diplomacy for a long time and rose to a position of importance in such regions as the Levant, on the eastern Mediterranean shores, and southeastern Europe. This was the result of the special position which France occupied in the late Ottoman Empire, and that position could be traced to the early Crusades, in which French warriors and institutions played a dominant role.

French economic and diplomatic interests appreciated the importance of the *internationale* of the French language. It is easier tô do business with a country whose tongue one understands, and it is also easier to follow its diplomatic leadership. The bulk of French cultural work abroad was carried out by the Bureau des Oeuvres Français à l' Etranger (Office of French Affairs Abroad) of the French Foreign Office. After World War II this work was greatly expanded under the Direction Générale des Relations Culturelles (General Directorate of Cultural Relations)—which was also under the Foreign Office—working in conjunction with the Ministry of National Education. All the major cultural activities are covered by this work: teaching of the language, exchange of students, libraries, theatres, art exhibitions, etc. In key positions abroad there are also French institutes, which operate on an academic level. And there is the Alliance Française, a private organization operating with the support of the French government to promote the knowledge of language and letters.

As the driving power of France began to ebb and that of the English-speaking world developed into a tidal wave, English revealed a winning trend, replacing French as the first foreign tongue in many parts of the world. Much-maligned Hollywood had a hand in shaping this trend. Certain American slang words became the public property of millions.

With the emergence of the age of dictators, the thoughts of the democratic countries turned to linking education to strategy. The British Council was founded in 1934 to encourage the study of

English in foreign countries, especially in South America, Portugal, the Balkans, and, naturally, the Middle East, land of petroleum and of the Suez Canal.

The Council was originally a private enterprise but was subsequently nationalized; its Royal Charter provided that it was to develop and foster cultural relations between the United Kingdom and other countries for the benefit of the British Commonwealth of Nations.

The United States was not among the first nations to act in this field. It was only in 1939 that our Department of State established its Division of Cultural Relations, under the direction of Ben M. Cherrington, head of the Social Science Foundation of the University of Denver. Cultural relations were to be reciprocal and diplomatic purposes were to be ignored. The United States was ready to teach other countries what it knew for the benefit of all, and it wanted also to learn from others. "Cultural exchanges," said Professor Cherrington, "should involve the direct participation of the people and institutions concerned."[4]

Eventually other cultural organizations were set up in the United States for reciprocal education. One of them was the Division of Inter-American Educational Relations in the Office of Education, under the sponsorship of Commissioner John W. Studebaker; another was the Inter-Departmental Committee on Cultural and Scientific Co-operation; still another was the Institute of Inter-American Affairs, previously called the Office of the Co-ordinator of Inter-American Affairs. Throughout the world the United States established libraries and information centers, which, in many places, turned out to be the only public libraries open to everybody without any special formalities. Thus a veritable revolution was brought about in the habits of the reading public in various parts of the world.

Pioneers in International Education. Not all attempts at international education served national purposes. The Children's Workshop Committee at Bilthoven, Holland, founded by Kees Boeke, was a notable example of those that did not.[5] The children of the community came from many lands. The Committee attempted to

[4] Quoted in Emil Lengyel, "Aid to World Peace," *Journal of Educational Sociology*, Vol. XX, No. 9 (May 1947), pp. 566 ff.

[5] Adolph Meyer, *op. cit.*, pp. 585-586.

do away with artificial boundaries of petrified institutions between man and man. It observed the individual, not his nationality, and sought to restore to him his original—as distinguished from national—attitude toward his fellow men.

An outstanding pioneer was Paul Geheeb, of the Oldenwaldschule of Germany, where children of many lands lived in self-constituted families which treated nationality merely as incidental and not essential. An attempt was made to lay the basis of a new type of citizenship, *Weltbürgerschaft:* citizenship of the world.

When Hitler came, Geheeb decided to leave. He moved to Switzerland, where he founded l'Ecole de l'Humanité, the School of Humanity, on the outskirts of Geneva. From there he moved to the more rural settings of Morat and Schwarzsee, in the canton of Fribourg. His idea was to create a pilot plant of the school of the future, where teachers and pupils should work as members of the same family. All cultures should promote international good will. The apparent incompatibility of some cultures, he averred, was the vestige of the aristocratic way of life, which set up caste barriers. Only when these were disregarded would democracy become a living reality.

EDUCATION DURING WORLD WAR II

The problem of postwar education for a sounder world was broached by the Allies while World War II was still in full swing. As early as 1942 a Conference of the Allied Ministers of Education met in London under the chairmanship of the head of the British Board of Education. The participants were ten European nations occupied by the Reich.[6] The British Commonwealth of Nations and the International Labor Office were represented by observers. The conference worked largely through commissions engaged in the detailed studies of special questions. More ambitious plans had to be abandoned and the Conference focused its attention on the technical problems of restoring educational services after the war. An Inter-Allied Book Center was created to organize collections of books published since the war. The Commission on Books and

[6] William G. Carr, *Only by Understanding: Education and International Organization* (New York: Foreign Policy Association, May-June 1945, No. 52), p. 62.

Periodicals set out to encourage the production of certain books. A Commission on Films and Visual Aids was also set up. The Commission on the Protection and Restoration of Cultural Material collected information which it made available to British and American agencies—the Roberts Commission and the MacMillan Committee—responsible for returning looted art objects, archives, manuscripts, and precious books.

Subsequently the United States announced its intention to cooperate with the Conference, and the State Department sent a delegation to London in April 1944. It helped to draft a constitution for a United Nations Organization for Educational and Cultural Reconstruction.[7] The draft contained a statement of the reasons for international cooperation in educational reconstruction, a definition of its functions, and provisions on the structure of the organization.

In the early discussions about the United Nations, its political functions monopolized attention. Again it was thought—as it had been thought a quarter of a century before, when the League was in the crucible—that the best way to assure peace was to set up agencies for the settlement of international disputes. Little attention was paid to the deeper causes of those disputes and to curing those causes, rather than the disease itself. Little attention was paid in those early days to the economic and social causes of conflicts among the nations, let alone the causes that are conceived in the minds of man. It took some time before the Economic and Social Council of the UN achieved the importance it has today. It took even more time before the need for an educational and cultural agency of the United Nations was fully recognized.

Numerous organizations were interested in such an agency, including the Educational Policies Commission of the NEA, which urged the establishment of a permanent international body for education with greater powers than those possessed by any League of Nations body. The same conclusion was reached by the Institute of International Education, the National Council for the Social Studies, the International Education Assembly, the Joint Commission of the Council for Education in World Citizenship, etc.

An important announcement on this subject was made from San Francisco by Archibald MacLeish, well-known poet and former

[7] William G. Carr, *op. cit.* pp. 64-65.

Librarian of Congress, who was then Assistant Secretary of State. A charter for a United Nations agency for education and cultural development was being discussed informally with the Conference of Allied Ministers of Education and with the other members of the Big Five, he advised. The hope was expressed that a conference on the subject would take place following the conclusion of the San Francisco United Nations Conference on International Organization. Joint Resolutions in the Senate and the House were passed unanimously in favor of such an organization, with the proviso, however, that it must not interfere with domestic policies in education. This was the start of UNESCO.

UNESCO

In the autumn of 1945 the United Nations Educational, Scientific and Cultural Organization, UNESCO, was founded, with the participation of forty-three nations whose delegates met in London. Its famed preamble proclaimed: "Since wars begin in the minds of man, it is in the minds of man that the defenses of peace must be constructed." In order for men to be able to construct those defenses of peace, they must be permitted the unrestricted pursuit of objective truth and they must have the means to engage in the free exchange of ideas.

Some of the means by which this world-wide program would be executed included large-scale international student exchange as well as the exchange of ideas dealing with educational, scientific, and cultural advances of all nations through all media of communication. Other means of cultural advance included the global exchange and purchase of books and of educational materials not only in the major languages but also in tongues little known in the West; an all-out attack on illiteracy; and aid to war-devastated lands to repair and increase their educational means.

UNESCO began to propagate the idea of internationalism. Under a leadership which, although not invariably inspired, was well-meaning, it drew up a large program, the extent of which was well illustrated by its Director General at the Fourth Session of its General Conference at Paris, late in 1949. The Director General, Jaime Torres Bodet, Mexican statesman and educator, listed among UNESCO activities educational seminars in key regions; a pilot project in Haiti (which, incidentally, did not turn out to be a success); educational missions to the Philippines, Thailand, and Afghanistan; a book plan for soft-currency countries (countries whose money was not convertible into dollars) to obtain books and periodicals in hard-currency countries; social-science associations as instruments of international collaboration; study and observation missions in comparative law, social psychology, and many other fields.

UNESCO also proposed to help create a Council of Medical Science. It proposed the convocation of an International Congress of Mathematicians and an International Union for the Protection of Nature and was prepared to sign a contract with the International Council of Music to work on behalf of that organization. UNESCO was also ready to help publish fine-arts reviews, to turn its attention to workers' education, to promote exchange programs, to organize teams for school broadcasts, to build up documentary material for the historians, etc., etc.

"In the present disorganized state of fundamental education," the Director General stated, "one of the most useful steps UNESCO can take is to create a center of training and production which can provide students and specialists with intensive and speedier training, while at the same time insuring the output of teaching material."

The program of UNESCO only a few years ago, in 1948, filled fifty pages. But for the fiscal year 1951 the organization received from its fifty-nine member countries only $8,149,985—$700,000 less than in the preceding year. This appropriation was an almost invisible fraction of one percent of the sums the members spent on arms.

In 1949, the Director General of the organization pointed to another one of its weaknesses when he asked: "There are a number of national commissions, but how many of them meet regularly? How many have attempted to start local branches, and how many answer our inquiries or endeavor to carry out our program?" Four years after the foundation of UNESCO he said: "For the most part, UNESCO is still a blueprint." That statement is true even today.

This is the situation despite the fact that at the outset UNESCO did attract the most public-spirited persons one could wish for.

Great scholars and famous scientists were bursting with ideas for the propagation of a world-mind. It was clearly shown that here was a vast untilled field.

Critics of UNESCO usually focus their criticism on two points. First, UNESCO may not intervene in matters that are essentially within the domestic jurisdiction of the member states. Would the Nazis' notorious hate propaganda against "inferior" neighbors be considered an essentially domestic issue? Secondly, UNESCO is said to be handicapped by the absence of the Soviet Union, which seems to hold the organization useless since it fails to operate within the framework of Marxian dialectical materialism. The validity of this second criticism is subject to serious doubt.

THE UNITED STATES AND EDUCATIONAL INTERNATIONALISM

America has had a large number of workers in the field of international education in the past, but generally speaking this country has been too busy with domestic problems to devote much time to outside issues. Just the same, let us remember that American schools in the Middle East were very important in raising the level of education and introducing new ideas.

At the end of World War II it became patent that the United States was cast for the leading role in the international field. The other great Western countries were weakened because of their participation in two vastly destructive conflicts. This nation, on the other hand, has come out of two world wars stronger and more prosperous than ever. The unique event occurred that one country with not more than some 7 percent of the population of the world was producing close to 50 percent of the industrial products of our globe. This nation was now in the very midst of international events.

The armed forces of the United States were stationed now in nearly all parts of the world. There were American bases in countries with which most Americans were familiar only through motion pictures, if at all. America's diplomatic representation became truly global. This nation was now represented not only in inaccessible parts of the Middle East but also in the darkest parts of Africa and Asia. American businessmen and engineers were scattered in all parts of the Old World.

In order to do justice to this new role, a more extensive knowledge of the world became necessary. Furthermore, the United States served as a mentor to former enemy nations called upon to deal with a large variety of civilian problems. Add to this the need for specialists in the ways of the countries with which the United States entered into special relations in the course of the years—through the Marshall Plan; through the Truman Doctrine of aiding Turkey and Greece to maintain their independence; through the North Atlantic Treaty association and the resulting Mutual Defense Pact against the policies of the Soviet Union; and through the "Point Four" program of President Truman for the development of backward countries.

Americans Abroad. In 1949 the United States had about 183,000 civilian employees working outside the country—one half in U. S. possessions and the other half in foreign lands.[8] These people were attached to diplomatic missions, at bases, assigned to the armed services, on special jobs. Many thousands of Americans were employed in private work abroad, as salesmen, journalists, teachers, technicians.

American Economic Interests in Foreign Lands. After World War II the United States came to occupy a position in the world which was unique in modern times—and perhaps for all times. Its productive capacity increased tremendously during two wars, whereas the productive capacities of the leading foreign countries declined, largely because of devastation and the depletion of monetary reserves. The vast quantities of goods produced in the United States could not all be sold there. In order to sell abroad, one must be versed in the ways of foreign people. Foreign traders are usually more international-minded than domestic traders.

Reciprocal Educational Agreements. The newly acquired position of the United States made it necessary from a national point of view to take a deeper interest in internationalism in education. The latter term, of course, means several things to several people. In its broadest meaning it stands for the belief in "One World"— or, as it was once expressed in this country, "One World or None." In a more restricted sense it means a deep and sympathetic interest in the other people of the world—the belief that even though

[8] Vera Micheles Dean, "How U. S. Foreign Policy Is Made," *Foreign Policy Reports,* Vol. XXV, No. 10 (Oct. 1, 1949), p. 118.

the One World idea may be long in taking shape, the interests of the various parts of the world are interconnected.

The first step in internationalism in education is to acquaint ourselves with the ways of other people and to stop looking at them as exotic curiosities. We must familiarize ourselves with their past histories, so that we may learn why they respond to challenges in different ways. Another step in internationalism is to look at ourselves critically, from a point of view which is broader than the purely nationalistic. From this critical analysis comes the recognition that no country is infallible. We make mistakes occasionally, and they should be recognized as such. Still another way of internationalism is to help other people learn our ways. Thus they can learn from us and we in turn may learn from them. Let us not forget that the very best analyses of our own governments have come from visitors to our shores, such as the immortal Alexis de Tocqueville, author of *Democracy in America*, and James Bryce, author of *The American Commonwealth*.

Among the attempts at internationalism in education, cultural exchanges may play an important part. At the end of 1950, some 29,000 foreign students were enrolled in American schools of higher learning, an increase of three thousand over the preceding year. In the first part of the same year, some 36,500 American students were studying in foreign schools of higher learning—17,000 more than in the preceding year. This is a clear indication of a significant trend, which the government-sponsored G.I.'s do not fully explain.

It should be pointed out here that student exchanges are not necessarily promoting internationalism in education. Much depends on the type of people who are being sent and the type of milieu into which they got. It was customary between the two world wars, for example, for authoritarian countries to send their students to the United States. In many cases these students did not become imbued with democratic ideals but, on the contrary, spread the idea of totalitarianism. American students sent on exchange scholarships into these countries frequently came back as admirers of the "strong men" of those nations.

We do not know how China was affected by the fact that a very large number of her students came to us for about a quarter of a century. Possibly the scale of exchanges was not large enough to make an appreciable impact on the native ways of life. It is also possible that the greatest impression was made on the foreign students by the display of indiscriminate nationalism. In the company of foreign visitors it is supposed to be a patriotic obligation to show only the best features of one's own country. No wonder students leave the place of their studies with distorted notions. Many of the foreign students in America were financed by private groups such as the Rotary International, the English-Speaking Union, the American-Scandinavian Foundation, and college fraternities. The United States sponsored a "two-way passage" exchange of students, partly through the sale of American surplus property left abroad after the end of the war. The country purchasing our war supplies could pay for them in part by underwriting the education of American students in that country and financing the travel expenses of its own exchange scholars in the United States.

Three types of activity were included in the program: graduate study, teaching, and research. Scholars in each of these categories received maintenance, tuition, and travel and incidental expenses. A United States Education Foundation was to be established in each of the participating countries to recommend programs. A Board of Foreign Scholarships was set up in the United States, which designated the Institute of International Education, the U. S. Office of Education, and the Conference Board of Associated Research Councils to select the candidates. It was expected that about three thousand persons would qualify under this so-called Fulbright Act.

Internationalism in education was furthered by the mighty groundswell of student travel abroad. This travel was promoted in part by commercial travel agencies which chartered means of transportation, especially airplanes, and thus reduced costs for each student; in part by nonprofit study-tour organizations, which operated the way travel agencies do but without profits accruing on equity capital; and in part by schools of higher learning.

Great impetus was given also to the creation of so-called "workshops" abroad, each engaged in the study of a special problem, such as the operation of the Marshall Plan, or the social, economic, and political life of a country, a region, or several countries. Generally, students were to receive regular academic credit for work in these workshops. Most of the workshops operated during the summer, thus taking the place of a full summer session.

Internationalism in education was also to be promoted by new courses in schools, mostly on the academic level, devoted to the study of foreign countries, their people, and their mores. Many such courses were launched during World War II, when it was felt that the United States should know far more about its allies, particularly about the Soviet Union. Courses were set up to study not only Russian history and political institutions but also the Russian language. Some of America's leading universities set up Russian departments and Russian institutes then and also after the war, when it became even more obvious that we should know more about that country. Harvard University began the publication of a series of authoritative books on various aspects of Soviet life.

The United Nations also invited the attention of the people of the United States. Universities and high schools launched projects in studying the UN and the people of this world organization.

It was also an encouraging trend that the schools began to take an interest in the foreign policy of the United States and other countries, in the State Department, in the diplomatic service, etc.[9]

After the war, "The Voice of America," attached to the State Department, became an instrument for disseminating the American point of view abroad. It was not as effective, possibly, as the BBC of Great Britain or the Soviet broadcasts, because of the lack of experience in this type of work in this country and also because of the limited knowledge of foreign ways.

The United States was thrust deeper into the international field when American troops occupied zones in Germany, Austria, Japan, and the southern part of Korea. It was thought to be one of the missions of the occupation forces to stimulate interest in the democratic processes through education. This was not easy, especially in Germany, where the bulk of the teaching staffs was discredited by too wholehearted cooperation with the defunct Nazi regime. Also the task was hard because of the havoc wrought in the larger cities by air attacks. New teaching staffs had to be created, textbooks produced, plants and equipment constructed. After nearly five years of occupation, it was the view of most impartial observers that the American efforts at education in the Reich were not signally

[9] Cf. Emil Lengyel, *America's Role in World Affairs*, in "American Way Series," ed. by S. P. McCutchen (New York: Harper & Brothers, 1946; rev. ed., 1950).

successful. This was due partly to the general world situation and partly to overlapping jurisdictions, but mostly to inadequate appropriations. Also, it was strongly felt by competent observers that the people assigned to this important task were often selected because of their total colorlessness in political matters and not because of their qualifications as educators or administrators.

GREAT BRITAIN AND EDUCATIONAL INTERNATIONALISM

We have seen that long before World War II the British Council was formed to spread knowledge of Britain abroad. After the war, the attempts of the United Kingdom to advertise itself and to promote a measure of internationalism in education became more important. In 1947 the Educational Interchange Council was launched to promote educational exchanges with selected foreign countries, of which Austria was the first.[10] The Council sent British students to foreign countries and foreign students to Britain, the visits ranging in length from three weeks to a year. Foreign workers were brought to England to attend workers' colleges, and teachers, youth leaders, adult educationists and trade unionists were to attend special holiday courses.

The British government itself helped through direct assistance for educational and other cultural visits, exchanges with other European countries, scholarships, grants for the rebuilding of libraries, distribution of books and films. It subsidized British orchestras, actors, and speakers abroad. The British Council sent exhibitions on foreign tours—for example, the Town and Country Planning and the English Theatrical Design displays. It subsidized foreign tours for the very popular Sadler's Wells Ballet and published the British Medical Bulletin to keep practitioners in other lands in touch with latest developments in Britain. And there was, of course, the BBC European Service.

It is generally recognized that the British Council has been exceptionally successful, and there are several reasons for its success. The Council gives people what they need: up-to-date, reliable information in a large number of fields. It conveys the impression of being absolutely sincere and not addicted to exaggeration. More

[10] *Britain and Cultural Reconstruction in Europe* (New York: British Information Services, August 1948).

important, perhaps, than all this, the personnel of the British Council is excellent—very polite, helpful, sympathetic, and well versed in the ways of the country. Also, the British Council seems to have adequate financial resources at its call.

OTHER PLANS FOR EDUCATIONAL INTERNATIONALISM

One of the best ideas to promote internationalism in education was that of the International Voluntary Work Camps, in which young people from all over Europe and sometimes elsewhere engage in socially constructive work during the summer holidays. These camps were set up with the cooperation of UNESCO, the American Friends' Service, national governments, youth movements, and private organizations. They are in operation in a dozen countries, from Britain to Greece. The camps are engaged in such varied activities as social work, farming, and building canals, hostels, youth centers, and playgrounds. Their main function is to bring together young people from a large number of countries, to have them work and play together, so that they may learn the advantages of helping instead of killing one another.

The Geneva Institute of International Studies, under the direction of Professor William F. Rappard, has been recognized as a leader in the field of internationalism in education. International study courses have been set up by a number of British universities, too— London, Oxford, Leeds, Birmingham, and St. Andrews, among others.

In Germany, too, the idea of internationalism has taken some hold. A special feature of the German movement is the *Studententreffen* or *Studentenwerk*. Special organizations connected with universities are set up to solve problems linked to international attitudes. Several of these projects were launched after World War II within the framework of summer university or seminar work. Among the more notable programs are those of Göttingen, Freiburg, Munich, Mainz, and Kiel Universities; they have special courses on economic, political, and social problems, language, literature, and the sciences. One of the most interesting of these ventures is in Austria, at Oesterreichisches College, in Alpbach. There the *Europäisches Forum* was founded in 1945, immediately after the end of the war, to engage in what the founders described as *übernationale geistige Zusammenarbeit,* supranational intellectual cooperation. The project was intended for scholars, artists, and all other people who want to find an intellectual meeting ground in a world rent by destructive forces.

A word must be said also about plans to establish one or more world universities, in which internationalism will be the guiding spirit. The first articulate postwar expression of this idea was propagated by the American-European Friendship Society, which lent its aid to the idea of the Czech author J. Urzidil that one or more world universities be founded.

Several such plans were launched subsequently. The most serious of these was the "College of Europe" in Bruges, Belgium. A "pilot plant" was in operation in 1949, with a student body of fifty. The school was expected to be in full operation in 1950. The object of the College of Europe was stated as follows: to provide European university graduates with a broad European education, a synthesis of the national educations. The United Nations showed great interest in the project, announcing that its graduates would enjoy priority in UN appointments. A similar object animated the Conference of European Culture, an integral part of the European Movement idea, which met in Lausanne early in 1950. The European Movement is a nongovernmental organization for European unity, largely the outgrowth of the working committee established by Winston Churchill in 1947. Mr. Churchill became the honorary president of the European Movement, and Paul-Henri Spaak, of Belgium, became the copresident. The cultural section of the Movement met under Salvador de Madariaga, celebrated Spanish author.

The Soviet Union had claimed to be the pioneer of an international system in which loyalty to the workers of the world was to take precedence over loyalty to one's own country, in the way loyalty to France had superseded allegiance to the Frenchman's *petite patrie*—Gironde, Savoie, Artois—after the Revolution. Recent developments do not bear out this hope. On the contrary, the Soviet Union, parading as the great land of international socialism, seems to be suppressing the smaller countries on its peripheries, following the well-established pattern of aggressive imperialism.

In the eastern-European belt, the Soviet language began to forge to the fore, displacing English, German, and French. History books were revised to eulogize the Soviet Union or simply translated from the Russian.[11] History was subjected to the treatment of Marxian dialectics, and the authors felt impelled at every turn to point out to what extent historic events did conform or failed to conform to Marx's theories. The books also revealed a highly critical attitude toward Germans in the past, even when these books were German translations intended for use in the Russian zone of Germany. The critical attitude was pronounced not only toward such highly conservative leaders as Chancellor Bismarck but toward the German people as a whole.

In connection with the Boxer Rebellion, for example, the authors of one book[12] make the following statement: "The Germans distinguished themselves through particular atrocities." The Kaiser is reported to have admonished his troops to take no prisoners, so that "not a single Chinese dare look askance at a German for a thousand years." On the same page of the book, the Germans are said to have been engaged in the complete extermination of the Africans in the Reich colonies. At another point the authors quote a nineteenth-century French newspaper: "The Germans are not only barbarians but also proud of being just that. They gloat over the fact that they have stepped back fifteen centuries into Germany's early days."

There are few precedents for such methods of teaching history. Is this method bound to provoke the readers to extremes of nationalist resentment or is this an effective way to combat German supernationalism? The answer to these questions can be provided only by time.

TOWARD A NEW INTERNATIONALISM

In reflecting upon the trend of times, one recalls Plato's sage words in *The Republic* to the effect that the character of education is determined by the theories of psychology, politics, ethics, culture, and social organization of the people, and that education cannot be discussed in a vacuum. In that case, education in a world dominated by nations must remain nationalistic, and international education must grow out of internationalism.

[11] A good illustration of this type of book is W. M. Chwostow and L. I. Subok, *Geschichte der Neuzeit, 1870-1918* (Berlin and Leipzig: Volk und Wissen, 1949).

[12] *Ibid.*

It was I. L. Kandel who wrote, "It is obvious that any trend towards the development of international understanding or world-mindedness is determined primarily by national emotions or attitudes which, although they often override the logical demands of the age, are at once the results and explanations of the character of the educational system."[13]

Sir Michael Sadler, one-time Vice-Chancellor of Leeds and Master of University College, wrote: "A national system of education is a living thing, the outcome of forgotten struggles and difficulties and 'of battles long ago.' It has in it some of the workings of national life."[14]

The history of humanity holds no precedent for the hold the nation exerts on the destiny of man. It lays claim to all his body and all his soul. The closest parallel is the tremendously strong hold that the church once had on the individual; yet people did dare to defy that hold and they did go to the stake with proud steps.

Internationalism is not something that may be brought about overnight, or even in the course of a few years. It will have to break down some of the most formidable taboos before it can assert itself. It is often said that the trend of the world is in the direction of a constantly expanding field of loyalties. The line of development is well known. It began with the human pack, and today we have reached the stage of the nation. There is no reason why man's political organization should call a halt at this point. Perhaps the next step will be the regional organization. In Europe we may discern the beginning of this tendency in the creation of Benelux. But how halting are the steps of this well-meaning group.

It is understood, of course, that internationalism is not meant to be opposed to the real concept of nationalism. The time may come when nationalism will be incomprehensible without the international setting. Pluralism in the ways of man is not a new departure. After all, we are not only Americans but also members of families and worshipers in churches. It is conceivable that the best type of Americanism will be recognized as the kind which employs the

[13] I. L. Kandel, *Comparative Education* (Boston: Houghton Mifflin Company, 1933), p. 14.

[14] I. L. Kandel, quoting a lecture by Sir Michael Sadler, in "University Departments of Education," *Universities Quarterly*, Vol. III (May 1949), pp. 704-705.

tolerance preached so often and practiced so little in relations with other countries. The measure today is the nation but the measure in the thinking of the most constructive interpreters of social institutions must be Man.

This does not mean that we, as nationals of a country, must abandon all our sovereignty. After all, we as citizens of a nation have not abandoned our own individual sovereignty. On the contrary, we claim that we can develop our special qualities as individuals only within the nation. We should be able to develop our best national qualities within the international commonwealth. Educators wield a tremendous power for good or evil through their choice of the seeds they implant in the hearts of the young.

Internationalism in education is an appropriate term only if it helps create a broader pattern for human relations. The accent is on the human species and not on the political form of human groups. The objection may be raised that human evolution needs the challenge of competition. That is true. But even though we no longer stab one another in the back on street corners as our feudal ancestors did, we are operating within the framework of competitive institutions. The challenge man needs is amply provided by the forces of nature. The larger part of the globe still defies man, in arctic tundras, in rain-drenched tropical forests, in the vast aridity of deserts, and in the frustrating world of swamps. These challenges call for positive answers testing both the ingenuity and endurance of man.

Naturally, internationalism in education can hardly be a hothouse product. In matters of social organization we deal with deeply rooted customs, superstitious fear of change, vested interests, inertia, and the scarcity of inspired leadership. If past history provides a pattern, the path of the future winds across intermediary regions. Nations may not combine promptly into a single global unit.

At the same time, our power to act must not be paralyzed by historic patterns. In the present critical period, the past may not be the ideal guide for an understanding of the future. In the past the urgency for action was never as great as it is today. Man should be capable of breaking traditional patterns in the face of an impending doom.

Internationalism does not mean, of course, that a country such as Costa Rica weighs as heavily in the scale of importance as, for example, the United States. Glib talk about the sovereign equality of all nations is not to be taken too seriously. But Costa Rica—to cling to our illustration—has as much right to cultivate her special cultural ways as the United States. Internationalism is a synonym for humanism, with the emphasis on what is universal in man—his striving for self-expression within the larger community and for its ultimate benefit. National contributions must not be glossed over by internationalism in education. On the contrary, they will be stressed, just as the individual's contributions are stressed in democratic society. But those contributions will be cherished as part of man's larger heritage and not as a nation's jealously guarded monopoly.

BIBLIOGRAPHY

BARKER, ERNEST, *National Character and the Factors in Its Formation* (New York: Harper & Brothers, 1937). A thoughtful, well-written book, which gives due weight to education.

BARNES, HARRY ELMER, *An Intellectual and Cultural History of the Western World* (New York: Random House, Inc., 1937). An encyclopedic book. Throughout the narrative, the importance of various forms of education is stressed.

CARR, WILLIAM G., "International Frontiers in Education," *Annals of the American Academy of Political and Social Science* (September 1944). Contains chapters on the most significant developments in education in the world of today.

———, *Only by Understanding: Education and International Organization* (Foreign Policy Association, Headline Series, No. 52, May-June 1945). Particularly detailed about international agencies of education.

COUNTS, G. S., and N. P. LODGE, *I Want to Be Like Stalin* (New York: The John Day Company, 1947). Translated from the Russian *Pedagogika* of B. P. Yesipov and N. K. Goncharov. Education in the shadow of dialectical materialism.

DEWEY, JOHN, *Democracy and Education* (New York: The Macmillan Company, 1916). An introduction to the philosophy of education. Treats also theory, systems, and the significance of the geographical factor in education.

DUGGAN, STEPHEN, and BETTY DRURY, *The Rescue of Science and Learning* (New York: The Macmillan Company, 1948). The story of the Emergency Committee in Aid of Displaced Foreign Scholars, by the chairman and executive secretary.

HART, JOSEPH K., *A Social Interpretation of Education* (New York: Henry Holt & Company, Inc., 1929). The author is a former professor of education at Teachers College, Columbia University, who has written extensively on education and democracy, creative moments in education, and education in an age of power.

HAYES, CARLTON J., *Essays on Nationalism* (New York: The Macmillan Company, 1926). The author is an educator and former American ambassador who has shown special interest in nationalism and education, as well as in the next step.

Journal of Educational Sociology, Social Studies Issue, Vol. XX, No. 9 (May 1947). Written by members of the Social Studies Department of the New York University School of Education, on various aspects of teaching social studies, including aids to international education.

KANDEL, I. L., *Comparative Education* (Boston: Houghton Mifflin Company, 1933). Description and analysis of the educational systems of Britain, France, Germany, Russia, and the United States, by one of the foremost workers in the field.

MANN, ERIKA, *School for Barbarians* (New York: Modern Age Books, Inc., 1938). Miseducation under the Nazis for intolerance and aggression.

MELBY, ERNEST O., ed., *Mobilizing Educational Resources*, Sixth Yearbook of the John Dewey Society (New York: Harper & Brothers, 1943). Includes a chapter on needed new patterns of control by George S. Counts.

MERRIAM, CHARLES EDWARD, *The Making of Citizens* (Chicago: University of Chicago Press, 1931). A comparative study of the methods of civic training in selected countries, against the background of national settings and social conditions. A highly cherished book in the field.

MEYER, ADOLPH E., *The Development of Education in the Twentieth Century*, 2nd ed. (New York: Prentice-Hall, Inc., 1949). An account of national systems of education in key countries.

MONROE, PAUL, ed., *A Cyclopaedia of Education*, 5 vols. (New York: The Macmillan Company, 1918-1919). Compiled with the assistance of more than a thousand contributors. With maps, diagrams, plates, illustrations, and portraits.

——— *Essays in Comparative Education*, 2 vols. (New York: Teachers College, Columbia University, Vol. I, 1927; Vol. II, 1932; rev. ed., 1933). Addresses, essays, and lectures by a former president of Robert College, Istanbul, who has also written reports on education in the Near East and China.

NORTHROP, F. S. C., *The Meeting of East and West* (New York: The Macmillan Company, 1946). A philosophic study of the differences between East and West, with suggestions on how to reconcile the differences.

REISNER, EDWARD H., *Nationalism and Education Since 1789* (New York: The Macmillan Company, 1922). A history of modern education in its setting of sociopolitical developments by an author deeply interested in religious values. The book is an elaboration of a syllabus for a course in the history of education, originally published by Teachers College.

SANDIFORD, PETER, ed., *Comparative Education* (New York: E. P. Dutton & Company, Inc., 1918). Studies of the educational systems of six modern countries, by H. W. Foght, A. H. Hope, I. L. Kandel, and W. Russell.

SELIGMAN, E. R. A., and ALVIN JOHNSON, eds., *Encyclopaedia of the Social Sciences*, 15 vols. (New York: The Macmillan Company, 1930-1935). While covering the entire social-science field, this encyclopedia pays due attention to international education.

ULICH, ROBERT, *History of Educational Thought* (New York: American Book Company, 1945). By an author who sought to condense three thousand years of educational wisdom.

WHEELER, W. REGINALD, and others, eds., *The Foreign Student in America* (New York: Association Press, 1925). A study by a commission to survey foreign students in the United States. The foreign student is studied against his native background, efforts on his behalf, and the activities of students who returned to their homelands.

WOODY, THOMAS, *New Minds: New Men?* (New York: The Macmillan Company, 1932). A book about the emergence of the Soviet citizen, by an author who has also written on the educational views of Britain and France, as well as on the history of the education of women.

ZIEMER, GREGOR, *Education for Death* (New York: Oxford University Press, 1941). An account of education in Nazi Germany.

ZINK, H., *American Military Government in Germany* (New York: The Macmillan Company, 1947). Includes material on education in occupied Germany.

Index

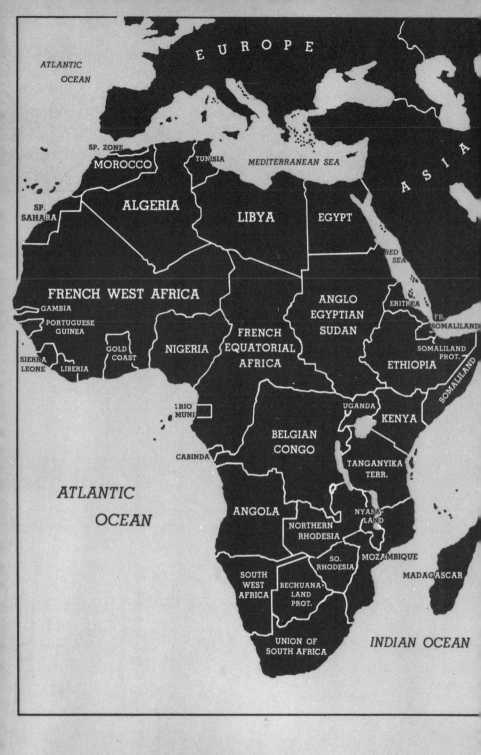